Experiments in Knowing

To judge rightly we need to bear both in mind, never to forget the numbers when thinking of the percentages, nor the percentages when thinking of the numbers. This last is difficult to those whose daily experience or whose imagination brings vividly before them the trials and sorrows of individual lives. . . . In intensity of feeling such as this, and not in statistics, lies the power to move the world. But by statistics must this power be guided if it would move the world aright.

Booth, *Poverty*, 1902–3

A man [*sic*] is but what he knoweth. The mind itself is but an accident to knowledge, for knowledge is a double of that which is. The truth of being, and the truth of knowing, is all one.

Bacon, *Essays*, 1625

It may be the World will judge it a fault in me, that I oppose so many eminent and ingenious Writers, but I do it not out of a contradictory or wrangling nature, but out of an endeavour to find out truth, according to that proportion of sense and reason Nature has bestowed upon me.

Cavendish, *Observations upon Experimental Philosophy*, 1666

Experiments in Knowing

Gender and Method in the Social Sciences

Ann Oakley

Polity Press

First published in 2000 by Polity Press
in association with Blackwell Publishers Ltd.

Reprinted 2005

Polity Press
65 Bridge Street
Cambridge CB2 1UR, UK

Polity Press
350 Main Street
Malden, MA 02148, USA

ISBN 0-7456-2256-9
ISBN 0-7456-2257-7 (pbk)

A catalogue record for this book is available from the British Library and has been applied for from the Library of Congress.

Typeset in 10 on 11 pt Ehrhardt
by Ace Filmsetting Ltd, Frome, Somerset
Printed and bound in Great Britain by Marston Book Services Limited, Oxford

This book is printed on acid-free paper.

For further information on Polity, visit our website: www.polity.co.uk

Contents

Acknowledgements

There are many debts associated with a book of this kind. First of all, I must thank the Swedish Collegium for Advanced Studies in the Social Sciences for giving me the time and space to begin the book; the Medical Research Council for providing a Senior Research Leave Award which has enabled me to pursue questions about methodology; and my colleagues at the Social Science Research Unit for many stimulating discussions and general support. Thanks particularly to Jackie Lee, Sandra Stone and Linda Attwell for important 'housework' tasks, especially the getting of references; to Angela Harden for knowing where to look in electronic databases; and to Sandy Oliver and Greet Peersman for reading and commenting on drafts in a way which can only be described as completely beyond the call of duty.

Friends world-wide have helped in numerous ways, including chasing obscure literature. There are many librarians without whom this book would have been poorer; thanks to them as important behind-the-scenes people. Iain Chalmers, Harvey Goldstein, Helen Roberts and Bill Silverman also read the manuscript for me and gave me invaluable comments. My biggest debt is to Iain Chalmers; not just for spotting more minor mistakes than anybody else, but for supplying me with material, arguing with me, and forcing me to rethink difficult issues, and convincing me (during those dark moments from which every author suffers) that the project of this book was worth undertaking.

Of course, none of these people is reponsible for the book's final form.

I am grateful to David Held at Polity Press for understanding what kind of book I wanted to write; and to Björn Wittrock for steering me in the right direction. More thanks (and apologies) than usual are due to my family and friends, who have had to put up with an unreasonable number of absences of various kinds.

Versions of parts of the book have appeared in five published papers: 'Experimentation in social science: the case of health promotion', *Social Sciences in Health*, 4(2)(1998):73–89; 'Public policy experimentation: lessons from

America', *Policy Studies*, 19(2)(1998):93–114; 'Science, gender and women's liberation: an argument against postmodernism', *Women's Studies International Forum* 21(2)(1998):133–46; 'Gender, methodology and people's ways of knowing: some problems with feminism and the paradigm debate in social science', *Sociology*, 32(4)(1998):707–31; and 'Experimentation and social interventions: a forgotten but important history', *British Medical Journal*, 316(1998): 1239–42.

I am grateful to the following for permission to reproduce copyright material: The Estate of Antoine Saint-Exupéry and Harcourt Brace (figure 3.1); the University of Chicago Press (figures 3.3 and 8.1); Basil Blackwell (figure 3.2); Musée d'Orsay, Paris (figure 4.1); *The Observer* newspaper (figure 11.1); and *Cochrane News* (figure 13.1).

Ann Oakley

Author's Note

Figures in the tables have been rounded up, so percentages may not equal 100 percent in all cases.

References in the text to modern editions of early works mainly cite the modern date, with the date of original publication given in the bibliography.

Part I

Modern Problems

1

Who Knows?

Every book that has ever been written proceeds on at least two levels. The first is that of the ideas which are presented. The second level pertains to the developmental process.

Bakan, *The Duality of Human Existence*

Oakley makes sense only to Oakley.

Pawson, *A Measure for Measures*

This is a book about the history and sociology of different ways of knowing. It is also about the manner in which gender – the cultural construction of femininity and masculinity – has intersected with these processes. My main argument goes as follows: that in the methodological literature today, the 'quantitative'/'qualitative' dichotomy functions chiefly as a gendered ideological representation; that within this gendering of methodology, experimental methods are seen as the most 'quantitative' and therefore as the most masculine; that these processes of methodological development and gendering cannot be separated from the ways in which both science and social science developed, and the social relations in which they were embedded; and that the goal of an emancipatory (social) science calls for us to abandon sterile word-games and concentrate on the business in hand, which is how to develop the most reliable and democratic ways of knowing, both in order to bridge the gap between ourselves and others, and to ensure that those who intervene in other people's lives do so with the most benefit and the least harm.

This issue of the basis on which such interventions are made, the claims that surround them, and the consequences which flow from them is a particularly critical one in terms of the genesis of this book. We live in a world full of 'experts' – doctors, teachers, social workers, politicians, economists, health educators, psychotherapists, lawyers, etc., not to mention a huge range of voluntary organizations and other groups – who all claim to know how to improve our lives. Some of them may do, but how do we (or they) know? This question is, I believe, one which receives far too little attention. Feminist social science has been a particularly important recent strand in the critique of experimental and 'quantitative' ways of knowing. But it seems to me that women and feminism need the service of these methods (and, indeed, depend on them in crucial ways in their everyday lives).

What is true of feminism and women is, of course, true of people generally. An alternative way to frame this is to suggest that the goal of would-be knowers is the elimination of as much bias or distortion as is possible in what it is that counts as knowledge. This means a meticulous, systematic, transparent, sensitive striving for descriptions of 'reality' that satisfy not primarily knowers' needs for professional and scientific recognition, but the much more generous task of helping human beings to make informed decisions about how best to lead their lives.

The book follows the dictate of the original positivist Auguste Comte, who advised that, 'It is true that a science cannot be completely understood without a knowledge of how it arose' (Comte 1853:24). What it presents is a discussion of how the definition of ways of knowing has constantly been interlaced with who is doing the defining, and about how the patterning of all of this has followed certain fundamental divisions existing in the wider culture. One of the implications of this argument is that some ways of knowing have traditionally occupied spaces at the edge of the dominant vision, the same kinds of spaces as are filled by the lives and experiences of the socially marginalized, including women. Thus, neither methods nor methodology can be understood *except* in the context of gendered social relations. Understanding this involves a mapping of how gender, women, nature and knowledge have been constructed both inside and outside all forms of science.

This first chapter takes a step back from the rest of the book and sets its project in its own social context – of the circumstances in which the book came to be conceived and written.

The project of the book

Experiments in Knowing was conceived in early 1997, when I had the good fortune to be the guest for several months of the Swedish Collegium for Advanced Study in the Social Sciences. SCASSS is an exhilarating institution, set up in 1985 with Swedish government money to bring together groups of academics from within Scandinavia and further afield to share for a term or so at a time a life of thinking and writing free from other distractions. It was difficult to know how to make the best use of my Swedish opportunity. What I decided is that I would spend my time trying to find out why in the world of science and social science today research methods – ways of knowing – tend to be described in different and opposed ways as 'qualitative' and 'quantitative'.[1]

Much has been written about this debate, but, as Martyn Hammersley (1989:4) observes, its history is strikingly neglected. The *oppositional* use of the terms 'qualitative' and 'quantitative' is relatively modern. It is, moreover, a use which seems to engender a great deal of emotion, with the two words flagging whole sets of associations, only some of which generally have anything directly to do with the topic being discussed. 'Quantitative' also includes 'experimental'; 'experimentation' is 'at the far end of the quantitative scale' (McKie 1996:7), and it, too, is a concept that seems to provoke considerable indignation. One of the 'founding fathers' of sociology, Herbert Spencer, put it well when he wrote in his *Autobiography*: 'While words are necessary aids to all thoughts save very simple ones, they are impediments to correct thinking. Every word carries with it a cluster of associations determined by its most familiar uses, and these associations, often inappropriate to the particular case in which the word is being used, distort more or less the image it calls up' (Spencer 1904:300). Since the modern 'paradigm war' between 'quantitative' and 'qualitative' methods is the starting-point for this book, the next chapter takes a closer look at some of its manifestations, at how the proponents of the two positions align themselves, and what the essence of the dispute might reasonably be considered to be.

Part of my Swedish project was an attempt to integrate my two interests in methodology and gender. The onset of second-wave feminism in the late 1960s and early 1970s injected a new awareness of bias into many disciplines (see e.g. Bowles and Duelli Klein 1983; Millman and Kanter 1975). In social science, one response was the elevation of 'qualitative' methods over others as the route to reshaping knowledge in a more egalitarian format. 'Quantitative' methods were early deemed 'hard', while 'qualitative' ones were considered 'soft' (Zelditch 1962). As this dichotomy immediately buys into a whole set of others, including 'masculinity' and 'femininity', it suggests that the division in methodology is, in some sense, just another epiphenomenon of the structural duality of male and female. But just how are ways of knowing and gendered ways of being related? What were the events and processes that connected them historically? This theme of gender runs throughout the book, although there are particular points (for example, chapters 2 and 3 on modern methodological issues, and chapters 4 and 6 on the development of social science) where it is more salient than others. In linking gender and methodology, I chose to focus on the field of women and health research. Health research presents a special case, methodologically speaking, since it bridges the two ways of knowing, with both medical and social scientists applying to it their own favoured approaches. Although the book draws on a wide literature, much of it American, some of the discussion inevitably reflects the UK scene.

Experiences and meanings

SCASSS is housed in a villa in Kåbo, a residential suburb of Uppsala. Uppsala lies north-west of Stockholm, and is the site of Sweden's oldest university, founded in 1477. The town owes its modernization to King Gustavus Adolphus (of the Thirty Years' War) and his daughter Christina in the seventeenth century; Christina reappears later in this book through her alliance with the

French philosopher René Descartes. Uppsala is dominated by the twin spires of the (originally thirteenth-century) cathedral, which can be glimpsed long before IKEA on the bus ride from the airport; equally magisterial is the huge red castle which sits on the hill looking down over the famous botanical gardens. Uppsala is where the botanist Carl Linnaeus produced his classification of the entire world of plants in terms of eighteenth-century human gender stereotypes; it is also known as an important manufacturing centre for bicycles and as the birthplace of Ingmar Bergman.

I posted 40 kilos of books ahead to myself and set off for SCASSS towards the end of January 1997. The apartment provided for me was well-sited, in central Uppsala, but the first thing I noticed was its smell. This turned out (eventually) to be due to the refrigerator defrosting itself over many years into the concrete floor, and thus setting in motion a most threatening (and offensive) form of rot. I had some problems convincing my colleagues at SCASSS that the qualitative nature of my experience of the apartment derived from something measurably real. But after they had been lured back there for champagne (a 'smell' party), consensus was happily reached that what was wrong lay outside rather than inside my head.

SCASSS lent me a bicycle with which I moved, not exactly effortlessly, between apartment, office and swimming bath. It snowed much of the time. I kept a diary. A few weeks after my arrival, I wrote:

'There's really no beginning to the day, because I wake several times in the night with the half-known fragments of dreams in a web of limbs and bedding which I at first think are not my own; and I get up to adjust the blind so I can see what the weather is doing: does the ground shine with a treacly black glaze, or is it downy with the fluff of freshly fallen snow? Will I skate or slide or fall or walk in the morning? How many clothes should I wear? What will happen to me?

Understandably, the Swedes are preoccupied by the weather. I've been here a month now, and the temperature has moved from about -5 to +5, but most of the time it hovers around zero. It's most important to quantify the weather. Mr Svensson, in whose apartment I'm living, has a thermometer fixed to the outside of his bedroom window. In the office to which I make my perilous journey each morning, there's a more modern thermometer which offers readings in both fahrenheit and celsius; Celsius was born in a house not far from here.

I watch myself as I live; observing; measuring; coding; classifying and trying to come to terms with the different meanings that emerge from this process. I am the qualitative knower, and also the quantitative one. I have swum 14 times in the central swimming bath in Uppsala: 30 lengths each time, except for the time when I felt particularly miserable and did 40 in an effort to raise some endorphins. That's 430 lengths. By the time I go in June what will it be? 2200, 3200? Is the number of lengths I do caused by my mood, or do other factors explain it – for example, the presence of alternative forms of evening entertainment or the number of anti-social male swimmers in the fast lane?

One of the surprises about Sweden is what dreadful swimmers many Swedes are. A view under the water, courtesy of my Boots goggles, reveals an awful lot of untidily arranged limbs. It's more of a cultural ritual than exercise. On the other hand, I've learnt that this qualitative indicator coexists with a real quantitative one. A lot of Swedes have awfully long legs and just as you think they've finished, they haven't, and wham, there's a Swedish foot in your face. Even the sauna isn't serious. Beautiful young Swedish bodies, tanned and blonde, with neatly tailored Vs of pubic hair, wander in and out, only staying long enough to warm up after their swim or to dry their costumes on the rail round the sauna coals. One woman was even eating an apple in the sauna the other day, and another was reading a book. It's not my idea of a sauna, but it is theirs.

I am outside myself all the time, and inside myself: the knower and the known. In the evenings I walk from my apartment to the swimming bath, alongside and across the Fyris river which streaks through Uppsala, a most welcome landmark for the spatially challenged like me. I count the bridges between the apartment and the swimming bath: 1, 2, 3, 4. The river was frozen when I came, now the ice is only patchy. Under the bridges in the dark water the ducks quack, but nobody feeds them. The melting of the snow which is, no doubt, only temporary, reveals faults in the landscape: a wine bottle on an ice floe; cracks in the surface of the road. Walking is an art – or a science. You have to look down all the time, and you must concentrate on putting one foot in front of the other. Each foot has to be down squarely without pushing too much, and then picked up again vertically without allowing any horizontal slippage. Of course you must have the right footwear, with enough crevices and ridges on the sole. It's no use looking round at things or engaging in conversation with yourself or someone else; distraction comes before a fall.

Then there's the observation of the ground itself. What I previously thought of as undifferentiated snow and ice isn't so any more. There are the streaks of ice that shine in the morning sunlight or the light of bicycles: they are to be avoided. Glaze is death. There are the great grey lumps of old snow and dirt which can be ridden over, like little hills. A new dusting of snow is worst, because of what it hides from view. This is why the Eskimos have multiple words for snow, and why people who live in forests can't speak only of 'green'. Being in an environment means that your concepts are shaped by it.[2]

So I live what I write about and I write about what I live.

When I came out of SCASSS last night, at about half past seven, it had been dark for nearly 3 hours. The sky above the pine forest held a low slung crescent moon coiled in a corona of vivid blue and pink. It made me think of a fertilized human egg sticking its tendrils into the walls of its mother's womb. I walked in the pine forest the other day, using the Swedish technique, passing several Swedish mums with heavily garbed toddlers and expansive old-fashioned pushchairs lined with sheepskins the colour of honey. I wonder what it's like to be a mother here? With the sheepskins and the daycare and the apparent absence of all those nasties we have at home – violent men and punitive welfare benefits, sexually marauding politicians and little boys with axes to grind (much the same thing).

I expect there are surveys which would answer that question for me. But there are very few surveys which can compare these issues across countries. Anne-Marie, a methodologist from Belgium, has left in my room a list of statements she wants me to score on how I think men and women would answer for five different countries. Then she'll give us the real answer at her seminar. But is there anything that will convey the texture of the experience – of being a mother and walking through the pine forest in Kåbo, Uppsala, Sweden's cathedral city, on a not-quite-snowing day in February 1997?

I got lost in the forest. I came out on a road I didn't recognize; scanning the landscape for familiar sights revealed none. But I had a map, creased and much folded in my pocket, and although not all the roads were marked on it, enough were, and so I found my way safely back to the white enclosure of my office, with its pale marine lino and the clean cut lines of its pine furniture – the chair with its rounded arms and blue cushions, the computer table with the bits that come out but aren't quite clever enough to hold all the books from which I want to take notes, the smooth (but not now so tidy) pine desk, and the office chair with its wheels so I can waltz across the floor from desk to bookshelf and back again, making my own music.

I remember TS Eliot:

"There is no end, but addition: the trailing/ Consequence of further days and hours,/ While emotion takes to itself the emotionless/ Years of living among the breakage . . . / We had the experience but missed the meaning,/ And approach to the meaning restores the experience/ In a different form, beyond any meaning/ We can assign to happiness."

We live through experiences, rather than in them. And we can't live in anyone else's. That's the great puzzle: none of us will ever know what it's like to be anyone else. History and now and Sweden (to paraphrase TS Eliot), and this English woman sitting in a chair. Her hair is wet from swimming and she wears white trainers on her feet. She smiles as she writes. This is because writing gives her pleasure. The words slip out of her pen like the pink-gold Fyris river, freed of its ice-floes, rushing out to sea; like a child who can't wait to leave the house and play. The words fix themselves on the page and become something; they are real, really there. But how easy it is to slip between 'I' and 'she'. If I can objectify myself, what does this say about our ability to objectify others? Am I right about any of this? Who knows?'

Different ways of knowing

Everybody thinks they know certain things, but debating what knowledge is and how to reach it has traditionally lain in the domain of 'experts'. Among the different ways we have of knowing about the world outside ourselves are autobiography and fiction. Autobiography can provide a startling insider view of phenomena otherwise classified in quite different terms. An example is New Zealand writer Janet Frame's account of her labelling as mentally disordered in her celebrated *An Angel at My Table*:

The six weeks I spent at Seacliff hospital in a world I'd never known among people whose existences I never thought possible, became for me a concentrated course in the horrors of insanity and the dwelling-place of those judged insane, separating me for ever from the former acceptable realities and assurances of everyday life. From my first moment there I knew that I could not turn back to my usual life or forget what I saw at Seacliff. I felt as if my life were overturned by this sudden division of people into 'ordinary' people in the street, and these 'secret' people whom few had seen or talked to but whom many spoke of with derision, laughter, fear. I saw people with their eyes staring like the eyes of hurricanes surrounded here by whirling unseen and unheard commotion . . . There was a personal geographical, even linguistic exclusiveness in this community of the insane, who yet had no legal or personal external identity – no clothes of their own to wear, no handbags, purses, no possessions but a temporary bed to sleep in with a locker beside it, and a room to sit in and stare, called the dayroom. (Frame 1990:193)

Once released from hospital, Frame found she needed a medical certificate in order to claim sickness benefit:

My visit to the Seacliff doctor . . . brought its own bewilderment, for the medical certificate stated: Nature of Illness; *Schizophrenia*.

At home I announced, half with pride, half with fear, 'I've got *Shizofreenier*' . . . It seemed to spell my doom, as if I had emerged from a chrysalis, the natural human state, into another kind of creature, and even if there were parts of me that were familiar to human beings, my gradual deterioration would lead me further and further away, and in the end not even my family would know me.

In the last of the shining Willowglen summer these feelings of doom came only briefly as passing clouds block the sun. I knew that I was shy, inclined to be fearful, and even more so after my six weeks of being in hospital and seeing what I had seen around me, that I was absorbed in the world of imagination, but I also knew that I was totally present in the 'real' world and whatever shadow lay over me, lay only in the writing on the medical certificate. (Frame 1990:196)

This was not Frame's only experience of being deemed insane, and she wrote another book, *Faces in the Water* (1980), which is a fictionalized account of these various mental health episodes. Fiction is another way of knowing. A book such as Marie Cardinal's *Devotion and Disorder* may tell us more about the psychological reality of drug addiction than 'quantitative' surveys or epidemiological studies of the social and risk factors involved in drug addiction. The mother in *Devotion and Disorder*, Elsa Labbé, is an academic psychologist, but she finds it impossible to write about her experiences with her drug-addicted daughter using her normal scientific language – 'That's not the kind of writing for what I want to express' (Cardinal 1991:3). She hires a ghost-writer to put together a narrative about how she discovered her daughter's addiction and helped her to overcome it. The account opens with Elsa returning from a stay in the USA to find her Paris flat reduced to a state of vomit- and syringe-strewn disorder by her daughter Laure and Laure's friends. This is the first she has known that Laure is ill:

Laure was caught up in heroin; she was under its spell, bewitched by it. She was reasonable, though; she wanted to stop shooting up, and she would stop – each new hit was the last . . .

Ever since Laure had become hooked, she no longer measured time in days or hours; she measured it in hits. Time consisted of one hit after another, and between one hit and another there was virtually no time, just a rush, a few moments. The rest of her existence was not time, it was a slow descent, it was starting to think about the next hit, it was running around after some smack with withdrawal on her heels . . . It passed quickly.

Laure did not realise quite how quickly . . . She was trapped in a separate world, one with its own internal logic and constraints so powerful that she had forgotten what it was like outside. She had no idea what Elsa was going through; she simply could not imagine it. She didn't know that three days had gone by.

During those three days Elsa didn't know how to deal with time. She was dependent on her daughter, who was not there, who was lost, who was perhaps dead. How could she endure the stagnation, the powerlessness? . . .

So she continued to organise, put things away, clean up. This time she went at the flat calmly, obstinately, as she had gone at her research and everything else in her life. In this meticulous, systematic, almost academic, industrious, yet curious way of hers, she tried to discover how the drug addicts who had lived in her flat had been organised. . . . She was going to have to learn and understand, if she wanted to be able to help Laure. *(Cardinal 1991:41–2)*

One can compare what we, the readers, are able to absorb about the quality of Elsa's and Laure's and Janet Frame's experiences from these accounts with what is to be learnt from the more academic and scientific kinds of accounts that Elsa rejected. Take the next example, a study of the effect on women with breast cancer of different drug regimens:

In a trial of postoperative adjuvant chemotherapy women with primary breast cancer and spread to one or more axillary nodes were randomised to receive a six-month course of either the single agent chlorambucil or the five-drug combination of chlorambucil, methotrexate, fluorouracil, vincristine, and adriamycin. On completing the treatment 47 patients were asked to fill in questionnaires at home on the side effects of their treatment and its influence on the quality of their life. Side effects including nausea, vomiting, malaise, and alopecia had been severe enough to interfere with their lifestyle in 9 (42%) of the patients who had received the single agent and 19 (79%) of those who had received multiple-drug treatment. Various other side effects were reported by a few patients. Seven (29%) of the patients who had received the multiple-drug schedule voluntarily added that the treatment had been 'unbearable' or 'could never be gone through again'.

The proportion of patients who had experienced severe side effects while receiving the treatment was considerable; hence adjuvant chemotherapy is justifiable only if it will substantially improve a patient's prognosis. *(Palmer et al. 1980: 1594)*

Through the dense medical jargon we can glimpse real people suffering real pain. Documenting how people 'respond' to medical therapies can be, as in this case, an important prod to reconsidering the use of these. The point of the larger study referred to in the abstract above was not, of course, to find out what it is like having breast cancer, but how the different drugs compared in preventing its recurrence. This is a very particular kind of research question. Other academic and scientific research uses another kind of method:

> Increasing attention has been paid to the health effects of women's smoking (Chollat-Traquet, 1992). While lung cancer mortality among men in Britain has been declining since the 1970s, it is still rising among women. In Scotland, female deaths from lung cancer have exceeded those from breast cancer since 1984, and in certain areas of northern England, lung cancer has recently overtaken breast cancer as the main cause of female cancer death (CRC, 1992) ... Maternal smoking during pregnancy and infancy is seen as a major risk factor for childhood morbidity and mortality. It has been linked to a greater risk of miscarriage and of [fetal] death during the latter stages of pregnancy and the first week of life. It is also linked to low birth-weight, to sudden infant death syndrome and to a range of health problems affecting the physical growth and educational development of young children (Gillies and Wakefield, 1993) ...
>
> Smoking among young women is a habit acquired by White women. Among White women, higher rates of cigarette smoking are reported among women born in Ireland than among UK-born women. Rates are also higher among women living in Northern Ireland, Wales and Scotland than among women in England (Barker et al., 1989; OPCS, 1992). Reported rates of smoking among young Asian and African-Caribbean women are low, although there is some evidence which points to an increase in smoking prevalence among young African-Caribbean women (Oakley et al., 1992). These patterns are repeated in adulthood. *(Graham 1994:105, 107)*

Here 'facts' are drawn from observations made about large numbers of people – women who smoke and women who do not smoke, smoking women with children, non-smoking women with children, etc., in order to map the social correlates and health implications of women's smoking. The data are second-hand, and the people who provided these are kept, apparently, at a distance. Neither this way of knowing nor the framing of experimental methodology in the previous example suggest a particular sensitivity to the perspectives of the people who take part in research. One origin of the move towards 'qualitative' research was a desire to democratize the research process by enabling the voices of people as research participants to be heard. The following voice comes from a study of frail elderly people in London carried out several years ago:

> Mrs B in Inner City exemplified the stoical approach. She was talking about the history of her disability, and in answer to a question about whether she had a calliper on her other leg, she said: 'No. Later on they tried to give me one but I couldn't use it because my foot sticks out. .... I had a knee cap removed ... so that means I've got no knee cap on and it hurts ... I've got arthritis in my knee and my hip but I've had a new hip, in 1981, 82. .... Of course I've got arthritis in my shoulder ... so I can only lift it like that. .... I get electricity going up my

arm, terrible. But that's what people say to me, "You're always cheerful, how
can you be cheerful?" I said, "Look, I've seen people worse than what I am . . .
so why be miserable? If you're miserable, no-one wants to talk to you, they won't
want anything to do with you, why not have a laugh and a joke?"'

   Mrs B constructed herself as an expert on her own body, though almost as if
she were referring to a mechanical object which had gone wrong. It is strangely
'disembodied' talk reminiscent of much of the medical discourse to which she
has been subjected. But becoming an 'expert' in this way allowed her some
distance between herself and the powerlessness associated with the identity as an
invalid. *(Hey 1994:30–1)*

Mrs B offers comments on her situation, and it is not difficult to picture the
person behind the words. The researcher interprets Mrs B's account in a
certain way, which perhaps reflects what she (the researcher) reads into it,
rather than necessarily what Mrs B herself might say (though we do not know
about this, and can only surmise what Mrs B would think of her talk being
described as 'disembodied').

   Autobiographical and fictional accounts clearly differ from academic ones,
in that they focus on the quality (and quantity) of particular individual experiences. We cannot know from what Janet Frame or Marie Cardinal say whether
the stories they tell are unique or not; we do not know how common such
events and patterns were among other young women in New Zealand and
Paris at the time. But similar questions can also be raised about stories such as
Mrs B's. By comparison with these ways of knowing, the breast cancer drug
trial and the facts about women's smoking suggest a more broadly based knowledge about the treatment of women with breast cancer and patterns of smoking among women. But is this just because they are presented in a certain way?
Is it because they come from a tradition in which the power of numbers, of
'hard' data and experimental 'trials', acts to reinforce the ascribed and enacted
power of experts to tell us what knowledge 'is'?

A 'factual' journey

Modern debates about ways of knowing represent only a small fragment of the
much longer effort to understand and give meaning to the social and natural
world. This book is the record of one particular journey into the history of
how ways of knowing have been defined. It is simultaneously an excursion into
the origins of science and social science as the two main repositories of 'quantitative'/'experimental' and 'qualitative' methods. While it may seem self-
evident that the former belong to science, and the latter to social science, these
equations are actually part of the puzzle to be explained. This is particularly so
when one considers the sociology of science literature, which tells us that both
scientific and sociological theory are exercises of the imagination (Lakatos and
Musgrave 1970; Pickering 1992); the informal organization of science is a
significant determinant of scientific 'discovery' (Latour and Woolgar 1979);
and the concern with falsifiability, which is generally considered the hallmark

of science, is missing in much scientific work. As Barnes (1974:47–8) has noted: 'Scientific activity is simply unintelligible in terms of distinctive general conventions; scientific knowledge claims have not been sifted by the application of a single set of general standards. That the opposite is so often thought to be the case is a result of pure conviction, rather than detailed examination of scientific activity as it is conceived and performed.'

Another absolutely key consideration here is that experimental methods were used in the infancy of social science, and, indeed, for much longer, and contrary to the stereotyped images of the methodological divide (see chapters 8, 9 and 10). It is often supposed that social science, and especially sociology, arose like a phoenix from the ashes of old 'scientific' ways of knowing with distinctively new ones. This is not what happened. Social science in its beginning was modelled quite narrowly on natural science. It was only later, under a variety of pressures to diversify, that a codification within social science of 'the scientific method' developed which allowed social scientists to set themselves up in opposition to it. The 'straw man' aspect of this (and gender was crucial here as everywhere else) has been responsible for a good deal of methodological and other miscommunication. The story about the development of social science is told in more detail in chapters 6 and 8.

In developing my argument, I have drawn on diverse literatures, from psychoanalytic interpretations of Cartesian dualism and late nineteenth-century uses of the survey method, to histories of the idea of chance and the professionalization of sociology following the Germanic tradition in North American higher education in the early twentieth century.[3] While I have often stressed the particular personalities of the scientists and social scientists who are key actors in the story, because these provide interesting vignettes of historical moments, there is also a sense in which the story is not personality-dependent: the American sociologist William Ogburn, proposing the notion that social conditions are an important determinant of great ideas, said (of science) that 'The inference to be drawn [from history] . . . is, for instance, that the discovery of the calculus was not dependent upon Newton; for if Newton had died, it would have been discovered by Leibniz. And . . . if neither Leibniz nor Newton had lived, it would still have been discovered by some other mathematician' (Ogburn 1964:37).

One woman's journey

One difficulty about the subject-matter of this book is that I myself have a certain involvement in, and even complicity with, the problem. This is an exaggerated version of what Bakan, in the first quote at the head of this chapter, refers to as 'the developmental process' that goes into the writing of a book (Bakan 1966:13). To put it in terms of the paradigm argument, I began by singing the praises of 'qualitative' research, of in-depth interviewing and observation as ultimately more truthful ways of knowing, and I have ended up advocating the use of 'quantitative' and experimental methods as providing what is often a sounder basis for claiming that we know anything.[4] What is going on here? Did I have some sort of strange conversion experience?

In his *The Scientific Image*, Bas van Fraassen talks about how he was converted to scientific realism, 'the position that scientific theory construction aims to give us a literally true story of what the world is like' (1980:9). His change of mind was, he said,

> a sudden occurrence, taking me unawares when I was reading Aquinas. Like Saul on the road to Damascus, I was struck by a blinding light, and I saw. What I saw was that the medieval attempts to prove the existence of God have modern analogues demonstrating the correctness of scientific realism.
>
> Indeed, exactly where the invalidity of the proofs of God's existence is most obvious, the truth of scientific realism veritably springs to the eye. Paley described a watch found, running perfectly and keeping time, on a deserted heath. Can you conceive, he asked, of a watch without a watchmaker? And the twentieth-century reader is blasé enough to answer: Yes, I can. But think again, gentle reader: can you conceive of a watch keeping time *without clockworks inside?*' *(van Fraassen 1980:204)*

Van Fraassen describes something of the transition in my own thinking here, but for me there was no blinding light. My own journey through the landscape of methods was a much more gradual experience than the biblical one.

In the late 1960s and early 1970s I interviewed women about housework, and analysed what they said as providing a basis for a conceptual and political shift – towards including domestic labour in definitions of what work means and how it affects workers in modern society. The book I published about the housework study (Oakley 1974) opened with a chapter entitled 'The invisible woman: sexism in sociology', which was written as an afterthought at the request of the publisher. The publisher was quite right: it was important to see the sociological neglect of housework within the framework of a misogynist social science that had ignored, or distorted, critical aspects of women's situation. The housework research, in the course of which I became a feminist, was followed by another project on women's transition to motherhood (Oakley 1979, 1980). Again this deployed in-depth interviewing, in order to follow a sample of urban women through the joys and vicissitudes of pregnancy and birth in an era when reproduction had become increasingly medicalized and mechanized. One of my most quoted publications, 'Interviewing women: a contradiction in terms?' (Oakley 1981) came directly out of the transition to motherhood research. This took the textbook model of social science interviewing and showed how interviewing in practice, especially a woman interviewing other women, did not easily fit the uncomfortable ideal-type mould of the interviewer as impersonal data-collector and the interviewee as subservient data-provider. My paper on this fed into an emerging and highly vocal literature on social science and women which took much previous work to task for its lack of awareness of gender issues, and was hailed as creating 'postpositivist, new paradigm studies' (Goldberger 1996:339). Within this literature 'qualitative' research was unambiguously highlighted as the preferred paradigm. Some of the dimensions of the feminist 'position' on methodology are explored in the next chapter, while chapter 3 examines in more detail the propositions of feminism and other 'isms' about the qualitative paradigm being an alternative, and inherently better, way of knowing. It argues that there are problems of credibility about 'qualitative' ways of knowing that are not compensated for by their political correctness, and which may, indeed, have been veiled by it.

This is where things get complicated. I describe the feminist critique of 'quantitative' methods and 'malestream' social science as though I were outside it; but in fact that is not the case, I was (am) very much inside it. I am proud to own up to having made a certain kind of contribution to academic women's studies through my work on housework, motherhood, research methods and a sort of stubborn insistence on the difference between biological sex and social gender. My contributions to feminist social science have been both much-quoted and much-criticized. The second quote at the head of this chapter comes from one such criticism. In a discussion of 'the social relations of the interview', Ray Pawson, proponent of an alternative paradigm of 'realistic evaluation' (see chapter 2), observes about my paper on interviewing women, that

> it could be said that there is a very fine line between 'involvement' and 'crusading' . . . the need for personal involvement can be overdrawn. In Oakley's hands it renders the detached, scientific (and hence masculine) interviewing of women as a contradiction in terms. We are well down the path to solipsism here, and in a world in which only men can interview men, scientists understand scientists, fascists involve with fascists, and Oakley makes sense only to Oakley. *(Pawson 1989:320)*

One does, of course, tend to make better sense to oneself than to other people. While the charge against feminist social science of political bias more often comes with a man's voice, feminists have also rightly taken me to task for ignoring both class dimensions of the interviewer–interviewee relationship in 'qualitative' research and the danger that assumptions of 'sisterhood' may mask other forms of exploitation (see e.g. Edwards 1990; Finch 1984; Ribbens 1989; Stacey 1988).

It is as a 'qualitative' feminist sociologist that my work is most often referenced (see e.g. Reid 1983; Spender 1985). In 1985, in a preface to the new edition of *The Sociology of Housework*, I wrote:

> The predominant paradigm today is one that favours rational knowledge over intuitive wisdom, and quantitative rather than qualitative forms of knowledge; it is one based on the unquestioned validity of Descartes' famed mind–body dualism, one that presupposes a mechanical division between emotional and material existence. This paradigm emerged between 1500 and 1700 in Western culture when intellectual and commercial development supplanted the notion of an organic and spiritual universe with an alternative idea of the world – of all living matter – as a mechanical structure. The 'Age of the Scientific Revolution' bred an obsession with measurement and objectification that in the modern era have

become synonymous both with an exploitation of nature, and with the exploitation of women.

There are many signs of the growing misfit between this mechanical paradigm
and the dynamics of the world to which it must constantly be applied as a
putative explanation. (p. x)

At this time I evidently took at face value the story documented in later
chapters of this book – that the concern with measurement and control underlying 'quantitative'/experimental ways of knowing developed as part of the
same social processes which enable men to exercise power over women. This
case is dissected in chapters 5 and 7. But while there is a historical association
between quantification and masculinity, the problem is that it is not so simple.

By 1984 I had started work on a study of a different kind, one which used
the common-sense reflection (often treated as a technical nuisance by (social)
scientists – see chapter 9) that all research constitutes an intervention of some
kind. This new study, which was on the topic of social support and pregnancy,
was prompted directly by my experience of interviewing as both a social relationship and form of action; one may never definitively say that the data
produced through interviewing are not shaped in some way by the manner of
their production. The social support and pregnancy study was an attempt to
capitalize on, instead of apologize for, the social action effect of interviewing
by seeing whether it could help women have healthier babies. This may sound
a fairly way-out idea (and certainly some of the research-funders I approached
at the time thought so), but my enthusiasm for it was also derived from a
considerable amount of evidence, since added to, about the importance of
stress in making people less healthy and the health-promoting effects of social
support (see Oakley 1992b).

Was this study 'qualitative' or 'quantitative'? It was 'qualitative' in using in-
depth interviewing as a means of encouraging narratives from research participants about their experiences. As a small pilot study for what I hoped would
be a much larger study later,[5] I was not much concerned with numbers –
probably not nearly as much as I had actually been in the housework study,
where the women's accounts of their lives jostle for attention with 2 x 2 tables
and tests of statistical significance (an important motive was an attempt to
calculate the length of housewives' working week in order to put domestic
labour in the language of the paid labour market and the economics of the
Gross Domestic Product). When I published the housework study, I was
slated in certain quarters both for using tests of significance and percentages
and for being a feminist, although the same people who made one sort of
criticism usually did not make the other (as the two might have seemed politically, if not logically, in conflict with one another). One of the volumes which
reported the transition to motherhood study (Oakley 1980) also made much
use of statistical tests as a way of arriving at a model of childbirth as a human
experience – one which challenges the human capacity to respond unprepared,
immediately and constructively to new and often painful experiences. In this
book I argued the opposite of what people probably expected me to argue: I

suggested that women's reactions to childbirth could best be understood by seeing them as people rather than as women. As this is my most neglected book, I have often speculated that my use of the 'quantitative' mode was what put people off.

My work on social support grew out of a new institutional affiliation; in 1979 I had taken a part-time job in a unit in Oxford which was doing medical and epidemiological research on reproduction and the maternity services. Social science was in a minority position in this unit, and I found myself exposed there to a different research tradition in which quantification and especially prospective experimental studies dominated the scene. Although my 'training' as a social scientist informed me that such approaches were unlikely to get at the really important forms of truth – such as how people feel and see the world – I did, none the less, find the reason for the focus on these methods quite powerful and important. It was apparent at this time, the late 1970s, that women having babies were increasingly being subjected to forms of health care practice – for example, induction of labour, Caesarean section, and heavily routinized antenatal care – which might not be in their or their babies' best interests. These potentially damaging effects flowed from the largely unscientific character of modern medicine – what Ivan Illich (1975) termed 'medical nemesis', the widespread illusion that doctors know what they are doing. On the contrary, medical practitioners very often decide what to do on the basis of educated guesswork, preference, tradition, material resources or fear of litigation, rather than because this or that procedure has been shown to be safe and effective. Neither intention nor skill have much to do with it; well-intentioned and skilful doctors can still make serious mistakes, because their generalizations about what works may be fanciful rather than factual, and may not take sufficient account of systematic observations encompassing the cumulative evidence of many cases. This move in the genesis of modern medicine away from a focus on the individual 'patient' to the evidence provided by a series of cases is discussed further in chapter 7.

Under the influence of the health care research being conducted in the Oxford unit, I became aware of a crucial, under-appreciated phenomenon which is fundamental to one of the main arguments developed in this book. This is the difference between 'controlled' and 'uncontrolled' experimentation. Uncontrolled experimentation is what usually happens in professional practice. Professionals do what they think is best, without necessarily having any evidence to support it. This kind of experimentation is not only normal behaviour, it is 'the dominant mode of innovation in professional practice' (I. Chalmers 1986:162). Controlled experimentation, on the other hand, happens within the context of a formal research study, whose design is likely to provide an answer to the question being asked: does this treatment/intervention work or not? Medicine's prime way of knowing, the randomised controlled trial (RCT), evolved as an alternative to the uncontrolled experimentation of 'normal' practice, and as offering answers to questions about effectiveness and safety which individual doctors cannot answer from the experience of individual cases.

Chapters 7 and 8 have more to say about the way in which RCTs developed. An RCT is simply an experiment ('trial') which tests alternative ways of handling a situation. Sometimes an intervention is tested against what would have happened had it not been used; sometimes different interventions are compared. The most efficient way to do this is to compare the effects of the intervention in one group of people with what happens to another group of people who are as alike as possible to the first group of people but who do not get the intervention. Only thus can rival hypotheses explaining the 'effects' of the intervention – such as age, social class, or the impact of the passage of time itself – be ruled out. The no-intervention group in such a trial is called, in something of a misnomer, the 'control' group; in French it is more accurately described as a 'witness' group. Of all the various ways of deciding which research participants should belong to which group, random allocation – tossing a coin or the play of chance – has been shown to be the most effective and easiest way of generating socially comparable groups. Random allocation is, in this sense, merely a convenient methodological device – like the use of a tape recorder for interviewing. Attempts to 'match' on variables known to be associated with the problem one is studying – for example, social class and the risk of a baby dying around the time of birth – turn out to be extremely complicated in practice. For researchers must know about *all* such factors before doing the matching in order to get it right, and such perfect knowledge is hardly possible. Examples of studies which tried matching can be found later in this book, in chapter 8; and some of the lessons of *non*-random allocation appear in chapters 9 and 10.

When first exposed to RCTs as a way of knowing, I was more impressed by faults in their design than by the potential they had to offer. One considerable problem was that in some trials half the people taking part – those in the control group – were unaware that they were part of a research study. This approach, known as the 'Zelen' design (1979), was promoted to overcome precisely that logic which had attracted me to the health-promoting value of socially supportive interviewing in the first place: the recognition that all research is an intervention which may change what is being studied. People who know they are part of a research study may behave differently as a consequence. While it would be impossible to convince people who are being interviewed in a 'qualitative' research project that they are not taking part in research, this is at least theoretically possible in the context of a controlled trial. Moreover, since the object of a trial is to quantify the effects attributable to an intervention, keeping those who do not have it in ignorance of their role as research 'subjects' has the important scientific function of enhancing the chances of significant differences being found.

My medical and epidemiological colleagues and I argued about the ethics of the Zelen method. It was by then a well-established precept of feminist social research that research participants should be fully included in the research process; they should help to set the research agenda, should know what the research was about, and have an opportunity to influence its design, analysis and dissemination. I struggled to reconcile these principles with the way I saw (some) experimental research being carried out. But at the same time, I could see the very real advantages for women of being protected from the adverse consequences of medical technology, either by being in the control groups of RCTs (of interventions which later proved to be damaging) or generally by taking part in trials whose object was to contribute to the evidence base of medicine.

One question began to frame itself in my mind: why did experimental methods appear only to belong to natural science and to doctors? Why did they not seem to be owned equally by social science and other groups of professionals – for example, social workers, teachers and those involved in criminal justice and crime prevention? What was so special about these professions that made them immune to the need to show that their interventions in other people's lives worked and did more good than harm? This was an example of a double standard. Medicine had to prove it knew what it was doing, but not other professions, which could shelter behind a language of 'qualitative' evaluation that set entirely different standards for their performance.

I also began to see the feminist critique of 'quantitative' methods in a somewhat different light. Perhaps the anti-quantitative and anti-experimental bent of these critiques was tantamount to throwing the baby out with the bathwater? Just as sociology ought to be refashioned so as to provide a sociology *for* women which begins from everyday experience and is free from prejudicial stereotypes, as Dorothy Smith (1988) and other feminist sociologists went on to argue, so also there would seem to be a strong case for an experimentation for women – an activity in which women themselves would actively participate and strive for the goal of an emancipatory social science.[6] As to 'quantitative' methods more generally, the very charting of women's oppression required quantification, surely: we needed figures for women's schooling and education *vis-à-vis* that of men, the distribution and work of women in the paid and unpaid labour markets, women's earnings, the burden of health problems and so forth, in order to say to what extent the situations of men and women were (are) structurally differentiated.

Over the last few years academic feminism has mostly moved in quite a different direction from these 'realist' propositions. Much early feminist work was over-dominated by the perspectives of white, middle-class women; the realization of this has produced the over-reaction that neither feminism nor women really exist. There are only feminisms and different social groups of women, with distinct, though sometimes overlapping interests. The useful concept of gender as a descriptor of socially constructed differences between the sexes has itself been relegated to an old-fashioned 'positivist' past. We live in a world of multiple constructed and constantly shifting meanings. Nothing is certain, and nothing can be known for sure. Reality itself has gone the way of gender; we can know little more than our individual experiences, and pursuing truth in the old quintessential way is an exercise doomed to failure on procedural as well as political grounds (see e.g. Butler 1991; Irigaray 1985a; Kristeva 1981; Young 1997). In these allegations, post-modern feminism is part of a broader intellectual movement which disposes of that very everyday reality in which people's lives are grounded.

My unhappiness with these arguments is one of the driving forces behind this book. It is one of my premises that most people operate as though reality does exist. It is only academics who make a living arguing the opposite. Commenting on the proceedings of a conference on social science held in 1983, Paul Meehl said:

> As to realism, I have never met any scientist who, when doing science, held to a phenomenologist or idealist view; and I cannot force myself to take a nonrealist view seriously even when I work at it. So I begin with the presupposition that the external world is really there, there is a difference between the world and my view of it, and the business of science is to get my view in harmony with the way the world really is to the extent that is possible. There is no reason for us to have a phobia about the word 'truth'. *(Meehl 1986:322)*

Meehl observes that labelling is an uninteresting pursuit; it is

> pointless to argue about these matters and mentally unhealthy for a social scientist to get involved in the semantic hassle as to whether he [*sic*] is engaged in science or not. It would be desirable to strike that question (perhaps even the very term 'science') from the methodological vocabulary. . . . In addition to being hygienic, this would conduce to greater intellectual honesty because it would force us, instead of warding off semantic attacks by administrators or skeptical intellectual laymen [*sic*] with an antiscience bias, simply to ask the question, 'To what extent does this discipline contain knowledge that brings some sort of credentials with it?' Whether there is any kind of credentialed knowledge that is not, in some carefully specified sense, 'scientific' knowledge is an interesting philosophical query. *(Ibid.: 317)*

When I embarked on a randomised controlled trial of social support and pregnancy in 1985, it was with all the zeal of a Columbus discovering America by accident, and it was certainly with the purpose of trying to put into practice some of the recommendations about integrating 'qualitative' and 'quantitative'/experimental methods that I arrive at (by a different route) at the end of this book. My intention was also to address the problem that many trials in medicine were done without proper attention to the rights of the people who took part in them, an issue that is developed at greater length in chapter 11. By the early 1990s I had also started another programme of work, establishing a database of social interventions, which was intended to parallel the efforts of health scientists to learn cumulatively from the multiplicity of experiments that have been done, but many of which are likely to be unknown to the next person who does one. I and my colleagues began to do a series of systematic reviews which looked at how a variety of social interventions in the health promotion field had been evaluated – sex education for young people, social interventions for populations at risk of contracting HIV/AIDS, accident prevention for older people, health promotion initiatives in the work-place, and anti-smoking interventions for young people (Oakley et al. 1995a, 1995b, 1996;

Oakley and Fullerton 1995; Peersman et al. 1998). In all these reviews we were shocked to discover how often on the basis of scanty or non-existent evidence reputable researchers argued that something works.

Publishing the results of such 'quantitative' and experimental work has gained me another kind of reputation – what the informants in one case-study call 'this Oakleyesque view' of 'gold-standard-copper-bottomed-man-in-a-white-coat-randomised-control-trial evaluations' (Bonell 1999:216, 223).[7] In this new representation, I have become the quantitative tyrant, the missionary of logical positivism, the uncompromising advocate of an impossible and inappropriate way of knowing. Most importantly, I am seen as having deserted the 'qualitative' camp – or, at least, of having suffered a temporary loss of consciousness. This is how Julia Brannen (1992:25) puts it:

> A current example of a qualitative researcher turning her hand to quantitative research is provided by Oakley who was previously rooted in the qualitative tradition. The project was a large scale quantitative investigation of the effects of social support on low birth weight . . . However since the research was also concerned with the evaluation of support and an exploration of the nature of support it included a qualitative component.

The stereotyping of methodological positions which goes on is also well illustrated by a recent interview in the *Journal of Contemporary Health* (Leavey 1997), where the interviewer's questioning relentlessly tried to make me agree that highlighting 'qualitative' methods remains the leading priority. In a seminar I gave during my stay in Sweden, at the Department of Sociology in Uppsala, the two positions were used to turn me into a literally split personality, as the commentator on my talk desperately produced evidence from my previous writings of 'the old Oakley' (a persona she much preferred), which she then contrasted with 'the new Oakley' (asking me to account for the difference).

In my own view, feminism is as much a part of the 'new' Oakley as the 'old' one, and so is the belief in ways of knowing that allow the voices of research participants to be heard above the (generally) louder noise of the researcher's own. Self-labelling as a feminist means only that one declares one's values, whereas the dominant tradition is not to do so. If all those whose work demonstrates (albeit unconsciously) a masculine perspective had to declare themselves 'masculinists', the world would be a very different place. As regards ways of knowing, I have never advocated 'qualitative' to the exclusion of 'quantitative' work, or the other way around, and I certainly do not do so now. The goal – and here I anticipate chapters 12 and 13 – is a democratization of ways of knowing (along the lines originally settled by feminist social scientists), and also a synthesis of these, so that the focus is on choosing the right method for the research question. I believe there are particularly urgent issues for feminist social scientists and for social scientists and social policy analysts generally about including well-designed prospective experimental studies as part of what is considered to be the legitimate tool-kit of students of the social world. The evidence of the 'buried' history of social experimentation contained in chapters 8, 9 and 10 offers a particularly cogent case for considering how experimental ways of knowing could be used more often and to greater effect.

Conclusion, and preface to the rest of the book

In a recent paper on the study of women and the construction of knowing, Patrizia Romito (1997) observes that 'gender analysis' is an essential condition for creating epistemological breaks with 'commonsense knowledge'. She makes this observation in relation to the shifting of the ground that has taken place over the last twenty-five years in reconceptualizing women's work as hard labour, in showing how cultural ambivalences about pregnancy have informed and distorted the medical treatment of child-bearing women, and in making it plain that there is no natural bond which yokes women to motherhood. A similar epistemological process has gone into the making of this book. Breaking with prejudices and reconstructing the object of research requires a different way of seeing, in the light of which common-sense knowledge is reconstructed as a form of bias. My argument that current disputes about ways of knowing are about very much more than technical issues concerning the best methods for tackling particular research questions can only be made once the sense of the 'quantitative'/'qualitative' divide has itself been fractured. Reframing this as an ideological representation enables us to see beneath the surface to what else is going on. The part gender plays in this is crucial, both as a tool for disturbing common-sense understandings and as a concept for systematizing the interwoven social processes which make up the history of 'experiments in knowing'.

2

Paradigm Wars

Is there anything more to be said about the paradigm wars? . . . What one sees is a musty stale-mate over first principles . . . experimentalists still manipulate and control, realists prefer to muse on causal configurations, constructivists choose empathy and negotiation, auditors balance costs with benefits, post-modernists lounge playfully in linguistic ellipses . . .

> Pawson and Tilley, 'Caring communities, paradigm polemics, design debates'

In addition, there appears to be a connection between gender and style of knowing.

> Reinharz, *On Becoming a Social Scientist*

This book argues that taking today's methodological quarrels at face value oversimplifies their significance. If we study their history, we can see that they are not merely competing and adjudicable claims about the best way to know, but something a good deal more than this. This chapter takes a closer look at paradigm arguments. It tracks the origins of the modern attack on 'quantitative' and experimental ways of knowing, and pays special attention to feminist positions on methodology which have valorized the 'qualitative' above the 'quantitative', but have by no means been alone in doing so. In health promotion, an apparently disparate field, very similar arguments are put about the inapplicability of experimental methods to the social domain. This points to the wider gendering of methodology itself as a fundamental, but covert, feature of paradigm warfare.

The warfare proceeds on a number of levels. Researchers presenting the results of their research often feel it necessary to claim their adherence to one or other camp as part of establishing their academic and political credentials. The methods textbooks are less didactic, but prone to follow the same distinction (see e.g. Blaikie 1993; Coole 1976; Creswell 1994). At the level of applications for research funding, proponents of 'quantitative' and 'qualitative' methods

frequently do not feel themselves to be on equal ground; insinuating dichotomies abound, with 'qualitative' researchers in the position of poor cousins,
accused of being 'unscientific' and 'anecdotal' (Green and Britten 1998; F.
Baum 1993). Especially in health services research, it is the contribution of
'qualitative' methods which needs to be drawn to people's attention (see Chard
et al. 1997; Popay and Williams 1998). A form circulated to peer reviewers for
the National Health Service Research and Development programme in the
UK invites reviewers to align themselves with one of two checklists of 'quantitative' and 'qualitative' methods;[1] significantly, familiarity with one sort of
method is assumed to rule out knowledge of the other.

Conflict between paradigms is also evident in different academic and practice fields; in the (mainly American) literature on evaluation; in discussions
about the relevance of evidence-based approaches to social interventions; in
domains which border on medicine, such as nursing and health promotion;
and last, but definitely not least, in the sizable literature produced since the
late 1960s on the possibility of a feminist social science. While there are accounts addressing the problem of competing paradigms *within* each of these
fields, few links have been made *between* them. For example, nurse-research-
ers' defence of qualitative methods has rarely been attached to the feminist
argument about the political 'oppressiveness' of quantification; what health
promotion practitioners say about the difficulty of using experimental methods
makes virtually no reference to the reaction against these described in the
American literature on evaluation over the last twenty years (or to the considerable record of their successful use – see chapters 8 and 9); the discussion of
how important 'lay' views ought to be in the 'new' public health and the
consequent call for 'qualitative' methods neglect the prominence that feminist
social researchers gave to exactly the same issues some years ago; and researchers in social welfare, education, criminology and health promotion are all
prone individually to argue against systematic experimentation in apparent
ignorance that others are also doing so in very similar terms.

Why *do* people argue about paradigms? What do today's paradigm wars tell
us about the methodological legacy we have inherited from the past – why
these sorts of arguments *appear to make sense* in the first place?

Of paradigms, and all who sail in them

Table 2.1 brings together a number of attempts to describe characteristics of
the two methodological paradigms. There are twenty-four attributes in the
table, which considerably exceeds the number given in individual lists.[2] The
labels for the two paradigms at the top of the table – '(logical) positivist'/
'scientific'/'quantitative' versus 'naturalist'/'interpretivist'/'qualitative' – reflect
the descriptions that most often appear in the literature. 'Empiricism',
'enumerative induction', 'rationalistic', 'functionalist', 'objectivist', a 'natural
science'/ 'medical'/ 'biomedical' 'model', and (most recently) 'foundationalist'
are other terms applied to one side of the divide; while 'analytic induction',

'constructivist', 'ethnographic' and 'subjectivist' also feature on the other (F. Baum 1993; Brannen 1992:5; Bryman 1992; Davies and Macdonald 1998b; Guba 1990; Hammersley 1995; Hoshmand 1989; Manicas 1987; Stanley and Wise 1993).

Reading through the table, one can be fairly persuaded that what we have here are two contrasting accounts of how it is that people 'know'. While researchers in one camp think they are studying the real world, which consists of things it is feasible to try to find out about, those in the other dispute the idea that there is a single reality to be known, and regard the pursuit of 'hard data' as impractical and unachievable. What for one side is a set of 'facts' is for the other a complex and impenetrable kaleidoscope of heavily constructed social meanings. Researchers in one paradigm leap in with all the faith derived from (something called) logical positivism that they will (providing they specify and measure and count enough) indeed be able to establish the truth; whereas their counterparts in the other paradigm walk much more lightly, aware of the constantly shifting ground of human social interaction and identity, and doggedly bound to the apparently more modest goal of reproducing faithfully and democratically whatever it is they think they may have found.

The following parable told by Ernest Gellner some years ago sums up one way of framing the disagreement:

> A quarter of a century or so ago there was a well-known eccentric who used to accost passers-by on Prince's Street and ask them – are you sane? If any replied Yes, he would retort – ah, but can you *prove* it? And, as they could not, he proceeded triumphantly to show them that *he* at any rate could prove his sanity, by producing his own certificate of discharge from a mental hospital. *(Gellner 1979:41)*

How *does* one judge the sanity of different sorts of evidence? In a bureaucratic and literate culture, what is written down in documentary records (the certificate of discharge from the mental hospital) may seem more trustworthy than people's own labelling of themselves, but of course questions need to be asked about what such 'facts' signify.

The term 'paradigm' became fashionable following the widely-read work of Thomas Kuhn on how science and scientific revolutions happen. As a graduate student in theoretical physics in the 1940s, Kuhn's chance contact with a history of science course exposed a gulf between the representation and the experience of science as it is actually done. Later on he was struck by the way in which sociologists openly argued about legitimate ways of studying problems (the paradigm war before it got named as such). His conviction that 'natural' scientists did not possess any firmer answer to the questions that were bothering sociologists led him to devise the notion of 'paradigms' as 'universally recognized scientific achievements that for a time provide model problems and solutions to a community of practitioners' (Kuhn 1962:x).

Kuhn was writing about science, not about social science, which he saw (partly under the influence of the early methodological arguments he heard)

Table 2.1   The warring paradigms

	'(logical) positivist', 'scientific', 'quantitative', 'positivism'	'naturalist', 'interpretivist', 'qualitative'
Aims	Testing hypotheses/ generalizing	Generating hypotheses/ describing
Purpose	Verification	Discovery
Approach	Top-down	Bottom-up
Preferred technique	Quantitative	Qualitative
Research strategy	Structured	Unstructured
Stance	Reductionist/inferential/ hypothetico-deductive/ outcome-oriented/ exclusively rational/ oriented to prediction and control	Expansionist/exploratory/ inductive/process-oriented/ rational and intuitive/ oriented to understanding
Method	Counting/obtrusive and controlled measurement (surveys, experiments, case-control studies, statistical records, structured observations, content analysis)	Observing (participant observation, in-depth interviewing, action research, case-studies, life history methods, focus groups)
Implementation of method	Decided a priori	Decided in field setting
Values	Value-free	Value-bound
Instrument	Physical device/pencil and paper	The researcher
Researcher's stance	Outsider	Insider
Relationship of researcher and 'subject'	Distant/independent	Close/interactive and inseparable
Setting	'Laboratory'	'Nature'
Data	Hard, reliable, replicable	Rich, deep, valid
Data type	Reports of attitudes and actions	Feeling, behaviour, thoughts, actions as experienced or witnessed
Data analysis	Specified in advance	Worked out during the study
Analytic units	Predefined variables	Patterns and natural events

Table 2.1 *cont'd.*

	'(logical) positivist', 'scientific', 'quantitative', 'positivism'	*'naturalist', 'interpretivist', 'qualitative'*
Quality criterion	Rigour/proof/evidence/ statistical significance	Relevance/plausibility/ illustrativeness/ responsiveness to subjects' experiences
Source of theory	A priori	Grounded
Relationship between theory and research	Confirmation	Emergent
Causal links	Real causes exist	Causes and effects cannot be distinguished
Nature of truth statements	Time- and context-free generalizations are possible	Only time- and context-bound working hypotheses are possible
Image of reality	Singular/tangible/ fragmentable/static/ external	Multiple/holistic/dynamic/ socially constructed
Research product	Stresses validity of research findings for scholarly community	Stresses meaningfulness of research findings to both scholarly and user communities

Sources: Bryman 1988:84; Guba and Lincoln 1981:57, 65; Lincoln and Guba 1985:37; Reichardt and Cook 1979:10; Reinharz 1984:11–15; W. A. Silverman 1985:138; Tones 1996:6.

as intrinsically 'pre-paradigmatic'. But this did not stop social scientists from enthusiastically taking up his idea of paradigms, whilst not being totally clear what they were. Indeed, Kuhn himself apparently used the term in twenty-one different ways.[3] In his later reflections on the original text, Kuhn gave primacy to the 'sociological' meaning of paradigm: paradigms are sets of standards to which practitioners can always refer: habits, puzzle-solving devices and ways of seeing: 'what the members of a scientific community share, *and*, conversely, a scientific community consists of men [sic] who share a paradigm' (Kuhn 1996:176). This reversal of the order is important: for paradigms are not only produced from the *doing* of scientific work, they also play a key role in *providing* covert reference points; paradigms bind people together in a shared commitment to their discipline. In Michael Patton's definition, 'paradigms are deeply embedded in the socialization of adherents and practitioners; paradigms tell them what is important, legitimate, and reasonable. Paradigms are also normative, *telling the practitioner what to do'* (Patton 1978:203; italics added).

One danger of calling research methods 'paradigms' and setting them firmly in opposite camps is that reasonable disagreements tend to sharpen in 'hard-and-fast and mutually exclusive alternatives' (Bulmer 1986:186). Much of the methodological literature does, indeed, assume that the two paradigms represent mutually antagonistic ideal-types. As George Lundberg, the American social scientist who defended 'quantitative' methods in the 1930s, observed, 'Sociologists at present dissipate a great deal of energy in dramatic attacks upon stereotypes, the contents of which are at best badly understood and at worst purely imaginary' (Lundberg 1933:298). But most of the designations that appear in one column of table 2.1 can be found in the other when actual instances of research are examined. For example, 'qualitative' researchers make considerable use of quantification, if not actually by enumerating, then by using terms such as 'most', 'all', 'some', 'frequently' and so on. Lundberg drove this point home neatly when he took issue with Znaniecki, the 'qualitative' author of *The Polish Peasant*, and defender of non-statistical sociology:

> The current idea seems to be that if one uses pencil and paper, especially squared paper, and if one uses numerical symbols, especially Arabic notation, one is using quantitative methods. If, however, one discusses masses of data with concepts of 'more' and 'less' instead of formal numbers, and if one indulges in the most complicated correlations but without algebraic symbols, then one is not using quantitative methods. *(Lundberg 1964:59–60)*

The terms 'experimental' and 'quantitative', although linked on an ideological level, are often taken to mean the same thing, and both are conflated with others, such as 'statistical' and 'mathematical'. But, as Meehl has argued:

> One can proceed experimentally without being quantitative; one can be quantitative in the sense of statistical counts without having a mathematical model for the causal structure underlying the processes; one could be highly quantitative, both in the sense of statistics of observations and in the sense of the postulated causal model being formalized in differential equations, and not be capable of experimenting at all, as in astronomy. Even worse is the conflation of the word 'empirical' to mean 'experimental and quantitative', a tendentious mistake that begins by failing to look up the word in Webster. *(Meehl 1986:317; on 'empirical', see Brewin 1994)*

'Quantitative' research can study feelings and emotions, and structured questionnaires and surveys can be so written that they encourage detailed accounts of people's experiences. As Cathy Marsh (1984:94) has observed, 'reducing' such data through coding 'is doing no more than describing it, making the rules of description in this manner as explicit as possible', and variables constructed through coding rules need to be interpreted theoretically before they can be useful. The 'obtrusive' nature of 'positivist' research is not necessarily replaced by the 'unobtrusive' character of in-depth interviewing. Controlled experimental studies may include attention to processes and collect 'qualitative' data from research participants (see below, chapter 9; Oakley 1992b; Peersman et al. 1998); there is even a tradition of 'N-of-1' trials in which the point at issue is not about generalizing from a large quantity of 'subjects', but how *an individual* reacts to different treatment strategies (Guyatt et al. 1986; Mahon et al. 1995).[4]

But pointing out the ways in which the actual practices of research defy the neatly opposing descriptors of 'quantitative' and 'qualitative' is not really what the war is about. The lists of qualities in table 2.1 signify not so much a disagreement about techniques, as 'essentially divergent clusters of epidemiological assumptions' (Bryman 1988:5). It is on the level of theories about what knowledge is – ways of framing both knowledge and the means of obtaining it, and how knowers are seen in relation to what is known – that adherents of the two paradigms face each other with such a determined lack of comprehension.

The sources from which the descriptions in table 2.1 are taken include a sociological analysis of the 'quantitative'/ 'qualitative' divide (Bryman 1988); a defence of 'qualitative' sociology (W. A. Silverman 1985); a feminist autobiographical account of research methods (Reinharz 1984); a discussion of health promotion research (Tones 1996); and three texts from the American evaluation literature (Guba and Lincoln 1981; Lincoln and Guba 1985; Reichardt and Cook 1979), two of these by evaluators who have progressively argued for a greater attention within the evaluation industry to 'qualitative' methods. One of the most striking features of some of these accounts, and of much of the relevant literature, is the defence of 'qualitative' methods against what are perceived to be the excesses of the other side. The two sides in the paradigm war do not have equal strength. 'Quantitative' methodologists much less commonly defend what they do.[5] This may be because they feel sufficiently secure not to bother, and this, in turn, may be taken as an indication of how quantification remains the more powerful tradition (Krug and Hepworth 1997). John Seidel, who invented the Ethnograph computer software program for analysing qualitative data, observed that although his program only did more quickly what had previously been done with 'pen, paper, cards and scissors and large amounts of floor space', none the less, using the computer gave him enhanced credibility with his quantitative colleagues (Qureshi 1992:101).

So why is the 'qualitative' paradigm the underdog, the alternative, the querulous voice trying to make itself heard?

Positivism as a form of abuse

Many anti-quantitative versions of the paradigm war give a good deal of attention to positivism (so-called), which comes in for much attack. In a defence of the life history approach to social science, Daniel Bertaux (1981:30) put it like this: 'I understood . . . that the scientificity of sociology is a *myth*. If there is such a thing as sociological *knowledge*, the way to reach it is not through quantitative methodology. And the main obstacle towards it is precisely the belief in sociology as a *science*. In a word: *positivism*.' Bertaux does not define positivism. Indeed, references to it (italicized in all the quotations below) are usually startling for their vagueness. Health promotion has many examples:

> . . . the health promotion movement has tended to be preoccupied with a search for indicators. This search too readily invites a recapitulation of essentially *positivist* logics. *(Stevenson and Burke 1991:283)*

> The biomedical model perceives health in an individual reductionist way. . . . Using the credibility of the medico-scientific paradigm it perceives effectiveness and quality only in *positivist* and empiricist terms *(Davies and Macdonald 1998a:209)*

> The biomedical model is firmly within a *positivist* paradigm. It is based on the belief that phenomena can be reduced to their constituent parts. *(F. Baum 1993:9)*

So too does feminist social science:

> *Positivism* describes social reality as objectively constituted, and so accepts that there is one 'true' reality. . . . *Positivism* sees what is studied as an 'object'. . . . Both as feminists and as social scientists we find each of these aspects of *positivism* objectionable. *(Stanley and Wise 1983:113)*

> I was still trying to work within an 'a priori' *positivist* structure of validation and categorization, and subconsciously fitting the data into a neat theoretical framework of patriarchy and power. *(Parr 1998:97)*

> A corollary of the reflexivity of feminist and other critical theory is that it requires a much broader construal than *positivism* accepts of the process of theoretical investigation. *(Jaggar 1983:148)*

> . . . *positivist* science is based on the tenet of value-free objectivity. . . . This contrasts sharply with the ways feminist research has been described. *(Wolf 1996:4)*

Phillips (1992:95) sums up the way in which positivism is often referred to:

> Nowadays the term 'positivist' is widely used as a generalized term of abuse. As a literal designator it has ceased to have any useful function – those philosophers to whom the term accurately applies have long since shuffled off this mortal coil, while any living social scientists who either bandy the term around, or are the recipients of it as an abusive label, are so confused about what it means that, while the word is full of sound and fury, it signifies nothing.
> The anti-positivist vigilantes, who realize nothing of this, still claim to see positivists everywhere. . . . The general fantasy is that anyone who is impressed by the sciences as a pinnacle or achievement of human knowledge, anyone who uses statistics or numerical data, anyone who believes that hypotheses need to be substantially warranted, anyone who is a realist (another unanalyzed but clearly derogatory word) is thereby a positivist.

However you look at it, positivism is the work of the devil. Almost no one is willing to call themselves a positivist.[6] Rather like the term 'paradigm', it matters little how 'positivism' is actually defined. Multiple usages of this term – at least twelve – have also been identified. As Halfpenny (1982:11) has observed, anti-positivists use the term with sets of meanings ('loosely and indiscriminately to describe all sorts of disfavoured forms of inquiry') which are different from the meanings implied by those who call themselves positivists, among whom there are further differences, according to positivism's intellectual history. Positivism's many usages embody five main themes: the belief that how scientists know is also how social scientists know; that only observable things can be included in valid knowledge; that theory is a compendium of empirically established facts; that knowledge is formed deductively by extracting specific propositions from general accounts; and that the act of trying to know ought to be carried out in such a way that the knower's own value position is removed from the process (Bryman 1988:14–15).

When did the war start?

In his *Quantity and Quality in Social Research* Alan Bryman notes (1988:3) that it is difficult to say exactly when the modern paradigm war first took off. George Lundberg's words quoted earlier suggest that it has been going on in some form or other for some time. The first quote at the head of this chapter comes from a paper published by two anti-experimental social scientists in 1998, and what it conveys is a sense of weariness about the longevity of the argument.

Although the main orientation of early social science was, as we shall see, 'quantitative', Weber (1947a) gave a cogent account of the importance of 'verstehen' – of subjective meaning and interpretive understanding – although this does not mean that his work was free from a concern with hierarchy and domination (see Bologh 1990).[7] Alfred Schutz published his *The Phenomenology of the Social World* in 1932. The work of Herbert Blumer and others at Chicago in the 1920s and 1930s had established a unique tradition of 'qualitative' research (see Hammersley 1989), which provided a fertile ground for disputes with those who espoused more traditional 'scientific' approaches to knowledge-gathering.

But, apart from the American arguments, there was little sign of the paradigm war in the general methodological and professional literature before the 1960s. It was after that time that groups of social scientists seemed to develop a special sensitivity to the charge that the methodology of social science was, or should be, modelled on that of natural science. Why did the 'qualitative' paradigm only really emerge then? Part of the explanation is the radical critique of science, which challenged the impact of its growth, along with that of technology and commercialization, on intellectual and artistic values. A key point was that the equation of science with knowledge made any critique of science itself impossible (how could one know anything that lay outside knowledge) (see Rose and Rose 1976)?

Such critiques of science placed a good deal of emphasis on science's social relations as following a logic of domination-subordination which effectively hid, or distorted, the experiences of the 'oppressed'. This point echoed emerging perspectives in social science which took similar issue with quantification and its effects in closing off from view not only the experiences of 'ordinary' people, but what these could tell social scientists about the way in which society itself was constructed. Rival factions developed in social science around the issue of how society as the subject of social science should be conceptualized; on one side were the structuralists, the functionalists and the Marxists, and on the other, the interactionists, phenomenologists and ethnomethodologists. Cicourel's *Method and Measurement in Sociology* questioned 'the mathematical and measurement systems currently used in social research', using the term 'quantofrenia' in 1964 (Cicourel 1964:2). Glaser and Strauss's 1967 manual *The Discovery of Grounded Theory* was a key text, tying the fascinating but drowning minutiae of 'qualitative' data to the respectable scientific task of generating theory (and in the process giving thousands of 'qualitative' researchers a promising new piece of methodological jargon – grounded theory – to use in their doctoral theses and research grant applications).[8] Garfinkel's invention, in 1967, of the term 'ethnomethodology' to describe a focus on the way in which people make the social world sensible to or for themselves, was another key event.[9] These texts were followed by a spate of books on qualitative methods (see e.g. Fletcher 1974; Lofland 1971; Schatzman and Strauss 1973).

Bryman suggests that one reason for the emergence of the 'qualitative' paradigm was widespread dissatisfaction with the products of the 'quantitative' one. This response is certainly detectable in the American evaluation literature, though in that case it happened later, in the late 1970s and early 1980s, and was very much part of that society's attempt to use systematic experimentation in the social field on a grand scale (see chapter 10). But in both the UK and the USA, the paradigm war was hugely energized by the arrival in the late 1960s of feminism as a social movement which infiltrated academia and also had a great deal to say about methodology.

Women and the three p's

The 'second wave' of the women's movement was born in the mid-1960s in the USA out of the radicalism of the civil rights, student and peace movements; rumours of an emerging women's movement first reached the UK in 1967. The first feminist social science texts appeared in the early 1970s. It was immediately apparent that one of the things feminist social scientists wanted to take issue with was the domination of men in the academy; this was a matter of statistics – there were (and are) far more men in senior positions – but it was also a matter of the way in which men's perspectives took precedence over women's in shaping academic subject-matter and ways of knowing. The statistical dominance of men and the use of 'quantitative' methods may not have been *intrinsically* related; but they were seen to coexist in a (more or less) unconscious conspiratorial alliance. Moreover, it was clear that 'quantitative' methods were often used in such a way that women's experiences and voices were absent; women were not included in research samples at all, or the questions asked were inappropriate to women's lives, or the information women gave was downgraded in an effort to produce research findings which fitted with men's lives; or other aspects of a 'quantitative' methodology subtly (or not so subtly) distorted social experience by forcing it into artificial, 'man-made' categories (Bowles and Duelli Klein 1983; Sherman and Beck 1979; Stanley and Wise 1983).

Methodology featured as one of six thematic critiques in Millman and Kanter's *Another Voice: feminist perspectives on social life and social science* (1975a), one of the first collections of feminist critiques. 'Certain methodologies (frequently quantitative) and research situations (such as having male social scientists studying worlds involving women)', Millman and Kanter ventured, 'may systematically prevent the elicitation of certain kinds of information, yet this undiscovered information may be the most important for explaining the phenomenon being studied' (p. xv). Dale Spender's *Men's Studies Modified* (1981) contained chapters called 'The oldest, the most established, the most quantitative of the social sciences – and the most dominated by men: the impact of feminism on economics' and 'Dirty fingers, grime and slap heaps: purity and the scientific ethic'. *Theories of Women's Studies* (1983), edited by Gloria Bowles and Renate Duelli Klein, devoted six of its fifteen chapters to methodological themes. Duelli Klein (1983) talked about 'paradigms' for feminist research, arguing for a methodology 'that allows for women studying women in an interactive process without the artificial object/subject split between researcher and researched (which is by definition inherent in any approach to knowledge that praises its "neutrality" and "objectivity")'. DuBois (1983) introduced the notion of 'passionate scholarship'. Mies (1983:120–1) argued that following 'the decisive methodological postulate of positivist social science research' drives women mad by forcing them to repress their own experiences of sexism.

Arguments against the 'quantitative' paradigm quickly became an established part of the feminist 'case'. These were accompanied by texts celebrating the alternative 'qualitative' paradigm (see e.g. Bowles and Duelli Klein 1983; H. Roberts 1981; Stanley and Wise 1983). It soon became obvious that being a good feminist meant using 'qualitative' methods, and apologizing if, for one reason or another, one lapsed into 'quantitative' ones. Most significantly, feminist scholarship highlighted the way in which many other dualistic forms of thinking, seeing and knowing paralleled the 'quantitative–qualitative' 'divide': some of these are listed in table 2.2.

These dualisms designate far more profound cultural processes than scientists' and academics' mere accounts of research methods, of course. They stand as indicators of precisely those systematic relationships between socioeconomic structures and forms of thought that have traditionally defined some

Table 2.2 Significant dualisms

Hard	Soft
Masculine	Feminine
Public	Private
Rational	Intuitive
Intellect	Emotion
Scientific	Artistic
Social	Natural
Control	Understanding
Experiment	Observation
Objective	Subjective
Separation	Fusion
Repression	Expression
Autonomy	Dependence
Voice	Silence

groups as powerless and excluded them from the social mainstream (Bakan 1966; Zaretsky 1976). Their cumulative effect, so far as women are concerned, has been to privilege male experiences and standpoints and to constitute women, as Simone de Beauvoir had said considerably earlier, as 'the Other'.

The feminist critique contested the 'quantitative' paradigm on a number of specific grounds, including that it often implicitly supports sexist values; its data are superficial and overgeneralized; it is unable to capture 'subjective'[10] meaning; relations between researcher and researched are intrinsically exploitative; and quantitative research is not used to overcome social problems. At points this case tends to merge with that against mainstream/'malestream' social science generally (see e.g. Eichler 1988). But it also levels three specific charges against 'quantitative' research: the case against *positivism*, referred to above; the case against *power*; and the case against *p values*, or the use of statistical techniques as a means of asserting the validity of research findings.

Positive fictions

The most extreme forms of feminist anti-positivism settled on 'objectivity' as a synonym. 'Objectivity' calls up other terms: 'object', 'objectification', and 'objectionable', suggesting that treating people as objects of research is an objectionable habit resulting in inevitable feelings of objectification (see Haslanger 1993). In some of these discourses, the difference between 'fact' and 'fiction' even disappeared completely, so that 'truth' and 'objectivity' became the same thing as 'lies' and 'subjectivity'; the loop was then neatly closed by redefining 'objectivity' as 'male subjectivity' (Stanley and Wise

1983; Caplan 1988). It was argued that objectivity in research methodology was nothing more or less than 'an excuse for a power relationship every bit as obscene as the power relationship that leads women to be sexually assaulted, murdered, and otherwise treated as mere objects' (Stanley and Wise 1983:169).

Liz Stanley and Sue Wise's *Breaking Out* had its origin in their experience of receiving hundreds of obscene telephone calls from men when their telephone number was advertised, during the 1970s, as the contact for a lesbian group. The book's starting-point was personal experience as research data, and it contended, among many other things, that feminist social scientists needed to break down the artificial divide between 'research' and 'life'. *Breaking Out* was published, as Stanley and Wise discuss in a later edition (1993), at a particular historical moment when academic feminism was struggling to make its voice heard. In its concern to establish and contest masculine bias in the academy, feminism was in danger of putting over the traditional masculine view of the researched as objects, and of using positivist methods to assert the subjection of women. Can one use the master's tools to knock down (and then rebuild) 'his' house?

In their revised text ten years on, Stanley and Wise adopt a position they call 'fractured foundationalism'. By this they mean that they consider there to be a social reality, 'which members of society construct as having objective existence above and beyond competing constructions and interpretations of it' (Stanley and Wise 1993:9). The fractures in the foundationalism are the result of a 'feminist ontology' which is concerned with 'rejecting Cartesian binary ways of understanding the relationship between the body, the mind and emotions'. Stanley and Wise continue:

> The 'masculinist' ontology associated with Cartesian dualisms and foundationalism sees all of reality as characterized by two opposing principles, those of masculinity and femininity (or rather maleness and femaleness) and their working out through science and nature, reason and emotion, objectivity and subjectivity and so on; the very grounds of reality are presupposed in binary and gendered terms. And these opposing principles are seen as both symbiotically related and necessary to each other *and* as existing in relations of super- and subordination, with the feminine supportive of the masculine. *(Stanley and Wise 1993:194)*

Feminist perspectives on reality and research practice call for a repudiation, on political grounds, of such forms of thought. Supporting the rationale for the rejection of foundationalism/positivism is the association between it and 'the scientific method', which is to be condemned on political grounds. Science props up 'the fantasy of a calculable universe where everything operates according to quantifiable laws', a fantasy which is 'central to the calculating project of bourgeois democracy and the strategies of global domination' (Walkerdine 1989:208). Or as Hilary Rose puts it in her *Love, Power and Knowledge* (1994:3–4), existing science and technology are 'locked into the contemporary forms of capitalism and imperialism as systems of domination'; and it is the frightening intimacy of this relationship which produces the feminist denunciation of science and technology 'as monolithically and irretrievably male'.

The power of knowing

When social science imitates natural science, the resulting delusion is that the barriers between researcher and researched keep researchers 'safe from involvement or risk' (Reinharz 1984:368). Involvement and risk are the other side of bias; what from within the 'quantitative' paradigm are seen as safeguards against the imposition on research data of the researchers' own viewpoints, outside it become naive (even dangerous) disengagement. The idea of a world to be known about implies a knower; the knower is the expert, and the known are the objects of someone else's knowledge, rather than their own. This is where power comes in. The notion of expertise, intrinsic to the 'quantitative' model of how research is done, means a hierarchy of power relations; where there are the powerful, there are also the powerless. Feminism, by contrast, is democratic; all women (people) are equal. It follows that, when involved in research, feminist knowers must reject 'any mode of explanation which requires or sanctions the imposition upon the female subject [sic] of the theorist's own views' (Elshtain 1981:303).

This moral obligation lies at the heart of feminism: to treat others as one would oneself wish to be treated. Feminist research shares with feminism as a political movement the ideal of emancipation; academic research, social science, sociology should thus be *for* women, not *of* or *about* them (D. E. Smith 1979). Hierarchy in research produces invalid data; democratic relations, on the other hand, offer a guarantee of validity (see Acker et al. 1983). This emphasis on the need for equal relations in the research process got feminist social scientists into something of a tangle, which is explored in the next chapter. It eventually led to a *rapprochement* which did acknowledge the existence of a power differential between those who do research and those who participate in it, although a lasting effect on the technical language occurred here, as research 'subjects' came to be renamed research 'participants'.[11]

The sin of p values

As David Silverman put it in his *Qualitative Methodology and Sociology* (1985:138), 'Since the 1960s, a story has got about that no good sociologist should dirty his [sic] hands with numbers.' Whether the reaction of male sociologists followed the injunctions levelled by feminist ones against the corrupting effects of numbers, or the other way around, feminist social science certainly added its collective voice to other 'isms' and 'ologies' suggesting that there was more to life than numbers. While the feminist critique of the 'quantitative' paradigm accepts that 'qualitative' studies need to use some numbers for 'directional orientation', the weight of the argument is against numbers and statistics on the grounds that these tend, once again, to obscure 'subjective' meaning (see e.g. Leininger 1994). Feminist qualitative researchers argue that the p's they are interested in do not concern the probabilistic logic of statistical p values, but the value of people, and that the value of people is only to be understood by studying their experiences directly (Sidell 1993). The whole idea of enumeration and statistical tests does, however, carry an even greater ideological significance: their use is seen as a device for emphasizing masculinity, a 'machismo' activity in which the manipulation of variables creates artificially 'controlled' realities (J. Bernard 1973) in an 'unpleasantly exaggerated masculine style of control' (Millman and Kanter 1975b: xvi). 'Patriarchal' measurements are deemed 'artificial' and 'abstract' (S. Griffin 1980:107); the underlying drive of the quantitative method is an urge to predict and control linked to men's desire to dominate, to exert power over people and nature; ultimately, therefore, this way of knowing is simply a veritable 'exercise in masculinity' (McCormack 1981:3). One element here is the acculturation of women, which remains antithetical to mathematical literacy (Kramer and Lehman 1990). It is not so much that girls are brought up to be afraid of numbers, but that their schooling does not reward them as it does boys for mathematical achievement (Walden and Walkerdine 1981; Walkerdine 1989).

The rape of empiricist research

In her account of a journey through methods, the feminist social scientist Shulamit Reinharz used her own experience as a case-study to illustrate features of different research techniques, and particularly problems with 'quantitative' research.

After college, Reinharz took a research assistant post on a survey being carried out at Columbia's Bureau of Applied Social Research of the public education system in Washington, D.C. It was a large-budget study, with two rather distant project directors who displayed little involvement in the research question (or the research process); the part she was hired to work on was a study of teachers' attitudes conducted by means of self-administered questionnaires. Expecting a thorough training in survey research, Reinharz found herself instead treated as a 'Jane-of-all-trades' – clerk, secretary, coder, errand-girl, confidante, as well as junior researcher. Her questions about why the method had been chosen met with an uncomprehending rehearsal of the 'ritual of survey empiricism' with its 'virtue of strict adherence to scientific procedure' and its 'mechanical repetition': 'The questionnaire-construction procedure was as mechanized as the computer that analyzed the responses. . . . The study lacked organic qualities. It did not stem from an attempt to get the whole truth but rather from an attempt to extricate from people something that had the appearance of meaning' (Reinharz 1984:66, 71). Data were collected from teachers cajoled through a series of ritualized promises: filling in this questionnaire will help improve the school system, your opinions are important to us, your answers will be confidential. All this, felt Reinharz, added up to a 'rape model' of research: 'The researchers take, hit and run. They intrude into their subjects' [*sic*] privacy, disrupt their perceptions, utilize false pretences, manipulate the relationship, and give little or nothing in return' (Reinharz 1984:95). A final blow was that before the study was completed, the school board in Washington decided to implement a new educational policy without waiting for the research results.

Reinharz went on to work on a study involving participant observation of friendships between patients in mental hospitals. This promised more direct contact with research participants and more accountability to them. However, it proved at least as difficult in practice as the survey study, although in different ways: the problems were how to present the research in a meaningful way without giving the game away; how to resist 'going native' – over-identification with hospital staff; and how to study 'naturalistically' the interactions of 'inmates', given that these were tightly controlled by staff. Reinharz moved on from this to a team research project studying the impact on family life of intermittent terrorist bombardment in an Israeli town; here 'collaborative' research yielded its own tensions, as the different disciplines all fought for ownership of the project. It seemed from these experiences that 'qualitative' research was not such an obvious answer after all to the disadvantages of the 'quantitative' kind.

Experimenting on people

The feminist case

The apex of the feminist critique of quantitative methods is reached when we come to experimental studies. Here lies the *real* difference between natural and social science (DuBois 1983:107). Experiments are inherently 'objectifying' and alienating; the 'rigid control' and 'manipulation' of variables that happens in experiments is a 'male' and 'agentic' way of knowing which takes no account of the subjectivity of experience (in the 'good' sense of this term):

> . . . in the human *experiment* much of what goes on is simply ignored . . . the researcher has the illusion of creating history at the moment. *(Sherif 1987:45; emphasis added)*

> *Experiments* are designed to predict human behavior and to analyze it quantitatively. . . . The methodology produces explanations of personality and of social structure that take into account neither the consciousness of the subjects studied nor the meanings and interpretations of their experiences for these subjects. *(Code 1991:34; emphasis added)*

> It is the *experimental* sciences that . . . have been the major focus of feminist criticism of contemporary technoscience. *(H. Rose 1994:86; emphasis added)*

Reinharz argues that scientists who use experimental methods do so not principally because they are committed to minimizing bias in hypothesis-testing, but because they want to play out a 'fantasy of control over the other (the subject)' (Reinharz 1984:115). Significantly, the feminist anti-experimental critique fastens almost wholly on psychology and medicine as the repository of this method, ignoring altogether the tradition of social science experimentation.[12]

The most explicit discussion of experimentation occurs (unsurprisingly) in the context of work on feminist science. Here it is argued that 'the scientific or experimental method' converts reality into 'mathematical entities modeled on the physical universe', with all bodies, whether human or animal, being seen as machines (Donovan 1989:361). The gentler nature of the observational sciences is contrasted with the 'controlled violence' of the experimental ones (H. Rose 1994:88) – another version of Reinharz's 'rape' model. Feminist accounts of the origins of science have also pointed to the use of metaphors of rape and torture in extracting nature's secrets, nature, being female, is thereby aligned with women in a forcible complicity to the malignant experimental purposes of male scientists. In a famous passage, the feminist philosopher of science Sandra Harding once likened Newton's mechanics to 'a rape manual' because understanding nature as a woman who could (should) be raped was fundamental to the new conceptions of scientific inquiry which arose in the seventeenth century (Harding 1986:113).[13] Like 'quantitative' research methods, experimental science can be seen as constituting a 'super-masculinisation' of rational knowledge (Harding 1991); it reproduces the forms of masculine thought and behaviour simply because it is an essential expression of it (Haste 1993; Keller 1990).

Anti-trialists in health promotion

The identification of experimental methods as the most extreme and objectionable manifestation of the 'quantitative' paradigm is not restricted to feminist social science. In the health promotion and social science fields more generally, the attack is more tempered, but it is still prominent:

Scientific experiments demand rigorous conditions, standardization of environments and precision of procedure. For the evaluation of health promotion programmes working with communities, however, conditions such as these will not be present. *(Downie et al. 1996:92; emphasis added)*

Definitions of the type of evidence that is regarded to be of 'good' quality have been inherited from medical and scientific moves toward the *experimental* evaluation of clinical efficacy. This may not always be the most appropriate way of measuring the impact of health promotion. *(Meyrick and Swann 1998:8; emphasis added)*

... unlike much biomedical research where statistical and causal relations are often more readily unravelled by *experimental* techniques, social-survey based research interested in environmental, sociological and psychological variables related to lifestyles and behavioural changes are [sic] often more opaque, contingent and sometimes just simply impossible to relate to a causal view of the world. *(Burrows et al. 1995:243; emphasis added)*

In such fields as health promotion and health services research, the anti-experimental case achieves a particular refinement; the loose concept of 'experiment' is equated with the precise, but none the less highly emotively charged, term 'randomised controlled trial'. This is regarded as the absolute epitome of the 'biomedical, logical-positivist paradigm' (Macdonald and Davies 1998:9):

> The *randomized controlled trial* is often an inappropriate and potentially mislead-ing means of evaluating . . . health promotion initiatives. *(WHO European Work-ing Group on Health Promotion Evaluation 1998:11)*

> The difficulties with using the *randomised control* research design with health promotion activities are well rehearsed: it is very expensive; allocation of people to randomised groups . . . is difficult . . . The design works best with single factor interventions . . . and it raises ethical issues about informed consent. *(Learmonth and Watson 1997:9–10; reproduced by permission of the authors)*

All these assertions present testable options; we can look at where and how health promotion interventions have been evaluated and judge whether or not the assertions make sense or not.[14] But within health promotion the anti-experimental arguments have gone a good deal further than in the feminist critique; they have been taken into the more specialized realm of debates about whether RCTs represent a gold standard against which all other experimental and non-experimental designs must be found wanting.[15] This debate centres on the idea of evidence-based medicine that has taken root in some circles over the last 10 years, but is strongly resisted in others (see Carr-Hill 1995; Oakley 1998a; Pope and Mays 1993; see chapter 13).[16] In this context, opposition to experimental ways of knowing functions not only as an extension in *extremis* of the anti-quantitative argument, but as a more technical discourse about the relationship between different 'trustworthiness' criteria, forms of bias, and the credibility of evidence yielded by research. It is also bound up with another struggle, that between 'social science methods' and 'medical' ones on the par-ticularly contested terrain of health care research (see Meyer and Sandall 1997). Social scientists, seeing themselves as the defenders of a 'social' model of health and illness, insist that doctors need to listen to patients, and that this foregrounding of 'lay' views must necessarily undermine 'the dominance of quantitative and statistical methods' (Williams and Popay 1997:68).

The post -isms

Repudiating positivism, quantification and experimentation (however these terms are understood) as these critiques do, they insert something else in their place: a list of 'post -isms': post-positivism, post-structuralism, post-modernism – the terminology varies. What the terms are intended to describe can be somewhat difficult to get hold of, and the differences between them are mostly clear only to their special advocates. Like the terms they are intended to replace, the 'post -isms' call up a good deal of emotion: 'Reactions to the issues raised under the contentious signs of "postmodernity", "postmodernism" and the "postmodern" are rarely sober, measured or thoughtful' (Smart 1993:11–12). Their main referent is a world-view which specifies either that reality itself is dead or that there is simply too much of it to be grasped by any one attempt to know. What can be known rarely extends further than the solipsism of individual experience set in delimited social contexts; but this is not of much consequence, because the whole project of desiring to know in order to understand, predict, control and even change is doomed anyway. Post-modernism refers to the cultural transformations undergone by Western societies since the Second World War; these include the emergence of a global economy, the weakening of radical politics, a disenchantment with rationality as bringing about freedom, widespread optimism about technology, the promotion of 'popular culture', and a sense of the problematic relationship between language and what it is taken to mean. Social science itself can be viewed as part of the modernist project, which means that post-modernism brings in its wake an inevitable focus on the false journeys which the 'quantitative' paradigm induces us to take. In some readings, post-modernism even queries the project of sociology itself, for the social may in the end be no more real than anything else (Baudrillard 1988).

These links between the 'post -isms' and the status of knowledge and ways of knowing mean that it is hardly surprising to see the former quoted as reasons why the old ways no longer work. Health promotion, for example, can be seen as a 'late modernist' project, representing new forms of social mediation; in contrast to medicine, it is 'non-institutional; multi-sectoral; multi-disciplinary . . . and conducted only with the active participation of groups and social networks' (Burrows et al. 1995:242). Similar arguments, differently framed, are present in the feminist critique; indeed, feminism can be argued to be the 'quantum physics of postmodernism' (Lather 1988). As Mary Hawkesworth has explained it:

> Feminist postmodernism rejects the very possibility of *a* truth about reality. Feminist postmodernists use the 'situatedness' of each finite observer in a particular socio-political, historical context to challenge the plausibility of claims that any perspective on the world could escape partiality . . . feminist postmodernists advocate a profound skepticism regarding universal (or universalizing) claims about the existence, nature, and powers of reason . . . they urge instead the development of a commitment to plurality and the play of difference. *(Hawkesworth 1989:535–6)*

Gender, methodology and identity

The war between the paradigms goes on, despite the efforts of many to resolve it. Paradigms need sustaining communities to uphold them; without these, they wither and die. The paradigm of 'qualitative' methods can be seen as an organizing platform for disparate groups of social scientists who are opposed in different ways to 'positivist' research methods. Constructing such a paradigm injects their efforts to repudiate positivism with a sense of solidarity; this then becomes a shared campaign against something seen to have inescapably damaging consequences for what counts as knowledge. Such a campaign counters any threat of internal divisiveness, supports practitioner morale, and provides a ready-made technical language. In an exactly parallel way, one can see how the organization of feminist social science around the misogyny of 'quantitative' methods gave it a distinctive agenda around which to infiltrate the patriarchal academy.

The claims of both the health promotion movement and feminist social scientists preferentially to own the 'qualitative' paradigm can be seen as part of their own professionalizing agendas. Professionalization restricts scientific vision, leading to a resistance to paradigm change (Kreft and Brown 1998). Both feminism and health promotion operate in worlds of hegemony – patriarchy and medicine – which push them to extremes in an effort to make their voices heard. Similar arguments apply to nursing research, which, in embracing 'qualitative' methods, hopes to make a distinctive contribution to understanding health care problems which doctors will be forced to recognize. All three of these groups – nurses, health promotion practitioners/researchers and feminist social scientists – occupy socially marginalized positions. They are 'the Other'.

But the issue of professional identity is the most superficial of the two main conclusions to emerge from this chapter. The more fundamental one concerns the framing of the methodological dispute as an ideological representation. What we have in the contest between the paradigms is another form of the war between the sexes, or rather genders: the 'quantitative–qualitative' dichotomy functions chiefly as a gendered description of ways of knowing. The 'qualitative' is the soft, the unreliable, the feminine, the private – the world of 'subjective' experience. The 'quantitative' and the experimental are hard, reliable, masculine, public: they are about 'objectivity'. Gender here refers not only to men and women as social groups; it also functions as a more general metaphor for the powerful and the powerless. This is why 'qualitative' methods are advocated for research on/with many less powerful groups: women, children, the disabled, ethnic minorities, travellers, patients, homosexuals – all who are excluded from the mainstream of white, male, able-bodied culture.

Seen in this way, it is evident that we cannot expect the paradigm argument to make much sense on a practical, technical level. Although one may easily show that the two sorts of research methods are not 'really' opposed, that in practice many people use a mix of methods, and so on, as ideological representations, the paradigms have to be, and must remain, opposed. This, then, raises for us a most basic question: one about the material and ideological processes that have given rise to the gendering of ways of knowing. This chapter has also thrown up a lot of other intriguing and poorly answered questions: what is positivism, and where did it come from? What are Cartesian dualisms, and why do they matter? Why did social science in its beginnings imitate natural science? If natural science stands as an inappropriate model for social science, what will do instead? What is so suspect about enumeration? Why are experimental ways of knowing so often contested? Were they really invented by medicine? Is research (what kind of research?) really about control? How can we trust what we know, including what we know as a result of using 'qualitative' techniques? There are no easy answers, but asking the questions is a fascinating business: the business of the rest of this book. We begin by taking a closer look, in the next chapter, at the rhetoric and practices of 'qualitative' enquiry.

3

Hearing the Grass Grow

If we had a keen vision and feeling of all ordinary human life, it would be like hearing the grass grow and the squirrel's heart beat, and we should die of that roar which lies on the other side of silence.

Eliot, *Middlemarch*

To the professional positivist this seems like chaos. The voices and material lead the researchers in unpredictable, uncontrollable directions. This is indeed not a controlled experiment.

Okely, 'Thinking through fieldwork'

This chapter examines in more detail some central issues about the validity and reliability of 'qualitative' research. It picks up on some of the contentions of the case against 'quantitative' methods which were discussed in the previous chapter: is it true that a research method based on listening to the silent necessarily builds a more valid knowledge? How can we distinguish 'good' from 'bad' 'qualitative' research? What are the strengths and weaknesses of using limited, non-representative samples? Do multiple methods of data collection invariably help the search for valid research findings? Do 'qualitative' methods really dissolve power and preserve the privacy and integrity of research participants – are they really more 'ethical'?

The eye of the beholder

Antoine de Saint-Exupéry's classic work *The Little Prince* opens with an account of how as a child the author drew a picture of a boa constrictor digesting an elephant (figure 3.1). When he showed this to the adults in his social circle, they could only see a hat. But the young artist retained his flair for imagination as an adult, so that when he became a pilot and his plane broke down in the middle of the Sahara desert, and a little prince from asteroid B-612 appeared

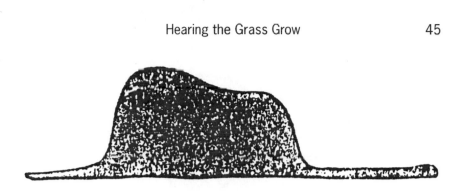

Figure 3.1   A boa constrictor digesting an elephant, or a hat.
From de Saint-Exupéry 1974:7, © Editions Gallimard.

and asked him to draw a sheep, he was not at all surprised. The little prince told him that asteroid B-612 had only once been seen through a telescope, by a Turkish astronomer in 1909. The astronomer had presented his finding to the International Astronomical Congress, but no one had believed him, because he was wearing Turkish costume at the time. When he repeated the presentation eleven years later minus the Turkish costume, it was well received.

Aside from being a classic of children's literature, the narrative of *The Little Prince* conveys two points about research rather well: first, that what is seen is shaped by the eye of the beholder; and second, that the credibility of research findings depends in part on the social standing of researchers. Figures 3.2 and 3.3 extend the point about the variability of perception: whose vision is the true one? The animal shown in figure 3.2 entered the epistemological literature via the reflections of Wittgenstein in his *Philosophical Investigations* (1997:194–5). The figure of 'duck-rabbit'[1] was used by Wittgenstein to convey the message that seeing and interpreting are different activities; that what people see is affected by what they already know about the underlying pattern. The figure appears quite unequivocally to be a duck until one's attention is drawn to the small indentation on the right which marks the rabbit's mouth. Now the duck's beak becomes the rabbit's ears. The third example, figure 3.3, is the well-known Müller–Lyer diagram. Most residents of a '"carpentered" culture' (Campbell 1988b:362) will say that the horizontal line in (a) is longer than the one in (b). But use of a ruler will reverse this perception, and (b) turns out to be longer than (a).

It could, of course, be argued that figures 3.1–3.3 *are* inherently ambiguous. It is reasonable to see a hat and a duck rather than a boa constrictor and a rabbit; the trick of vision that leads to line (a) seeming longer than line (b) would deceive most people. Other visual representations, such as photographs, offer a greater degree of verisimilitude by comparison. But this is not necessarily the case. In the early photographs of American Indians, for example, photographers clothed and posed their subjects according to how they thought Indians *ought* to

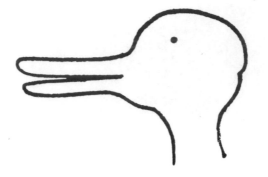

Figure 3.2   'Duck-rabbit'. From Wittgenstein 1997:194.
Reproduced by permission of Blackwell Publishers.

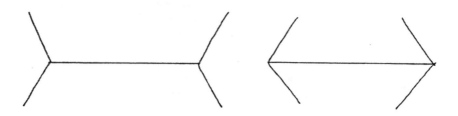

Figure 3.3   The Müller–Lyer diagram.
From D. T. Campbell 1988b:362. © 1988 by the University of Chicago. Reproduced by permission of the University of Chicago Press.

look (Scherer 1975; see also Becker 1979). Some degree of 'posing' is a feature of much modern photography. If we 'triangulated' (see below) the frequency of smiling suggested by photographs, on the one hand, with the conclusions of observational data, on the other, the two sets of results would probably be considerably out of line with one another: people smile because this is expected when photographs are taken. Methods of recording reality produce representations which are mediated by the recording activity itself. We are left with the question of how far these representations correspond to the 'truth' from which they were derived. While this is a question to be asked about all research, it is particularly pertinent to 'qualitative' enquiry, which does not aim to be 'representative' in the same way as 'quantitative' research.

As the aphorism goes, the findings of 'quantitative' research may be reliable but not valid, while the opposite may be the case for 'qualitative' studies:

validity is all, and reliability very much a secondary issue. 'Validity' here means the extent to which the research 'findings' truly correspond to the 'reality' from which they were drawn; 'reliability' refers to the repeatability of the findings – will the same researcher obtain the same data again, and/or will different researchers treat the data in the same way? (Galtung 1967:121).

Hearing the silent

Giving voice to the silent has been a dominant feminist metaphor. Tillie Olsen celebrated the history of women writers in a book called *Silences* (1978). Feminist sociologists such as Dorothy Smith (1988) refer extensively to the metaphor of 'silencing'; one of the earliest collections of feminist social science essays in the USA was called *Another Voice* (Millman and Kanter 1975a). The quotation from George Eliot's *Middlemarch* at the head of this chapter (1872:189) makes the important link between the silencing of particular voices, on the one hand, and the material contexts in which silencing is embedded, on the other. Those of us whose experiences and labours are most closely bound up with responsibility for the everyday world are least likely to be considered as having something important to say. What George Eliot is commenting on in the quotation from *Middlemarch* is the state of the young, passionate Dorothea Brooke's feelings after six weeks of marriage to the dry, over-intellectual clergyman Mr Casaubon. The couple are honeymooning in Rome, whose delights provoke in Dorothea a wealth of fresh observations; these contrast with the 'lifeless embalmment of knowledge' she finds in her husband. Dorothea's feelings seem to her unauthenticated; the marriage acts as a metaphor for the clash of 'qualitative' and 'quantitative' approaches.

The methods of 'qualitative' research – interviews, observations, focus groups, life histories – are notable for the closeness they require between researcher and researched. The two sides of the research process exist in the same plane, face to face. In-depth interviews are the face-to-face method *par excellence*, and so have been the chosen method for feminist researchers.[2] Interviews imitate conversations; they hold out the promise of mutual listening. Many of the reasons for preferring a 'qualitative' approach centred on in-depth interviews are the obverse of the objections which feminist critiques have levelled against 'quantitative' methods: the advantages of 'connected' as distinct from 'separated' knowing, dissolution of the artificial boundaries between knower and known, the opportunity to ground knowledge in concrete social contexts and experiences.

Gender and generalization

Women's Ways of Knowing by Mary Belenky and colleagues, first published in 1986, rapidly rose to fame as an exemplary feminist research project. It is a study which meets many of the criteria for a feminist 'qualitative' project:

loosely structured interviewing, sensitivity to interviewees' concepts and forms of thought; a concern with grounding women's experiences in the material circumstances of their lives. The analysis provided is appealing. It resonates on the ideological level with feminist precepts, and thus also with those personal aspects of women's experiences which those precepts represent. But it does present us with a number of problems, many of which concern the general credibility of 'qualitative' research studies.

The book is, as the title suggests, a study of how women know and the ways of knowing that are valued by women. It was hailed as making a significant contribution to the growing literature on women's distinctive, but traditionally silenced, ways of being, knowing, thinking and feeling, a literature initiated by Carol Gilligan's study of moral choice, *In a Different Voice* (1982). Whereas Gilligan's argument was that mainstream theories of psychological development ignore the particular parameters and processes relevant to women's lives, Belenky and colleagues focused on the ways in which education as an institution has traditionally disregarded the special orientation of women to education. In their study they describe five epistemological perspectives from which they say the women they interviewed viewed and knew the world: silence, received knowledge, subjective knowledge, procedural knowledge, and constructed knowledge.

The interviews in the study were largely unstructured, allowing the women to talk about and around a range of topics broadly defined as of interest to the research team. Questions such as: 'What does being a woman mean to you?', 'What do you care about, think about?' and 'How do you know what is right/true?' were asked (Belenky et al. 1986:231, 234), along with others derived from previous work on moral and cognitive development. The interviews ranged from two to five hours long, and resulted in 5,000 pages of transcribed text. Parts of the transcripts were scored by coders 'blind' to who the women were;[3] the rest of the material was analysed contextually, using a laborious process involving multiple readings, copying of quotations and categorizing of themes: 'The very process of recopying the women's words, reading them with our eyes, typing them with our fingers, remembering the sounds of the voices when the words were first spoken,' say Belenky and colleagues, 'helped us to hear meanings in the words that had previously gone unattended' (Belenky et al. 1986:17). This process of 'immersing' oneself in the data is generally considered to be an important feature of 'qualitative' research.

There were 135 women in Belenky et al.'s sample, which was not random but intentionally chosen to represent certain groups of women. Ninety of the 135 were enrolled in six different kinds of educational institutions, and were selected after discussion with staff for being 'representative' in terms of age, interests, commitment and educational/academic performance; twenty-five of the ninety had previously been interviewed by a member of the research team for another project. The remaining forty-five women came from three different family agencies: an organization working with teenage mothers; a network of self-help groups for parents with a history of child abuse and family violence; and a children's health programme. How the interviewed women were selected from the three agencies is not clear, and no information is given about the social backgrounds of the sampled women as a whole.

Most significantly, Belenky and colleagues chose to listen only to women. They approached their subjects with a disposition to search for certain themes: in this case, how the institutions of the family and education impose on women a particular kind of silencing, within which, like the youthful Dorothea Casaubon, women can find it difficult to hear the authenticity of their own voices. In defence of their research strategy, they offer the following: 'The male experience has been so powerfully articulated that we believed we would hear the patterns in women's voices more clearly if we held at bay the powerful templates men have etched in the literature and in our minds' (Belenky et al. 1986:9). They did have some comparative material available, however: a study carried out some years earlier by William Perry and colleagues on the epistemological development of predominantly male students at Harvard (Perry 1970). But despite the references to the Perry data, the analysis seems to have proceeded without much cross-reference to the male students' ways of knowing; these data were in any case gathered some 20 years earlier and from a single-institution sample. Belenky and colleagues do note that the women in their study were 'on the whole less privileged in terms of social class' (Belenky et al. 1986:44) than the men in Perry's study. The results of their study showed that 'almost half' of the sample fell into the 'subjective' knowledge category; there were 'only two or three' in the 'silence' category (Belenky et al. 1986:55, 23); and the distribution of the sample across the other types of knowing is not given. 'We recognize', say Belenky and colleagues, 'that these five ways of knowing are not necessarily fixed, exhaustive or universal categories . . . that similar categories can be found in men's thinking, and . . . that other people might organize their observations differently' (Belenky et al. 1986:15).[4]

Another book about women, *Social Origins of Depression* by George Brown and Tirril Harris, published a decade earlier in 1976, provides a different illustration of some of the same problems. The methodology of the Brown and Harris study had a very different orientation from that of the Belenky et al. study; the research described in the book is part of a major programme of work undertaken by Brown and his colleagues aimed at documenting the causal associations between stressful life events and circumstances, on the one hand, and mental and physical health, on the other. The core of their methodology is an approach to collecting data from individuals which separates, so far as is possible, the 'subjective' meanings of these data from the 'objective' meanings they are given by a systematic, standardized coding framework developed by researchers and applied to all similar events, circumstances and states, whatever their personal meaning. 'Subjective' meanings are seen as one of many possible sources of bias interrupting the identification of causal relationships rather than, as in the Belenky et al. study, the very stuff of the research itself.

Social Origins of Depression is a meticulous account, based on highly structured interviewing and psychiatric assessment, of the relationship between life events and emotional well-being in a sample of 458 working-class women living in south London. The 'vulnerability factors' which make depression more likely, as identified in the Brown and Harris study (death of a parent in childhood, three or more young children, lack of a confiding relationship, no employment outside the home), have made an important contribution to understanding the links between life circumstances and depression, and have become part of the technical vocabulary of the socio-psychiatric literature. However, Brown and Harris's claims to have established the social roots of depression are made on the basis of empirical data collected only from women. They decided to focus on women because women are more prone to depression than men, and they are also, crucially, more likely to be at home during the day and be willing to submit themselves to lengthy interviews (Brown and Harris 1976:21–2).

This approach leaves the door open to the crucial objection that, were Brown and Harris to have studied men, they might have come away with a different map of the relationships between people's lives and their mental health. There are strong reasons why this might be so. For example, there is much research which shows that men's responses to difficult situations *are* different from women's; they are less likely to 'internalize', to feel adverse events as an injury to self-esteem; the whole pattern of illness and mortality is gender-differentiated in ways and for reasons that, despite a great deal of research, remain largely mysterious (Briscoe 1985; Jenkins 1985; Meddin 1986; Verbrugge 1986; Viney et al. 1985).

These proved but ill-understood differences derive from the fact that gender is not simply a property of individuals, but a set of interactive processes whose influence needs to be accounted for in any research process. Part of the feminist academic project has been to demonstrate the biases embedded in research findings if the influence of gender is ignored. Gender operates by linking biology to social structure in systematically patterned and unequal ways. Men and women appear to be different because they occupy different social positions and 'enjoy' different life-chances. Thus, analyses of research 'findings' which control for variables related to social position generally result in the disappearance of most so-called sex or gender differences (Walker 1984; see also Crawford 1989). Where research is carried out with socially similar samples of males and females, the conclusions that can plausibly be drawn about gender differences may be very different from research which depends on single sex samples only. The best way to derive unwarranted conclusions about one sex (or about human beings in general) is to omit the other. This is similar to the conclusion discussed later in this book that the best way to prove that something works is to omit a comparison situation. What we have here is not a conflict between 'quantitative' and 'qualitative' ways of knowing, but an epistemological error that can be present in *both* ways of knowing.

Women's ways of ageing

The literature on the menopause, a uniquely female experience,[5] provides a third illustration of how misleading it can be to derive research findings from limited samples using research methods which give considerable power to the researcher's own interpretive disposition. For most of its history, the menopause has been socially stereotyped as a negative event. In eighteenth and nineteenth-century Europe, physicians took the view that the menopause was inevitably a period of decay (Grossman and Bart 1979). In the 1990s middle-aged women are thought to suffer from many health problems caused by the menopause, an 'oestrogen deficiency disease'; these symptoms include hot flushes, sweating, tiredness, joint and muscle pains, insomnia, nervousness, weight gain, headaches, back pain, irritability, mood swings, frequent and/or involuntary urination, depression, forgetfulness, low self-esteem, palpitations, dizziness, shortness of breath, loss of feeling in hands and feet, lack of energy, and a phenomenon known as 'restless legs' (Holte 1991; Kaufert et al. 1988; Oldenhave et al. 1993). Of course, the first thing to be said about this formidable list of symptoms is that it is promulgated by a medical profession and a pharmaceutical industry which has a vested interest in women's ill health – in defining women as sick when they may not be, and in prescribing medical remedies when they may not be needed. The medicalization of the menopause has, indeed, been significantly driven by the pharmaceutical industry in Europe and North America, which decided in the late 1930s to make middle-aged women the main targets for the sale of newly synthesized hormones (Oudshoorn 1994). Accounts of their experiences by women themselves, gathered by 'qualitative' researchers such as Emily Martin, present an alternative 'cultural grammar' from the one conveyed by medical representations. This stresses the release of energy and potential that often accompanies the menopause. Within such a grammar, hot flushes are best represented as an experience of embarrassment shaped by a culture in which there is a profound conceptual association between power, rationality and coolness (Martin 1987). Think, for instance, of the metaphors of 'losing one's cool' or not being 'real cool' or getting 'hot under the collar', all of which link emotionality and heat with lack of power.

The underlying epistemological error is potentially the same, however: most of the 'findings' on the experiences of middle-aged women come from studies of women without any comparison group of similarly aged men. The health problems experienced by women are attributed to their being women, without any alternative explanation being considered. In the few studies that do look at health in middle age in both sexes, all the above symptoms except for hot flushes and sweating have been found to be just as common among men (Bungay et al. 1980; Holte 1991; M. Hunter 1990).[6] It is also possible that a number of these symptoms are experienced relatively commonly in the pre-menopausal years, but until this question is asked in a research study, we will not know the answer.

There are patterned differences between groups of women in the extent to which they view the menopause as an illness. Women with manual occupations or those with no paid employment outside the home are most likely to perceive it as troublesome (Martin 1987:170). Table 3.1 illustrates the general point about gender and social circumstances. The data are taken from a large national survey of 9,000 people, the Health and Life Styles survey, carried out in England, Wales and Scotland in 1984–5. Looking at the last two columns of

Table 3.1   Social class and health, men and women aged 40–59

	Social class					
	I, II, IIINM		IIIM, IV, V			
	women %	men %	women %	men %	all women %	all men %
Good/excellent	32	37	25	32	29	35
Poor/very poor	28	23	30	27	29	25
Good but unfit	11	9	14	12	13	11
Good but poor psycho-social health	12	8	13	8	13	8
High illness without disease*	12	7	16	10	14	9
'Silent' disease**	8	15	6	10	7	13

* No disease declared, but a high rate of illness.
** Chronic disease declared without accompanying illness.
Source: Taken from Blaxter 1990:63, table 5.1 (based on 1,301 women, 1,070 men)

the table, one might conclude that women have generally poorer health than men. However, the previous four columns show that in most cases the *direction of the social class difference* is the same for women as for men. Health is related to occupation and to material circumstances, and the distribution of women between occupations is different from that of men. For example, in the UK in 1996 40 per cent fewer employed women than employed men worked full-time, and over half of all employed women, but less than a quarter of employed men, worked in clerical, secretarial, sales and 'personal and protective service' occupations (Macintyre and Hunt 1997; see also Arber and Ginn 1993). Unfortunately the existence of two separate research traditions, one looking at social class and health, the other at gender and health, has meant very little exploration of the ways in which socio-economic position, gender and health interact. Generally it seems that social class differences in indicators of health and illness are often stronger for men than for women. Sometimes the direction of these may be reversed; thus women's body mass index decreases with higher socio-economic position, while men's increases (Macintyre and Hunt 1997).

Looking and finding

It is generally true that what people look for they will find, and that what they are not looking for will probably escape them. Thus, Brown and Harris 'found' causal relationships between social adversity and mental health, and Belenky and colleagues 'found' distinctively female approaches to knowledge. This serendipitous nature of research findings is neatly illustrated by a subtopic which concerned both research teams: child abuse.

A later study by Brown and colleagues (Bifulco et al. 1991) 'found' that being sexually abused as a child emerged as an important vulnerability factor explaining a significant amount of the variation in depression found in the earlier study. Abuse had not been part of the structured interview agenda used in the first study; the later study was done at a time when child abuse and sexual abuse were both in the news. Had a less structured approach been used in the earlier study, it is possible, of course, that some women would have made some sort of reference to abuse. Like Brown and Harris, Belenky and colleagues lighted on the variable of child abuse only when it became part of the media political agenda. Half-way through their study they included a question about it: 'One of the things that we have been finding is that many women were sexually abused at some time in their lives, even as children. Studies have shown that a large percentage of women have been victims of sexual or physical abuse. Has this ever happened to you?' Seventy-five women answered this question, providing 'alarming' 'statistics': 52 per cent said they had been sexually abused; around one in four reported incest in childhood (Belenky et al. 1986:233, 58–9). These figures for sexual abuse are considerably higher than those found in other studies (see Astbury 1996). The relative 'over-estimate' may have had something to do with the 'leading' tone of the question asked and/or with the particular nature of the sample.[7] Such findings suggest the alarming possibility that at least some of 'hearing the silent' may consist of projecting someone's else's imagined reality.[8]

Trustworthiness and its enemies

The basic question is the credibility of research findings or, as one 'qualitative' researcher has put it: 'The soundness of qualitative methodology is the most urgent challenge for those researchers interested in the growth of qualitative inquiry' (Morse 1994a:4). There are three issues here: how 'qualitative' research is done, how it is described, and how its audience is able to decide whether or not its findings are trustworthy.

Reporting research

Judgements of the validity of research can only be made, of course, on the basis of published or otherwise publicly available accounts. One may therefore be judging not so much the quality of the study itself, but the quality of the way it is reported. John Lofland from the University of California carried out an analysis of the reporting of 'qualitative' studies in the early 1970s. His basic data were the papers submitted for publication to a journal and the reports of evaluators asked to assess these papers. Using these data, Lofland discerned five different dimensions and twelve different styles of evaluating and report-ing which reflect different attitudes and practices in the field of 'qualitative' research as a whole. For example, the 'Protocol' style involves an author beginning a paper with a few paragraphs about his or her topic being an important social problem, or aspect of social life, or whatever, and then going on to provide a lengthy set of interview transcripts. The underlying assumption here is either that 'the significance of the raw materials is so obvious as to require no further work on the author's part or that the material is so interesting that it renders superfluous any framing by the author' (Lofland 1974:104). In the 'Then They Do This' style, on the other hand, reports are organized around multiple citations of direct observations with little attempt at analysis or synthesis but with much quotation from 'ungrammatical', 'free-flowing' field notes.

The point here is that the evaluated reports in Lofland's survey were alike in their 'qualitative' data collection methods, but they exhibited enormous diversity in styles of reporting and analysis. He concluded that 'qualitative' research is distinct among all forms of enquiry 'in the degree to which its practitioners lack a public, shared, and codified conception of how what they do is done, and how what they report should be formulated' (Lofland 1974:101). His explanation for this state of affairs refers to a dominant conception within social science of 'qualitative' methods as exploration and discovery devices – a general 'ideological celebration of creativity' which provides a mandate for reporting anything social in virtually any manner whatsoever. So 'qualitative' research can be considered 'organizationally and technologically the most individualized and primitive of research genres' (Lofland 1974:110). On this view, anyone can do it. All you need is yourself, some people to watch or talk to, and pen and paper. Another name for this is 'blitzkrieg ethnography': quick forays into research fields by people who use the terminology of 'qualitative' or ethnographic research but misuse its tools by acting as if a deep understanding of something can be gained and transmitted without too much time or difficulty (Rist 1980). It was, perhaps, bound to follow that as 'qualitative' research came increasingly into vogue in the 1970s, committed ethnographers would object that their trade was being plied by people who did not really understand it and were not trained to do it.

Whether training makes a difference is one of many unanswered questions. All research, however conducted, and within whichever paradigm, involves 'an imaginative and creative leap from observed data to synthesis, hypothesis, and generalization' (Dreher 1994:295). The problem lies in how we, the audience, are able to track the nature of that leap. It has been suggested that asking 'qualitative' researchers to account for the processes involved may be like asking a centipede to consider how it is that it is able to move all its legs at the same time: faced with such an epigenetic enquiry, the centipede is simply paralysed (Sandelowski 1994:47).

Magic and myth in ethnography

When Malinowski wrote his account of the trading system operated by South Sea Islanders, *Argonauts of the Western Pacific* (1922), he was well aware that he needed to give some account of how he arrived at the conclusions he did.

'What is then this ethnographer's magic', he asked rhetorically, 'by which he is able to evoke the real spirit of the natives, the true picture of tribal life?' (Malinowski 1922:6). The answer was that the 'magic' inhered in the 'patient and systematic' application of the rules of common sense and scientific principles. Any good ethnography, says Malinowski, has to be based on three principles: the pursuit of scientific aims, living among the natives, and using certain methodological procedures in setting down the rules and regulations of native cultures. Prime among these is the method of 'statistic documentation by concrete evidence' (Malinowski 1922:17), whereby the ethnographer attempts to infer underlying patterns from collected data, where necessary going beyond the surface impressions provided by native informants. Malinowski is in no doubt that the central problem is one of trustworthiness: 'an Ethnographer, who wishes to be trusted, must show clearly and concisely . . . which are his own direct observations, and which the indirect information that form the bases of his account' (Malinowski 1922:15).

Margaret Mead's *Coming of Age in Samoa*, published six years after Malinowski's *Argonauts*, is the most widely read of all anthropological books; it has been translated into sixteen languages, including Urdu and Serbo-Croatian (Tiffany and Adams 1985:27). When Mead sailed for Samoa in 1925 with six notebooks, a portable typewriter and a small Kodak camera, she knew, by her own admission, very little about fieldwork. Her professor and doctoral supervisor, Frank Boas, the intellectual leader of American cultural anthropology at the time, told her she should spend her time sitting around listening to people, but need not bother with any kind of study of the culture as a whole, since this had already been done (Mead 1972:156–7, 147–8). Mead went to Samoa to study female adolescence, because Boas wanted her to; he had a hypothesis that adolescent rebellion in America was due to modern conditions, and did not occur in 'primitive society'. Boas's theory was part of a wider debate about nature versus nurture which had reached one of its recurrent peaks in the 1920s. Other cultures constitute 'natural experiments' in the society–biology relationship, so that studying them can theoretically provide an answer to the question as to whether nature or nurture has the upper hand in shaping human conduct. As Mead herself put it in the case of Samoa, 'Here are the proper conditions for an experiment; the developing girl is a constant factor in America and in Samoa; the civilisation of America and the civilisation of Samoa are different' (Mead 1928:108–9).

Mead's fieldwork in Samoa was concentrated on three villages close to one another. She lived there, in a community of about 600 people, for six months as a member of a group of unmarried girls.[9] The community included sixty-eight girls aged between nine and twenty (Mead 1928:144–5), twenty-five of whom she got to know well. As a result, she concluded that adolescence in Samoa is not marked out or experienced as a difficult period in women's lives. But Mead's Samoan study is probably best known for her conclusions about the place of sex in Samoan adolescence. The image of easy love affairs under the palm trees for which the study is famous derives from Mead's description of a culture which she portrayed as untrammelled by the kind of moral constraints and double standards characteristic of American society at the time. For Samoan girls, as for Samoans generally, sex, said Mead, was 'a natural pleasurable thing' (Mead 1928:112); it was accepted and expected that unmarried girls would have active sex lives, and sexuality did not constitute any kind of moral battleground, either for them or for adults.

Mead's interpretation of Samoan adolescence has since been contested in a much-publicized book called *Margaret Mead and Samoa: the making and unmaking of anthropological myth* published in 1983 by Derek Freeman. In this book Freeman alleges that Mead acquired an incorrect view of Samoan culture because as a woman she was excluded from any participation in Samoan political life, because she was based in a Western household,[10] because she lacked systematic training, because she used an unsystematic, 'homespun' approach to studying the complex problem Boas had set her, and, most of all, because when she went to Samoa, she was already committed to the theory of cultural relativism: she found what she expected to find. Freeman highlights the different view of Samoa he felt was revealed by his own fieldwork. Freeman's Samoa is far from being the romantic paradise attributed to Mead's account; instead it is a competitive masculine society rife with violence and unacknowledged tensions of all kinds. Freeman's research was done in a different village on a different island. A third Samoan ethnographer, Lowell Holmes (1957, 1983) conducted a restudy of Mead's original research in the same village, and concluded that her findings were substantially correct. Further fieldwork in the early 1970s by a fourth anthropologist, Eleanor Gerber, seemingly uncovered a culture considerably stricter about sexual matters than the one Mead had described. This dissonance was explained by Gerber's informants as a consequence of their parents and grandparents simply telling Mead lies in order to tease (or please?) her (Gerber 1975; Freeman 1983:108).

Female anthropologists can penetrate aspects of unfamiliar cultures which are inaccessible to male anthropologists, and vice versa. Freeman and Holmes had privileged access to male informants and to the domain of politics and political rivalries, whereas Mead concentrated on the world of Samoan women. But there is more to it than the sex/gender of informants. As Sharon Tiffany and Kathleen Adams argue in their *The Wild Woman: an inquiry into the anthropology of an idea* (1985), the 'scientific' façade of anthropology hides anthropologists' participation in an ideology of 'the Other' and a view of women which together make some interpretations more likely than others. Forms of thought dominant in Europe in the nineteenth century conceived of women as closer to nature and of other cultures as verging on savagery; fragments from this world-view are liable to influence anthropological 'findings'. Mead's Samoa portrayed women as self-confident and actively and unashamedly sexual; Freeman's vision is inspired by a different view of women, one in which they are dehumanized sex objects. Another factor, of course, is that considerable time had passed between Mead's original observations and the later ones.[11] But whatever else the Mead–Freeman debate is, it is not an example of the deliberate falsification of results – a charge against which Mead's daughter, Mary Catherine Bateson, had to defend her mother after Freeman's book was published (Bateson 1983). It is, instead, best read as an example of the 'untrustworthiness' of 'uncontrolled findings' (Lincoln and Guba 1985:289). While the diversity of the world's cultures provides an experimental laboratory for the anthropologist, the relatively inaccessible processes of anthropological enquiry are quite different from those of a controlled experiment (as the second quotation which heads this chapter (Okely 1994:20) notes).

Ways of judging

What happens when we try to spell out criteria which might be used for judging the trustworthiness of 'qualitative' enquiries? Table 3.2 gives four different lists of criteria compiled by different researchers who have looked at this issue.

While some degree of overlap is clear from a quick reading of the table, there are also issues picked up in one list which are not reflected in the others. There is considerable variety in the language used to describe the criteria. Words such as 'clear', 'adequate', 'careful' and 'systematic' are often used, sometimes in an interchangeable sense, although they are not strictly interchangeable (one may be 'clear' without being 'systematic', for example). Unpacking the various standards suggested in table 3.2 into their component parts gives forty-six distinguishably different criteria. Twenty-eight of these occur in only one of the lists, ten in two, and six in three; only two are common to all four lists (clear description of the sample and how it was recruited, and an adequate description of how the findings/analytic framework are derived from the data).[12]

Reaching agreement on what criteria to include in assessing the validity of 'qualitative' research is clearly not an easy task. Many of the criteria in table 3.2 involve making judgements about whether or not a standard has actually been satisfied; for example, what constitutes an 'adequate' description of fieldwork methods or an 'adequate' description of data analysis, or an 'adequate' description of the context (column 3, points 7 and 12, and column 1, point 11); what is 'sufficient original evidence' (column 2, point 11, and column 4, point 17), and how 'clear' do criteria (column 4, point 3), definitions of problems and purposes (column 1, points 3 and 6) or descriptions (column 3, points 1,3 and 4, column 2, points 2,5 and 7) have to be in order to persuade the assessor that they are clear enough?

Audit and other trails

The lists of criteria in table 3.2 are predicated on an important assumption: that 'qualitative' research *is* the same sort of enquiry as 'quantitative' research, about which such questions of trustworthiness are regularly asked. There are those who would argue the opposite case:

Table 3.2 Four examples of 'quantitative' criteria for judging the trustworthiness of 'qualitative' research

Cobb and Hagemaster 1987	Mays and Pope 1995	Boulton et al. 1996	Medical Sociology Group 1996
1. Understanding of qualitive paradigm	1. Explicit account of theoretical framework and methods stated	1. Clear aim(s)	1. Research methods appropriate to research questions
2. Appropriate references cited	2. Clear description of context	2. Qualitative approach appropriate	2. Clear connection to existing body of knowledge
3. Problem clearly defined	3. Clear description and justification of sampling strategy	3. Clear description of sample	3. Clear criteria for sample selection and data collection and analysis
4. Scope of question manageable within study time frame	4. Theoretically comprehensive sampling strategy to ensure generalizability of conceptual analyses	4. Clear description of recruitment	4. Theoretical justification for selection of cases
5. Purpose is discovery/ description/theory building/ illustration	5. Clear description of fieldwork methods	5. Adequate description of sample characteristics	5. Sensitivity of methods matches needs of research questions
6. Study purpose clearly stated	6. Independent inspection of evidence possible	6. Adequate and appropriate final sample	6. Relationship between researcher and subjects considered, and research explained to 'subjects'
7. Inclusion of literature review if appropriate	7. Clear description and theoretical justification of data analysis procedures	7. Adequate description of fieldwork	7. Systematic data-collection and record-keeping

8. Reference to accepted analytic procedures

9. Systematic analysis

10. Adequate discussion of how findings derived from data

11. Adequate discussion of evidence for and against researcher's arguments

12. Measures taken to test validity of findings

13. Steps taken to see if analysis is comprehensible to participants

14. Clear contextualization of research

15. Systematic presentation of data

16. Clear distinction made between data and interpretation

8. Adequate description of data collection methods

9. Systematic data collection

10. Sensitive data collection

11. Careful records of data

12. Adequate description of data analysis

13. Evidence provided to support analysis

14. Sufficient original material presented

15. Evidence that supporting material is representative

16. Evidence of efforts to establish validity

8. Analysis repeated by more than one researcher to ensure reliability

9. Use of quantitative evidence to test qualitative conclusions where appropriate

10. Evidence of seeking out contradictory observations

11. Sufficient original evidence presented to satisfy reader of relation between interpretation and evidence

8. Literature review sufficiently comprehensive

9. Major concepts defined

10. Appropriate initial framework

11. Context adequately described

12. Plan for gaining entrée given

13. Researcher–respondent relationship understood

14. Role of researcher apparent

15. Issues of qualitative study sampling adequately addressed

16. Characteristics of sample outlined

Table 3.2 *cont'd.*

Cobb and Hagemaster 1987	Mays and Pope 1995	Boulton et al. 1996	Medical Sociology Group 1996
17. Knowledge of qualitative research strategies demonstrated		17. Evidence of efforts to establish reliability	17. Sufficient original evidence presented to satisfy reader of relationship between evidence and conclusions
18. Plan for organizing/retrieving data outlined		18. Study located in broader context	18. Clear statement of author's own position
19. Framework for analysis stated			19. Credible and appropriate results
20. Problems of validity and reliability addressed			
21. Demonstration of how framework is derived from data.			
22. Understanding of ethical issues			
23. Importance of study to subject area outlined			

Except at a very high level of abstraction, *it is fruitless to try to set standards* for qualitative research per se. (*Howe and Eisenhart 1990:4; emphasis added*)

The greatest concern today is that many qualitative researchers are using quantitative criteria to interpret, explain, and support their research findings without realizing *the questionable practice* or the inappropriateness of such efforts. Using quantitative criteria to evaluate qualitative studies is clearly inconsistent with the philosophy, purposes, and goals of each paradigm. *(Leininger 1994:97; emphasis added)*

According to this logic, the 'truth' that is sought through 'qualitative' research is a special kind of truth: as 'socially and historically conditioned agreement' (J.K. Smith 1984:380). What is true is simply what people at the time can agree is true or trustworthy. Such a position disputes the 'ontological creed' of the 'positivist' 'paradigm' – that the object of social research is to find out how things really are. 'Reality' can only be a property of a mental framework, and what counts as knowledge can only be a human construction. If 'reality' does not exist, then establishing how best to assess whether research findings adequately represent this must be a senseless task.

Some aspects of the argument about applying standards of trustworthiness across research 'paradigms' remind me of a discussion that took place in the early 1980s in a medical research unit where I was then working. The subject was a proposed study to investigate the accuracy with which pregnant women's experiences of fetal well-being predicted health problems in their babies. The method being suggested was one in which women would be asked to quantify their experiences of the ways in which babies moved in the womb by counting the number of movements per unit of time on a regular daily basis; these observations would be recorded, and the relationship between them and the babies' state of health would be looked at. Dissenting voices argued that mothers' feelings about the health of fetuses were 'qualitative' in nature and could not be quantified in this way. In seeking to impose one way of knowing on another, the proposed methodology was simply an improper translation between incommensurable languages. Moreover, as it was already known that there was a problem in getting health professionals to take mothers' anxieties about their fetuses seriously, this was the bit of the predictive chain that really needed attention.[13]

If criteria derived from a 'foundationalist' standpoint should not be used, then what alternatives are there? One suggested solution is that of the 'audit trail'. This model is derived from the process of checking financial accounts, and depends on access not only to the raw data but also to all data reduction and analysis products (field notes, notes about theories and concepts), processes and products of data synthesis (themes, definitions, findings), process notes (methodological procedures, etc.), material relating to 'intentions and dispositions' (the original proposal, personal notes about the research) and 'instrument-development information' (how the interview schedules etc. were developed). A fully developed audit trail is a detailed, laborious and time-consuming process involving a sequence of predetermined stages and resulting in an 'attestation' that the auditor found (or did not find) evidence that the results of the research can be trusted (see Halpern 1983; see also Lincoln and Guba 1985:319–27). But what may appear to be a relatively straightforward process in theory can prove more awkward in practice. For example, in an audit of an evaluation carried out by two auditors of a child care information and referral service in the USA, the two auditors could not agree as to whether the evaluation had been well done (Greene at al. 1988). Much depends on judgement. The audit concept does not itself, therefore, dispense with the need for a set of agreed standards.

Non-foundational criteria?

So what alternative criteria might be used to determine trustworthiness in 'qualitative' enquiry? Table 3.3 compares four sets of proposals made by those who argue that special criteria are needed to establish the trustworthiness of 'qualitative' research findings. Those shown in the first column come from the work of Egon Guba and Yvonne Lincoln in the USA, who have been at the forefront of the effort to establish standards for 'qualitative' research. Their work stemmed from the rise in 'qualitative' research papers published in education journals in the late 1970s; the editors of these journals were at a loss as to how to judge the rigour of these studies. The result was the set of 'trustworthiness' criteria shown in table 3.3. The other lists were produced by 'qualitative' researchers who have all given some thought to how the credibility of their enquiries might be judged.

Like table 3.2 above, the criteria proposed in the four lists in table 3.3 have some overlap and some differences. A total of twenty-five different criteria can be identified. Of these, thirteen appear once and eleven twice: one (the collection of 'thick' data) appears in three lists, but none in four.[14] 'Thick' data/description is a popular notion among 'qualitative' researchers. The term was devised by philosopher Gilbert Ryle, and was adapted to anthropology by Geertz (1973); what it means is a detailed and literal description of the entity being studied, including interpreting the meaning of descriptive data in terms of cultural norms and values (Guba and Lincoln 1981:119).

A comparison of the two tables does, however, suggest that the 'qualitative' criteria are not strikingly different from the 'quantitative' ones. That is, the former represent an adaptation of the latter, but the issues each are intended to address are the same.[15]

Checking with members

Two of the lists in table 3.3 suggest that taking data/interpretations back to the people from whom they came in the first place ought to be part of the attempt to establish trustworthiness. This is not a new idea; Alfred Schutz's 'postulate of adequacy' required that scientific propositions be understandable to community members, because if scientific and common-sense thinking are not overlapping terrains, then science must have got something wrong (Schutz 1967). The implication is that if one's research participants agree with the interpretations which constitute the research 'findings', then more confidence can be had in their reliability. This kind of iterative process, in which the researched join forces with the researchers in a collaborative effort to give birth to the research product, is also a feature of the feminist argument for 'qualitative' research. It is an essential aspect of the case for decreasing the power differences between researcher and researched; neither party should dominate either the process of deciding who should take part in research or that of determining what the research 'means'.

An early experiment in 'member checking' which pre-dated the feminist call for more democratic practices is the study of 'dual-career families' carried out by Rhona and Robert Rapoport in the late 1960s. The book of this name, published in 1971, described the lives and experiences of five British families in which both spouses were employed in professional careers and were also parents. The intention of the research (which included interviews with a total of sixteen couples) was to look at similarities and differences in the ways such families cope with the demands of their careers and their family lives, at strengths and weaknesses of the dual-career family pattern, and at the extent to which it may serve the interests of men and women rather differently. Both partners were interviewed a minimum of four times over a period of two years. On one of these occasions the couples were given for discussion a write-up of their particular 'case'. The five couples whose cases were detailed in the book were given a further opportunity to comment on the material the Rapoports wanted to publish. 'The feedback of the reports to the couples', they say, 'was regarded partly as an ethical requirement and partly as a validity check. For populations of the kind studied . . . we assumed that their own perceptions together with ours would provide the most valid approximation of "the truth"' (Rapoport and Rapoport 1971:324). It was not a straightforward matter. The initial feedback proved 'a point of some tension'. The couples had spoken freely – many of them said more freely than they would have talked to their best friends – and this sometimes brought into the open elements that had not been explicit, either to themselves or to each other, before. Such tensions were of much interest to the researchers, and of course highly relevant to the purpose of the research. But in order to satisfy the research participants, most of them had to be excised. Getting the consent of the five couples who were the focus of the detailed case-studies was even more difficult. Partly because they felt they might be recognized, but also because of a general feeling of embarrassment, they exercised 'quite severely' their right to veto the inclusion of certain materials. Interestingly, the men wanted to excise more than the women did – in part, it seems, because of a general view that such research on family life is really women's business anyway (Rapoport and Rapoport 1976).[16] Two of the five case-studies ended up so truncated that they were nearly dropped from the final version, which certainly reads in places as an account which has been 'sanitized' by the omission of anything remotely conflictual or controversial.

Table 3.3 Four examples of 'qualitative' criteria for judging the trustworthiness of 'qualitative' research

Lincoln and Guba 1989	Leininger 1994	Muecke 1994	Popay et al. 1998
Credibility 1. Prolonged engagement (at the enquiry site to establish rapport and immerse the researcher in the culture to be studied)	1. *Credibility* – ensuring that the researcher uses active listening, reflection and empathic understanding to grasp what is 'true' to informants in their lived environment	1. The research interprets one social group to the large society or another society	1. The privileging of 'subjective meaning' – the research illuminates the subjective meaning, actions and context of those being researched
2. Persistent observation (sufficient observation to collect data relevant to the research topic)	2. *Confirmability* – repeated direct participatory and documented evidence observed or obtained from primary sources	2. The research participants would find the research an honest and caring description of them in their situation	2. Responsiveness to social context – the research design is adaptable/responsive to real-life settings
3. Peer debriefing (discussing the research with a disinterested peer)	3. *Meaning-in-context* – understanding data within holistic contexts (participants' environments)	3. The conceptual orientation of the researcher is acknowledged and coherently linked to the data	3. Purposive sampling – the sample produces the knowledge necessary to understand participants' location in structures and processes
4. Negative case analysis (revising hypotheses until they account for all known cases)	4. *Recurrent patterning* – using repeated experiences, events, etc. to identify patterns of sequenced behaviour	4. The relationship between the researcher and the researched is explicitly assessed for its influence on the data	4. Adequate description – the reader can interpret the meaning and context of what is researched

5. Progressive subjectivity (the researcher monitors her/his own construction/biases

6. Member checks (checking data with research participants)

Transferability
7. Using 'thick description' to establish the transferability of the findings to other settings

Dependability
8. Ensuring that the research process is trackable and documentable

Confirmability
9. Ensuring that data can be tracked back to their sources and that the logic connecting data and interpretations is explicit

5. *Saturation* – full immersion by the researcher in the phenomena being studied; getting 'thick' data to know fully what is being studied

6. *Transferability* – examining general similarities of findings in similar environmental situations

5. The anonymity and integrity of research participants are protected

6. The sources of the data are sufficiently clear for the reader to assess the adequacy appropriateness and breadth of coverage of the data

7. 'Thick description' is used to explore and contrast diverse sources of data

8. Data were obtained from a variety of sources

9. Data were gathered accumulatively and cyclically leading to reformulation of questions

10. The research narrative is competent literature

5. Data quality – different sources of knowledge about the same issues are compared

6. Theoretical and conceptual adequacy – the research describes the process of moving from the data to their interpretation

7. Typicality – claims are made for logical rather than probabilistic generalizations

But, unsurprisingly, it is in the feminist research literature that we find the most fully developed examples of 'member checks'. These also uncover flaws in the logic underlying the process. A much-quoted example is the study by Joan Acker and colleagues of women's transitions into the labour market. 'We were convinced', they said, 'that middle-aged women who had spent most of their lives as wives and mothers had been ignored by much of the [women's] movement and we hoped that we might give voice to some of their perspectives' (Acker et al. 1983:426). Using unstructured in-depth interviews, Acker and colleagues studied sixty-five women, following a subgroup of thirty for up to five years. During this process they showed much of their written material to the women concerned. 'We have to admit to some reluctance', they acknowledged, 'to share our interpretations with those who, we expected, would be upset by them. There was a potential conflict between our feminist frame of reference and their interpretations of their own lives. Our solution to this conflict was not to include them as active participants in the analysis of our research.' A particular problem was women who were not in employment and who defined themselves as 'very independent' but whom the researchers viewed as both structurally and personally dependent. Acker and colleagues concluded that they had not solved the problem of how to do research democratically, in line with a feminist ethos, and that it is hard to avoid the position of researchers as those with 'the power to define'.

Perhaps it is always easier to preach than to practice. Ethnographic research, as Judith Stacey, among others, has observed, appears to be ideally suited to the requirements of feminist research, because the very closeness of researcher to researched suggests a dissolution of the traditional researcher–researched hierarchy. But after two and a half years of trying to do ethnographic fieldwork in a feminist way, Stacey found herself 'wondering whether the appearance of greater respect for and equality with research subjects in the ethnographic approach masks a deeper, more dangerous form of exploitation' (Stacey 1988:22). She frequently found herself in a position of knowing things about informants that they did not know she knew. How do you check with research participants the validity of data which they would not approve of you having in the first place? In one particular case, of the disclosure of a closet lesbian relationship, Stacey felt obliged to leave this out of her ethnographic account. While feminist ethical principles suggested that she respect her research participant who wanted it left out, deciding to do this resulted in a distortion of the 'truth' reported in the final write-up of the study (as well as colluding with the traditional homophobic silencing of lesbian experience).

Everything informants share with researchers is ultimately grist for the researchers' mill. All research represents an intrusion and intervention into a pre-existing system of relationships; thus, taking research data back to the researched is an example of a social event rather than a scientific test (Bloor 1997).

Triangulation

For many 'qualitative' researchers, another answer to the problem of establishing credibility for 'qualitative' research is called 'triangulation'. The term comes originally from broadcasting; radio triangulation means determining the point of origin of a radio broadcast by using directional antennae set up at the two ends of a known baseline. A triangle is then created by measuring the angle at which each antenna receives the most powerful signal; using geometry, the source can be pin-pointed (Lincoln and Guba 1985:305). Applied to research methods, the idea is usually that taking data from several sources will increase one's chances of being able to establish trustworthy results. As Michael Patton (1980:329) phrases it, 'There are basically two kinds of triangulation that contribute to verification and validation of qualitative analysis: (1) checking out the consistency of findings generated by different data-collection methods and (2) checking out the consistency of different data sources within the same method.' The aim is verification, not falsification (or both). 'Triangulation' is a term which makes many ill-specified appearances in research grant applications, creating the illusion that researchers have at hand a ready-made technique for dealing with disbelievers. But what happens in practice, when triangulation is tried, rather than merely appealed to, is that data from different sources or collected using different methods may conflict.

One example of this is a study of women's experiences of the menopause. A survey of 1,713 Finnish women carried out by Hemminki and colleagues provided the opportunity to compare the pictures gained of menopause symptoms in answers to a structured and an open-ended question (Hemminki et al. 1995). The structured question listed seventeen health problems, and asked the women to say which they had experienced in the last two weeks. The open-ended question enquired what symptoms the women had experienced *which they regarded as linked to the menopause*. The three symptoms most commonly ticked in answer to the structured question were tiredness, hot flushes and backache; the three most commonly reported answers to the open-ended question were perspiration, hot flushes and irritability. Table 3.4 shows the percentages of women reporting the most commonly mentioned symptoms in both sets of answers.

If one took the first set of answers only, menopause would appear to pose health problems for significant numbers of women. But, judged by the second set of answers, menopause is an altogether less troublesome experience. Even hot flushes are cited as menopause symptoms by less than a third of women. Which is the true answer?

A second example comes from the childbirth field. Health professionals and medical researchers are often sceptical about the extent to which women can be trusted to remember correctly aspects of their childbirth experiences. They assume that medical case-notes are more reliable. An experimental study of social support in pregnancy provided an opportunity to look at this and other methodological issues, since data were collected from medical notes and from mothers, using both self-administered questionnaires and semi-structured

Table 3.4 Women's answers to a structured and an open-ended question about menopause symptoms

	Structured question N = 436 (%)	Open-ended question N = 303 (%)
Tiredness	45	9
Hot flushes	41	40
Headache	35	4
Joint/muscle aches	24	6
Vertigo	24	7
Sleeplessness	22	15
Depression	21	13
Irritability	19	18

Source: Adapted from Hemminki et al. 1995:83 (women aged 50–4)

interviews. Table 3.5 shows the extent of 'agreement' between medical notes and mothers on certain key features of pregnancy and motherhood. The table can be read two ways: either that there is more than 90 per cent agreement between the two sources for most items, or that there is significant disagreement, particularly for the last item, neonatal problems (where the medical notes were more likely to record problems than the mothers were). Perhaps most surprising are the 3 per cent of cases where there was disagreement about the baby's sex; these represent fifteen instances in which mothers said the sex of the baby they had given birth to was different from the sex recorded in the hospital case-notes.

Table 3.5 Agreement between hospital records and mothers* on questions about pregnancy and the baby's condition

	Hospital and mother:	
	Agree (%)	Disagree (%)
No. of previous pregnancies	91	9
Bleeding in pregnancy	95	5
Baby's sex	97	3
Neonatal problems	81	19

* Mothers' information taken from home interviews for number of previous pregnancies, and from postal questionnaires for other items
Based on N = 467.
Source: Oakley et al. 1990:479

Table 3.6 Number of cigarettes smoked daily at the beginning of pregnancy as reported in hospital records and by mothers in home interviews and postal questionnaires

No. of cigarettes smoked	Hospital records (%)	Home interviews (%)	Postal questionnaires (%)
1–9	23	21	11
10–19	57	57	42
20 or more	20	22	47
Total	100	100	100

Based on N = 75 women
Source: Oakley et al. 1990:483

Table 3.6 comes from the same study. It shows data relating to the incidence of smoking in pregnancy from three sources – medical notes, interviews and questionnaires – for the same group of women. The figures derived from medical records and home interviews (with research midwives) are very similar. But estimates of cigarette smoking are significantly higher in the self-administered questionnaires. Actually, the mean number of cigarettes smoked went from 11.7 in medical notes to 13.0 in the home interviews to 16.6 in the postal questionnaires. What does this mean? Given the moral reprobation that smoking in pregnancy induces in some people, especially health professionals, it is reasonable to suppose that the answers mothers gave in the questionnaires were the 'true' ones. It is easier to tell the truth to an anonymous sheet of paper than face-to-face to someone who is likely to have a reaction (visible or hidden) to this piece of information. Such an explanation, however, does not work in relation to the discrepant instances of babies' sex in the previous table. Here, the most likely explanation is either incorrect recording by health professionals[17] or confusing layout of the questionnaire (or even incorrect data extraction by the researchers).

The third example comes from an investigation of the health status of older women. Moyra Sidell used three approaches to collect data on this: national mortality and morbidity statistics; data from two large-scale sample surveys; and in-depth interviews with thirty older women. What she found was 'a mass of paradox and downright contradictory evidence', with the 'hard' data giving a picture of older women living a long time with a high burden of disease and constantly going to doctors; the 'medium-textured' data yielding a more optimistic picture as regards subjective health perceptions; and the 'soft' data demonstrating much resilience and stamina, with women rarely taking to their beds and being extremely reluctant to use the health services. Sidell ends up viewing with nostalgia the days of 'methodological puritanism' when 'You were not required to perform intellectual contortions, and we qualitative types didn't have to do our sums' (Sidell 1993:117–18).

In other words, using multiple methods does not lead to sounder explanations in simple additive fashion. It may even be the case that 'the neat dovetailing of the pieces of a research puzzle should be cause for suspicion. Unanimity may be the hallmark of work in which the avenues to other explanations have been closed off prematurely' (Trend 1979:68). This conclusion was reached in an attempt to synthesize 'qualitative' and 'quantitative' data collected in a large-scale study conducted in the USA in the 1970s of the effects on low income families of housing allowances (see chapter 9). In this study, the two sorts of data could not easily be reconciled. 'Quantitative' impact data pointed to the programme being a success, but observational data suggested the opposite conclusion.

Differences between data sources have received a good deal of attention under the heading of 'validity' in questionnaire and interview research. For example, studies reported by William Belson used two interviews (an 'ordinary' and an 'intensive' one) separated by a short time period in order to find out how research participants actually interpreted particular questions. More than two-thirds did not interpret the questions as the questioner intended (Belson 1986). A famous example was the chocolate study. This was commissioned by confectionery manufacturers, who suspected that their market information was inaccurate. A sample of 295 adults in London were double interviewed (by market research and 'specially trained' interviewers) about their purchases of twelve chocolate products over the seven days preceding the interview. Comparing the two sets of data showed that the number of products bought in the week before the interviews was a fifth larger in the market research data; for particular products (notably Fry's Chocolate Cream), this made a 50 per cent difference to estimates of their market share. The discrepancies between the two sets of results were due to those questioned interpreting the time period idiosyncratically, being reluctant to say 'no' to the interviewer all the time, wanting to impress her/him, not taking the interview seriously, or simply forgetting what they had bought (Belson 1966).

Deceiving the sane

The interviewed can deceive their interviewers, intentionally or by simple omission. Deception is probably pervasive in all forms of research. Although the contentions of 'qualitative' researchers would have them possess the moral edge here – face-to-face methods supposedly lacking the objectifying distance of 'quantitative'/experimental ones – yet tensions exist between the principle of democracy and the very goal of research as producing warrantable knowledge.

Gellner's story about the man who could prove he was sane, whereas most people are unable to do so (see chapter 2), raises many questions, one of which concerns the ability of medical professionals to identify correctly sanity and insanity. D. L. Rosenhan (1973) put this to the test by conducting a small experiment in which eight sane people gained admission to twelve different hospitals on the East and West coasts of the USA. These 'pseudo-patients' included the researcher, psychologists, a painter and a housewife. They all contacted the hospitals complaining that they could hear voices telling them their lives were empty and hollow. Apart from inventing these voices and using pseudonyms, they gave medical staff accurate details of their life histories. Once admitted to hospital, they dropped the pretence of psychiatric symptoms and behaved normally. Part of the deal was that, if they were successful in getting into hospital, it was up to them to negotiate their own release.

Length of hospital stay ranged from seven to fifty-two days, with an average of nineteen days; around seven minutes a day on average was spent with medical staff; some 2,100 pills of many varieties were prescribed (only two were swallowed, the rest being pocketed or consigned to the lavatory, a common practice among 'real' patients). None of the medical staff correctly identified sanity, and all the pseudo-patients were released with diagnoses of schizophrenia.[18] The experiment was instructive in demonstrating how strong the bias is among doctors to make 'type II' errors – to call healthy people sick. But was the deception justified?

Laud Humphreys' study of homosexual encounters in public places, *Tearoom Trade* (1970), is often cited as the classic example of this particular dilemma in research practice. The preface to the book, by the sociologist Lee Rainwater, calls *Tearoom Trade* part of the great tradition of studies of city life going back to Henry Mayhew. Humphreys' study made an important contribution to criminological knowledge in correcting the view then prevailing that the anonymous sexual encounters of 'lavatory homosexuality' were the province of the single and lonely. Most of the men Humphreys observed were married and predominantly heterosexual. But the only way he was able to know this was because he noted down the registration numbers of cars belonging to men he observed in such encounters, and with the help of 'friendly policemen' tracked down their addresses. He then interviewed the men, ostensibly for a study of health which had nothing to do with his own study. Humphreys, in real life an Episcopalian minister, pretended to be a gay man in order to do his research:[19] 'I am convinced', he says, 'that there is only *one* way to watch highly discreditable behaviour and that is to pretend to be in the same boat with those engaging in it' (Humphreys 1970:25).

Most research using 'qualitative' methods does not give rise to quite the ethical dilemmas represented by *Tearoom Trade*. But participant observation, as Shulamit Reinharz found (see chapter 2) is likely always to carry an element of 'dishonest' social interaction, and methods such as life histories, interviews and focus groups do not *in themselves* guarantee greater participation of research 'subjects' in developing the product of the research.[20]

Conclusion

In the war between 'quantitative' and 'qualitative' paradigms, 'qualitative' research is, as we saw in chapter 2, the alternative paradigm fighting for a
general democratization of ways of knowing. This chapter has looked at some
of its key contentions: that listening intensively to the silent as subjects of
research produces a more authentic, and hence reliable, knowledge; that generalizations about knowledge can proceed from highly limited research samples; that asking questions produces honest and trustworthy answers; that
consensual standards for 'good', 'qualitative' research can be specified; that
sharing research findings with the researched is an uncontentious exercise; that
the products of 'qualitative' research can be verified using data from different
sources or methods; that 'qualitative' research is inherently less deceptive than
the 'quantitative' or experimental kind. All these contentions are problematic.
The language of paradigms beguiles us into thinking that the alliance between
'qualitative' enquiry and the world of the social will somehow guarantee that
such research is both ethically and scientifically 'better' at representing people's interests. But in-depth interviewing and ethnographic observations may
only bring us nearer to the truths that flourish inside researchers' heads. The
laudable goal of feminist research, to do away with the traditional 'objectification'
of research participants, may itself be a contradiction in terms: however one
looks at it, from within whichever paradigm, researchers *are* the ones with 'the
power to define'. While 'qualitative' research may have problems of credibility,
so does 'quantitative' research. Indeed, as I shall argue later, these are to a
large extent the *same* problems. One might reasonably argue that the distinguishing mark of all 'good' research is the awareness and acknowledgement of
error, and that what flows from this is the necessity of establishing procedures
which will minimize the effect such errors may have on what counts as knowledge.

Part II

A Brief History of Methodology

4

Cartesian Nightmares

> I thereby concluded that I was a substance, of which the whole essence or nature consists in thinking . . . so that this 'I', that it is to say, the mind, by which I am what I am, is entirely distinct from the body.
>
> Descartes, *Discourse on the Method*

> Science and femininity share an intimate history, shaped as they both have been by similar social, political and economic forces.
>
> Schiebinger, *The Mind Has No Sex*

Modern methodological combats set up the quantitative orientation of 'natural' science as the enemy of social enquiry. But, as we saw in chapter 2, this rhetorical opposition raises far more questions than it answers. One of the most basic of these questions concerns the 'nature' of science itself. What is science, and where did it come from? Are its methods and social relations inherently oppressive, as some of its modern critics would argue? This chapter takes a new look at the emergence of an emphasis on empirical evidence and experimental methodology in early science. It argues that the emancipatory potential of these tenets was limited by the age they were born into; one in which ideas about gender shaped both women's exclusion from knowledge and how knowledge and nature were themselves conceived. 'Scientific' ways of knowing developed within a set of pre-existing dualisms which generated the conclusion that, so far as the liberation of the less powerful is concerned, science must almost always be an evil impulse.

The origins of what we today call 'science' and 'the scientific method' are inseparably bound up with the changed relationship between human beings and the social and natural world which developed in Europe in the period from the late fifteenth to the late seventeenth centuries. This period saw an intellectual revolution which laid down the foundations of twentieth-century world-views. It was, signally, a revolution in which thinking about astronomy, about the human body, about the principles of mechanics and about human society were all interconnected in a fervour of enthusiasm for discarding old theistic and metaphysical ideologies, and turning instead to the new products of 'man's' reason. Underlying this epistemological shift were new forms of social relations; the hierarchies of absolute monarchy and serf labour gave way to the incipient democracy of a society characterized by the free labour of craftsmen and independent peasants (although that of women would take considerably longer to gain acceptance). These changes did not mean that the birth of modern science was an egalitarian process – although, as we shall see, an empirically based science *was* a startlingly democratic idea, for it opened the gates of valid knowledge to anyone who was willing to put ideas to a practical test. It was not simply the case that women were excluded from the processes of intellectual development (although most of them were), but, rather, that 'science' was absorbed into, and in turn helped to infuse, a cultural division of labour which opposed masculinity and scientific activity to the passivity of feminine nature. The resulting 'masculinization' of science underwrites the methodological paradigm divisions of the late twentieth century. It and, most significantly, reactions against it are among the most important, but ill-recognized, legacies we have inherited from the historical development of modern science.

Man as the centre of all things

The key figures were born in Poland, England, Italy and France between 1473 and 1643. Nicolaus Copernicus (1473–1543) came from a Polish merchant family, and studied liberal arts, medicine and the law and worked as a church administrator before being introduced to the fascinations of astronomy by a mathematics professor, Domenico Maria de Novara, in whose home he lived. His *De Revolutionibus Orbium Coelestium* (On the Revolutions of the Celestial Spheres) put forward the iconoclastic view that the Earth spins on its axis and revolves annually around the Sun. This theory of heliocentrism was in fact an old idea, having been propounded some 1,800 years earlier by Aristarchus of Samos (*c*.320–250 BC) (Sharratt 1994:32). Copernicus's book was published by a Lutheran printer in Nuremberg, Germany, just before his death. It did not cause any particular stir at the time, partly because a preface was added reframing the Copernican observations as merely speculative, but also because in some important ways Copernicus himself did not see his ideas as a challenge to the received wisdom of the time.[1] The Copernican 'revolution' was not instituted by Copernicus himself, but by those who followed him – the Danish astronomer Tycho Brahe (1546–1601) and his young colleague Johann Kepler (1571–1630), and, most notably of course, in the well-known story, by Galileo (1564–1642), whose battles against the received authority of the Papal Church have provided an enduring metaphor for freedom of enquiry.

There are two key points about the original Copernican vision, one ideological and one methodological. On the ideological front, considerable damage was done to 'man's'[2] self-centred world-view by the downgrading of the Earth to the subservient status of a planet under the control of solar forces. Secondly, and more centrally in terms of the story being told in this book, Copernicus initiated a critical challenge to accepted ideas about the basis on which human beings know anything about themselves or the world. His theory about planetary movements was derived from actual observations; 'Ye Galileans, why stand ye gazing up into heaven?' (Acts I:II) was, significantly, the text used by a hostile preacher in Florence in 1614 (V. H. H. Green 1952:52). It was Galileo's actual observations which led him to confront, as misleading, existing ideas about the organization of the cosmos. The accepted procedure at the time was to describe the universe in terms that fitted the schema and principles laid down in biblical and other authoritative sources. (Martin Luther heard about Copernicus's view even before the book was published, and condemned it on the grounds that the Bible said that the Earth was fixed and the Sun moved (Cohen 1985a:51)). This was a 'system' of knowledge that was essentially anti-empirical; it depended for its credibility on people being willing to forgo any study of experiential data in favour of essentially untestable (and therefore unchallengeable) notions about the way the world 'is'.

Fifteenth-century astronomers inherited their understanding of the universe from ancient Greek astronomers, from Aristotle and from Ptolemy. Writing in AD 150, Ptolemy found the idea of a moving Earth 'quite laughable' (Sharratt 1994:8). The Ptolemaic system was intended to be a 'model' of the universe, not a 'true' picture. It was a complex model involving a set of mathematical techniques and geometrical devices which were designed to serve a pre-defined positional map; the question was not how the theory was derived from the observations, but how any observations could be rendered (mathematically) concordant with the theory. This approach, like others throughout different domains of knowledge, was supported by the framework of Aristotelianism, which dominated the intellectual life of Europe from about the middle of the eleventh to about the middle of the fifteenth century. Aristotelian philosophy and logic were taught in most European universities, and were widely understood to provide a comprehensive approach to all knowledge. It was also, most critically, one which was entirely in line with Christian thought. Aristotelianism was the main element in the philosophical/theological movement known as Scholasticism, whose principal aim was the use of human reason to understand Christian revelation. The point was not to analyse how observed facts related to preconceived ideas, but to make observation and experience the servants of theism. The only valid path to knowledge was the study and interpretation of ancient authors, whose wisdom was thought to be so much greater than anything modern scholars could devise. A central plank in the Aristotelian worldview was that heavy bodies move downwards in a straight line towards the centre of the universe – the Earth – whereas light ones move away, also in a straight line. These presuppositions were rooted in the theory of the elements: the four spheres of earth, water, fire and air constitute the whole elementary world beneath the Moon. What happens beyond the Moon is endless repetition without progress or decay and this is because the heavens make up a fifth element, which is an imperishable and incorruptible substance. The same laws do not apply to the cosmos beyond our own world. The task of physics and philosophy is to explain motion, since bodies at rest in their natural place are only what is to be expected. Aristotelian 'science' was anti-empirical both in theory and in practice: although Aristotle's main occupation was that of an observational biologist, he neither advocated nor carried out any experiments or observations as ways of checking his theories.

Galileo Galilei, schooled in Aristotelianism at the University of Pisa in the early 1580s, discovered that it would not do as a method of scientific enquiry. His model for disputing received wisdom was his father's[3] work as a musician; Vincenzo Galilei had played a significant role in the musical revolution which transformed medieval polyphony into the harmonic system we recognize as 'classical' music today. His son, who went to Pisa to study medicine, left without a degree. In one of those many (probably) apocryphal stories that attend the lives of the famous, Galileo is reported to have observed, in a moment of boredom during a church service, the movements of a great hanging lamp in the cathedral at Pisa. He noticed that the time the swing took was the same whether it followed a wide or a narrow arc. Thus he discovered a scientific law governing all pendulum motion; the time taken to perform a swing is independent of its amplitude (Kline 1972:212). Galileo returned to Pisa several years later as professor of mathematics, to feature in another apocryphal story about dropping weights from the leaning tower of Pisa (the fact that it leaned was not actually germane to the case). Whatever actually happened on this occasion[4] preceded the non-renewal of Galileo's appointment at Pisa; the Aristotelian academicians were displeased with him. This was one of a series of personal misfortunes which beset him, and which can be attributed directly to the challenge his work represented to the entire academic establishment, because it countered the theism of received doctrines about what constitutes knowledge and reliable methods of acquiring it.

Galileo came to support the Copernican theory primarily through his observations and analysis of the motion of the tides (an immobile Earth could not explain the existence of tides). He made a great many 'discoveries', but is remembered primarily for his work on the laws of motion, methods for relating mathematics to experience, and the science of the experimental method. After Pisa, he went to Padua, where, in 1609, he heard news of a new optical instrument, the spyglass or telescope, which had been developed in Holland.[5] By the spring of 1609 spyglasses were being sold along the banks of the Seine in Paris, and they reached Italy in the summer. At the end of August, Galileo delivered to the Doge in Venice an instrument which magnified eight or nine times and would be of great military use, since it would permit the viewing of enemy ships some two hours earlier than would be possible with the naked eye. He offered it free, but, since he was chronically short of money, dropped a hint that life tenure and an increased salary would be appreciated – he got both (Sharratt 1994:15).

Some of what Galileo saw with his telescope was reported in *The Starry Messenger*[6] published in 1610. He saw the Moon, with its mountains; he saw the rotating Sun with its spots, the phases of Venus, and assemblages of faint

stars which no one had seen before; and he saw Jupiter with its four moons –
a discovery of enormous consequence, since, if Jupiter could revolve without
losing its four moons, this destroyed the prevailing objection that the Earth
could not itself be a moving object because such motion would cause it to shed
its moon, too. These discoveries showed people what the heavens were really
like. They also confirmed the essence of the Copernican vision – that the Earth
went round the Sun, and is a planet like other planets.[7] By 1610 the first
rumours of revolt were heard; Jupiter's moons had to be illusions caused by
faulty glasses or atmospheric vapours; Galileo had, in any case, stolen the
telescope from the Dutch. Galileo's appeal to Kepler, the Imperial Astronomer in Prague, who replied to the effect that Galileo was nothing less than a
new Columbus, made very little difference to Galileo's subsequent persecution
for upholding the heretical Copernican world-view. The better financial deal
he concluded for himself after the visit to Venice freed him to write his later
works, including *Discourse on Floating Bodies* (1612), *Letters on Sunspots* (1613)
and his *Dialogue Concerning Two Chief World Systems*, which was finally published in 1632 after a prolonged struggle. From 1616 Galileo's works were
subjected to censorship; the Inquisition in Rome decided that there should be
an end to the false doctrine of the mobility of the Earth.[8] The publication of
the *Dialogue* provoked a special Papal commission. Galileo was summoned to
appear before the Inquisition in 1633, where he was condemned for heresy, a
judgement only formally reversed by Pope John Paul II in 1992.

This is not the place to recite the details of Galileo's fight against, and
condemnation by, the Church for developing a science that did not accord
with biblical interpretation, except to note that it remains the archetypal example of how difficult it can be to free the pursuit of knowledge and ways of
knowing (however defined) from the constraints of strongly held beliefs. Pre-
Copernican cosmology actually owed as much to pagan theism as to Christian
theology (V. H. H. Green 1952), but its accordance or otherwise with the
biblical scriptures was not really the point. The point was that people wanted
to believe what they had always believed rather than to have their eyes (almost
literally) opened to new forms and methods of acquiring knowledge. Full
responsibility for Galileo's fate cannot be laid at the door of the Roman Catholic Church; equally culpable were his colleagues, the philosophy professors,
who first complained to the theologians about their dislike of his new science,
which it helped their cause to caricature as religious heresy.

Words, beliefs and revolutions

It is Galileo's qualifications in the area of the science of experimentation which
most fit him for the title of 'the founder of modern science' (see Cohen 1985b).
He argued that 'sensate experiences and necessary demonstrations' must always take precedence over philosophical or theological dogmas (Cohen
1985b:142). Galileo's use of the term 'experiment' rehabilitated it from an
earlier Renaissance usage as 'natural magic' – the province of alchemists, whose

secretive exercises with multifarious substances made them vulnerable to attack by those who were developing a more modern view of science as an openly accountable activity. What Galileo said was that questions – for example, about the motion of falling bodies – could only be adequately answered by performing an experiment – that is, by setting up an intervention in nature and by studying what happened using mathematics. This combination of the experimental and mathematical techniques of description and analysis constituted the essence of the method of knowing that was produced by the 'scientific revolution'.[9] This revolution paralleled that of the Renaissance[10] in giving birth to the modern world; both were essential intellectual precursors of what came to be called the Enlightenment,[11] a term redolent of that very emergence from darkness and unthinking dependence on authority exemplified by Galilean science.

Science and the scientific method, as these evolved during 'the scientific revolution', rested on two things above all else: the power of human reason and an appeal to experience of the world as the only valid basis for all knowledge. These, too, informed the outlook of Enlightenment thinkers, and in turn gave rise to that spirit of enquiry which included discovering the 'laws' of the social world, and which later led to the birth of social science. Central to the new concept of science was the idea of the self-motivated universe – a world in which physical matter moved for natural rather than supernatural reasons. As C. Hill (1974:176) has noted, 'It is difficult for us to appreciate the intellectual revolution involved in assuming that matter – the planets, the blood – might move of itself without being pushed around by an angel or a spirit.' The French mathematician Jean le Rond d'Alembert (1717–83) referred to the new outlook, which crossed many different areas of enquiry, thus in 1759: 'The discovery and application of a new method of philosophizing, the kind of enthusiasm which accompanies discoveries, a certain exaltation of ideas which the spectacle of the universe produces in us – all these causes have brought about a lively fermentation of minds' (cited in Hankins 1985:1). The social context for d'Alembert's fermentation included the political struggles in England and France, and the rise of Puritanism, with its emphasis on the singularity of (religious) experience and its celebration of science as a progressive force (Kearney 1974).

One of the problems (fascinations?) of history is that words, as well as events, people, places and things, change their meaning. What we call 'science' was termed 'natural' philosophy in the sixteenth and seventeenth centuries. Natural philosophy, divorced from other kinds of philosophy, stood precisely for that new enterprise which challenged the medieval university with its inbred metaphysical theism, although it also continued to dispute such 'traditional' philosophical issues as the existence of the soul and the freedom of the will. It was not until the work of Isaac Newton (1642–1727) that 'experimental philosophy' broke off decisively from the rest of philosophy. 'Physics' in the seventeenth and eighteenth centuries did not mean what it does now; it meant the science of causes and effects in both living and non-living things, and it included medicine, physiology, heat and magnetism.[12] Physics overlapped with mathematics, and mathematics included astronomy, optics, hydraulics, geography, navigation, surveying and fortification. Chemistry was part of medicine, but it also merged with natural history, the main domain of which was the classification of nature; so it covered, too, the modern sciences of zoology, botany, geology and meteorology. The study of heat belonged to chemistry as well as to physics. Biology, like sociology, was a nineteenth-century invention. Most important of all, 'science' (*scientia* in Latin) did not mean science at all; it was the generic term for knowledge (from *scire*, 'to know').[13] The Latin term *philosophia* was closest to the modern meaning of 'science'. But it meant, literally, 'love of wisdom'. Thus, this term too could be read comprehensively as concerned with the pursuit of valid knowledge in whatever sphere. These changed and changing meanings are more than superficial linguistic issues, for what they point to is an understanding of the *generic* character of knowledge and ways of obtaining it. The implicit importance of this in the work of Copernicus, Galileo, Kepler and other 'natural' scientists can best be seen by looking at the way the new scientific ideas were taken forward by two great codifiers of method whose thinking has directed the subsequent development of all forms of science – Francis Bacon (1561–1626) and René Descartes (1596–1650).

Experience and experiment: Baconian science

In England as late as the eighteenth and early nineteenth centuries, 'experiment' and 'science' were used generally to mean respectively 'based on experience' and 'system of knowledge': an experiment was simply organized thought founded on solid experience. Francis Bacon, the 'founder of modern empiricism',[14] was largely responsible for developing this notion of the experimental method and its place in science. His work gave rise to a view of 'good' science as 'methodized' experience, technologically exploitable and harnessed to social needs (Pérez-Ramos 1996).

Bacon was a contemporary of Galileo. There is no evidence they actually met, but Bacon refers approvingly to Galileo in his texts, and there are clear connections between their ideas of how 'man' is to study Nature and 'penetrate' her secrets. Bacon's questions about how knowledge can be derived from experience produced a novel methodological doctrine about access to reality, which not only informed subsequent thinking in natural science, but was repeated by virtually all those who speculated on the methodological stance of the new social science in the late eighteenth and nineteenth centuries. He is also known as the initiator of the inductive method, according to which conclusions about future events are drawn on the basis of repeated past observations. He was fundamentally a materialist, although he never made any scientific discoveries himself, and in his writings largely ignored the Copernican revolution.

Like Galileo, Bacon recognized during his university studies the barrenness of much current Scholastic philosophy. His subsequent resolve was to take the methods and products of natural philosophy, 'the great mother of the sciences' (Bacon 1994:89) into the real world. This process involved mounting venomous attacks on traditional academic knowledge and philosophy; Bacon called Greek 'wisdom' 'merely the boyhood of knowledge . . . good at chattering, but immature and unable to generate', dismissing the rest as mere alchemy, having a 'foundation in imposture, in auricular traditions and obscurity' (Bacon 1994:8; 1625:279). These old traditions were among the many 'idols' which obscured human understanding: 'So much then for the several kinds of idols and their trappings, which must be steadily and sternly disowned and renounced,' he wrote, 'and the understanding entirely rid and purged of them, so that the entry into the kingdom of man, which is founded on the sciences, may be like the entry into the kingdom of heaven' (Bacon 1994:77). Bacon dubbed traditional academic knowledge 'idols of the theatre', because it was like 'stage plays creating fictitious and imaginary worlds' (Bacon 1994:56). Much of his ridicule of Aristotelianism amounts to a sustained exposition of the sources of what we would today call 'bias'. His classification of the various sorts of idols (Bacon 1994:53–68) makes very modern reading.

Francis Bacon had the good fortune to be born into a well-connected family – his father was Lord Keeper to Elizabeth I – but the misfortune to be left without much money when his father died, which meant that, like Galileo, he spent a good part of his life trying to curry favour with those who could help him politically and financially. He had a distinguished career as a lawyer and a statesman, becoming a Member of Parliament at the age of twenty-three and holding a series of prized public appointments before becoming Lord Chancellor in 1618. He was a multi-talented, egocentric individual, known for his wit, dry humour, halitosis, liking for 'stable boys', pursuit of power and status, and lavish expenditure (despite his chronic shortage of money). He was also given to deep introspection about his own financial, political and health problems (Jardine and Stewart 1998). His political scheming eventually fell apart, and he was accused of taking bribes (he admitted receiving gifts, but argued that these did not affect his judgement). He was fined £40,000 and imprisoned in the Tower of London for corruption; when released, he was debarred from further public office, so devoted himself full-time to research and writing. Magnanimously, though with his usual degree of self-interest, he offered the King a digest of the laws, a history of Great Britain, and biographies of Tudor monarchs. He did, in fact, complete a history of Henry VII, and also wrote a 'History of the Winds' (*Historia Ventorum*) and a 'History of Life and Death' (*Historia Vitae et Mortis*), and translated his earlier *Advancement of Learning* into Latin. While driving in Highgate, North London, in the winter of 1626, it occurred to him to see what effect the cold had on the putrefaction of the flesh; so he stopped his carriage, bought a hen from 'a cottage woman', stuffed it with snow, caught a cold, and died some days later at a friend's house nearby.[15]

Bacon's *Advancement of Learning*, originally published in 1605, was the first significant philosophical book to be published in English. Dedicated to King James (a man known for his 'backward-directed classical learning' (Eiseley 1961:41)), it aimed to be 'a small globe of the intellectual world', examining prevailing views about knowledge and its customary divisions (Bacon 1965:221). Although predominantly pious and conservative in tone, the *Advancement of Learning* puts forward a critique of the way 'men have withdrawn themselves too much from the contemplation of nature, and the observations of experience' (Bacon 1965:33), setting out the method of discovery (instead of imagination or supposition) as the essential route to knowledge. These precepts are fully developed in Bacon's best-known work, his *Novum Organon,* which first appeared in 1620. *Organon* is a Greek word meaning 'instrument', often used to mean 'instrument of reasoning'. The *Novum Organon* was part of an ambitious Baconian project which he called the 'Great Instauration' (*instauratio* means 'a fresh start'), and intended to be a comprehensive study of the whole of human knowledge.

A memorable passage in the preface to the *Novum* outlines Bacon's general approach to his grand project:

> And our journey has always to be made by the uncertain light of the sense, now shining forth, now hidden, through the forests of experience and particulars. In such a difficult pass there is no hope to be had from human judgement acting by its own power alone, nor from some lucky turn of chance. For no excellence of wit, however great, nor repeated throws of the dice of experiment[16] can overcome these obstacles. Our steps must be guided by a thread, and the whole way from the very first perceptions of the senses must be laid down on a sure plan. *(Bacon 1994:12–13)*

Bacon's 'sure plan' was the method of systematic observation and experiment, which he saw as applicable to all 'sciences', including those governing human political relations. He chose this approach as an important guard against the errors of the old Aristotelianism. The inductive method he proposed would use reason to generate theory from facts, rather than the other way around. Another reason for choosing it was the fallibility of the human senses. The senses could deceive, for example, on the size, distance or speed of objects, because of 'the familiarity of the object, or for other reasons ... For the evidence and information given us by the sense has reference always to man,' points out Bacon, 'not to the universe; and it is a great mistake to say that the sense is a measure of things.' Most importantly, in terms of Bacon's proposed methodological solution, the culpability of the senses leads to a search for aids to overcoming false inferences, and thus directly to the advantages of the experiment: 'For the subtlety of experiments is far greater than that of the sense itself ... (I am speaking of those experiments that are skilfully and expertly thought out and framed for the purpose of the inquiry.)' Bacon quickly added. 'I do not therefore attach much importance to the immediate and natural perception of the sense; but I arrange it so that the sense judges only the experiment' (Bacon 1994:22).

Like Galileo, Bacon was here rescuing the notion of an experiment from its associations with the activities of alchemists, who used it to build 'a fantastic philosophy having regard to few things' (Bacon 1994:62). An experiment in

Baconian language meant attention to experience, but it also meant something more than that: 'There remains simple experience which, if taken as it comes, is called accident; if it is deliberately sought, it is called experiment' (Bacon 1994:91). An experiment was 'a correct and regular procedure' (Bacon 1994:78) – a way of organizing experience so that it was most likely to inform rather than mislead. It was also a labour-saving device; observing nature was a very hit-and-miss affair; one could spend a lifetime watching and not see two sticks rub together to make a fire. The man of science ought, therefore, to mess around a little: 'Nature is an actress with a prodigious repertoire: give her an opportunity to perform' (Medawar 1982:94). This meaning of experiment was closely allied to Bacon's proposition about the inductive method as a means of analysing Nature 'by proper rejections and exclusions' rather than by means of simple enumeration, which he called 'childish' and 'precarious' because it is 'open to danger from a contradictory instance, and it generally makes its pronouncements on too few things' (Bacon 1994:111).[17] These remarks about sample size (as we would call it) are one of many ways in which Bacon anticipated many of the problems and possibilities of scientific methodology which were taken up by later thinkers.

Nightmares of consciousness: Cartesian dualism

The Frenchman René Descartes was born the year before Bacon published his first volume of essays. While the contrasts between Baconian empiricism and Cartesian rationalism have often been highlighted, the shared ground in terms of concepts of knowledge and how this is best acquired is striking (Jordanova 1989:25). Originally a mathematician, Descartes is credited with the discovery of coordinate geometry, as well as being 'the father of modern philosophy'. Much of his personal life is a mystery, largely because he himself was almost pathologically secretive about it (Vrooman 1970). He was the fourth child of Jeanne Brochard; his father, Joachim, was a lawyer in the provincial parliament at Rennes. His mother died having her fifth child (who also died), when René was fourteen months old; he was subsequently looked after by his grandmother and a nurse. At the age of ten he was sent to a Jesuit boarding-school, where his education, like Bacon's at Cambridge, put him off dessicated Scholasticism forever. He later studied law at Poitiers, his mother's birthplace, but he became increasingly dissatisfied with the world of books. During the years 1614–18 there is little trace of his activities, though there is evidence that he did get his law diploma and that he spent a certain amount of time gambling in Paris, where his knowledge of mathematics apparently came in useful as a way of trying to systematize the role of chance (Vrooman 1970:46). In 1618 he went to Holland to join Prince Maurice of Nassau's army as a volunteer for the Protestant cause against the Spanish-Austrian monarchy. He never fought, however, and was never paid, using his time instead to study mathematical problems and write a treatise on music with a young doctor, Isaac Beeckman. In 1619 he left Holland and enlisted as an engineer in the Bavarian army.

Cartesian philosophy was born during the cold winter of 1619–20, which Descartes spent alone in a small room heated by a stove on the outskirts of Ulm on the Danube. Here he reviewed systematically all his knowledge, and came to doubt even his own existence. He arrived rapidly at the conclusion that most of his education was not about knowledge at all. In this state of ignorance, he realized that he could be certain only about what he knew mathematically. It came to him then, almost as a vision, that all knowledge, all science, was a unity; his particular project must therefore be to extend mathematical certainty to other fields. At the age of twenty-three, what he had found was, he said, 'the foundations of a marvellous science'.

Descartes turned to reason as a way of overcoming the depression born of doubt. He must indeed have been in something of a morbid state at the time, living in self-imposed solitary confinement with nothing but the contents of his own mind to survey. He was troubled by nightmares, and there is a story about three in particular, which occurred on the night of 10–11 November 1619. The story comes to us not in Descartes' own words, but from his first biographer, Adrien Baillet, whose account was probably drawn directly from Descartes' own notebooks (Cottingham 1986:9). The dreams are about phantoms and whirlwinds, melons, thunder, weakness on the right side of the body, dictionaries, poems, and not knowing what to do in life, and they have been subject to multiple interpretations, by Freud among others, who said he was inclined to accept Descartes' own view of them, which was essentially that they were divinely inspired, although also laced with various symbolisms to do with sins of his past life, the charms of solitude, etc.[18]

In part 4 of his *Discourse*, Descartes tells the well-known story of how he resolved this mood of intense anxiety and doubt. 'I do not know if I ought to tell you about the first meditations I pursued there,' he begins tentatively, referring to his sojourn in the stove-heated room,

> ... as I wanted to concentrate solely on the search for truth, I thought I ought to do just the opposite, and reject as being absolutely false everything in which I could suppose the slightest reason for doubt ... I resolved to pretend that nothing which had ever entered my mind was any more true than the illusions of my dreams. But immediately afterwards I became aware that, while I decided thus to think that everything was false, it followed necessarily that I who thought thus must be something; and observing that this truth; *I think, therefore I am*, was so certain and so evident ... that I could accept it without scruple as the first principle of the philosophy I was seeking. *(Descartes 1968:53–4)*

The essence of Descartes' project was to turn away from unobserved and unobservable entities, basing knowledge instead on the only things that can be known reliably – the self and the world as experienced by the self. The months following his 'vision' were spent studying the different sciences – geometry, algebra, astrology, astronomy, optics – in an effort to establish their commonalities. He later settled in Holland, where he was daily surrounded by evidence of 'man's' success in using science to harness Nature – land reclaimed from the sea, canals and windmills. Here, interspersed with further university study, he started to prepare a treatise called *Le Monde*. The treatise was almost finished in 1633, when he heard that Galileo had been condemned by the Church 'for nothing other than wanting to establish the movement of the earth', as he phrased it, incredulously (cited in Vrooman 1970:84). Fearful for his own fate – though probably unreasonably so, given the less orthodox cultural milieu of Holland and the religiously respectful nature of his own philosophical speculations – he put *Le Monde* aside, and worked instead on his *Philosophical Essays*, one part of which consisted of his famous *Discourse on the Method of Rightly Conducting the Reason and Seeking Truth in the Sciences*. This was finally published in 1637, when Descartes was forty, after years of hesitation and complicated arrangements with printers (Descartes was fussy, and wanted attractive type and high-quality paper for his long-awaited progeny).

The *Discourse* was a unique combination of science and philosophy, autobiography and history. Its theist conformism would have impressed many of the traditional philosophers whose works Descartes criticized. He ranked the certainty of God along with that of mathematics, and argued the existence of God from the inability of human beings to construct the idea of perfection without divine help. His substitution of the Copernican theory of the universe for a peculiar theory of vortices, according to which space is entirely filled with matter whirling about the sun, was hardly founded on the rules of method he himself advanced. The *Discourse* is in many ways an incoherent little book, summarizing an intellectual journey, rather than articulating the details of a new approach to knowledge and science. For a man given to secrecy, the book is in some ways surprisingly revealing; much of it travels the ground of his 1619–20 psychological journey. Only a short section of the book is actually devoted to method. Using the logic of mathematics, Descartes describes in part 2 how he derived four rules of method which he considered as valid for all the sciences: never to accept anything as true that one does not know to be 'evidently' so; to divide up problems into their component parts; to think systematically, proceeding from the simple to the complex; and 'to make such complete enumerations and such general reviews' that one can be sure to have omitted nothing (Descartes 1968:41).

Aside from the derivation of existence from consciousness, Descartes is best known (and much chided) today for something called 'Cartesian dualism' (see the quote from the *Discourse* (1968:54) at the head of this chapter), and for the associated idea that all living things have the quality of machines. These ideas are set forth most fully in his other works, particularly the *Meditations on First Philosophy* (1641) and *The Principles of Philosophy* (1644). The full title of the *Meditations* is *Meditations on the First Philosophy in Which the Existence of God and the real Distinction between the Soul and the Body of Man are Demonstrated*. Again, Descartes' method is to expose the reader to the apparent logic of his own thought processes, which evidently had particular difficulty in grasping as certain anything outside themselves. This included the body in particular, and bodies and objects in general: 'If I chance to look out of a window on to men passing in the street,' Descartes observes despairingly, 'I do not fail to say, on seeing them, that I see men . . . and yet, what do I see from this window, other than hats and cloaks, which can cover ghosts or dummies who move only by means of springs? . . . I judge them to be really men . . . by the sole power of judgement which resides in my mind . . . ' (Descartes 1968:110). During a detailed discussion in *The Principles of Philosophy* of the nature of matter, Descartes makes a central distinction between quantity – which can be known reliably, since it concerns the occupation of space, and may thus be characterized geometrically – and other aspects of matter such as hardness and colour, which only tell us what something is 'like'. For example:

> when we say that we perceive colours in objects, this is really just the same as saying that we perceive something in objects whose nature we do not know, but which produces in us a certain . . . sensation which we call the sensation of colour. *(Descartes 1985:70)*

Proponents of the modern quantitative–qualitative paradigm divide might well see in this distinction the philosophical origin of the second-class citizenship which has often been assigned to 'qualitative' data.

Central to the Cartesian schema is the thesis that human beings are made of two distinct substances: one thinking, the other corporeal. Thought is independent of the body, and the body is basically a machine – though a better one than all others, since it is made by God. In his unfinished work *Description of the Human Body*, Descartes wrote:

> I shall try to give such a full account of the entire bodily machine that we will have no more reason to think that it is our soul which produces in it the movements which we know by experience are not controlled by our will than we have reason to think that there is a soul in a clock which makes it tell the time. *(Descartes 1985:1.315)*

Descartes did not succeed in this particular project; like Bacon, he died of a cold. He caught his as a result of tutoring a prominent and unusual woman, Queen Christina of Sweden (1626–89), in mathematics and natural philosophy. Queen Christina, crowned 'king' of Sweden in 1650, received an education more typical of a man; she is one of many independent women throughout history of whom it was said that she must really have been a man, or at least a hermaphrodite (Schiebinger 1989:47; Weininger 1975:81–4).[19] Christina was a voracious learner; she spoke five languages fluently and possessed an excellent library, and she used her royal position to patronize learned men. She invited Descartes to Sweden in 1649 with a grandiose plan for him, which involved getting him naturalized and making him a member of the Swedish nobility, then providing him with an estate and a pension and encouraging him to set up, and become director of, the first academy of learned men. In January 1650 she invited him to give her classes at five o'clock in the morning three times a week; the early hour, combined with the cold, led to an inflammation of the lungs from which he died.[20] During his illness he memorably referred to his body as 'a prison' (Vrooman 1970:246), and the subsequent arguments about the disposal of his body had an equal poignancy. It took sixteen years for the Swedish government to agree to ship his remains back to France, where they were moved around several times before ending up in the cemetery of St Germain des Prés. As to Christina, she abdicated four years later, tired of the constraints of monarchy; she then left Sweden, converted to Catholicism in Brussels, and entered Rome on horseback in the costume of an Amazon.

Knowing men?

There is another story in all this – a narrative not unrelated to Descartes' fate at the hands of a challenging woman – which weaves its way between and underneath all the other themes. It is a sub-plot concerning the social relations of men and women in early modern Europe, and the ways in which these helped to shape the methodology of science that was developed by Copernicus, Galileo, Bacon, Descartes, and by others at the same time and later. The context for this sub-plot is that the shedding of the Aristotelian world-view reflected a predicament which derived from a broad social crisis about the citizenship of human beings in a natural universe.

The sixteenth and seventeenth centuries were a time of food crises, wars, plagues and poverty; hunger and famine marked the lives of the poor, and chronic disease and virulent epidemics those of poor and rich alike. The mid-seventeenth century was a particular time of social instability; there were revolts, uprisings or revolutions across Europe, in England, France, the Netherlands, Catalonia, Portugal, Italy and elsewhere. The significance of this cultural context for the discoveries discussed above concerns the manner in which these disturbances fractured an old equilibrium that existed between human beings and nature. What the scientific revolution dissolved was an organic cosmology in which the Earth was a living organism, and human beings were conjoined seamlessly with it. In this cosmology, there was no necessary divide between the natural and the supernatural, and the Earth and Nature featured principally as a nurturing mother (Aries 1983; Merchant 1982). But when the men of science started questioning the scientific basis of received wisdom, the old image of a beneficent and wise female Nature was slowly but surely transformed into an altogether different image: that of 'a disorderly and chaotic realm to be subdued and controlled' (Merchant 1982:127). Most people were semi-literate, steeped in religious conviction, and had their 'gaze turned backward in wonder upon the Greco-Roman past' (Eiseley 1961:31). In the sixteenth and seventeenth centuries the Nature in which they were embedded appeared to be letting people down; the birth of science, happening at the same time, and largely under the midwifery of men, gave rise to a telling and influential lexicon of Man the knower probing female Nature for her secrets.

This argument about masculine methodology and feminine subject-matter, which is put most forcibly by Carolyn Merchant in her book *The Death of Nature* (1982), leads to a somewhat different reading of thinkers such as Bacon and Descartes from that which celebrates them as harbingers of intellectual enlightenment. Such a reading highlights the gendered contours of Baconian and Cartesian thought. In describing his scientific method, Bacon, for example, is given to a gendered language and imagery; Aristotelian philosophy is described as a female offspring – passive and weak; in the *Novum Organon*, the metaphors are of nature as female and knowledge as power (Bacon 1994:29). The grand programme of his *instauratio* was designed to restore to man the mastery over nature which was lost at the fall of Adam. Bacon talks about how his work of separating out the nature of things and the nature of mind means that he will have 'prepared and adorned the bridal chamber of the mind and the universe' (Bacon 1994:23). In these images nature is treated as a female who can be known only through mechanical interventions – by dissection and experiment. One of the complaints Bacon made about Aristotle was that Aristotle was merely a voyeur in relation to Nature, whereas what was needed was that one should capture and control her. In his famous essay 'The masculine birth of time' (1608) Bacon argued that only his new experimental philosophy would enable mankind to thus enslave Nature. What is relevant to such imagery is the cultural context of witchcraft persecution, and contemporary disputes about whether women could be considered people at all. The period from 1540 to 1620 was a time of intense speculation about this, with many tracts being published for and against a socio-biological view of women as 'naturally' inferior subjects (see Oakley 1972a).[21]

Bacon's *New Atlantis* (1626) is a fictional fragment of a mechanistic utopia which anticipates the formation of scientific academies. In this community there is no politics – everything is decided by science and scientists. This view reflected the programmatic plans, held by Bacon and his circle, for science as the vanguard of an expanding and well-ordered economy. The research institute of the New Atlantis, 'Solomon's House', has enclosures where beasts and birds are kept for purposes of experimentation – the testing of medicines and surgery, and the alteration and creation of species. This is a society which is a patriarchy *par excellence*; families are governed by men, and women are nearly invisible behind glass partitions. 'Here, in bold sexual imagery', comments Merchant (1982:171), 'is the key feature of the modern experimental method – constraint of nature in the laboratory, dissection by hand and mind, and the penetration of hidden secrets – language still used today in praising a scientist's "hard facts", "penetrating mind", or the "thrust of his argument".'

There is a clear continuity between the conceptions of an interventionist masculinist science in the writings of Bacon and others and the later institutionalization of science. When the Royal Society was founded in London in 1662, its founders explicitly acknowledged their debt to Bacon's *New Atlantis* vision (Leiss 1972:46). In 1802, Sir Humphrey Davy, later President of the same Royal Society, spoke of the benefits of science in giving 'the man of science' 'powers which . . . have enabled him to modify and change the beings surrounding him, and by his experiments to interrogate nature with power, not simply as a scholar, passive and seeking only to understand her operations, but rather as a master, active with his own instruments' (Davy 1802:16; see H. Rose 1994: ch. 6).

On its most superficial level, Bacon's gendered imagery can be read as a misogynist view of the new science's domineering relations with female nature, an inscription of metaphors of gender divisions directly on to ways of knowing. Yet, in some ways Bacon's imagery is more complex. He called his subject, natural philosophy, 'the great mother of all the sciences', and complained that many demoted it to 'the highly undignified role of a maidservant' (Bacon 1994: 89). As Evelyn Fox Keller has pointed out, one of his quarrels with the ancients was that their teaching discouraged receptivity; truth must enter the mind from without in a kind of hermaphroditic marriage between mind and nature. The mind can only know by submitting itself to what nature has to say: 'Experiment expresses the spirit of action, of a "doing" devoted to "finding out"' (Keller 1980:302).

Oppressive sexual metaphors can also be found in Descartes' writing. He, like Bacon, spoke of knowledge making men 'the masters and possessors of nature' (Descartes 1968; *Discourse on the Method*, part 4). But Descartes went further in transforming the organic female cosmos and all living things into mechanical systems. This view reaches its extreme in Hobbesian philosophy, where the human soul, will, brain and appetites are all reduced to mechanical matter, and society itself has acquired a mechanical structure as the only solution to the problem of *social* disorder.

All this also provides another interpretation of Descartes' famous dreams. Instead of standing as 'a symbol of the seventeenth century rationalist project', they are demoted to the status of masculine anxiety about separation from the mother – the real mother, as well as Mother Nature. This argument is put most strongly by Susan Bordo (1987), whose approach is influenced by Evelyn Fox Keller's work on the gendering of science in the seventeenth century (Keller 1985). Both Bordo and Keller draw on Nancy Chodorow's use of object relations theory to explain why men brought up in a mother-centred child-rearing structure are likely to develop a particular type of masculine personality in which 'objectivity' functions as a denial of connection with women (Chodorow 1978). We know, of course, that Descartes was separated from his own mother as a young child.[22] Psychoanalytic interpretations might therefore see Descartes as having suffered from what Easlea (1981:57) calls 'penile insecurity'. He appears to have had less than straightforward relationships with women. He corresponded for a number of years with Princess Elizabeth of Bohemia, another talented royal female who was interested in learning anything Descartes could teach her. Elizabeth seems to have been more interested in actually meeting Descartes than he was in meeting her – he is rumoured to have moved house to avoid her too-frequent visits (Vrooman 1970). Queen Christina interrogated him about his relationship with Elizabeth, who suffered from repeated depressions and other ailments, and required constant reassurance from Descartes. He never married ('He was too wise a man to encumber himself with a wife,' says John Aubrey in his racy portraits of seventeenth-century figures in *Brief Lives*), but he did have a six-year non-residential relationship with a Dutch domestic servant called Helen. They had a child together, Francine; Descartes, man of secrecy that he was, wrote the date of her conception on the flyleaf of a book (Vrooman 1970:138), and expressed considerable tenderness towards her. She died of scarlet fever, aged five.[23]

The passions of *The Blazing-World*

Descartes' ideas about mind and body did not go uncontested at the time. A singular opponent of Cartesian dualism was Margaret Cavendish (1623–73), a woman with little education who, like many others later, realized that thought was free, and women 'may as well read in our Closets, as Men in their Colleges' (Cavendish 1655: preface, no page number given).

Margaret Cavendish wrote plays, poems, essays, a collection of stories called *Nature's Pictures* (1656), which is one of the earliest examples of published fiction in English, a biography of her husband and a number of philosophical works, including *Observations upon Experimental Philosophy* (1666) and *Grounds of Natural Philosophy* (1668). She published eleven books and two collections of plays, was the first woman in England to write primarily for publication, and the first to publish scientific works. She was born into a large, well-off political family in Colchester; her father died when she was young, and her mother set Margaret and her sisters an example by becoming an efficient manager of the family estates (at a time when women were not allowed to be the legal guardians of their children). As with most women at the time, Margaret's education was neglected and left to an 'ancient decayed gentlewoman', who plied her with *Aesop's Fables* and set her to embroider the alphabet on linen samplers. During the Civil War, the family was suspected of housing Cavaliers; the house was ransacked and they were imprisoned. Margaret subsequently became a maid of honour to Queen Henrietta, and followed the court retinue to France, where she fell in love with William Cavendish, Earl of Newcastle, one of the richest men in England, a favourite of the Queen, a playwright and military strategist, a womanizer and thirty years older than Margaret. At first the Cavendishes lived in relative poverty, exiled in France, but they then returned to England where they had to spend long periods of time apart, and Margaret took to writing poetry by candlelight to ward off insomnia. The marriage was childless, a state that inspired various unsavoury medical treatments including the administration of rams' excrement. It gave Margaret plenty of time to study and write, although another remedy urged on her for childlessness was giving up books, in accordance with dominant and long-lived theories about the competition between the brain and the womb.

Margaret Cavendish was frankly ambitious to make her name by writing, but also appallingly shy. The public criticism her writings engendered was not helped by her habit of refusing to edit her work, on the grounds that she did not enjoy this activity. She became increasingly radical, writing in *The World's Olio* (1655, The preface to the reader):

> True it is, our sex make great complaints, that men from their first creation
> usurped a supremacy to themselves, although we were made equal by nature,
> which tyrannical government they have kept ever since, so that we could never
> come to be free, but rather more and more enslaved, using us either like chil-
> dren, fools or subjects.

Men, she said, 'would fain bury us in their houses and beds, as in a grave; the
truth is, we live like bats or owls, labour like beasts, and dye like worms'
(Cavendish 1662:225). The fact that her husband's permission was required
for publication of her books must have added to these feminist indignities. Her
interest in natural philosophy began when she was living in Paris and met
Descartes and Hobbes; she saw it as a chance to infiltrate a masculine field.
She entertained Descartes to dinner, but could not converse with him, due to
the lack of a shared language. She claims to have spoken no more than twenty
words to Hobbes, and to have informed all these eminent men that women are
as difficult to know as the universe it/herself (K. Jones 1988).

In her books Margaret Cavendish used plain language, as a reaction against
the obscurantism of male philosophers, who, she said, might as well have
written in Latin; she defined her philosophy as 'real' and distinct from the
'philosophy of discourse and disputation' (Cavendish 1666: preface and p. 16).
Her view was that all corporeal matter is both subject and agent, and that the
natural and social worlds and mind and body are joined in a fundamental
unity. She took issue with Descartes' notion of matter being moved by God,
and disputed the idea of man acquiring power over nature since he was part of
it (and a prejudiced part, moreover, since he ignored the views of other animals). These extraordinarily modern ideas were joined by a criticism of experimental methods for flawed measuring instruments and a divorce from practical
policy issues; for example, she condemned the activity of inspecting bees through
a microscope as unlikely to produce more honey (Cavendish 1664:147).

This was an era of utopias. Margaret Cavendish's utopia, portrayed in *The
Description of a New Blazing-World* (1666), begins, like Bacon's *New Atlantis*,
with a shipwreck. A travelling merchant has fallen in love with a young lady,
and borne her off in a boat; the boat sails into an icy sea, and the merchant and
his seamen all die, being men and therefore quite unable to withstand the cold.
The boat sails on to another land, where the young lady is rescued by creatures
shaped like bears, who show her 'all civility and kindness imaginable', and who
take her on ships of gold driven by a wind engine on a magical journey through
cities made of marble, alabaster, agate, amber and coral until they reach the
Emperor of the Blazing World, who lives in paradise, equipped with a bed-
chamber decorated with jet walls, a black marble floor, and a mother-of-pearl
ceiling, and an Imperial State room paved with green diamonds. There are few
laws in the Blazing World, and only one religion; like many later female utopias,
it is a world so well ordered 'that it could not be mended; for it was governed
without secret and deceiving policy; neither was there any ambition, factions,
malicious detractions, civil dissensions, or home-bred quarrels, divisions in Religion, foreign Wars, etc, but all the people lived in a peaceful society'.

The Emperor at first wants to worship the young lady, but she explains she is mortal, so he makes her his wife instead. She then becomes a great matron of the arts and sciences, and carries on many conversations with experimental philosophers, astronomers, chemists, physicians, politicians and immaterial spirits, all of which act as a thinly masked vehicle for Margaret Cavendish's own views and dreams. The format provides a neatly reversed model of usual practice: men are the servants of an all-knowing female ruler. The Empress asks for a 'famous writer' to help her make sense of all this; the spirits reject Galileo, Descartes, Hobbes, etc., on the grounds that they are too 'self-conceited' to be of much use, and recommend instead a woman called the Duchess of Newcastle. Thus Margaret Cavendish, the author, duly arrives in her Blazing World, complaining that the spirits should have known about her handwriting, which is notoriously bad. Consulting the spirits, she is conveniently advised to create a world of her own theories, rather than expound those of others with which she does not agree. Later on, she takes the Empress back to her own terrestrial world, including to Nottinghamshire, where the Empress is most impressed by Sherwood Forest; the two of them end up inhabiting the soul of the Duke of Cavendish, and all three have a most enjoyable time.

The Description of a New World Called the Blazing-World is a literarily fantastic book, combining romance with what has been hailed as the origins of modern science fiction. Its central narrative is about a woman's effortless rise to absolute power. The book celebrates both women's liberty and the emancipatory power of utopian speculation (Cavendish 1992). As Hilary Rose has noted, Cavendish's utopia was written partly as a complaint against the Royal Society, which excluded her, as a woman. She was allowed to attend a meeting once, where she witnessed experiments performed by Robert Boyle and Robert Hooke on the weighing of air and the dissolving of mutton in sulphuric acid; her appearance, with six attendants, threw the meeting into confusion, and was not received well (Mahl and Koon 1977:138). But Margaret Cavendish also wrote The *Blazing-World*, more positively, '*for* a new scientific community where love and the acquisition and production of knowledge are reconciled, and where the lines between nature and culture are softened' (H. Rose 1994:210). Unsurprisingly, perhaps, the book was not well received at the time, being taken as final evidence of the Duchess's insanity (they called her 'Mad Madge'). She died suddenly at fifty, outlived by her husband, having suffered from partially self-induced ill health for some years (she ate little, and exercised even less).

The emotional body and other problems

Modern methodologists find in Cartesianism the original parameters of the mind–body dualism and the subservience of 'qualitative' to 'quantitative' data. However, these accusations may owe more to 'Cartesian legend' and the intellectual needs of modern philosophers than to what Descartes actually said

(Baker and Morris 1996). What Descartes said was that bodies and their properties are objects of sense perception, but minds and theirs are not. Although mind and body are 'substantially united', the interaction between the two is 'rationally unintelligible' – it is impossible to know at first hand what is going on.

But the mythology of Cartesian dualism, like other such legends, is what substantially counts. To Descartes we may also trace another enemy of modern social science: the distinction, further developed in the work of John Locke, between 'primary' and 'secondary' qualities. 'Primary' qualities are those that 'really' inhere in objects which occupy space in the external world; 'secondary' qualities are those human beings (variously) perceive as inhering in them (see Cottingham 1986:141–3). This ordering of qualities is the historical predecessor of that hierarchy of 'quantitative' and 'qualitative' data which has emerged to occupy methodological debates in the twentieth century. Another significant legacy of the scientific revolution is the neglect within social science (and science in general) of human emotions. As a recent text puts it:

> The roots of this neglect lie deeply buried in western thought . . . emotions have tended to be dismissed as private, 'irrational', inner sensations, which have been tied, historically, to women's 'dangerous desires' and 'hysterical bodies' . . . the dominant view . . . seems to have been that emotions need to be 'tamed', 'harnessed' or 'driven out' by the steady (male) hand of reason . . . ' *(Williams and Bendelow 1998:xv)*

Seen from this viewpoint, the project of male rationality as pursued by Descartes and others becomes, of course, wholly 'unreasonable' (Seidler 1998).

The idea of emotions as passions which constitute confused and therefore potentially misleading modes of perceiving reality is clearly present in both Bacon's and Descartes' writings. In his *Novum Organon* Bacon is dismissive of the 'contaminating' effect of emotion: 'The human understanding is not a dry light', he wrote, 'but is infused by desire and emotion, which give rise to "wishful science".' Bacon's view of emotion partly stereotyped it as a potential source of all those errors from which he was so anxious to free knowledge by means of a new, empirically based methodology: 'For man prefers to believe what he wants to be true,' he goes on:

> He therefore rejects difficulties, being impatient of inquiry; sober things, because they restrict his hope; deeper parts of Nature, because of his superstition; the light of experience, because of his arrogance and pride, lest his mind should seem to concern itself with things mean and transitory; things that are strange and contrary to all expectation, because of common opinion. In short, *emotion in numerous, often imperceptible ways pervades and infects the understanding. (Bacon 1994:59–60; emphasis added)*

Descartes was also notable for his dismissal of emotion as undesirable, though he did write a treatise entitled *On the Passions of the Soul* for Princess Elizabeth. Elizabeth asked him to define the passions; he replied that it was difficult to enumerate them (see Voss 1989:xvi). The treatise was an expression of Descartes' conviction that the disruptive effect of the emotions could be controlled through reason; published in 1649, a few weeks after his death, it probably partly represents his own struggles to defeat the depression arising from his own imminent mortality. In a letter to Elizabeth, he expressed the canonical view that 'True philosophy teaches that even amid the saddest disasters and most bitter pains a man can always be content, provided that he knows how to use his reason' (Descartes 1970:180). The disturbing influence of the emotions on knowledge is a viewpoint most fully developed in the work of later philosophers such as Spinoza. Kant came out definitively on the side of gendering when he remarked that women's philosophy is to feel, not to reason. The heritage of the same idea can, significantly, be found in the work of Condorcet, one of the originators of the idea of social science in the late eighteenth century. Condorcet praised the methods of natural science as enabling social scientists 'to study human society *as unemotionally* as we study the society of beavers or of bees' (cited in Schapiro 1934:117; emphasis added).[24]

Science unveils the secrets of female nature

In her *Observations upon Experimental Philosophy*, Margaret Cavendish noted that the idea of knowledge as female was being taken over by the new philosophers, 'so great is grown the self-conceit of the Masculine, and the disregard of the Female Sex' (Cavendish 1666:2). She was here referring to an old idea of science/knowledge as female which pre-dated the scientific revolution and the development of those ideas and methods which led to social science.[25] The imagery of science was female for many centuries. In Cesare Ripa's *Iconologia* (1593) the Renaissance bible of iconography, *scientia* was portrayed as a woman in stately robes; physical science appeared as a goddess with a globe of the earth at her feet; geometry was a woman holding a plumb line and a compass; and female astrology wore a crown of stars (Schiebinger 1989:122; see Jordanova 1989). Most abstract realms or virtues were depicted as feminine. As Ripa pointed out, these gendered depictions suit 'the way we speak' (cited in Warner 1985:65): abstract nouns are feminine in Latin, Italian, French and German. However, as Schiebinger (1989:132) points out, the grammatical observation merely pushes the question one stage further back, since the historical origins of grammatical gender remain for the most part unexplained.[26]

The rendering of science as feminine cannot, of course, be dismissed as mere iconography; the example of Margaret Cavendish and many others proves that. The protests of such women, who made important contributions to scientific thinking, point to a significant set of social transformations which began to happen with the establishment of Baconian science and the Cartesian method. These included the development of medicine as an increasingly interventionist practice; the institutionalization of both science and medicine; moves to exclude women from independent activity outside the domestic realm; and the associated growth of mercantile capitalism, with its decisive separation of private and public spheres. All these transformations involve complex histories beyond the scope of this book. Together they created the well-known doctrine of sexual complementarity which justifies inequality largely by an appeal to the supposed biological necessity of women's caring work.[27] An opposition between science and femininity was a cornerstone of sexual complementarity theory: 'By embedding the theory of sexual difference in the theory of separate spheres, complementarians cemented the association of masculinity with science' (Schiebinger 1989:237).

These transformations, together with their justifying ideologies, helped to construct a situation in which, by the end of the nineteenth century, feminine nature came to be understood as yielding its secrets to masculine science. Decisive moments in this transition were delivered by Paracelsus (1493–1541), Andreas Vesalius (1514–64) and William Harvey (1578–1657). Paracelsus, the son of a Swiss-German physician,[28] began the movement to make medicine an empirically based science by denouncing organized religion and classical scholarship, and marking his disagreement with Galenic medicine by refusing to take the normal oath of allegiance to it when appointed municipal physician and professor at Basel in 1527. Galenic theories of the body dominated the life sciences just as Aristotelianism held sway in natural philosophy.[29] Paracelsus, whose life overlapped with that of Copernicus, contended that diseases, which have their own particular bodily location and symptomatology, have causes external to the individual body.

Vesalius's great work *De Humani Corporis Fabrica* was published the same year as Copernicus's *De Revolutionibus Orbium Coelestium*. Born in Brussels, he studied at Padua, and suffered the same condemnation by Galenists as Galileo did at the hands of the Aristotelian professors. Like Galileo, he was sentenced by the Inquisition; but his crime was the contribution to medicine for which he is chiefly recognized today – the habit of dissecting the human body, of 'experimenting' on it, as a method for establishing how bodies actually work. Most of the corpses he examined were those of convicted criminals, although the frontispiece of his 1543 treatise shows a female body; a particular obsession with the female corpse developed later, in the eighteenth and nineteenth centuries, and was associated with a cultural eroticization of death as part of nature (Aries 1982; Jordanova 1989). In urging physicians to undertake their own dissections and experiments, Vesalius was issuing a revolutionary plea for medical theories to be based on evidence – evidence, moreover, which could only be obtained from plundering the secrets of the human corpse. The imagery of the early dissectors is almost a literal representation of the atomism of the body as a machine which is to be found in Cartesian thinking.

The 'discovery' within Western science of the circulation of the blood was reported in William Harvey's *Exercitatio Anatomica de Motu Cordis et Sanguinis* (1628), and is often cited as one of the best exemplars of a revolutionary moment in science. Harvey, dubbed 'the greatest of England's experimental scientists' (Keynes 1966:1), came from obscure Kentish origins, and little is known about his private life beyond the fact that his wife Elizabeth had a tame parrot; according to Aubrey's *Brief Lives*, he may also have been the first

Englishman to be addicted to coffee. Like Vesalius and many others, Harvey studied at the University of Padua, a great centre of intellectual and scientific activity, where students elected their own teachers and chose their own courses of instruction; Galileo was a young professor there at the time. Harvey's work constituted a systematic debunking of Galenic and Aristotelian ideas; he, like Bacon, dismissed, as part of a strategy of discreditation, the whole of ancient learning as contemplative and passive and, above all, *feminine*. The dedication of *De Motu Cordis*, to Charles I, contained the imagery of the heart as a sun and a symbol of kingly power; it well illustrates the transference of models and ideas across different subject-matters which was characteristic of the intellectual revolution of the sixteenth and seventeenth centuries. Harvey was actually rather nervous about challenging accepted authority, and was lecturing on the principles of cardiovascular circulation some twelve years before he put them into print (C. Hill 1974). He planned an ambitious programme of work based on original investigations into the workings of the human body. At the heart of this programme was also the idea of the experiment; it was his work that established biology and physiology as experimentally based sciences.

Figure 4.1 depicts a famous statue made in 1899 in France. The statue, which is called 'Nature unveiling herself before science', shows a young half-naked, half-veiled woman, in a modest, downward-looking posture, being looked at (it is presumed) by masculine viewers, who cherish the expectation that as a result of their own interventions in, and with, Nature, even more will be revealed. The imagery and reality of the male scientist penetrating nature also comes to be accompanied in the medical sphere by that of the male doctor dissecting, and otherwise experimenting on, the bodies of women. The nineteenth century experimental physiologist Claude Bernard described 'Nature as a woman, who must be forced to unveil herself when attacked by the experimenter' (cited in Lansbury 1985:48). It was the Swedish natural scientist Carl Linnaeus (1707–78) who coined the term 'homo sapiens' – man the knower – to distinguish human beings from apes. From the late eighteenth century on, we see a steady decline of the feminine icon in scientific culture. Kant banished from critical philosophy metaphysics, 'queen of all the sciences', as 'a matron outcast and forsaken' (Kant 1855:viii). In terms of modern arguments about science and social science, it is undoubtedly no accident that the sciences acquired a queen once more when Auguste Comte invented sociology (see chapter 6).

Another kind of utopia

The foundations of the modern world were laid in the sixteenth and seventeenth centuries, and these include the origins of modern views about knowledge in both natural and social domains. In many ways the most remarkable aspect of the modern world-view is this idea that scientific knowledge can be used at will by 'man' to 'master' and exploit nature for 'his' own ends. But,

Figure 4.1 Nature unveiling herself before science.
By Louis Ernest Barrias; *La Nature se dévoilant devant la Science* 1899, in the collections of the Musée d'Orsay, Paris, and reproduced by permission.

however one reads the work of those with whose names the scientific revolution is associated, it is hard to doubt the intention of rationality they saw as powering their endeavours. That the knowledge and methodologies they produced say as much about the prevailing social structure (which was hierarchical in ways other than being sexist) is also hardly surprising.[30] What we can see from the vantage-point of the twentieth century is how the re-definition of the Earth as mere matter laid the groundwork for our current technological exploitation and ecological spoilage of it; but to most sixteenth- and seventeenth-century thinkers science promised human progress, and it would have been inconceivable for them to have seen it as an instrument of destruction.

The scientific revolution and the 'Enlightenment' movement are, in this and other ways, capable of many interpretations. The Enlightenment can also be seen as the disenchantment of the world and the subjection of its peoples to the 'mass deception' of the culture industry (Horkheimer and Adorno 1972). Others have argued that much of the history of Western philosophy can itself be interpreted as a defence against the operations of chance; certainty as a controlling principle in 'man's' knowledge of the universe is a preferable option (Dewey 1980). Similarly, the project of using reason to construct knowledge can also be interpreted in different ways. Whilst it operated to characterize women as 'unreasonable' and, later on, to debar them from the institutionalized practices of science and medicine, some women at the time found it extremely useful to appeal to the idea of reason as supporting arguments for women's equality with men (see Atherton 1993). Psychoanalytic accounts of Cartesian science de-emphasize Descartes' desire to provide methodological tools for women, particularly by writing in the vernacular, which would make what he had to say more accessible to them (see Atherton 1993; Vrooman 1970:91). Paracelsus lectured in his vernacular German instead of Latin; Galileo also wrote in his own language, Italian, because he wanted to appeal to a wider audience; Newton wrote in English for the same reason.

The idea that Descartes turned to science in order to vanquish the uncomfortable emotions associated with women can as well be applied to others, such as Isaac Newton, whose depressive and schizoid traits have been attributed to maternal rejection in early infancy, although they also helped to foster an obsessional concentration on method and science (Storr 1985). While at Cambridge, Newton was preoccupied with sin, and set up in business as an unfriendly small-time loan shark; a later psychotic breakdown was precipitated by an infatuation with a young, Swiss mathematician, Nicholas Fatio de Duillier, but may also have had something to do with the lead and mercury Newton imbibed during his alchemical operations.[31]

Newton, a highly secretive man, spent much of his life studying and experimenting, isolated from the rest of the world. Born after his father died, on Christmas Day, in the family home at Woolsthorpe in Lincolnshire, Newton had the misfortune to watch his mother marry an aged rector, Barnabas Smith, and depart with him to live in another village, leaving Isaac, then aged three, to be brought up by his grandmother.[32] Isaac loathed his stepfather, and his mother's return, eight years later, with two half-sisters and a half-brother,

Smith's children, did not help. At school in nearby Grantham, he lived with an apothecary from whom he learnt the tools of his lifelong fascination with alchemy. As well as the *Principia Mathematica*, he left more than a million words on alchemy in coded Latin. In this sense he was, as his biographer, the economist J. M. Keynes put it, 'the last of the magicians', rather than the first of the modern scientists (Keynes 1947, cited in White 1998:3).

Reason and the vernacularization of philosophical language acted as democratic devices; another was the whole idea of the experiment. In discarding the appeal to authority and religious faith as the basis for knowledge and replacing this with the principle of the experiment, the domain of knowledge was opened up to all comers – at least in theory: people 'could put any statement and theory to the test of controlled experience ... The simplest and humblest student could now test ... the theory or laws put forth by the greatest scientist' (Cohen 1985b:79). In this sense, the methodology of experimentation is an instrument of democratization, rendering knowledge both open and (theoretically) accountable. Indeed, the twentieth-century practice of evidence-based medicine can be glimpsed in the pages of Bacon's *New Atlantis*, for all its patriarchal faults. But it appears even more clearly in another contemporary utopia, *The Kingdom of Macaria* (Anon. 1641),[33] an anonymous tract targeted at the Puritan leaders of the Long Parliament in England, a few days after they assembled for their second session in October 1641.

The Kingdom of Macaria addressed to the new parliament a comprehensive plea for action on social reform. It outlined a programme of social policy and economic reform based on the principles of experimental science, using the format of a dialogue between a scholar and a traveller, who brings stories of a place, Macaria, where 'they have not half so much trouble as they have in these European countreyes'. Macaria, so named after the Greek word for 'happiness',[34] was governed by one Great Council, which met briefly once a year, and five sub-Councils responsible for husbandry, fishing, trade by land, trade by sea and the new plantations, all of which had the power to make laws. One twentieth of all wealth in Macaria was spent on environmental improvement. The health of the Macarians was maintained by 'an house, or Colledge of experience, where they deliver out yeerly such medicines as they find out by experience'. New cures were debated publicly, and were accepted only when agreed to be effective. When the scholar in the dialogue responds to the traveller's tales by complaining that surely this is 'against Physicians', he is told that Macaria has solved this particular problem by integrating religion and medicine: 'cure animarum' and 'cure corporum' have been combined in the same person, and parsons in Macaria have absorbed the functions of doctors,[35] thus pursuing a religion which 'consists not in taking notice of severall opinions and sects, but is made up of infallible tenets, which may be proved by invincible arguments, and such as will abide the grand test of extreme dispute' (Anon. 1641:2, 14–15).

The authorship of *The Kingdom of Macaria* has been credited to either Gabriel Plattes, an English writer on mining and husbandry, or Samuel Hartlib, a central figure in the English educational renaissance, who was born in Polish

Prussia in 1600 and came to England in 1625.[36] Hartlib's main interest was in reforming education at both school and university level; he was an early pioneer of state comprehensive education. Plattes was an active inventor, an experimenter, who wrote widely on the uses of Baconian experimental philosophy to the study of such subjects as metal refining and methods for undertaking chemical analysis. He developed a plan for the state regulation of technology and economic innovation; his ideas exemplified the unprecedented wave of concern with social planning which accompanied the Puritan revolution. Plattes was supported financially by Hartlib during his last years (though not altogether satisfactorily, since he is reported to have died of starvation) (see Webster 1974a:375).

Conclusion

What we face here is a fundamental paradox between the idea of open, accountable, empirically based knowledge, on the one hand, and a system of thought which is deeply oppressive towards women and anything to which they are seen to be attached, on the other. The transformations in knowledge and methodology referred to in this chapter owed much to the increasing secularization of society – to the decline in the power of the Papacy and the rise of other forms of power embodied in the nation-state. Baconian and Cartesian philosophy embraced within it, at least in theory, the realm of social relations, but it was left to others, particularly Bacon's friend Thomas Hobbes and also to the French positivist thinker Auguste Comte – to develop the philosophical basis of the Baconian programme into a system of social science, and to bring the Cartesian version of mind into the modern age by giving it a more decisively materialist base. As S. P. Turner (1986:10) notes: 'The obscure promise that Bacon's realism held out to the social sciences was the possibility of the systematic repudiation, replacement, and correction of our present beliefs about human kind and society.' The process of realizing this promise dissolved into fragments the original unity of science and the scientific method; the result was today's apparently irreconcilable views – science as quantitative and experimental, social science as qualitative and observational. The first step in this was the growth of mercantilism and international trade, which imposed a quantitative logic on the new science and on its extensions to the social realm; the implications of this are explored more fully in the next chapter.

5

Mean Values

The properties of number, alone among all known phenomena, are, in the most rigorous sense, properties of all things whatever. All things are not coloured, or ponderable, or even extended; but all things are numerable.

Mill, *A System of Logic*

Why should the kind of success achieved in the study of stars, molecules or cells have come to seem an attractive model for research on human societies?

Porter, *Trust in Numbers*

The history of mathematics, statistics and quantification can be told at great length and in different ways; the account in this chapter settles on the work of a few individuals and a few themes as a way of providing a linking narrative between the story of science told in the last chapter and the emergence of what we would recognize as social science, which comes next. The question addressed in the chapter is really one about why quantification came to be regarded as so important a feature of the scientific method. How can this be explained, and what consequences does it suggest for the genesis of a more *social* science? If numbers are about 'objectivity', then where does this leave subjectivity? The chapter argues that quantification was promoted by male methodologists and was imposed on an existing hierarchical system of social relations, with the result that using numbers to contain feeling became as much a formula for ways of knowing as it is for a patriarchal social world.

According to that renowned methodologist, J. S. Mill, in the first quote at the head of this chapter, all things have the quality of numerability, and this may be all they have in common. From Copernicus onwards, the codification of the scientific method depended on mathematics as a tool for describing the 'laws' of nature. Mathematics had an especially important role to play in demonstrating how both metaphysical and theological world-views and individual human experience may (differently) generate misleading accounts of how nature works. It was thus the science of numbers which rescued human beings both from the pitfalls of theological certainty and from the solipsism of individual experience: the Earth does not fail to spin on its axis, or move round the Sun, just because people do not *feel* it to do so. While this observation, which is about rejecting the evidence of the senses, was an important facilitator of understanding how the natural universe works, it was to breed a long legacy of trouble for the methodology of the social sciences, whose proponents, because of their subject–matter, had ultimately to regard the experiences of individual human beings as essential data.

The technology of numbers

'Social mathematics', so named by the French methodologist Condorcet, had become one of two distinct branches of moral science by the early nineteenth century (the other was history – the chronology of human social development). 'Moral' science was regarded as synonymous with the study of the social. Social science thus absorbed, unthinkingly in the beginning, the idea that quantification is the prime method for establishing social facts – and indeed, the whole notion of 'facts' as being what social science is about.

Significant schools of sociological thought in the twentieth century have contested this point of view, taking apart the natural science model of enquiry as inappropriate to understanding the social world. Sociologists have also taken a hard look at the operations of science itself, and have found a sizable gap between what science says it does, and what it actually does – a gap not unlike the difference between what men say they do in the home and what they actually do. (This analogy is more than trivial, if we take into account science as a system of patriarchal relations.) In just the same way, the sociological framework can be used to posit fundamental questions about the common assumption that quantitative methods have achieved power and prestige in the modern world because these are proven, successful ways of knowing – they merely crossed the disciplinary divide between the natural and the social as part of the evolutionary process of modern knowledge-development. As Theodore Porter suggests, in the second quotation from his book *Trust in Numbers* at the head of this chapter, the ascendancy of numbers constitutes a research subject in its own right. Quantification is a social technology; what it raises is all the same kinds of problems associated with other technologies. Technology does not come from nowhere, or take the form it does by accident; it is ineluctably shaped by the social and economic setting which gives rise to it. It meets certain needs; but these are not everyone's needs. Technology may always seem to be some 'man's' dream, but all sorts of unanticipated consequences flow from the implementation of technologies in specific social circumstances, and some of these are likely to damage the very goals those technologies were designed to promote.

The first part of the story about the rise of quantification is about mathematics as the carrier of the main burden of scientific reasoning and the core of all the major theories of physical science. To the Renaissance scientist, mathematics held the key to nature's behaviour. This conviction began to take hold in the twelfth century, and is said to have come from the Arabs, who got it from the Greeks (Kline 1972). The interest of many methodologists in optics (both Hobbes and Descartes wrote treatises on this subject) stemmed from the belief that divine light is the cause of all phenomena; thus the mathematical laws of optics formed the true laws of nature. Chapter 4 described some of the close overlaps between mathematics and the codification of the scientific method; Galileo spoke for many when he expressed the opinion that God wrote the world in the language of mathematics (Hacking 1990:5). Many of the pioneers of scientific method and methodology were trained and practising mathematicians, including Copernicus, Descartes, Newton (and Auguste Comte – see chapter 6). The very expression 'Scientific Revolution' was coined by mathematicians, to whom it seemed that mathematics was the greatest revolutionizing force ever (Hankins 1985:1). This vision was most perfectly encoded in Newton's famous work, *The Mathematical Principles of Natural Philosophy* (1687), which summed up the importance of the mathematical vision to the whole scientific project, proving that everything can be subjected to the same calculus of quantity – the 'abstract' relationships of numbers.

The three methodologists whose work and lives appear below are not the only ones who helped to shape the quantitative basis of social science, but all three are distinguished for making explicit the argument that the method of knowing which depends on mathematics and which deals in the coinage of measurable facts is *the* way of studying the social domain.

From social mathematics to social science

The precursors of social science followed scientific thinkers in adopting the mathematical model of knowledge production. Thomas Hobbes (1588–1679)[1] is better known today for his political theory than for his embryonic 'social mathematics'; but he was one of the first to see that the combination of empiricism and mathematics had the potential to offer an understanding of the 'laws' of society, as well as those of nature. As Manicas puts it in his *A History and Philosophy of the Social Sciences*, (1987: 28) 'it was Hobbes ... who really put the whole business in motion'.[2]

Hobbes led a colourful and argumentative life, being much occupied by English politics during the time when Stuart England was rife with unrest, as Charles I fought with his Parliament for the power to rule as an absolute monarch. Not very much is known about Hobbes's personal life. He is said to have lacked emotional warmth, though to have been a reasonably reliable friend to those in need. Like Descartes, he had a 'natural' daughter, for whom he provided (Taylor 1908:25). It is to Hobbes that we owe the beginnings of the modern distinction between 'science' and 'philosophy'. But while he introduced this distinction, he maintained that the main requirement in both is correct reasoning. What correct reasoning means is computation –

adding and subtracting. For example, the idea of a human being is a compound of the concepts rational, animate and body; subtracting 'rational' leaves one with the definition of an animal. A second modern element in Hobbesian thought is the notion that philosophy ought above all to be *useful*: 'The end of know-ledge is power,' he wrote, 'and . . . the scope of all speculation is the perform-ing of some action, or thing to be done' (Hobbes 1656:i.6). He was particularly impressed by the potential of what he called 'philosophy' to avoid war – men did not want to engage in war; they did so, he argued, in ignorance of the true causes of war and peace. He concluded that only a scientific understanding of social laws can provide the means for a health-promoting public policy.

Like Newton, Hobbes was born prematurely – his mother is said to have been shocked by the news of the approaching Armada.[3] His father was a somewhat disreputable clergyman. Hobbes went early to Oxford, where he, like others, dismissed Aristotelian logic, and apparently spent much of his time capturing jackdaws and visiting map shops, where he was particularly taken by the parts on maps labelled 'terra incognita'. After Oxford, he began a lifelong association with a branch of the Cavendish family – not the one that contained 'mad Madge' (see chapter 4), but the Devonshire Cavendishes. He was given a position as tutor to the young William Cavendish; when the Cavendishes ran out of money, he worked for a time for another wealthy family, and then later returned to the Cavendish fold. Through these connections, Hobbes was in-troduced to many key thinkers, including Galileo, Descartes, William Harvey and Francis Bacon, whose secretary he became for a short time during the period of Bacon's fall from grace; Bacon claimed that Hobbes was one of the few people who understood his philosophy.

Hobbes spent his early years mainly reading history, romances, poetry and plays; he translated Thucydides' *History of the Peloponnesian Wars* in order to warn people of the dangers of not supporting the sovereign. His later, famous *Leviathan* (1651) was written mainly as an extension of this position, while he was in exile in France tutoring the future Charles II in mathematics. It was not until 1630, when he was in his forties, that Hobbes read Pythagoras and Euclid by accident during an idle moment. Thereafter geometry became his paradigm of science. He was a materialist, like Descartes, but quarrelled badly with him, writing one of six sets of objections to Descartes' *Meditations*, and taking the view that Descartes would have done better to have stuck to mathematics – he might then have avoided getting stuck down the blind alley of believing in immaterial souls. A specific bone of contention between them was that Hobbes said he came up with the Cartesian theory of vision (that colour does not inhere in objects, but is caused by the effect of the object on the optical nerves) before Descartes (see chapter 4).

Hobbes's *The Elements of Philosophy* was written in the 1640s and 1650s. It consists of three parts: 'of Body', which presents the principles of the new science of motion; 'of Man', which extends these principles to human physiol-ogy and psychology; and 'of the Body Politic', an elaboration of the same principles in ethics, politics and social relations. The subject-matter in all these three spheres is bodies; there are 'two chief kinds of bodies' which are very different from one another, but which 'offer themselves to such as search after their generation and properties; one whereof being the work of nature, is called a *natural body*, the other is called a *commonwealth*, and is made by the wills and agreements of men. And from these spring the two parts of philosophy, called *natural* and *civil*' (Hobbes 1656:11). What the whole added up to was an argument about the founding of social science in a set of corollaries derived from mechanics and mathematics. The opening paragraphs of Hobbes's *Leviathan* develop what was to become another highly influential metaphor in social science – that of biology as the ground-plan of social relations. Drawing on Harvey's work on the circulation of the blood and the body as a machine, Hobbes presents leviathan – the commonwealth or state – as an 'artificial man' with its various parts corresponding to the various bodily organs; sovereignty is the soul. Significantly for the development of a capitalist social system, money represented for Hobbes the blood circulating through the 'artificial man' of the state (with two modes of circulation, into the public coffers and out of them).

In the 1660s Hobbes became embroiled in another famous debate, with Robert Boyle about the usefulness of experimentation in science. Hobbes's view was that Boyle's experiments with an air pump (by means of which he attempted to prove the existence of a vacuum) were capable of different interpretations (one of which was that the equipment was faulty). Experimentation as such is an inadequate pathway to a better understanding of nature: what is needed is correct reasoning. He criticized the Royal Society for attempting to advance science through experimentation, rather than by deductive reasoning from general theories.[4] However, this anti-experimentalist line did him no good, and in fact led to substantial discredit, since he was swimming against the tide of a move towards experimentally-based science. By the time of his death, it has been noted, the word 'hypothesis' had become a term of abuse (Sorell 1996:102).

Our second 'social' methodologist is Marie-Jean-Antoine-Nicolas Caritat, Marquis de Condorcet (1743–94).[5] Condorcet, disciple of the great French mathematician d'Alembert, was himself a skilful mathematician, and another of those multi-talented players in the history of methodology. Condorcet promoted his vision of 'social mathematics' as steering French society through revolutionary times in the safe boat of rational decision-making. He believed that it was rational discussion – the power of reason, with mathematical calculation as its most precise expression – that would convince men to agree on what was in their, and society's, best interests.

Condorcet was an early opponent of slavery and a staunch advocate of women's rights; early in life he espoused the idea of *sensibilité*, or natural sympathy, on which ground he gave up sport and refused even to kill insects (E. S. Pearson 1978:425). Like Descartes, he tried to write accessibly so that women could read what he had to say. He supported universal suffrage, universal state education, social security for the poor, civil marriage and divorce and birth control, and he anticipated the United Nations in a plan for a World Council which would have the authority to adjudicate international disputes.

He opposed war, capital punishment, primogeniture and the civil and penal punishment of prostitutes and homosexuals (Bierstedt 1978). It was perhaps not surprising that he got himself into political trouble.

Condorcet defined the 'moral sciences' as all those which have as their object of study the human mind or the relations of 'men'; later he subdivided these into *sciences psychologiques* and *sciences sociales* (see Baker 1975:197–8). One of his minor claims to fame is as the probable originator of the term 'social science'; he used it in 1792 in a draft plan to the Committee on Public Instruction – in the singular, though the English translator put it into the plural (McDonald 1993:187; see also Baker 1975:viii and appendix B).[6] Much more substantially, he pioneered a unique combination of scientific methodology and commitment to evidence-based social reform, acknowledging debts to Bacon and to the British empiricists Locke, Berkeley and Hume, but especially to Hume (1711–76), whose arguments about the nature of proof and about the mental character of causal relationships (things human beings perceive, rather than things simply existing 'out there') resonated with Condorcet's own thinking.

Condorcet was born in 1743 of a poor noble father and a wealthy bourgeois mother. His father died when he was four, and his mother, an intensely pious woman, dedicated her son to the Virgin and dressed him in the white petticoats of a girl until he was eight – with what effect we do not know (E. S. Pearson 1978:424). He received a Jesuit education, and at sixteen upset his family by declining a military career and choosing mathematics instead. He published his first book on calculus at the age of twenty-two, and was elected to the French Academy of Science at twenty-six, later becoming its permanent secretary, in which capacity he advocated an institutional organization of science that followed the lines outlined in Bacon's *New Atlantis*. He played important political and scientific roles in the ministry of his friend Turgot, the renowned economist, in the mid-1770s, including attempting a standardization of weights and measures and a project on the hydrodynamics of canal building, which would open up interior waterways from Paris to the Atlantic coast. The canal project led Condorcet to his first research on population and mortality, in the form of a study of the relative mortalities compared to others of people living in marshy districts around the canals (see Baker 1975:69).[7] This study probably prompted his suggestion, one of the earliest to be made, that what was needed was a national data bank of mortality records, coded by occupation and marital status.

Condorcet became increasingly preoccupied with 'the science of man' as he rose rapidly up the political hierarchy, becoming one of the Commissioners of the National Treasury and a member of the Legislative Assembly for Paris in 1791. Political troubles – he was condemned to death for criticizing the new constitution – eventually forced him to go into hiding in the Parisian home of a 'gallant' woman called Madame Vernet.[8] He fled from her house nine months later, disguised as a woman, when he feared for her safety following the passage of a new law which was punitive towards those who harboured enemies of the government (Bierstedt 1978:19). In the months when Condorcet was secreted away, his wife, Sophie Groucy, Marquise de Condorcet, herself a prominent left-wing political activist, kept herself, their daughter, her sick sister and an old governess by painting portraits, sometimes of the condemned in prison; when this failed as a source of income, she set up an underwear shop (E. S. Pearson 1978:446). She also translated Adam Smith's *Theory of Moral Sentiments*, a book which is more about such qualities as ambition, justice and duty than about emotions, which Smith denigrated on the traditional masculine grounds that their expression is 'indecent, loathsome and disagreeable' (A. Smith 1759:53). Condorcet was finally arrested, and died in police custody in 1794. According to E. S. Pearson (1978:448), while on the run, Condorcet made the mistake of going into an inn, claiming to be a carpenter, and ordering an omelette made of the mathematically exact number of a dozen eggs – far too many for a frugal labourer, thereby giving the game away. Among the various stories about the cause of Condorcet's death, the one favoured by Pearson (1978:449) is suicide, as a result of taking arsenic contained in a ring prepared for him by one of his friends.

It was in Madame Vernet's home that Condorcet, encouraged by Sophie, wrote his grand work *Esquisse d'un Tableau Historique des progrès de l'Esprit Humain* (Sketch of the Intellectual Progress of Mankind), which was published posthumously in 1795. The *Esquisse* was adopted by many as the authentic testament of the Enlightenment, and it inspired Saint-Simon and his student Comte to formulate their ideas of positive sociology. As a mathematician, Condorcet argued that mathematical methods were appropriate tools for studying society. 'Social mathematics' here meant political arithmetic: statistics as social facts. He applied the calculus of probability (see chapter 7) to a broad range of social topics, including the relationship between 'life-style' and duration of life, and other social factors affecting health and mortality.

One of the many lessons of Condorcet's life was the one that re-emerges in chapter 10: that the diffusion of scientific thinking into politics is fostered best when close personal links exist between scientists and politicians. Turgot, appointed Controller-General (Minister of Finance) by Louis XVI in 1774 to deal with the impending financial crisis, moved in intellectual circles, and took a number of steps to ensure that policy-making was informed by science. For example, he appointed a commission on epidemics to investigate a cattle plague; the commission's work resulted in the establishment of the Royal Society of Medicine. He also saw the relationship between the challenge of constitutional reform in France and Condorcet's calculus of probabilities (see Matthews 1995). Condorcet's *Essay on the Application of Analysis to the Probability of Decisions Obtained by a Plurality of Votes* (1785) tried to solve a problem of political arithmetic which had been around for some time. The question was one about the conditions needed for the probability of tribunal decisions being true, and thus high enough to justify the faith of all citizens in accepting such decisions. This exercise demonstrated Condorcet's faith in a mathematically-driven reason as the basis for peaceful and successful social relations.

Adolphe Quételet (1796–1874),[9] the third prominent methodologist to take forward the programme of a mathematically-based social science, was born in what later became Belgium two years after Condorcet's premature death. He also trained as a mathematician, but learnt astronomy and meteorology from the master scientists of the age in Paris. Like Condorcet and other innovators, he practised a wide range of talents, writing poetry and the libretto of an opera; and he is said to have founded more statistical organizations than anyone else in the nineteenth century (Stigler 1986:102). His main occupation in Belgium was that of astronomer and meteorologist at the Royal Observatory in Brussels, but he gained an international reputation as a statistician and a founder of the new field of social science. For Quételet, Condorcet's 'social mathematics' was 'social physics', but it shared the same key features of being a rigorous quantified investigation of the laws of society that would equal the achievements of eighteenth-century astronomers (here Quételet was influenced by his main wage-earning occupation). He wrote:

> First of all, statistics gathers numbers; these numbers, collected on a large scale with care and prudence, have revealed interesting facts and have led to the surmising of laws which rule the moral and intellectual world, much like those that govern the material world; it is all these laws together which appear to me to constitute *social physics*, a science still in its infancy, but one which daily becomes incontestably more important and will ultimately rank among those sciences from which man will most benefit. *(Quételet 1837:485–6)*

It was in a dispute between Quételet and Comte about how to name the new territory of social physics, that the term 'sociology' was born (see chapter 6).

Quételet's early statistical work involved population research and planning for a national census in Belgium, during which he was much impressed by the inaccuracy of previous population estimates and the need to apply more rigorous scientific principles which would not make the mistake of assuming a misleading homogeneity in social data. His particular contribution was applying probability to the measurement of uncertainty in the social sciences. In this he built on the work of the French mathematician and astronomer Pierre Simon Laplace (1749–1827), who had devised the method of community sampling ('random' sampling, though he did not call it that) in order to determine the rate of births in the population, and who made the startlingly important observation in relation to judging the effectiveness of medical treatments that the best method 'will manifest itself more and more in the measure that the number [of observations] is increased' (cited in Matthews 1995:100).

Quételet's own major contributions were the 'normal distribution' – the notion that all naturally occurring distributions of data follow a 'normal' curve – and the concept of 'the average man' as a way of summarizing statistical data. This concept was crucially important in the development of a mathematical social science; its acceptance was aided by its resonance with the egalitarian ideas prominent in nineteenth-century French political thought, given that it appeared to capture both the democratic ideal and the apparent precision of scientific thought (Stigler 1986:171), though it also bought into notions of gender inequality. Quételet used the masculine pronoun without comment, although he did include data on real men and women (some of it consisting of measurements of the human body taken by Renaissance artists, including Leonardo da Vinci, Dürer and Michelangelo (Kline 1972:394)). However, the essential building block of his idea of 'the average man' consisted of measurements carried out on male army conscripts.[10]

Quételet was particularly impressed by the relevance to a science-based medical practice of his statistical breakthrough: how else, he argued, could a physician determine whether someone was really ill or not, except by comparing their condition to that of 'the average man'? 'Every physician, in forming such calculations,' he argued, 'refers to the existing documents on the science, or to his own experience; which is only a similar estimate to that which we wish to make on a greater scale and with more accuracy' (Quételet 1962:99). It is no accident that the cogitations of the early methodologists should so often have settled on the practice of medicine as an exemplar of the need for exact quantification and greater scientific precision (this strand in the story is continued in chapter 7). During this period, the late eighteenth and early nineteenth centuries, medicine was itself in a process of transition from art to science. Debates in the early 1800s about the value of different treatments hinged on two issues: the need to control the play of chance in attributing cause and effect and the importance of more, rather than fewer, numbers as a guard against invalid inferences. When the statistician Pierre-Charles-Alexandre Louis advocated his 'numerical method' (statistical comparison) as a more reliable way of determining the effects of treatment, he incurred the wrath of many doctors, who maintained a case that looks very like the later feminist one: that each patient is an individual, whose situation and history can only be taken into account during a clinical interview; thus the value of 'aggregative thinking' destroys the essential, individualized basis of the medical art (Desrosières 1991). This was a turning-point for the medical profession, poised between contrasting visions of professional legitimacy: humanitarian healer or empirical scientist? The argument was that reducing people to numbers cancels out personal knowledge. This was not Louis' intention: 'it is not sufficient to count in order to know the relation between the facts,' he responded, 'and in employing the numerical method without discernment, either one can arrive at absurd results, or results that experience does not verify' (Louis 1837:25).

The use of medicine as a case-study signifies a subterranean cultural association between the notions of professional expertise, objectivity and the impersonality (or depersonalization, as some would put it) afforded by the technology of numbers. Medicine needed quantification to acquire credibility as a science – not because this is what science means, but because this is what it had come to mean. In the same way, the professional identity of the early social scientists was inextricably bound up with the ideology and practice of quantification.

Statistics and the state

Around 1800 most European countries began to institutionalize efforts to cen-
tralize information about the population in the form of national statistical
bureaux (Clark 1973). This is another aspect of the move towards quantification:
the use by the state of numbers as a way of knowing about (and therefore
controlling) its citizens.

As M. Greenwood notes (1948:21), it is hard to believe that no one in the
ancient world studied demography arithmetically. The Romans enumerated
citizens (the word *census* is Latin). The Domesday Book is notable for the
absence of any estimate of population numbers; but it did offer some kind of
quantitative map to inform government. According to Karl Pearson's detailed history of statistics, the adjective *statisticus* first came into vogue in the
seventeenth century. Its origin was the Italian word *statista*, meaning 'the
man concerned with reasoning about the state', and the first trace of statistics
in the modern sense is to be found in the activities of a fourteenth-century
Florentine priest who determined the sex ratio in his parish by setting aside
a black bean every time a boy was born, and a white one for every female
birth.[11] 'Statistics' as a discipline is commonly said to have begun in seventeenth-century Germany with the work of Hermann Conring, a theologian
and philosopher who also had the distinction of being physician to the noto-
rious Queen Christina of Sweden. In 1752 another scholar called Gottfried
Achenwall, a Professor of Philosophy at Göttingen, used the word *statistik* to
indicate a specialized branch of knowledge concerned with the collection of
'remarkable facts about the state' (E. S. Pearson 1978:2; Hacking 1990:25; see
also Clark 1973).

The British counterpart to 'statistik'/'statisticus' was the political arithmetic of John Graunt (1620–74) and William Petty (1623–87).[12] The story of
John Graunt and his work on the Bills of Mortality is well known. One of the
best accounts of his joint work with Petty is given by Major Greenwood
(1880–1949), an influential statistician in his own right.[13] As Greenwood
notes, biographical material about Graunt is sparse. Graunt, like Petty, was
born in Hampshire. His father traded in haberdashery, and brought his son
up to the same trade. Graunt taught himself Latin and French, becoming a
self-made intellectual as well as a wealthy merchant. According to John Aubrey's
Brief Lives, he converted to Catholicism, and had one son, who died in
Persia, and a daughter, who became a nun in Ghent. His fame as the father
of statistics flows from a small volume entitled *Natural and Political Observations, made upon the Bills of Mortality*, which was published in 1661. The
London Bills were kept regularly from 1603 on as records of medical events
in the different London parishes, and were published annually on the Thurs-
day before Christmas Day. Their original purpose was to warn the sovereign
of the need to move to clean air. But Graunt, wanting something to do in his
spare time, and building on his 'Shop-Arithmetick' (Cohen 1994b:166), saw
and exploited the Bills of Mortality as a 'tables of discovery' – a source of

original and generalizable data about the population, which could form part of that natural history of 'man' anticipated by Bacon (Baker 1975:198; Kline 1972:387).

What Graunt had to work with was sixty years' worth of numbers about males and females christened and buried and the causes of death, under about sixty headings (but not sex-differentiated). The method he used in his analysis was not academic mathematics such as theoretical geometry, but business mathematics or accountancy. What he spotted in the data were surprising regularities; for example, the excess of male over female births, and differences between the life chances of town- and country-dwellers. The conclusions he drew were not always the obvious ones; the sex ratio at birth, for instance, taken in combination with men's tendency to die from occupational hazards and military service, provided the lesson that monogamy must be the natural form of marriage. As Pearson notes, an extraordinary number of modern statistical and epidemiological problems are to be found in Graunt's text, including the expectation of life at different ages, the effects of urban and rural life on health, and the difficulty of acquiring reliable data on 'shameful' health problems ('French pox' or syphilis in Graunt's day).

At some point Graunt met William Petty, who provided the academic side of a highly fruitful collaboration. Petty was the son of a clothier, but he received more formal education than Graunt, went into the Navy, travelled in Europe (meeting Hobbes on the way), qualified as a doctor, and became a Professor of Anatomy at Oxford. When he first taught anatomy (an unusual subject at the time), he did so using a body 'he brought by water from Reading . . . some way pickled or preserved' (Aubrey 1982:242). He bought estates in Ireland, where he started ironworks, lead mines, sea fisheries and other industries, and was made Surveyor-General of that country by Charles II, who knighted him. He was a man of great ingenuity and verve, inventing a copying machine in 1648 and an unsinkable boat in 1663. His published works include a *Treatise on Taxes* (1662) and *Political Arithmetic* (1691). His work in this latter field demonstrated an understanding of how to calculate fertility rates and an accurate grasp of the principles of a life table (a table showing survivorship at different ages based on age-specific mortality data). He also asked some impertinent and modern questions about whether doctors decreased or increased mortality[14] and whether the use of medicines was any more effective than the play of chance (see M. Greenwood 1948:16).

The products of Graunt and Petty's intellectual partnership have earned them a secure place in the history of medical statistics and epidemiology. But this obscures their more fundamental contribution, which was to pioneer application of the numerical method to the phenomena of human society, and, most importantly, to harness this to the needs of government and the state: social knowledge, in the sense in which they sought it, primarily concerned what happened to bodies as Cartesian extensions of matter in space. Moreover, the purpose of this social knowledge had a modern tinge to it; it was not 'academic' – gathered for its own sake and the self-serving interests of scholars – but pragmatic: to serve the cause of scientific medicine and the state. Graunt, in particular, argued that the art of government would always be deficient without an adequate basis of quantitative data.

Numbers, technology and power

Numbers, as Porter (1995) persuasively argues, form strategies of communication which impose distance and impersonality on what would formerly have been familiar relationships: 'most crucially, reliance on numbers and quantitative manipulation minimizes the need for intimate knowledge and personal trust'. Thus, 'Quantification is well suited for communication that goes beyond the boundaries of locality and community. A highly disciplined discourse helps to produce knowledge independent of the particular people who make it' (Porter 1995:ix). Taken in conjunction with the rise of professionalization in modern society, this produces a situation in which expertise is increasingly inseparable from objectivity. In turn, objectivity is associated with the reduction of everything to that mathematical code which Galileo saw as the God-given language of the universe. There is also a conceptual link with the idea of validity: the most valid knowledge becomes that produced, or described, using numbers. The Latin root of 'validity' means 'power'; the circle is thus complete, as the power of some people to know more, or better, than others both inheres in and derives from knowledge expressed numerically.

The emphasis on precision created the frame of mind which made the inventions of the Industrial Revolution possible. The growth of abstract numerical calculations is a feature of an increasingly complex society. As Hacking (1990:5) has commented:

> The avalanche of numbers . . . and the invention of normalcy are embedded in the grander topics of the Industrial Revolution. The acquisition of numbers by the populace, and the professional lust for precision in measurement, were driven by familiar themes of manufacture, mining, trade, health, railways, war, empire.

When the young, bored Galileo whiled away time by studying the great swinging lamp in Pisa Cathedral, he had no watch with which to check his observation that the time of the swing was independent of the breadth of the arc through which the lamp swung; instead, he used the pulse of his heart (Kline 1972:213). The Renaissance was marked by a new awareness of the passing of time; the pendulum clock came into being soon after Galileo's observation, and during the same period as the microscope, the thermometer and the telescope. The old boundaries of time – the rising and setting of the Sun, the seasons, the appetites of humans and animals, the pacing of human reproduction – no longer served the time-keeping needs of a society in which time meant fixed moments, shared and understood by everybody. Church and state began to set times for things – a time to pay taxes, a time to pray. Later on, industrialized time in factories, schools and offices became an indispensable means of social regulation.

When the English diarist Samuel Pepys remarked that as a senior civil servant in charge of the Royal Navy he had to sit up half the night in order to learn his eight times table (C. Evans 1983:11), he was complaining about the rise of a new strategy of communication which effectively separated professional expertise from personal experience and relationships. The same notion – that numbers rendered objective what would otherwise be subjective – informed the rise of the social survey during the nineteenth century. This primarily 'quantitative' method of investigation, it has been argued, enabled middle-class philanthropists to maintain a distance from the object of their gaze, whilst dealing with their anxieties about the social transformations they saw all around them, most of which they did not understand. Many such studies were done on what would later be called 'deviant' sub-groups of the population – vagrants, prostitutes, the insane, the diseased. An important underlying notion was that enumeration and classification would ensure control.[15] In this sense, the mathematical model of understanding, which presumes that problems, in order to be solved, must be broken down into their component parts, reflects fundamental mechanical principles of capitalism, with its hierarchical divisions of labour and devotion to monetary goals.

The rise of quantification was part of a professional abandonment of reliance on expert judgement in favour of standardized rules that could be communicated between unknown people, across continents, and so forth, thereby diminishing the human element in knowledge production. The work of people such as Condorcet was formed in, and influenced by, the cultural context of a society in transition from forms of social relations that depended on particularistic notions and the primacy of personal and community experience to those organized instead around the centralization of decision making and the contractual principles of mercantile capitalism.

Once again, medicine provides the exemplary case-study of the way in which the logic of quantification in its technological mode also serves to impose distance between professionals and clients. Since the late nineteenth century, the growth of new mechanical and pharmacological ways of knowing what is going on inside human bodies has neatly bypassed the need for people themselves to tell doctors what they think is going on. For example, when upper-class pregnant women first started to consult doctors in the late nineteenth century, doctors relied on mothers to know about the fetus inside the female body. But today, in many hospitals, the existence of a pregnancy is confirmed only by ultrasonic examination and/or by urine tests, and any information offered by women about whether, and when, they became pregnant is regarded as unnecessary and unreliable (see Oakley 1994).

Information about bodies produced by medical technology has a numerical form: the computer print-out from the electronic fetal heart-rate recording machine, the laboratory estimation of the levels of hormones in blood and urine. Interestingly, just as nineteenth-century doctors resisted numbers, so they also disliked technological forms of diagnosis as detracting from their individualized expertise. For instance, the new technology of stethoscopes for listening to patients' hearts was just about acceptable, because only the physician could hear the sound the stethoscope produced – the results were not available as 'objective' data for anyone else to hear or challenge (Reiser 1978). But stethoscopes had another value; they removed the need for doctors to have physical contact with patients. While the early stethoscopes were rigid and notoriously difficult for obese doctors to use, the introduction of flexible stethoscopes in the 1830s meant that doctors could effectively keep their distance (and could also examine patients whose modesty ruled out actual physical contact). This is one of countless examples of a technology bringing unforeseen consequences in its train.

'Hard' times

We can see the acceptance of all these ideas about positive social facts and enumeration in Charles Dickens's novel *Hard Times,* which was first published in 1854, a few years after Mill's celebration of numbers in *A System of Logic.* The central character of *Hard Times* is Thomas Gradgrind, a self-made business man with political ambitions. Gradgrind's main interest in life is 'Facts'. He is a man 'with a rule and a pair of scales, and the multiplication table always in his pocket ... ready to weigh and measure any parcel of human nature and tell you exactly what it comes to' (Dickens 1854:8). Gradgrind lives in a red-brick industrial Midlands city called Coketown with five little Gradgrinds and Mrs Gradgrind, 'a little, thin, white, pink-eyed bundle of shawls', whose destiny it is to be dominated by her husband's 'ological' interests: 'Ologies of all kinds, from morning to night. If there is any ology left, of any description, that has not been worn to rags in this house, all I can say is, I hope I shall never hear its name' (Dickens 1854:24, 266).[16] Gradgrind's office is his observatory, and it is full of statistical books. Even his house is built according to mathematical principles: it is 'A calculated, cast up, balanced and proved house', with the same number of windows on each side, and 'A lawn and garden and an infant avenue, all ruled straight like a botanical account book ... mechanical lifts for the housemaids ... everything that heart could desire'. Coketown itself is 'a triumph of fact': 'everything was fact between the lying-in hospital and the cemetery, and what you couldn't state in figures ... was not, and never should be, world without end, Amen' (Dickens 1854:33–4). Thomas Gradgrind's obsession with measurement gave rise to the term 'gradgrindism', used to refer to an inhumane fervour for numbers and the currency of economic costs (see e.g. Abrams 1968:22).

Unsurprisingly, the five little Gradgrinds are brought up in the same mathematical and 'ological' spirit as breathes life into their father; he has perpetually lectured them about facts since their earliest years, and has encouraged them in habits of definition and classification. The story told in the book is one about Gradgrind's come-uppance, as two of his children repay his efforts by thieving and making a miserable marriage respectively, and a warm-hearted circus girl called Sissy, who is quite unable even to define a horse and even more unable to pronounce the word 'statistics', proves an incomparable support. But it is particularly in the dialogues between Gradgrind and his daughter Louisa that Dickens plays out the conflict between 'Fact' and 'Feeling', revealing the book's deeper narrative, which is about the domination of modern life by science, economics and technology and the repressive supremacy of 'hard facts'. (It is no accident that Gradgrind used to be a wholesale *hardware* manufacturer; his house is called *Stone* Lodge.)

When Mr Bounderby, Gradgrind's banking friend, proposes to Louisa, it is at first not obvious to her that she ought to marry him. Her father sets in front of her the case, partly based on statistical evidence, that she should. Louisa is still not persuaded:

> 'Father, I have often thought that life is very short.' –
> This was so distinctly one of his subjects that he interposed – 'It is short, no doubt, my dear. Still, the average duration of human life is proved to have increased of late years. The calculations of various life assurance and annuity offices, among other figures which cannot go wrong, have established the fact.'
> 'I speak of my own life, father.'
> 'Oh indeed? Still,' said Mr. Gradgrind, 'I need not point out to you, Louisa, that it is governed by the laws which govern lives in aggregate.' *(Dickens 1854:135)*

Such unhelpful remarks do not encourage Louisa to avoid her troubled fate. One night, sometime later, when she is married to Mr Bounderby and having problems with him, she comes to visit her father:

> 'What is it? I conjure you, Louisa, tell me what is the matter' . . .
> 'Father, you have trained me from my cradle.'
> 'Yes, Louisa.'
> 'I curse the hour in which I was born to such a destiny.'
> He looked at her in doubt and dread, vacantly repeating, 'Curse the hour? Curse the hour?'
> 'How could you give me life, and take from me all the inappreciable things that raise it from the state of conscious death? Where are the graces of my soul? Where are the sentiments of my heart? What have you done, O father, what have you done, with the garden that should have bloomed once, in this great wilderness here!' *(Dickens 1854:286)*

Louisa is, of course, clutching her breast as she says this. That it should be a woman who articulates the importance of feeling and of the *quality* of life entirely fits with the discovery of 'qualitative' social science by feminist social scientists in the late twentieth century. Moreover, Louisa's appeal to emotion, her feeling that her education in 'Facts' omitted all that is important in human life, echoes the mental crises that affected many of the key figures in the history of methodology, including J. S. Mill himself. The figure of Thomas Gradgrind was actually modelled directly on J. S. Mill's father, James Mill, whose political economy and utilitarian philosophy were well known to Dickens,[17] and had led him to educate his own son exactly in the manner of the little Gradgrinds (or, rather, the other way around) (Lepenies 1988:112).[18]

What Dickens illustrates in the fable of *Hard Times* is precisely the function of objectivity, defined in Mill's numerical terms, as a struggle against subjectivity. What is implicit in the Cartesian discovery of reason's ability to control emotion – recourse to numbers – becomes an explicit *modus operandi* in early social science. Mrs Gradgrind, with all her appealing weakness, stands for the feminine, for 'Feeling', as against 'Fact'.

It would be easy to conclude from the above account that there were no women advancing the case for quantification as a modern approach to society. But the struggles of seventeenth-century philosopher and writer Margaret Cavendish to make her mark on the public world, referred to in the last chapter, were replicated by those of many women before and since. Florence Nightingale's (1820–1910) efforts to emancipate herself from restricted views of women's sphere are especially legendary. What is less often recognized is that Nightingale's reputation as the 'lady of the lamp' inventing scientific nursing on the battlefields of the Crimean War hides another, less well-known existence as a 'passionate statistician' (K. Pearson 1924:414). Nightingale had pleaded with her family to be taught mathematics, and had carried out many private statistical studies of health. After she came back from the Crimea, she made no more public appearances and attended no more public functions; many people assumed she was dead. But she was labouring away quietly and relentlessly, with a determination to use statistics to reform public health, including that of the Army, a special concern of hers after she had witnessed the high casualty rates of British soldiers on the battlefields of the Crimea.

Nightingale's *Notes on Matters affecting the Health, Efficiency, and Hospital Administration of the British Army* (1858) was packed with figures, tables and statistical comparisons, and was published only a few years after Dickens penned his condemnation of masculine 'gradgrindism'. Personally collecting the necessary figures, she had shown that mortality inside army barracks in peacetime was twice that of the population living outside, despite the fact that those recruited to the army had been passed by medical examination as strong and fit. She became the expert on anything and everything to do with the social and administrative conditions of the Army, including inventing a cost-accounting system for the Army Medical Services which was introduced in the early 1860s and was still going strong in 1947 (Woodham-Smith 1950).

Nightingale anticipated national health surveys by many years in recommending the addition of information on sickness to the 1861 Census, was well aware of the need to 'control' for social background in interpreting health data, and observant about the critical effect on health of housing and other social conditions: 'In Life Insurance and such like societies,' she wrote, 'were they instead of having the person examined by the medical man, to have the houses, conditions, ways of life, of these persons examined, at how much truer results would they arrive!' (Nightingale 1969:123). Her *Introductory Notes on Lying-in Institutions* (1871) is a careful, pioneering analysis of why childbirth deaths were higher in institutions than at home – and higher in lying-in institutions, including the one she had established for training midwives – than in workhouses. In all this endeavour she worked with the innovative government statistician William Farr, and through him met Adolphe Quételet sometime in the mid-1860s. Quételet sent Nightingale a copy of the 1869 edition of his *Physique sociale*, and she was much impressed, maintaining a correspondence with him until he died in 1874.[19]

Madame de Staël (1766–1817) was a contemporary of Condorcet's. Like Florence Nightingale, but in a different way, her achievements in the fields of methodology, politics and philosophy have been overshadowed by the attention given to another aspect of her life – the many colourful liaisons she enjoyed with leading political and philosophical figures of the time. She was born Anne-Louis-Germaine Necker to a well-connected banker, later Louis XVI's Minister of Finance, and an independent, well-educated mother who was determined that her daughter should become a 'living encyclopaedia' of mathematics, theology, languages, history and geography (Besser 1994:2). Her parents tried to marry her off to the English politician William Pitt, but Germaine would have none of it, so they compromised on a middle-aged, financially dissolute Swedish baron, Eric-Magnus de Staël-Holstein. Madame de Staël established a famous salon in Paris which attracted diplomats, politicians, aristocrats and writers, and expressed her disappointment with marriage in a number of verse plays and other writings. She later fell in love with Comte Louis de Narbonne, rumoured to be the incestuous son of Louis XV and his daughter Adélaïde, and had two more children by him; there followed the series of other liaisons with prominent political figures for which she is well-known, culminating in a marriage to a soldier half her age, by whom she had a child (at the age of forty-six) who later married the granddaughter of her lover Narbonne.

In 1788 de Staël published a literary volume on the work of Rousseau, *Lettres sur les écrits et le caractère de JJ Rousseau*, the first of an impressive series of works which spanned and united her various 'passions' – for politics, philosophies and methodologies of knowledge, science, literature, the study of social relationships, and women's rights – at a time when most women who managed to write and to publish their writings were limited to poetry and romance. She argued that nature and society had disinherited women, criticized the double moral standard applied to men and women, and memorably noted of her own work 'another kind of attack, capable of endless repetition . . . blaming me, as a woman, for writing and thinking' *(On Literature Considered in its Relationship to Social Institutions* (1800); Folkenflik 1987:173). Her close friends called her too masculine; contemporary abuse deemed her 'hermaphrodite', 'prostitute' and 'witch' (Besser 1994:139). De Staël's *Influence of the Passions* (1796) dissected the basic paradox with which the social sciences deal – that individuals themselves may be unpredictable, but there are still regularities in social behaviour; and she argued the Condorcetian case that a society whose government followed 'geometrically true principles' would be a peaceful society. Bonaparte was at first an ally, then banished her to exile. She also corresponded with Thomas Jefferson, President of the United States, about foreign policy (and tried to persuade him to abolish slavery), wrote a book about suicide, *Reflections on Suicide* (1813), which anticipated the later work by Durkheim, and an informative political treatise, *Consideration of the Principal Events of the French Revolution* (see Besser 1994; McDonald 1993:189–93).

Conclusion

By the end of the nineteenth century, science and social science had come to mean the use of quantitative methods to discover the laws governing the organic and inorganic worlds. The early 'pre-sociologists' such as Condorcet, Quételet and Hobbes took a decisive stand on the principle articulated by Mill, and before Mill by other scientists and methodologists, that everything worth anything could be represented by a number. This model of quantification reflected cultural moves towards a number-driven and increasingly technological society and cultural linkages between the pursuit of objectivity and claims to professional expertise. But if numbers, in embryonic social science, were the measure of all things, they were so for a laudable (if ultimately unattainable) purpose: that affairs of social policy might be settled by reference to firm evidence, just as matters of natural science were. In utopia there is no place for the chaos of differing opinions; it would take the long evolution of social science for these to be embraced, along with other 'subjective' data, as legitimate subject-matter.

6

Imagining Social Science

The problem of sociology is that, although it may imitate the natural sciences, it can never become a true natural science of society: but if it abandons its scientific orientation it draws perilously close to literature.
Lepenies, *Between Literature and Science*

From the flight of emotion away from the service of God to the service of man, and from the current faith in the scientific method, I drew the inference that the most hopeful form of social service was the craft of a social investigator.
Webb, *My Apprenticeship*

The paradigm divide in research methodology today casts social scientists as the enemies of natural scientists. The main grounds for this are that positivism is dead (and ought never to have been alive), and that quantification and experimentation rob human beings of their subjectivity by turning them into objects of scientific gaze. These contentions rest on a particular view of social science (and of natural science), which is itself socially located. Moreover, all such debates sooner or later raise the question of historical origins. Where did social science come from, and what kind of science was it? The story told in this chapter unfolds two critical dialogues. The first is between the ideas of sociology/social science, social reform and socialism; while these are not the same as each other, they share an overlapping history. The second dialogue continues the story begun in chapter 4 of the terms 'experience' and 'experiment'; the shifting relationship between these two notions mirrors the relationship between the two sorts of science themselves.

It is within this second dialectic that an enduring problem for social science is also located: for, if social science is something different from science, how can we be sure about its difference from fiction? These questions themselves feed into the underlying question of gender and its relation to methodological divisions. It is no historical accident that all the 'great' methodologists of social science were male. The naming of social science as a discipline followed two logics already successfully associated with masculinity: that of science's penetration of the feminine natural universe and the ideas of evolutionary biology and natural selection. These provided the essential blueprint for the new understandings of the social world which were demanded by the social and economic dislocations of the nineteenth century.

Beatrice Potter discovers positivism

At the age of twenty eight, Beatrice Webb, née Potter (1858–1943), the youngest but one of nine daughters of Gloucestershire industrial magnate Richard Potter, felt her life was over. Beatrice was expected to lead the life of a Victorian lady, occupied solely with domestic and 'society' duties. But her happiest hours were those stolen from such duties and spent reading books about philosophical and social issues. These gave her the feeling that if only she could devote herself to one subject, she might be able to *do something*. What saved Beatrice was the discovery of this something – social science. It was social science, together with its British twin, eugenics, which rescued her and her contemporaries from the 'perpetual state of ferment' which characterized an age bent on questioning all received wisdom (Seymour-Jones 1993:44). Two men were especially instrumental in her salvation: an old family friend, one of the founding fathers of sociology, 'the incessantly ratiocinating philosopher' Herbert Spencer (Webb 1938:39), and Beatrice's cousin, Charles Booth (1840–1916), who devoted eighteen years at his own expense to the first modern social investigation of poverty, (published in seventeen volumes in 1902–3).

Herbert Spencer (1820–1903) first encouraged the young Beatrice's interest in social issues, and it was he who urged her to take up the 'craft' of social investigation. He told her she reminded him of George Eliot, another close friend of his,[1] whom he advised to write fiction (Webb 1938:47; Spencer 1904: 38).[2] Brought up in total ignorance of 'the world of labour', Beatrice took her first step as a social investigator in 1883, when she went to live, disguised as a Yorkshire farmer's daughter, with poor relations of her mother's, mill-hands in East Lancashire, in order to find out more about the everyday lives of working people.[3] The following year she took up a role as a rent-collector in the East End of London. This was a charitable duty inherited from her sister Kate on Kate's marriage; it involved selecting suitable tenants for a tenement block which had been built to rehouse displaced working-class families at the instigation of the housing reformer Octavia Hill, and making sure they paid their rents on time. The tenement work afforded troubling insights of the kind Beatrice had not formerly had into the exigencies of working-class life:

> The meeting places, there is something grotesquely coarse in this, are the water closets! Boys and girls crowd on these landings – they are the only lighted places in the buildings – to gamble and flirt. The lady collectors are an altogether superficial thing. Undoubtedly their gentleness and kindness bring light into

many homes: but what are they in face of this collective brutality, heaped up together in infectious contact; adding to each other's dirt, physical and moral? *(Webb 1938:325)*

Her work as a tenement-manager led Beatrice to ponder the nature of charitable and other endeavours. She began to form a view, which she would later develop in her partnership with Sidney Webb, that social reform was in all essential respects analogous with scientific experimentation: '"Experimenting in the lives of other people, how cold-blooded!" I hear some reader object,' she wrote:

> Is it necessary to explain that such 'experimenting' cannot be avoided; that all administration, whether from the motive of profit-making or from that of public service, whether of the factory or the mine, of the elementary school or the post office, of the co-operative society or the Trade Union . . . necessarily amounts to nothing less than 'experimenting in the lives of other people'. *(Webb 1938:387)*

It was a logical step for Beatrice to offer, in 1886, to help cousin 'Charlie' with his poverty enquiries. Even with three paid secretaries, these threatened to swamp him.[4] Working for Booth, Beatrice again resorted to disguise, this time as a 'plain trouser hand' in a series of East End workshops, so as to gain a better understanding of the so-called sweating system, whereby middlemen expropriated profits from the labour of men and women working in often appalling conditions for very low rates of pay. Beatrice's strategy was an early example of the use of participant observation to complement 'quantitative' enquiry. Booth himself later copied Beatrice's example, spending some time lodging in three households in his classes 'C, D and E', and apparently enjoying their habits of life better than those of his own social circle, aside from the fleas. Neither Charles Booth nor Beatrice Potter were honest with their informants, disguising from them their real purpose. Beatrice's disguise proved particularly difficult to maintain when her co-workers observed that she was a dreadful needlewoman and was better suited to giving orders than taking them (Webb 1938: 367, 10).

Beatrice Potter's experience as a social investigator for Charles Booth's poverty study confirmed her faith in the application of the scientific method to social issues. It also helped to transform her into a socialist. She developed a deep mistrust for the Darwinism of those such as Spencer, her old mentor, who saw the hierarchies of power embedded in the capitalist system merely as part of the 'natural order of things', and who stubbornly treated 'suggestive hypotheses' as 'proven laws' (Webb 1938:319).[5] To her, all social facts were things to be discovered and then questioned; the scientific method was the means to this all-important end. When her father died in 1892, she married Sidney Webb, entering into the well-known partnership of dedication to socialist and social science causes which produced some twenty volumes of research on social institutions, and helped to found the London School of Economics and the British Labour Party.

Comte and the new religion of social science

Beatrice Webb's reading as a young woman included the entire works of a French social philosopher called Auguste Comte, which she and her sister Margaret ordered from the London Library. From Comte, she took the 'alternative religion' of humanity; above all, what she absorbed was the message of altruism as the highest human mission to be attained (Seymour-Jones 1993:69).

Comte (1798–1857), like the other precursors of sociology, originally made his living teaching mathematics, and then became secretary to the entrepreneur Comte Henri de Saint-Simon (1760–1825). Saint-Simon, dubbed the founder of French socialism, was a nobleman and an adventurer, by turns a soldier in the American Revolution, a canal-builder, a speculator in confiscated church properties, a stage-coach operator and a textile manufacturer. At the age of forty-one he decided to devote himself exclusively to social reform, a project he embarked on by inviting leading thinkers of the day to sumptuous dinners in his home. Saint-Simon saw scientific knowledge as rescuing society from the intellectual and moral chaos which followed the French Revolution, when legislators drafted one plan after another in ignorance of social conditions. 'Science' here included a natural science of society, which would discover laws of social behaviour and so establish valid ways of settling disputes about social policy. The basis of Saint-Simon's methodology was Baconian empiricism: sensation was the only means to knowledge, and theories had to be tested against observable facts. These ideas influenced many later social science developments, including those of Comte, Durkheim and Marx. Marx was introduced to them by his father-in-law, and made full use in his writings of the terms 'positive' and 'positive science'.

Comte's own mammoth six-volume work, *Cours de philosophie positive* (1877), owed much to Saint-Simon, to the social philosophy of Condorcet, and, indeed, to lines of speculation about the problem of order and change in human society that went back a long way in the history of Western thought. In so far as Comte's central achievement was to articulate the spirit of the age, this does not, of course, give him 'property rights in it' (Abrams 1968:55). Social science was not simply born in the mid-nineteenth century; rather, its naming and conceptual organization followed traditions of thought which go back as far as the fifth century BC. As Lynn McDonald notes in her *The Early Origins of the Social Sciences*, the orthodox narrative of social science's founding fathers denies the contribution to its ideas and practices of significant women. The 'secret history' of the social sciences contains the activities of women such as Harriet Taylor, Harriet Martineau, Florence Nightingale, Jane Addams and Beatrice Webb. The official story also turns its back on an entire history of analytic thinking about social issues and a productive interchange between all forms of 'science'. For example, the very term 'cosmos', used to describe the ordering of the universe, was adopted from the 'social' field of housekeeping and gardening.

But Comte's work remains the most often-quoted representation of positivism

today. The first English translation of the *Cours* was undertaken by the writer
and feminist Harriet Martineau (1802–76). In her Preface to the (freely) translated edition of *The Positive Philosophy of Auguste Comte*, Martineau writes of her
motivation to make Comte's work accessible 'to the largest number of intelligent
readers': like Beatrice Webb, she notes how people seem to be 'adrift' in 'un-
sound speculation' and 'moral uncertainty and depression'; what they need to
save them is the 'firm foundation of knowledge', which is what Comte's philosophy can offer. Martineau was in no doubt that by the end of the century his work
would be recognized as 'one of its chief honours' (Martineau 1853:vii–viii).

Martineau was an unknown young woman when her first writings popular-
izing the new ideas about political economy began to appear in the 1830s; she
later published such books as *Illustrations of Taxation* (1834), *Society in America*
(1837), and *Household Education* (1849). Cecil Woodham-Smith, Florence Nightingale's biographer, uncharitably described Martineau as 'the daughter of an
unsuccessful sugar refiner, deaf, sickly, physically unattractive, and born without the sense of taste or smell' (Woodham-Smith 1950:255). Nightingale and
Martineau knew one another, but fell out over feminism, with Nightingale
forbidding Martineau to cite any of her work to further feminist causes.
Martineau was a passionate defender of women's rights, particularly to education (see Walters 1976). She and her sister were taught at home. 'Blue-
stockingism' was something to be avoided: 'it was not thought proper for
young ladies to study very conspicuously; and especially with pen in hand'
(Martineau 1877:1.200). Like Nightingale, she suffered from bad health. In
her *Autobiography*, she chronicled the price paid in illness and depression for
making her own way in the world, from inauspicious beginnings in a cheerless
household, where even her wet-nurse reputedly had no milk (see Porter and
Porter 1988). Martineau's espousal of positivism followed her apparent 'cure'
through mesmerism from a long-standing gynaecological disorder, which had
caused her to lie on a sofa in Tynemouth for five years.[6]

'My mind,' Martineau had noted of her childhood, 'considered dull and
unobservant and unwieldy by my family, was desperately methodical' (Martineau
1877: 1.35). Her 1838 text, *How to Observe Morals and Manners*, is one of the
first accounts of how to undertake social observation using systematic methods. 'A child does not catch a goldfish in water at the first trial, however good
his eyes may be, and however clear the water,' wrote Martineau (1838:1–2);
'. . . knowledge and method are necessary to enable him to take what is actually before his eyes, and under his hand . . . the powers of observation must be
trained.' She particularly advised against taking notes during interviews (afterwards was much better), and recommended the use of what we would now call
'topic guides'.

The list of antecedents named in the work Martineau translated, Comte's
Cours de philosophie positive, indicates that he wanted his contribution to be
read as a marriage of Baconian scientific reasoning and Cartesian certainty,
combined with the progressive social visions of Condorcet and the other 'En-
cyclopaedists' (S. P. Turner 1986). The *Cours* outlines a famous evolutionary
framework for the development of sociology:

From the study of the development of human intelligence, in all directions, and through all time, the discovery arises of a great fundamental law, to which it is necessarily subject, and which has a solid foundation of proof, both in the facts of our organisation and in our historical experience. The law is this:- that each of our leading conceptions, – each branch of our knowledge, – passes successively through three different theoretical conditions: the Theological, or fictitious; the Metaphysical, or abstract; and the Scientific or positive.

In this third stage, 'the mind has given over the vain search after Absolute notions, the origin and destination of the universe, and the causes of phenomena, and applies itself to the study of their laws, – that is, their invariable relations of succession and resemblance' (Comte 1853:1.1–2).

For Comte, sociology, originally called 'social physics' (following Quételet), was simply the last in a line of sciences to go through the three successive stages of knowledge: 'Now that the human mind has grasped celestial and terrestrial physics, – mechanical and chemical; organic physics, both vegetable and animal, – there remains one science, to fill up the series of sciences of observation, – social physics. This is what men have now most need of' (Comte 1853: 1.7). Social physics represented the most concrete end of a linear trajectory which began with the most abstract science – astronomy. He called it 'the queen of the sciences', deliberately contesting the Enlightenment naming of the natural sciences as *hautes sciences*. Most significantly for the subsequent fate of positivism in social science, Comte saw the development of sociology as entailing exactly the same methods of exact observation and analysis as prevailed in the 'lower' sciences. These methods were observation, experiment and comparison. Of experiment, he wrote:

It might be supposed beforehand that the second method of investigation, Experiment, must be wholly inapplicable in Social Science; but we shall find that the science is not entirely deprived of this resource, though it must be one of inferior value. (*Comte 1853:2.100*)

Comte regarded himself as a kind of high priest of humanity, and positivism as a humanitarian religion (which is one reason why those such as Beatrice Webb could espouse his ideas with such passion). The preface to the first volume of the French edition records why Comte chose the term 'positive philosophy' as against the more obvious alternative, 'natural philosophy': namely because the latter term fails to embrace all phenomena, particularly the social (see Lenzer 1975a:xlviii). The term 'positivism' meant something in the real, as distinct from the theoretical, world; a 'positive law' was thus one passed by a legislature or a king, as opposed to the 'divine' or 'natural' laws associated with religious beliefs. As Comte's translator, Martineau, explained it in a letter to her mesmerist, positive philosophy was simply 'the philosophy of fact, as arising from the earliest true science, and rehabilitated by Bacon's expositions of its principles' (Martineau 1877:3.323). 'Positive' facts came from empirical observation rather than mental conjecture; 'empirical' is derived from *empeiria*, the Greek word for 'experience' (McDonald

1993:15).[7] Until the eighteenth century, 'experience' was interchangeable with 'experiment'; the two words come from the common Latin root *experiri*, 'to try', or 'put to the test' (cf. modern French, in which *expérience* and *expérimentale* continue to have overlapping meanings[8]). 'Experience' became a conscious test or trial, and thus a consciousness of what has been tested or tried (R. Williams 1983). The focus of knowledge on experience in this sense was the argument of the Vienna Circle, a group of scientists, philosophers and mathematicians who worked together in the 1920s. They argued that only knowledge based on experience can constitute a legitimate science, that facts and values ought to be separated in what counts as knowledge, and that the scientific method applies across all disciplines (Kolakowski 1972).

Experiential knowing replaced idealist knowing. The emphasis within positivist thought on observation and experience made it an attractive philosophy for Victorians who found themselves rejecting orthodox religion; the idea of a regulated and discoverable social system and a secular religion of humanity appealed as a replacement set of beliefs. This transition was helped by the almost fanatical faith in the scientific method which prevailed in the latter decades of the nineteenth century; science, with its synthesis of observation and experiment, hypothesis and verification, was seen as promising the solution of all social problems. As Stephen Turner puts it in his *The Search for a Methodology of Social Science*, one absolutely critical aspect of social science's adoption of the methods of the natural sciences at the time was that the two forms of science were 'coparticipants in the struggle between theism and science' (1986: 6).

A short note on terms

The term 'social science' appears to have originated with Condorcet in the 1790s. From there it spread to Britain and the German-speaking countries, where it came gradually to replace the older terms 'moral philosophy', 'moral science' and 'political arithmetic' (McDonald 1993:18; Senn 1958; Wittrock et al. 1997a:2). 'Science' at the time was used to refer to any systematic study, irrespective of subject-matter (D. Ross 1991). The term 'sociology' itself is credited to Comte,[9] who selected this 'bastard' name (it combines a Latin beginning with a Greek ending) in response to a complaint that Quételet had plagiarized his own term 'social physics'. The two men were involved in a long-running dispute about names for the new discipline. Comte's ultimate choice of 'sociology' was made in the confident belief that the term was so ugly that no statistician would ever want to steal it (Lottin 1912). But the naming dispute had another significance; it marked the bifurcation of the new 'moral' science into separate numerical and historicist terrains. Social statistics represented one way forward. The remaining, contested, challenge was to determine what should occupy the space of a predominantly non-statistical sociology.

From experiment to experience

The English philosopher J. S. Mill's *A System of Logic* (1843) is generally seen as *the* foundational text for social science methodology. Mill (1806–73), son of the Scottish philosopher James Mill, was the archetypal infant prodigy who could read Greek at the age of three; he combined philosophy with a dedication to radical reform, becoming the author of the much-quoted *The Subjection of Women* (1869). Mill first read Comte in the 1820s, when emerging from a profound mental 'crisis' not unlike that of Descartes in its central realization of how little one may know as a result of formal education. Mill immediately recognized an affinity between his thinking and that of Comte, although 'I already regarded the methods of physical sciences as the proper models for political [science]', he noted (Mill 1981:173). Reading volume 6 of Comte's *Cours* in 1842 led Mill to make substantial revisions to book 6 of his own *A System of Logic*. Although the two men never met, they corresponded for several years until a disagreement about the status of philosophy drove them apart (McRae 1974).

'Logic' in the title of *A System of Logic* did not stand for abstract reasoning; what it referred to was the question of evidence: how we know that something is true. 'Logic is not the science of Belief,' inscribed Mill, 'but the science of Proof, or Evidence. In so far as belief professes to be founded in proof, the office of logic is to supply a test for ascertaining whether or not the belief is well grounded ... without evidence in the proper sense of the word, logic has nothing to do' (Mill 1843, 1973–4 edn, books 1–111:9). *A System of Logic* brought together all the various strands of Enlightenment arguments for social science: that there are social laws, just as there are physical ones, and that the aims of the social sciences must therefore resemble those of the physical ones. But Mill's particular stance on the applicability of natural science methods to social science proved a decisive moment for the subsequent history of social science in one particular respect which is thematic to the story being told in this book. Baconian science had incorporated the idea of active intervention as a method for acquiring reliable knowledge. Mill rejected two approaches as inappropriate for the emerging social sciences: abstract geometrical procedures and the idea of the experiment in the Baconian sense. What Mill called 'the Method of Difference' – a procedure involving two instances 'which tally in every particular respect except the one which is the subject of social inquiry' – simply does not apply in social science. 'The first difficulty which meets us in the attempt to apply experimental methods for ascertaining the laws of social phenomena,' he declared,

> is that we are without the means of making artificial experiments. Even if we could contrive experiments at leisure, and try them without limit, we should do so under immense disadvantage; both from the impossibility of ascertaining and taking note of all the facts of each case, and because (those facts being in a perpetual state of change) before sufficient time had elapsed to ascertain the result of the experiment, some material circumstances would always have ceased to be the same. *(Mill 1973–4:881–2)*

Mill's position on experimentation interrupted the Baconian link with experience. Much of European social science thereafter went on to develop an emphasis on *experience* as something quite different from *experimentation*. However, despite Comte's own embrace of the unity of science, the Baconian scientific method as revised by Mill is less evident in his work than in that of his countryman, Émile Durkheim, who was born the year after Comte died. Durkheim (1858–1917) came from a close-knit orthodox Jewish family of rabbinical scholars in Lorraine, but gave up any ambition to take up the rabbinate himself in his youth through the influence of 'a Catholic instructress' (Alpert 1961:15). He trained as a teacher, completed a thesis in Latin on Montesquieu, decided in the early 1880s to devote himself to the scientific study of social phenomena, and was appointed as the first full professor of social science at the University of Bordeaux in 1896.

Durkheim first read Comte in the early 1880s, before he named his own interest as sociology; the new subject was in considerable disrepute among French philosophers at the time (Lukes 1973). He acknowledged a debt to Comte for establishing that social laws are akin to natural ones, and that the methods for discovering each are identical; positive philosophy was in this sense exactly the same thing as sociology. One of Durkheim's main achievements was to rework the Comtean framework, separating it from Comte's dubious global theory of historical change (Giddens 1978). Durkheim's elaboration of social facts as both external and constraining took the positivist standpoint as applied to the social world to its logical conclusion.[10]

It was thus Durkheim, rather than Descartes, who inserted the most intractable wedge between mind and body; there can be nothing more external than *his* view of social facts. In the Durkheimian narrative, social facts have the same status as the facts which constitute the data of the physical sciences; most critically, their existence is seen as independent of individual psychology. Quételet's notion of the average man as more real and more general than any particular individual strongly influenced Durkheim's view of social facts, though he also took issue with Quételet for the social determinism implied in the Quételetian concept (Desrosières 1991:202; S. P. Turner 1986:84).

In chapter 2 of his *The Rules of Sociological Method* (1895), which is concerned with the observation of social facts, Durkheim refers back to Bacon's idols – 'illusions that distort the real aspect of things'. If idols interrupt the process of acquiring reliable knowledge in the natural sciences, says Durkheim, they must be even more of a problem in sociology, where prejudices are especially likely to be substituted for social facts, since everyone has their own ideas about law, morality, the family, the state and so forth. He takes Comte to task for not going beyond the notion that *ideas* are the proper subject of sociological study. For example, the *idea* of continuous intellectual evolution embedded in the Comtean idea of three stages is merely an assumption: 'it cannot be said to exist at all'. Similarly, Herbert Spencer's definition of society as distinguished by the presence of co-operation among individuals must be dismissed as anti-empirical: it 'defines as a thing that which is merely an idea'; one would need to study all societies and to establish that all are characterized by co-operation in order to accept that Spencer was right. The pronounced ideological tinge of most social theory drove Durkheim to insist that all observable data are things; only things can be observed; and ideas can therefore be studied only in their 'phenomenal reality' (Durkheim 1938:19, 21, 27).

Chapter 6 of *The Rules* is occupied with questions of cause in social science, and follows Mill's injunction about active experimentation not being among the sociologist's methodological tools:

> We have only one way to demonstrate that a given phenomenon is the cause of another, viz., to compare the cases in which they are simultaneously present or absent, to see if the variations they present in these different combinations of circumstances indicate that one depends on the other. When they can be artificially produced at the will of the observer, the method is that of experiment. . . . Since . . . social phenomena evidently escape the control of the experimenter, the comparative method is the only one suited to sociology. *(Durkheim 1938:125)*[11]

Herbert Spencer, Beatrice Webb's childhood friend, was Durkheim's other main intellectual progenitor. Spencer's works were read avidly in France, which was overcome by an 'epidemic of Spencerianism' at the end of the nineteenth century (Alpert 1961:33). It was George Eliot who first gave Spencer a copy of Mill's *A System of Logic* (Spencer 1904:487), and who first told him about Comte's work; she had discovered positivism in 1851, read Comte's work systematically, and later met him in Paris (Simon 1963). Spencer, originally a civil engineer, was a 'gentleman' social scientist, able to devote himself to sociology because of a small private income; he complained endlessly about money, and would have liked a proper job, but was unable to get one (see Spencer 1904). His qualifications for calling himself a sociologist were weak – he read little, and never did any empirical work. He specialized in that form of morbid introspection associated with the multiple psychological crises of the Victorians. He complained that he worked for only three hours a day because of 'cerebral congestion' and used 'ear stoppers' and morphia to get any sleep at all. His first book, *Social Statics* (1850), was published nine years before Darwin's *Origin of Species*. Thereafter his work largely expounded the creed of social Darwinism in relation to every branch of science; his *The Study of Sociology* described sociology simply as 'the study of Evolution in its most complex form' (1903:385). Spencer's writings helped to make terms such as 'sociology', 'structure' and 'function' popular, but his addiction to abstract theory and speculation, as well as morphia, led George Eliot to tell him, 'you have such a passion for generalising, you even fish with a generalisation' (Spencer 1904:203); one of the two inventions celebrated in appendices to his *Autobiography* (1904) was a new fishing rod joint (the other was an invalid bed).

Spencer's work was produced on the later side of a significant division in the history of social science methodology which occurred in the 1870s (S. P. Turner 1986). Before this, Comte, Quételet, Mill and others laid down the basic framework of a positivist social science dedicated to using the scientific method in order to discover social laws. After this, those interested in the project of social science had to contend increasingly with social Darwinism. This broke the earlier consensus among those whose work not only shared key ideas but was linked through common social networks. Mill and Comte were friends (though they never actually met): in a letter to his friend the Scottish philosopher Alexander Bain, Mill called Comte's *Cours* 'very nearly the grandest work of the age' (Simon 1963:174). Spencer and Comte had an antagonistic relationship; when they first met in Paris, Comte advised Spencer to find a wife in order to cure his depressions, but Spencer declined to take this advice (Peel 1971); he also refused to recognize that Comte had made any significant contribution to establishing sociology as a science. Mill criticized Spencer, who generally took criticism badly (S. P. Turner 1986:29, 93). The importance of Spencer's sociology lay mainly in the need for subsequent sociologists, especially in Britain, to mount a defence against him, particularly against his derivation of policy conclusions directly from the laws of natural selection with little reference to empirical data (see Abrams 1968).

Beyond the particular efforts of sociology's different 'founding fathers' to map out their terrain, there is another significant theme. This concerns the whole project of separating the realms of the social and the natural and of establishing a specific science for each. Science as systematic study had evolved in association with a masculine crisis of understanding and control; the scientific method promised the taming of a wayward feminine nature. Social science was similarly powered by the need to understand and take charge of a rapidly changing society. But what interfered with a simple transference of the epistemology of science to social science was the different gendering of the social and natural worlds. Man-the-knower and woman-the-known-about was a formula that worked better for the physical than the social sciences. It was the very humanity of 'men' – their co-conspiracy in the social project – that posed such a problem for social science methodology.

Like Descartes and Bacon, Spencer, Mill, Booth and Comte all suffered from psychological crises. Booth's crisis was precipitated by reading Comte, so overwhelming was the notion of an alternative religion. His moral dilemma was that of a rich man in a world of class inequality; it was a dilemma he faced, literally, on a daily basis, as his walk from his home to his shipbuilding yard took him through the material realities of poverty. What Darwinism and positivism offered jointly was the conclusion that God had not ordained poverty and that science could be used to root out and treat its causes. The evolutionists had crises too, including Darwin himself and Galton, the founder of the eugenics movement, and Max Weber (1864–1920), whose views on 'verstehen', though often misquoted (see Platt 1985) none the less mark him out as an early advocate of a qualitative social science. Spencer blamed his personal difficulties on poor physique and lack of affection as a child. The crises of Mill and Comte were associated with a superfluity of feeling; these personal problems, along with their differing views about women, featured as prominent topics in a long-running correspondence. After one of his crises, Mill decided that reason rather than emotion ought to provide the guiding principle of life, and he castigated Comte as an example of a scholar who lost the capacity for systematic thought the more he discovered feeling (Lepenies 1988:107). Both men had intense spiritual and intellectual liaisons with women: Mill with Harriet Taylor, the feminist wife of a wealthy London merchant, and Comte with Clotilde de Vaux, the novel-writing sister and eventual convert to positivism of one of his pupils. The question of how much Mill's work owed directly to Harriet Taylor's influence remains unresolved (see McDonald 1993:262–3; P. Rose 1984); but there is no doubt that her ideas and her feminism influenced him, and that much of the work which bears his name would not have been the same without her. Mill's essay on *The Subjection of Women*, published after Harriet's death in 1869, is a passionate defence of women's rights. Comte himself thought women men's natural inferiors, incapable of abstract reasoning and of any public achievement, though the veneration he expressed for Clotilde somewhat contradicted this. Significantly, one aim of his positivist philosophy was to institute a harmony between public and private life. For Charles Booth a woman, his wife Mary Macaulay (Beatrice Webb's cousin), was also the mainstay of his life and work; apart from taking care of his domestic life, Mary acted as 'universal critic and amanuensis', reading and often rewriting every page he wrote (Simey and Simey 1960:54).

What we see here are the struggles of men involved in giving birth to a 'feminine' science; that science which would subject the softer social world of existence to the same rigorous scrutiny as the older sciences afforded the world of nature. It was a struggle both to claim ownership and to reject identification. Some degree of ownership was necessary to establish professional authority; but in so far as the domain of the social resolutely resisted absorption into the subject-matter of science proper, there was always the danger of its advocates themselves being taken over by the world of feeling and experience.

The problem of what to do with the experience of emotion existed not only in the personal lives of the founding fathers of social science methodology, but within social science itself. As positivism in its various forms became the new religion, not everyone was convinced that the heart should be sacrificed to the head, or that the old religion should be supplanted by the new one of reason. The battle between rationality and feeling, between experiment and experience, was played out on the terrain of social science. Hence we have the intellectual theorizing of Spencer and Comte, and to a lesser extent of Durkheim (who at least tested his ideas against statistical facts, as in his classic study *Suicide*, but who was none the less regarded in some quarters as a proponent of 'bad metaphysics in search of an empirical alibi' (Lasserre, cited in Lepenies 1988:77)).

From the mid-nineteenth century on, the new social science and the old art of novel-writing fought a further battle to provide the key orientation to the problem of living in industrial society. What novels offered was the opportunity for social observation and grounded experience which the formulae of science decreed were inappropriate (Dickens's novel *Hard Times*, quoted at the end of the last chapter, is a good example of this). Beatrice Webb, early convinced by the scientific method, complained that she had to turn to fiction – to Balzac and Browning, Fielding and Flaubert, Thackeray and Goethe –

and George Eliot – in order to understand men and women in their social environment (Webb 1938:161, 167). People at the time observed that Eliot brought the dead systems of Comte, Spencer and J. S. Mill to life in her novels (Lepenies 1988:200). Virginia Woolf reluctantly recognized the synergism between her fiction and the work of Beatrice Webb, a woman whom she intensely disliked. The French writer Honoré de Balzac described himself as a doctor of social science; his *Comédie humaine* narrowly missed being called *Études sociales*. Proust talked of presenting a 'sociology' of Combray and the Faubourg Saint-Germain in his majestic *À la recherche du temps perdu*. The English novelist H. G. Wells, addressing the Sociological Society in 1906, outlined a case against 'scientific' sociology which sounds very like the later attack of qualitative epistemologists, with counting, measuring and classifying procedures rejected as ignoring precisely that uniqueness of individuals which constituted the stuff of fiction. 'Now what is called the scientific method', pronounced Wells, 'is the method of ignoring individualities; and, like many mathematical conventions, its great practical convenience is no proof whatever of its final truth.' On the contrary, it can be regarded as deceitful precisely because it ignores the 'objective truth' of individual experience (Wells 1907:361).

'Bettering the Condition of the Poor'

The other great motive which fuelled the fire of social science was that of social reform. Those who created the new science of society felt they were living through a time of profound social dislocation which necessitated new modes of analysis and action. The French, Industrial and urban revolutions caused huge changes in traditional relations of class and gender, demanding new tools and new modes of understanding. The social problem of the labouring masses in factories and mills created anxiety and apprehension among the upper and middle classes; the liberal reform sentiment provided a convenient channel for this. One consequence was the creation of a new 'science of the poor', with an emphasis both on finding out the exact facts of the state of the poor, and on doing something effective to improve this. 'Scientific philanthropy' led to a practical social science and later to 'scientific' social work (Yeo 1996).

The Society for Bettering the Condition of the Poor was founded by Sir Thomas Bernard, an evangelical philanthropist, in 1796. The Society appealed to science as providing more reliable solutions than older forms of charity to the problem of poverty. Unlike early social science, these attempts to systematize philanthropy were intimately associated with religious beliefs; in the aftermath of the French Revolution, irreligion did not appeal to those members of the ruling classes who were drawn to philanthropy. However, as with social science, the emphasis on the facts of experience as a way of producing social knowledge had a socialist ring about it. The term 'survey', like the term 'statistics', was originally associated with the activities of the state making inventories of its possessions. From the late eighteenth century the survey underwent a slow process of democratization; the first national census in 1801 and the door-to-door statistical surveys carried out by the voluntary statistical societies of the 1830s (see Elesh 1972) gave little priority to the experiences of the surveyed, but the pioneer work of Henry Mayhew in the mid- and Charles Booth in the late nineteenth century was significantly 'qualitative' in nature.

Mayhew (1812–87), a successful novelist, published his classic social survey, *London Labour and the London Poor*, in 1851–62. Mayhew notes the uniqueness of his project:

> It surely may be considered curious as being the first attempt to publish the history of a people, from the lips of the people themselves – giving a literal description of their labour, their earnings, their trials and their sufferings, in their own 'unvarnished' language; and to pourtray [*sic*] the condition of their homes and their families by personal observation of the places, and direct communion with the individuals. *(Mayhew 1851:iii)*

An example is the section on water supply and drainage, in which Mayhew included a table comparing the percentages to be found in three poor, middle-class and rich parishes of damp houses, those with 'drains emitting offensive smells', those with water-closets and those with cesspools. But he also approached the topic another way, by looking at the experiences of the men employed to empty the cesspools and manage the sewage system. One question to which he wanted an answer was about the number of rats in the sewers: '"Why, sir," said one flusherman, "as to the number of rats, it ain't possible to say. There hasn't been a census (laughing) taken of them"' (Mayhew 1851:431).

One of the original motives for the poverty research undertaken by Charles Booth was to win an argument with Henry Hyndman, a 'top-hatted Etonian' and socialist associate of Marx's, who maintained that a quarter of people in the East End of London lived in poverty (Simey and Simey 1960; see Cole 1972:105). When the facts from his survey began to be aggregated, Booth was surprised to find that the figure established by his poverty enquiries was nearer one-third. Booth obtained some of his information from School Board visitors' reports, but he also carried out detailed case-studies, and did much of the institutional interviewing; as Philip Abrams (1968:24) has pointed out, only about one-third of *The Life and Labour of the People of London* is 'quantitative'. Booth's reports contain much fascinating detail on the *practice* of social science methodology. For instance, his book on the East End drew on forty-six notebooks containing information on every household with children in 3,400 streets: 'Our books are mines of information,' observed Booth. 'They have been referred to again and again at each stage of our work. So valuable have they proved in unforeseen ways that I only regret they were not more slowly and deliberately prepared.' He also noted the problems inherent in triangulation (him or his assistants recording impressions on the streets, which were also surveyed by the School Board visitors), interviewer variability (some of the School Board visitors were more 'trustworthy' than others), and the need always to envision the human experiences behind the percentages: 'To judge rightly we need . . . never to forget the numbers when thinking of the percentages, nor the percentages when thinking of the numbers' (C. Booth 1891:598).

Mayhew's and Booth's practices of the social survey are considerably at odds with the characterization of surveys to be found in the 'anti-quantitative' paradigm today. Harriet Martineau (1838), Florence Nightingale (1860) and Beatrice Webb (1938) had all shown themselves to be sensitive to the requirements of a more 'qualitative' social science. While it is undoubtedly true that a significant inspiration for the survey method was 'men's' desire to count facts about working-class life as a way of coming to terms with a changing social world, the extent to which these efforts ignored everyday life from the standpoint of the urban poor has been exaggerated (see Graham 1983). Surveys could be a way of interposing social distance between middle-class investigators and the socially marginal objects of their censorial gaze – the unemployed, manual workers, prostitutes, the insane. But the survey method, in certain hands, could also offer a means of incorporating the subjective viewpoints of studied groups. Like many British 'sociologists' at the time, Booth was ambivalent about quantification. But he also knew that a weakness of his method was the difficulty of generalizing from a non-random sample. 'I have . . . assumed that as is the condition of the tested part . . . so is the condition of the whole population,' he noted (C. Booth 1891:5); the key word was *assumed*. By the time Seebohm Rowntree's second survey of York was published in 1941, the method of random sampling devised by A. L. Bowley (1869–1957), the first statistician to be appointed to the newly founded London School of Economics in 1895, had arrived to rescue social survey work from this particular black hole (see Bowley 1915); *Poverty and Progress: a second social survey of York* contains an interesting chapter examining how the York results would have differed[12] had Bowley's random sampling method been used (see Bowley 1915).[13] So far as the motive of aiding the cause of practical social reform was concerned, what was essential here was that the poverty surveys not only yielded evidence of the *extent* of poverty, but revealed its structural regularities – its links with unemployment, wage rates and poor housing – thereby demonstrating that poverty was socially determined rather than, as some eugenists would have it, flowing from some incurable biological defect.

The National Association for the Promotion of Social Science, formed in 1857, represented a conglomerate of reform groups held together by a common belief in the capabilities of a practical social science to outline effective ways of resolving social problems. A list of the founding members of the Association contains little evidence of expertise in empirical social research, but many names of merchants, industrialists, barristers, magistrates, doctors, clergymen, MPs, social workers, engineers, educators and civil servants. When set up, it had five 'departments': law amendment, education, crime, public health and social economy. The chief focus was on identifying and instituting suitable reforms for particular social problems; there was very little interest in their theoretical or analytic significance (Abrams 1968:46). The term 'experiment' in this context simply meant the results of institutions or legislation as reported by the people who administered them.

Cultures of institutionalization

Social science was not the same thing everywhere. Between 1750 and 1850 many of the central assumptions, concepts and terms of social science were developed and named, some of these building on considerably longer traditions of reflection about the social world (Wittrock et al. 1997b; Wagner et al. 1991a, 1991b). But an equally important process, especially in terms of understanding the background to today's paradigm divide, was the way in which social science was incorporated into *institutional* structures and practices. 'Institutionalization' here means the existence of commonly held and binding norms governing the status, collective identity and practices of a discipline or profession (Cole 1972). In order for new fields to develop and take hold, three prerequisites are generally necessary: intellectual innovation – 'some sort of paradigm'; talented individuals to promote this; and institutional support (Clark 1973). There were key differences between countries with respect to the third of these factors. Crucial to the different pathways of development were the uneven development of industrial capitalism, which was linked with different formulations of 'the social question' and a variety of state responses to this; differences between higher education and welfare systems; and the fate of the natural sciences under industrialization (see Manicas 1987; Wittrock and Wagner 1996).

The later institutionalization of social science in Britain is partly explained by its association with social reform (see Oberschall 1972a); it took until the end of the Second World War for British sociology to achieve a separate institutional existence (Bulmer 1991). The willingness of politicians and administrators to apply statistics directly to social issues meant that establishing sociology as an organized academic field was a much less pressing matter in Britain than elsewhere. Moreover, because the British higher education system was 'severely vocational' (Abrams 1968:101), there was a limited supply of potential recruits for the new social science/sociology. When the Sociological Society was formed in 1903, many of those most active in it were wealthy male eugenists with careers elsewhere (others, like H. G. Wells, were writers with a scientific interest in socialism); the Society had, in any case, to compete with the much more successfully networked Eugenics Education Society. The British form of Spencerianism led directly to eugenics as 'applied sociology', and to both social biology and social medicine. The British class system, itself linked to the dominance of eugenic thought in social science, meant that simple, unsupported political responses to social problems tended to be taken up with relative ease. Simply, there was not as much need for a 'positivist' social science in Britain as there was in other countries.

Terry Clark's (1973) study of the institutionalization of sociology in France shows how features of the higher education system there systematically encouraged the dominance of the Durkheimian tradition in modern sociology at the expense of other groupings, particularly the social statisticians. The strong academic leaning of the French university system, with its emphasis on the more theoretical and less empirical forms of social philosophy, offered a more receptive ground for those, such as Durkheim, who brought an acceptably formal academic background and social qualifications as members of the petty bourgeoisie along with novel ideas about the academic status of social facts. In Germany, by contrast, sociologically inclined academics could fit into the existing disciplines of history, economics, law, religion and philosophy with relative ease, since these established disciplines were very broadly defined. In the early years of the twentieth century, traditionalists within the university system tended to oppose sociology *de novo*, suspicious of its foreign and socialist origins. In this institutional framework, the links between sociology and social research were tenuous; later attempts at integration were interrupted by Hitlerian hostility from the 1920s on (Oberschall 1972b).

'In contrast to the difficulties of establishing sociology as an autonomous academic discipline in Europe,' notes Oberschall (1972a:187), 'its institutionalisation in the United States can only be described as a smashing success.' The American experience provides an interesting historical lesson in the pre-eminence of material factors and the distinctly lesser importance of ideas. Its 'smashing success' cannot be attributed to the American social scientists' invention of new intellectual schemata; on the contrary, as Albion Small put it in 1924, 'The true story of the American sociological movement would be a treatment of the theme: *Up from Amateurism*' (1924:347). The critical factors in the success of American social science were, rather, the rapid expansion of higher education in the United States around the turn of the century and the resources put into academic social science by upwardly mobile men whose entrée into the university system would have been obstructed by the established disciplines, and whose energetically pursued status interests gave them an almost 'obsessive' concern with academic legitimation (Oberschall 1972a:189).

Conclusion

The outcome of these different developments was a definite weakness in the energy, orientation and expertise of sociology in Britain in the early years of the twentieth century, as compared to continental Europe and North America. This applies particularly to the ownership by social science of experimental methods. The more recent legacy of this tradition has been an almost complete lack of any practice of large-scale social experimentation in Britain. As Martin Bulmer has noted (1991:160), this absence stands out in any comparison of American and British research in the post-Second World War era, and it 'requires some explanation'. The story told in this chapter provides a partial answer.

The tension notable within early European social science between imitating the natural sciences and being content with the 'social reality' novel is reflected in some aspects of the quantitative versus qualitative paradigm debate today. 'Detached objectivity' faces conscious subjectivity across the academic–fiction divide, as well as over the garden fence of logical positivism. Sociology as an art-form rather than the practice of science remains a contended position today. English literary criticism has a tradition of advancing the view that novels see further and better than the 'misplaced rationality' of social science (Lepenies 1988:13). The two cultures of art and science can both be described as 'ways of living with one's own experience' (Bruner 1966:5–6); many significant sociological contributions to knowledge more closely resemble art and literature than they do 'the scientific method' (Nisbet 1976:7). Imagination is important to both sociology and art; the creative linking of private and public issues is at the heart of both (Wright Mills 1959).

Max Weber, in his *Science as Vocation*, highlighted an interesting but forgotten relationship between experiment in science and creative activity:

> The experiment is a means of reliably controlling experience. Without it, present-day empirical science would be impossible. . . . But to raise the experiment to a principle of research was the achievement of the Renaissance. They were the great innovators in art, who were the pioneers of experiment. Leonardo and his like and, above all, the sixteenth-century experimenters in music with the experimental pianos . . . From these circles the experiment entered science, especially through Galileo, and it entered theory through Bacon. *(Weber 1947b:141–2)*

The emphasis on experience is one of the main themes at issue here; but it is, as Yeo (1996) comments, not only the place of experience as such which is the subject of debate; the question of *whose* experience most counts in both sociological and fictional ways of knowing needs constantly to be asked. Gender and class are understudied axes of difference in all forms of enquiry. Gendered divisions in the separation of social from natural science are responsible for some of its most notable weaknesses, although in the hermeneutics of postmodernism, not to mention other 'isms', they also undoubtedly contribute to some of its strengths.

7

Chance is a Fine Thing

> The Elimination of Chance is effected by the Calculus of Probabilities, a powerful but dangerous instrument . . . Formulae founded upon games of chance are to be transferred with caution to real life.
>
> Edgeworth, *Logic of Statistics*

> It has been often recognised that any probability statement, being a rigorous statement involving uncertainty, has less factual content than an assertion of certain fact would have, and at the same time has more factual content than a statement of complete ignorance.
>
> Fisher, *Statistical Methods and Scientific Inference*

The Rothamsted Experimental Station for Agricultural Research in Harpenden, twenty-five miles north of London, was originally a manor farm belonging to the family of John Bennett Lawes. In the 1830s Lawes, who had taken a chemistry degree at Cambridge, turned one of the barns into a laboratory in order to find out why bone products did not appear to work successfully as manure on the kind of heavy loam and clay soil which was to be found in the area. As a result of this work, he developed and patented an agricultural fertilizer, using the proceeds to set up an 'Experimental Station' which would pursue further research on agricultural productivity.[1] The Rothamsted Research Station's main claim to fame derives from the later residency there of another Cambridge graduate, Ronald Aylmer Fisher (1890–1962), who was recruited to Rothamsted in 1919, and who is credited as the originator of that prototypical, much-loved and much-hated experimental method, the randomised controlled trial.

This chapter examines this particular history in more detail. It traces 'Fisher's' creation of the randomised controlled trial to a fundamental and long-lived aspect of 'man's' attempt to understand himself and the universe: the idea of chance. Things happen that we do not make happen. God or scientific 'laws' may be deemed responsible for some of these, but it is also apparent that our lives are subject to random happenings – things that might quite well happen in another way or at another time or to someone else and with entirely different consequences. The enquiring mind wants to gain control over all this: what principles govern the operation of chance? How can we turn these to our advantage?

Fisher's first major impact at Rothamsted occurred over a cup of tea. Regular afternoon tea had been introduced there in 1906 when the first woman joined the staff; no one had much idea how to treat a woman member of staff, but it was felt that she must have tea, so from the day of Miss W. Brenchley's arrival, tea and Bath Oliver biscuits were offered at four o'clock every afternoon. On this particular day, soon after Fisher's appointment, he drew a cup of tea from the urn and offered it to the woman beside him, Dr B. Muriel Bristol, an algologist (the experiment of having a woman on the staff had clearly been a success). But Dr Bristol refused the cup Fisher offered her, on the grounds that she preferred tea into which the milk had been put first. Joan Fisher Box, Fisher's daughter, takes up the story:

'Nonsense,' returned Fisher, smiling, 'Surely it makes no difference.' But she maintained, with emphasis, that of course it did. From just behind, a voice suggested, 'Let's test her.' It was William Roach, who was not long afterward to marry Miss Bristol. Immediately, they embarked on the preliminaries of the experiment, Roach assisting with the cups and exulting that Miss Bristol divined correctly more than enough of those cups into which tea had been poured first to prove her case. (*Box 1978:134*)[2]

The tea episode reappeared in Fisher's *The Design of Experiments* (1935) as the initiation of the whole project for which he and the Rothamsted Research Station are most famous – the story of randomised controlled trials. Although Fisher is often portrayed as the 'inventor' of these,[3] like most 'inventions', the modern history of experimental methods is better described as a process of cumulative, serendipitous and sometimes wayward knowledge which is marked by particular moments of synthesis and advance. Moreover, this history is not restricted to one 'discipline'. Prospective experimental studies using randomly generated control groups were the unplanned outcome of a lengthy developmental process in psychophysics, psychology and education, as well as medicine. Dr Bristol's refusal of tea that afternoon in the Hertfordshire countryside undoubtedly sparked off a train of thought in Fisher's head. But Fisher was a man of his times, and those times were much occupied with the problem of establishing cause and effect, especially as regards situations of human intervention, and particularly with respect to the stubbornly intractable problem of distinguishing the relative strengths of nature and nurture as influences on the conduct of all living things, including plants. These issues of the time had already led others in agriculture, medicine, education and the emerging social sciences to some of the same conclusions as Fisher later synthesized about the requirements of well-designed experiments.

The fiction of monkeys and other laws

As we saw in chapter 4, experiments in the sense of controlled observations had already demarcated science from philosophy by the seventeenth century, and in the nineteenth century the experimental method was regarded by many as marking the boundary between 'natural' and 'moral' science. Further developments in experimental methods followed from the gradual revolution in 'men's' understanding of chance, more formally represented in terms of probability theory and applied both to the 'laws' of the universe and the behaviour of people.

Chance is a central concept in the design of RCTs. Two features – the use of control or comparison groups and of random allocation – are essentially methods for dealing with the unknown. It is usual *not* to know the full range of factors impinging on any outcome that is the subject of research; it is also usual to be *uncertain* about the extent to which the validity of any inferences that may be made about cause and effect may be disturbed by the play of chance. Because of this central role of chance in modern ideas of experimental methods, it was necessary for an understanding of the concept of chance itself to pre-date their 'invention'. The fundamental question, in the words of the nineteenth-century mathematician Francis Edgeworth (whose views on chance are quoted at the head of this chapter), is: 'under what circumstances does a difference in figures correspond to a difference of fact [?]' (Stigler 1986: 308). The same question underlies the invention of the 'random' sample (with which the concept of random allocation in RCTs is often confused);[4] samples derived 'at random' from a wider population are more likely to form a valid basis for generalizations about that population than samples chosen by other means.

The modern history of the experimental method – that way of knowing which lies at the extreme end of the 'quantitative'/'qualitative' divide – involves two linked issues. The first is understanding the play of chance and how this affects events and processes in both the natural and the social domains. The second is the emergence of a specific methodological technique – that of random allocation – as a way of imposing an artificial control on the operations of chance, with the aim of securing a more reliable knowledge. As the second quotation at the head of this chapter, from Fisher, acknowledges, it is not that statements about knowledge produced as a result of rigorously designed experimental studies are necessarily to be regarded as 'true'. But what they can provide is a *measure of the degree of uncertainty* attached to such statements. Of course, it almost goes without saying that the epistemological uncertainties of post-modernism played no part in this history of the way experimental methods developed in the late nineteenth and early twentieth centuries. For the most part, these were informed by an uncompromising commitment to the positivist revolution instituted by Comte and taken up so enthusiastically by the early social scientists.

Chance only becomes useful as a way of understanding the universe once this is seen as non-determined: when the future is viewed as controlled by the past, and when it is thought that both are determined by universal, God-made laws, chance as a concept is literally inconceivable. This was, by and large, the case until the end of the nineteenth century. By then, and as Ian Hacking puts it in his *The Taming of Chance*, developments in statistical and philosophical thinking about probability meant that the concept of chance 'had attained the respectability of a Victorian valet, ready to be the loyal servant of the natural, biological and social sciences' (Hacking 1990:2). The promotion of chance to a newly respectable status was hastened by the Darwinian emphasis on random-ness in evolution (uncomfortable as this notion was for those who believed in a divinely ordered universe). Another major transformation accounting for the new appreciation of chance was the one described in chapter 6 – the move towards enumeration as a method of social accounting and a device for assert-ing 'professional' authority. Counting revealed regularities – 'laws' – that came to be understood as features of social, as well as natural, systems, rather than symptoms of divine providence. Thus, Durkheim, for example, in his classic study of suicide (1897), traced apparently individual self-destructive acts to pathologies of the social system.

William Farr (1807–83), appointed as 'compiler of abstracts' in the first General Register Office for England and Wales in 1838, spoke of the 'laws' of life and death. Born in rural poverty in Shropshire, Farr's medical education was sponsored by a local patron, and his interest in vital statistics came at a time when nations were waking up to the need for information on the quantity and quality of their populations. The main problem was the absence of efficient data coding and collection systems. Farr introduced his own classification for the causes of death, endeavoured to improve the census as a source of data on sickness and health, and introduced the modern analysis of mortality by occu-pation in a form which remains essentially unchanged today (Alderson 1983; McDowall 1983). In an early paper, Farr campaigned against the potentially misleading character of evidence based solely on individual experience: 'Public health may be promoted by placing the medical institutions of the country on a liberal scientific basis,' he ventured; 'by medical societies co-operating to collect statistical observations; and by medical writers renouncing the notion that a science can be founded upon the limited experience of an individual' (Farr 1837:601). Like many innovative thinkers in these fields, Farr struggled to put a name to what he did, calling it 'nosometry' – measuring on the basis of a classification (nosology) of disease. Interestingly, much of the early work on mortality statistics, a key medium for working out probability theory, was driven by the interests of the insurance industry which needed accurate data for calculating life annuities (Hacking 1990:49); the interests of insurance also prompted the later twentieth-century refinement of computing the probabili-ties of different mortality rates in different social classes.[5]

The originator of the apocryphal story about monkeys writing books by chance was the astronomer Arthur Stanley Eddington (1882–1944), who is reported to have remarked that an army of monkeys strumming on typewriters '*might*' write all the books in the British Museum. The chances of this happen-ing have been calculated as overwhelmingly larger than the number of atoms in the universe (Peterson 1998:ix–x). But the point is that, if it did happen, it would be erroneous for anyone to suppose either that the monkeys had intended to do it or that they understood what they were writing.

In other guises, chance is an old and familiar idea. Casting lots is an ancient way of avoiding personal responsibility. For example, in AD 73, the rebellious sect of Sicarii in the Judaean desert was about to be overcome by Roman troops; the men first murdered their wives and children, and then drew lots to choose one man who would kill the other nine and then himself. The idea that using lots is a fair method of resource allocation crops up in biblical and talmudic literature; for example, Proverbs 18:18: 'The lot causeth contentions to cease, and parteth between the mighty.' The land of Israel was divided between the tribes using lots, and lots were drawn for the scapegoat on the Day of Atonement, and for other sacrificial and judicial purposes. When a single person needed to be selected from a larger group, a form of what we would today call 'cluster randomisation' was used: a tribe was selected from all tribes, then a family from all families, then an individual (Bennett 1998). Rulers and political leaders have been chosen in the same way: for instance, in ancient Athens, and for the 'election' of the Tibetan Dalai Lama rather more recently (see Fienberg 1971). Lots were cast to select human sacrifices to ancient Scandinavian gods; although the rhetoric in this case was one of giving everyone an equal chance of being favoured, it is doubtful whether the victims saw it quite in that light.[6]

Games and gambling are also ancient human activities. Cubic dice with different numbers of dots on their surfaces have been found among the artefacts of classical Greece and Iron Age settlements in Northern Europe; more than 2,000 years BC, nobles in the Sumerian city of Ur in the Middle East played with tetrahedral dice made of ivory or lapis lazuli. The use of chance in these situations ensures fairness – that no one can turn the game to their advantage. Coin tossing probably has an equally long history. The belief that a tossed coin will land heads and tails an equal number of times has been tested – by a bored prisoner of war in Germany, who counted 5,067 heads in 10,000 coin tosses; by mathematician Karl Pearson (1857–1936), who made it to an exhausting 24,000 tosses with 12,012 heads; and, before both of them, by the French naturalist Georges-Louis Leclerc (1707–88), who tossed 4,040 times, getting 2,048 heads (Peterson 1998:4).[7]

Gambling with dice was fertile ground for some of the earliest speculations along the road to modern probability theory. A Florentine correspondence arising from a commentary on Dante in the late sixteenth century pursued the question of how to interpret particular series of falls of dice (E. S. Pearson 1978). French and German philosophers became involved, including Abraham de Moivre (1667–1754), whose *Doctrine of Chances* (1718) offered a method for calculating the effects of chance. De Moivre, a physicist turned mathematician, was a close friend of Isaac Newton; although well respected by other scientists at the time, he lived in poverty, making his living advising gamblers and underwriters from Slaughter's Coffee House in London's Covent Garden. Other significant contributions to the early development of probability theory were made by the Dutch Bernoulli family (especially James Bernoulli's *Ars Conjectandi* (1713)) and by another Dutchman, Nicholas Struyck (1687–1769), whose first work, published in 1716, was entitled *Calculation of the Chances in Games, by aid of Arithmetic and Algebra, together with a Memoir on Lotteries and Interest*. Struyck was among the first to observe that women live longer than men, reaching this conclusion by examining data on the productivity of life annuities sold (he found it was better to invest in women).

Inventing experimental design

As we saw in chapters 5 and 6, the 'social physics' that emerged in the nineteenth century as a rigorous quantitative investigation of the laws of society provided the basis for a new social science. But the same set of notions also established the groundwork for modern experimental design, both within and outside social science. Experimental psychology, dating from the mid-nineteenth century, inherited some of its concerns from the older sciences, particularly astronomy. A dominant concern in early experimental psychology was the study of reaction times. This dates back to the observations made by the British Astronomer Royal, Nevil Maskelyne, in 1796. Eighteenth-century observatories measured time by determining the moment at which stars and planets crossed the meridian. To do this, they used a specially designed telescope fitted with a number of equidistant parallel wires; the middle wire was set to coincide with the plane of the meridian. The astronomer on duty focused on a particular star and recorded the times at which the star crossed each of the wires; the average of the different times then gave the moment at which the star crossed the meridian. Maskelyne noticed that the times recorded by his assistant, David Kinnebrook, were systematically eight-tenths of a second slower than his own. Since he could find no explanation for this, he fired the unfortunate Kinnebrook. But the episode provided data for later work on inter-observer variation which showed that the habit of different observers recording different observations is the rule rather than the exception (Bessel 1876) (psychology later dubbed it 'the method of average error').

The German physicist Gustav Theodor Fechner (1801–87) developed research on individual sensation and perception through the study of lifted weights; his *Elemente der Psychophysik* (1860) is hailed as the predecessor of Fisher's *Design of Experiments*. Fechner began by studying medicine, but found his interest in the identity of mind and matter was not well accommodated within it. He turned to physics, where his work on the galvanic battery earned him a professorship of physics. Like many other men in the history of methodology, a period of illness and personal crisis (including three years of partial blindness) led to a change of direction – in Fechner's case, to the founding and naming of the subject of 'psychophysics' (Stigler 1986:243).

Between 1845 and 1849 Fechner personally lifted weights more than 67,000 times (Dehue 1997:655). In these experiments, a subject, usually Fechner himself, was given two boxes, and asked in a series of trials to name the heavier. The proportion of right judgements indicated sensitivity to real weight differences, and this was represented in a curve of variance. One element that was missing from Fechner's otherwise careful and systematic observations was the use of randomisation to control the influence of extraneous factors. He was the experimenter and also the one experimented on; he knew the weights of the different boxes he was asking himself to assess and the order in which they would be presented. In the early 1870s, a group at Tübingen improved on this design by deciding that it takes two to experiment: an experimenter and an observer. Further, the observer's expectations should be challenged by the insertion of 'control' or 'deception' trials (Dehue 1997). The device of artificial randomisation was first introduced into psychology experiments by Charles Sanders Peirce (1839–1914), the prolific and 'iconoclastic American philosopher' (Hacking 1990:11) in the 1880s, working with his student, the psychologist Joseph Jastrow of duck-rabbit fame (see chapter 3). Peirce's father was taught by Nathaniel Bowditch, who translated the French mathematician Laplace, whose role in developing the calculus of probabilities was probably more important than anyone else's. Peirce spent thirty years measuring and improving measuring devices as a US Government employee on the Coast Survey, whose goal was mapping the contours of the new land. He took up Fechner's problem of discerning weight differences and responded to a challenge Fechner had set: that there is a threshold below which small differences in weight will not be perceived by anyone. Peirce's opposing hypothesis was that there is, instead, a *continuum* of decreasing accuracy.

The experiments set up by Peirce and Jastrow in 1883–4 improved on Fechner's by 'blinding' the subjects, so that they did not know whether they were being presented with heavier or lighter weights, and by using an artificial randomiser (consisting of two packs of playing cards – Jastrow later suggested that throwing dice could work as well) to determine the sequence of the trials set (Dehue 1997; Hacking 1990:205). According to historian of statistical ideas Stephen Stigler (1978:248), these experiments are the first 'performed according to a precise, mathematically sound randomization scheme'. Recognizing the disturbances that could be introduced into experiments by the play of chance, Peirce and Jastrow used the notion of random allocation to gain a new level of control.[8] Somewhat mysteriously, however, the use of artificial randomisers was slow to be taken up by other experimenters in psychology. However, well before the first medical trial built on Fisherian principles, experiments using randomisation had become an accepted methodological technique within psychology (see McNemar 1940).

Simultaneously, in quite a different arena, that of the study of telepathy, researchers were reaching similar conclusions about the principles it was desirable to follow in conducting experimental studies. The Society for Psychical Research, founded in London in 1882, carried out many experiments on thought transference using randomisation, though not named as such (Hacking 1988). A Parisian physiologist, Charles Richet, applied the method of probabilities to the study of thought transference, in order to assess the likelihood of any apparent successes being due to chance; Richet's first experiments along these lines were conducted in 1884, contemporaneously with those of Peirce and Jastrow.

Later, between 1912 and 1917, experimental research methods applied to psychic phenomena were extended with the work of the American psychologist John Edgar Coover (1872–1938). Coover began life as a telegraphist with the Union Pacific Railway and publisher of a local county newspaper (Dehue 1997). In tens of thousands of trials in which 'agents' were asked to image cards or objects and 'reagents' to guess what these were, Coover instituted the use of 'control experiments'. In these, in contrast to the ordinary run of such experiments, reagents were asked to guess what the cards or objects were, but agents did not look at the cards or objects at all. It was decided on a random basis, using a dice, whether the trial would be 'regular' or 'control'. Randomisation was used here to determine the order of experimental conditions, rather than the distribution of 'reagents' to different research groups.

According to Ian Hacking (1988:449), this is the origin of the term 'control' or 'controlled' experiment. The term has other significant historical roots – in accountancy. In the later nineteenth century, a 'counter-roll' was a duplicate register or account made to verify an official account (Boring 1954). And, as with probably all such 'firsts', the practice was considerably older than the concept. In 1648 the French mathematician and physicist Blaise Pascal (1623–62) directed a physics experiment which led directly to the design of the modern barometer, hydraulic press and syringe. The experiment involved two glass tubes containing mercury and inverted with their lower open ends in a bath of mercury. It was known that glass tubes treated thus would display a vacuum in the upper part of the tube; Pascal's hypothesis was that the vacuum was created by the weight of the atmosphere pressing down on the mercury in the dish; if this were so, one would expect the vacuum to expand with increased altitude (the weight of the air would be less, and thus the mercury column shorter). The experiment was carried out on a 3,000-foot-high mountain, the Puy-de-Dôme, near Clermont-Ferrand, by Pascal's brother-in-law, attended by three clergy and three 'laymen'. Instead of just taking both tubes up the mountain, they cleverly left one at the bottom to act as a 'control' (plus one cleric in attendance to watch it constantly) (Boring 1954). Pascal's hypothesis was supported, though few people believed him at the time.

Medical experiments

The use of artificial randomisers, originally developed in psychology and psychophysics, also crept into the science of educational administration in the 1920s and 1930s (see Dehue 1997; also chapter 8). But in none of these fields did randomised experiments receive anything like the same sustained attention as a technology of evaluation as they did in medicine (Hacking 1988).

Today RCTs are quite unequivocally associated with medicine, as the method of choice – the 'gold standard' – for evaluating the effectiveness of different health care treatments. The apocryphal 'first' RCT of a medical treatment was

sponsored by the Medical Research Council in Britain in 1946. It was published in the *British Medical Journal* in 1948, and celebrated as ushering in the
first half century of RCTs in a special edition of that journal in 1998. The
1946 MRC trial was not, however, the first such attempt rigorously to control
the play of chance in arriving at estimates of the effectiveness of different
treatments in the medical field.[9] There had, for example, been an earlier controlled trial of 'gold therapy' for treating pulmonary tuberculosis in the USA
in 1931 (Sutherland 1960:47) and another of anti-diphtheria serum in Den-
mark in the late 1890s (Fibiger 1898). In the mid-sixteenth century, around
1545, Ambroise Paré had tested the use of onions as a dressing for wounds by
treating parts of wounds with onions and either leaving others alone or treating them with alternative remedies (D. W. Singer 1924). In the late eighteenth
century, the 'mesmerism' which apparently saved Comte's English translator,
Harriet Martineau, from a life recumbent on a sofa, had been subjected to a
trial in which some subjects were blinded and others were not; the treatment
did not have positive effects (Lavoisier and Franklin 1784). The eighteenth
century saw an 'authenticated example of a therapeutic experiment with matched
controls' (F. H. K. Green 1954:1087) carried out by James Lind. Fruit had
been used sporadically for some 200 years to prevent the affliction of scurvy
among sailors. Lind took twelve patients with scurvy on board a boat called
the *Salisbury*, 'their cases as similar as I could have them' – all suffered from
'putrid gums, the spots and lassitude, with weakness of their knees'. Two were
given a quart of cider a day, another two twenty-five 'gutts of elixir vitriol'
three times a day, two others had two spoonfuls of vinegar thrice daily, two
drank at least half a pint of sea water daily, two had a concoction three times
a day of spices 'recommended by a hospital surgeon', and two were given daily
two oranges and one lemon. It was the last treatment that produced 'the most
sudden and visible good', so much so that one of the two subjects was fit for
duty after six days, and the other was so much improved that he was asked to
nurse the rest of the patients (Bradford Hill 1962:4–5; W. A. Silverman 1985:7).
Like many such pieces of research, Lind's findings were not immediately
translated into practice; it was not until 1795 (the experiment took place in
1747) that lemon juice was issued regularly to Royal Navy ships (F. H. K.
Green 1954).

The Hungarian obstetrician Ignaz Semmelweiss's famous discovery of the
importance of hand-washing in preventing childbirth deaths was made as a
result of a 'natural' controlled trial. In the large Viennese maternity hospital in
which Semmelweiss worked, an Imperial Decree in 1840 had assigned students by sex to different clinics, with patients allocated to the two clinics on
the basis of the day of the week on which they were admitted. The clinic run
by male students had three times as many maternal deaths, mainly from puer-
peral fever, as the female-run clinic. The male students, who were training to
become obstetricians, began their days in the post-mortem room, unlike the
female students, who were training for midwifery, and were not expected to
examine the dead. The men went straight from the post-mortem room to the
wards, where they did vaginal examinations on live patients without first wash-

ing their hands. Semmelweiss's trial, begun in 1847, used existing admission practices, which amounted to alternate, rather than random, allocation,[10] in order to test the effects on maternal death rates of hand-washing in chloride of lime. The result was an equalization of the death rates in the two clinics at the lower level (see Codell Carter 1983).

Other doctors were slow to believe in the effectiveness of Semmelweiss's remedy, partly because he waited thirteen years to publish his results and only did so shortly before being admitted to a mental asylum with a terminal mental illness.[11] Another factor was that the processes whereby dirty hands caused mothers to die were not understood; antisepsis became part of routine practice only in the 1880s with James Lister's discovery of bacteria.[12]

The method of alternate allocation was also used in a trial that immediately preceded the 1946 MRC one – a trial of a substance called patulin as a cure for the common cold. A small trial in the Navy had suggested that this worked; aware of the problem of generalizing from small numbers, the MRC funded a further, much larger study. This included over 100,000 people with colds in factories, post offices and schools. It ran early in 1944, and showed that patulin was not the answer (Patulin Clinical Trials Committee 1944). Alternate, rather than random, allocation may have been recommended in this and other trials around this time at the instigation of Austin Bradford Hill (1897–1991), the statistician whose name is coupled with that of Fisher's in developing modern trial techniques. Bradford Hill apparently thought doctors would find alternate allocation easier to understand than randomisation (I. Chalmers 1997a).

The subject of the 1946 MRC trial was streptomycin, a new drug for treating pulmonary tuberculosis. This was, at the time, the main cause of death among young adults in Europe and the USA. Preliminary use of streptomycin, mainly in America, suggested that it might help. But only a small amount was available in Britain, so the MRC decided that random allocation was the fairest way of rationing it, and that this approach would also lead to a definite answer about the drug's value. Young adults in the London area with definite infection were randomised by sealed envelopes containing allocations derived from tables of random numbers either to receive streptomycin or bed-rest only (this was the established treatment at the time). The aim of the trial was to compare the variability in outcome *expected* in bed-rest treated patients with the *observed* outcome in the drug-treated patients. The key question was, what reason is there to think that the group of drug-treated patients might not have experienced better survival even without the drug? Of fifty-five patients given streptomycin, fifty-one were alive after six months' treatment, compared to thirty-eight of the fifty-two allocated bed-rest alone (table 7.1). Calculations showed that such a variation in survival would be expected to occur by chance less often than once in a hundred.

The situation today, in which many doctors accept[13] the judgements arising from RCTs rather than their own, represents a complete volte-face from the earlier medical tradition which held sway for many centuries; it was the strength of this tradition which, as we saw in chapter 5, fuelled medical resistance to the use of quantification in medical practice. The wisdom of the individual

Table 7.1 The streptomycin trial: assessments at six months

Radiological assessment	Streptomycin group (%)	Control group (%)
Considerable improvement	51	8
Moderate/slight improvement	18	25
No change	4	6
Moderate/slight deterioration	9	23
Considerable deterioration	11	11
Deaths	7	27
Total	100	100

Based on N=55, streptomycin group, N=52, control group.
Source: taken from Bradford Hill 1962:51.

physician in choosing the right treatment for the individual patient had to be paramount. Blood-letting is often quoted as an alarming example of professional certainty. Many doctors in the nineteenth century and before were enthusiastic about blood-letting as a cure for most diseases. The pinnacle of the blood-letting era was probably between 1815 and 1835 in Paris, when a physician called François Joseph Victor Broussais (1772–1838) recommended the frequent use of blood-letting in accordance with his theory of medicine which attributed all disease to either too much fluid or too little. The French novelist de Balzac makes many references to Broussais in his novels; in his 1839 *La Comédie du diable*, for instance, a man in hell pleads for light punishment because he has already been treated with leeches by Broussais.[14]

Most importantly, in terms of the arguments of this chapter, how could doctors at the time have been expected to know that leeches did not work as a panacea for most health problems? There had been isolated suggestions, such as the one recorded by Jean Baptiste van Helmont in 1662, that the fashion for blood-letting needed to be put to the test; van Helmont proposed that lots should be cast in order to determine who should be bled and who should not (van Helmont 1662). But the formal development of experimental designs for evaluating the effectiveness of medical experiments followed debates in the nineteenth century about the applications and limitations of the 'numerical method'. This method allowed series of cases to be counted in which patients received, or did not receive, particular treatments, with the aim of arriving at conclusions about therapeutic effectiveness. For example, as regards leeches, sceptics at the time noted that the number of deaths in Paris rose steadily with the application of Broussais's favourite therapy. One such sceptic, Pierre-Charles-Alexandre Louis (1787–1872), undertook a series of statistical evaluations of blood-letting. Louis had trained in medicine at Rheims and Paris, and had then spent a period in Russia, where he became physician to the Czar and had to deal with an epidemic of diphtheria, which made him realize how fragile the evidence base of medicine really was. In a study of blood-letting as a therapy for typhoid fever, he found that thirty-nine out of fifty-nine fatal cases had been bled, with a mean disease duration of 25.5 days compared to 28 days for those not bled; this suggested that blood-letting may have hastened death. Other case series convinced him that blood-letting did, indeed, render death more likely (Louis 1836:19). Louis's principal contribution to scientific medicine was the value of aggregative thinking. This, he argued, should bring to an end the 'romantic' notions of physicians and their 'kind of divining power' (Louis 1836:57–8). His conclusions with respect to blood-letting therapy could not have been popular with the leech industry, which was a considerable one – Broussais reportedly used 100,000 a year; France, having exhausted its own leech supplies by 1827, imported over 33 million a year, mainly from Bohemia and Hungary (Rangachari 1997).

While some physicians held out even against the argument that a series of cases was more informative than a single one, experimental physiologists were putting forward the view that only laboratory experimentation on living organisms could really make medicine scientific. The most famous of the experimental physiologists was Claude Bernard (1813–78). Medicine, according to Bernard, was not a passive observational science, as Louis would have it, but an active interventionist and experimental one. J. Rosser Matthews in his *Quantification and the Quest for Medical Certainty* summarizes the difference between the two viewpoints:

> The contrast between Louis and Bernard's view of science can be seen as a function of a much more fundamental disagreement; they had contrasting views of what constituted 'objective' knowledge. For Louis, the idiosyncratic individual (which his clinical opponents admired) must be rejected for the 'objective' knowledge that emerged at the level of the population. For Bernard, any conclusions based on population thinking must be rejected because such results constituted merely statistical or probabilistic knowledge; they did not possess the 'objective' determinism of conclusions based on experimental investigation of the individual living organism. *(Matthews 1995:74)*

One of the things this debate was about was whether medicine should be a science like other sciences, or whether it should follow the more intuitive methods of the 'moral' sciences. It also represents, in microcosm, today's opposition between 'qualitative' and experimental methods as the most 'soft' and most 'hard' research methods. But what is fascinating is that during this period – the first half of the nineteenth century – both viewpoints were argued from different camps within both medicine and physiology.

An interest in eugenics

No history of experimental methods or the development of modern statistics is complete without an understanding of how both bear an intimate relationship with one of the most influential of all social movements: eugenics. The belief that some human beings are more socially desirable than others because of their genetic endowment has a long, deeply rooted and continuing history. In the nineteenth and twentieth centuries the eugenics movement has taken the form of a broadly based organization embracing a wide range of positions on social and medical policy, from the sterilization of the unfit to family allowances for mothers. There have been eugenics societies in many countries. In Britain, the movement was patronized mainly by the upper classes, so much so that its critics deemed it 'an apology for snobbery, selfishness and class arrogance' (Searle 1979:164). From the viewpoint of the history of science, and as Donald MacKenzie (1976) has argued, the eugenics movement is an important example of the relationship between scientific ideas and the interests and purposes of social groups. Modern psychometric testing was developed primarily by men with eugenic convictions, such as Galton, Charles Spearman and Cyril Burt; eugenist assumptions are also built into modern statistical tests.

When R. A. Fisher went to work at the Rothamsted Agricultural Research Station in 1919, he was himself a committed eugenist. Like many, he was impressed by Nietzsche and Nietzschean ideas of superman. He believed that the environment had a negligible influence (though, significantly, he also thought that what influence it did have was randomly distributed). As a Cambridge undergraduate, he helped to found a local branch of the Eugenics Society there in 1911; its records show that he was very active in it (Mazumdar 1992). In the debate about the sterilization of the 'feeble-minded' that raged in the early decades of the twentieth century, Fisher used mathematics to affirm the eugenist position, calculating that sterilization would reduce the incidence of feeble-mindedness in the next generation by 36 per cent (Kevles 1985:165).[15] He wrote a book on *The Genetical Theory of Natural Selection* (1930) which he dedicated to Darwin's son, Leonard, who sponsored the book for publication under the auspices of the Eugenics Society after it was rejected for publication by the Royal Society. Fisher himself was turned down for war service because of his poor eyesight (this must have been upsetting for one who subscribed to the eugenic creed); he tried farming for a while, before going to Rothamsted. An aspect of his eugenist philosophy was the belief that eugenists would marry better than other people, be cleverer, more beautiful and have more children. He himself married a seventeen-year-old, Ruth Eileen Grattan-Guinness, the daughter of an evangelical preacher. Mrs Fisher had problems believing in God and turned to 'Ron' as a substitute (Box 1978). She bore him eight children (Fisher believed that the professional classes destroyed their racial stock by using birth control – a friend said of him, 'he was the only man I knew to practice eugenics' (Kevles 1985:350)), and uncomplainingly ran his household with little domestic help, entertained his colleagues, looked after his experimental animals, read the newspapers to him every day, and listened to him talking about his work in the bath every evening for many years before leaving him for a more congenial existence beyond the eugenic ideal.

Eugenics was a term coined by the 'founding father' of modern statistics, Francis Galton (1822–1911); it comes from a Greek root meaning 'noble in heredity'. Galton, a cousin of Charles Darwin's, was one of the last 'gentlemen scientists' (Stigler 1986: 266), an occupation made possible by the substantial inheritance left Galton by his father's death in 1844. Galton subsequently abandoned medicine, which he had been studying, and turned to a variety of pursuits, including travel, psychology, education, the study of fingerprints and meteorology; he was, according to his student and biographer, Karl Pearson (another eugenist), until his death 'a boy who must try his powers on all things that came his way' (1924:67). In the Lake District in 1841 Galton was stimulated by meeting a party of ordnance surveyors at the top of Scawfell to develop a 'hand heliostat' – an instrument for flashing sun signals which could be carried in the pocket. In 1849 he designed a 'printing electric telegraph' thereby anticipating the later invention of the telephone; in 1862 he developed the outlines of a system of decimal coinage for England. Galton's fascination with empirical data got him into particular trouble when he applied it to the efficacy of prayer. It struck him when looking at the expectation of life of various occupational groups that the clergy, who ought to live a long time, being a far more 'prayerful class' than others, did not do so; neither did members of royal families, who must surely be more consistently prayed for than anyone else (K. Pearson 1924:116).[16]

Galton is reported to have said, 'whenever you can, count' (K. Pearson 1924:340); counting was a personal obsession. He once estimated the total bulk of gold in the world, computed its volume, and worked out that it would occupy 3,053 cubic feet, or 94 cubic feet less than the room in which he did the calculation; while having his portrait painted, he counted the strokes of the artist's brush (K. Pearson 1924:21). During his travels in Africa, he measured Hottentot women with a sextant. In England he was given to counting the number of fidgets in the audiences of meetings he attended, and he developed no fewer than five portable counting devices, called 'registrators' (K. Pearson 1924:340). Anticipating the later importance of tea in the development of experimental research designs, he tested 'severely the patience of Mrs Galton' by carrying out experiments with the 'flavour, freshness, body and softness' of tea morning and evening for many months in 1859. Even in the presence of visitors, he insisted on weighing the tea and inserting a thermometer into the teapot (K. Pearson 1924:456–8).

Galton's interest in eugenics was prompted by his own personal experience: 'I had been immensely impressed', he wrote in his *Memories of My Life* (1909:288) 'by many obvious cases of heredity among the Cambridge men who were at the University about my own time.' Also influential was his cousin Charles Darwin's *Origin of Species*, the reading of which, he declared, had formed a real crisis in his life, freeing him from all his old superstitions, as if from a nightmare. Under these two influences, Galton wrote *Hereditary Genius* (1892), which attempted to show that talent runs in families. Darwin himself hailed it as converting him to a eugenic view of intelligence – he said he had never in all his life read anything 'more interesting and original' (K. Pearson 1914:6). In this work Galton took up Quételet's method of the normal distribution, and began to develop the idea of statistical regression towards the mean as a strategy for demonstrating the importance of genetic inheritance. He also wrote an unpublished novel, *Kantsaywhere*, whose theme is an island run on eugenic lines by a Eugenic College – there are examinations for fitness; only the fit can marry; and the rest are segregated or deported.[17]

Galton's work on statistics and eugenics was taken up by Karl Pearson (1857–1936), 'a man with an unquenchable ambition for scholarly recognition and the kind of drive and determination that had taken Hannibal over the Alps and Marco Polo to China' (Stigler 1986:266). According to the biography written by his son Egon, Pearson was born of 'yeoman stock' in Yorkshire to a barrister father (his mother, as is the general tendency, being unmentioned). After a degree in mathematics at Cambridge, Pearson took off for Germany, like many young men of his time. There he studied physics, metaphysics, Roman law and German history, on which he became an expert. He also became a socialist (though of an atypical, eugenist kind), and came back to England to lecture on Marx in Soho (E. S. Pearson 1938). Unlike many other eugenists, Pearson was in favour of the education of women. He considered this an issue that ought to be settled by science, although he did worry about the eugenic consequences of educated women declining to bear children, which would put the future of the nation at the mercy of lower-grade working-class stock. Also unlike many other eugenists, Pearson managed to put into practice by breeding three children (Galton had none) the eugenist doctrine that any economically efficient nation needed a sufficient store of well-bred people. Pearson's breeding was, of course, with the aid of his wife, a woman called Maria Sharpe whom Pearson met in the company of the famous feminist writer Olive Schreiner at a small club he founded in 1885 to discuss the mutual position of men and women.

In 1884, at the age of twenty-seven, Pearson accepted a chair in applied mathematics and mechanics at University College, where his main function was to teach mathematics to engineering students. It seems that he at first resisted the notion that Galton's statistics should be applied to 'sociological' topics. But in 1903 he set up a Biometric laboratory in London dedicated to the collection of eugenic statistics. The aim of the Laboratory, as Pearson himself described it some years later, was 'to train statisticians as men of science . . . to convert statistics in this country from being the playing field of *dilettanti* and controversialists into a serious branch of science' (quoted in E. S. Pearson 1938:53). This arduous endeavour meant criticizing 'erroneous processes' in many fields, including medicine, anthropology, craniometry, psychology, criminology, biology and sociology. In 1906 Pearson also took over the Eugenics Records Office founded two years before by Galton at University College. In 1911 the two departments were combined to form a Department of Applied Statistics, with Pearson as its director and the first Galton Professor of Eugenics, a title apparently selected in direct response to the abortive attempts Florence Nightingale made in the last years of her life to persuade Galton of the need for some sort of chair in applied social science (Diamond and Stone 1981. See also ch. 8).

By the 1890s, Pearson was giving lectures on the laws of chance which emphasized questions of logic and controlled experiments. His notes for lecture 3, 'The laws of chance', in 1892 included the following:

> Two methods of deducing laws: Theory and Experiment. Former must start from some results of observation; we must appeal to statistics or experiment somewhere, e.g. if only in the 'principle of the equal distribution of ignorance'. Complexity of mathematical theory based on minimum appeal to experiment. Easier method in the case of an elementary discussion seems to be to appeal to a maximum of experimental evidence, and a minimum of calculation. . . . Nature of experimental evidence. I *Artificial experiments*. These resemble 'games of chance', and the chances are fixed by the experimenter as exactly as possible beforehand. examples: (a) Tossing of Coins, (b) Roulette Results, (c) Lotteries. *(Quoted in E. S. Pearson 1838:147)*

Pearson's work on skew curves and on regression analysis was an important inspiration for the introduction of statistical methods to social science. This process was helped on its way by the work of the mathematician Francis Edgeworth, a distant cousin of Galton's, who came to mathematics from an education in classics and commercial law. Edgeworth's main project was to adapt the statistical method of the theory of errors to the quantification of uncertainty in the social sciences. His contribution to modern statistics was to develop methods for testing for differences between sub-populations fitted to Quételet's normal curve by using estimates of variability.

Applying statistics of chance

Like others before and after him, Pearson was impressed by the extent to which medicine would benefit from more knowledge of modern statistical methods. This was well demonstrated in a debate that took place in the early 1900s about the value of inoculation against typhoid fever. The bacteriologist Almroth Wright (1861–1947) had developed a serum against typhoid fever while working at the Royal Army Medical College in Netley, Hampshire, in the 1890s. From the late 1890s he began to immunize soldiers going to India. When the War Office questioned this practice in 1902, Wright responded by publishing his results in *A Short Treatise on Anti-Typhoid Inoculation* (1904); in this he noted two requirements for credible statistical evidence: first, that there should be a control group, 'which ought to correspond with the inoculated group in all points save only in the circumstances of inoculation'; and, second, that exact numerical records of morbidity and mortality needed to be kept for both groups (Matthews 1995:98). The War Office invited Pearson to pronounce on the significance of Wright's data. Pearson concluded that the effectiveness of Wright's serum had not been demonstrated, and recommended a clinical trial in which every second man in a regiment of 800 would be inoculated (K. Pearson 1904). Such a trial never happened, because the War Office advisory board considered that the method of alternate allocation was unethical in relation to what was essentially a voluntary procedure (Matthews 1995).

Major Greenwood, one of Pearson's medical students and another well-known member of the British Eugenics Society, took forward the proselytization of statistical methods in medicine. Greenwood had taken up an appointment at the London School of Hygiene and Tropical Medicine in 1927, and Bradford Hill, one of Greenwood's protégés,[18] joined him there in 1933 as Reader in Epidemiology and Vital Statistics. Hill, who himself had had TB, acted as the statistical adviser on the streptomycin trial in 1946. A collection of papers written by Hill at the invitation of the editor of the medical journal *The Lancet*, later published as *Principles of Medical Statistics*, advocated clinical trials as the principal source of statistically reliable conclusions about medical treatments. In this he wrote of the advantages of random allocation in the following terms: first, 'it ensures that neither our personal idiosyncrasies (our likes or dislikes consciously or unwittingly applied) nor our lack of balanced judgement has entered into the construction of the different treatment groups – *the allocation has been outside our control*'; second, 'it removes the danger, inherent in an allocation based upon personal judgement, that believing we may be biased in our judgements we endeavour to allow for that bias'; and third, 'the sternest critic is unable to say when we eventually dash into print that quite probably the groups were differentially biased through our predilections or through our stupidity . . . the random method of allocation removes all responsibility from the clinical observer' (Bradford Hill 1962:10, emphasis added). 'Hill's trial' was recognized almost instantly on both sides of the Atlantic as a new and exemplary model of how to conduct a well-designed trial to answer questions about therapeutic effectiveness. It had been designed to imitate closely Fisher's agricultural experiments, using the mathematical techniques of analysis developed for small sample problems in agricultural research (W. A. Silverman 1980:134).

Fisher's original role at Rothamsted was to analyse the historical data on crop yields collected since Lawes first converted one of his barns to study fertilizers in the 1830s. Comparative experiments in agriculture using matched plots had a long history, with their first systematic use dating from the agricultural reform movement in the eighteenth century (Hacking 1988). Danish agricultural researchers had conducted experiments using sophisticated experimental designs, including 'systematic' squares, as early as 1872. R. A. Fisher refers to these in his *The Design of Experiments* (1935:78–80), tracing *their* origin to a Norwegian named Knut Vik. Most of Lawes's experiments at Rothamsted had been carried out in the field named the 'Broadwalk', which, from 1852 on, had been divided into long strips seventeen feet wide, half an acre each. The same wheat variety would be sown all over the field, but each strip would be dressed with different treatments, and there would commonly be two control strips, one left unfertilized and one treated with farmyard manure. Making sense of the historical data was complicated by the fact that different varieties of wheat had been used for different periods of time. Fisher identified three kinds of variation in crop yield: annual variation, variation due to soil deterioration and variation resulting from another group of 'slow changes'. There were two peaks, around 1860 and in the late 1890s, in all the yields.

Fisher's explanation was the competition of weeds; wheat was known to be very sensitive to weed growth, and the field had been repeatedly sown year after year. He had to look elsewhere to account for the peaks and falls; the decline in the 1870s was traced to the loss of boy weeders following the 1870 Education Act, which put boys in school instead, and that of 1900 with the death of John Lawes, who had been an obsessive weeder (Mazumdar 1992:118).[19]

Fisher's interest in the effects of the soil on crop yields, together with his background in Mendelian genetics, led to his development of the statistical technique of the analysis of variance, a method for comparing means. The underlying idea was to allow for the simultaneous action of several different causes; the variance produced by all the causal factors acting together was the sum of the individual variances resulting from each on its own. This technique quickly became an established tool in agricultural experiments. But the statistical developments for which Fisher is best known concern how he dealt with the play of chance in these experiments. The basic analytical problem he faced with the Rothamsted data was quantifying the effects of the environment on productivity. These might be *assumed* to be random (to operate unselectively on all crops, however treated); but a sounder approach was to design the experiments in the first place so as to make sure that the environmental effects *were* random. He tried this out first in an experiment which looked at the effect of farmyard manure and different fertilizers on twelve varieties of potato. All twelve varieties were planted in a random manner on two plots, one manured and one unmanured, in triple rows of sulphate-fertilized, chloride-fertilized and unfertilized. This plan foreshadowed the method of randomisation by the Latin square which makes possible a general test of the statistical significance of experimental differences – that is, a disentangling of the 'true' effect from the effects (and errors) which might be due to chance. In a Latin square arrangement, all the experimental treatments are equally represented in each geographical subdivision.

There is no doubt that Fisher knew about the forty-year history of randomisation in parapsychology (Hacking 1988:450), though he did not take this field of study seriously (Box 1978). Interestingly, as regards the link between eugenics and statistics, Fisher's experience with these agricultural experiments led him away from the traditional eugenic emphasis on the negligible importance of the environment. It was clear that the opposite was the case when it came to crops; the quality and quantity of the soil they grew in were all-important. As a member of the Eugenics Society's Research Committee, Fisher thus urged the importance of a control group in research, such as that by Ernest Lidbetter on pauperism. Lidbetter, originally a relieving officer in a workhouse, had been trying for many years to demonstrate the view held by many in the Eugenics Society that pauperism was an inherited deficiency rather than an economic accident, and that its cure was therefore restricted breeding.

This was an episode in another long history, that of the eugenic study of problem families (see e.g. G. Jones 1986). The pauper study, started in the early 1900s, was resumed in 1923 when Lidbetter took a census of the 1,174 paupers in his old East End parish of Bethnal Green. The Council of the Eugenics Society urged Lidbetter to have a control sample before arriving at conclusions about the special characteristics of paupers as a social group, although it was unclear about how such a sample might be found. Fisher particularly battered away at the control group problem. Under the influence of the experiments at Rothamsted, his own thinking was now focused on the effects of the environment in determining agricultural yields, and this was clearly applicable to the problem of determining the causes of pauperism. Fisher attacked Lidbetter for being generally unscientific (see Mazumdar 1992: ch. 3). The control group problem was never solved, and Lidbetter's study was eventually published in 1933, as a 'vast compendium of genealogical data' (Kevles 1985:114) which concluded, unscientifically but in line with much eugenic thinking, that the poor constitute a biological class of their own.

Chance and true science

The new conceptualizations described in this chapter of the role of chance in the fates of living beings were derived both from general changes in world-views and from movements within particular disciplines. Individually, psychology, education, medicine and, as we shall see in the next chapter, sociology, had to come to terms with the human vulnerability to chance occurrences. This bedevils both consciously directed attempts to change behaviour and the striving for causal understanding. No longer divinely regulated and ordered, the twentieth-century universe calls for forms of knowing other than blind faith.

Medicine is singled out for attention in the historiography of RCTs not because it was the only discipline that struggled with these issues, but for other reasons. As a set of interventions in people's lives, those of medicine probably have more capacity than those of other professions to kill and cause serious injury. Certainly most of the critical methodological and scientific moments cited in medicine are those in the 'life or death' category. But the equation between RCTs and medicine was also made because of the role the new scientific medicine was coming to play in post-Victorian society. Medicine came to represent some kind of apotheosis of modern science: the expert application to the human body and mind of the kind of systematic, privileged knowledge which ordinary citizens could not easily be expected to grasp.

This new framing of medicine, and within it the motif of scientific experimentation, is exemplified in Sinclair Lewis's classic novel *Arrowsmith*, first published in 1924. *Arrowsmith* is often quoted for its fictional representation of some of the moral dilemmas involved in experimental research.[20] The idea for the novel came from a chance meeting in 1922 between Lewis and a young bacteriologist at the Rockefeller Institute, Paul de Kruif, who had attacked the pretensions of some American doctors in a series of articles in the *Century Magazine*. De Kruif's attack focused on the slipshod and worthless nature of most medical research. His commitment to scientific medicine and the newly

evolving canons of systematic research gave Lewis the outline of his novel and
the biography of its main character, Martin Arrowsmith. The novel charts
Arrowsmith's career, beginning with his medical studies at the University of
'Winnemac' in the 'slightly Midwestern city of Zenith' under the suitably
German Professor Gottlieb. Gottlieb experiments with anthrax germs on guinea-
pigs, eschews the profit motive, goes to work on a squeaky bicycle, follows the
biometrical edicts of Karl Pearson, and is above all 'an elaborately careful
worker, a maker of long rows of figures, always realizing the presence of
uncontrollable variables' (Lewis 1925:123). It is from Gottlieb that Arrowsmith
learns

> the trick of using the word 'control' in reference to the person or animal or
> chemical left untreated during an experiment. . . . When a physician boasted of
> his success with this drug or that electric cabinet, Gottlieb always snorted,
> 'Where was your control?' . . . Now Martin began to mouth it – control, control,
> control, where's your control? . . . till most of his fellows and a few of his
> instructors desired to lynch him. *(Lewis 1925:40–1)*

After practising in 'Wheatsylvania' and working as a public health doctor in
the 'great city of Nautilus' as assistant to the unbelievably named Dr Almus
Pickerbaugh (with his even more unbelievably named children Orchid, Ver-
bena, Daisy, Jonquil, Hibisca, Narcissa, Arbuta and Gladioli), Arrowsmith
realizes that important scientific work is not done on the political platforms of
public health campaigning. He goes to work for the Rouncefield Clinic, a
clean, commercial factory, but finds this disappointing too. He is then offered
a research position at the McGurk Institute (a thinly veiled Rockefeller Institute) under, once again, Professor Gottlieb. Here Arrowsmith meets the great
challenge of his career, the discovery of a 'phage' which is potentially a cure
for bubonic plague. It is agreed that Arrowsmith's phage will be tested on a
West Indian island called St Hubert, where there is currently an epidemic.
Gottlieb entrusts him with the task of giving the phage to half the patients and
withholding it from the other half as controls. But this proves more difficult
than it sounds. The 'shopkeeping lords' of St Hubert are against a test in
which (as they see it) half of them might die needlessly; the Governor delivers
to Arrowsmith a speech against 'you Yankee vivisectionists';[21] and the general
view is that experiments belong in the laboratory, not in the real world. '"I'm
not a sentimentalist; I'm a scientist!"' boasts Arrowsmith in response. But
'They snarled at him in the streets now; small boys called him names and
threw stones. They had heard that he was wilfully withholding their salvation.
The citizens came in committees to beg him to heal their children' (Lewis
1925:382).

Arrowsmith manages to hold out, and in one parish he divides the population into two equal parts, injecting one with the phage, the other not. Unfortunately, the untreated community is attacked by the plague much more heavily
than the treated one. After his own wife dies from the plague, he turns his
back on the lessons of Professor Gottlieb and succumbs to giving the phage to

everyone. When the epidemic eventually subsides, he is hailed as a hero for saving lives, but returns to New York with scientifically worthless data.

In *Arrowsmith* the rigorous German scientist is the hero, representing the new religion of uncertainty. One of Gottlieb's speeches proclaims on 'the religion of a scientist': 'the scientist is . . . so religious that he will not accept quarter-truths, because they are an insult to his faith,' pronounces Gottlieb:

> He speaks no meaner of the ridiculous faith-healers and chiropractors than he does of the doctors that want to snatch our science before it is tested and rush around hoping they heal people. . . . He is the only real revolutionary, the authentic scientist, because he alone knows how liddle he knows. *(Lewis 1925: 278–9)*

But the young, idealistic doctor who experiences the conflict between the new scientific principles of experimental trials and the moral anguish of treating people as 'controls' is another kind of hero. He represents the tension between two ways of knowing which have come to be divided – experience and experiment. What experience teaches are the lessons of attending and responding to what is happening in the here-and-now; experiment, on the other hand, introduces the caution of understanding that present appearances can be deceptive, and that the path to reliable knowledge must, consequently, pick a very particular way through these. In *Arrowsmith* the experiment is seen at the very point at which it is emerging from the laboratory into ordinary social settings, which are replete with human problems. In this sense, the novel fictionalizes the birth of a new scientific medicine, with all its attendant modern language of experimental methods and control groups (Rosenberg 1976). It is also no accident that the women in the novel are all dimly lit, background figures; wives, mothers, mistresses, housekeepers – they represent that very domain of everyday life, of feeling, whose appearances can be so deceptive, and against which the scientific model of knowing must pit its superior *modus operandi*.

Conclusion

Today's technology of the randomised controlled trial is rooted in much older and more universalist attempts to understand the place and play of chance in both the social and natural worlds. Such efforts were not restricted to the domain of medicine, as the modern historiography of RCTs would often have us believe. Indeed, the struggle to come to terms with the idea and implications of a chancy universe involves the history of how the different sciences underwent a gradual process of disentanglement, and came to be defined as separate. To the eighteenth- or nineteenth-century mathematician, astronomer, philosopher or social analyst, science was a unity. Laplace, Poisson, Quételet, Galton and their ilk did not distinguish between the problems of the biological body and those of the social system in working out their theories about how to deal with chance. While the most lasting push towards RCTs as the prototypical technology of chance occurred in medicine, this owes more to the story of what has happened to medicine and to other disciplines since their 'discovery' than it does to the prior history of ideas about chance.

The story told in this chapter is uniformly one of male achievements. The key players are male; the performance is one about the development of men's understanding of the role of chance as applied to the natural and social worlds. Chance itself has a role analogous to that of female nature in the Cartesian revolution, being conceived as a wayward, unpredictable force with an unnerving tendency to disrupt the cerebral operations of man. In order for men to grasp with any sincerity the true nature of relationships between events, chance itself must be rendered captive; it must be fenced in with numbers and equations; it must be defined, measured and controlled. This gendering of statistical knowledge and techniques as ideological processes was substantially helped by the alliance with eugenics. Although perhaps not inherently sexist, most eugenic philosophies and practices have not in fact viewed women as equal citizens. The early work of Galton's Biometric Laboratory focused on the measurement of brain size and intelligence. Craniometry was the first sociobiological theory to be 'supported' by quantitative data: the smaller brains of women, Negroes, apes and children were irrefutable proof of white male supremacy (Gould 1981; Schiebinger 1993). In eugenist thinking, women featured exclusively as the transmitters of hereditary ability (MacKenzie 1976). As E. S. Pearson noted (1978:221), the history of statistics omits sisters, wives and mothers, which makes it very difficult to understand the true pedigree of male scientific achievement.

As the later use of RCTs in and outside medicine demonstrates, this way of knowing is not always as simple as it might at first appear. Some of its intricacies which have constituted fuel for the anti-trialists are examined in more detail in chapter 11. Many, however, were noted from the outset. The problem of personal preference, and its potentially biasing effects on what subsequently happens, was recognized in an important early challenge to randomised design, that of the 'Bayesian' school. Thomas Bayes (1702–1761), a Nonconformist English clergyman, left his *An Essay towards Solving a Problem in the Doctrine of Chances* to be published posthumously by a friend. Its origin, like its writer's life, is somewhat obscure (see E. S. Pearson 1978). But Bayes's challenge was to arrive at a method which would give the probability of an event, taking into account past personal experience of it; the object was to form an initial assessment of one's personal beliefs about a subject and then to modify this in the light of experience, so arriving at a theoretical analysis modelled by the calculus of probability and a theory of personal utility.

The potential difficulty – faced by Martin Arrowsmith on the plagued island of St Hubert – of withholding from the control group in an RCT what might transpire to be an effective treatment was discussed at the time of the streptomycin trial. The fact that randomisation acted as a democratic rationing device for a scarce resource was viewed as containing the ethical problem (Mainland 1950). The objection that trials treat people like objects was discussed by Bradford Hill himself in a 1952 lecture, referring to the criticism that trials lead to 'the replacement of humanistic and clinical values by mathematical formulae' with the result that subjects are degraded 'from human beings to bricks in a column, dots in a field, or tadpoles in a pool' (1962:42). As Hill said, the emotive rhetoric of this complaint must contend with the requirement of advancing human knowledge. It is difficult to arrive at knowledge in any other way except by controlling the wayward influences of chance. Once the operations of chance have been recognized, ways of knowing can never be the same again; chance, like women and like nature, must be put firmly in its place.

Part III

Experiments and their Enemies

8

Experimental Sociology: The Early Years

We need men not afraid to work, who will get busy with the adding
machine and the logarithms, and give us exact studies, such as we get in
the . . . laboratories. Sociology can be an exact, quantitative science, if we
get industrious men interested in it.

Giddings, *Inductive Sociology*

The question, therefore, would seem to be imminent and inescapable:
Why cannot sociologists utilize the technique of the controlled experiment?

Carr, 'Experimental Sociology'

Today, experimental studies are usually seen as belonging quite unequivocally
to medicine and 'science', with other ways of knowing appropriated by students of 'the social'. But in order to make this division persuasive, a selective
rendering of history has been necessary – one in which social science, and
especially sociology, arrived on the scene in the twentieth century to rescue
knowledge from the mistaken techniques of quantification and experimentation. The trouble with this story is that it ignores a significant history of
experimentation *within* social science. This chapter looks at some of this early
history. Since North America was the main site for the early experimental
social science, this bit of the story is a continuation of chapter 6 – the steady
but uneven evolution of social science itself. It is also an important precursor
to the next episode of the story, in chapter 9, which discusses the full-blown
use of RCTs in large-scale social experimentation – the so-called golden age of
evaluation in the United States which spanned the decades from the 1960s to
the 1980s.

A central underlying argument is one about the desirability of evidence about the effectiveness of all kinds of interventions in people's lives. Choices between alternative therapies might seem particularly stark in medicine, but actually such choices exist in relation to a very wide range of interventions. As one commentator on the relevance to future research of 'Bradford Hill's' streptomycin trial (see chapter 7) noted, 'modern statistical principles are not something that we can take or leave as we wish, for they comprise the logic of the investigator in *all fields*' (Mainland 1950:929; emphasis added). Bradford Hill himself certainly saw 'his' method of the RCT as being useful much more generally outside clinical medicine – for example, in the area of crime prevention. 'I do not, let me hasten to say,' he observed,

> envisage the judge with the black cap . . . upon one side of the bench and upon the other Bradford Hill's Random Sampling Numbers. But I would believe that a very serious study ought to be made of the possibilities of controlled experimentation in this setting as compared with the present uncontrolled and, largely, uninformative experimentation. *(Bradford Hill 1962:181)*

Archie Cochrane, after whom the Cochrane Collaboration is named, wondered much the same thing. He was working on the epidemiology of tuberculosis in the Rhonda Valley at a Medical Research Unit in Cardiff when the 'first' randomised controlled trial was published. It made him wonder how other aspects of medicine would stand up to such scrutiny, and, indeed, how all sorts of interventions would fare when evaluated outside the normal framework of 'essentially subjective observations'. Some years later, Cochrane recruited a sociologist to his staff, and embarked on trying to apply the method to a number of social problems, including flogging, which had been popular in the boys' public school he had attended in middle England (he had wondered at the time about its effectiveness). A case-control study in Rhonda secondary schools suggested that caning was ineffective as a deterrent to smoking, but Cochrane feared that randomising caning would not be an acceptable experiment to most school heads. Instead, he randomised detention and a reprimand from a senior teacher as cures for lateness, finding the latter more effective. Turning his attention next to crime prevention, Cochrane floated the idea of randomising social workers to families containing delinquent children; but this was immediately turned down as impractical (Cochrane 1989).[1]

Experimental education

Much of the early work applying these ideas about systematic evaluation took place in education. In the late 1890s and early 1900s educational researchers in the United States were tangling with the problem of evaluating different approaches to promoting educational performance. The wider context for these efforts was the much-discussed Progressive Era in America, with its weariness of *laissez-faire* politics and call for centralized government intervention. The drive was for such intervention to be based on carefully collected facts and evidence of administrative efficiency and effectiveness. The 'cult of efficiency' and the motif of scientific management facilitated a transfer of methodological expertise from psychology to education; as we saw in chapter 7, social researchers had introduced experimental tests using random control groups well before the turn of the century.

The leading figure in educational experimentation was Edward L. Thorndike, a psychologist and educational researcher at Columbia University. Together with his colleague Robert S. Woodworth, Thorndike carried out a series of tests in 1901 looking at the impact of training on students' 'mental function'; the difficulty of working out, using simple before-and-after comparisons, what the effects of training actually *were* led them to suggest incorporating a group of students who would be given no special training, but would be tested at the same time points as the students exposed to training (Thorndike and Woodworth 1901). This was a direct transfer of the functional slant and methodological principles developed in psychophysics and psychology research by Fechner, Peirce and others. Thorndike's vision was of a science of educational practice based on experimentation; he wanted to provide teachers with tested principles and procedures so that they did not have to rely on intuition, chance or talent (see Eisner 1979). This vision had its followers; by 1916 some 14 per cent of experiments reported in the *Journal of Educational Psychology* employed control groups (Danzinger 1990). A transfer of methodological learning across the Atlantic was also evidently occurring at this time, as the British researcher W. H. Winch deployed control groups several years later in his experiments on the transferability of memory skills. Winch wanted to know whether teaching children poetry would make them better historians or geographers. He divided groups of thirteen-year-old middle- and working-class girls into two, based on teacher assessments and the girls' marks in a pre-test which involved trying to recall passages from a history or geography book. In each experiment, one group of girls then had lessons in learning poetry, while the other proceeded as usual. The results were claimed to 'strengthen the case of those who wish children to learn much poetry' (Winch 1908:293).

Schools are natural laboratories. This key feature of educational research was noted by Campbell and Boruch in the 1970s in a paper discussing the design deficiencies of many of the compensatory education interventions (which come later in the educational research story). 'Pupils are arbitrarily fed doses of education,' observed Campbell and Boruch. 'They assemble regularly for this process. What is being taught them is arbitrarily varied all the time. There is therefore a laboratory in which the treatment can be arbitrarily changed without difficulty' (Campbell and Boruch 1975:205). The emphasis on the value of experiment in educational research which emerged in the early years of the twentieth century was not new, as Robert Rusk pointed out in his *Experimental Education*, published in 1919; more than a century before, the Edgeworths'[2] *Practical Education* (1798) contained the opinion that the art of education should be converted into an experimental science. Rusk himself referred to the method of Winch – 'equivalent or parallel groups' – as being 'extensively applied in educational experiments' because of its superiority in tackling the problem of determining the difference between changes due to educational intervention and those proceeding from 'natural development' (Rusk 1919:10–11). 'It may be asked,' he went on optimistically, 'how the new method will affect the position of the teacher. It will deliver him [sic] from the tyranny of tradition and the caprice of the faddist, and bring him under the servitude of his science' (Rusk 1919:5).

Another early series of educational experiments, conducted by Earl Hudelson in Minnesota in the early 1920s, examined class size, a thorny subject which continues to preoccupy educational researchers today (most of whom reject the usefulness of an experimental research design[3]). Hudelson carried out fifty-nine experiments involving 108 classes and 6,059 students. His method was to 'embed' matched pairs of students within small and large classes, using the same instructor, text and method of instruction for both sets of classes (Hudelson 1928). (He found a slight advantage in favour of larger classes, a result which is somewhat out of line with later research, and which may signal the well-known difficulty of 'matching' accurately.) Similarly, Marvin Pittman's doctoral thesis at the University of Columbia used what he termed 'the equivalent groups method' to answer a question dear to the heart of American school administrators, teachers and taxpayers at the time: did supervision of schools pay in terms of improved educational outcomes? Pittman 'arbitrarily' selected fifteen experimental and twenty-five control schools in Brown County, South Dakota, and looked at the impact on a wide range of outcomes of subjecting schools and teachers to a programme of systematic supervision. The programme included observation of classroom instruction, 'democratic teachers' meetings' and 'the development of a community consciousness on the part of rural communities' (Pittman 1921:19). Most of the schools were one-teacher schools, and the teachers were usually young, with limited training and experience. A weakness of the experiment was that Pittman himself provided the intervention, which took place during a winter of subzero temperatures when many of the country roads could only be traversed with sleighs. Strengths of his evaluation design were the collection of qualitative data from children, parents and teachers, including asking the teachers what they thought it was about the intervention which worked (on twelve out of thirteen standardized tests the experimental children seemingly did better than the control children).

In none of these early experiments, however, were the control groups selected randomly. Selection of experimental and control group participants using the principle of chance is described in W. A. McCall's *How to Experiment in Education*, published in 1923. McCall was a student of Edward Thorndike's; the two had worked together a few years earlier on a study testing the effects of fresh and recirculated air on children's performance, in which McCall had suggested choosing the research groups randomly. McCall's text outlined a comprehensive theory as to why more and more rigorous experimentation was needed in education. He estimated that well–designed research to improve teaching methods could save $134,680,000,000,000, or 790 times the cost of the First World War over the next 100 generations of American students. McCall's description of random allocation adds a further item to the growing inventory of studies which pre-date the first 'official' application of the RCT design in the 1946 streptomycin trial. It went as follows:

> Representativeness [of research subjects] can be secured by making a chance selection from the total group, or a chance selection from a chance portion of the total group. . . . Just as representativeness can be secured by the method of chance, so equivalence may be secured by chance. . . . One method of equating by chance is to mix the names of the subjects to be used. Half may be drawn at random. This half will constitute one group while the other half will constitute the other group. *(McCall 1923:38–41)*

McCall's recipe for random allocation was offered in the context of a critical analysis of all types of research design. He took a Comtean view of its evolution; the first stage through which methods of determining truth pass is that of *authority*; the second is *speculation*; the third and best is *hypothesis* and *experimentation*. Within the experimental armoury 'the equivalent groups method' had a great deal to recommend it, but the problem was just *how* to select equivalent groups (well illustrated in studies such as Hudelson's). Having come down on the side of random allocation, McCall went on to observe that a method which is *supposed* to be random may not be in practice. His example was the lottery for military conscription conducted by the War Department; numbers were written on paper and enclosed in capsules, but the longer numbers weighed more because of the additional ink deposit, so tended to sink to the bottom and be drawn last.[4] Unfortunately, McCall became ill with tuberculosis in 1927, and when he resumed work, he concentrated his energies on designing educational tests and working with Chinese universities, rather than on helping other educational psychologists to use the more rigorous evaluation methods he had described in his book (Dehue 1997).

As Julian Stanley (1966:224) has noted, these methodological innovations in educational research were 'ingenious from the standpoints of both design and substance'. But they did not sustain their early promise, as other leading educationalists besides McCall also increasingly migrated into the field of educational testing, leaving experimental research largely to the psychologists. The wave of enthusiasm in education for rigorously designed experiments did, however, leave the important legacy of a textbook, Lindquist's *Statistical Analysis in Educational Research* (1940), which had the explicit purpose of 'translating' Fisher's *The Design of Experiments* and *Statistical Methods for Research Workers* into 'a language and notation familiar to the student of education' (Lindquist 1940:iv). Lindquist's underlying mission was the same as McCall's had been – to improve educational research design. His book contains a detailed description (24–9) of how the principle of random selection should be used in educational research.

Despite these efforts, the educational experiments reported in the late 1920s, 1930s and 1940s mostly did not build on McCall's description of randomly generated control groups, though they continued to wave the flag of controlled experiments. There was, for example, a controlled trial of the effect of 'motion pictures' on children's dental care (F. N. Freeman 1933), and another of integrated health education in a New York school (Gillis 1927); a set of studies carried out at Pennsylvania State College in 1932 looking at 'character education' also used the matched group design to estimate the effects of such interventions as morality discussions and Latin and economic geography on pupils' ethical judgements and 'international-mindedness'. (Talking about morality was said to make little difference to ethical judgements, whereas learning Latin made more; geographical instruction targeted at developing 'a feeling of intimacy for people of distant lands' was said to be followed by more positive attitudes (Campbell and Stover 1933:245; Meek 1933; Robb and Faust 1933).)

It was the continuation of poorly designed experimental studies that led Julian Stanley in 1957, like McCall in 1923, to argue for more and better controlled experimentation in school settings. He himself reported two controlled experiments, one of speech instruction and one of role playing and attitudes to world government, which were unable to detect any intervention effects. What happened in educational evaluation was a move away from experimental methods, on the grounds that these 'frequently failed to produce results which were statistically significant' (N. Williams 1981:73). This flight from the 'wrong' answers yielded by well-designed experimental studies is a recurrent theme in the history of social intervention evaluation. Writing in 1972, N. L. Gage of Stanford University commented on the wave of pessimism that had greeted the many experimental studies in education which had come up with 'no difference' findings; neither this nor that method of instruction seemed to be superior; characteristics of teachers appeared unrelated to student outcomes. 'The early years of research on teaching have not paid off in solid, replicable, meaningful results of considerable theoretical or practical value. Positive and significant results have seldom been forthcoming' he concluded (Gage 1972:114). A few years later Eisner's summary was even more gloomy: 'if educational practitioners *had* to base their educational practices on hard data we would have to close our schools' (Eisner 1979:180).

Chapin's 'projected design'

Francis Stuart Chapin (1888–1974) did more than any other single American social scientist to proselytize and practice the use of experimental methods.[5] Like many of the other early pioneers of sociology in America, Chapin came from a family of pastors, but he upset family tradition by taking an engineering degree. His uncle, to whom he was close, was an eminent paediatrician, with connections to the eugenics movement and a strong interest in 'modern scientific management' and fact-driven social reform. Chapin went to Columbia University for the last year of his degree. Columbia was at that time (1909) the centre of scientific sociology in the United States. It housed people such as John Dewey (who urged the application of the natural science model of evaluation to public policy) and the experimentally-minded Edward Thorndike, whose work Chapin much admired; also William Ogburn, a sociologist whose primary interest was in developing quantitative methods in the social sciences, and the anthropologist Franz Boas, who was concerned to make anthropology more of a factual exercise than it had been hitherto (he was famous locally for his difficult courses in statistics (Hoxie et al. 1955)).

After leaving Columbia, Chapin organized a new school of social work at Smith College, and then went in 1922 as Professor of Sociology and Director of Social Work to the University of Minnesota. Here he built up a department of distinguished academics, including Pitrim Sorokin,[6] who had recently emigrated from Russia; Edwin Sutherland, the criminologist; and George Lundberg, who would carry Chapin's arguments for a scientific sociology into the 1940s and beyond. Chapin's pre-eminence in American sociology is indicated by a long list of institutional connections: he was a moving spirit behind the formation of the Social Science Research Council in 1924, and edited the Council-sponsored *Social Science Abstracts*; he was president of the American Sociological Society in 1935, a leading organizer of the Sociological Research Association in 1936, advisory editor of the *American Journal of Sociology*, contributing editor of *Sociometry*, and co-editor of the *American Sociological Review* from 1944 to 1946. Among his colleagues, Chapin had something of a reputation for austere, emotionless and humourless quantification. Its zenith was the 'living-room scales' he developed in 1927-8 as a method of measuring social class; household items such as books, floor coverings, lights, heaters and clocks were all awarded points; a electric light earned eight points, a hardwood floor ten, while a kerosene heater or a sewing machine *cost* two. The resulting classification was truly 'objective'. Like Galton, his passion for order and measurement infected everything; he filed jokes alphabetically, kept meticulous diaries, and in the oil-painting he took up the year his mother died experimented systematically with different techniques. He planned his retirement home on the basis of weather data, the distances from his several children, and the proximity of facilities such as shops and a well-stocked fish-pond.[7]

Chapin's early works – *An Introduction to the Study of Societal Evolution* (1913) and *Historical Introduction to Social Economy* (1917) – were celebrations of rational intelligence in which sociologists, like chemists, studied problems by breaking them down into their component parts. His textbook *Field Work and Social Research* (1920) was one of the first 'modern' guides to how to do research; it brought research methods fully into the twentieth century with discussions of random sampling and even a photograph of a punch card. Chapin began to be interested in experimental methods more directly around 1916. His book *Experimental Designs in Sociological Research*, published in 1947, brought together accounts of nine experimental studies carried out over a number of years by Chapin and some of his students. These are prefaced by an explanation of how experimental designs in social relations work and a sustained plea, which echoes McCall's earlier one in education, for sociologists to take these more seriously: 'Experiment is simply observation under controlled conditions,' observes Chapin reasonably. But reason is not in the ascendant in this debate: 'It may be stated as a truism that just as soon as the sociologist passes from the method of passive observation to active interference . . . he [*sic*] begins to encounter a stiffening resistance.' This resistance stems from a kind of abhorrence which hangs round the idea of experimentation, despite the fact that the state experiments 'endlessly and thoughtlessly' with people's lives and welfare all the time. But this is not *recognized* as experimentation – it is regarded as normal practice, or what Chapin calls '*blind* trial and error'. The point of an experimental sociology is to use '*overt* trial and error' to 'facilitate the discovery of cause-and-effect relationships in society', using this knowledge for the rational guidance of social change (F. S. Chapin 1947:viii, 1, 4, 26).

Chapin listed three sorts of research design under the heading 'experimental', of which only one – '*a projected design*' – is the *prospective* experimental study using a control group which was beginning its modern career in medical evaluation around the time his book was published. His criterion of inclusion for the nine studies was that they had all been set in a 'normal community' context; enough was already known, he argued, about doing experimental studies in laboratory situations such as the classroom, but because people cited the limitations of such studies in community settings, it was worth taking a closer look at some of them 'in the hope that thereby the way may be pointed to devices that can be used to overcome these limitations' (Chapin 1947:ix).

Four studies

Four of the nine studies used the 'projected design'. The first of these was Stuart Dodd's *A Controlled Experiment on Rural Hygiene in Syria* (1934). Dodd wanted to evaluate the effects of a rural hygiene programme (including water boiling) on families' health practices. The recipients were forty families in the Arab village of Jib Ramli. A control village was selected using nine variables (sanitary conditions, geography, etc.) to attempt comparability with the experimental village. In both villages families' hygiene practices were assessed before and after a two-year period of instruction by a travelling clinic in the experimental village. The hygiene score of experimental families went up from 253 to 304 points, and that of control families from 241 to 286. Dodd concluded that this form of health promotion did not appear to make much of a difference; there may have been seepage of the hygiene instruction from the experimental to the control village. Chapin pointed out that the two villages did not consist of comparable populations in the first place.

Dodd himself went a great deal further down the quantitative route than any other social scientist at the time in his book *Dimensions of Society: a quantitative systematics for the social sciences* (1942). In this he proposed that the whole of sociology and social relations could be reduced to one single formula – $S = _s(T;I;L;P)_s^s$ [8] – what he called the 'S theory'. This extremist version of quantitative social science probably did not help win the case for scientific sociology against the arguments of those who suspected it of a base reductionism.

Chapin's second study examined the effects of rehousing on the living conditions and social life of 'slum families' in Minneapolis. A group of 108 families were selected in 1939 from among those being rehoused to be the experimental group; and 131 families from the waiting list were taken as the control group. A complicated matching process ensued, which removed a number of families from the study because they could not be paired with others. This study, for which Chapin himself was the principal investigator, gave him an opportunity to flex his intellectual muscles with respect to the famous 'living-room scales'. The study results were interpreted as showing no statistically significant changes in morale or general adjustment, but greater changes in social status and social participation among rehoused families (Chapin 1938).

Thirdly, there was a study by Reuben Hill (1944) which looked at the effects on social adjustment of encouraging university students to engage in (certain kinds of) extra-curricular activities. The research sample was 1,306 freshmen [sic] in the College of Letters and Sciences at the University of Wisconsin in 1940. Using an alphabetical list, every other name was taken for the experimental group; the rest became the control group. Then the groups were 'matched' on fifteen factors, resulting in a final sample of 226 each in experimental and control groups. The intervention consisted of counselling interviews by two members of staff in the Division of Social Education, who directed students into 'suitable' activities. Drop-out in both groups was substantial. At the end of the study, the investigator viewed the results as favouring the initial hypothesis but not confirming it: differences in social adjustment between experimental and control groups were small.

Lastly, in his list of prospective experimental studies, Chapin included a study from a different field – that of juvenile delinquency. The focus of this study was on integrating 'normal' and 'problem'[9] children (boys aged 10–14) in a programme of 'controlled activity' which included classes in art, woodwork, metal and leather work, and games of various kinds organized by trained group leaders 'blind' to which children were which. The 'problem' boys were drawn from 'official sources' and the 'normal' ones from school records in underprivileged areas. Again matching was used to attempt to create comparable groups, which resulted in abandoning some of the sample; there was also the usual further loss to follow-up. The original sample was 155 in each group, but results were based on only twenty and eighteen of the experimental and control samples respectively. The dubious conclusion derived from these attenuated data was that experimental boys had become 'significantly' less problematic (Shulman 1945).

A theoretical solution

In the final chapter of his *Experimental Designs*, Chapin highlighted some of the problems thrown up by these studies, including the difficulty of adequate matching which was experienced in all four. Referring to Lindquist's (1940) textbook, he made it clear that he knew what the answer was:

'Randomization is theoretically the solution. .... The procedure is to select a
sample at random from the population to be studied. This sample may then be
divided at random into the experimental group, which is to receive the social
program, and the control group, which is excluded from the program. *(F. S.
Chapin 1947:166)*[10]

The main problem Chapin saw with this approach was this one: 'Who ever
heard of a director of . . . relief or of public housing willing to court the public
criticism that would develop if it became known that selection for treatment or
exclusion was made on a random basis?' (F. S. Chapin 1947:168). Chapin
himself had confronted this difficulty in his housing research. What it meant,
in his view, was that the use of randomisation in experimental studies of social
programme evaluation would have to wait until the public administrators were
behind the idea. This moment in the history of methodology was to arrive in
the United States some twenty years later (see chapter 9).

The case of Columbia

There are always different possible kinds and levels of explanation for intellectual developments. In Chapin's case, several influences seem clear: the engineering background, the medical eugenist uncle, the combined sociology–social
work department at Minnesota which pushed sociology locally in a practical
direction, the example of Thorndike and others who were already thinking
experimentally. A decisive moment occurred when Chapin read Karl Pearson's
Grammar of Science (1892, republished with new chapters on statistics in 1911);
the core of science was evidently not *material* but *method*. Pearson's work was
very influential in the 'inductive' and 'statistical' sociology for which the work
of Giddings and others at Columbia was known. While at Columbia, Chapin
himself was a member of the FHG (Franklin H. Giddings) club, which drew
inspiration directly from Pearson and from H. T. Buckle, whose populariza-
tion of Spencerian evolutionary ideas was more widely read, particularly in
America, than Spencer's own work (S. P. Turner 1986:219; see Buckle 1859).
    Giddings (1855–1931), one of the 'founding fathers' of sociology in the
United States, was appointed to Columbia in 1892, not as the Professor of
Sociology that the Faculty of Political Science wanted, but as a mere lecturer.[11]
His background was marked by two features many of the other early sociologists shared: a father who worked in religion,[12] and training in the physical
sciences. Giddings traced his own interest in sociology to a copy of the *Popular
Science Monthly* which fell into his hands as a young man – it contained the
first chapter of Spencer's *The Study of Sociology* (Odum 1951:46). Giddings
re-defined Comte's three states (the theological, metaphysical and positive) as
speculative, observational and 'metrical' (Giddings 1901; see Turner and Turner
1990). Columbia, equipped with an up-to-date statistical laboratory and modern computational facilities, was a congenial home for the direction in which
he wanted to steer sociology, which was unambiguously that of a quantitative

science; his masculinist ambitions in this direction are given in the first quotation at the head of this chapter.

Columbia was obviously an exciting place to be for anyone with an incipient interest in collecting solid data on the effectiveness of different types of social intervention, and in the process not coincidentally strengthening the credibility of social science, or, as Ernest Greenwood (1945:31) put it, ridding 'themselves of the odium in which sociology was held by its opponents' through 'a grand rush to borrow from the physical sciences their peculiar techniques'. The eugenic strand was in evidence again: Giddings was proud of his dolichocephalic skull, thought that social reformers constituted the most efficient and superior social class, and believed that blond Aryans were the only possessors of genius and culture, and was not popular among the Columbian faculty for his anti-Semitic remarks. Another influence on the direction of social science at Columbia was Henry Ludwell Moore, a 'brilliant and nervous' mathematical economist who went to Columbia in 1902 from a position at Smith College (where Chapin was later to work). Moore's importance was methodological; he advocated the application of the methods of quantitative biology to economics and sociology. According to Oberschall (1972a:230) both Chapin and Ogburn learnt their mathematical-statistical techniques directly from Moore. Here was another direct link with the eugenist statistical movement which preceded Fisher's development of experimental methods in agriculture and medicine; Moore paid special attention to the work of Galton and Pearson, whose laboratories in London he visited frequently.[13] Unsurprisingly, Columbia would later prove a fertile ground for Fisherian ideas – these were developed by Harold Hotelling, another Columbia professor, in the 1930s (T. W. Anderson 1955:251; Dorfman 1955; Hoxie et al. 1955:76).

A slightly shadowy contributor to the profile of experimental sociology at Columbia is Ernest Greenwood, who also worked there, and whose pioneering *Experimental Sociology: a study in method* was published two years before Chapin's book on the same subject. It is more of a theoretical discussion than Chapin's, defending 'the basic logic which is one in all experimental study' against the attacks of the anti-behaviourists (E. Greenwood 1945:31). What Chapin called 'projective' designs appear as 'projected simultaneous experiments' in Greenwood's book. He discusses twenty-three of these, using some of the same examples as Chapin: fourteen were educational experiments, three involved health promotion, one was Chapin's housing study, two were studies of anti-racist interventions, two of interventions to change the political process, and one rather unique (and possibly unethical) study of the effect of home environment on intelligence. In this last study, one member of 130 pairs of siblings was allocated[14] to a 'superior' and the other to an 'inferior' home for a period of seven years on average; the children were tested on IQ before and after a considerable period in their new homes, and the 'superior' group was found to have gained nine points more in intelligence (Freeman et al. n.d.). One of the anti-racist interventions also deployed an unusual level of intervention; forty-six graduate students in education were invited to spend two weekends in

Harlem in the homes of black families, and their 'attitudes towards Negroes' were assessed before and after; members of a 'matched' control group were also tested, but were not given the benefit of exposure to 'Negro' culture. According to the results of something called the Hinckley Scale of Attitude Toward the Negro, those who had spent time in Harlem were distinctly less racist eleven months later (F. T. Smith n.d.; see Murphy et al. 1937:958–72).

Chapter 6 of Greenwood's text, 'The technique of control in experimental sociology' is mostly given over to a discussion of how to maximize the control to be derived from matching. Only after fifteen pages do we come to a section headed 'Control through randomization'. Here Greenwood refers to J. S. Mill's position on the experimental method as inappropriate for social science, declaring it inadmissible because the problem of securing adequate matching is a problem for *all* science. It was R. A. Fisher, contends Greenwood, who in his *The Design of Experiments* (1935) 'delivered experimental social science from the hopeless fate to which Mill had relegated it' by seeing how the constructive use of chance could yield a solution to the matching problem. For Greenwood, however, randomisation is only slightly more than the 'theoretical' solution proposed by Chapin; rather than being an alternative to matching, it should be used only when the matching process breaks down.

'Laboratory' studies in politics and social welfare

There were few topics during the 1920s, 1930s and 1940s the American vision of experimental social science did not shelter under its all-encompassing wing. The concept of 'laboratory' work as an essential adjunct to the teaching of sociology became popular; hence, for example: 'Rural sociology ... can be taught by the laboratory method with the same facility and profitableness as the physical sciences' (Melvin 1925:261). 'Laboratory' sociology here meant principally the systematic collection of social facts, modelled purposively on natural science methods of investigation. Hornell Hart of the University of Iowa described the laboratory method as having two basic characteristics: 'first, the development of apparatus for the accurate observation, measurement, recording and enumeration of data; and second, the development of methods for controlling all variables except the one under investigation' (Hart 1921:372). Sociology students seemed especially liable to find themselves enlisted in experimental studies. At the University of Washington, for instance, the phenomenon of labour unrest during the 1930s provoked Selden Menefee to test the effectiveness of different forms of strike propaganda. He divided 406 students enrolled in introductory sociology courses into five groups;[15] four groups heard different sorts of propaganda taken from current newspaper articles about the strike problem, and one group acted as a control. The finding that students generally followed the particular propaganda line put to them prompted Menefee to worry about the overall anti-labour bias of much of the American press at the time (Menefee 1938).

Of the four studies discussed briefly below, the second – the Cambridge–

Somerville study of a social work intervention – has become relatively well known as an example of an evaluation which came up with surprising results. The third and fourth examples illustrate the dissemination of the approach of controlled experimentation through the social welfare/crime prevention field. The first study applied a common-sense notion – that giving people information about something will help them to appreciate its importance – in the field of electoral behaviour.

Voting behaviour in Chicago

In 1927 Harold Gosnell at the University of Chicago published a ground-breaking study which followed the new tradition of controlled experimentation in educational research by applying this method to getting people to vote. Declining interest in voting had been noted among the American electorate since the late 1890s. One response in the run-up to the presidential election of 1924 was the organization by lawyers, business men, civic societies, energetic women's groups and others of country-wide 'Get Out the Vote' clubs. The National League of Women Voters arranged house-to-house canvasses; over two million Boy Scouts were enlisted to disseminate the message; the newspapers, radio, theatre and public lectures all joined in the struggle to remind citizens of their privilege and duty to vote. But did all this effort make any difference? It was true that in some states a higher proportion of the electorate voted in 1924, but was this because of, or despite, the 'Get Out the Vote' movement?

Gosnell's study sought hard evidence on the effectiveness of campaigns to increase voting by studying a sample of Chicago citizens both in the 1924 presidential election and a local election the following year. It built on the revelations of an earlier study of non-voting, which had shown that many people did not vote because they could not find the polling place, had failed to register, were new to the area, or had never voted before (Merriam and Gosnell 1924). Twelve districts of Chicago were selected for the study as being representative of the different ethnic and economic communities of the city; demographic and electoral data were collected by interviewers on all 6,000 people living in these districts before the 1924 presidential election. The sample was then divided into experimental and control groups on the basis of the housing block in which people lived.[16] The intervention consisted of mailed non-partisan information about the voting process sent out before the official registration days, delivered in English, Polish, Czech and Italian, the languages spoken in those districts (figure 8.1 shows how streets were allocated and the text of the notices sent out).

When the registration lists were examined, it was found that 42 per cent of those sent the information had registered, compared to 34 per cent who had not received it. But there was little difference in actual voting behaviour at the national election: 92 per cent versus 91 per cent. The non-partisan information appeal was repeated before a February 1925 aldermanic election, which

Map of precinct containing experimental and control group

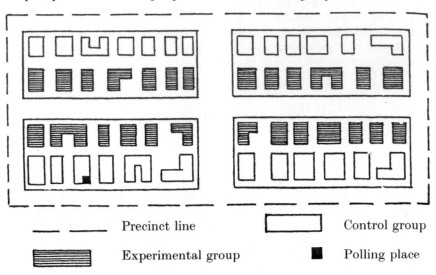

_____ _____ Precinct line   [   ] Control group

▨▨▨▨▨▨ Experimental group   ■ Polling place

NOTICE TO REGISTER

You cannot vote November 4 unless you register now. It makes no difference whether you were registered before or not; *you must register again* if you wish to vote for President, United States Senator, or Governor.

Registration Days will be *Saturday, October 4*, and *Tuesday, October 14*. You can register at your polling place on either of those days from 8:00 a.m. to 9:00 p.m. Your polling place is located at

In case you expect to be out of the city on both of these days, you can get your name on the new register by making application at the Election Commissioners' Office 308 City Hall anytime after October 4 and not later than noon October 13.

Figure 8.1   Allocation of houses to experimental and control groups and notice to registrar in Gosnell's 1927 study of voting behaviour in Chicago.
Source: Gosnell 1927:18, 25. © 1927 by the University of Chicago. Reproduced by permission of the University of Chicago Press.

resulted in 57 per cent of the experimental group and 48 per cent of the control group voting. A particularly interesting aspect of this study was the use of 'watchers' who were assigned to observe voting behaviour in each of the precincts; their observations were found invaluable in interpreting the results.

Troublesome boys in Cambridge and Somerville

The Cambridge–Somerville Youth Study was launched in 1937 by a medical doctor, Richard Clarke Cabot (1868–1939). Cabot, Professor of Social Ethics and Clinical Medicine at Harvard University, had started out as a specialist in blood diseases, but had quickly become dissatisfied with the limitations of clinical medicine and turned his attention to wider therapeutic efforts. He established medical social work in the USA in 1905; in 1931, when he was elected President of the National Council of Social Work, Dr Cabot took social workers to task for their failure to base their work on anything other than 'faith' and 'assertion'. A review of the delinquency prevention literature had shown no evidence for the reforming power of most social programmes aimed at reducing crime (see Glueck and Glueck 1959). Some social workers noted the lack of evidence for the effectiveness of social work and the need for more reliable methods for testing different approaches (see Glueck 1936). Cabot's contrary hypothesis was 'that the influence of skilled and directed friendship on the part of a continuously available counsellor may succeed in preventing delinquency in boys' (Powers and Witmer 1951:vii).

When Dr Cabot retired from Harvard in 1934, he drew up the plan for the experiment, which was based on the intervention of 'sustained friendly counselling' over a ten-year period to boys at risk of becoming delinquent.[17] Unfortunately he died before the experiment really took off, and its direction was taken over by Dr Edwin Powers, one of the original ten counsellors who worked on the study, and later Deputy Commissioner of Corrections in Massachusetts. The study collected a drowning 22,000 pages of single-spaced data, and has been much quoted as an example of a social intervention with unanticipated damaging effects – as making the case *par excellence* for rigorous evaluation. The two densely populated and economically deteriorating Northeastern towns of Cambridge and Somerville were selected by Dr Cabot for the study – these were the years of the Great Depression. Schools, churches, social agencies and police departments in the two cities were asked to nominate boys under twelve known to be 'difficult' or 'bad'.[18] A committee of three experts inspected the resulting information and placed each boy on an eleven-point scale of likely delinquency. Two psychologists then matched the boys in pairs on a number of variables (including health, intellect, home background, neighbourhood and delinquency prognosis); as each two boys were paired, a coin was tossed to determine which of them would receive the intervention.

In all, 325 boys were entered into the intervention between November 1937 and May 1939, with the same number in the control group. It is unclear what boys and their families were told about the study, but at their first contact, 33 per cent were said to be eager to be included, 25 per cent wanted to hear more about it, 16 per cent were indifferent, 25 per cent suspicious, and 1 per cent would have nothing to do with it (Powers and Witmer 1951:107–9). In 1941 the case-load for the counsellors became too high, so sixty-five boys considered not to need the service, together with their matched controls were 'retired'. Petrol shortages and other dislocations due to war (including boys enlisting for military service) left seventy-five pairs who continued in the study until it officially ended in 1945. The average length of treatment was four years, 10 months, starting at age ten and a half years; on average the counsellors visited twice a month. Most of the counsellors were men with social work training who used (then) fashionable casework techniques. What happened under the heading of the intervention was variable; most of the boys had regular medical examinations; around forty were seen by psychiatrists; ninety-three had academic tutoring; twenty-four were put in foster homes; many were encouraged to attend church and become members of community organizations such as Scouts and/or the YMCA; later in the study boys were encouraged to attend a centre where woodwork classes and other group work went on; in many instances, the family rather than simply the boy was the target of professional advice.

All the boys had 'interim' outcome data collected on them in 1941–2 and 1943 via personality tests, interviews and delinquency statistics. These data suggested poorer outcomes for the intervention group, despite the fact that more than half these boys expressed positive views about the intervention:

> Mr B came down to the house . . . He took me to the circus. He was trying to keep me off the street and he took me to camp, baseball games. They were very good men. *(Powers and Witmer 1951:160)*

> It was a good organisation. . . . They helped some of the kids out of their trouble. Something they couldn't speak to their parents about. *(159)*

In 1946 when the crime figures were compared again, forty-nine boys in the intervention and forty-nine in the control group had made at least one appearance before the Crime Prevention Bureau, but sixty-five and fifty-two respectively had made two or more such appearances (Powers and Witmer 1951:324). These results were interpreted as 'almost totally discouraging' (McCord and McCord 1959:7). A later follow-up in 1955 did not alter this picture; more intervention group boys had been convicted of more crimes: see table 8.1. There was no evidence that longer treatments were of more benefit (53 per cent of boys treated for more than six years were convicted, compared to 32 per cent treated for less); nor was the restriction of treatment to one counsellor more effective (43 per cent compared to 44 per cent).[19] A further follow-up study was conducted in 1975 of 506 men from the original population who could still be found; 42 per cent of the treatment and 32 per cent of the control group had experienced 'undesirable' outcomes, defined as criminal conviction,

Table 8.1 Number of boys convicted [number of convictions] for various crimes in the Cambridge–Somerville Study 1938–55.

Type of crime	Intervention	Control
Property	86 [212]	77 [224]
Person	14 [17]	15 [20]
Sex	12 [14]	15 [17]
Drunkenness	46 [72]	37 [83]
Traffic	70 [171]	67 [127]

Source: Taken from McCord and McCord 1959:22.

death before aged thirty-five, alcoholism, schizophrenia and manic depression (McCord 1981).

What the Cambridge–Somerville Study actually found has been widely debated. Do the findings prove that social work is harmful? It was noted that *all* the boys in the study turned out better than expected.[20] Since most of the counsellors were trained social workers, and there was substantial turnover among them, Dr Cabot's original theory about the healing effects of sustained friendship provided on a one-to-one basis probably had not been tested. Thus, a number of sub-analyses were carried out. The only one of the original ten counsellors who was not a social worker (she was a 'motherly' nurse) appeared to have markedly more positive effects than the others (she was also the only one to keep almost her whole case-load) (Powers and Witmer 1951:x–xi). It did seem as though the female counsellors were more effective, especially for the older boys (McCord and McCord 1959:30). This prompted the evaluators to look for boys for whom the intervention had proceeded along the lines Dr Cabot had planned;[21] among the twelve they found, six had committed crimes, compared to eleven out of twelve in their matched pairs (McCord and McCord 1959:38). These numbers may be suggestive, but they are of course far too small to warrant generalization.

Dr Helen Witmer, in charge of the evaluation, regarded the results as damning the whole notion of applying a 'medical' evaluation design to the social world; social problems are not medical disorders, she argued, and social interventions are far more variable commodities than drugs:

> To give a great variety of services to a great variety of boys. . . . is no more a scientific experiment than a medical one would be in which different kinds of medicine were given to patients suffering from different kinds of disorders.
> *(Powers and Witmer 1951:343)*

Against this, it was noted that, had there not been a control group, the fact that two-thirds of the boys avoided delinquency would have been attributed to the success of the intervention (Powers and Witmer 1951:320); the decline in criminality observed after the age of twenty-one would also have been so attributed (McCord and McCord 1959:22).

Boys behaving badly in New Jersey

The prevention of delinquency was the aim of another study in the social welfare field. Highfields, a guidance centre for the 'rehabilitation of juvenile delinquents', was established by the state of New Jersey in 1950 as offering a programme that would utilize all the latest findings of behavioural research. It was the brain-child of a sociologist and a psychologist who had met during the war, and who unusually planned an evaluation of the effectiveness of the Highfields approach as an integral part of the programme (spurred on in this endeavour by the 'shocking' lack of evaluation of many past delinquency prevention projects). The evaluation was directed by H. Ashley Weeks, a professor of sociology at New York University; it assessed the progress of sixteen- to seventeen-year-old boys sent to the Short-Term Treatment for Youthful Offenders Program at Highfields, compared to that of boys who went to a more traditional state reformatory. The basic principles of the Highfields programme were small-group living, no outward signs of incarceration or control, paid work on some constructive project, relative freedom of movement in the local community, and 'guided group interaction sessions'.

The original research plan was for juvenile court judges in the four largest New Jersey counties to send to a diagnostic centre all male first offenders aged sixteen to eighteen who were serious enough offenders to be sent to the state reformatory; these young men would then be assessed, and those with serious pathology, 'inferior mentality' or a record of only minor offences would be excluded from the research sample. The diagnostic centre would 'select every other individual at random' – one for the reformatory, one for Highfields, and make this recommendation to the sentencing judge. If the judge did not follow the recommendation, these individuals would be dropped from the sample. In practice, however, this plan collapsed, partly because of the difficulty of getting enough staff at the diagnostic centre to do it, and partly for (in a frustratingly coy phrase) 'administrative reasons' (Weeks 1958:140).[22] The result was use of the 'matched pair' design. The results of the study showed that one year after release, 17 per cent of the young men who had attended the Highfields programme had re-offended, compared to 49 per cent from the state reformatory. There was evidence that judges sent to Highfields young men whom they *thought* would benefit from treatment there, and the Highfields sample did come from somewhat more advantaged backgrounds. Weeks argues that this was not enough fully to explain the relatively large difference in re-offending rates; while acknowledging the failure of the randomisation plan as a 'misfortune', he was concerned (understandably) to rescue what was an ambitious study from the pitfalls of a weak evaluation design which could hardly be laid wholly at the door of the research team.

Girls at Vocational High

Most of the literature on delinquency prevention, including the above two examples, focuses on problems of misbehaviour among young men. One notable exception, and another early controlled trial, is a study carried out with 'problematic' adolescent girls at a vocational high school in New York.

The *Girls at Vocational High* study began in the mid-1950s. Four successive cohorts of new recruits to the school, a citywide vocational school which served mainly girls, were screened for signs of 'potential deviance',[23] and the resulting pool was randomised[24] either to be referred to a social work agency which provided casework or group counselling, or to school life as usual. The social work agency was the Youth Consultation Service (YCS), which had specialized in offering social work help to troubled girls in Manhattan, the Bronx and suburban New York for more than fifty years, and was currently involved with about 200 clients a year. The study was initiated by the YCS, which was concerned about the difficulties it experienced in trying to make and maintain contact with young women perceived as having school difficulties referred to it by the New York City Youth Board.

About a quarter of each yearly cohort at Vocational High was identified as potentially having problems; 189 girls were assigned to YCS, and 192 to the control sample. The researchers and YCS decided to include both school performance and behaviour and what happened to the girls out of school as outcomes of the experiment; the latter covered 'out-of-wedlock' pregnancy and delinquency. There were also measures of general attitudes and aspirations, of social relationships and of personality and social adjustment, designed to get at how many girls in the experimental and control groups had 'healthy personalities' at the end of the experiment. These data were collected during the girls' first month at Vocational High and at the end of each school year.

Around 95 per cent of experimental group girls did get some social work 'treatment'. No differences were detected in educational outcomes (completing high school, achieving 'normal' grades, highest grade obtained, teacher ratings of performance and behaviour). There was a 7 per cent difference (56 per cent versus 49 per cent) in the proportions attending high school for four years or more, and a slightly smaller proportion of experimental group girls (52 per cent versus 56 per cent) were suspended or discharged from school. Truancy rates showed a small, statistically non-significant difference in favour of the intervention (24 per cent versus 32 per cent). As regards health and social outcomes, there were, again, small differences, with experimental group girls being slightly less likely to have health problems, to have low emotional well-being, and to have a pregnancy recorded (10 per cent versus 12 per cent). Girls in the experimental group were more likely than those in the control group to say that they had a significant opportunity to talk with adults about things that bothered them (95 per cent versus 74 per cent). Fewer (11 per cent versus 31 per cent) said they wanted more of this.

Interestingly, the judgements of the social workers involved were that only about 2 per cent of the girls referred to them really benefited from the intervention. The researchers concluded that

> no strong indications of effect are found and the conclusion must be stated in the negative when it is asked whether social work intervention with potential problem high school girls was in this instance effective. *(Meyer et al. 1965:180)*

They did, however, stress the positive achievements of the project (which are certainly marked by comparison with the Highfields study) in successfully carrying out a research design involving random assignment and requiring the active co-operation of both a social welfare agency and a school.

These four studies illuminate different aspects of social science experimentation. Gosnell's study shows the efficacy of relatively simple interventions and the value of conducting a well-designed evaluation which builds on what in today's jargon would be termed a 'needs assessment' or 'pilot qualitative work'. The Cambridge–Somerville study, on the other hand, demonstrates the need to take social intervention evaluation seriously in order to protect the public from its sometimes harmful effects. The Highfields study is an example of the harmful effects on study design of resistances to randomisation; as Chapin declared in his book, though a simple idea, it often evokes complex issues when researchers try to operationalize it. The fourth example, by Meyer and colleagues of a social work intervention with young women, shows that randomised controlled trials *can* be mounted successfully in complex social settings, but with the result that intervention effects may sometimes be neither clearly in one direction or the other.

The Hawthorne effect

One problem in the Gosnell study was to try to prevent households in the control group getting hold of the information about voting sent to experimental group households. This notion of a 'no-intervention control group' is one of the most frequently cited obstacles to the use of experimental methods for evaluating social interventions. It is impossible to get very far in any discussion of this without coming across something called 'the Hawthorne effect'. The Hawthorne effect was born in the same period when sociology was pursuing its vision of a more quantitative and experimentally based science.

The origin of the term is a series of experiments carried out at the Hawthorne works of the Western Electric factory in Chicago. Beginning in 1924, managers at these works collaborated with Elton Mayo and his colleagues at the Harvard Business School on a series of experiments concerned with worker productivity. The most famous of the experiments were the lighting experiments and those conducted in the relay assembly room. The lighting experiments were funded by electrical manufacturers and utilities, who hoped to see higher standards of lighting incorporated into industrial codes as a result of scientific research. In the best known of these tests, two groups of coil-winders at the Western Electric factory were matched for skill and average productivity, and were assigned to different sections of a divided test room. The control group worked under a steady illumination of eleven-foot candles, while the experimental group was subjected to increasingly lower levels of lighting. Productivity increased slightly in both groups, with the experimental group complaining only when they could hardly see at all.

The relay assembly room, the site of the other best known of the Hawthorne experiments, was a place of particularly monotonous, and particularly female, work. Work in this room was the result of the development of machine-switching, automated telephone exchanges, which required the large-scale production of new equipment – relays – involving multiple, detailed manufacturing operations. Most of these could be done by machine, but some had to be done by hand; thus the speed of individual workers determined total productivity. The relay assembly room experiments took place over five years, and involved six women (called 'girls' in the main reports of the research and often in secondary reports as well; see e.g. Madge 1963; Roethlisberger 1941; Roethlisberger and Dickson 1939) The women's working lives were closely observed by two researchers, and they were asked to provide detailed documentation of their non-work lives, including hours of sleep and dietary and leisure patterns, and were subjected to regular physical examinations. Various aspects of working conditions were manipulated by the researchers; production increased more or less consistently. It also continued to do so when working conditions were allowed to revert to their pre-test state.

The lesson drawn from these and the other Hawthorne experiments was that the informal social relations of work and the attitudes and expectations of the workers are more important determinants of output than mechanical or material aspects of working conditions. This conclusion was described by one of the researchers as 'the great *éclaircissement*, the new illumination' to come from the research (Roethlisberger 1941:15) (no pun intended). It was held up as just the kind of astonishing scientific discovery that challenges all previous assumptions and which justifies experimental research in the first place. Since productivity seemed to be more or less equally affected whatever test group workers were in, and however their working conditions were altered, a further conclusion was that some, at least, of the changed behaviour must be caused by the effect of being studied. This came to be known and cited by millions of researchers, students and teachers in the social and medical sciences thereafter as 'the Hawthorne effect'.

The effect on research participants of taking part in research is an important theme of this book; it is a critical issue in almost all kinds of research, including in medical research, where it is often misleadingly known as the 'placebo' effect, a word that owes its origin to an erroneous Latin translation of the Hebrew Bible (Aronson 1999).[25] But whereas 'the Hawthorne effect' exists, it now seems likely that the Hawthorne experiments did not establish it.

Significantly, none of the original reports included the raw data. When Richard Franke and James Kaul visited the Hawthorne plant in 1976–7 and borrowed the original data for re-analysis, they found that some 90 per cent of the variance in quantity and quality of workers' output could be accounted for by the variables manipulated by the researchers (Franke and Kaul 1978). Moreover, awareness of the importance of social relations and psychological variables pre-dated the main experiments, rather than being a product of them. In addition, the relay assembly room experiments were not quite what they seemed. A major confrontation between researchers and researched developed over the level of conversation permitted, and the two most 'disruptive' women were removed from the experiment and replaced with two more malleable and productive workers (Gillespie 1988).[26] Elton Mayo examined the records of the 'disruptive' women and declared them 'Bolshevik' and 'paranoid', interpreting the low haemoglobin levels which showed up on the physical tests as indicating psychological disturbance and organic disability. Conversely, the records kept of the women's conversations make it evident that they had a clearheaded appreciation of certain aspects of the experiment, particularly the looser managerial supervision and increase in wages – a small-group incentive – that had accompanied their assignment to it. Again, Mayo dismissed these as 'emotional' responses.

The frontiers of (social) science

American efforts to establish an autonomous sociology depended on a particularly unambiguous articulation of social science as science, one which stressed prediction and control as its underlying rationale. The first 'founding fathers' of American sociology – Giddings, Albion Small, Lester Ward and William Graham Sumner – were all committed to scientific sociology. The first department of sociology in the world was established at the University of Chicago under the leadership of Albion Small in 1892. The incorporation of social research among the tasks of academic sociology first took place at Chicago in the 1920s. Under Small and his colleagues, professional sociology became *method* more than anything else.

The Chicago emphasis on method was different from the direction methodology took at Columbia, but both schools were dedicated to the canons of objectivity, rigour and empiricism, and the same pioneering spirit infused both. The American frontier ideology rendered these sociologists 'frontiersmen' themselves, 'breaking new grounds, clearing new vistas, blazing new trails, discovering new areas, defending themselves from attack, pushing on again and founding new dynasties with their students and followers' (Odum 1951:75). The frontier spirit was saturated with a particular view of society – American society – and it was one that ensured an instant sympathy with the methods of the natural scientists. As de Tocqueville noted in his famous exposé of *Democracy in America* (1835), America was the laboratory experiment in democratic politics and social relations.

[It] *had to be* the supreme living social laboratory, challenging the new science to set its frame of reference not only for the study of American society and for the attainment of a democratic order, but for initiating new scientific ways of measuring societal phenomena, analyzing results, and testing them in a new world laboratory. *(Odum 1951:55; emphasis original)*

America was also a virtual case-study in the Comtean law of evolutionary stages: theocracy in the seventeenth century, abstract theories of political rights in the eighteenth, science and industrialism in the nineteenth. It exemplified and 'proved' these, giving an empirical basis to the Comtean science of positivism. At the same time, early American sociology took its cue from Comte in defining the new science as one about 'man', with women decisively relegated to a constitutionally inferior and domesticated role (see Schwendiger and Schwendiger 1971). The science of sociology performed an extra ideological function here in designating an unequal sphere for women.

When an Arkansas sociology professor pleaded in 1935 for an evaluation of President Roosevelt's New Deal programmes, the metaphor of America as the evolved laboratory was exactly the model he had in mind. The clarion call of A. S. Stephan's paper, 'Prospects and Possibilities: The New Deal and the New Social Research', was sounded in its opening statement that 'Mankind in a test-tube is the hope and aim of social science.' Stephan argued that 'The promise of a more exact knowledge of human relations must come from a development of experimental methods that will approximate in precision the techniques of the laboratory scientists.' He thought that this prospect was brought closer by the policies of the New Deal, which would allow a more efficient use of the experimental method in social science research (Stephan 1935:515). Like many others, Stephan referred to Sinclair Lewis's novel *Arrowsmith* as laying down the standard for evaluating preventive interventions, and he happily anticipated application of this method to criminal justice and alcohol prohibition policies, to rehousing and slum clearance, to the effects of industry on rural communities, and to almost anything else one could imagine. Within this new world laboratory of America, there were also the more succinct experiments of the utopian communities;[27] Chapin used these in his book to introduce the whole notion of a social experiment. If the whole country and communities could be laboratories, just like classrooms, then so could cities. In the statement setting out the remit for the new Chair of Sociology at Columbia, Giddings stated unequivocally that 'the city is the natural laboratory of social science' (cited in Odum 1951:61; see also Ogburn 1930). In 1928 a professor of political science at the University of the City of Toledo spelt out the case for students of government using the experimental method – what, after all, is the subject-matter of political science, if not growing organisms, just like biology, and what is a city, if not a clone of the starfish as the subject of biological laboratory work? (O. G. Jones 1928). The metaphor of laboratories and experiments was everywhere. In Chicago itself, the city was said to be 'one of the most complete social laboratories in the world', and the university itself was to be regarded as nothing more or less than a successful experiment (quoted in Fitzpatrick 1990:41, 28).

This aping of 'the scientific method' by sociology was aided by the industrialization of the physical sciences themselves, and by the explosion of practical applications for science within a *laissez-faire* political economy. For the early pioneers of scientific sociology, what science provided was a bridge between evangelical and secular modes of social reform. Science was not religion, of course, but it did offer a set of elevated values – selflessness, truth and spiritual dedication – which mimicked those of religion and provided a contrast with the blatantly materialistic rationales of other careers. In Charles Rosenberg's exploration of the role of science in American social thought, the analysis and arguments borrowed from science feature as 'an increasingly plausible idiom in which to formulate – and in that sense to control emotionally – almost every aspect of an inexorably modernizing world' (Rosenberg 1976:7). Private charitable organizations such as the Rockefeller Foundation, which entered the scene in a substantial way in the 1920s, turned to the new social science precisely for the idiom of science it offered – the promise of distance from political controversy combined with a real prospect for controlled social change (D. Ross 1991). The dominant reference group for university social scientists was clearly the professional scientific community, with quantitative techniques in the ascendant.

The drive to follow other sciences in defining all phenomena as observable and measurable was a theme in Lowell Juilliard Carr's paper on experimental sociology, from which the second quotation at the head of this chapter is taken (Carr 1929:65). Carr noted that American sociologists were rapidly moving from the philosophical to the empirical in their thinking, and that recent advances in, for example, social psychology carried an implied challenge to sociologists to 'push on beyond the empirical level to the level of definitely controlled experiment' (Carr 1929:63). Carr's paper reported on the success of the new experimental sociology course at the University of Michigan – one of many initiated at about that time; a 'partial survey' conducted by Brearley (1931) located twenty-six universities and colleges across the United States offering courses in experimental or laboratory sociology. This training of students in the methods of social experimentation was a key resource in later developments on the American evaluation scene from the 1960s on. Of course, not everyone used the term 'experimental' in the same way; Brearley distinguished a number of differing usages: a *controlled* experiment of the sort we would mean by that term today, various types of *uncontrolled* experiment, the *demonstration* of theories or hypotheses, *'natural'* experiments, the *comparative* method, and learning by personal contact or *experience*.[28]

The relationship between social science and social reform also developed distinctively in the United States. Sociology developed much more rapidly in the USA than in the UK, with much of the early effort at the graduate level. A survey carried out by Luther Bernard on behalf of the *American Journal of Sociology* in 1909 found 337 colleges and universities offering 1,044 courses. The early institutionalization of American sociology, combined with the lack of easy channels of political influence and the religious backgrounds of many of the early sociologists, led to a unique alliance between social reformers and academic sociology (Oberschall 1972a). Through its religious connection, American sociology was shot through with a belief in the power of human action to change social conditions and bring about the Kingdom of God on earth; the Christian economist Richard Ely, in the first graduate social science programme in the United States, taught that the state was an instrument given by God to man for the purpose of human improvement. The brief which Ely laid down as a founder member of the American Economic Association included viewing the state 'as an agency whose positive assistance is one of the indispensable conditions of human progress' (Ely 1938:140). This view of economics made it a natural collaborator with sociology and social reform, and was another key building block underpinning the later 'golden era' of evaluation in the United States.

Moribund Britain?

In America, metaphors of sociological 'laboratories' served to stress the co-participation of social science in promulgating the rhetoric of detached objectivity. In Britain, the idea of detached objectivity had flourished among physical scientists in the nineteenth century as part of their claim to professional status, chiefly as a way of dissociating themselves from practical, commercially oriented work. But in the early twentieth century this stance was less attractive to social scientists in Britain than it was to those in America and Germany, where the idea of detached objectivity had a potentially useful role to play in protecting academics from victimization for political views (see Yeo 1996). Richard Ely was one of those so threatened in the United States in the 1890s; in front of the University of Wisconsin Board of Regents in 1894 he recanted his radicalism, declaring himself a conservative after all (Sklar 1991). Such experiences of persecution must have made the emphasis on a true 'science' of the social appear a safe haven indeed.

An American social scientist, Ernest Harper, who visited England in the late 1930s, found it in a 'rather undeveloped and even moribund condition'. He was impressed by the fact that there was only one chair in sociology (at the London School of Economics); Bernard's survey some thirty years earlier had yielded fifty-five full-time and 372 part-time sociology professors in the USA (L. L. Bernard 1909).[29] Harper found that in the UK there was little theoretical, research or teaching work of any quality, and that the standard of publication in the academic journals was low (Harper 1943).[30] Much so-called social science masqueraded as social work. Harper particularly noted that in the UK there was no teaching about 'the laboratory method', recently introduced in his own country in courses labelled 'experimental sociology'. The field was dominated by the Fabianism and social survey mode of the London School of Economics, founded by the Webbs and their friends in 1895. The class backgrounds and social relations of those involved in the School's work gave them a close connection to government, and freed them from the need their American counterparts felt to establish a secure academic status as scientists (Bulmer 1982). In the 1940s, 1950s and 1960s the British tradition of social accounting, social policy and community studies continued unchecked by any of the concerns that had led to the development of an experimental social science in America.

Sidney and Beatrice Webb's *Methods of Social Study*, published in 1932, was one of the first attempts to provide a blueprint for the actual *doing* of social science research.[31] In a section called 'The use of experiment' towards the end of their book, the Webbs reveal their ignorance of developments in American social science by declaring that it is practically impossible for sociologists to experiment in the sense that physical scientists do. This, however, did not stop them from an interesting peroration on the theme of society as the experimenter *par excellence* (the same viewpoint as taken by the American experimental social scientists):

> Every finance minister in every country tries a sociological experiment . . . every time he imposes a new tax or remits an old one. . . . The laws and administrative departments regulating the employment of labour or the supply of pure water, unadulterated food, and authentic drugs, like those providing the social services . . . represent a whole series of experiments.

What this means is that there is

> far more experimenting and experimenting on a vastly greater scale, continuously carried on in the world sociological laboratory in which we all live, than by the numerous but relatively small physical, chemical and biological laboratories that have been established within it. *(Webb and Webb 1932:223–4)*

Although the Webbs both understood the nature of uncontrolled experimentation that makes up normal social relations and appreciated the design of 'The experiment' in natural science, the intellectual soil that nourished these understandings in Britain simply did not encourage the kind of connection between them that many social scientists in the United States were daily putting into practice.

But history is full of missed opportunities, and the history of ways of knowing is no exception. Florence Nightingale, that 'passionate statistician', re-established contact when she was over ninety with Sir Francis Galton, whom she had corresponded with earlier, with a scheme for teaching Quételet's subject of social physics at the University of Oxford and endowing a professorship there. She mentioned a number of subjects about which 'we appear hardly to know anything', including the results of Forster's Education Act of 1870. In a letter to Galton she wrote:

> We sweep annually into our Elementary Schools hundreds of thousands of children, spending millions of money ... Do we know: (i) What proportion of children forget their whole education after leaving school . . . ? (ii) What are the

results in the lives and conduct of children in after life who don't forget all they
have been taught?

After this, she moved on quickly to criminology: does going to prison deter
crime? what effect does education have on it? Then there was the question of
poverty and its intergenerational transmission. What effect do workhouses
have on children? And what about India – are the social conditions there
improving or not? How has British domination affected native trades and
Indian education? 'I have no time to make my letter any shorter,' Nightingale
observed (one can almost hear her sighing),

> although these are but a very few instances. . . . You remember what Quételet
> wrote . . . Put down what you expect from such and such legislation; after ——
> yrs, see where it has given you what you expected, and where it has failed. But
> you change your laws and your administering of them so fast, and without
> inquiry after results past or present, that it is all experiment, see-saw, doctri-
> naire, a shuttlecock between two battledores.

Galton responded poorly to Florence's proposals. He disliked professors, and
thought Quételet had achieved almost nothing of the promise of his *Physique
sociale*. A codicil added to Nightingale's will revoked the £2,000 she had left to
endow a chair, citing her disagreement with Galton. She especially feared that
if the project were still to go ahead in anything like its original form, her
money would be used for medical research, 'endowing some bacillus or mi-
crobe' (E. R. Cook 1913:2.400).

There was historical continuity between this turning away from the possibility of an applied social science that would address leading policy questions
and the debates that featured in British social science around the turn of the
century. When H. G. Wells referred in 1907 to the growing contingent of
people who believed that sociology was not a science, arguing that all the
paraphernalia of quantification were essentially 'deceitful', he called Comte
and Spencer 'pseudo-scientific interlopers' and wrote (as if directly mindful of
Nightingale's aspirations):

> What to do with the pariah dogs of Constantinople, what to do with the tramps
> who sleep in the London parks, how to organize a soup kitchen or a Bible coffee
> van, how to prevent ignorant people who have nothing else to do getting drunk
> in beer houses, are no doubt serious questions for the practical administrator . . .
> but they have no more to do with sociology than the erection of a temporary
> hospital after the collision of two trains has to do with railway engineers. *(Wells
> 1907:369)*

The German connection

The association of American social science with the German tradition was
another critical influence on its more favourable attitude towards experimental

methods. Albion Small's *Origins of Sociology*, published in 1924, celebrates the German historical legacy in positivist social science, going as far as to identify the origins of modern social science with the tradition of German theories of government. Small (1854–1926) himself spent two years studying in Germany (after his three years at a theological seminary), where he was much impressed by the views of elite German scholars about scientific truths as a basis for enlightened public policy. Most of the 9,000 Americans who studied in Germany between 1820 and 1920 were studying social sciences (Berelson 1960; Herbst 1965); these included Richard Ely, E. A. Ross, Robert Ezra Park, E. R. A. Seligman, Richmond Mayo Smith, W. I. Thomas and Lester Ward. William Graham Sumner (1840–1910), later Professor of Political and Social Science at Yale in 1872, also studied in Germany, but his degree was in theology. The anthropologist Franz Boas was born and educated in Germany. In his autobiography, Ely noted that it was considered 'a matter of course' that after his first degree at Columbia he, like many others, would go to Germany to study; when he went in 1872, he wrote, 'I sail to Germany in Quest of the Truth' (Ely 1938:36). As 'young rebel' economists, they found the 'new and living' economics being taught in German universities a great contrast to the sterile versions purveyed in their own country.

As Oleson and Voss have observed (1979:x), the experiences of these scholars in German laboratories and seminars and their 'intense involvement in the objective analysis of a precisely defined area of study' left a permanent imprint on the subsequent development of American social science. So, too, did the immersion in German academic misogyny: US graduate schools were patterned after German universities, which had never admitted women, and it was only in the 1890s that the first female doctoral students graduated in both countries (Rossiter 1982). American *social* science was modelled on German practice and ideas, because science itself was, at its best, Germanic. 'Were we not constantly nursed at the breast of Germany,' wrote the doctor George Beard (the discoverer of neurasthenia[32]) in 1882, 'both England and America would long since have starved to death scientifically' (Beard 1882:66–7). But although the German connection was significant in strengthening the move towards adoption of the experimental method in sociology, it later acquired a more sinister interpretation by those who saw it as conflicting with humane moral values.

Counter-arguments

The early days of experimental social science were beset by paradigm arguments in much the same way as it is now; some of the counter-claims against 'scientific' sociology made at the time even have a distinctly modern ring about them. The favoured term of the anti-experimentalists in the 1930s was 'behaviorism'. This term was used in much the same way as 'positivism' is today. 'It is strange and somewhat amusing,' noted Read Bain of Miami University in 1931, that simple words like behavior and its derivatives should become so highly charged with emotion in so short a time. . . . Some sociologists seem to think behaviorism is of the Devil. . . . Others seem to think behaviorism is . . . the magic formula which has only to be shouted to insure scientific salvation.

Bain argued that behaviourism was simply a 'method of procedure', and the notion that it discounted the importance of subjective experience was sheer rubbish (Bain 1931:155, 157).

On Bain's side was George Lundberg (1895–1966), a student of Chapin's at Columbia and tutor to Stuart Dodd of Syrian health promotion and S-theory fame. Lundberg's commitment was to the use of a scientific sociology for social reform. His early work on methods reflected the state of American sociology as he found it at the time – marked by the philosophical position that human social behaviour was irredeemably beyond the reach of natural science methods. Lundberg launched a polemic attack on this, using the very language of a pioneer trail-blazer: 'To undertake scientific work in a jungle,' he observed,

> it may be necessary first to hack out . . . a clearing for a cabin in which scientists can work. It may be necessary occasionally to widen that clearing, and finally to take an occasional potshot against the former inhabitants of the area who hang around the periphery disturbing or interfering with one's scientific work. *(Quoted in Odum 1951:209)*

Lundberg noted the tendency of opponents of science in sociology to make ridiculous assumptions about science itself – 'the highly exaggerated notion of the perfectness of natural science methods is responsible for much of the doubt as to their applicability in sociology' – and about what might go on under the heading of 'scientific sociology' – 'No recent sociologist has to my knowledge ever proposed or attempted to put a specimen of sociological phenomena in a test tube for analysis or attempted to weigh or measure them with the instruments of the physics laboratory' (this was perhaps slightly contrary to the Arkansas professor's view of mankind). Behaviourism had become 'little more than an epithet designating almost any theory disliked or not understood'. Those who used this epithet also frequently referred to the 'alleged frightful complexity of sociological problems', calling up the term 'gestalt' from psychology to describe the need to preserve 'the situation of the whole' and on the theory 'that the antidote should come from the same source [psychology] as the original poison – behaviorism' (Lundberg 1933:299–300, 302). Lundberg hit the nail on the head of the central argument of the anti-behaviourists, that social phenomena could not be studied using the same methods as natural phenomena because they were different. Of course all phenomena are different. But the key question is one about *means* of knowing; are these fundamentally different in the case of social phenomena as compared with physical phenomena? Furthermore, the attack on behaviourism and natural science methods was not really an attack on the methods themselves, 'but an attack on what nobody defends, namely defective methods of whatever kind'. In the end, and most tellingly, 'If we do not "imitate" the methods of science in sociology, we shall assuredly "imitate" the methods of philosophy, metaphysics, theology, astrology' – and what would happen then? (Lundberg 1933:315–16).

The 1930s version of the methodological paradigm divide owed a good deal to the competition between Chicago and Columbia as alternative bright stars in the firmament of the new subject of sociology. Although Robert Park and others at Chicago shared with their Columbia colleagues the concept of cities as laboratories, they drew rather different conclusions about the methods to be used in studying them, preferring to emphasize the quality, rather than the quantity, of life. At Chicago, the influential work of Jane Addams (1860–1935) at Hull House was much closer to the British tradition of carefully crafted local studies, and academics there were more inclined to believe in the value of this sort of evidence than in the 'scientism' of the Columbia school (House 1993). Although there were differences, it is interesting to note, however, that the reputation for pioneering 'participant observation' methods held by the Chicago school is something of a *post hoc* attribution; most of the leading studies depended heavily on documentary analysis, and their authors were unfamiliar with the term 'participant observer'[33] until later (Hammersley 1989; House 1993).

When Ogburn moved to Chicago from Columbia in 1927, he found himself neatly caught in the prevailing version of the methodological paradigm divide. At Columbia he had developed work on statistics started by Giddings; in his new home he introduced more instruction in statistics, and generally became an advocate of the survey method. There were departmental debates in which Blumer and Burgess spoke on behalf of the case-study, and Ogburn and Stouffer defended survey methods (Bryant 1985; on Stouffer, see ch. 9). Ogburn's new faculty vented their antagonism to his 'science without concepts' (Bannister 1987:176). The more he advocated 'instrumental positivism', the more they resisted. The brand of sociology for which the Chicago school eventually became famous was fine-tuned 'qualitative' investigation inspired by anthropology or high-quality journalism: studies such as Nels Anderson's *The Hobo* (1923) and Robert and Helen Lynd's *Middletown* (1929), which culminated in the rallying cry against 'scientism' of Herbert Blumer's symbolic interactionism; this sowed the seeds of the entire modern insistence on the primacy of 'qualitative' methods (Blumer 1937). Thereafter, whenever reaction against 'scientism' set in, the 'qualitative' sociologists would be ready with their alternative ways of knowing (D. Ross 1979). Meanwhile, the Columbia tradition continued on a quite different trajectory, which eventually led to the appointment of an aptly named 'Quételet Professor of Social Sciences' in the persona of Paul Lazarsfeld, a German-trained psychologist and mathematician, whose view of a unified science inspired a well-known corpus of quantitative research.

The sin of 'scientism' and the sociology of gender

Viewing the beginnings of experimental sociology in its wider cultural context, it is clear that (whatever the merits and demerits of the method itself) there was an implicit historical linkage between the 'new' sociology, the pursuit of objectivity and the masculine intellectual tradition. Almost none of the cast of characters who have appeared in this chapter were women. That is partly because women were in a minority and at a disadvantage in science as the institutional idiom within which social science developed. The practice of science as rigorous, rational, impersonal, masculine, competitive and unemotional conflicted with prevailing stereotypes linking women to soft, delicate, emotional, non-competitive and nurturing behaviours: women in science therefore constituted a contradiction in terms (Rossiter 1982). A separate labour market developed for women in science in the 1880s and 1890s, which became politicized around 1910 with the arrival of suffragism. It was a woman scientist, Helen Thompson, later Woolley, who fired an early salvo against the doctrine of men and women's separate spheres in 1898 when she pointed out that psychological characterizations of men and women as different had never been put to a valid experimental test. As part of her Ph.D. research, she gave a battery of tests to twenty-five male and twenty-five female students, finding minimal differences (the men were better at manual dexterity and physical strength and the women at memory and sense perception – but Thompson attributed these differences to upbringing) (see Rossiter 1982:102). The discipline of psychology was particularly sexist. In 1904 Edward Titchener of Cornell University formed the Society of Experimental Psychologists, from which women were formally excluded until 1929 (Boring 1938). Titchener's view, as expressed in a letter to a colleague in 1904, was of 'an experimental club . . . the men moving about and handling (apparatus), the visited lab to do the work, no women, smoking allowed, plenty of frank criticism and discussions, the whole atmosphere experimental, the youngsters taken in on an equality with the men who have arrived' (quoted in Furumoto 1988:94). The imposition of Titchener's view on a whole generation of experimental psychologists excluded women from the informal communication networks important in research, and deprived the discipline of women's input. Moreover, the meetings of the Society were secret, and no publications of its proceedings were allowed.

Like European sociology, sociology in America had no 'founding mothers'. The masculinization of American social science during this period is strikingly illustrated in Howard Odum's history of American sociology, where the photographs included between pages 104 and 105 of presidents of the American Sociological Society and editors of the American sociological journals show fifty-four (mostly unsmiling, balding and suited) men and one woman; the exception was Katharine Jocher, editor of *Social Forces*. Although Jane Addams won the Nobel Peace Prize, this seems to have been insufficient to gain her much of a mention in the history of social science (McDonald 1993:298). Addams, the daughter of a Quaker senator and mill-owner, visited London's East End on a post-college trip to Europe in the 1880s, and was impressed by the Toynbee Hall Settlement's work for the poor. Hull House in Chicago, which Addams founded, followed the Toynbee Hall model, but minus the traditional elitism of charity work. Addams was a radical thinker, opposed to hierarchy, academia, war and patriarchy. Her circle of influential friends included the Webbs, who stayed at Hull House in 1893 (Addams smoked cigarettes to keep Beatrice Webb company), the social philosopher John Dewey, G. H. Mead, the feminist writer Charlotte Perkins Gilman, and a number of men of the Chicago school, especially Albion Small and E. W. Burgess (Deegan 1988).

As a settlement for the socially marginalized, Hull House was an exemplar for many male social scientists of the sociological laboratory (Woods 1923). It had co-operative apartments for women residents, men's and women's clubs, education classes, a coffee-house, gym, crèche, nursery, music school, theatre and art gallery; the women who resided there were dedicated to a new way of living, in which women's personal and professional lives were interconnected. But it was Hull House's empirical work, surveying in great detail the local community – modelled after Charles Booth, but with the added motive of empowering the local community – which was enormously influential in Chicago sociology. *Hull House Maps and Papers*, published in 1895, was an exhaustive, fine-tuned and numerative account of the local neighbourhood, documenting the living and working conditions of its eighteen national groups, and paying particular attention to class and ethnic exploitation. It established the use of mapping as a statistical technique to reveal patterns of social interaction, and formed the prototype for much which became known subsequently as Chicago sociology: Wirth's *The Ghetto* (1928), Park and colleagues' *The City* (1925), Anderson's *The Hobo* (1923), Thrasher's *The Gang* (1927) and Zorbaugh's *The Gold Coast and the Slums* (1929). Although Addams was considered the leading sociologist of her time, and Hull House, rather than the university, the leading sociological institution in Chicago, histories of Chicago sociology refer to her work and that of her colleagues as social reform rather than social science (see e.g Faris 1967). Collecting data of the kind Addams and her friends specialized in was regarded by the men of the Chicago school as women's work and as inherently non-sociological (see Sklar 1991).

They called her 'St Jane', a back-handed compliment denigrating her intellectual contribution by emphasizing the conventional feminine quality of angelic altruism. (Florence Nightingale's reputation was constructed in the same way.) The women students attracted to social science in these early years were, indeed, likely to be sidelined into social work (House 1993). Later on at Chicago, in 1920, the women sociologists interested in social reform were all moved from the Department of Sociology to the Social Work School, leaving an all-male department to concentrate on the really important issues. This sidelining of the early women social scientists in America into social welfare projects, and within that into those concerning the position of women, served its usual purpose of eclipsing them from official histories. There is no mention in Odum's 'official' history, for example, of Caroline Dall, who was a co-founder of the American Social Science Association (ASSA), or of the fact that in the mid-1870s nearly half the ASSA board were women. In Odum's book, Addams gets no separate extended treatment of the kind afforded to forty male sociologists, appearing instead in 'A roll call of allied workers' which merely notes her place and date of birth, the Hull House association, and her author-ship of *The Spirit of Youth and the City Streets* 'and of a half dozen other distinguished volumes' (Odum 1951:399).

The treatment accorded to Jane Addams both at the time and later was repeated for other crusading women in American social science. Ellen Fitzpatrick's (1990) account of four of these – Sophonisba Breckinridge, Edith Abbott, Katharine Davis and Frances Kellor (all students at Chicago in the 1890s and early 1900s) – shows how crucial, but poorly acknowledged, was the contribution of these and other women in divorcing academic science from popular enquiry and establishing the scientific basis of modern social welfare policy. Abbott and Breckinridge worked with Jane Addams at Hull House, and helped to establish the first graduate school of social work at the University of Chicago. Kellor specialized in criminology, and set up her own anthropomet-ric measurement laboratory in order to test (and disprove) prevailing eugenic theories about the inheritance of criminality, particularly among women. In 1901 she published a book called *Experimental Sociology* based on her research into criminality, especially her visits to prisons in the South, where her obser-vations about the treatment of black offenders made horrifying reading. Davis's early career was also devoted to criminology. She became the first superin-tendent of the New York State Reformatory for Women at Bedford Hills, and set up a research centre there. She was a leading figure in prison reform, campaigning for a more 'rational' approach. Later in her career she pioneered the study of human sexuality, and published a book based on a questionnaire study, *Factors in the Sex Life of Twenty-two Hundred Women* (1929), many years before Kinsey and his colleagues turned female sexuality into a scientific subject (Kinsey et al. 1953). The women in Davis's book admitted to a range of sexual practices and feelings, including homosexuality, which considerably strained conventional views of female sexuality.

But gender – the cultural construction of femininity and masculinity, within and beyond methodology – is not simply a matter of charting where the men and women *are*, and how their particular achievements fitted into the academic and other frameworks of the time. It is also a matter of seeing how their social positioning feeds into and off whatever else is happening in society. The same conditions which led to the development of separate academic professions in America also provided the foundations of the drive towards 'scientism'. Given the prevailing sociology of men's and women's social positions, strengthening the methodological programme of social science by emphasizing its capacity to experiment translated into an expression of *masculine* ambition for status and prestige. This argument is developed most strongly by Roger Bannister in his *Sociology and Scientism* (1987). The story Bannister tells situates the effort to make sociology more experimental and thus 'scientific' within the framework of a masculine desire for 'efficiency' and 'social control'. This desire can be seen as fuelled by a number of sources: the fear of social fragmentation in American society generally, and specifically in the lead up to the First World War; a social-psychological status crisis associated with the rural/small town/ Protestant backgrounds of the early male sociologists; and programmatic de-

nial of the role of personal values and emotions, partly in response to a growing hardening of the gender differentiation of labour at a time when feminism
was making one of its recurrent and male anxiety-provoking appearances on
the social scene. What Bannister calls interchangeably 'objectivism', 'behaviourism' and 'scientism' reappears in this interpretation in the new guise of
boys behaving badly and also playing God: for, 'by reifying experience in the
manner of behaviorism', he observes, 'the objectivist gained control over self
and others, in effect having the exquisite pleasure of playing God while denying His existence' (Bannister 1987:233).

There is no doubt that the form the early experimental social science took in
America did emphasize rationality, control and facts at the expense of the
expression of emotion and feeling. Part of the rationale behind injecting science into sociology was to remove the distorting effects of personal judgements and ethical standards, behind which usually lies strong feeling. Chapin's
initial interest in science identified it as a source of the intellectual equipment
by means of which the untrustworthy lessons of tradition and habit could be
transcended; emotionalism and the ascendancy of local interests would, he
believed, be replaced by a firm commitment to rationality and evidence. Ogburn
talked of the need for social scientists 'to crush out emotion' (D. Ross 1991:431).
He, like other pioneers of scientific sociology, sought an outlet in his personal
life for the emotion that had no place in his professional one; in his case it was
exotic travel; for Chapin it was painting; Giddings wrote poetry. There is
equally no doubt that some of the men who pushed for a quantitative and
'controlling' version of social science led highly sexist and chaotic lives. Prime
among these was Luther Lee Bernard, protégé of Chapin, proponent of sociological behaviourism, and womanizer on 'a grand scale' (Bannister 1991:40).
Bernard's marriage to the sociologist and, later, feminist Jessie Bernard, en-
capsulated in intimate terms the struggle between subjectivity and objectivity,
emotion and intellect, and private and public. Jessie Bernard's experience was
of accepting the professional ideal and its standard of objectivity (in the 1930s
she developed what she called 'a mania for measurement') as a necessary path
to career advancement in a man's world, but of finding such standards crip-
pling as regards women's interior sense of self-worth. The science of sociology
meant mastery and control – masculinity and therefore the denial of woman-
hood. Luther Bernard not only held misogynist academic views about women,
but throughout their stormy marriage subjected Jessie to his string of affairs
with other women, detailing, like Chapin with his sitting-room scales and
Galton his wife's tea-making, all the times and other measurements of these
encounters, right down to the minutiae of arousal, ejaculation and orgasm. Not
surprisingly, when Jessie Bernard discovered feminism in the 1960s, she deemed
sexism 'a brilliant term' for describing what it is that women have to suffer
both personally and professionally at the hands of men (J. Bernard 1971:36).

For Bannister, and also for Dorothy Ross, who argues a similar line in her
The Origins of American Social Science (1991), the case for this kind of psychological interpretation of the move towards quantification and experimentation
in American social science is fuelled by their own evident dislike for such a

social science.[34] Ross takes the view that the aim of 'scientism' has been to 'establish prediction and control of the historical world'; the resultant tech niques have been used

> to manipulate such things as the money supply, consumer choices, votes, and reme-
> dial social therapies . . . Blind to what cannot be measured, they are often blind to
> the human and social consequences of their use. The manipulators of social scientific
> technique, intent on instrumental rationality, cannot notice the qualitative human
> world their techniques are constructing and destroying *(D. Ross 1991:472)*

These are strong words. What they point to is the impossibility of viewing these early efforts to construct a scientific and experimental sociology through anything other than the refractive prism of modern methodological arguments – the present is, after all, made up of the past. The view, widely held today, that there is something almost immoral about experimentation in the social field colours the interpretation of methodological development in the past.

Conclusion

The modern defence of 'qualitative' social science and the related attack on 'positivism' are partly responsible for the hiding from view of an extensive history of social science experimentation. The method of prospective experi-mental studies with control groups emerged in a number of different fields as a technique for tackling a range of disciplinary, policy and practice questions. First, the strategy of a control group, and then the device of random allocation came on the scene as answers to problems of attributing cause-and-effect for which no other procedure of comparable strength could be found. Of course, this was a fledgling history, and many mistakes were made, but the very range of the effort – across the fields of education, social welfare, the law, housing, health promotion and health care – is testimony to the widely acknowledged need for better evidence about the effects of interventions in people's lives.

The stress on an experimental and 'quantitative' social science developed in a context of cross-cutting issues as regards gender. Women as well as men measured and experimented, but their efforts were increasingly seen as out of place. In turn, the 'hard' science with which they had been associated acquired a masculine gender which was then affirmed by wider institutional and cul-tural pressures.

The history of early social experimentation, like all histories, has an impor-tance in its own right. But the other main importance of the early experimen-tal efforts was in creating the academic expertise for a more sustained and broadly based attempt to take the methodology of experimentation out into the public policy domain. America's 'golden age of evaluation' – the subject of the next chapter – would not have been possible without the trials and errors of the 'frontiersmen'.

9

Of NITs and LIFE and Other Things

Systematic experimentation is a radical new strategy of social reform. The key word is 'systematic'. 'Experiment' has been loosely used in recent years as a synonym for 'new' or 'innovative'. Governments and foundations have promoted hundreds of 'experimental' programs, but no one has been following a strategy of systematic experimentation.

Rivlin, *Systematic Thinking for Social Action*

It should be recognised that the strategy of social experimentation necessarily implies that many of the policies under examination will not work.

Gramlich and Koshel, *Educational Performance Contracting*

Carmen Rodriguez emigrated to New York from Puerto Rico when she was six; fifteen years later, her family returned to Puerto Rico but Carmen stayed in the USA, moving to Springfield, Massachusetts. Her marriage broke up, but she supported her two young children and also her brother by working in the Government's Head Start programme and by receiving benefits under the largest welfare entitlement scheme – Aid to Families with Dependent Children (AFDC). In Springfield, Carmen and her family lived in a new apartment, part of a public housing project; they liked the neighbourhood, although it was sometimes noisy and prone to vandalism. But at least the rent of $38 a month on an annual income of $4,600 was one they could afford.

In 1973 Carmen was recruited into a large government research study which was looking at the effect of cash housing allowances on the supply of adequate housing in twelve metropolitan areas. She was one of many thousands of Americans who took part in a series of national public policy experiments carried out between 1968 and 1990. As the Webbs had noted in the 1930s,

society is the greatest experimenter of all: every piece of government policy
constitutes an experimental intervention in the lives of citizens. But uniquely
in the USA between the mid-1960s and the late 1980s, this *uncontrolled* experimentation gave way to a new model of *controlled* experimentation. Instead of
new policies being introduced merely on the presumption that they would
work as intended, policy-makers developed a shared commitment to the importance of well-designed evaluation in sorting out effective from ineffective
interventions.

   The research which Carmen Rodriguez took part in was the outcome of a
Presidential Committee (the Kaiser Committee) which a few years earlier had
examined the problem of urban housing and had debated the introduction of
housing allowances. Instead of just deciding one way or the other, the Committee proposed *an experiment* to determine the effectiveness of this approach.
A basic principle of the Experimental Housing Allowance Program (EHAP),
as it was called, was that cash housing allowances provided by local government agencies should be given to people so that they could make individual
efforts to improve their housing. Effectively this added up to the privatization
of housing stock improvement – the off-loading on to individual initiative of
federal and state government responsibility. So far as Carmen Rodriguez was
concerned, participation in the EHAP meant that she was eligible for a housing allowance (calculated in her case at $82 a month), only if she moved out of
her public housing project and found somewhere else to live. She looked at
about thirty apartments, most of which were too far away from her work, too
expensive, or in bad condition. Searching for new housing was difficult, since
she felt that landlords discriminated against her for the double jeopardy of
being Hispanic and a welfare recipient. Finally she found somewhere the other
end of town, with a rent of $75 a month, although she had to pay utility bills
on top of this, and had to fight with the landlord to provide kitchen cupboards
and a fridge. After moving to the new apartment, Carmen and her children
missed their own neighbourhood, and often went back there to shop. However, she learnt a lot from EHAP staff about the rental housing market and
about her legal rights; she felt the programme staff respected her privacy,
unlike those in welfare offices, and were helpful – though they did not provide
the practical help in apartment-hunting which she really needed. The following year Carmen increased her working hours, and her housing allowance was
reduced; she found a new apartment back in the old area.[1]

Standards of gold in a golden age

This period in America when public policy iniatives were made the subject of
systematic experimentation was known as the 'golden age' of evaluation. The
golden age was, moreover, dominated by the 'gold standard' of the randomised
controlled trial which became over this period 'the ruling paradigm for evaluation research' (Rossi and Wright 1984:334). The policies evaluated in the
large-scale policy experiments varied, but all were targeted at cost-consuming

social problems: poor families on welfare, young people who achieved little academically or who dropped out of school, the unemployed and hard-to-employ, drug-users, criminals and repeat offenders. There is an enormous literature on these experiments (although, strikingly, much of it is unknown in the UK). Much of the literature is 'quantitative', dominated not only by numbers but by mathematical formulae and economic and statistical modelling techniques; case-studies such as that of Carmen Rodriguez are relatively hard to find. There are competing interpretations of what the experiments 'prove', both in policy and methodological terms. But it is at least possible to draw one conclusion: that in these years the model of randomised controlled trials enjoyed a period of successful large-scale use in social settings. The examples which are described in this chapter, of *how* it was used, certainly invalidate modern methodological arguments about the impossibility of using this approach in the social domain. But there are other lessons to be gathered too; this chapter discusses some of them.[2]

Wars of various kinds

In order for the golden age to come about, two factors had first to coalesce: the technical capacity to *do* experiments and the political will to *sponsor* them. The first social experiments carried out in the USA demonstrated the more experimental bent that social science was taking there; they also, most critically, provided the building blocks for the later golden age. The decisive spur to the application of RCTs in national policy programmes came from an unexpected quarter, the US Department of Defense. Samuel Stouffer and colleagues' well-known research with the American Army used the device of randomised controls to evaluate the impact of different propaganda techniques. Stouffer, a student of Ogburn's at Chicago, became technical director of the US Army's Research Branch in 1941. There he oversaw more than 170 different research studies. The research programme Stouffer negotiated with the Army had controlled experiments at its very heart. He pointed out that the Army was accustomed to experimentation; for example, the introduction of a new type of boot had been preceded by a controlled experiment, so why should other sorts of policies and practices not be similarly tested before being adopted routinely? (Stouffer et al. 1949; see Bryant 1985 and Madge 1963 for discussions).

Among the experiments conducted by Stouffer and his team was one of the impact on soldiers of a film series *Why We Fight*; soldiers were randomly assigned either to see the films or not (this created considerable suspicion as to why only some of them were being invited to watch movies) (see Dehue 1997). Another experiment in 1945 assessed different ways of raising the morale of troops affected by what they perceived as the imminent end of the war. The attitudes of eight quartermaster training companies were surveyed; a week later eight platoons (one chosen at random from each company) were exposed to one set of arguments, while another group of eight, similarly chosen, heard another set, and a third group received no propaganda. All the men filled in another survey afterwards. Presenting for-and-against arguments rather than just a single set of arguments was found to be more effective for the men with most education and for those opposed to a particular point of view (Hovland et al. 1949).

This 'scientific' approach to settling differences of opinion about what works spread outwards from the Department of Defense to other government agencies in the years after the war. One feature of Defense Department operations was something called the planning–programming–budgeting (PPB) approach, which spelt out a scientific basis for policy decisions, including the use of systematic comparison. In 1965 President Johnson ordered that the same approach be applied to all government departments. This sowed the seeds of what Nathan (1988) has called the 'evaluation research movement'. In the years from 1964 to 1968 Johnson also launched the famous 'War on Poverty' and 'Great Society' programmes. These were a response to the widespread recognition in the USA that welfare services were in a mess. There was an administratively complex and inefficient patchwork of different programmes, mostly designed in the 1930s to protect certain groups against certain types of financial insecurity. Income loss due to retirement, disability and death of 'the breadwinner' fell under the remit of the social security system; unemployment compensation protected some workers; public assistance programmes supposedly covered other vulnerable groups. Many programmes were administered differently in different states, and supplied varying levels of cover. Problems were especially rife in AFDC, one of the main welfare programmes (the one used by Carmen Rodriguez), and called by a later American president 'inequitable, inefficient and inadequate' (Lynn 1980:82). The prime objective of AFDC was to help lone-mother families; average monthly payments ran from $83 in New York to $14 in Mississippi (Lynn 1980:98). Because fewer than half of all states extended AFDC to families with unemployed or low-earning fathers, millions of poor children were excluded from the welfare system, and a perverse incentive operated in many states for men to increase family income by leaving their families, and for women to avoid marriage because they would lose welfare benefits. As in the UK around the same time, there was a system in place which cut off welfare benefits for women if there was any suspicion of a man in the house (irrespective of whether or not he was making any financial contribution) (Rivlin 1971).

The welfare mess was conjoined with rapidly rising service costs: the bill for all public aid programmes, including AFDC, rose from $5 to $160 billion between 1950 and 1979 (Shadish et al. 1991:22). But it was also abundantly clear that existing welfare services were not meeting the challenge of rising poverty and inequality. In 1966 about 30 million American citizens were officially defined as poor (Orshansky 1968). While it was clear that something ought to be done, it was less clear what. Into this knowledge gap stepped the notion of systematic experimentation as a logistical answer: different approaches to welfare policy could be tested, in order to see whether or not they worked. This would offer a more scientific and rational basis for public policy than educated (or ignorant) guesses. The move towards systematic experimentation was undoubtedly partly driven by fiscal conservatism; it was recognized that spending on social programmes needed to have in-built accountability, or their cost effectiveness would simply never be known.

The first federal programme to require evaluation was the juvenile delinquency programme enacted by Congress in 1962; there followed the Elementary and Secondary Education Act, which provided substantial federal aid for poor students, and the Economic Opportunity Act (1964), which introduced many programmes for other disadvantaged groups: both laws mandated evaluation (usually set at 1 per cent of programme spending) (D. T. Campbell 1979). In 1967, the General Accounting Office was required by amendments to the Economic Opportunity Act to evaluate anti-poverty programmes; this was followed in 1970 by the Legislative Reorganization Act which further required the evaluation of programme results and the development of staff capacity for detailed cost–benefit analysis. By three years later there had been forty separate legislative acts mandating programme evaluation; six specified the percentage of funds to be allocated to evaluation, and eight spelt out the kinds of data collection required (General Accounting Office 1972; Haveman 1987). In 1964 the Office of Economic Opportunity (OEO) was set up to develop strategies for a government attack on the poverty problem. It was staffed by 'a particularly creative and dedicated group of young economists' (D. T. Campbell 1979:80), and it was the OEO which would sponsor some of the large-scale social experiments.

The evaluation industry and its tools

On the technical capability side, America's history of quantitative social science came into its own during the golden age. But it also needed to be supplemented with the more exact tools for experimental evaluation. These were supplied largely by one man – Donald Campbell (1916–97). Campbell, known as 'the father of scientific evaluation', spent a good part of his professional life as a missionary for the experimental method, though he actually started out working on a turkey ranch. An article on the psychological novel (Stendhal and Dostoevsky) in a popular magazine led him to choose psychology as his field of study, and he spent many years in mainstream psychology, including a period at the University of Chicago, an important home of 'behavioural science' (see chapter 8), before he realized that what he was really trying to do was to take the methods of laboratory science out into the real world.[3] Campbell's 1969 paper, 'Reforms as experiments', 'probably the single most influential article in the evaluation field' (Rossi and Freeman 1993:29), enlarged the Webbs' point about nations being perpetually engaged in experimentation. 'The United States and other modern nations should be ready for an experimental approach to social reform,' Campbell opened. But there was still far too much hiding under the cloak of ignorance; too many stakeholders exhibited a lamentable prior commitment to the correctness of reforms – and all this added up to what Campbell frankly called a 'morass of obfuscation and self-deception' (D.

T. Campbell 1969:409, 426). What was innovative about Campbell's stance was the linking of social reform with systematic experimentation; policies to ameliorate human welfare should ideally be indistinguishable from evaluations using randomised control groups which would assess the translation of laudable aims into reality. The effect of this union between methodological technique and reformist impulse was to make social experimentation with random assignment[4] 'unique' to the United States; no other Western countries adopted the same approach to public policy evaluation (Nathan 1988).

One of the things Campbell's self-set task – extending the model of 'laboratory experimentation' into field settings – entailed was a careful look at the methodological and political challenges commonly confronted by evaluators and the provision of guidelines as to how these might best be avoided. His 1969 paper listed fifteen 'internal' and 'external' challenges to validity which evaluators needed to look out for – a list updated from an earlier one published in the 'evaluation manual' Campbell wrote with Julian Stanley. Campbell and Stanley's classic *Experimental and Quasi-Experimental Designs for Research* (1966) provided evaluators with a ready-made tool-kit – a taxonomy of research designs which, most importantly, highlighted the reduction in validity problems achievable through use of the randomised controlled trial design. It launched what has been called 'the social experimentation school', attracting the interest of other subsequently well-known names to the evaluation field, including Robert Boruch, Lee Sechrest, Edward Suchman, Thomas Cook, Charles Reichardt, William Shadish and David Cordray (House 1993).

In 1971 the American Social Science Research Council, recognizing the drift towards a more experimentally-based public policy, appointed a committee to summarize available knowledge about how randomised experiments might be used in the developing field of social programme evaluation. Committee members included Campbell, Robert Boruch (who continues to be active in this field today) and other prominent social experimenters such as Henry Riecken, Albert Rees and Walter Williams. The committee acknowledged in its report the crucial need to obtain reliable knowledge about the effectiveness of various means for attaining desired social goals. Having reviewed the evidence, it considered that systematic experimentation was applicable to 'nearly every social setting and nearly every kind of social intervention with which a policymaker may be concerned'. Tongue in cheek, it went on to point out an important advantage of systematic experimentation – its role as a 'labor-saving device' for settling arguments about the effects of intervention, thereby allowing 'statesmen and the concerned public to spend their time more usefully making value judgements' (Riecken and Boruch 1974:2–3, 8, 10).

The result was a new high-growth industry of private firms, academic departments and research centres all specializing in evaluation research. One prominent organization was the Brookings Institution in Washington, formed in 1927 as a non-partisan, independent organization with a mission to provide a direct input into governmental decision-making. Its founder, Robert Brookings, an 'eccentric, and talkative entrepreneur', started out as an amateur violinist before becoming compulsively launched on a series of capitalist enterprises and then having a breakdown (as we have seen, a common event in the history of methodology). He was advised to rescue himself by becoming a philanthropist instead. The Brookings Institution was set up in the aftermath of the First World War, when it became obvious that public officials operated under conditions of almost complete ignorance when it came to making major economic decisions. The institution formed 'a kind of university without students, where learned men of high reputation contribute expertise to current discussions on public policy' (Critchlow 1985:4). It published a series of high-quality reports on the American experiments, one of which, written by a senior economics fellow at Brookings, Alice Rivlin, is a thoughtful exposition of the logic underlying social experimentation: *Systematic Thinking for Social Action* (1971); the first quotation at the head of this chapter comes from Rivlin's book (1971:87).[5]

Many other new administrative agencies were set up to handle this new industry of evaluation, employing teams of economists, psychologists, educationalists, political scientists and sociologists. A survey carried out by the US General Accounting Office in 1982 of federal evaluation activities uncovered 228 different evaluation organizations spending about $180 million in the fiscal year 1980 and producing in that year a total of 2,362 evaluations (Shadish et al. 1991:26–7). Private firms such as the Rand Corporation, Abt Associates and Mathematica Policy Research, which were all involved in the studies described in this chapter, hugely expanded their evaluation capabilities. The OEO established its own 'research think tank' – the Institute for Research on Poverty at the University of Wisconsin, with a budget of over $1 million in 1970, to undertake basic and applied social science research on 'the nature, causes and cures of poverty' (Haveman 1987:202). Between 1969 and 1972 federal spending on evaluation increased from $17 million to $100 million. Evaluation had become big business. Many new associations and journals concentrating on evaluation were established; the term 'evaluator' came to signal a particular kind of professional identity, which fell in between the traditions of university-based academic and market research work.

Products of the golden age

The first 'genuine' social policy experiment to be born of this unique marriage between technical capability and political commitment was the New Jersey–Pennsylvania Negative Income Tax (NIT) experiment. It was 'genuine' in the sense that it instituted a social programme as an experimental 'treatment' accorded to certain people and 'withheld' from a socially equivalent control group; it was thus the first large-scale attempt at social experimentation using the randomised controlled trial model of evaluation. As a model, the New Jersey–Pennsylvania NIT experiment was rapidly taken up by others in the OEO, the Department of Health, Education and Welfare (DHEW) and the Department of Housing and Urban Development (HUD).

Table 9.1 gives basic information about this experiment and about twelve others, all conducted over the same period using a similar design.[6] Four of the studies in table 9.1 are income experiments; one is an experimental housing allowance scheme; two are programmes for supporting disadvantaged workers; two are interventions for ex-prisoners; one is a study of health insurance; and three are educational interventions aimed respectively at pre-school children, contracting out education to private firms, and young people who drop out of school.

'A pathbreaking piece of social science research'

According to Martin Bulmer (1986:161) the idea of negative income tax was first suggested in 1943 in Britain by a stalwart member of the upper classes devoted to charitable causes, Lady Juliet Rhys-Williams. Some years later, in 1956, Lady Rhys-Williams, a friend of Harold Macmillan, sent him a proposal for a negative income tax when Macmillan was Chancellor of the Exchequer (A. S. Williams 1997:202). During the 1940s economist Milton Friedman at the University of Minnesota also had the same idea; Friedman's proposal caught on among liberal economists when he later publicized it in his book *Capitalism and Freedom* (1962). Joseph Kershaw, the first planning officer at the newly created OEO advocated a negative income tax in 1965 (Rivlin 1971:22). The idea was that poor families, instead of paying income tax, should receive tax credits, and that these credits would be available in principle to all families. This proposal was supported by many liberal economists, both in and outside government; the idea was attractive for its administrative simplicity, but it also appealed to 'the standard economist's notion' (Lynn 1980:91) of maximizing the play of market forces. In 1967 President Johnson set up a task force to explore the idea.

The original proposal to carry out an experiment was submitted to the OEO by Heather Ross, a graduate student in economics at the Massachusetts Institute of Technology who had been working at the Brookings Institution. Ross proposed to randomise 1,000 Washington families either to receive negative income tax or not (H. L. Ross 1970). The proposal was turned down; but the idea had taken hold (Rossi and Lyall 1976:8). OEO subsequently commissioned Mathematica Policy Research through the Institute of Research on Poverty to design, implement and evaluate a test of the effects of a negative income tax policy. The main intended focus was work incentives. This was because there were long-standing policy concerns that bringing poor families out of poverty through state aid would result in a disinclination to work; or, as one Mississippi senator tellingly phrased it, if poor families received income support, 'Who will want to iron our shirts?' (Rossi and Wright 1984:338).

Much of the sociological interest of the American experiments is omitted from the official write-ups of the programmes; most of the interesting events happen between the lines. But in the case of the original NIT experiment, Ross wrote a doctoral dissertation on the background and design of the study which provides a detailed account of much of the thinking and negotiation which went into it (H. L. Ross 1970). Particularly fascinating aspects of this

Table 9.1 Controlled trials of social programmes carried out in the United States 1962–91

Title (funder)	Year and location	Aim	Study population (no. of participants)	Design	Outcomes assessed
Income maintenance experiments					
New Jersey–Pennsylvania NIT experiment (OEO, DHEW)	1968–72, three sites in New Jersey, one in Pennsylvania	To study effects on work incentives of NIT	Intact families headed by married men aged 21–58 with family income <150% poverty level (N = 1,216 families)	Random allocation to eight intervention and one control group	Labour force participation; consumption expenditure; health and family behaviour; school attendance
Rural NIT experiment (OEO, DHEW, Ford Foundation)	1970–72, two sites in North Carolina and Iowa	To replicate the NJ–Penn. experiment in poor rural areas and with non-intact families with either female or male heads	Families with incomes <150% of poverty level and either female or male heads aged 21–58 (N = 809 families)	Stratified random allocation to five intervention and one control group	Labour force participation; consumption expenditure; health and family behaviour; school attendance
Gary income maintenance experiment (DHEW)	1971–4, one site, Gary, Ind.	To study effects on labour force participation and other family	Black lone-mother families with heads aged 18–58 and at	Stratified random allocation to four intervention and one control group	Labour force participation; consumption expenditure;

		behaviours of different levels and forms of income maintenance, daycare subsidies and information/ referral services	least one dependent child (N = 1,799 families)		health and family behaviour; school attendance; social and psychological attitudes
Denver–Seattle income maintenance experiments (DHEW)	1970–91, two sites: Denver, Seattle	To study effects on labour force participation and other household behaviours of different levels and forms of income maintenance, job counselling and training subsidies	Families with either female or male heads aged 21–58 (N = 2,042 families)	Stratified random allocation into eighty-four experimental cells using different combinations of support levels, tax rates, etc., and one control group	Labour force participation; consumption expenditure; health and family behaviour; school attendance
Housing allowances Experimental housing allowance programme (Demand experiment) (HUD)	1978–80, two sites: Allegheny Co., Penn. and Maricopa Co., Ariz.	To study effects on households' behaviour of different forms of housing allowances and estimate cost effectiveness	Low income households living in rented housing (N = 2,241 households)	Stratified random allocation to seventeen intervention groups using different housing allowance formulae and two control groups	Quality of housing; housing consumption behaviour; mobility

Table 9.1 cont'd.

Title (funder)	Year and location	Aim	Study population (no. of participants)	Design	Outcomes assessed
Supported workers programmes					
Supported Work Program (Manpower Demonstration Research Corporation)	1975–8, ten sites, Atlanta, Chicago, Hartford, Jersey City, Newark, New York, Oakland, Philadelphia, San Francisco, Wisconsin	To study effects and costs of a supported work environment offered to disadvantaged workers	AFDC recipients with youngest child six or more; ex-alcoholics; ex-offenders; ex-addicts; young people 17–20 with poor school/delinquency record (N = 6,616)	Random allocation to one intervention and one control group	Labour force participation; hours worked; total earnings
Texas Worker Adjustment Program (Texas Dept. of Community Affairs)	1984–5, three sites in Houston and El Paso, Co.	To study effects and costs of a combination of job search assistance and occupational skills training for displaced workers	Unemployed/made redundant recipients of unemployment insurance, older and non-English-speaking workers (N = 2,259)	Random allocation into two intervention and one control group on one site and one intervention and one control group on two sites	Earnings; unemployment; unemployment benefits
Penal experiments					
Living Insurance for ex-prisoners (LIFE) (Dept. of Labor)	1971–4, one site, Baltimore	To study effects on rearrests and labour force	Prisoners aged 45 or less released from Maryland	Stratified random allocation to three intervention	Arrests and convictions by type of offence;

Study	Dates and sites	Purpose	Population (N)	Design	Outcomes measured
		participation of different levels of post-release payment and job assistance schemes	State prisons at high risk of reoffending and returning to live in Baltimore (N = 432)	groups (payments only, counselling and placement only, both combined) and one control group	labour force participation; health and living arrangements
Transitional Aid Research Project (TARP) (Dept. of Labor)	1975–7, two sites, Texas and Georgia	To study effects on rearrests and labour force participation of different levels of post-release payment and job assistance schemes	Prisoners released from Texas and Georgia State prisons returning to live in Texas and Georgia near employment security offices (N = 3,982)	Stratified random allocation to four intervention groups using combinations of different payment levels and tax rates (three groups) and job placement services (one group) plus two control groups	Arrests and convictions by type of offence; labour force participation; health and living arrangements
Health Insurance Rand Corporation Health Insurance Study[a] (OEO)	1974–82, six sites, Dayton, Oh., Charleston and Georgetown Co., S. C., Fitchburg and Franklin Co., Mass., Seattle	Families with annual income <$54,000 excluding children under 14 and people over 61 and disabled unable to work (N = 5,840 people in N = 2,754 families)	To study effects on health outcomes and health care use of different methods of health insurance	Stratified random allocation to fourteen experimental insurance plans (one free service plan, three 'catastrophic' plans under which families paid 95% of all health bills up to a ceiling; ten intermediate cost-	Use of health services (including dental, psychological and preventive); health status; social contacts; health perceptions; health habits; risk factors

Table 9.1 Cont'd.

Title (funder)	Year and location	Aim	Study population (no. of participants)	Design	Outcomes assessed
				sharing plans); an additional experimental group of families assigned to a group prepaid practice plan in Seattle and a group (non-randomised) from the same population	
Educational experiments The Perry Preschool project (US Office of Education; National Institute of Mental Health; Rosenberg Foundation; the Levi-Strauss Foundation of San Francisco; the	1962–5, Ypsilanti, Mich.; follow-ups in 1973–7, 1977–81, 1985–9	To help children acquire the intellectual strengths they need in school	Black children in low socio-economic status families scoring in the range 70–85 on the Stanford–Binet scale, born 1958–62 and living in the attendance area	Pairs of children matched on initial IQ scores, sex and socio-economic status, 'arbitrarily' assigned to experimental and control groups	IQ and school achievement; special educational placement; grade retention; parental satisfaction with school performance; relationship with

Carnegie Corporation; the Ford Foundation; US Department of Health and Human Services; the Spencer Foundation)			of the Perry Elementary School (N = 123)	parents; delinquency; value attached to schooling; time spent on homework; self-rated ability (at follow-ups) reproductive history; crime; educational achievement; social and health service use; future plans; health; employment; marital status
Educational Performance Contracting (OEO)	1970–1, twenty sites, Alaska, Arizona, California (2), Connecticut, Florida, Georgia, Indiana, Kansas, Maine (2), Michigan, Mississippi, Nevada, New York, Pennsylvania, Tennessee, Texas (2) Washington	To study effects on students' reading and mathematics proficiency of private firms providing additional reading and mathematics, instruction in public schools	Students in school grades 1–3 and 7–9 scoring below national standards on reading and mathematics in twenty school districts with 80% of population at poverty level income (N = 24,000)	Academically deficient schools in volunteer school districts assigned to experimental group, less academically deficient to control group[b]
				Performance on reading and mathematics tests; parental attitudes

Table 9.1 Cont'd.

Title (funder)	Year and location	Aim	Study population (no. of participants)	Design	Outcomes assessed
Youth Entitlement Program (Dept. of Labor)	1978–80, eight sites, Baltimore, Cincinnati, Denver, rural areas in Mississippi (experimental), Cleveland, Louisville, Phoenix, other rural areas in Mississippi	To study effects and costs of a job guarantee programme designed to encourage young people to complete high school	Young people aged 16–19 enrolled in high school and from families on cash welfare assistance/ at or below poverty level (N = 6,667)	'Matching' of four experimental and four comparison sites	School and labour market behaviour

[a] The design of the Rand Study (like many of the others in this table) was complex; the above figures are derived from Brook et al. 1983 and Manning et al. 1984.

[b] In some cases this order was reversed, when the most deficient school was too small or for other reasons (Gramlich and Koshel 1975:19).

Sources of information: Income maintenance experiments: Ferber and Hirsch 1982; Kehrer 1978; Kehrer and Wolin 1979; Mallar 1977; Maynard 1977; Maynard and Murnane 1981; Robins et al. 1980; Rossi and Lyall 1976; Shadish et al. 1991; Experimental housing allowances: Bradbury and Downs 1981; Friedman and Weinberg 1983c; Jackson and Mohr 1986; Struyk and Bendick 1981; Supported workers' programmes: Bloom 1990; Ferber and Hirsch 1982; Manpower Demonstration Research Corporation 1980; Penal experiments: Berk et al. 1980; Rossi et al. 1980; Zeisel 1982; Health insurance: Brook et al. 1983; Ferber and Hirsch 1982; Manning et al. 1984; Educational experiments: Berrueta-Clement et al. 1984; Schweinhart and Weikart 1980; Schweinhart et al. 1993 (Perry Preschool Study); Gramlich and Koshel 1975 (Educational Performance Contracting); Ferber and Hirsch 1982; Mandel and Solnick 1979 (Youth Entitlement Program).

account are the discussions of the focus on 'normal' nuclear families, participant consent and the complications introduced by the changes in welfare
services that happened coincidentally in the course of the experiment and
which considerably muddied the experimental waters.

The tender document written by Mathematica Inc. for organizations to
conduct the New Jersey–Pennsylvania experiment, originally known as 'The
Graduated Work Incentive Experiment', described it as 'a large, long-range
investigation, funded by the Office of Economic Opportunity, into the effects
of a universal income supplementation programme on the lives of low-income
families in the urban United States. It is *a pathbreaking piece of social science
research which promises to provide unique guidance in the rational planning of
social and economic policy*' (H. L. Ross 1970:91; emphasis added). New Jersey
was selected as the original site for the experiment because it had sympathetic
welfare administrators, and it was one of few heavily populated industrial
states without an AFDC plan covering unemployed male family heads. The
target population selected for the study was intact low-income families headed
by married men (an experiment focusing on male-headed families would not
compete with existing welfare services). There was much discussion about the
guarantee levels and tax rates which would be used; those eventually picked
were negotiated with local stakeholders (though not the families who would
take part in the experiment). Recruitment of families started in 1968; when the
experiment ended in 1972, 1,216 families had been randomly assigned to one
of eight different intervention groups or a control group. The intervention
groups were offered different levels of income support, calculated using combinations of values of two variables: the poverty level (25 per cent above, at
poverty level, and 25 per cent and 50 per cent below) and the tax rate (30 per
cent, 50 per cent and 70 per cent) (in practice, only eight of the twelve possible
combinations were used). Families were offered support for three years; the
average level was $90–100 per week. Data on the effects of the different levels
of support were collected through monthly income reports, internal revenue
and social service records, and by quarterly interviews with the families. Although the prime focus of the experiment was the effect on work incentives,
other outcomes of interest on which information was collected included family
expenditure patterns, health and educational attainment.

The New Jersey–Pennsylvania NIT experiment has yielded a huge amount
of literature, and there has been considerable debate about what the findings
actually are (see e.g. Pechman and Timpane 1975; Rossi and Lyall 1976). But
it is clear that little evidence of a substantive effect on labour force participation as a result of income support was detected. The results of the experiment
were summed up by two commentators as follows: 'What we did learn from
the experiment was that for that small portion of the poverty population in
male-headed, eastern, urban industrial families 1) there is no evidence of massive reductions in work effort attributable to a negative income tax although 2)
the modest responses that do occur are differentiated in both direction and
magnitude by race and sex' (Rossi and Lyall 1976:189). Men in the intervention groups worked on average just over two hours a week less than those in

the control group. There were considerable (unanticipated) differences by gender and ethnicity, with Spanish-speaking men reducing their work hours by an average of seven, and wives cutting theirs by 23 per cent (a figure that had little impact on the overall result, as women's average working week was only four hours) (Ferber and Hirsch 1982:61). There were few observable effects of the programme on other outcomes such as health, fertility and school attendance.

Among the other conclusions to be drawn from the analysis were that an improvement in housing standards and an increase in home ownership were major effects of the programme. These findings would later cause some embarrassment to evaluators, since the later experiment on housing allowances (see below), which was directly targeted at precisely these goals, came up with disappointing results by comparison. A second effect which attracted comment was also found in the other income experiments: an impact on 'family stability'. Intervention families were more likely than control families to become 'female-headed' during the course of the experiment (Watts and Rees 1977). These findings on family breakup were to put an important nail in the coffin of the whole idea of negative income tax. Senator Daniel Moynihan, chairman of the welfare subcommittee of the Senate Finance Committee in 1978, interrogated the scientists who had been involved in the experiment, and concluded by siding with the conservatives in assessing its social policy findings as 'calamitous' largely for this reason (Hunt 1985:292).

Other income experiments

One obvious limitation of the New Jersey–Pennsylvania experiment was its restriction to (originally) intact families with male wage-earners living in urban areas. For this reason, OEO and DHEW decided to sponsor three additional experiments. The first, the rural experiment, replicated the New Jersey–Pennsylvania model in a black rural county in North Carolina and a poor white farming community in Iowa, and included all families, whether intact and male-'headed' or not. The second experiment concentrated on a social group of particular policy concern: black female-headed families. This was carried out in Gary, Indiana, and it added a new component to the income support calculation: different levels of child care subsidy (100 per cent, 80 per cent, 60 per cent and 35 per cent of cost). The third experiment, conducted in Denver and Seattle, was the largest and most ambitious, adding job counselling and training subsidies to the intervention package, and testing different lengths of support: three, five and twenty years (a fifth of the Denver sample was allocated to the twenty-year group). It also included child care subsidies for all experimental group families similar to those obtainable for AFDC recipients, but available irrespective of income level (Munson et al. 1980). The different variables fed into the intervention equations in the Denver–Seattle experiment produced a complex total of eighty-four different experimental 'cells'.

The findings of the three additional experiments were generally similar to those of the original one – a small reduction in labour force participation for men, a larger one for women. In the rural experiment, hardly any effect could be detected; in Gary the effect was a 7 per cent reduction in working hours for men and a 17 per cent reduction for women, and female 'heads' who switched from AFDC to NIT reduced their work hours by 5 per cent (Kehrer 1978). The Denver–Seattle experiment found the largest effects: a 9 per cent reduction for men, 20 per cent for wives, and 25 per cent for female 'heads' of households. There were also larger effects in the five-year than the three-year intervention group, some evidence of an effect in reducing work in adult children in the experimental families, but not much evidence that child care subsidies in the form they were offered had an impact on economic outcomes (Ferber and Hirsch 1982; Munson et al. 1980; Robins et al. 1980; West 1980). Results with respect to the non-work outcomes analysed were mixed. School performance of elementary school children improved in North Carolina but no similar effect could be found in Iowa in the Rural experiment (there was also no evidence of an effect in high school students (Maynard 1977)). In the Gary experiment, the younger children in intervention families had higher reading scores, an effect that was more pronounced with the longer interventions and in poorer families (Maynard and Murnane 1981). A positive effect on school attendance for male teenagers was noted, but was not found for female ones (Kehrer 1978). Intervention families were more likely 'to reduce medical debt', to spend more on clothes, medicine and car repairs, to become home-owners, and to use social services less often (Ferber and Hirsch 1982). There was apparently a lower incidence of sub-optimal birth weight among babies born to women with high-risk pregnancies; this finding was attributed to the effect of increased income in paying for medical care and better nutrition. However, it, like other findings reported for some of the experiments, represented something of a data-dredging effort, and sub-group analysis suggested that the birth weight 'effect' only operated for the highest-risk mothers; for low-risk mothers, the effect actually went the other way (Kehrer and Wolin 1979). A surprising finding was that less than 5 per cent of eligible families took up the day care subsidy, though, unsurprisingly, more did so at the higher subsidy levels and when there was no attached requirement that the mothers take paid employment. In the Denver–Seattle experiment, reimbursing half of training costs resulted in a substantial increase in schooling among men and even more so among women. An unanticipated finding which, as in the original NIT experiment, much impressed policy-makers was the considerably higher rate of marital dissolution among intervention families (Ferber and Hirsch 1982; Groeneveld et al. 1980; Kehrer 1978).

Donald Campbell's comment on the four NIT experiments was, predictably, laudatory: 'It is to me amazing', he observed, 'that our nation achieved, for a while at least, this great willingness to deliberately "experiment" with policy alternatives using the best of scientific methods.' He liked to shock audiences by proclaiming the New Jersey experiment 'the greatest example of applied social science since the Russian Revolution' (D. T. Campbell 1979:80–1).[7]

Experimenting with housing allowances

The project in which Carmen Rodriguez took part was one of a series of experiments which took another approach to improving the lives of the poor: giving them money to improve their housing. The state of confusion in the housing policy field was much the same as in the welfare system generally. For many years successive congresses and administrations had pursued similar housing goals with diverse policies. Housing expenditure constituted about a third of total public assistance and social security expenditure, which made any more effective method of improving the housing of the poor directly relevant to welfare reform (Isler 1981:268). The Kaiser Committee had argued that a housing allowance scheme should first be evaluated in a national experiment which would examine its impact on housing markets and people's housing behaviour, and would then reach some conclusion about whether this was a sensible way to go about improving the stock of adequate housing for poor people.

Cash allowances were defined as monthly payments provided to 'a family that has been determined to be unable to afford a decent home in a suitable living environment'. (The wording 'has been determined' is significant in view of many of the issues about user participation which the American experiments raised.) (Carlson and Heinberg 1978:1). Housing allowances, or 'rent certificates' in the older terminology, had been debated since the 1930s; in the early 1950s a predecessor of the Kaiser Committee had decided they would be degrading to recipients and would not add to the housing supply. The policy shift in the direction of housing allowances came with the Housing and Urban Development Act of 1965, which set up new housing programmes incorporating the principle of income-related subsidies (Carlson and Heinberg 1978). The change of government (from Johnson to Nixon) brought an influx of new officials to the Office of Management and Budget and HUD, who saw a housing allowance scheme as consistent with the Republican goal of boosting the contribution of the private market to public policy programmes. A key role was played by the Assistant Secretary for Research and Technology at HUD, Harold Finger, who was impressed by the income experiments and wanted to repeat this model in the housing field (Bendick and Struyk 1981). Congress gave a legislative directive to HUD to start the EHAP in 1970 with an earmarked budget of $20 million (Friedman and Weinberg 1983a). Conceived as a 'far-ranging social experiment', EHAP's basic purpose was to provide policy-makers with the information they needed to make informed decisions about the future of housing programmes (Carlson and Heinberg 1978). Particular policy concerns were the possibility of massive price inflation and the impact of cash allowances on racially segregated housing patterns which were prevalent in many American cities. The EHAP involved more than 25,000 households, at an eventual cost of nearly $200 million (Friedman and Weinberg 1983b). At about twenty-four times the cost of the New Jersey–Pennsylvania experiment, this made it the most expensive and ambitious of all the national social experiments.

The 'Demand experiment' listed in table 9.1 is one of three components of the EHAP. It was the only one to use a randomised controlled design, and it focused on the housing behaviour of individual households. A second component of the EHAP, the 'Supply experiment', examined the impact of housing allowances on the market for housing in two metropolitan areas in Wisconsin and Indiana. No control sites were used. A third component of the experimental housing programme – the one that included the case-study data from which Carmen Rodriguez's story is drawn – examined the role of agencies which would be candidates for administering a national system of housing allowances. Eight agencies were selected, and given individual quotas for the number of households to whom allowances could be paid (using one of the housing gap formulae) over a two-year period. Their administration of the allowance scheme was monitored by HUD and evaluated by Abt Associates. As the intention was to collect data on the efficiency with which different agencies ran the project, control sites were again not included.

The 'Demand experiment' was restricted to low-income families living in rented housing in Allegheny County, Pennsylvania, and Maricopa County, Arizona. Eligible families were randomised to seventeen intervention and two control groups, using, as in the income maintenance experiments, combinations of different values of a number of variables. Eleven of the intervention groups had their housing allowances calculated according to a formula based on the difference between the cost of modest standard housing and a fraction of the household's income (the housing gap formula); in five groups the calculation was based on a 'per cent of rent' formula; one group received an 'unconstrained' cash allowance. Significantly for the outcomes of the experiment, a direct housing improvement incentive was included in the housing gap formula 'treatments', and families living in housing which was classified as substandard had to bring their homes up to the required standard *before* they received their allowances. The average payment made was about $69 per month (Allen et al. 1981:10). The housing standards included an index of crowding, amount of light and heat, hot and cold running water, functioning electrical outlets and windows that could be opened. Some three-quarters of eligible families were found to live in substandard housing and therefore had this 'improvement' condition attached to the offer of a housing allowance (Watts 1981). Information on what happened to participating families was collected by interview six, twelve and twenty-four months after enrolment.

A major finding of all three housing allowance experiments was the unwillingness of families to upgrade their housing (either by repairs or by moving) when told to do so as part of a research study. Many families complained that they liked their current homes and neighbourhoods and did not want to move (Schnare 1981). The discrimination encountered by Carmen Rodriguez was multiplied many times; finding new housing was especially difficult for disadvantaged families who lacked their own transport (Cronin and Rasmussen 1981). Families did not move any more often than they would have done ordinarily; those who did move mostly stuck to established geographic patterns (Carlson and Heinberg 1978). Only about a third of eligible households ever got any allowances; for many the cost of participation was simply too high (Carter et al. 1983). Enrolment was only about 58 per cent overall; families with the worst housing had the lowest participation rates. In the 'Demand experiment', the participation rate for the 'housing gap' groups which had to bring their housing up to a certain standard was 38 per cent compared to 84 per cent for groups where no such condition was attached (Kennedy 1983).

Partly for this reason, the 'Demand experiment' produced only a very modest housing effect: an 8 per cent rise in housing consumption and an increase from about one-half to four-fifths in households living in 'standard quality' dwellings (Mulford 1983:164). Analysing the data was complicated by the fact that the size of the 'unconstrained' sample had deliberately been kept small, on the grounds that this was effectively an income support intervention, and questions about the impact of this were being answered in the income maintenance experiments. However, it did seem as though unconstrained income transfer produced more or less the same increases in housing consumption as the constrained conditions operating in the 'housing gap' groups. There was little evidence of any effect on racial and economic integration, although families who moved were more likely to move to neighbourhoods with less dense concentrations of low-income and minority families. Among black intervention group families who moved, the percentage of neighbours who were black declined by 4 per cent, whereas among control black families who moved, it increased by 6 per cent. It was argued by some that apparently small differences in moving patterns might have a substantial effect on the integration versus segregation of neighbourhoods (Aaron 1981:74). There was no observable effect on the market in terms of the massive price inflation some policymakers had feared (Mills and Sullivan 1981). Somewhat paradoxically, in view of the political background to the experiment, some commentators concluded that the difficulties in finding new housing encountered by Carmen Rodriguez and many others who took part in the project constituted a forceful argument for the 'old' approach of increasing publicly owned housing (Kennedy 1983).

Supporting work

Yet another approach to welfare reform which was tried in the golden age was the direct provision of services not linked to any kind of cash incentives. In 1962 the Kennedy government enacted legislation to provide counselling, job training and other rehabilitative services to able-bodied welfare recipients. Two of the experiments listed in table 9.1 were designed to examine the effects in terms of employment and earnings that might be secured through different support strategies.

The Supported Work Program was launched in 1974 by the Manpower Demonstration Research Corporation, an organization set up with the backing of the Ford Foundation and five federal agencies, including the Department of Labor, DHEW and HUD. It was the first major employment programme to be evaluated using an RCT design, and had developed originally from a programme for ex-addicts set up by the Vera Institute of Justice in New York City in 1972, which was said to have yielded 'promising' findings (Manpower Demonstration Research Corporation 1980:17). The focus was on a mix of groups with traditionally high unemployment rates: AFDC women, out-of-school youth, ex-offenders and ex-drug addicts. The basic objective was to provide a package of help that would enable these vulnerable groups to attach themselves more effectively to the world of paid work. Peer support (working in teams of four to seven people), graduated stress (tightening work rules about, for example, punctuality gradually over time) and close supervision (by supervisors matched where possible with participants' social and ethnic backgrounds) were the key programme characteristics. This work support package was provided for twelve or eighteen months in the different sites.

Fieldwork in fifteen different cities and rural areas started in 1975 and ran to the end of 1978. Some 10,000 people in total passed through the Supported Work Program, mainly young, male, black non-high-school graduates with one or more dependants. Most of the programme evaluation was done simply by looking at the experiences of the participants at the different sites, but Mathematica Policy Research and the Institute for Research on Poverty were commissioned to select and monitor a control group. Random assignment to the intervention or a control group was carried out at ten of the fifteen sites. It was intended that intervention and control group participants should be interviewed every nine months from the start of the programme, with some being followed up for three years. Data were collected from state wage and unemployment records and from brief telephone surveys (and occasionally interviews) with study participants a year after recruitment.

Results from the experimental supported work sites showed increases in labour force participation and earnings for AFDC women, and some increase for ex-addicts, but there was no evidence of any effect for ex-offenders or young people. Indeed, an analysis of the youth component of the study (along with other similar interventions for young people carried out around the same time) concluded that the design of the study made it possible to say with confidence that there had been no effect on employment rates, hours of work, wage rates or welfare dependency in this age-group (Betsey et al. 1985:144). Crime amongst ex-addicts, but not amongst ex-offenders or young people, appeared to have fallen. A detailed cost–benefit analysis showed that the benefits for AFDC women and ex-addicts far outweighed programme costs (Manpower Demonstration Research Corporation 1980).

The background to the second approach to supporting workers in table 9.1 – the Texas Worker Adjustment Program – was the Job Training Partnership Act passed in 1983, which provided considerable funds for a variety of 'displaced worker' programmes. Little was known about the effectiveness of these, and there was increasing disenchantment with the efforts of non-experimental studies to evaluate their impact. In 1985 two national advisory committees looking at employment and training programmes recommended RCT designs (Bloom 1990:33). The Texas Project, an RCT, was implemented by the Texas Department of Community Affairs at three sites in 1984–5. Its aim was to evaluate a mix of job search assistance and occupational skills training for unemployed people with poor chances of returning to work: those made redundant, long-term recipients of unemployment insurance benefits, older and non-English-speaking workers. The theory under test was that this approach would expedite re-employment in jobs that minimized wage loss. Abt Associates was again the programme contractor. Eligible people in one site were randomised to two intervention groups (job search assistance, job search assistance, plus occupational skills training) and one control group, and at the remaining two sites to a combined job search and skills intervention and a control group. Altogether, 1,445 people were included in the intervention, and 814 served as control participants. The major outcomes of interest were earnings, unemployment and receipt of unemployment benefit; data were derived from state wage and unemployment records, and from a five-minute telephone survey with study participants carried out a year after recruitment, supplemented by a brief face-to-face interview where necessary.

Most of the people who took part in the Texas project were men with one or more dependants who had lost relatively well-paying jobs; the length of the intervention varied from ten to seventeen weeks. Results with respect to earnings showed an 8 per cent treatment group advantage for men, and a 32 per cent advantage for women; the employment advantage was near zero for men and 6 per cent for women; men and women in the intervention arm of the study received 14 per cent less in unemployment benefit; and no evidence could be found that adding occupational skills training to job search assistance was of benefit in terms of the study outcomes.

LIFE and TARP

Two of the experiments listed in table 9.1 involved ex-prisoners. As with the housing and income maintenance experiments, there had been intense policy debate over a number of years about appropriate and effective ways of reducing further crime among ex-prisoners. Vocational training programmes in prisons had been tried, but these did not appear to have any effect (Taggart 1972). The prime mover in the Living Insurance for ex-Prisoners (LIFE) and the Transitional Aid Research Project (TARP) experiments was Howard Rosen, Director of Research and Development at the Employment and Training Administration. Rosen wanted to test the proposal then being discussed in policy circles that repeat offending would be reduced if released prisoners were given some form of basic income support. Qualitative research showed that many ex-prisoners experienced a long period of unemployment post-release, and that most had few financial resources to help them through this period (at Rikers prison in New York, 'gate' money in 1970 was twenty-five cents and a bologna sandwich) (Rossi et al. 1980:23).

The LIFE experiment began in Baltimore in 1971, with a target group of men aged forty-five or under with multiple convictions, released from Maryland state prisons and returning to live in Baltimore. Heroin and alcohol addicts were excluded. Responsibility for the study was given to a non-profit research organization, the Bureau of Social Science Research in Washington. Stratified randomisation (by length of work experience, age and marital status) was used to create four groups: three intervention groups, which received payments of $60 a week for thirteen weeks, payments plus job counselling and placement services, and counselling and placement services only, and a fourth, no-intervention control group. The men were interviewed immediately post-release and monthly for a year (and were paid $5 plus expenses for each interview). These interviews, plus court records, provided both process and outcome data. The main outcome used was arrest. When the data were ana-lysed, it was found that members of the groups receiving financial aid were 7 per cent less likely to be arrested in the post-release year and 8 per cent less likely to commit theft offences than members of the other groups. Arrests for other kinds of crime did not appear to be affected. A second-year follow-up indicated that the arrest differential was maintained. An effect on work disin-centives of the payments was also searched for, but not found. There was no apparent effect of the intensive job counselling and placement programme on either employment or re-arrests (Rossi et al. 1980).

These results were regarded in policy circles as interesting, but not convinc-ing. The numbers of people involved in the experiment had been small, and the intensive effort put into the programme by the research team would be unlikely to be duplicated in a state or federally administered scheme. Thus, further research was recommended. The Department of Labor designed the Transitional Aid Research Project (TARP), an experiment carried out in Texas and Georgia largely because these had computerized criminal justice systems and large prison populations and were willing to accept the principle of randomisation. Sample sizes were calculated on the expectation derived from the results of the LIFE experiment that financial aid would reduce property crime arrests by one-quarter (a 5 per cent difference between intervention and control groups). The TARP experiment began in 1975. Stratified randomisation (by sex, age, rural/urban residence, etc.) of both male and female ex-prisoners was used to create six groups: four intervention groups (payment for thirteen weeks at 100 per cent tax rate; payment for 26 weeks at 100 per cent tax rate; payment for 13 weeks at 25 per cent tax rate; job placement services) and two control groups (one given regular interviews, the other not). As in the LIFE study, paid interviews were carried out regularly throughout the post-release year (every three months).

The findings of the TARP experiment have been much debated. Straight-forward analysis of outcomes following the procedure used in the LIFE study – comparing the benefit groups with the non-benefit groups – showed that arrests overall were actually somewhat *higher* among ex-prisoners receiving benefit: 44.4 per cent compared to 42.0 per cent. The difference with respect to property-related arrests was even larger: 25.7 per cent versus 21.6 per cent (Rossi et al. 1980:93–4). In order to explain these findings, the researchers developed a complicated theory of 'counterbalancing' effects. As employment rates were also different in the two groups (20 and 25.2 weeks in the post-release year in the benefit and non-benefit groups respectively), the theory was that, because of the links between unemployment and crime, arrest rates had not been lowered: since the financial benefits had led to increased unemployment, they had also increased crime. It was thus concluded that the effectiveness of a policy of providing financial support to ex-prisoners could not be dismissed on the evidence of the experiment, and that further research was needed on ways of 'stripping the work-disincentive effects from transitional financial aid' (Rossi et al. 1980:283).

Dissenting voices put another view. As one of the analysts of the housing allowance experiments put it, the great advantage of the RCT design is 'its ability to provide relatively model-free estimates of impact' (Kennedy 1983:53). Complex statistical modelling should be unnecessary when there is good comparability between intervention and control groups and sufficient statistical power to compare outcomes across groups. In the TARP evaluation, search for a theory that would explain the findings in terms consistent with the original hypothesis (that payments to ex-prisoners would reduce crime) required complex structural equations – what Cronbach (1982:285) called 'heroic methods of data analysis'. These ignored the fundamental distinction between the strength of experimental and the relative weakness of non-experimental evidence (Zeisel 1982).[8]

Insuring health

The United States has 'enjoyed' a prolonged debate about the financing of the health care system. As with welfare services, it is widely agreed that there are problems with the existing health care system; it is one of the costliest in the world, and it serves to promote, rather than prevent, health disparities between different social groups (see e.g. Inlander et al. 1988; Navarro 1976). In the USA, the example of the UK's 'socialized medicine' as it is called has caused much dispute between those who argue that health care free at the point of use is a basic human right and those who consider that this right is likely to be abused, causing further escalating health care costs. The Rand Corporation's Health Insurance Study was designed to answer some of these questions about the relationship between differently financed health care systems and health care behaviour. It had, like the other experiments, a pragmatic objective: to provide decision-makers with dependable information which they could use to consider the development of national health insurance legislation. The study shared with the housing allowance study the rationale of seeing what would happen if the costs of improved welfare (housing or health) were shifted on to individuals themselves; both studies, like most of the large experiments, reflected ideologically the American attachment to private enterprise.

The Health Insurance Study was designed in response to a call for proposals put out by the OEO in 1971; the Rand Corporation and Mathematica were chosen to do the work. A pilot study was started in 1973 in Dayton, Ohio, to test out families' willingness to take part in such an experiment; the main study began there the following year, and a further five sites were added in 1975. The experiment tested fifteen different strategies in a complex design, which involved stratified randomisation of families at the six sites to fourteen different plans, and an extension of the experiment in Seattle, where the additional approach of prepaid group health care was also evaluated. The fourteen insurance plans were: (1) a free plan, where families received all services without charge; (2) an individual-deductible plan, which entailed families paying 95 per cent of the cost of outpatient care up to $150 per person per year, with all other care being free; (3) nine co-insurance plans, under which families paid 25 or 50 per cent of all health care used until 5, 10 or 15 per cent of income, or $1,000 had been spent, whichever was less;[9] and (4) three further income-related 'catastrophic' plans under which families paid 95 per cent of all bills, again up to 5, 10 or 15 per cent of income, or $1,000, whichever was less.[10] The extended experiment in Seattle enrolled a further group of families in a prepaid group practice system. This increasingly popular approach to the financing of health care limited families' health care expenditure, and was hailed in some circles as an important method of cost containment, since it also seemed to produce lower hospital admission rates. However, this conclusion about the role of Health Maintenance Organizations, as they were called, was unreliable, since people using such systems were obviously self-selected, and so may have been healthier in the first place.

Estimates in 1978 put the cost of the Rand health insurance experiment up to 1981 at $63 million, of which $14.7 million would be paid to families (Ferber and Hirsch 1982:136). The experiment was designed to be as realistic as possible in its population representativeness and geographical coverage and the fact that families could choose their own doctors. It came as something of a surprise to the researchers (and proved something of a methodological problem) that many families actually spent nothing on medical care. Eligibility was restricted to families with an annual income of less than $54,000 (at 1982 prices); people over sixty-one and those who were disabled and unable to work (and therefore eligible for Medicare) were excluded. Children under fourteen were omitted from the major analyses, which were carried out on 2,754 families. Most families were randomised to three-year but some to five-year enrolment.[11] Measures of health at enrolment and exit from the study included physical functioning, 'role functioning' (e.g. 'Does your health keep you from working at a job, doing work around the house, or going to school?'), mental health, social contacts and health perceptions. Functional vision was measured, along with weight, serum cholesterol, blood pressure and smoking, and these factors were combined in a 'risk of dying' index.[12] These medical tests were carried out on 60 per cent of the sample at enrolment and 100 per cent at exit; the other data were collected using self-administered questionnaires.

A large number of publications resulted from the Rand experiment, reporting a variety of both non-effects and effects in different directions for different population groups. Unsurprisingly, and as in most of the other experiments, families' willingness to take part reflected a preference for randomisation to the most generous plans. Of those offered free care, 92 per cent agreed, and only 0.4 per cent dropped out thereafter; the 'catastrophic' plans, on the other hand, recruited only 75 per cent of randomized families, and 11 per cent of these dropped out during the study. One of the main questions that the researchers asked of the data was whether free care improved health more than the other plans. For most of the measures used, the answer seemed to be no. The exceptions were vision, blood pressure and anaemia among children; people randomised to the free plan were more likely to have 'corrected far vision' and lower diastolic blood pressure, and children with anaemia were much less likely to have it at the end of the study if their families were enrolled in a non-cost-sharing plan. These improvements were largest among low-income and high-risk people. A second major question regarding whether free care increases the use of health care, got a yes. Those who shared the costs of care were nearly one-third less likely than free-care groups to see a physician for minor symptoms (Shapiro et al. 1986). There were about a third fewer out-patient visits and hospitalizations among families assigned to the cost-sharing plans. Children in families on cost-sharing plans were 22 per cent less likely to seek and receive care (G. M. Anderson et al. 1991). 'We found', concluded the researchers, 'that the more people had to pay for medical care, the less of it they used' (Brook et al. 1983:1432). The extended experiment in Seattle produced similar results, with families assigned to a prepaid group practice scheme having a rate of hospital admission about 40 per cent lower than those offered free care.

An Office of Technology Assessment (OTA) report on the Rand Health Insurance Study advised caution about generalizing from these results. Its conclusions were that 'coinsurance deters individuals from seeking all types of care, even potentially effective treatment'. The general finding of less health service use with payment schemes was hardly surprising, given that people will generally use services less often if they have to pay for them. The OTA report deemed the health results of the experiment 'largely inconclusive' (Office of Technology Assessment 1993:4–5). This is because there is no direct relationship between health service use and health status. The report points out that the long-term effects of cost-sharing are unknown. However, the Rand study did, suggestively, find a decrease in cervical cancer smears among women and immunizations in children when the costs of health care were partly or wholly borne by families.

Experimenting with education

As we saw in chapter 8, educational researchers were among the first to use systematic experimentation to settle intra-professional disputes about effective teaching methods. Education, in its broadest sense, was another obvious candidate for a programme of experiments designed to test different approaches to welfare reform.

Preschool education

During the 1960s and 1970s many early childhood initiatives were launched in the USA with the aim of improving outcomes for socially disadvantaged children. There were at least thirty separate federal educational and training programmes for low-income populations in America (Levin 1978). One of the main objectives of these programmes was to increase the basic cognitive skills of disadvantaged children. The most famous of these initiatives, Head Start, which consisted originally mainly of six- to eight-week summer programmes sponsored by school systems, churches and community action agencies, had expanded to 13,000 different sites by 1967, with an operating budget four years later of about $360 million (McDill et al. 1972).

Head Start was set up following the 1964 Economic Opportunity Act, which included the authorization of grants for developing day care projects within community action programmes. The Elementary and Secondary Education Act of 1965 settled on day care as a prime anti-poverty strategy, and provided for substantial investment in day care for educationally deprived children living in poor communities. At the time, about one in four American mothers of preschool children worked, and mothers' views made it clear that care in day care centres came a close second to care provided by fathers or other relatives, but there was not nearly enough of it (Lynn 1980).

The Perry Preschool Project, in which day care was a major component, has the distinction of having the longest period of follow-up (currently to age twenty-seven) of all the early intervention projects. Its inception pre-dated the War on Poverty/Great Society initiatives by a few years, and arose from local dissatisfaction with the way school services were meeting the needs of disadvantaged children. The study's originator was David Weikart, a public school administrator and school psychologist, who has remained associated with the project. The study's location, Ypsilanti, was one of the worst congested slum areas in Michigan with high school failure and crime rates; the intention of the project, as originally stated, was 'to help children acquire the intellectual strengths they would need in school' (Schweinhart and Weikart 1980:22). This was interpreted as involving a wide range of outcomes, from children's tested IQs to parental views about children's adjustment, use of special educational services and school behaviour. In the follow-ups at ages fifteen, nineteen and twenty-seven, the outcomes expanded further to include use of health and social services, relationships between parents and children, self-concepts, use of time, reproductive history, delinquency and crime, marital status and living arrangements, income, car ownership and community activities, as well as cognitive ability, educational achievement, aspirations and employment.

All the children in the Study were black,[13] and the criteria for being admitted to the study were that they lived in the neighbourhood of the Perry Elementary School, came from families of low socio-economic status, and had initial scores on the Stanford–Binet IQ test of 70–85; this put them in the then prevailing borderline category of 'educable mentally retarded'. In all, 131 children were invited to participate in the study; the parents of three refused; and five dropped out early on.[14] Those who agreed to take part were assigned by a process of matching and coin tossing[15] either to the services normally provided in the neighbourhood or to a programme consisting of twelve and a half hours weekly of preschool attendance plus one and a half hours weekly of home visits (during which they and their mothers were involved in 'educational' activities). The intervention ran for thirty weeks a year; some children received it for one year, others for two. Recruitment started in 1962, of children born in 1958–9, and continued until 1965 for children born in 1962. Data on what happened to the children were collected, including IQ tests at ages 3–10 and 14, school achievement tests at 7–11 and 14, rating scales completed by teachers in four grades, school records, and interviews with parents at the start of the study and eleven years later, when the young people themselves were also interviewed; later follow-ups involved more interviews with traceable members of the sample and police and court records.

Early results from the Perry study's mix of part-time preschool education and home visits showed an increase in cognitive ability scores of twelve points for the experimental group over the control group at the end of the first and second years. However, three years later the scores had equalized and remained so thereafter. Teachers rated the experimental group children more highly on school motivation at elementary school. By age fifteen more striking differences emerged on a number of measures, including school achievement in reading and arithmetic, use of special educational services, the value attached to schooling, time spent on homework, self-rated cognitive ability and future educational aspirations. Especially notable in this array of outcomes which could be attributed to the input of the preschool programme were lower rates of 'deviant' behaviour at school (a particular concern of David Weikart and the other local educational administrators who had initiated the project) and delinquent behaviour. This pattern was repeated at age nineteen, when 121 of the original sample of 123 were interviewed. At this point, 31 per cent and 51 per cent had records of being detained or arrested. Employment was 59 per cent in the experimental and 32 per cent in the control group; 67 per cent of the experimental group, but only 49 per cent of the control group, had graduated from high school; 38 per cent and 21 per cent went on to college or vocational training; 16 per cent and 28 per cent had spent time in special education; and among the twenty-five young women who had been in the preschool programme there were seventeen pregnancies and/or births, compared with twenty-eight among the twenty-four young women in the control group (Berrueta-Clement et al. 1984).

The follow-up at age twenty-seven involved 117 of the original sample, and continued the trend of the age nineteen findings, with significantly higher levels of education, monthly earnings and rates of home ownership, and lower rates of social service use and criminality for 'programme graduates'. Economic cost–benefit analysis showed that 'Over the lifetimes of the participants, the preschool program returns to the public an estimated $7.16 for every dollar invested' (Schweinhart et al. 1993:xviii).

The evidence from the Perry Preschool Project is stronger than that from many evaluations of most other early childhood interventions because of the design used, which was deliberately an attempt to follow Campbell and Stanley's precepts for experimental research (Schweinhart et al. 1980:21). Along with a small number of other evaluations of such interventions, the Perry study provides convincing grounds for investing in resources for children, especially as a strategy for reducing social and personal problems later in life (see Zoritch et al. 1998). The Perry study was also marked by an unusually low attrition rate. This was partly attributable to low natural migration out of the area, but more importantly to the interviewers going to 'extraordinary lengths' to locate and interview as many participants as possible (Berrueta-Clement et al. 1984:100). The findings that early improvement in IQ scores tended to wash out over time duplicated those of other early childhood interventions. Results from the Perry study formed the basis for legislation supporting preschool education in a number of states, and were also used to support the case for continued funding of Head Start. This and its extension programme Follow Through had always suffered from problems in their original design which meant that *post hoc* attempts at evaluation yielded unreliable evidence of effectiveness (see R. B. Anderson et al. 1978; Cicirelli et al. 1969; Gilbert et al. 1975; Stebbins et al. 1978). These design problems almost certainly made both Head Start and Follow Through look less effective than they in fact were (see Campbell and Erlebacher 1970).

Educational performance contracting

The experiment sponsored by the OEO with contracting out teaching in public schools to private firms – the second educational experiment in table 9.1 – was partly a response to criticisms voiced about the earlier interventions in compensatory education, Head Start and Follow Through, which had used such a weak evaluation design that interpretation of their effects was extremely difficult, leading to charges that 'innocent' children had been used as 'guinea pigs' (Rivlin 1971:84). This OEO project was designed to investigate the theory that paying private firms on a performance-related basis was a more effective way than normal public school teaching of raising the basic academic standard of socially disadvantaged and underachieving pupils.[16]

The idea itself was an old one; from 1863 for some thirty years the English state education system had based grants to schools on pupil attainment and attendance figures. In the USA a private firm, Dorset Educational Systems, hit the headlines in the late 1960s with its claims that scores of educationally disadvantaged students in Texarkana, Arkansas, had doubled or tripled since the firm had signed an incentive contract with the local school board.[17] As a result, more than 200 other school districts were thinking of trying the same system. Incentive contracting also fitted well with the notions of accountability being expressed at federal government level.

In the OEO experiment, invitations were sent to school districts which had expressed an interest in trying performance contracting. After screening to

meet the project eligibility criteria of poverty, academic underachievement and
the availability of reliable test data, twenty-two districts were selected – four
dropped out during negotiations. The eighteen districts were divided up between six private firms which had tendered for the performance contracts.
Later on, two further districts were included with an added intervention of
teacher incentives. In each district a control school was selected, the next most
academically underachieving; this 'violation' of the usual standard for random
allocation was recognized at the time, but defended on the grounds that the
group differences turned out to be small (see Gramlich and Koshel 1975:21).
The students who took part in the experiment were the most underachieving
in six school grades: 100 in each grade for the control schools, 150 for the
experimental schools (to allow for drop-outs and replacements). All the students were tested at the beginning of the school year and again at the end;
questionnaires were given to parents. Students in the experimental schools
received an hour's additional teaching in reading and mathematics every day
from the private firms. Firms received payments on the basis of how much
students gained in the academic year; there was no payment for students who
did not improve, an average of $75 for one grade improvement and an average
of $8 for every 0.1 grade improvement above this. The payments were not
generous, reflecting the firms' confidence that they would be successful, and
the appeal of taking part in an experiment as providing valuable publicity.

Results were disappointing; gains attributable to the intervention were much
less than everyone involved in the experiment had expected. Differences between experimental and control schools were small; in reading the students did
slightly better, but in mathematics they did worse. On subjects outside the
experiment, control students also did better, suggesting that teachers in these
schools felt threatened by performance contracting, so generally tried harder.[18]
Significantly, as in the Youth Entitlement Program, qualitative interviews with
local school personnel during the experiment showed that most of them believed
the experiment was working well. Following the results, which were more or
less universally acknowledged as disastrous, there was an abrupt turn-around in
the fashion for performance contracting. Only one of the twenty sites which
took part in the OEO experiment subsequently signed a performance contract;
by 1975 there were none in operation (Gramlich and Koshel 1975:165).

Youth entitlement

The third educational programme in table 9.1, the Youth Entitlement Program, was mandated by Congress, launched in 1978 and managed, like the
Supported Work Program, by the Manpower Demonstration Research Corporation. Its background was the Youth Employment and Demonstration Projects
Act (YEDPA) of 1977. This mandated a substantial increase in spending by
federal government on youth employment and training programmes; $600
million was spent over the four years (1978–81) of YEDPA activities. The
legislation included a clause specifying that some of the money had to be spent

on testing 'the relative efficacy of different ways of dealing with these [youth employment problems] in different local contexts' (quoted in Betsey et al. 1985:vii). Many different initiatives were sponsored and evaluated under the Act. One of these was the Youth Entitlement Program, which set up a demonstration project providing subsidized employment for economically disadvantaged young people. The idea was to guarantee jobs (part-time during the school year, full-time over the summer) in order to encourage such young people to complete their secondary education. The educational target was seen as a mediating factor *en route* to better employment opportunities. Congress set aside $222 million for the programme, which ran from 1978 to 1980. Seventeen sites across the United States were enrolled in the programme. The larger sites received grants from $8.5 million to $23 million to recruit between 3,000 and 8,000 young people each; the smaller sites recruited between 200 and 1,000 young people for $750,000 to $1.25 million. Eligible young people had to be aged 16–19 and come from low-income families. As with the Supported Work Program, many of the estimates of effect were derived simply by examining the school and labour market records of the participants. However, four sites were matched with a similar four 'non-entitlement' sites, and interviews with parents and young people were conducted at these sites.

Preliminary results suggested higher return-to-school rates among young drop-outs in the four entitlement sites (Ferber and Hirsch 1982). A more detailed look at two sites showed that among sixteen-year-olds, 24 per cent in the experimental group and 30 per cent in the control group went back to school in the first six months; among seventeen-year-olds the figures were 20 per cent and 14 per cent. The figures for 'persistence in school' among those who were theoretically attending were very similar for both groups. This hardly constituted strong evidence of an effect. Interestingly, interviews with school administrators showed a 'strong, intuitive feeling' that the Youth Entitlement Program was having an effect, especially on young people who were on the verge of dropping out of school (Mandel and Solnick 1979:v). This is one example of the kind of conflict discussed in chapter 3 which may be revealed by 'triangulating' data from different sources; triangulated data which all suggest the same answer are one thing, but how to decide on the 'right' answer when the messages conflict is a different matter altogether.

Later analyses concluded that the programme 'was not effective in increasing school retention' (Betsey et al. 1985:15), although there was some evidence that white youths benefited more than black ones (Farkas et al. 1984), and that young women benefited more than young men (Simms 1985). Margaret Simms, who looked specifically at the role of young women in the YEDPA programmes, found that women were generally underrepresented, more likely than the young men to be assigned to work experience and classroom training than to on-the-job training or public service employment activities, and more likely to be assigned traditional female occupations. Moreover, data collection and analysis in these programmes paid very little attention to their possible impact on non-employment outcomes, including child-bearing, which could well have been important for the women.

The Youth Entitlement Program was one of the few YEDPA projects com-missioned to have been evaluated in such a way that any conclusions could be reached about effectiveness. The general failure to take the evaluation challenge seriously resulted in the YEDPA efforts being brought to a premature close in 1981. A review by the National Research Council commissioned by the US Department of Labor two years later concluded that for the most part YEDPA activities had consisted of 'poor research on hastily constructed programs' with too short periods of post-programme follow-up (usually three to eight months), and a failure to make 'sufficient use of random assignment in defining partici-pant and control groups' (Betsey et al. 1985:5, 18). Robert Boruch, a leading figure in the evaluation industry, who wrote an appendix to the National Re-search Council's review, was particularly damning about the quality of the evalu-ation, pointing out that more than 70 per cent of reports of YEDPA programmes had to be rejected by the Review Committee as methodologically flawed; fur-ther, none of those which claimed to have randomised experimental and control groups described how these had been set up.[19]

Conclusion

Systematic social experimentation, as noted by Gramlich and Koshel (1975:65) in the second quotation at the head of this chapter, always carries the risk that what is being tried may be shown not to work. Even worse, it may do more harm than good. Of course, 'failing' to find benefit and demonstrating harm where such harm exists both form part of the logic of the method of systematic experimentation itself. The possibility of unintended harm is precisely why interventions need to be subjected to such scrutiny.

Some of the ways in which the academic and policy communities reacted to the American experiments are discussed in the next chapter. Both the experi-ments themselves and reactions to them form part of the background to to-day's dismissal of experimental methods as irrelevant to social science and impractical ways of settling social policy questions.

The theme of gender runs through the story of this and the next chapter in two particular ways. The first is that the women who took part in the experi-ments were often not treated and did not react in the same way as the men; for the most part, they changed their behaviour more, particularly in the work incentive experiments. This reflects the very different attachment that women and men have to the worlds of paid work and the caring work that goes on at home. But the second, and more fundamental, way in which gender was relevant is in terms of methodology; most of the experiments carried out during the golden age were driven by male economists who had little respect for the contribution which might have been made to the design, implementa-tion and analysis of these studies by what were by then decisively seen as softer, sociological methods. It was not women *per se* who were the problem, but the way in which femininity had come to be constituted in the domain of methodology.

10

Lessons from America

Given the focus and recent proliferation of field experiments, it seems appropriate to try and collect, sort out, and capitalize on these experiments so that we can stop condemning experimenters to repeat history.

Dennis, *Implementing Randomized Field Experiments*

Those of us who were engaged in evaluation research in the 1960s and 1970s were dismayed by the results. We seemed to be messengers of gloom and doom.

Weiss, 'Evaluating social programs'

This chapter considers reactions to the findings of the large American experiments discussed in the last chapter. What did people think these experiments meant, and how were these responses reflected in policy and subsequent research? How, with hindsight, might the results of the experiments be interpreted today? Learning from the American endeavours is especially important, as the first quote at the head of this chapter (Dennis 1988:10) intimates, if we are to avoid repeating history in ways that are wasteful of time, effort and human ingenuity. A deeper level of questions concerns the significance of this particular moment in the history of methodology, in the long-drawn-out battle between the protagonists of different kinds of science and the division of ways of knowing along ideologically gendered lines. Can the American experience with the 'method of natural science' be seen as definitively establishing its relevance to social issues? Or does it demonstrate the difficulties that are bound to arise?

Evaluation works!

One absolutely critical message yielded by the golden era of programme evaluation in America is that this model of evaluation does *itself* work. The American experiments proved beyond any reasonable doubt that prospective experimental studies with control groups selected using random methods *are* feasible ways of evaluating social interventions. The main obstacles to rigorous evaluation of public policy and other social interventions do not lie with the research designs themselves (although in most cases these could have been improved); nor do any such problems inhere in the settings in which these evaluations are done: neither is the public intrinsically unwilling to participate. In so far as there *are* generic problems with the application of this method to the social world, these are at the level of policy making, practitioners and service-providers, and research capability.

But this conclusion coexists with a rather different one that was drawn in some research and policy circles at the time. Most of the experiments described in the previous chapter were greeted as having failed to produce any significant effects. It was apparently the case that the Negative Income Tax experiments demonstrated little impact on work disincentives; the Experimental Housing Allowance Program made little difference to housing consumption or housing stock; the Supporting Workers initiatives produced only small increases in employment or earnings; in the penal experiments, the minor effects on re-arrests in the LIFE study were reversed in the TARP experiment; in the Rand Corporation Health Insurance Study cost-sharing insurance seemed to reduce health care use, but there was little evidence of any impact on people's health; the Youth Entitlement Program did not encourage young people to stay in school; and contracting out education to private firms failed to confirm the positive impact which had been claimed in an earlier nonexperimental study. Some of the findings could even be put in the 'doing harm rather than good' category: these included the re-arrest figures in the TARP experiment, the results for sixteen-year-olds in the Youth Entitlement Program, and the apparently 'negative' effects on family breakup noted in the NIT experiments. If the purpose of systematic social experimentation is to produce positive effects, then, among the experiments discussed in chapter 9, only the Perry Preschool Project appears to rescue the golden age of evaluation from the charge that a great deal of money was spent to find nothing of much consequence at all.

Whatever the designers and supporters of the American experiments hoped for, one major lesson they drew was, as Rossi and Wright (1984:341) put it, 'that it is extremely difficult to design programs that produce noticeable effects in any desired direction'. The apparent 'zero effects' of the national experiments were regarded as devastating by many of the social reformers who had hoped to show that the Great Society programmes would make an appreciable difference to the lot of the poor. In the second quotation at the head of this chapter (Weiss 1987:41), Carol Weiss, an evaluator with a sociological background who took part in some of the studies described in chapter 9, reflects on how the initial enthusiasm and commitment of the evaluation community to systematic experimentation was transmuted into despair and despondency when few concrete findings seemed to emerge. As the results sank in, there were even those who recommended that in future, because of the zero effects problem, policy-makers should *not* submit their favoured programmes to systematic evaluation, but rather should simply introduce them, on the old-fashioned assumption that what was believed in would work. To put it baldly, 'if you advocate a particular policy reform or innovation, do not press to have it tested' (Burtless and Haveman 1984:128).

The meaning of 'zero' effects

There is an important distinction to be made between no evidence of effect and evidence of no effect. The two are frequently confused, so that studies which yield no evidence of effect are assumed instead to have produced evidence of no effect (Altman and Bland 1995). A critical issue here is sample size. The chances of finding a statistically significant effect for an intervention are increased with large sample sizes, which means that they are decreased with smaller ones. Many experiments, including some of those carried out in America's golden age, simply did not have sufficient numbers of participants to have a reasonable chance of showing even a modest effect. Furthermore, even with sufficient numbers, modest or small effects are the rule rather than the exception in well-designed evaluations (Peto 1987). Thus the expectation, held by the evaluators of the American social programmes, that 'their' interventions would have dramatic effects, was probably an unreasonable one.

But these conclusions are derived from a considerable amount of experience with trials since the 1970s, which was not available at the time. Then there was little substantive counter-experience with which to contest the 'doom and gloom' message. Consequently, responses to the 'zero effects' finding helped to create a general backlash in the United States against the use of applied economics and systematic evaluation in government. Consulting the evaluators as a way of determining effective public policy went out of fashion; policy evaluation came to be regarded as a difficult art, rather than an exact science. A classic statement of this position is Henry Aaron's *Politics and the Professors: the Great Society in perspective* (1978). As a high-level official on the planning and evaluation staff of the US Department of Health, Education and Welfare in the 1960s, and also a senior fellow at the Brookings Institution, Aaron was close to much of the evaluation effort expended in the golden age. His book is profoundly pessimistic about the ability of evaluation research to contribute effectively to the policy-making process. In part he blames this on the political complexities surrounding the War on Poverty/Great Society initiative, with which the evaluation efforts described in the last chapter were inextricably intertwined; when the political process caused expectations about winning the War on Poverty to crash, it brought down systematic evaluation as well.

A fundamental question concerns the delicate politics of the research–policy relationship. Aaron pointed out that the rational model of systematic experimentation, whereby policy-makers wait for the results of evaluation before acting, was the exception, rather than the rule. Conversely, some of the most equivocal results formed the basis for policy initiatives. For instance, Head

Start, the early intervention initiative for disadvantaged children, which was widely seen as weakened by poor evaluation design, was none the less hailed as politically robust, and was taken by many as evidence that government intervention in the lives of young children would pay measurable dividends later on (Weiss 1991). According to Aaron, a significant underlying theme here is the 'profoundly conservative tendency' of formal evaluation: by raising awkward questions about effectiveness, it tends to slow the pace of reform. As Weiss (1972:126) has observed, the fact that evaluation results tend to be interpreted as negative 'has the effect of undermining reformers and innovative programs. Barnacle-encrusted programs – many of which would profit from a long, clear look – sit by unexamined.'

Evaluation is the child of scepticism, but faith and even prejudice are much more common philosophical positions inside, as well as outside, politics. Another aspect of the backlash against the 'zero effects conclusion' of the Great Society programmes was definitely a conservative one: a move against 'throwing money at social problems' – at the very idea that government intervention is an appropriate strategy for reducing inequalities. The findings of the experiments fuelled the conservative notion that 'coddling' people was wrong. This message was articulated most fully in the response of another evaluator, Charles Murray, whose book *Losing Ground: American social policy 1950–1980* (1984), takes the cynical view that the ineffectiveness of government investment in welfare programmes revealed during the golden age is a sign, not of the value of systematic evaluation but, rather, of the counter-productive nature of doing things for people who ought, instead, to be helping themselves. In the period from 1968 to 1980 in the USA, which saw the discovery of structural poverty, the emergence of various minority rights movements, and the launching of many of the big social programmes, the proportion of Americans living in poverty – 13 per cent – did not shift. Murray especially slated the 'new frontiersmen' of the OEO for their naïve idealism and for contributing to a largely self-serving and introspective industry – that of evaluation.

The economists and the social scientists went to Washington in order to provide the level of proof the structuralists in the OEO felt they needed to convince the President that government intervention was the only way to win the War on Poverty. The NIT experiments, as the first of the Great Society programmes, bore the main weight of this expectation. They were driven by believers convinced that welfare would not, as the folk belief put it, make people 'shiftless'. But faith cannot work miracles. 'With rigor and in enormous detail,' observes Murray, 'the scientists validated not the sponsors' hopes but their fears. The results were more or less what the popular wisdom said they would be' (Murray 1984:150). The reason why the experiments did not work, says Murray, is because social interventions of this kind are the wrong approach; they encourage dependency and at times misguided, mechanistic responses to what is on offer. Against Murray, it could be argued that the forms of social intervention tried in the American experiments were hardly radical. They fitted conservative convictions in substituting market-like incentives (for example, housing allowances conditional on individuals upgrading their housing) for more traditional welfare state policies (for example, subsidized public housing) (Wagner and Wollmann 1986). The interventions tested were thus inherently unlikely to have the capacity to tackle the poverty problem in any serious way.

Although on the whole, neither of the two main predicted results – cutbacks in social programme funding or the direct translation of evaluation findings into policy – followed the 'disappointing' findings which were seen to be generated by the golden age, there *were* some examples of programme findings being used directly to influence government spending or policy change. The results of the Seattle and Denver income maintenance experiments, which showed significant decreases in work activity among women and those in longer-term plans, became available around the time when the Carter administration was putting together a package of welfare reform legislation, and the research findings were used to reduce projected costs by cutting back the plan (Nathan 1988). In the LIFE experiment, policy changes directly followed the experimental findings in some states; in California legislation was passed extending unemployment benefit to released prisoners from 1978 (Rossi et al. 1980:46). Early findings from the Perry Preschool Project were used to secure additional funding for early intervention strategies in the lives of disadvantaged children. But in the main linkages between the evaluations of social experiments and the policy process were not straightforward. In the time lapse between the start of an experiment and its results, policy agendas often changed. In the case of the Rand Health Insurance Study, for example, the Ford administration put forward a health insurance bill 'prematurely', before the results of the experiment were known. In the national income policy field, congressional and presidential interest in the idea of negative income tax peaked in the early 1970s, well before the experimental results were available. In fact, Nixon's sponsorship of a 'Family Assistance Plan', which embodied the idea of a negative income tax, was announced at the same time as the first payments in the New Jersey–Pennsylvania income experiment were made – an example of 'research following reality' (Nathan 1988:54).

The golden age of evaluation in America was followed by a downgrading of the role which policy analysis and evaluation play in the policy-making process. The Nixon administration abolished the OEO and much of the structure of the planning–programming–budgeting system. The Carter administration attempted a minor regeneration of the notion of evidence-based public policy, but got insufficient presidential support. Under Reagan, as under Thatcher in the UK, there was an overwhelming conservative antagonism to social science research, which was suspected of an old-fashioned alliance with socialism (Kirkpatrick 1984). This hardly helped the cause of policy evaluation. When Reagan's government dismantled the federal welfare programmes, evaluation research departments received severe cuts in staff and budgets (Haveman 1987). In both the USA and the UK during this period, there was a strong ideological shift away from government intervention and in favour of the privatized profit motive, although this was also allied with a confused and confusing rhetoric about 'community care'.

Methodological lessons

Some very specific methodological lessons about the *way* in which systematic social experimentation is done can be abstracted from the American experience. Six key points are discussed briefly below: the problem of social complexity, the role of research participants, what constitutes a 'control' group; costs of social experiments, the meaning of multi-disciplinarity in research, and matters of gender (again).

The complexity of social settings

While the complexity of social settings is an argument in favour of RCTs,[1] it is this very complexity that may also get in the way of evaluation. For example, critical aspects of the policy context may change for exogenous reasons while an experiment is under way. During the TARP evaluation, the Governor of Georgia issued an order shortening sentences for some prisoners, and this upset the mix of people being recruited into the experiment (Rossi et al. 1980:79). One year into the New Jersey–Pennsylvania experiment, a statewide welfare plan was introduced aiding two-parent welfare families on a more generous basis than several of the NIT plans being tested. Levels of the experimental payments were altered, but the change in the design was one of the arguments used for the need to undertake further experiments (Nathan 1988:53).

The complexity of the social contexts in which programmes are evaluated means that it is easier to assess simple than complex interventions. Some of the American experiments could be criticized for having been too ambitious; they tried to test too many interventions within the framework of a single study. The most complex of all was the Denver–Seattle income experiment, which boasted a total of eighty-four different experimental 'cells'. The resulting analytic headache certainly obscured the importance of simple intervention–control comparisons, and detracted from the value of asking and answering straightforward questions about the effects of offering guaranteed income to socially disadvantaged households.[2]

Involving research participants

There are important issues about people's willingness to take part in any study using human 'subjects'. Low participation rates were a problem in many of the American experiments. Little thought seems to have been given to what would-be participants should be told about the research, to the relationship between the 'informed consent' and randomisation processes, and to whether people, once enrolled, would stay in their allocated group. The problem is illustrated in the New Jersey–Pennsylvania NIT experiment, in which refusal either before or after randomisation resulted in only 8 per cent of the initial random sample of households ending up in the study; later on a further 25 per cent of the control group and 16 per cent of the intervention participants dropped out (Ferber and Hirsch 1982:60). Both high rates of drop-out and higher rates in the control than the intervention group make it difficult to draw reliable conclusions about the effects of the intervention.

It is difficult to interpret the findings of experiments without knowing what people were told about the research. Most of the American experiments assigned people to study groups before asking for their consent, and most used the 'Zelen' design,[3] in which only those assigned to the intervention group(s) were told they were part of a study which was testing the way a new programme works. Attrition was a problem in evaluations using this design, partly because randomisation preceded consent; had it been the other way around, fewer people might have dropped out because they would have taken a decision that they wanted to take part (D. T. Campbell 1979). It was important that people understood the rules. But many did not. In the New Jersey–Pennsylvania NIT experiment, for example, many people were at a loss to know what the experimenters expected of them: 'Particularly vexing was the fact that a large number of families initially misinterpreted the instructions and reported take home pay[4] instead of gross pay, with the result that much of the initial wage data had to be discarded for the analysis' (Ferber and Hirsch 1980:57). The explanation as to why the findings of the Gary experiment on family stability were out of line with those of the other NIT experiments may well have been that the information process followed in Gary led many couples to believe that they would actually lose their benefits if they split up (Murray 1984). Thus, what the experiments actually showed cannot be disentangled from the experiences of those who took part.[5]

In the reports of most of the American experiments, the thousands of people who took part in them appear mainly as numbers, rather than as individuals with their own stories. The discrepancy between the 'ethnographic' and the 'quantitative' approaches is well illustrated in the report of the EHAP study, where four case-studies contained in an appendix throw more light on the implementation of the programme than most of the preceding chapters (Struyk and Bendick 1981: appendix D). Respecting the autonomy of research participants means taking their views and experiences seriously, seeing them as at the centre of the research process and as holding the keys to both the success of the experiment and the interpretation of the data. The only experiment to have explicitly identified the importance of linking process and outcome data is the Supported Work Program (Hollister et al. 1979). The only social experiments to place the views and experiences of the target group at centre stage in designing the experiment were the LIFE and TARP evaluations. Both were preceded by a needs assessment and by thorough pilot testing of design and measurement issues. In the LIFE evaluation, a feasibility study for an RCT was carried out in 1970 in New York, which resulted in significant changes to the proposed design; the experiences of the men who took part shaped the decision to restrict the income support to thirteen weeks and to add a job placement component.

Had such careful pilot work been done in the other experiments, some of the problems they ran into might have been avoided. For example, in the NIT experiments, some households randomised to be offered income support refused because they did not want to accept what they saw as charity. This was also a problem in the EHAP study, where 'welfare stigma' deterred especially older people and 'the working poor' (Carlson and Heinberg 1978). The low take-up of housing allowances was partly explained by the fact that because of the conditions attached, families had to move in order to secure their allowances. About a third of families living in 'ineligible' units did not even look for new housing; when interviewed, they said they liked their current homes and neighbourhoods, and moving was too much trouble (Schnare 1981:143). The importance of structural and political constraints also emerges in these data; a considerable proportion of households complained of racial discrimination and/ or discrimination against children in the housing market (Cronin and Rasmussen 1981:127). Searching for new housing was especially difficult for the most disadvantaged families, who lacked their own transport (Cronin and Rasmussen 1981:129; Schnare 1983:143).

The status of control groups

The model of 'laboratory experimentation' represented by the RCT is sometimes held to be compromised by the impossibility of creating no-intervention control groups. In the real world of negative income tax, housing allowances, preschool day care or post-prison payments, it is unlikely that some people in the control arm of social experiments will not realize that that is where they are, even if the 'Zelen' design is used. In the EHAP study and in the income experiments, experimental and control group participants were informed about their own group but not about the other; but since randomization was done by households rather than by neighbourhoods, a control group household could well find itself living next to an intervention group household. There are reports of control families leaving the New Jersey–Pennsylvania NIT study on discovering that their neighbours were receiving allowances that they were not (Wortman et al. 1976).

Control group participants are usually involved in providing information to the research team. But such an involvement also constitutes an intervention, thereby altering the status of the control group as standing entirely outside the dynamics of the research process. In some of the experiments the level of intervention experienced by the control group was quite substantial; for example, monthly reports and quarterly interviews in the income maintenance and housing experiments. In the housing experiment control families were paid at the rate of $10 for each monthly report and $25 for each interview (intervention families were not paid). This much-vaunted 'Hawthorne effect' was recognized as a problem; in the Gary income maintenance experiment, the TARP evaluation and the demand EHAP experiment, there were two control groups; in the Gary experiment one was asked to provide more regular and more frequent information than the other one; one control group in the TARP evaluation provided no direct information at all; and one of the two control groups in the housing study received 'an informational treatment' (an invitation to five housing information sessions, with a payment of $10 for attending each session). Yet analyses of these different 'control interventions' do not figure at all in the main reports of the experiments.[6] If control group participants felt themselves to be part of an experiment, this might well have acted to reduce the size of any outcome differences between intervention and control groups, and thus to have lowered the chances of the experiment being seen as 'successful' in the sense of producing measurably positive outcomes.[7]

This problem has its own technical literature, that devoted to what is called 'pre-test sensitization' – the tendency of data-collecting from control group research participants to affect their behaviour (see e.g. Campbell and Stanley 1966; Lana 1969; Welch and Wahlberg 1970). One analysis of pre-test effects in 134 randomised studies of educational, psychological and social interventions compared studies using and not using pre-tests, and found a statistically significant effect of pre-testing on outcomes (Willson and Putnam 1983). One solution to this problem is the design suggested by Richard Solomon (1949), in which both experimental and control groups are divided (randomly), with half of the participants in each being pre-tested and half not. Solomon originally developed this method for studying the effectiveness of teaching methods. Comparing studies using the new method with the 'traditional' one (pre-test and post-test for all experimental and control group participants), he showed that pre-testing 'erroneously underrated' the effectiveness of teaching procedures (Solomon 1949:145).

An expensive form of evaluation?

One response to the American experience with systematic social experiments is linked to the 'zero effects' problem: many people complained that, not only were few effects found, but a lot of money was spent in the process. The bill for the four income maintenance experiments came to $65 million (D. T. Campbell 1979:80); the EHAP demand experiment cost $31 million (Jackson and Mohr 1986); the Supported Workers Program came out at $82.4 million (Ferber and Hirsch 1982); the total cost of the Rand Health Insurance Study to 1981 was $63 million (Ferber and Hirsch 1982).[8] By comparison, the intervention in the Perry Preschool Project was cheap, costing a mere $747,504 (Barnett 1993:150).

It is difficult to verify claims about the greater expense of well-designed experimental studies, because most evaluations, whether experimental or not, provide little information about costs. An indication of this is that, of the 500 presentations made to the annual meeting of the American Evaluation Association in 1986, only two collected any data on costs (Levin 1987). In one set of studies of career education programmes which did provide 'hard' data, the shift from co-variance analysis to randomised testing as a research design increased the evaluation budget by less than 1 per cent (Boruch 1975:111). In another educational study, of a high school physics programme (see below), carrying out a national randomised field study cost less than $10,000 more than a local non-randomised investigation would have done (Welch et al. 1969). As Levin (1987) argues, competent cost–benefit analysis may be particularly important in estimating the value of social programmes when effect sizes are small, because even small effects may have relatively large benefits in relation to costs. Especially when the cost of the routine service is high (for example, imprisonment or health care), any experiment which demonstrates even small percentage cost savings adds up to the saving of a great deal of money overall (Berk et al. 1985).

The figures for the total costs of the American experiments include payments to individuals, many of which would have been made in a similar form if the experiment had not been conducted. Thus, in the New Jersey–Pennsylvania NIT experiment, payments made up $2.4 million of the total cost of $7.8 million; of the $160 million total bill for the housing experiments, some $80 million consisted of payments to families, which would have been made under existing federal statutes anyway; in the Rand Health Insurance Study, payments made up $14.7 million out of the total of $63 million (Ferber and Hirsch 1982). As Riecken and Boruch note, there is no intrinsic logic to the argument that social experiments should be cheaper than those in medicine and physical science (which may incur considerable costs). It is 'unwise public policy to save dollars at the risk of having to rely upon undependable knowledge' (Riecken and Boruch 1974:38). The 'institutional learning' which occurs as part of the experimental process may independently produce important cost savings. One example from the housing experiments is that data collected during the course of these were used by HUD to reset fees paid to local housing authorities at 8.5 per cent of fair market rents rather than the 10 per cent they had been getting; this added up to a saving of $25 million per year. A direct result of the income experiments was the system of monthly retrospective reporting, which subsequent research showed to reduce the administrative costs of welfare offices by 4 per cent. Extrapolated to the national level, this saving would have amounted to nearly $300 million per year, which would in turn mean that the income experiments would have paid for themselves in less than three months (Aaron 1981).

The challenge of multi-disciplinary research

On the surface, most of the American experiments involved a range of social science expertise. In practice, however, most were dominated by economists (Haveman 1987). The sociologists in the experiments felt somewhat alienated. They and the social psychologists occupied a peripheral position; the economists who designed the experiments had a very low regard for the sociologists' skills and potential input; they would have preferred not to have them on board at all (Rossi and Lyall 1976:170–1).

This neglect of sociological input was all the more serious because none of the economists had any experience of conducting experiments in field settings, whereas some of the sociologists and social psychologists did. Some of the data analysis problems might have been avoided with a greater and earlier involvement of sociologists; these included the tendency to treat social groups as homogeneous and stereotyped cultures. Lee Rainwater, a sociologist who had done important interview studies with American families, later complained that the NIT experiments almost totally neglected the study of social behaviour (Rainwater 1987). As one of the evaluators in the housing allowances project noted, 'The point is that policy depends not only on simple outcomes but on the much richer stories that explain and describe these outcomes in terms of the motivations and perceptions involved' (Kennedy 1983:54). In the housing experiments, many such (unanticipated) stories emerged about the collusion between tenants and landlords which developed as people strove artificially to raise their allowance payments by demonstrating increased rents and sharing the additional allowance payments with their landlords (Aaron 1981:82).

One very important result of the intellectual domination by economists was the emphasis on a narrow range of outcomes. Social interventions of the kind trialled in the American experiments have the potential to affect many interrelated aspects of people's lives, including physical and mental health, material resources, social support, relationships, living arrangements, reproduction, service use, educational achievement and occupational behaviour. Although it was agreed formally that the NIT experiments would include some outcomes aside from labour supply responses, such as health status and work satisfaction, economists regarded others, such as family relationships and alienation, as frankly ridiculous (Rossi and Lyall 1976:171), and in practice a very restricted range of outcome data was collected in most of the experiments. A notable exception was the Perry Preschool Project, which collected long-term outcome data on an impressive range of outcomes. Some health data were collected in the income experiments, but little prominence was given to these in the analysis. The TARP, LIFE and EHAP studies ignored health altogether (see Connor et al., in press). This was a particularly striking omission in the EHAP study, since there was considerable existing evidence that efforts to improve people's housing would also have an impact on health; in 1962 (some years before the EHAP study was planned) Wilner and colleagues had reviewed forty studies, of which thirty-three had a major focus on some aspect of health; their own study of 'Negro' families in Baltimore carried out in the mid-1950s suggested that moving out of slums into new housing was a major route to health improvement (Wilner et al. 1962).

Gender matters again

The American experiments were driven by particular methodological notions about how social experiments should be done. Use of a relatively rigid applied economics model of social experimentation was allied to a mistrust of 'softer' sociological thinking; both weakened the contribution to knowledge that the experiments were able to make. These are also themes in the story of gendered methodology being told in this book. Historically, 'qualitative' methods have belonged to a research and policy underclass, and have been seen by the dominant 'quantitative' players as inferior routes to understanding.

Evaluation itself was an 'overwhelmingly male' field in the late 1960s, when many of the American experiments were first conceived (House 1993:23). The reliance on a masculinist applied economics infused the experiments with distorting normative ideas about how people live. The main focus of the experiments listed in table 9.1 was men. Where women were included, they were fitted into an analytic framework derived from men's lives, with the classic division between work outside the home and family life inside it. The consequences of this were many. For example, in the New Jersey–Pennsylvania NIT experiment, with its focus on labour supply responses, 'work response' was defined narrowly as 'working' or not and hours worked (Berk and Rossi 1976). Had the concept of 'work' included unpaid domestic labour, the results of the experiment would have been turned on their head, since the apparently greater 'work' disincentive effect for women was related to their domestic 'work' responsibilities in the household. If these 'work' hours had gone into the equation, the effect of guaranteed income would have been to make women work more, not less.

The chief policy concern of most of the evaluators was men as the main 'breadwinners' – as 'heads' of intact nuclear families containing women and children as dependants. The family was implicitly seen as a system of hierarchical power relations. This spectre of the 'normal' nuclear family haunted the experimenters' files as community after community turned out not to have enough of them: it was more normal not to be normal.[9] A significant aspect of the design that slipped their attention was that the model of male-headed, wife-dependent nuclear family life was particularly inappropriate for many of the ethnic minority communities targeted by the experiments. The unanticipated effects of some of the interventions on family breakup also suggested power inequalities at the heart of American family life which seemed to take the investigators entirely by surprise; these constitute an interesting lesson in gender-blindness, because a disposition to favour intact families at any price appears to have prevented some researchers and policy-makers from understanding that channelling more resources to women may enable them to make the positive choice of leaving inhospitable and even violent marriages.[10] This was strange, considering the availability of social science evidence at the time (in the form of 'qualitative' studies) which painted a very unequal picture of American family life. It should not have surprised anyone to discover that more material resources might be liberating for women, or that the incentives offered by such resources had different implications for women's attachment to the labour force, given their extensive caring responsibilities. The trade-off in terms of real-life obligations and what was offered experimentally was simply very different for the women and the men.

Interestingly, Ross, whose proposal for an RCT of a 'graduated work incentive experiment' set off the golden age of evaluation, initially defended the 'primary interest' in intact male-headed families. This was criticized at the time for being discriminatory and biased against female-headed families, which were prominent in the poverty population but excluded from the programme. But Ross later changed her mind when the study findings showed that poverty was particularly, and increasingly, rife in 'incomplete family units' (see H. L. Ross 1970:35–6, 102–3). The implications of the pro-family bias of some of the experiments were serious. For example, it was an implicit assumption that focusing on work-eligible, male-headed families was a sensible evaluation strategy, since such units were likely to be most responsive to the disincentive effects of wage and tax rates. But there was actually no evidence supporting this assumption (Rossi and Lyall 1976). The emphasis on intact families meant that the analysis in the New Jersey–Pennsylvania experiment only included the 690 families which stayed together and completed the study; these represented only 57 per cent (690/1216) of the original sample (Ferber and Hirsch 1982:59).

A significant ill-considered question was who, really, was the focus of the experiments? In the income and housing allowances studies, randomisation was by household or family; but households and families are composed of different individuals, who may well (and did) react in different ways to what appears to be the same 'stimulus'.[11] Underlying the decision to focus on households rather than individuals was a presumption that households are democratic units, and that it makes sense to treat these as stable, integrated entities. In the NIT experiments, it was at least possible to trace effects in terms of the work behaviour of individuals within families. The EHAP study proved more of a methodological nightmare, since the design took no account of the tendency of households to change and dissolve. Other studies showed that households are not stable entities: even over a period of a few years, in the kind of population studied in the research, some 38 per cent of children would leave home, and some 8 per cent of couples would get divorced (Watts 1981:50). The assumption of household democracy was equally problematic. Within households, resources are often not simply 'pooled', and decision-making is not shared. Contemporary studies of family life (see e.g. Komarovsky 1967; Rainwater et al. 1959) showed that, particularly in the population groups studied in the experiments, this was far from being the case.

Setting a trend

The large American experiments were part of a general move towards systematic experiment in the social policy field. Many smaller trials of social interventions were also carried out over this period. In 1974, the report of the American Social Science Research Council Committee on Social Experimentation included an appendix listing forty-six controlled trials of social experiments spanning the fields of crime prevention, legal procedures, mental health, education, communication, fertility control, economics and research utilization (Riecken and Boruch 1974). Two further bibliographies from the same team

(Boruch 1974; Boruch et al. 1978) produced around the same time upped these totals to 109 and 350 (see table 10.1). A separate bibliography of educational experiments published in 1975 yielded a total of ninety-two (Campbell and Boruch 1975). These listings were intended to drive home the point that randomised controlled experiments in the social domain *were* being done. But they also illustrated a lesson learned later in systematic literature searches for health care evaluations, that what one finds is very much a product of how hard one looks. Not all the increases in citations between 1974 and 1978 in table 10.1 are accounted for by new studies done between these years; most were simply the product of looking harder.

While the complexity of some of the national experiments made interpretation difficult, by comparison, some of the studies listed by Boruch and colleagues put to the test hypotheses of attractive simplicity. Is it safe to release people before trial? Do police patrols reduce crime? Does providing therapy in prison prevent further crimes? Do educational programmes for children enhance literacy? Does watching television make people aggressive? Is safety belt education a way to promote safe driving? Do social workers help prevent illness in the elderly? Does including fathers in family therapy make any difference? Some of the experiments included in these lists also have important points to make in relation to some of the objections that followed in the wake of the large national experiments, particularly the argument that the results of trials are unlikely to enter the policy-making process in any straightforward way and the problem of generating findings that appear highly counter-intuitive to those who favour (and/or practise) the intervention under test.

The next section of this chapter looks at some examples of these smaller-scale attempts at experimental ways of knowing about effective policy interventions.

Table 10.1 Bibliographies of 'randomized field experiments': 1974 and 1978

Topic	1974	1978
Crime and delinquency	15	59
Legal procedures	7	11
Mental health rehabilitation	18	26
Education and training	37	97
Sociomedical and fertility control	15	69
Mass communication	6	6
Research methods	11	41
Traffic safety	–	6
Market research	–	4
Social welfare	–	18
Employment	–	13
Total	109	350

Sources: Taken from Boruch 1974; Boruch et al. 1978.

Experimenting with pre-trial release

The Manhattan Bail Bond experiment carried out in New York from 1961 to 1964 provides one example of the 'rational' research–policy relationship. This experiment was set up as a test of the hypothesis that many offenders could safely be released from prison pre-trial without bail. Its genesis was the humanitarian interest shown by a chemical engineer, Louis Schweitzer, in the problems of men imprisoned for many months awaiting trial for charges on which they would often be found innocent; they stayed in prison simply because they could not afford to pay bail. In the Manhattan Bail project, information was collected on prisoners awaiting trial who had not committed homicide or other serious crimes. Half of those considered by the project researchers to be suited to pre-trial release had recommendations along these lines submitted to the judge; the other half (randomly assigned) acted as a control group.[12] The result was that four times as many prisoners in the intervention group as in the control group were recommended for pre-trial release, and less than 1 per cent failed to appear for trial, a lower figure than for the control group (Arcs et al. 1963; Riecken and Boruch 1974).

The Manhattan experiment was followed by others in Washington, Missouri and Iowa, and its findings were quickly reflected in recommendations on pre-trial parole made by the Attorney-General (Botein 1965). A conference held in 1964 resulted in nearly half of all states attacking the bail problem; by 1965 pre-trial release programmes had been set up in eighteen states. Non-bail pre-trial release was extended to all five boroughs in New York City, and bail-free release was also written into the Bail Reform Act of 1966 (Riecken 1975; see also Botein 1965). 'The whole enterprise', noted one group of commentators, 'has been a most notable success' (Gilbert et al. 1975:79).

Patrolling Kansas City

The question of whether policing is effective is a bit like asking whether education or social work or medicine is effective. But, as with these other questions, there are specific aspects of what police do which *can* be put to the test. In the early 1970s a group of researchers at the Police Foundation worked with the Kansas City Police Department to test a common assumption of crime prevention, that the presence of police patrols on the streets deters criminals; the relationship was assumed to be a 'dose response' – the more patrols, the less crime. At the time about $2 billion was spent annually in America on maintaining and equipping patrol forces. The rise in crime and in police spending led criminologists and others to question the wisdom of routine patrolling. The initiative for the trial came from the Kansas City Police Department, which had the reputation for being one of the most progressive in the country. Fifteen patrol districts in Kansas City were divided (matching areas for demographic characteristics) into five groups of three; within each group, one patrol beat was randomly assigned[13] to be *reactive*, *control*, or *proactive*.

In the *reactive* areas, police were instructed only to respond to calls; normal patrolling practice was followed in the *control* areas – a police cruiser was available at all times; in the *proactive* areas, the police presence was increased to two or three times the normal level. The effects of these different practices were monitored by questioning residents, interviewing and observing police, and using police department and court records. The experiment ran for a year in 1972–3. On almost all measures, the data showed an equal incidence of crime in the three areas. The evaluation included interviews with police and people in the community, many of whom expressed the fear that crime would rise – although they also saw the main value of patrolling as creating a sense of security, rather than specifically preventing crime (Kelling et al. 1977).

The contribution of the study to policy was 'to cast grave doubt on the validity of a plausible (and expensive) idea *before* it became policy and also to suggest some rethinking of crime-control methods' (Boruch and Riecken 1975:8). The charge that the study showed the unimportance of the police in preventing crime was a message quickly picked up by the local media and by other researchers. Against this, the study's authors argued that they had shown only that 'the present patrol strategies do not necessarily produce the results many have unquestionably assumed they do in terms of crime prevention and feelings of security' (Kelling et al. 1974:534), and that a study 'which systematically modified levels of routine preventive patrol and which precisely measured the effect of such modifications over an entire year' was preferable to the kind of uncontrolled experimentation that happened in most police departments most of the time (Pate et al. 1975:319). As with many of the experiments, there were those who tried to take the study to pieces in order to call into question the validity of the conclusion that some were drawing – that the police are not as effective as many people think they are. But even its critics admitted that the experiment 'sparked a lively debate in police circles and has prompted others to want to test their own hypotheses' (Larson 1978:474).

Therapy for prisoners

Another policy issue current at the time was rehabilitation programmes for prisoners. These tended to be attacked by the right as over-protective and by the left as violating civil liberties. A trial by Kassebaum and colleagues (1971) in California compared the effectiveness of small- and large-group counselling with no counselling in order to test whether claims as to the effectiveness of 'soft' approaches could be confirmed. What was under test in the Californian study was a group counselling approach, popular in prisons, developed by Norman Fenton. This was based on Carl Rogers's nondirective therapy and certain tenets of Freudian psychology, and proposed that providing warm, supportive relationships with the kinds of authority figures men in prisons had often lacked as children (and which were held responsible for their criminality) would reduce re-offending.

Before doing their study, Kassebaum and colleagues examined the literature to find out what was known about correctional treatment programmes. They located a review by Walter Bailey of 100 studies published between 1940 and 1960; Bailey's (1961) finding was that most studies employed questionable research designs. Sponsored by the Department of Corrections, the Californian study ran for six years. It encountered considerable resistance from stakeholders (members of the parole board), who argued that it was unethical to withhold the treatment from some prisoners. Because some 12,000 inmates and hundreds of staff members were involved in counselling programmes, most people believed these worked, and a considerable amount of money had been invested in them (Kassebaum et al. 1971; D. A. Ward 1973).

The study was carried out at a new medium-security prison for men, California Men's Colony East (CMCE), 'a quadrangular prison comprised of four six-hundred-man units physically separated from each other but all surrounded by a double cyclone fence and eight gun towers' (D. A. Ward 1973:189). The quadrangles were the men's basic sleeping, eating, recreational and social units. In order to gain a sense of what life was like for the men in CMCE, the researchers began with some 'qualitative' interviews, talking to seventy-six randomly selected inmates about their experiences and views of prison life.[14] As the men arrived to fill the prison, they were randomly allocated[15] to the four quadrangles; those in one quadrangle made up the control group, and the others were assigned to different variants of the intervention programme.

The evaluators concentrated on four outcomes: norms about conforming (law-abiding) behaviour, hostility towards staff, violations of prison rules, and rates of return to prison. Data were collected from prison records, questionnaires, interviews, a psychological inventory and observations. The study included a three-year follow-up of around 1,000 men. On none of the study outcomes did the counselled men do better than those assigned to the control group. Indeed, the data suggested that on some scores control group men did better; they were more often employed post-prison than the counselled men, and they were also arrested less frequently and spent less time in prison. The results were regarded as disturbing for the professionals and administrators involved.[16] These findings came hard on the heels of another review of 231 evaluative studies of treatment for offenders which showed that there was very little evidence for *any* of the treatments currently on offer in American prisons having any effect on reducing the chances of repeat offences (Martinson 1970, cited in D. A. Ward 1973). The cumulative results helped those who wished to curtail prison spending on ineffective methods of rehabilitation.

Teaching physics

Although systematic evaluation of educational strategies has a longer history than most, this also means that it began to go out of vogue earlier than in other spheres. However, there remained some evaluators committed to this method in the educational field throughout the golden age.

In 1967–8 an experiment was conducted on the effectiveness of a new high school physics curriculum (Welch et al. 1969; Welch and Walberg 1972). Physics teaching was regarded as stale, and students were uninterested in taking up physics; in the wake of Sputnik, the Physical Science Study Committee in the United States developed a new up-to-date curriculum. Adoption of this in schools did not help the problem, however, as many students found it too difficult. A more popular alternative, Harvard Project Physics, was developed in order to present science as a way of knowing and living and achieving social progress. The evaluation was an unusual experiment in that it took place on the national level, and it was teachers who were randomly assigned their roles – as intervention or control – in the experiment. A random sample of 136 teachers was taken from the national list of physics teachers held by the National Science Teachers' Association. Out of those (124) who could be contacted, seventy-two accepted the invitation to take part in the experiment;[17] transfers, illnesses, etc. meant that the final sample consisted of thirty-four teaching the new curriculum, with nineteen making up the control group. Intervention teachers went on a six-week training course, and control teachers were given a two-day session (a morale-boosting event intended 'to reduce possible Hawthorne effects' (Cronbach 1982:61)).[18] The main outcomes looked at were cognitive performance (understanding) and course satisfaction – what the students felt about the way they had been taught. No difference between the two groups could be shown in cognitive performance, but the students who were taught the new curriculum more often found it enjoyable and an easier way of learning physics. This may, of course, have had something to do with the enthusiasm of the teachers for the new approach.

This contrast between the outcomes points to an important aspect of the way 'success' is measured in both social and medical interventions; it is often assumed that 'real' success equates with 'objective' measures, rather than with the self-reported experiences of intervention participants.[19] The Harvard Project Physics is also a good illustration of another recurrent issue in the experimentation field, which is the publication bias that may result from studies reporting few or no effects being less likely than others to see the light of day. The Harvard Project Physics researchers were unable to secure a publisher for a full-length report because the results seemed so unexciting (Cronbach 1982:60–1). This limited the influence Harvard Project Physics had on science education.

Radio mathematics

Most of the readily available reports of social experiments describe studies carried out in the developed world. The Radio Mathematics Project, established in 1973, investigated the teaching of primary-level mathematics by radio in a developing country. It was carried out in Nicaragua, and jointly sponsored by the Ministry of Public Education there and the United States Agency for International Development. The project radio lessons were broadcast in Spanish by the national radio station, and consisted of 150 thirty–minute lessons which involved children in a high level of activity; the lessons were accompanied by teachers' guides, student worksheets and materials to use before and after the broadcast lessons.

Fifty-four classrooms in the Nicaraguan departments of Masaya, Granada and Carazo took part in the study, with thirty classes assigned[20] to hear the radio lessons, and the others continuing with their usual teacher-provided instruction. The research budget included paying teachers to help with the experiment and training them to do so, and providing radios for the experimental schools (those without electricity were expected to supply their own batteries). Two major interruptions to the programme as planned were failures in power supply and political events which took over radio time. The observations carried out by researchers of control schools' mathematics teaching showed the poor level of educational resourcing prevailing in Nicaragua; there were few teaching aids, and in only one of the twenty-four control classes were textbooks available.

All the students in the Radio Mathematics study were tested before and after the radio teaching programme. Those who were assigned to hearing the radio programmes had on average consistently higher scores – twenty-five percentage points higher – than those who did not, with highest-ability students obtaining the highest scores (Searle et al. 1978; see also Searle et al. 1976).

Help the aged

In the early 1960s Margaret Blenkner and colleagues at the Institute of Welfare Research in New York designed a research study to look at the effectiveness of 'protective services' for older people living in their own homes. The study grew out of a pilot project run by the Community Service Society of New York. Blenkner and colleagues recognized that most evaluative research in social work had been of the *ex post facto* kind; there were few prospective experiments, and those there were often evaluated outcomes by choosing these after the research results were in. 'This is picking the winners after the race is run,' they noted, 'and as such is convincing only to those already convinced.' They saw their study as a 'radical departure' from this tradition, particularly in its use of random allocation of clients to experimental and control groups (Blenkner et al. 1964:6–7). People over sixty living in their own homes in areas of New York served by the Community Service Society were randomised to two experimental programmes with different levels of intensity, and were compared to a standard service control group. Neither of the experimental programmes was more effective than standard services in promoting physical health and survival.

The New York experiment, which was not widely disseminated in the usual social science/social welfare literature,[21] was the spur to a further study undertaken by the same research team, then relocated to the Benjamin Rose Institute in Ohio (Blenkner et al. 1974). In this study 'older people' were defined as aged sixty or over, and those included in the research were people considered to be mentally incapable of looking after themselves and without adequate family or other support. The model for the study was 'controlled clinical trials' in medicine (Blenkner et al. 1974:11). Out of 164 such individuals, seventy-six were randomly assigned to receive the intervention, which lasted a year and consisted of a wide range of services, from medical, psychiatric and legal to domestic and financial. Social workers were involved in providing casework services and in removing people to 'protective' settings when this was considered necessary. The outcomes of interest to Blenkner and colleagues were mental and physical functioning, 'contentment', use of assistance and support, survival and institutionalization; they confidently expected that the intervention would secure an improvement in most, if not all, of these outcomes. However, their expectations were dashed when it was shown that mortality and institutionalization were higher in the intervention group at both one- and three-year follow-ups, and that on the other 'softer' outcomes this group did not do as well as the control group either. Blenkner and colleagues judiciously advised, 'That the service provided . . . might have had a deleterious effect on some is a hypothesis that should be entertained in future research.' In a particularly thought-provoking sentence, they suggested that their data indicated a professional proneness 'to introduce the greatest change in lives least able to bear it' (Blenkner et al. 1974:157–8).

Since these results were so surprising to many who believed that social work was effective, a re-analysis of the original data was carried out by another team of researchers some years later (Dunkle et al. 1983). This showed some problems with the initial design (in which two non-randomly assigned experimental groups had been collapsed into one), but came up with no strong reason why the original findings should be regarded as invalid. The results of the Blenkner study added to others (see the Cambridge–Somerville example in chapter 8) which put a question mark over the intensive casework approach to social work intervention; this would later be confirmed by systematic reviews (see J. Fischer 1973; Macdonald and Sheldon 1992).

A significant footnote to the Blenkner study is that it also directly inspired what is probably the first controlled trial of social work to be carried out in the UK, by Matilda Goldberg and colleagues in London in the late 1960s. The report of the Goldberg study is unusual (for its time) in reviewing earlier relevant studies – six, including Blenkner's, all carried out in the USA and all yielding 'disappointing results' (Goldberg 1970:28).

Like Blenkner, Goldberg studied the effect of intensive casework help for a population of older people, many of whom were isolated and incapacitated.[22] As with Blenkner's study, most hypotheses about the beneficial effects of casework help were not supported by social and medical assessments carried out after ten months of intervention: no differences between intervention and control groups could be found in mortality, illness, self-care and social contacts, and it was only with respect to 'social needs', attitudes, interests, activities and 'consumer reactions' that the intervention group appeared to fare better. In the preface to the book reporting the study, the renowned social policy expert Richard Titmuss attached great value to these latter findings. He also noted a scepticism, which he held in common with much of the UK social policy community then and now, about the value of systematic experimentation (Titmuss 1970:15).

The power to tell the truth

One major result of the American experiments was to demonstrate over and over again how much easier it is to interpret the outcomes of experiments evaluated with control groups than those produced by uncontrolled evaluations. The comparative value of different research designs is most obvious in those experiments, such as the EHAP study, the Supported Workers Program, the Perry Preschool Project, and the Rand Health Insurance research, in which RCTs sat alongside pre–post designs. The weaknesses of the causal inferences about the effectiveness of early childhood interventions that could be drawn from non-RCT designs were particularly clear when the findings from Head Start and Follow Through were compared with those from the Perry Preschool Project. Both Head Start and Follow Through suffered from not using an RCT design. Intervention children were either followed on a pre- and post-test basis, or they were compared with other children 'matched' on several variables, although not, significantly, social background. Complex statistical procedures were used to try to get over the fact that what had happened to Head Start and Follow Through children was being compared with the situation of other children who were more advantaged to start with, but these procedures did not yield dependable results (see Campbell and Boruch 1975; Cicirelli 1977; J. W. Evans 1977; Levin 1978; McDill et al. 1972; Saxe and Fine 1981; Williams and Evans 1972). A major methodological moral abstracted from the American experiments was thus that 'Results can always be improved by omitting controls' (Muench, quoted in Light 1983:15).

Peter Rossi has condensed much of this learning experience about social experimentation into a set of 'laws' which, following the nineteenth-century fondness for taxonomy, he named after metallic substances of varying durability. The 'Iron' law of evaluation states that the expected value of any net impact of a large-scale social programme will be zero or close to zero. The second, 'stainless steel' law specifies that the more technically rigorous the evaluation, the more likely it is to show zero effects. The 'brass' and 'zinc' laws refer to the effect of social programmes in changing individual behaviour (low) and the tendency for only those programmes which are likely to fail to be evaluated; this, says Rossi, is the most optimistic of all the laws, since it highlights the fact that there *are* effective programmes, although we may not always (or often) know about them (Rossi 1987).

One way of learning methodological and other lessons is to look at individual studies; another is to put different studies together and examine what can be concluded, both about the state of evaluation in that field and about the quality of the evidence for and against different approaches. As experience with the experimental method applied to social topics accumulated in the United States, analyses began to be published which provided some handle on both these issues. The bibliography by Boruch and colleagues published in 1978 listed thirty-five such reviews in crime and delinquency, legal procedures, traffic safety, mental health, education, mass communication and research methods.

The aim of collecting studies together is research synthesis: putting different studies in the pot together and looking at what comes out. Some research synthesis proceeds to meta-analysis, when data from different studies are combined; the larger sample sizes produce more reliable estimates of effect. In the 1980s and 1990s this approach became popular in the medical field, but, like other aspects of experimental ways of knowing, research synthesis actually began life as a social science procedure. The use of quantitative procedures in integrative reviews was recommended by Gene Glass and his colleagues in the 1970s (Glass 1976; see also Glass et al. 1981). Their review of the effectiveness of psychotherapy (Smith and Glass 1977) attracted much attention in the psychology field. It would not have seemed strange reading to the researchers responsible for the study of counselling in that California prison. The work of Glass and his colleagues made it clear that most traditional literature reviews are not systematic, and that this matters. For example, they found more than 475 studies of the effects of psychotherapy, yet most literature reviews look at small numbers of studies, often fewer than forty. That they reach conflicting conclusions about the benefits of psychotherapy on this basis is hardly surprising (Smith and Glass 1977).

Methods of reviewing literature were also put under the microscope by social scientists wanting to improve the reliability of research methods. Cooper and Rosenthal (1980) compared the methods that university staff and students 'normally' use to assess papers with systematic 'statistical combinatorial procedures'. There were statistically significant differences between 'descriptive' and 'statistical' reviewers in the conclusions reached about seven papers on sex differences in task persistence ('statistical' reviewers were more likely to find a sex difference). These issues of differences in review methods and the selective nature of many literature reviews apply across all research fields, not just to experimental methods. They explain many apparent inconsistencies and contradictions between the accounts of knowledge given by different people (see also Light and Pillemer 1984).

One objective of research synthesis is to assess the quality of the research that has been done. The main messages that most of the reviews in the social intervention field in the USA came up with were that: many social interventions had not been evaluated at all; of those which had, most evaluations had failed to consider impact; of those which did, many were too poorly designed and/or too small in size to be expected to address the question of effectiveness; and where there were findings that did stand up, comparisons of well-designed and poorly-designed evaluations generally yielded the conclusion that effect sizes are reduced with stronger design. For example, Charles Logan's review of evaluation research in crime and delinquency, published in 1972,

Table 10.2 Research design and effectiveness claimed: two examples from delinquency and crime prevention research

| | Intervention | |
	'successful' (%)	'not successful' (%)
a) Logan 1972[a]		
Random control groups	27	73
Non-random control groups	50	50
No control groups	69	31
b) Wright and Dixon 1977[b]		
Random/matched control groups	25	75
Other control groups	51	49

[a] Based on 100 studies.
[b] Based on 96 studies.

analysed 100 studies, of which 26 per cent used an RCT design, 16 per cent had non-random control groups, and the rest had no control groups, at all. 'High' or 'good' success was claimed for 69 per cent of the studies without control groups, for 50 per cent of those with non-random control groups, and 27 per cent of RCTs (Logan 1972). A few years later William Wright and Michael Dixon (1977) reduced 6,000 abstracts of delinquency prevention and treatment interventions published before 1974 to ninety-six studies addressing effectiveness. Of those studies giving information about group assignment, 25 per cent using random or matched assignment reported only positive outcomes; this compared with 51 per cent of those using some other form of assignment (see table 10.2).

The results were very similar in a more broadly based look at the social programme evaluation literature carried out by Mark Lipsey and colleagues in 1985. They analysed a random sample of 175 studies reporting evaluations of any 'distinct program or policy designed and implemented to accomplish some social purpose' and presenting 'a more or less systematic assessment of at least some of the accomplishments of that program' (Lipsey et al. 1985:12). Of the 175 studies, 19 per cent were randomised experiments, 39 per cent were quasi-experiments (regression discontinuity or time series analyses, or experiments with non-equivalent comparison groups); the remainder were pre–post comparisons without control groups or had used some other non-experimental design. Methodological problems with many of the studies led Lipsey and colleagues to deem evaluation more of an art than a science. Particular problems were low statistical power (more than 90 per cent of the studies were unable to detect relatively modest effects which may have been humanly important), poorly specified outcome measures and inadequate information about what was done to whom – for example, 25 per cent failed to say how many people received the intervention, and 72 per cent were unclear about what the intervention was. Estimated effect size was also significantly greater in the non-randomised studies. In the course of this early research synthesis work, the conclusion later established in the medical field became clear: that there are significant differences between published and unpublished literature in the effects claimed for social interventions. In general, the two sources have 'opposite average effects', with published studies more often finding positive effects and unpublished studies being more likely to report negative ones or to find no difference (Glass et al. 1981; Rosenthal 1979; M. L. Smith 1980).

Another study of the way evaluation was done was funded by the Russell Sage Foundation and undertaken by Ilene Bernstein and Howard Freeman (1975). Their focus was 416 evaluations in progress sponsored by federal agencies. The review confirmed the tendency of evaluation to sideline sociologists; most projects were led by economists or psychologists (40 per cent); sociologists headed 12 per cent, and educationalists 11 per cent (Bernstein and Freeman 1975:45). As to evaluation quality, the main finding was that fewer than one in five evaluations followed 'accepted' procedures with respect to sampling, design and data analysis; many did not assess impact.[23] Most of the impact studies (67 per cent) did not use a randomised control group design. RCTs were particularly likely to be carried out for projects that lasted longer than eighteen months, were given to university evaluators who defined their major audiences as other researchers, and where evaluators and programme implementers had a degree of independence. Bernstein and Freeman conclude:

> From the standpoint of research quality, there is an obvious solution for improving evaluation research: have all studies undertaken in academic research centers, by PhD psychology professors . . . include a commitment that the research results much be published in refereed social science journals, provide funds only as grants and have them awarded on the basis of peer-review committee judgments, allow a time period of from three to five years for the planning and conduct of the research, have the grants monitored by federal officials with a high degree of social-science graduate training . . . and insist on the research being undertaken in collaboration with the action agency. *(Bernstein and Freeman 1975:135)*

Interestingly, much the same conclusions were reached by a UK study of the dissemination of public health research carried out twenty years later. The most successfully disseminated research had university involvement and investigators working in a stable, professionally supported environment (Gray et al. 1995).

Institutional location and political factors affect not only the design of evaluation studies, but the 'findings' they are claimed to generate. In a third review, Gordon and Morse (1975) looked for evaluation studies published between 1969 and 1973. Of the ninety-six they found, 76 per cent examined effectiveness. When the programme evaluator was organizationally affiliated to the programme being evaluated, the claimed 'success' rate was 58 per cent. This compared with 14 per cent for programmes where there was no such relationship between the evaluator and the programme ('failure' rates were 14 per cent and 29 per cent respectively).

The politics of research

All research is done in a political context. Research agendas are partly set by the priority attached to particular policy issues or solutions; what is fundable in one era may not be so in another. Likewise, research findings are not launched into a political vacuum. This is one reason why few are uncontentious, and why other kinds of explanations are required to answer the question of why some research findings get taken up with enthusiasm while others fall on deaf ears. It is clear from the American experience that the political will which encouraged use of experimental methods in policy evaluation was largely the *same* political will which placed many of the interventions under test at the top of the policy agenda. Policy-makers promoted evaluation of the programmes they wanted to see happen, not those they would rather not encourage. This had two consequences, one short-term, one long-term. In the short term, it strengthened the tendency for policy-makers to act in advance of the results of the experiments. The American experience suggests that RCTs of policy programmes are most appropriate when policy-makers are genuinely interested in the programme under test, when there is real uncertainty about how it works, and people are willing to wait for the results (Nathan 1988).

A well-known demonstration of the political bias which often greets research findings comes from the medical domain. It is Archie Cochrane's presentation of a trial of community versus hospital treatment for heart attack victims. Cochrane gave the data to a medical audience as showing a disadvantage for patients treated in the community by GPs; his medical colleagues responded by saying that the trial must be stopped at once, and that community treatment should be discontinued in favour of hospital coronary care units for all patients. Cochrane then explained that he had deceived his audience, and that the results were actually the other way round: it was better to be treated at home. The clinicians did not subsequently campaign for hospital treatment to be discontinued (Cochrane 1989).

Sometimes it is easy to see why a discredited intervention is continued – it serves some useful end so far as key stakeholders are concerned. Again, medicine provides multiple examples. One of these is the practice of electronic monitoring of the baby's heart (EFM) during labour, which began in the UK and the USA sometime in the 1960s. This replaces the traditional method of listening to the baby's heart through a stethoscope placed on the mother's abdomen with electronic monitoring by means of an electrode placed on its scalp. By the early 1970s, EFM was used routinely in some European and American hospitals (Wagner 1994). As with other such technologies, systematic evaluation was not carried out before the practice came into routine use,

but instead followed afterwards. By 1986 the results of six RCTs of electronic
monitoring compared with the traditional practice of listening to the baby's
heart with a wooden stethoscope had been published. Collectively, researchers
were unable to detect any difference in measures of babies' health or risk of
death with electronic monitoring. One trial, carried out in Dublin, reported
fewer seizures (fits) in new-born babies, although no effect on cerebral palsy
was detected. All six trials found higher rates of operative delivery and maternal infections after birth in the electronically monitored group – consequences
with implications of considerable pain and distress for mothers. 'One might
expect', ventured one reviewer of these findings, 'that the lack of evidence of
clear benefit would influence clinicians and hospital administrators to rely less
on EFM than they now do' (Simkin 1987:219). But, on the contrary, use of
EFM continued to rise. The reasons emerging from discussions with doctors
and midwives included the following: the financial interests of the manufacturing companies and the stockholders who vigorously promoted use of their
technology; freedom for staff, who felt more able to leave women alone in
labour; disagreement with the way the studies were done;[24] the objection that
in skilled hands EFM *must* work; and appeal to the possibility of legal action if
health care providers could not demonstrate that every available technology
had been used (regardless of whether safety and effectiveness had been established) (Keirse 1987; Simkin 1987) (see also chapter 11).[25]

People may say that they believe in the usefulness of research, but in practice make rather little use of it. A survey carried out in the late 1970s by
Nathan Caplan at the University of Michigan's Institute for Social Research
asked 204 civil servants their opinion of research findings. While most had a
very positive attitude to the potential policy contribution of social science
research, few could cite documented instances in which they had *actually used*
research, whereas almost half could recall occasions on which they purposely
disregarded or rejected relevant research findings in reaching policy decisions
(cited in Rein and White 1978). In 1980 Leviton and Boruch looked at a
sample of evaluation studies in education sponsored by the Office of Education
and other federal agencies; through painstaking detective work they tracked
pathways of influence which added up to 'numerous contributions [of evalua-
tion] to law, regulation, management and budgets' (Leviton and Boruch
1983:586). Whereas policy-makers sometimes found it difficult to point to
instances of decisions founded on research evidence, many were in no doubt
that research findings and ideas provided by research permeated their work
generally (Weiss 1991). These studies are part of a vast literature on the
'irrationality' of the research–policy relationship (see e.g. Bulmer 1986; Finch
1986; Heller 1986; Wagner et al. 1991a).

Shooting the messenger

When research fails to produce the findings people expect, a number of different things can happen. People may face up to the implications of the new

knowledge and adjust policies accordingly. Alternatively, it may be decided that the findings cannot be trusted – that there is something wrong with the evaluation method used. This was the dominant response to the so-called failure of the national experiments in America to deliver the findings that people wanted. What followed was a retreat in some circles to other methods of evaluation. As Weiss puts it: 'If evaluation was showing minimal effects for programs that many people believed were doing good, then there must be something wrong with the evaluations' (1987:43). This move away from systematic evaluation had already happened before, in the field of educational research,[26] and there are many individual examples of people finding research results unpalatable and dismissing them on the grounds of faulty method.[27]

A major outcome of the national experiments in the USA carried out from the 1960s to the 1980s was a revisionist school of evaluation methodology which dissected the methodological procedures of randomised experiments on the grounds that they could not be expected to show anything worthwhile anyway. Some proponents of this school were 'reformed number crunchers . . . reborn as qualitative researchers' (Rossi 1987:8); others, such as Robert Stake (1981), came from the ethnographic/qualitative stable in the first place, and welcomed the disenchantment being expressed with quantitative/experimental methods as liberating them and their preferred methods from an inferior place in the evaluation hierarchy. Prime advocates of the 'alternative paradigm' position in the American literature were Michael Patton (1980) and Egon Guba (Guba and Lincoln 1981). Lee Cronbach, an applied psychologist who trained with Ralph Tyler, a 'qualitative' evaluator in the 1930s, also reacted adversely to the direction that evaluation research was taking. Cronbach's career started early: he took the Stanford–Binet IQ test at age four with startling results, and graduated from university at eighteen with dual majors in mathematics and chemistry. He subsequently trained as a teacher, and worked on measurement theory in education (see Shadish et al. 1991:324–5). Starting out as an enthusiastic supporter of systematic social experimentation, he came to feel that the stress on randomised controlled studies was creating an 'unacceptable imbalance'. He set up the short-lived Stanford Evaluation Consortium in 1974 to combat the 'Fisherian model of narrowly-targeted stand-alone studies' and proposed an alternative route which would downplay the role of impact assessment and 'formal quantitative comparisons' (Cronbach 1982:xii–xiii, 19).[28]

Carol Weiss also changed her mind about the role which systematic experimentation could play in the policy-making process, urging social scientists to study social problems more directly (Weiss 1973; see Shadish et al. 1991:290–7). As a consequence of these changed positions, the dominance of quantitative methods came increasingly under attack in evaluation research during the 1970s and 1980s (T. D. Cook 1997; Jessor et al. 1996). As one of the attackers put it, 'The blanket acceptance of the quantitative paradigm as *the* model for evaluation research is being seriously questioned by the evaluation research community. This questioning has given rise to a changing climate' (Filstead 1979:39). A fashion mounted for qualitative evaluations which would take as their starting-point the experiences of the people at the receiving end of social interventions. There would be less of an attempt to measure impact. The notion of 'cause' itself became less interesting; post-modernism replaced the idea of the universe as knowable, as made up of discoverable, law-like processes, with an altogether more fluid and subjective set of ideas (Cronbach 1982). However, and significantly, it was noted that these 'alternative' evaluations would lack credibility in important places (Weiss 1987).

Conclusion

J. S. Mill, whose vision of social science uncompromisingly equated it with an *inability* to experiment, would undoubtedly have been most surprised to have found social science thus imitating its laboratory cousins; Florence Nightingale, pragmatic mistress of social problems that she was, would surely have welcomed the American experiments as healthy signs of a move towards evidence-based social policy; Beatrice Webb would probably have been rather overwhelmed by the translation of her 'society is the great experimenter' line into such major government-funded practice as was demonstrated during the golden age in the United States; Herbert Spencer and the grand evolutionary schemers of sociology might well have been rather disapproving, and it is certainly highly doubtful whether Comte would have seen his 'positivism' as extending thus far; those in America itself, such as Chapin and Greenwood and the Columbia school of quantitative sociology, who had most clearly foreshadowed the inclusion of systematic experimentation in the armoury of social science, and before them the great social mathematicians of continental Europe – Condorcet, Laplace and Quételet – would surely have rubbed their hands sore with glee; even further back, we can only guess at how Cartesian dualism and Baconian science might have related to this unique spectre of governments carrying out scientific experiments with social interventions, thus apparently throwing into confusion the boundaries of the two worlds of manipulable physical objects and conscious human experience.

From today's vantage-point, it is certainly possible to say that the primary lesson of the American experience is that rigorous evaluations of public policy and other social interventions *can* be done, but there are many respects in which they could have been done better than they were. A more broadly based social science approach, more ethnographic and process data, the testing of simpler interventions, and more attention to the expectations of the groups studied, particularly in relation to study design, would all have improved the capacity of the experiments to illuminate important policy questions. Since many of the programmes tested were far-reaching in their potential impact, more use of multiple outcomes would have increased their value. A particular missed opportunity concerns those experiments which did collect information on outcomes spanning the welfare, health and education fields, but did not report these data in detail, if at all.

No research method works quite as smoothly in practice as it does in text-

books, but there seems to be a particular impetus to reduce the real-life complications of systematic social experimentation to a simple message: *it does not
work*. The same conclusions are not drawn from reports of large-scale quantitative surveys, which just as often encounter problems (for example, attrition,
and/or unanswered or misunderstood questions), or for research designs which
focus on the collection of 'qualitative' data and can present severe challenges of
credibility (as we saw in chapter 3). It is impossible to understand why so
much 'irrational' disapprobation is exhibited towards experimental social research without also understanding the whole story of the gendering of methodology. This includes the political contexts which have 'contaminated' the
reputation of experimental research. That is one of the main arguments of this
book. The next chapter continues it, by looking at the fate of people who have
taken part in medical and social experiments.

11

The Rights of Animals and Other Creatures

A somewhat related political consideration is that frequently the prospect of experimentation . . . conjures up thoughts of Frankenstein's monster, inhuman physicians in concentration camps, and the Antivivisection League.
                                    Stanley, 'Controlled field experiments'

From the cultural feminist viewpoint, the domination of nature rooted in postmedieval, Western, male psychology, is the underlying cause of the mistreatment of animals as well as of the exploitation of women and the environment.
                                    Donovan, 'Animal rights and feminist theory'

Modern attitudes to experimental ways of knowing form part of the paradigm war described in chapter 2. In the social research community particularly, there are many who reject experimental methods on the grounds that there is something *inherently* objectionable about these. It is clear from such positions that the experimental method has come with a lot of ideological baggage. It is this baggage which helps to explain both current and past resistances to it. Ernest Greenwood, one of the pioneers of experimental sociology, called it 'this guinea pig complex'. He identified the main 'stumbling block' as lying in 'subjective and emotional elements' (1945:95).

This chapter examines the basis of some continuing resistances to experimental research design. One such resistance is rooted in the association that exists between the word 'experimentation' and the kinds of unethical and unscientific experiments that have been conducted in the name of eugenics. Experimental ways of knowing have suffered from this link; they have also, by extension, been tarnished with the general brush of the Nazi connection. Beyond these particular associations lies the grounding of an 'objective' social science in German methodology explored in chapter 8. A second unsavoury link is with vivisection, the use of animals in experiments. Thirdly, as regards gender – a major sub-theme of the story being told in this book – the historical gendering of method-ology has tended to align women with 'qualitative' research; in the same breath it has also opposed them to experimentation. This case is supported by exam-ples of women being especially maltreated as objects of experimental research.

One woman's story

Figure 11.1 shows the *Observer* headline which drew attention to the story of Evelyn Thomas, a university lecturer in biology, who had a mastectomy for

Evelyn Thomas (right) was not told she was part of an experiment on different treatments for breast cancer.
ADAM RAPHAEL examines the medical ethics of tests on patients without their informed consent.

How doctors' secret trials abused me

Figure 11.1 The troubling issue of consent.
From the *Observer*, 9 October 1988; reproduced by permission, The Observer ©.

breast cancer in 1982 at King's College Hospital in London. A few days after her operation, her suspicions were aroused when a woman with breast cancer in the next bed to hers was visited by a counsellor, while she herself was offered a breast prosthesis by 'a male fitter more used to fitting artificial limbs' (*Observer*, 9 October 1988). This episode was the beginning of extensive detective work on Evelyn Thomas's part, leading finally to the acknowledgement by the hospital that she had been entered into two controlled trials without her knowledge. One was of counselling and post-operative adjustment; those randomised to the no-counselling group were not told about the study. The second trial that Evelyn Thomas was unknowingly involved in compared the relatively new drug tamoxifen with standard chemotherapy. The researchers in this trial had argued against informed consent as causing unnecessary distress. In a piece published in the *British Medical Journal* in 1989, the researchers defended this decision, arguing that Evelyn Thomas had in fact been randomised to the group shown in a subsequent report published seven years after the study started to have been the best option (Baum et al. 1989).

Evelyn Thomas's experiences were published initially and anonymously in a journal concerned with medical ethics. The article was preceded by an editorial 'depicting the perpetrators as being equivalent to Nazi war criminals and the patient to a survivor of Auschwitz' (see Baum et al. 1989:251).

Nazi experimentation and the Nuremberg Code

It was the Nuremberg military tribunals held in Germany in 1946, in the aftermath of the Second World War, which first exposed many people to information about medical experiments that violated human rights. According to evidence presented at the tribunals, up to 200 German doctors had performed criminal experiments on both civilians and prisoners of war, as a result of which many people died (Nicholson 1986:3). The subsequent judgement of the tribunal, which became known as the Nuremberg Code, stated plainly that the voluntary consent of 'the human subject' is an essential prerequisite for all research. This was the first of many codes laying down principles of ethical research conduct; it formed the basis for the well-known Declaration of Helsinki in 1964 (see figure 11.2).

German National Socialism extolled eugenic and racist ideals, and these elements of its philosophy were linked into a world-wide eugenic movement which was particularly strong in Britain. During the 1920s and 1930s, before the true horrors of German National Socialism became known, R. A. Fisher, of random allocation fame, was an active and committed eugenist. At Cambridge as an undergraduate, where he founded a local branch of the eugenics society, he was a 'romantic and enthusiastic elitist' (Mazumdar 1992:102). He thought eugenists were cleverer, more beautiful and more scientific than other people (Fisher 1913–14). Fisher later worked on a bibliography of eugenics for the society, and was a member of its research committee from 1923, in which capacity he took part in a long-running, vituperative debate about a study of

1. Biomedical research involving human subjects must conform to generally accepted scientific principles and should be based on adequately performed laboratory and animal experimentation and on a thorough knowledge of the scientific literature.

2. The design and performance of each experimental procedure involving human subjects should be clearly formulated in an experimental protocol which should be transmitted to a specially appointed, independent committee for consideration, comment and guidance.

3. Biomedical research involving human subjects should be conducted only by scientifically qualified persons and under the supervision of a clinically competent medical person. The responsibility for the human subject must always rest with the medically qualified person and never rest on the subject of the research, even though the subject has given his or her consent.

4. Biomedical research involving human subjects cannot legitimately be carried out unless the importance of the objectives is in proportion to the inherent risk to the subject.

5. Every biomedical research project involving human subjects should be preceded by careful assessment of predictable risks in comparison with foreseeable benefits to the subject or to others. Concern for the interests of the subject must always prevail over the interests of science and society.

6. The right of the research subject to safeguard his or her integrity must always be respected. Every precaution should be taken to respect the privacy of the subject and to minimize the impact of the study on the subject's physical and mental integrity and on the personality of the subject.

7. Physicians should abstain from engaging in research projects involving human subjects unless they are satisfied that the hazards involved are believed to be predictable. Physicians should cease any investigation if the hazards are found to outweigh the potential benefits.

8. In publication of the results of his or her research, the physician is obliged to preserve the accuracy of the results. Reports of experimentation not in accordance with the principles laid down in this Declaration should not be accepted for publication.

9. In any research on human beings, each potential subject must be adequately informed of the aims, methods, anticipated benefits and potential hazards of the study and the discomfort it may entail; he or she should be informed that he or she is at liberty to abstain from participation in the study and that he or she is free to withdraw his or her consent to participation at any time. The physician should then obtain the subject's freely-given informed consent, preferably in writing.

10. When obtaining informed consent for the research project, the physician should be particularly cautious if the subject is in a dependent relationship to him or her or may consent under duress. In that case the informed consent should be obtained by a physician who is not engaged in the investigation and who is completely independent of this official relationship.

11. In case of legal incompetence, informed consent should be obtained from the legal guardian in accordance with national legislation. Where physical or mental incapacity makes it impossible to obtain informed consent, or when the subject is a minor, permission from the responsible relative replaces that of the subject in accordance with national legislation.

Whenever the minor child is in fact able to give a consent, the minor's consent must be obtained in addition to the consent of the minor's legal guardian.

12. The research protocol should always contain a statement of the ethical considerations involved and should indicate that the principles enunciated in the present Declaration are complied with.

Figure 11.2 Declaration of Helsinki: the international code of ethics for biomedical research. 10th World Medical Assembly 1964, revised 35th World Medical Assembly, Venice 1983.

social problem families in the East End started by E. J. Lidbetter, secretary to the research committee, in 1910 (see chapter 7). The study lacked a control group, which Fisher argued was necessary in order to take account of both biological and environmental variation: only thus might any reliable conclusions be drawn. In this way, eugenic disputes about the role of nurture and its interactions with nature lie at the heart of the history of the experimental method as it developed within medicine.

Of course, the Nazi experiments were not experiments in the sense of well-designed studies with control groups and consenting, informed research participants. But it is the connotations of the term 'experiment' – doing invasive and painful things to people's bodies without their consent – that are the issue here. Many eugenists were interested in eliminating the 'unfit' from society, either by preventing their births through selective sterilization or by killing them directly. The gas chambers used to kill Jews in Germany were originally built to gas unfit Germans; by mid-1941, some 50,000 Germans had met their deaths this way (Sharf 1964). Germany's sterilization law of 1933 was modelled on existing American legislation; the *Eugenics Review* in England published a translation of the German law, whose measures were widely supported by British eugenists (G. Jones 1986). However, British eugenists did not take the same view as the Nazis. In 1952, C. P. Blacker, a psychiatrist and secretary of the Eugenics Society from 1931 to 1952, told the society that during the Nuremberg tribunals he had been sent information about medical experiments carried out in the 1940s on living humans to find a cheap and quick method of sterilization; he had made it clear, he said, not only that British eugenists would not countenance this kind of research, but that it was 'unscientific' (Blacker 1952). None the less, the link between eugenics as a social movement and Nazi experimentation was an association from which it never recovered; in Britain, the Eugenics Society, significantly, tried to recover its reputation by sponsoring some of the first work on class inequalities in health (see Oakley 1996).

Animal liberation

Another phenomenon called up by the notion of 'experimentation' involves animals; the main referent here is the exploitative use of these in scientific research. Feminist writing on science makes particular use of the 'evidence' about animal experimentation to condemn the use of experimental methods (see e.g. H. Rose 1994:86–8). However, the allegation that experimentation is such an unpleasant procedure that it is akin to vivisection (even when no animals are involved) appears much earlier. Stuart Chapin, American pioneer of experimental sociology, referred to antivivisectionism in his discussion of obstacles to systematic social experiments in 1947: 'The line between permissible and forbidden subjects of experimentation is not sharply drawn,' Chapin commented. 'Even for worthy scientific ends, when it affects the lives of higher animals, experimentation is censured. In fact, there is now systematic opposition in the form of an organization of antivivisectionists' (F. S. Chapin 1947:5).[1]

In the nineteenth century and before, experimentation on live animals lay at the centre of medicine's claim to be scientific, identifying it thoroughly as a discipline that would not achieve knowledge merely through passive observation. This was part of its professionalizing agenda, a process designed to establish medicine as equal in status to the natural sciences. Physiologist Claude Bernard, who advocated active experimentation as the basis of a newly scientific medicine (see chapter 7), saw vivisection as a pathway which would enable 'men' to gain the power to control and change the process of life itself (Rupke 1987a). He argued that medicine required animal experimentation in order to make it scientific. Like others before him, Bernard envisaged the whole of nature as a woman who had to be subdued, stripped naked and probed by the experimenter in order for the secrets of life to be revealed. By the end of the nineteenth century, experimental physiology centred on the quantitative measurements of the laboratory had become the pre-eminent approach to nature (H. Rose 1995).

Physiologists used vivisection (the word comes from the Latin *vivus*, 'alive', and *secare*, 'to cut') to claim an equal professional status with the older sciences of physics and chemistry. Surgeons, in particular, had a difficult time raising their trade from its original lowly status as a manual occupation (the 'barber-surgeons'); learning from animal experiments provided a useful tool for claiming professional authority. Animals were not assigned any right to life, and were experimented on without anaesthetic. Descartes took the view that animals' bodies, like those of humans, could be regarded as machines, though animals differed from humans in lacking any non-corporeal principle. In this sense, Cartesian 'objectivism' established a theoretical justification for animal abuse (Donovan 1990). Sympathy for the plight of animals subjected to cruelty emerged slowly in the nineteenth century, much helped by the publication in 1877 of Anna Sewell's famous children's novel *Black Beauty*, which used the 'qualitative device' of a first-person narrative – the book is the 'autobiography' of a horse – to drive home the lesson that animals are sentient beings too.

As Peter Singer notes in his book *Animal Liberation* (1976), the concept of 'animal liberation' may sound like parody. Indeed, ideas about animal rights *were* once used to ridicule arguments about women's rights. Mary Wollstonecraft's pioneering *Vindication of the Rights of Woman*, published in 1792, was quickly followed by an anonymous publication called *Vindication of the Rights of Brutes*. The author, a Cambridge philosopher called Thomas Taylor, argued that it was just as absurd to claim that animals had rights as to suppose that women should have them; since the argument applied to animals was obviously absurd, so also must be the idea of women's rights. This is one of a number of critical historical links between feminism and antivivisection. In the first place, vivisection was a thoroughly male practice: until 1876, the date of the first British law regulating vivisection, women were not allowed to train as doctors. Men practised vivisection not only in the laboratory or the hospital, but in the home. The physician Marshall Hall set aside part of his home as a laboratory, keeping mice, hedgehogs, bats, birds, fishes, frogs, toads and snakes there (Manuel 1987). The wife of physiologist Claude Bernard was so upset by his habit of mutilating dogs in their kitchen that she set up an asylum for stray animals in Paris (E. S. Turner 1992). John Burdon Sanderson, first professor of physiology at Oxford University, kept a laboratory in a backroom of his elegant Bloomsbury house, despite privileged access to most of the laboratory space in London (see Kean 1998); and *his* estranged wife left her estate to animal homes (H. Rose 1994:87).

Secondly, in late Victorian society, direct links were made between scientists' violence to animals and men's violence to women (Kean 1998; H. Rose 1994). Jack the Ripper, who was responsible for the serial murders of prostitutes in East London in 1888, was suspected of being an experimental physiologist because of the way he mutilated women's bodies (Elston 1987). Women supported vivisection in numbers exceeded only by their support for suffrage societies, and they did so 'because the vivisected animal stood for vivisected woman: the woman strapped to the gynaecologist's table, the woman strapped and bound in the pornographic fiction of the period' (Lansbury 1985:x). Elizabeth Blackwell, the first woman to become a licensed medical practitioner, witnessed Bernard's experiments in Paris, and opposed vivisection partly on the grounds that women were increasingly being used in medical experiments. She had been particularly impressed by an event which occurred in 1847 during her training in New York, when she was asked to conduct a gynaecological examination on a working-class woman. In accordance with customary practice, the woman had been strapped to a frame with her feet in stirrups for the benefit of the gaze of attending medical students (Lansbury 1985).

In 1903, two young women, Louise Lind-af-Hageby and Liesa Schartau, enrolled at University College, London – one of Britain's most prominent vivisection sites – in order specifically to see and publicize the outrage of vivisectionists at work. Their book, *The Shambles of Science* (first published in 1903), is a colourful invective against the blood-stained 'priests' of vivisection, who not only inflicted pain and suffering on living animals but appeared to enjoy doing so. In their view, physiologists' use of live animals rendered the whole of medical science 'a stupendous fraud', and one incapable of penetrating the realm of the 'true and healthy' (Lind-af-Hageby and Schartau 1913:143–4). The first organized protest against animal experimentation took place in Florence in 1863. The target was a Professor Moritz Schiff, a German physiologist, accused of carrying out cruel experiments on hundreds of animals every year in his Florentine laboratory. The campaign organizer was the arch-antivivisectionist Frances Power Cobbe (1822–1904), who was enjoying a spell in the Florentine hills at the time (Guarnieri 1987). The earliest antivivisection societies, formed in 1875, were inspired not only by knowledge of how animals were being treated in laboratories, but much more fundamentally by a public concern over how the new physiology, and science and medicine generally, threatened to co-opt the moral framework of Victorian society, replacing religion with secular authority. Furthermore, women, as the traditional carers of people's moral sentiments, bodies and minds, felt themselves to be increasingly displaced by the new materialist medical science. Significantly, feminist antivivisectionists also included in their frame of reference the fates of working-class women, congregated in hospitals which were all too often used as giant teaching laboratories. In London, the Battersea Anti-Vivisection Hospital, set up to serve a very different clientele from the fashionable hospitals north of the Thames, advertised its treatment for 'the suffering poor' in a 1903 fund-raising leaflet as based on the principles of 'No vivisection in its schools, No vivisectors on its staff, No experiments on patients' (quoted in Kean 1998:154). Cobbe and others made direct links between vivisection and medical abuses of women; much of the death, ill health and misery of women, she said, could be attributed to the 'Human Vivisection' carried out by doctors 'too fond by half of the knife' (Cobbe 1894:544).

The antivivisection movement was widespread in Europe, but, perhaps significantly, in view of some aspects of the later history of experimentation, it established less ground and faded more quickly in German-speaking countries (Tröhler and Maehle 1987). Antivivisectionism overlapped in ideology and membership with other moral reform movements, notably the campaigns against compulsory vaccination and the Contagious Diseases Acts. These acts of 1864, 1866 and 1869 enforced compulsory medical inspection and detention of women suspected of prostitution. The 'control' of prostitution and disease through vaccination, as Mary Elston (1987) has pointed out, ruptured the old association between sin and disease. If sickness was the product of chance encounters with germs, and germs could be eradicated through science, what place could virtue have?

Guinea-pigs of various kinds

The bad press which medical experimental research has had in recent years follows in part from the history of its association with eugenic and anti-egalitarian ideologies. But other factors have also been important. One of these is unethical experimentation by some doctors on some groups of patients.

Professional practice is governed to some extent by the principle of secrecy: this is one of the meanings of 'professionalization' (Freidson 1970). It is thus hard to know how often health professionals and others experiment in the name of testing cherished hypotheses, and to what extent the experimented-on have, or have not, known about their status as research participants. Within social psychology, there has been a particular tradition of study involving deliberate deception – a disciplinary canon reproduced in many social psychology texts (Patten 1994). Until at least the 1970s, much psychology research depended on deliberately deceiving participants about the purpose of experiments (Collier et al. 1992).

Uncontrolled and unethical experimentation also involves deception – that an experiment is, in fact, taking place. The rise of modern gynaecology provides a particularly strong example of how 'advances' in medicine may be based on uncontrolled experimentation. In 1853 Dr L. P. Burnham of Lowell, Massachusetts, carried out the first successful hysterectomy in America. His operation was part of a move in the years from the mid-1840s to develop a new class of specialists who could intervene, often surgically, to correct the increasing 'deterioration' of women. The reasons for this deterioration were seen as moral and sexual. Women's physiology and sexuality were regarded as rendering them morally culpable; the cure for both physical and mental disorder was the gynaecologist's knife. Operations such as clitoridectomy (surgical removal of the clitoris) and oophorectomy (removal of the ovaries) were carried out with increasing frequency. But the worst scandal was the operations on black female slaves carried out by the 'father' of American gynaecology, J. Marion Sims. Sims, also known as 'the architect of the vagina' (Barker-Benfield 1976:91), invented numerous devices and procedures including the still-used Sims speculum,[2] was an enthusiastic castrator of women, and generally advocated active interference with women's sexual organs. He pioneered the surgical treatment of vesico-vaginal fistulae[3] on a series of black slaves whom he kept locked up for some years in a building in his backyard. Later on, with the development of anaesthesia and aseptic surgical procedures, Sims was able to apply to the bodies of white women the techniques he had practised on black slaves. When he expanded his backyard hut into a women's hospital, his first patients there were destitute Irish immigrants who endured as many as thirty operations in four years as he continued to 'perfect' his technique. Sims was also known for helping husbands with cases of female frigidity. He would go to the house several times a week and give the woman anaesthesia so that her husband could have intercourse with her. (Some of these women were most surprised to discover they were pregnant, since as far as they knew, they had not had sex. (Barker-Benfield 1976).)

Like the activities of the Nazi doctors, Sims's 'experiments' and those of other would-be gynaecologists at the time are, on one level, clearly nothing to do with the rights and wrongs of modern RCTs. But the ideological association, achieved via the shared notion of 'experimentation', has been profoundly influential. The ability of some people to do things to other people, whether in the name of research or not, invokes fundamental issues of power. The sexual division of labour and its accompanying ideology cannot be separated from the rest of what goes on in society. Nineteenth-century America may have been especially misogynous; but twentieth-century America and Britain remain socially hierarchical societies marked by sexism. It is this social context which makes abuse of the experimental method uncomfortably easy.

A more modern example is provided by the study of a New Zealand doctor called Herbert Green who in the early 1960s began to withhold treatment from women with cervical abnormalities. Dr Green, who held strong anti-abortion and pro-fertility views, was concerned about the destruction of young women's child-bearing potential through hysterectomies, then the main treatment for potential cervical cancer. He wanted to see how many women with cervical abnormalities would develop cancer if left untreated. In 1966 Green formalized his experiment by seeking permission from the medical committee of the

National Women's Hospital in Auckland to manage a group of women 'conservatively' (without removing their uteruses) in an attempt to prove that carcinoma-in-situ (CIS) (pre-cancerous changes in some cells in the cervix) is not an abnormality which leads to cancer. Another group of women would receive treatment; the decision about who would be treated and who would not would be taken by individual doctors. This experiment continued for more than twenty years until it was uncovered, through extensive detective work, by two women's health activists, Sandra Coney and Phyllida Bunkle (Coney 1988; see also Bunkle 1988).

It is unclear exactly how many women were involved in the 'unfortunate experiment' in New Zealand, as it was termed. The paper in the medical journal *Obstetrics and Gynecology* which drew Coney and Bunkle's attention to Dr Green's studies reported on 1,028 women diagnosed with CIS at National Women's Hospital between January 1955 and December 1976. The paper analysed the histories of 948 of these women, who had been followed up for between five and twenty-eight years (thirteen of the 1,028 had died, some were impossible to trace, and others were excluded from the analysis for a mixture of reasons). Out of the 948, 131 women had been 'conservatively' managed, with no, or minimal treatment: 22 per cent of these developed invasive cancer, and 6 per cent died. These figures compared with about 1 per cent of invasive cancers and less than 1 per cent of deaths in the 817 women who did receive treatment (McIndoe et al. 1984). It became clear subsequently that significant numbers of women had been omitted from this analysis (Cartwright Report 1988).

Many women had been asked to return to National Women's Hospital for dozens of repeat smears, only to develop and then to die of cancer. For example, one Maori mother of sixteen children came to the hospital with bleeding and had CIS diagnosed, with some micro-invasion of cancer. She was given no treatment and went on to have a seventeenth child. Two further smears produced the same results. When the next was due, the woman rang the hospital to say she could not afford to make the visit. Eight years later when she returned, she had obvious and visible cancer, and she died shortly afterwards (Coney 1988:105). A further consequence of Dr Green's researches was that in 1963, at his instigation, the hospital started to take smears from the vaginal vaults of new-born babies – he had a further theory that CIS was congenital. Dr Green lost interest after the first 200 new-born smears, because no evidence was emerging to support his theory, but no one told the nursing staff, who continued to take smears from a further 2,044 new-born babies (Coney 1988:209–13).

None of the women in the New Zealand study were told about the 'trial'; thus they had no chance to consider whether or not they wished to take the risk of remaining untreated (the parents of the babies were not informed either). The full details and lessons of the New Zealand experiment were investigated in a public enquiry held in 1988 chaired by a woman judge, Silvia Cartwright. The Cartwright enquiry took evidence from fifty-nine witnesses and thirty-one written submissions and examined 226 individual patient files;

the hearings amounted to 5,657 pages of transcript. The enquiry found that Green and his colleagues had acted unethically; they had abrogated the requirement to respect patients' rights for information and active consent laid down in the Nuremberg Code of 1947 and the Helsinki Declaration of 1964. Other damning indictments were that the so-called peer review system had failed – doctors and other staff who knew that something was wrong either kept quiet or protested ineffectively; and, as the report of the enquiry put it, 'the doctrine of clinical freedom was observed to a dangerous degree' (Cartwright Report 1988:171). Moreover, although the New Zealand study *was* a trial – of the hypothesis that CIS is self-curing – it ignored the principles of well-designed evaluation which had been clearly established in the medical field since the late 1940s (see chapter 7). Had Green assigned women at random to treatment or non-treatment (having first explained the study to them and asked them if they were willing to take part), he might at least have got an answer to his original question – what happens to cervical abnormalities which are left untreated.[4] As it was, the trial was not only unethical, but almost completely valueless as a piece of scientific research.

Some 15 per cent of the women in Dr Green's experiment were Maori, and many were socially disadvantaged.[5] Even more infamous than the New Zealand experiment is one in Tuskegee, which has come to symbolize racism in medical treatment and research. Beginning in 1932, and continuing for forty years, treatment was withheld from poor black men working as sharecroppers in Macon County, Alabama, diagnosed with syphilis. The question was the same as in the New Zealand cervical cancer study: what would happen to the disease if no treatment was offered? (J. H. Jones 1981). However, the difference between the two studies was that the prognosis of untreated syphilis was known, and there was a non-mutilating treatment available.

The New Zealand and Tuskegee studies are not isolated cases: there are many instances of unethical and unscientific experimentation, many of which have been conducted with socially disadvantaged 'subjects' (see Mastroianni et al. 1994; Pappworth 1967).[6] The legacy of such studies is that people from ethnic minority groups in America are especially reluctant to take part in research trials (Macready 1997). Many women also are suspicious about the ethics and motives of doctors who want them to take part in trials of different approaches to treatment. A review of studies of medical research and consent published in 1998 found evidence that up to one in five doctors enter people in trials without seeking consent, and between half and three-quarters of doctors consider that people in trials are not aware that this is the case (Edwards et al. 1998b).[7]

Who's afraid of the RCT?

Tamoxifen, one of the drugs given to Evelyn Thomas, is a synthetic anti-oestrogen which has been used since 1973. It has been the focus for continuing debate among women and user groups about the ethics and practice of breast cancer trials. The debate centres on three issues: what women should be told about such research; how women's experiences, including any effects of drug treatment, should be recorded and represented; and whether using tamoxifen to prevent cancer in otherwise healthy women (as opposed to targeting recurrences in women who have already had cancer) should be regarded as particularly contentious.

Tamoxifen's value in breast cancer is derived from its capacity to block the effect of oestrogen in those cancers which are oestrogen-dependent. Patient information leaflets telling women about tamoxifen commonly say that it has no or few side-effects; 75 per cent of women with breast cancer taking tamoxifen say they were told nothing about its side-effects (Editorial 1991). Many women, however, experience considerable side-effects when taking it. A fact sheet produced for one user group listed the following symptoms attributed to tamoxifen: indigestion, nausea, cessation or irregularity of periods, hot flushes, increased vaginal secretions, labial irritation, slowed hair and nail growth, thinning of the hair, weight gain, eye changes, headaches and skin rashes (Jeannie Campbell Breast Cancer Radiotherapy Appeal, n.d.). Women are also concerned about the changes in their voices which may occur on the drug; these are said to affect particularly the upper frequencies. When the singer Kathleen Ferrier was offered hormone treatment[8] for breast cancer over forty years ago, she was told by her doctor that there was a danger it would affect her voice. She declined the treatment on the grounds that her voice was a divine gift, and she wanted to go to the grave with it unaltered (Leonard 1988:229).

In 1992, four years after Evelyn Thomas's story was publicized, analysis of data from a number of trials did not demonstrate a clear advantage for tamoxifen (Early Breast Cancer Trialists' Collaborative Group 1992). A similar exercise in the USA in 1994 showed an excess of new primary tumours among women who took tamoxifen; these findings led to the drug being labelled 'carcinogenic' and to the recommendation that more than five years' treatment with tamoxifen is not advisable (Bulbrook 1996:389). Three trials of tamoxifen as a prevention strategy for women at high risk of breast cancer have come up with conflicting results. In a trial carried out in the UK involving 2,494 healthy women with a family history of breast cancer, no benefit of taking tamoxifen could be detected at six years follow-up (Powles et al. 1998). Similarly, in an Italian trial of 5,408 women followed up for four years, there was no evidence that tamoxifen was of benefit (Veronesi et al. 1998). However, a trial in the USA was halted when its interim results showed a 45 per cent lower incidence of breast cancer among women taking tamoxifen compared to those given placebos (Josefson 1998). Debate about these contrary results has highlighted issues such as the different risk profiles of the populations of women taking part in the trials, the smaller numbers in the European trials, and whether the US trial will result in mortality differences (Bruzzi 1998; Kmietowicz 1998). One major lesson is the need to combine all available data in order to arrive at the most reliable estimate of whether an intervention such as tamoxifen 'really' does make a difference; research synthesis offers the prospect of *cumulative* knowledge (see chapter 10).

The Medical Research Council withdrew its support for the UK trial in 1992 because of new evidence about liver tumours in rats, the poor quality of the patient information it was planned to provide, and concern about the recruitment of relatively low risk women (Rees 1992). There is still little reliable evidence about the long-term side-effects of tamoxifen, although there is evidence of an increase in cancer of the lining of the womb and blood-clotting disorders (Bruzzi 1998). Underlying the tamoxifen debate is the general medicalization of women's bodies; Dr Trevor Powles, the driving force behind the on-going tamoxifen trial, envisages one day being able to give middle-aged women a single pill containing a mix of hormones plus tamoxifen to overcome all menopausal problems, reproductive cancers, heart disease and osteoporosis (*Evening Standard*, 18 February 1992).

Recruitment to the UK tamoxifen trial was slower than the trialists wanted (*Independent*, 23 October 1997). This is symptomatic of the general problem that modern medical trialists have in persuading people to take part in their studies.[9] Recruitment to cancer trials, for example, is around the 10–25 per cent mark; that is, three-quarters or more of people considered by doctors 'eligible' to be trial participants decline the invitation to take part (Slevin et al. 1995; Tate et al. 1979). Refusal rates are on the increase; for instance, in 1984, 61 per cent of would-be participants in trials of lymphoma (a tumour of the lymph tissue) treatment agreed, but this had declined to 25 per cent by 1992 (Hancock et al. 1997).

These figures represent failure to the trialists, whose goal is simply to enrol as many people as possible in studies which they hope will answer questions about the effectiveness and safety of different treatments. But the bare statistics are fairly meaningless without some understanding of their background and context. How much information of what kind are people given about trials? What are their experiences and perceptions of research in general and of trials in particular? In striking contrast to the enormous volume of medical and social research carried out, the number of studies examining the attitudes and experiences of research participants in general is very small. This is particularly so with respect to trials (Snowden et al. 1997). But when we look at the scanty data on this subject, several key messages do emerge: first, much of the information given about trials is inadequate and inappropriate; second, and contrary to received medical wisdom, the lay public does not find it difficult to comprehend the design of RCTs once this is explained in non-mystifying terms; third, the idea of professional uncertainty (intrinsic to the ethical basis of an RCT) constitutes something of a stumbling block (surely professionals know what to do?); fourth, there may be a profound underlying resistance to the notion of subjecting fate to the 'whim' of chance. As the American paediatrician Bill Silverman (1980) has noted, the repugnance that some people feel about trusting chance rather than the fallibility of human beings is reminiscent of the outcry that followed Darwin's revelations about human evolution; many felt uncomfortable at the role chance played in Darwin's description of evolutionary processes.

The examples below come from the fields of gynaecological surgery, breast cancer research, treatments for new-born babies and day care for preschool children. They all illustrate how the wonderful simplicity of the RCT hailed by Archie Cochrane (Cochrane 1989:158; see chapter 8) becomes more complicated once it is applied to, and seen from the standpoint of, the people who are its experimental 'subjects'. What people understand may not be what researchers think they do; 'informed consent' is a shifting, complex process, rather than a discrete cognitive event.

Gynaecological surgery in Sweden

In the 1980s a trial was undertaken in Sweden of different treatments for women with inflammation of the fallopian tubes (Weström 1986). Taking part in the study meant that the women's medical diagnosis was established via laparoscopy – a minor operation carried out under general anaesthetic in which an optical instrument is inserted through a small slit in the abdomen, and a dye is blown up through the cervix into the fallopian tubes so that the doctor can examine their condition. After diagnosis, the women were randomised to different drug regimens. Three to four months after first becoming ill, they all had a second operation to determine the effects of the different treatments (whereas the first operation was carried out to diagnose the problem as a normal part of medical care, the second was part of the research protocol, and would not have happened without it). Eighteen months later those women who finished the study and who could be traced – forty-three of the original sixty-eight – were sent a questionnaire asking them how much they had known about the study.

Half the women had been given oral information, and half information both orally and in written form. Table 11.1 shows that whatever they were told, there were deficiencies in terms of what they said they had understood. Only about half felt the information had been adequate, knew that they could withdraw from the study at any time, or felt they had been able to weigh up the pros and cons before agreeing. One in five did not feel they had given consent, and about one in seven did not understand the aim of the study or appreciate that the second operation was part of the research process. The investigators concluded in this case also that the study had not followed the Declaration of Helsinki guidelines (Lynöe et al. 1991).

Studying breast cancer

Breast cancer is the most commonly diagnosed cancer in the world; about one in five of all cancers are breast cancers. In the UK, one in twelve women gets breast cancer; it is the single most common cause of death among women aged 40–55, accounting overall for about one in twenty deaths among all women (McPherson 1994). In 1992–3 a study was carried out at the Social Science Research Unit (SSRU) in London, funded by the Cancer Research Campaign, of women's and health professionals' attitudes to breast cancer treatment and

Table 11.1   Participation in a Swedish trial of gynaecological treatment: information and consent

	Yes (%)	No (%)	Cannot recall (%)
Knew aim of study	86	9	5
Knew meaning of participating	79	16	5
Knew they could withdraw	44	40	16
Received information about the study	98	2	0
Received adequate information	51	49	0
Gave consent	81	2	16
Weighed up pros and cons before agreeing	42	56	2
Knew purpose of second operation was for research	86	12	2

Based on N = 43 women.
Source: Taken from Lynöe et al. 1991

Table 11.2   The views of women treated for breast cancer and of health professionals about trial information and consent

	Women (%)	Professionals (%)
Doctor should put you in a trial without telling you/doctor alone should decide	6	0
Doctor should tell about choices, then decide	3	3
Doctor should discuss choices, then decide, taking patient's views into account	15	9
Decisions should be shared between doctor and patient	21	38
Patient should be informed, then left to decide	47	29
Complex	9	21

Based on N = 50 women and N = 40 health professionals.
Source: Alderson et al. 1994:117

Table 11.3 Women's understanding of the terminology of RCTs according to women and health professionals

	Randomisation (%)	Control group (%)	Double-blind (%)	Placebo (%)
Screened women:				
'haven't a clue'	49	47	79	42
'rough idea'	16	14	10	4
'fairly clear'/				
'know exactly'	34	36	8	51
[no reply]	1	3	3	3]
Treated women[a]:				
knew before	36	46	14	54
knew when explained	40	36	60	30
didn't know after				
explained	8	6	10	2
[other/no reply]	16	12	16	14]
Professionals:				
women generally understand				
term	19	4	5	40
concept	58	56	54	82

Based on N = 93 screened women, N = 50 treated women, N = 40 professionals.

[a] The options for the 'treated' are different from those of the 'screened' women in the table because it was assumed that they would already have been exposed to some discussion of research terms.

Source: Alderson et al. 1994:121–3

research. Information was gathered from forty health professionals, fifty women after surgery for primary breast cancer, and ninety-three women attending breast cancer screening services (Alderson et al. 1994).

Findings from the study with respect to breast cancer research included different perceptions of the need for research; more than twice as many of the professionals as of the screened women believed that more research about treatments was necessary. Women were considerably more optimistic than professionals (85 per cent versus 59 per cent) about research saving lives and reducing illness. Treated women and professionals were asked how they would feel about different options for taking part in treatment trials; table 11.2 shows that nearly half the women felt they alone should take the decision, whereas the professionals' single most preferred option was for what they thought of as a 'shared' decision-making process.

Table 11.3 shows how much the two groups of women knew about the terminology of RCTs and how much professionals thought they knew. One-third to two-fifths of the women understood 'randomisation' and 'control group'; around half were familiar with the term 'placebo'; 'double-blind' was more of a mystery. The question the professionals were asked was: 'Do you find that women generally tend to know these terms and know or easily grasp the concepts?' Measured by the standard of what the women themselves said, professionals *under*estimated the women's knowledge of the terms. One of the themes that emerged strongly from this research is that of altruism; 92 per cent of treated women gave helping other people as the main motive for taking part in research. As one woman said in answer to a question about whether she would agree to take part in an RCT of surgery:

> I would leave it up to them, once they'd explained everything to me. . . . I would go in for research, like these tablets I've agreed to take for a year. Somebody's got to try them out, it's got to be trial and error at the beginning or you would get nowhere fast. I mean if women hadn't tried things beforehand I wouldn't have had the treatment I had. *(Cited in Alderson et al. 1994:127)*

This view, that research contributes to knowledge, so altruism may in the end serve everyone's interests, is not uncommon (Elbourne 1987; Mattson et al. 1985). Similar findings emerged from an RCT of social support during pregnancy (Oakley 1990). Altruism is also a generally important, but under-recognized, motive for action (Titmuss 1997).

But taking part in a trial does mean forgoing the chance to make treatment choices on the basis of what feels personally to be the right or best thing to do. A breast care nurse interviewed for the SSRU breast cancer study phrased it like this:

> 'My dis-ease comes from an uncomfortable tension between . . . two main purposes. . . . At one end is Science, represented by the medical researchers and funders. They want to recruit large numbers into clinical trials to try to define once and for all the most effective treatment for early breast cancer. . . . On the other pole of the project are the here-and-now breast cancer patients and their perceived information needs. They are grappling with the diagnosis of a life-threatening disease . . . No wonder randomisation, with its attendant depersonalisation, is such a problem for women who feel threatened by the loss of their intrinsic selves anyway. Benefits for unknown women a generation away don't stand much chance against hanging on to something of self now. *(Cited in Alderson et al. 1994:149)*

This nurse's view is that the more informed women are, the less likely they are to agree to enter trials. If this is so, the tension for the trialists is between promoting informed consent and persuading enough people to take part in trials.

Consent, of course, is an issue not only in experimental studies, but in all forms of research. In the breast cancer research field, the commitment of women to helping health care professionals answer important questions about different forms of treatment was severely tested in the UK by the study of the Bristol Cancer Help Centre which hit the medical press and general media headlines in 1990. The Bristol Centre provided a programme of diet, counselling, meditation and alternative healing therapies for women with breast cancer, some of whom agreed to take part in a study of the benefits of this approach. The study used a matched 'case-control' design: women attending the centre were 'matched' with non-attenders who also had breast cancer. In September 1990, the medical researchers conducting the study published a paper in the *Lancet* suggesting that the women going to the centre were twice as likely to die. The women themselves were not told about this analysis, or warned beforehand of its publication. In response to the outcry that followed, the paper's authors re-analysed their data and found serious design flaws which invalidated the results claimed (Goodare 1996).

Trialling ECMO

The issue of whether would-be recruits to medical trials understand the implications of taking part may be more acute in situations of immediately life-threatening illness. Snowden and colleagues describe the experiences of parents in a randomised trial of different treatments for respiratory failure in new-born babies. The two treatments were 'conventional' management, using ventilatory support, and a newer treatment, Extra Corporeal Membrane Oxygenation (ECMO). This involves the insertion of cannulae into blood vessels in the neck; in the research it usually also meant transportation of very sick new-born babies, often without their parents, from the hospital where they were born to one of five specialist centres. At the time the trial was done (1993–4) ECMO was available in the UK only to parents who agreed to take part in the trial. Eighty centres and 185 babies participated; all the babies were severely ill. Eighty-four died – thirty in the ECMO and fifty-four in the conventional management group; and health problems when the babies were one year old were about evenly balanced between the two groups (UK Collaborative Trial Group 1996). Information about the study was given to parents at the time of their babies' illness by means of letters and leaflets, and doctors expanded on the written information. The research looking at parents' experiences used questionnaires and a qualitative study involving interviews with about one in ten of the families – in most cases both parents were interviewed, in some, mothers only. The interviews took place before the end of the trial, so no one knew the trial results at the time.

While all the parents responded to words such as 'random' and 'randomisation' as though they knew what they meant, it was unclear just what information they had been given, and their use of these terms in the interviews was often contradictory. Most parents felt that their baby was being selected or rejected for a treatment – ECMO – that might offer the only chance of survival. 'Randomisation' thus generally meant 'a gateway to the desired treatment, the point at which access was either given or denied. Use of the term . . . did not always signify that parents were aware of the element of chance inherent in the allocation of treatment' (Snowden et al. 1997:1343). Where chance *was* recognised, parents used analogies such as a lottery, tossing a coin, drawing a name from a hat and 'potluck' to describe the process. A small number of parents gave the reason for randomisation as being the need to avoid bias, have a comparison group, or ration scarce resources. About half accepted the need for the design, the rest disagreed; as one mother said:

> 'I suppose trials have to be a bit heartless, but you'd think that when the baby looks like they're dying, you'd think they'd just say . . . "Oh hell" you know "let's try the ECMO, see if it saves this baby" but with that sort of trial they can't do that can they? They have to say, "Well look, this baby looks like it's dying but I'm sorry it's getting conventional treatment and that's that."' *(Snowden et al. 1997:1346)*

Some parents came to terms with randomisation by seeing it as a guise for 'God's hand'. Others felt that randomisation was irresponsible medical practice: a trivial way of managing a serious situation. They were puzzled by the conflict between the design of a randomised trial and the general expectation that doctors will provide the best care for individual patients:

> 'I was thinking why is the computer making the decision? I wasn't sure if it was the actual computer making the decision or if it was somebody else but . . . it was odd. . . . They did explain at the time why which made it easier, but I still like thought well you know, why don't they just say "we'll do this" instead of "We may be doing this or we could do that."' *(Mother cited in Snowden et al. 1997:1344)*

Parents' feelings and understandings about the ECMO trial partly reflect how it was presented to them, and we do not know what information they were given (Robinson 1998). It is clear that some doctors expressed considerable enthusiasm for the new treatment. In addition, some parents were aware that ECMO was being used in other countries outside the context of a trial. It is thus hardly surprising that some were distressed by the idea that their babies would only have ECMO if 'the computer' said so.

Trials of day care

The effect on young children of being looked after by people other than their parents in centres outside the home has provided a much-plundered research topic in some developed countries for many years. A major driving force for this research tradition has been the theory of maternal deprivation developed by John Bowlby during and after the Second World War. The theory suggests that anything other than home-based maternal care is a definite second-best. So a mass of research has looked at the development and behaviour of children in day care, attempting to derive causal relationships linking type of care with what happens to children's health, welfare and development. Given that in most countries the children receiving day care are disproportionately socially disadvantaged, disentangling any negative effects of day care *per se* from other environmental influences has proved difficult; this has not, however, prevented some researchers from reaching some alarming conclusions (see e.g. Melhuish and Wolke 1991).

The design of most day care research is observational; that is, children in day care are studied for day care 'effects'. Less commonly, control groups of children not in day care are included, but there are usually problems of comparability: the children getting and not getting day care are often socially rather unalike [10] A recent review of day care research located eight randomised controlled trials, all carried out in the USA. These showed that day care promotes children's intelligence, development and school achievement; long-term follow-up demonstrates increased employment, lower teenage pregnancy rates, higher socio-economic status and decreased criminal behaviour. Added benefits include positive effects on mothers' education, employment and interaction with children (Zoritch et al. 1998). An RCT of day care is now under way in England (Roberts et al. 1997).

As a prelude to this, a pilot study was undertaken, which involved talking to parents in a deprived inner city area in London about their attitudes to day care and to the proposed RCT (Rajan and Turner 1997). Fifty interviews and five focus groups were carried out with parents. The researchers explained the design of the proposed research using and expanding on the idea of tossing a coin, or lottery balls, as well as using visual 'props' (for example, 'the tape recorder is the group that gets a day care place, the baby's bottle is the group that doesn't, now let's toss the coin and see which group your family would go into' etc.) (Rajan and Turner 1997). Then they asked how parents would feel about taking part. Half the parents said they were happy about randomisation:

'That's a fair way, a good way.'

'I think it's probably the only way to do it, in that what you are doing isn't looking at who is the most deserving of a day care place.' *(Parents quoted in Rajan and Turner 1997:51)*

These comments also referred to random allocation as being the fairest way of allocating a scarce resource – in this case, day care places, where demand far exceeds supply. Wortman and Rabinowitz (1979) carried out an RCT of 'merit, needs, first-come first-served' versus random principles of selection for special educational programmes. Most people thought the random principle the fairest method of deciding.

The findings on attitudes to RCTs were similar in the day care and breast cancer studies. Most (84 per cent) parents indicated a willingness to take part in research which would help families with young children generally. One aspect of the research design involved all the children getting extra health service attention – special checks from health visitors or paediatricians. Again, most (84 per cent) of the parents welcomed this, seeing 'the feedback from an outsider' as 'interesting' and/or 'reassuring' (Rajan and Turner 1997:42). Another planned aspect of the study was interviewing children; again most (78 per cent) parents thought this a good idea. Parent interviews were also for the most part an accepted aspect of the research, though mothers felt that fathers might be recalcitrant interviewees:

> 'They wouldn't mind. But mine wouldn't be much use.'

> 'He would say he's very busy, which is normally the excuse for anything they don't want to do'. *(Rajan and Turner 1997:46)*

Some of the same questions were asked in the two studies. In the day care study, 21 per cent of parents felt that the school head should decide whether children should be entered into a trial, either with or without informing the parents and taking their wishes into account; 64 per cent thought that decision-making should be shared; and 7 per cent said that parents alone should decide. Table 11.4 repeats the questions about RCT terminology asked in the breast cancer study. As in that study, considerable percentages of parents said they knew what the terms 'randomisation' (54 per cent) and 'control group' (50 per cent) meant. However, while some people said they knew a term, further discussion exposed some confusion. One mother who said she knew what a control group was later said: 'I would want to be completely in control of what type of care my child gets ... I wouldn't want my child to be in a group I had no control over' (Rajan and Turner 1997:41). In all, 40 per cent of parents were willing, 24 per cent were willing in principle (if contacted before their current day care arrangements had been made), and 36 per cent said they would refuse to take part. The questions and explanatory methods (using envelopes as props this time) were then repeated in a series of five focus groups. The focus group parents were generally more positive towards the planned trial, perhaps because they had more of an opportunity to discuss and work through the implications of the research design. Focus group and inter-

Table 11.4 Parents' understanding of the terminology of RCTs

	Randomisation (%)	Control group (%)
'Haven't a clue'	24	34
'Rough idea'	8	6
'Fairly clear'/'know exactly'	54	50
No reply	14	10

Based on N = 50.
Source: Rajan and Turner 1997:40

view data do not always agree (see Ward et al. 1991); this is an example of the 'negative' triangulation discussed in chapter 3. Some parents in the day care study were also quite sophisticated in spotting potential problems, such as the need for large enough numbers, the inability of the research to influence the behaviour of control group parents, and 'contamination' due to some families being offered day care places living next door to other families who were not. Recurrent themes were what would happen to families who really *needed* day care places, the importance of geographical accessibility and of nurseries fitting in with parental employment regimes, and parents' desires to choose the 'right' day care for their child. Some parents mentioned the need to avoid the 'objectification' of subjects which is associated in the public mind with some experimental research; as one father put it:

> 'one should have the opportunity to discuss the nature of the research, the nature of any observations of children . . . And if there were to be some kind of interaction involved in it, you know, what that was going to be like. Are they going to be treated . . . is someone going to go up to them with a cattle prod or something. Are they going to be put into a maze and be made to run round after white balls?' *(Unpublished interview, day care study)*

The sociology of randomisation

More research is now beginning to be done on attitudes to trials (see e.g. Edwards et al. 1998a, 1998b); this has even spawned a specialized instrument, the ARTQ – Attitudes to Randomised Trials Questionnaire (Fallowfield et al. 1998). The examples quoted above from the real world of experimental research involving men, women and children highlight several difficult dimensions of the research design.[11]

Believing in uncertainty

One difficulty is that all those involved in an RCT supposedly share equally a condition known as 'equipoise', in which there is genuine uncertainty about the effects of the intervention under test (see Edwards et al. 1998b). The people who provided information in the day care, breast cancer and ECMO studies were, for the most part, and understandably, fairly opinionated about what they wanted for themselves and their families. 'New' treatments such as ECMO are often hailed as miracle cures; there is a bias towards the publication of scientific papers showing that new treatments work better than older ones (Egger and Smith 1998). People's understanding of randomisation operates at different levels; an intellectual appreciation of its importance may conflict with a cognitive perception of those who get the 'desired' treatment being more deserving than others (Apsler and Friedman 1975). Some interventions, such as day care, may seem self-evidently beneficial (for those who want or need them, especially employed parents). The questions for many people asked to take part in such trials concern not only the effect of this intervention in curing or preventing health and other problems, but what else may be associated for them or their families with this intervention and its alternatives. Different forms of breast cancer treatment – types of surgery, radiotherapy and chemotherapy – for example, have different side-effects and different implications for people's everyday lives. Part-time day care is not the same thing as full-time day care, and a nursery which demands a complicated journey on two unreliable bus routes is not the same thing as one within a few minutes' walking distance. Since ECMO demanded the removal of the baby from the parents for the duration of the journey to the ECMO centre, this was one among many considerations parents in the trial had to take into account. Although it may be assumed that equipoise is easier for professionals, it is interesting to note that, in the breast cancer study, 75 per cent of the professionals interviewed thought this was not possible for them.

Control groups: are they fair?

A second problem relates to the whole notion of a control group as people who are essentially *uninvolved* in the testing of an intervention.

Even before they knew that ECMO was superior to conventional management, some parents in the ECMO trial felt distressed because their babies were not allocated the new treatment. Parents discussing the proposed day care trial were concerned that those families assigned to the control group, which would not be offered day care, would consequently suffer feelings of deprivation. Aside from the unpleasantness of this reaction for the people involved, what Cook and Campbell (1979) have termed 'resentful demoralization' has implications for the scientific value of trials. If these feelings affect the outcomes being studied in various ways, then the control group is not really a control group any more. It is simply another group of people subjected to a research intervention who are likely to be affected by it. Conclusions about differences between control and experimental group outcomes may thus be distorted.[12] For this reason, David Fetterman (1982) has suggested that it would be more accurate to describe a control group as a 'negative treatment' group. Fetterman was responsible for the ethnographic component in a study, involving random assignment, of a programme for disadvantaged minority youth; his interviews with programme directors suggested that they saw this as a considerable problem.

One way round this is the alternative design proposed by Marvin Zelen some years ago (1979), and referred to earlier in this book. The Zelen design randomises people before asking for their consent, and then only informs those allocated to the new or experimental treatment(s) that they are in a trial. Those assigned to the control group are not told. An example of this design is the trial of counselling in which breast cancer patient Evelyn Thomas was involved. This design has mainly been used for cancer trials in the USA, sometimes explicitly as a solution to the problem of too few women agreeing to take

Table 11.5 The views of women and health professionals about the Zelen method

	Treated women (%)	Screened women (%)	Professionals (%)
Should be told about being in control group	73	48	45
Need not be told	19	17	27
Depends/don't know	8	35	28
Should tell person about medical notes being used	52	46	_[a]
Need not tell person about medical notes being used	35	25	_[a]
Depends/don't know	13	29	_[a]

Based on N = 50 treated women, N = 93 screened women, N = 40 professionals.
[a] The question about medical notes was not asked of professionals.
Source: Alderson et al. 1994:120

part in a trial (see B. Fisher et al. 1985a and 1985b) or to speed up recruitment (Marquis 1986). It is controversial, chiefly because some people are deceived about the basis of treatment decisions – chance rather than doctors' individualized choices (Botros 1990; Kennedy 1988; Marquis 1986); there is the further problem that medical records of control group patients may be available without their knowledge to researchers.

Like many aspects of research design, the views of the researched about the Zelen approach have been largely ignored. The study by Alderson and colleagues included some questions about this method; the findings are shown in table 11.5. Between one-half and three-quarters of the women felt that people should be told that they are in a control group. Opinion about this was strongest among the treated women, who had more personal involvement with breast cancer research: nearly three-quarters thought people should be told. Professional opinion was more likely to be in favour of not informing the control group. With respect to disclosure of medical notes, about half the women felt this should not happen without people first being informed.

In an extension of their work on the ECMO trial, Snowden and colleagues also explored parents' attitudes towards the Zelen method using in-depth interviews. The method was first explained, and then parents whose babies were assigned to ECMO were asked to think about this method as if they had been asked for their consent for their babies to have ECMO, while those in the conventional management group were asked to think about their responses had they not been asked for consent. The two themes that emerged were the value of the Zelen method in protecting parents from harmful information (that their baby was not being considered for ECMO as a potentially life-saving treatment) and the counter-argument that it deprives people of rightful information. The parents were about evenly split. Significantly, more of those whose babies were allocated to the conventional management group were against the Zelen method. As this is the group which would not be informed in a Zelen–designed trial, Snowden and colleagues' study suggests that it may be least acceptable to those most affected by it.

The point of randomising a treatment is that there is uncertainty about the best thing to do. But in a Zelen–designed trial, people in the experimental group are effectively offered a choice between the experimental and control treatments, which negates the philosophical basis of the trial. Parents in the ECMO study observed this contradiction, and felt it was an impossible responsibility.

The problem of people knowing what they want

Human preferences are a scientific nightmare. As two health service researchers recently put it: 'A common problem in randomised controlled trials arises when patients . . . have such strong treatment preferences that they refuse randomisation' (Torgerson and Sibbald 1998:360). A study of attitudes towards a trial of colon cancer treatment found that only two out of twenty-two patients with a preference for the standard treatment were willing to enter the trial, whereas twenty-two out of thirty-six who wanted the new treatment agreed to take part (Llewellyn-Thomas et al. 1991). Under such circumstances, the people who do agree may not be representative, so the results of the trial will have limited generalizability. Persuading people who have preferences to take part may not be desirable, because those who get what they want will be pleased, and those who do not, as we saw above, will not be. Experiments in a different arena – with psychology students randomly assigned unpleasant or innocuous tests – show that far more of those assigned the unpleasant option are highly critical of those responsible for the experiment (Apsler 1972). Bearing in mind that other scientific inconvenience, the indissolubility of body and mind, anything a trial with these problems is purported to show may well be due to psychological effects rather than 'therapeutic efficacy' (McPherson et al. 1997). People may also drop out of trials when dissatisfied or demoralized, refusing to take the treatment or accept the intervention to which they have been allocated, and neglecting to provide necessary information. This can be a major problem.

The suggested solution here is a device called the 'patient preference' trial (Bradley 1993). In such a design people with preferences for one or another treatment are allowed to choose; those without preferences are randomised. This design is not widely used. One example is a trial of medical abortion (using drugs) versus surgical vacuum aspiration for women with early unwanted pregnancies (Henshaw et al. 1993). This study looked at acceptability to the women of the two procedures. Perhaps unsurprisingly, those who *chose* their method were equally likely to find it acceptable; but this was not the case for the randomised women, who had not indicated a preference: only 2 per cent of women randomised to vacuum aspiration said they would opt for a different method in future, whereas 22 per cent of those randomised to medical abortion said they would do so. These hypothetical future choices reflect different experiences with the two methods. But what, 'really', is the nature of the two experiences, given that women with and without initial preferences apparently describe them differently?

Wortman and colleagues (1976) explored some of the above issues in a series of studies with students offered an intervention (information and discount coupons for cultural activities) designed to improve their leisure opportunities. In the first study, students were told that a leisure-promoting intervention was to be offered on a randomised basis. In the second, those assigned either to get the intervention or not were simply told that they were to receive an intervention or provide questionnaire data only. The third study followed the same procedure as the second, except that students were later allowed to find out that people in the different groups were being treated differently. These students, particularly those in the 'control' group, were much more inclined than the others to be angry and negative towards the study and the researchers. A further experiment was then conducted in which students were informed about a randomised controlled study of additional teaching by advanced undergraduates. Half were told they could choose whether or not to volunteer for the study, and half that they would be randomised. Those who could choose were much more likely to say afterwards that the study was fair to those assigned to the control group, and that the scientific evaluation of the additional teaching justified depriving half the students of it.

Who wants RCTs?

Most research, whether social or medical, is initiated by researchers, rather than by the researched. Most research proceeds from the interests of researchers because researchers generally have more to gain from the research process: publications, external research grant income, points in academic research assessment exercises (I. Chalmers 1998). Experimental research can be argued to be in a somewhat special category here, in that its purpose is to arbitrate between competing interventions, and thus to work towards a solution which is as much (if not more) in the interests of the researched as of the researchers. But this construction of research makes the singular assumption that both parties in the research process agree on what is to be counted as evidence, and, moreover, that they share the same view about the important role of evidence in shaping medical practice. Such an assumption may well be incorrect.

Seeing the baby on the screen

Issues about informed consent to both treatment and research have probably been asked more often in the area of pregnancy and childbirth than in any other. As is frequently observed, pregnant women and their babies differ from most other health care 'patients' in that most of them are not sick in the first place. One type of information relevant to pregnant women concerns the results of trials of different approaches to treatment and diagnosis. The Midwives' Information and Resource Service (MIDIRS) and the NHS Centre for Reviews and Dissemination in the UK developed a series of informed choice leaflets for pregnant women summarizing this evidence.

One of these leaflets concerns the routine use of ultrasound as a screening/ diagnostic/monitoring procedure in pregnancy. Ultrasound imaging of unborn babies is a technology that originated in the research of Professor Ian Donald in Glasgow during the 1950s. 'Sonar', as Donald called it, was modelled on techniques used to detect submarines during the First World War. Its original use in women was to distinguish between different kinds of abdominal tumour; as medics are fond of saying, pregnancy is the commonest abdominal tumour in women. Between the early 1960s and the mid-1970s the use and applications of obstetric ultrasound grew rapidly, until it had acquired the status of routine procedure (Oakley 1984). Questions about its effectiveness and safety had been asked from the beginning, and were eventually addressed in a series of controlled trials.

The MIDIRS leaflet on ultrasound invites women to question having a routine ultrasound examination, and sums up the trial data as showing that the usefulness of routine ultrasound examinations in pregnancy has not yet been established, while there remains a question-mark about its safety. In a pilot study exploring reactions to these leaflets, a number of interesting findings emerged. First, health professionals, particularly ultrasonographers, were more likely than women to question the scientific status of the evidence and to raise concern about women's anxiety. Second, some of the professionals were reluctant to allow the pilot study in their hospitals. Third, women did not seem to be made more anxious by reading the leaflet. Finally, it appeared that reading the leaflet did not make them decide not to have ultrasound. What the women in the pilot study said made it clear that they were more interested in adequate feedback during the scan than in the proved effectiveness of routine ultrasound. The point of ultrasound for them was not necessarily what it was for the clinicians. Ultrasound has become a normal part of the experience of pregnancy; seeing the baby on the ultrasound screen is usually regarded as reassuring, and it is an experience in which partners can share. Thus, it has a *social* significance, quite apart from the place it holds in evidence-based medicine (Oliver et al. 1996).

Social support in labour

Whereas particular medical technologies may be the main focus of interest for health professionals, they form merely one aspect of experience for those at the receiving end. A striking illustration of this comes from research, discussed in chapter 10, on electronic fetal monitoring (EFM). One difference between this and the traditional method of monitoring the baby during labour – listening to its heart through a stethoscope placed on the mother's abdomen – is that stethoscope monitoring is intermittent, whereas electronic monitoring provides a continuous polygraph recording (assuming the machine does not break down). The Dublin RCT of the two approaches, carried out in 1981–3, used the Zelen design. Women were first randomised to the two approaches, and then those allocated to electronic monitoring were asked for their consent. The main trial outcomes concerned the survival and health of the baby at and after birth.

A sub-sample of 200 women (100 from each arm of the trial) were asked about their experiences. It was clear from this sub-study that the women given the 'new' technology did not find it more reassuring; what they did report was that they were slightly more likely than the other mothers to be left alone during labour, which they minded. Asked what was reassuring about events surrounding labour, the most prominent response was the nursing/midwifery staff (37 per cent), followed by not being left alone (22 per cent); method of monitoring hardly featured (Garcia et al. 1985). It is significant that these results were obtained in a study conducted at a hospital which at the time operated two somewhat contradictory policies; on the one hand, there was a considerable level of medical intervention in labour, and no labour was allowed to continue for more than twelve hours; on the other hand, all mothers were provided with a companion, usually a student midwife but sometimes a medical student, who stayed with them throughout labour as a source of support and encouragement. This second aspect of hospital policy is known to be particularly appreciated by mothers and to reduce the likelihood of medication for pain relief, operative delivery and the length of labour and to improve the baby's condition at birth (Hodnett 1999). From a research point of view, it may have masked differences between the two methods of monitoring (see chapter 10). But from the women's point of view, it could be argued that the main trial finding was the higher priority mothers attach to the 'technology' of social support.[13]

Conclusion

The modern use of RCTs in medicine and other fields carries with it substantial historical baggage. This includes the horrendous story of Nazi medical experimentation and many campaigns upholding the rights of the socially powerless not to be abused as research participants. Undercutting these individual stories are profound cultural associations between nature, women and animals, who have all fallen prey to the exploits of a male experimental medical science. Modern opposition to RCTs also derives, directly or indirectly, from some of the unethical and unscientific ways in which these studies have in practice been carried out, and the extent to which their designers have chosen not to respect the rights of people to know what is happening to them.

Thus, critics of medical RCTs, especially those in the field of women's health, are certainly justified in summoning history to their defence. Trials of social interventions cannot claim the moral high ground here, for many of these, too, have ignored the principle of fully-informed, consenting research participants. There are large gaps to be bridged between 'lay' and 'professional' understandings. Whether a better informed public will mean fewer trials, or the opposite, remains to be seen.[14] But it is likely that chance will continue to be the enemy of choice. Choice is what the user advocacy groups want and what 'social' research points to as desirable; but the method of well-designed experimental studies deploys chance to decide who gets what. Although the method can be translated into practice in many different ways, it may be that respecting rights is in the end unalterably at odds with science.

Part IV

Moving On

12

People's Ways of Knowing

I am seeking an end to androcentrism, not to systematic inquiry.
Harding, *The Science Question in Feminism*

Perhaps it is even time to go beyond the dialectic language of qualitative and quantitative methods.
Reichardt and Cook, 'Beyond qualitative *versus* quantitative methods'

The journey taken by this book has moved from today's paradigm wars, and the celebration of 'qualitative' methods as solutions to the problems exposed by the 'quantitative' kind, back into the history of the first attempts to frame ways of knowing that did not appeal to divine or magical authorities. It has traced the career trajectories of different ways of knowing, with a particular spotlight on the fate of methods which rely on active intervention to produce dependable knowledge. Science arose long before the systematic study of social relations – social science – was itself conceived. 'Man' – and it was, often, men – sought first to understand the natural world; it was only later that they self-consciously put human beings on the stage as the subject of study. Then it became clear that the act of knowing is an extremely complex endeavour; not only do different human beings know different things, bringing different values, beliefs and perceptions to what they know and how they know it, but the act of knowing and what is known are often irredeemably fused. Knowing is itself the problematic.

This chapter and the next try to bring together the various themes and arguments of the book. What does the history charted in these pages have to say about ways of knowing today? Both chapters focus on future challenges for social scientists and others who endorse the goals of a democratic social science and an evidence-based public policy. This chapter concentrates on issues around moving on from the methodological paradigm divide, using feminism and research on women's health, again, as an example. The final chapter takes up the notion of 'an experimenting society'.

'Disclosing relations not otherwise apparent'

A central human project in all forms of knowledge is knowing in order to predict, and thus to gain control in an uncertain universe. Knowing depends, crucially, although often only implicitly, in linking events, situations or actors in a causal chain: A gives rise to B, not only because A preceded B, but because A was the reason why B happened. Without A, B would not have happened, or would not have happened in the way it did. It is this causal chain which attracted mystics and alchemists and others who believed that the purpose of knowledge was to understand divine revelation. It is what drew the eyes of Copernicus and Galileo to the heavens, and the minds of Bacon and Descartes to consider what can be learnt from human experience. The efforts of Spencer and Mill and Comte and the other European thinkers in early social science were informed by the desire to put 'man's' knowledge of society on the same law-like basis as the science of the natural world; similarly, the wish to map the causal associations between how people live and what happens to them spurred the renowned surveyors of the social, such as Mayhew and Booth, and Chicago's 'Saint Jane', and the great public health reformers Graunt and Farr, who saw in the material roots of people's social relations the reasons for their unequal life chances. Dialectically, also, this vision of understanding the 'laws' which shape both social and natural domains has, throughout the history of methodology, powered criticisms by women such as Margaret Cavendish, Florence Nightingale and Harriet Martineau to the effect that what men and women know may be different because of their different social positions.

The idea and practice of experimentation is closely linked to the logic of causality. Trying something out – experimenting – is a way of putting to the test specific ideas about cause; if B happens after doing A, then perhaps B is caused by A. We all do this sort of thing every day. The philosopher John Dewey put it like this in his *The Quest for Certainty* (1980:85):

> The rudimentary prototype of experimental doing for the sake of knowing is found in ordinary procedures. When we are trying to make out the nature of a confused and unfamiliar object, we perform various acts with a view to establishing a new relationship to it, such as will bring to light qualities which will aid in understanding it. We turn it over, bring it into a better light, rattle and shake it, thump, push and press it, and so on.

Animals, as well as humans, experiment as part of their everyday life. 'Indeed the amoeba,' wrote Hornell Hart, an early advocate of social experiments,

> thrusting out experimental pseudopodia, is engaged in rudimentary scientific investigation of its environment. The amoeba, moreover, is more scientific than many a human student, for the amoeba sticks closer to the facts and avoids the logical errors of generalizations from biased data. *(Hart 1921:373)*

Traditional occupations based particularly on empirical procedures, such as cookery, gardening and midwifery, have made extended use of the principle of trying something and watching to see what happens: 'Children improperly cared for will not thrive; plants will not grow in just any soil or location; water will not boil in a refrigerator' (Code 1991:68). However, all this experimental playfulness, which so contributes to common-sense knowledge, does not necessarily lead to anything either systematic or shared. 'The important thing in the history of modern knowing', Dewey observes, 'is the reinforcement of these active doings by means of instruments, appliances and apparatus devised for the purposes of disclosing relations not otherwise apparent' (Dewey 1980:85). This redolent phrase, 'disclosing relations not otherwise apparent', is in many ways the hub of it all.

One highly significant aspect of experimental doing and knowing is that the world of everyday experimentation is also our 'ordinary qualitative world' our usual environment, full of things 'we see, handle, use, enjoy and suffer from' (Dewey 1980:100). Experimental and 'qualitative' ways of knowing are thus fused at ground level, in the everyday experience from which all knowledge comes. The 'quantitative' may even creep in there as well (see chapter 1). Seen from this vantage-point, the arguments of the paradigm warfarists, rehearsed in chapter 2, seem very silly. Why do people go on about 'quantitative' and 'experimental' and 'qualitative' methods as though these were inherently opposed, rather than simply being aspects of the way we all live in and make sense of the world?

This question brings us back to the starting-point of *Experiments in Knowing*. The answer is that people engage in paradigm arguments for understandable reasons. The three main ones are disciplinary identities – the positioning of different occupational/political groups around different perspectives on knowing and ways of knowing; the tainting of methods by what has been called a 'Nazi' view of experimentation – the notion that those who use experimental research methods, in whatever way, necessarily commit atrocities of one sort or another; and gender, or the infusion of cultural standards about femininity and masculinity into the framing of techniques of knowing. Gender functions in two ways here: first, in its more ordinary sense, as a source of signals to 'real' women about how their experiences may have been missed or maltreated within those knowledge procedures approved of by the dominant group; and second, in a less straightforward sense, as a metaphor for hierarchical structures of thought and social relations.

The question of identity

People belong to particular social groups, and invest a certain amount, socially and psychologically, in being members of those groups. Social scientists have marked out and defended their methodological territory, in exactly the same manner as all occupational groups. But they have also done so specifically in relation to natural scientists' definitions of ways of knowing. Within social science, there are those who have made their academic careers out of methodological warfare. Certain groups, notably feminists and health promotion researchers, have seen it as particularly important to defend an 'alternative' paradigm against what is perceived as the 'quantitative' logic of male/mainstream thought. Other kinds of scientists have been less embroiled in methodological paradigm arguments – they have been less on the attack, and certainly less on the defensive. All these 'positions' are the stakes of the paradigm war.

Had the original Baconian vision of science/knowledge as a unity triumphed (suitably stripped, of course, of its sexism), and had social science never set out on its separate disciplinary trajectory, we might not have been in the methodological trouble we are now. But we would probably have been in some other, equally interesting and difficult place.

Atrocious experiments

While experimental methods are largely rejected by social science today, the history revealed in earlier chapters of this book describes a different picture. Prospective controlled experimental studies – the very 'model' of the scientific method – were once *the* apparatus espoused by social scientists for the purpose of 'disclosing relations not otherwise apparent' in one particular but important area of research: estimating the impact of social interventions on people's lives. Most of this work took place in the USA, making it easy for the tradition of social science experimentation to drop out of the collective memory of European social science.

However, while social science experimentation disappeared from view, becoming instead a thing that never happened because, inherently, it was not possible, the experimental ways of science and medicine continued unabated. Research with human 'subjects' has sometimes been uninformed by ethical perspectives on the need to combine good science with treating research participants well. Through its own social origins, the whole notion of 'experimentation' became dreadfully bound up with eugenist ideas about the superior rights of some people to inherit the earth. This association, reinforced by the dependence of early medical science on the inferior rights of living animals not to be cut up and destroyed 'in the name of science', spelt, in certain important places, the political death knell of the experimental method. The future of experimentation was further damned by an unfortunate history of deliberate deception in psychological experiments. Although an established tradition of systematic social experimentation did not develop in continental Europe, the association in Germany between social science and 'a science of direct apprehension and intervention' led to the suggestion that Hitler himself might become a professor of organic sociology; this did not help dissociate the idea of an experimental social science from the eugenist creed (Lepenies 1988).

As a result of this cultural history, two disparate activities became ideologically linked: the use of animals and non-consenting human beings in uncontrolled experiments, on the one hand, and deploying, as a research technique, the methodology of prospective experimental studies with 'control' groups in order to gain reliable evidence about effectiveness, on the other. Uncontrolled unethical experiments are clearly deplorable; but these are not at all the same thing as well done, controlled experiments used to evaluate health care or social interventions.

Gender and other dualisms

As we saw in chapters 2 and 3, modern methodological arguments are all about dualisms: science and social science, 'quantitative' and 'qualitative', 'natural' and 'social', experimental and non-experimental. One of the arguments put forward in this book is that gender is the most fundamental and influential dualism of all. Gender has had a primary influence on the ways in which methodology has been seen and used.

The concept of 'gender' acquired its modern usage in the early 1970s as a way of differentiating between biological sex and more culturally variable forms of femininity and masculinity (Oakley 1972b; see also Oakley 1997). Methodology, gender and dualisms are much-discussed topics in the feminist epistemology and philosophy literature (see e.g. Antony and Witt 1993; Crawford and Gentry 1989; Fonow and Cook 1991; Garry and Pearsall 1989; Harding 1986). Logical dichotomies have been called essentially 'patriarchal' procedures, with dualistic thinking modelled on the perception that men and women are basically different. The habit of dualistic thought functions to prop up this perception, defending it against the competing view that men and women are also basically the same (Jaggar 1983; Jay 1981). One dualism fundamental to Western thought (though not propagated by Descartes in quite the way some have implied – see chapter 4) is that between 'subject' and 'object'. In *What Can She Know?*, Lorraine Code says:

> Feminist theorists have argued, persuasively, that dichotomous thinking is peculiarly characteristic of malestream thought . . . the idea that there are connections between these dichotomies and male intellectual hegemony is *prima facie* plausible just because of the fact that so many deeply entrenched dichotomies run parallel to a taken-for-granted male/female dichotomy, not just descriptively but evaluatively . . . The veneration of ideal objectivity and the concomitant denigration of subjectivity are manifestations of a 'sex/gender system' that structures all the other inequalities of western social arrangements and informs even those areas of life – such as 'objective' knowledge – that might seem to be gender-free. *(Code 1991:28, 67)*

Women's knowledge may be called, by others, hopelessly 'subjective' – this term being intended as an insult; ways of knowing that require attention to individual perspectives and circumstances may be described as 'qualitative', which, in this context, as used by opponents, is only a more polite way of saying 'subjective' (see the text by Belenky and colleagues (1986) discussed in chapter 3). As we saw in chapter 2, many feminist theorists view the subject/object dichotomy as basic to 'the scientific method'; scientists 'objectify', treating their research 'subjects' as mechanical atoms to be manipulated at will. The tendency to treat others as objects is paralleled in the psychological differentiation of men and women, with men specializing in an unfeeling rationality and women in a fused emotionality. Hence, the procedures of science must be dismissed out of hand. Alternatively, for women to enter the realm of 'the objective', deploying 'rationality' as a way of knowing, means denying their status as women and becoming 'honorary' men (Lloyd 1982). Reason can itself be compared to the male sex organ: linear, hard,[1] penetrating but impenetrable. Knowledge prioritizing evidence which can be 'seen' is merely a reflection of men's need to see and value their own external genitals, against the threat of women's, which cannot be 'seen' in at all the same way (Irigaray 1985a).[2]

Rejecting the whole notion of evidence would produce a considerable problem in everyday life, were it to be adopted consistently as a criterion of behaviour. Feminist social scientists who choose, with some degree of disciplinary pride, 'qualitative' methods because of the 'subjectivity' these give back to research participants, find themselves hoisted on a double petard. First, they are actually buying into the same troublesome dichotomies against which they protest. If these echo (are even caused by) the 'sex/gender system', then continuing to use them (even for the 'right' reasons) must surely reinforce the logic of this system. As Judith Grant (1993:191) has put it, 'Feminism is a rich tradition that has become completely obsessed with the fruitless quest for the authentic female experience.' 'Qualitative' research is not more authentically female or feminine than 'quantitative' research (and there are many examples of this in earlier chapters). It is not necessarily more ethical, either. Although issues about the rights and responsibilities of both researchers and the researched have most often been raised by the practitioners of 'qualitative' research, its operations are far from non-intrusive and non-hierarchical in their processes and consequences. Being interviewed, for example, may be a far-reaching intervention in someone's life. There is no such thing as 'simply' recording or publishing data. There must always be a selection; the critical issue is whether this is made according to the kinds of open and systematic criteria which other people can inspect, or not.

But the historical development of ways of knowing gave both 'qualitative' and 'quantitative' research sets of ideological associations which effectively linked the former to the interests of the underdog – to those whose position excludes them from mainstream power and authority, motivating them to construct knowledge from below, rather than above. Secondly, dividing 'qualitative' from 'quantitative' research perpetuates the continuing separation of two important traditions: that of systematic social enquiry, on the one hand, and that of an engagement with political and ethical issues concerning the knowers and the known, on the other. In this sense, a more appropriate goal is the one suggested in the first quotation at the head of this chapter (Harding

1986:10): an end to androcentricism, but the continuation of systematic enquiry.

Really?

The feminist writer Germaine Greer recently answered a question about what she thought of post-feminism by saying that it was hard to tell, since we are still in the pre-feminist era (Greer 1999). Unlike feminism, which had grass-roots beginnings, post-feminism was born in the academic world, where it has flourished mainly as a set of 'badly written and simplistic ideas that are little more than old-fashioned pluralism rewritten in a French accent' (Murray 1997:37). Much the same could be said about post-positivism, post-structuralism and post-modernism, which all arrived around the same time. If the object of knowledge is a more reliable understanding of the social and natural world, and if this depends partly on a process of cumulative learning, then we had a long way to go at the point at which these 'isms' arrived on the scene with their insistence that we might as well not bother, because there is no such thing as reality anyway.

The term 'gender' has fallen into the same sort of disrepute in some quarters as have 'positivism', 'knowledge', 'science', 'truth' and 'reality' (and 'feminism') (see e.g. Butler 1991; Curthoys 1997; Hood-Williams 1996; Irigarary 1985b). The over-arching belief here, shared by all these contemporary 'isms', including post-feminism, is that there is no independently existing real world; all knowledge is a kind of language game (although some 'discourses' have a seductive tendency to masquerade *as* knowledge); and there is, in particular, nothing special about the narratives of science. Indeed, these are eminently suspect, because of the anti-ecological uses to which scientific activity has been put in the modern world, and because scientific knowledge has historically been indistinguishable from the motives of 'man's domination of nature' (Leiss 1972).

There is no doubt that a lot of science has been 'bad' science. As regards the doing of research, the practice of much science, like that of much social science, has not treated research participants with openness, honesty and respect, and both have used methods which cannot be expected to deliver the answers to the questions they set out to address. In this sense 'scientific' and 'ethical' requirements of 'good' research are linked; it is unethical to ask people to take part in research which has been designed in such a way that it cannot answer the research question(s). Science has been an activity reserved largely for white, middle-class men (see Mitroff et al. 1977; H. Rose 1994; Rosser 1988; Rossiter 1982; Tuana 1989; Witt et al. 1989); social science has been dominated by 'founding fathers', who have presented selective masculinist theories and perspectives as gender-neutral disciplinary logic (see L. McDonald 1993; Oakley 1974). But the striking thing about post-modernism and post-feminism is their contention that there is something 'bad' about *all* science. What is bad is its misleading 'mythic account of universal and objective knowledge' (H. Rose 1993:204). On the contrary, knowers are located in specific political and historical contexts; everything they know is partial; there is no such thing as 'a putative unitary consciousness of the species' (Hawkesworth 1989:535).

This dispute about 'reality' versus 'realities' brings us back to some of the problematic canons of 'qualitative' methods. Joey Sprague and Mary Zimmerman (1989:75) put it like this:

> Even if it were possible to transparently reproduce the world view of the people we study, the adequacy of that world view for understanding society is limited. The emphasis on privileging the perspectives of women and other oppressed groups by struggling to detect and present them without mediation implies that the unmediated world views of our subjects [sic] constitute the best way to understand the world in which we live.

It is, after all, one of the purposes of research to move beyond individual world-views; this is its essential difference from fiction. 'Qualitative' research includes (usually) more than one 'case' for exactly the same reason: that what we seek are patterns, generalities, associations, that help us to understand 'what is going on'. Individual research participants are usually not in a position either to divulge or to see these patterns. For example, women who enjoy the experience of ultrasound scans in pregnancy, because they can see pictures of their babies on a screen, are not in a position to know about the results of well-designed experimental studies which challenge the effectiveness of ultrasound's routine use in pregnancy as a way of reducing baby deaths (Neilson 1999), and point to the malign possibility that ultrasound may have an effect on the developing fetal brain (Salvesen et al. 1993) (see chapter 11).

There are particular problems in viewing reality as entirely personal and contextual – 'subjective' in the polite use of that term – when the object is emancipation. If there are really no such things as 'facts' about the way people are treated, then there is also no such thing as discrimination or oppression. Post-modernism is inherently apolitical. It drives the enforced injustices of social inequality into the personal cupboard of privately experienced suffering. As Alison Assiter has phrased it:

> It is sometimes said that all one can do is tell stories, and one chooses the story one likes best. I believe that, in a world in which there are horrendous wars taking place, the environment is being destroyed, and there is mass starvation, this view is morally and politically reprehensible. *(Assiter 1996:5–6)*

The contention that there are no 'objective' realities would obliterate the purpose of feminist (and other) emancipatory political projects. Furthermore, and as Code (1991:45) has pointed out, under such a regime the findings of feminist research would themselves be disregarded as merely an 'idiosyncratic way of seeing the world, no better than any other way. They could even be dismissed as manifestations of ideological paranoia.' Such a possibility indeed seems quite likely, given the preoccupation in Western thought with women's proneness to 'hysteria' (Astbury 1996).

Quantification and experimentation for women?

Some years ago, the sociologist Dorothy Smith (1979) elaborated an important case for developing a sociology *for*, rather than *of*, women. Similar arguments apply to the need for rehabilitating and reshaping 'quantitative' and experimental ways of knowing within the techniques that can be used productively to map women's situation.

Without 'quantitative' methods, feminism as a political and social movement would not have got very far. Knowing about the oppression of women depends on an opportunity to examine their relative positions *vis-à-vis* men in the labour market, the health and welfare systems, political organizations and government, and the private world of the home and domestic relations. The form such knowledge has taken, its dissemination and responses to it, have varied in feminism's different historical eras. But in all of them there has been a theme of pointing beyond how individual women feel to the ways in which women as a group are slotted into, and treated by, prevailing social and economic structures. Similar arguments can, of course, be put about other emancipatory movements and impulses, including those involving ethnic minorities, children, older people and the inequalities of the class system. Setting injustices right first requires a factual map of what has gone wrong. In this sense, the argument for a return to old-fashioned quantification simply reiterates the visions of those who first promoted a 'positivist' science, such as Condorcet and Comte. For them, maps of the social world which rely on quantification provide an important path to enlightenment for ordinary people (see Glassner and Moreno 1989).

There is, as Helen Roberts (1990:1) has argued, nothing helpful in the current climate about 'An aversion to looking at figures or to understanding how they may be analysed and used'. Official statistics, survey data and longitudinal studies are all rich sources of information. One example is the light such data can throw on the common contention that women are more likely than men to be absent from work because of sickness. In 1982 the Equal Opportunities Commission (EOC) in Britain asked Sara Arber and her colleagues at the University of Surrey to assess the veracity of this belief using data from the General Household Survey, a multi-purpose household survey of around 25,000 people carried out annually in Britain. The researchers found that, overall, women's sickness absence was not higher than men's. Women were more likely to be absent for periods of one to three days, and men more likely to be absent for more than four days; the most marked gender difference was for absences of more than three months – 8 per cent of men and 3 per cent of women employed full-time. These analyses of gender and sickness absence were used by the Equal Opportunities Commission in leaflets sent to employers in an attempt to dispel the myth that women are unreliable workers. They also formed part of the evidence the commission used in a subsequent sex discrimination case against an insurance company which, like many others, was in the habit of charging higher health insurance premiums for women (despite not paying for care during normal pregnancy and childbirth) (Arber 1990).

Much research on health conditions shared by both sexes has focused on men, because women's bodies are seen by mainstream health researchers as a deviation from the male norm (Cotton 1990a, 1990b; Mastroianni et al. 1994). For example, the fact that women have menstrual cycles has been used as a reason for not including them as 'subjects' in drug trials. One survey in the USA in 1997 of 4,000 clinical trials found that a quarter excluded all women of child-bearing age (Josefson 1997); there is a thin line between protection and prohibition here. Drug trials may exclude women irrespective of whether the drug in question will be prescribed for them. Coronary heart disease is the major cause of death for older women in most industrialized countries (Wenger 1997); a study in the USA found that three-quarters of trials of cholesterol-lowering drugs were conducted with middle-aged men only, although half the prescriptions written for these drugs in the USA are for women over sixty (Wysowski et al. 1990). The Institute of Medicine in the United States commissioned a study of women and health research in 1992 (Mastroianni et al. 1994). One problem was the many studies that gave insufficient information about sex (or gender).[3] Gender bias was particularly evident in two areas: HIV/AIDS and heart disease. Several well-known heart disease studies looking at either treatment or prevention had no women at all in them (Mastroianni et al. 1994).[4] In Britain, a considerable amount of research on health differentials has gone on under the rubric of work on social class and health, which has been another effective device for ignoring women. Part of the explanation for this is the well-rehearsed problem (which merely pushes the issue one stage further back) of fitting women and their occupations (both paid and unpaid) into a schema originally invented for men and *their* occupations (Dex 1987; Osborn 1987).

Women may be underrepresented in experimental and 'quantitative' work on health, despite being major targets for health care interventions. Of course women have different bodies from men, but it is impossible to say how many of the interventions applied to women proceed from biological 'need' and how many from the perspectives of health care professionals on women as a gender group, or from some combination of one and/or the other of these and the effect on women's bodies of living in a gendered culture. One interesting repository for these arguments about nature and nurture is the debate about women's greater tendency, as compared to men, to suffer from psychological 'morbidity' which features in European and North American statistics (see e.g. Jenkins 1985; Verbrugge and Wingard 1987). Are women 'really' ill more often than men, or is this an artefact of their greater (culturally shaped) tendency to seek help and thus enter the rolls of the officially sick? Or are women ill because of their social roles? Does women's work make women sick? How much of women's illness is 'really' physical, and how much psychological? A particularly illuminating moment occurred in the history of research on women's health when one researcher noted that a commonly used instrument for assessing illness classified tiredness as a 'psychological' symptom. This was not how the women in her study (of mothers with young children) talked about it (Popay 1992).

So far as arguments about experimental research and women's health are concerned, the opposition to trials of many feminists, social scientists and qualitative researchers is especially troubling (see Oakley 1998a, 1998b, for detailed discussions). The health problems of women as a result of uncontrolled experimentation are legion. These include both over- and under-treatment of such diseases as breast and cervical cancer, high rates of hysterectomy and other forms of genital mutilation, and the 'medicalization' of women's bodies and minds through widespread prescription of psychotropic drugs. The international network of health care researchers, the Cochrane Collaboration (see chapter 13) had its origin in concerns about high and rising rates of surgical and other interventions in pregnancy and childbirth, many of which were subsequently shown to be unsupported by evidence of safety and effectiveness (I. Chalmers et al. 1989).

There are questions about the safety and effectiveness of many of the other health care interventions commonly prescribed for women, including psychotropic drugs, preconceptional health checks, fertility treatment, and hormone replacement therapy; and also about the various screening programmes targeted at them, including antenatal care, postnatal health visiting and parent education, cervical and breast screening, and screening for osteoporosis risk. All the screening programmes which women today are exhorted to use suffer from similar weaknesses – over-diagnosis of non-existent problems and under-diagnosis of 'real' ones (see Marshall et al. 1986; Oakley 1998b, 1999; Raffle 1996; Roberts 1989; Tucker et al. 1996). For instance, a detailed analysis of cervical cancer screening in one British town from 1988 to 1993 found that over 15,000 healthy women were incorrectly told they were at risk, and over 5,500 were investigated, with many being treated for a 'disease' that would never have troubled them, leaving them with lasting worries about cancer, not to mention concerns about future fertility and also other non-trivial issues such as life insurance (Raffle et al. 1995). Hormone replacement therapy, taken by about a third of all middle-aged women in Europe and the USA (Topo 1997), is a medication with unknown long-term effects. Rates of breast cancer are raised by 50 per cent in HRT users, and the risk of deep vein thrombosis and pulmonary embolism is two to four times as high (McPherson 1995; Wise 1996); there is no evidence that HRT does one of the things it is held out to do, which is to prevent heart disease, and some recent evidence indicates that it actually increases this risk (Hemminki and McPherson 1997; Josefson 1999).

Of course, it is hard to reconcile the importance of these issues to most women with the pronouncements of post-modernism that reality, and therefore real problems, do not exist. As Sandra Harding (1991:173) has observed, 'Meanwhile, women want to know about how their bodies really work' – just as they want to know about the social forces responsible for keeping them in poverty, for making men violent towards them, and so on.

What kinds of methodology do we need?

Many researchers recognize that the present situation with respect to methodology is unsatisfactory. Too much time and effort is going into paradigm
warfare. Neither 'qualitative' nor 'quantitative' methods on their own, as currently recommended, will do the job. Of course, the important thing is the
research question, but most research questions can be answered in different
ways. There is almost no discussion in mainstream social science (and certainly
very little in sociology) of experimental ways of knowing, although there are
signs that an informed debate is beginning. Similarly, the traditional exclusion
of 'qualitative' methods from health care research is now starting to be addressed (see e.g. Chard et al. 1997).

One of the things we need is a more critical, and ethical, approach to *all*
kinds of methodology. The philosopher Sandra Harding, who has written
widely on feminism and science, has proposed that 'a critical and self-reflexive
social science' should be the model for *all* science (Harding 1986:44).[5] In part
this conclusion is reached through sociological studies of science, which have
amply demonstrated that science is not the kind of activity it is often made out
to be. Science, as it is often thought of, is an ideological representation which
has lent itself particularly well to the kind of 'gendering' that has made it
complicit with the story of methodology told in this book. A fundamental
fault-line crept into the history of methodology when social science evolved in
the shadow of natural science as ideological representation; the problem was
not that social science tried to imitate physics (as the exemplar of laboratory
science), but that it imitated what physics was mistakenly thought to be (Kaplan
1965). Scientists rarely conform to 'canonical' versions of scientific activity,
enshrining the principle of straightforward applications of technical method.
Much science involves 'qualitative' knowing and even fusion between knower
and known (E. F. Keller 1983). It is often messy, non-linear, creative, contingent, pragmatic and 'experiential' – all the things 'qualitative' social science
research is celebrated as being. Decisions about what kinds of experiments to
do, which instruments to use, and what kinds of interpretations to make reflect
local conditions, circumstances, opportunities, beliefs and value systems (Knorr-
Cetina and Mulkay 1981; Latour and Woolgar 1979; Pickering 1992; Woolgar
1996).[6] Contrary to the accepted view, science does not proceed cumulatively
through replication – or at least, it does so no more than the social sciences
(Hedges 1987). Many scientific 'discoveries' were accidents; their discoverers
were after something else at the time. A lesser-known example than those
usually quoted is evidence for the 'big bang' theory of the origins of the
universe, which was stumbled on by two scientists who were trying to calibrate
a microwave communication antenna. Their efforts were disrupted by background noise, which turned out to be 'fossil evidence' of the moment at which
the universe came into being. They subsequently got the Nobel Prize for
Physics for this 'discovery' (Casti 1989:476).

To say that science, like social science, is a social product, is not at all the
same thing as subscribing to epistemological nihilism. Science may be socially

produced, but particular scientific conclusions may be more or less credible and trustworthy. All forms of science need to rid themselves of their systematic blindness to 'the ways in which their descriptions and explanations . . . are shaped by the origins and consequences of their research practices and by the interests, desires, and values promoted by such practices' (Harding 1991:15). All forms of science need to develop an awareness of how hidden partialities, including Eurocentrism and androcentrism, may lead to bias. People are not interchangeable as knowers, any more than they are as the known.[7] 'Quantitative' methods need to enshrine a greater respect for the perspectives of the people who contribute data. One of the things this may mean is less use of pre-prepared measuring and assessment scales, which often force people's experiences and views into places they do not want to go. 'Experimental' methods as used in the health care field have a particular history to shed with respect to the issue of treating research participants well; among other things, this will mean facing up to the tension that exists between the 'scientific' requirement of no-intervention control groups[8] and the ethical obligation to provide full information to would-be research participants about the research. 'Qualitative' methods could do with more self-criticism about the mediation of their research findings by partial, researcher-driven perspectives, and by more caution, openness and accountability in relation to the findings claimed. It is time to stop boasting that 'triangulation' and computer-based analysis are all that are required to establish the trustworthiness of 'qualitative' findings – just as it is time to give up the pretence that all that matters in experimental research are large sample sizes, adequately concealed allocation and competently executed statistical tests.

Getting rid of paradigms

One crucial strategy for bringing to a close our current paradigm war is to drop the language of 'quantitative' and 'qualitative' approaches altogether. These terms are relative, rather than absolute, in any case: 'quantitative' research often measures quality, and numbers are a frequent occurrence in 'qualitative' research. This book has argued that the main referent of the 'quantitative'/ 'qualitative' terminology is ideological; it serves to mark out contrasting sets of values and philosophical and political positions. In this sense, the language of 'quantitative' and 'qualitative' has always been distinctly unhelpful as a technical guide to research methods, and we would all be better off without it.

Dissolving the paradigms, instead of choosing between them, is not a new idea, although there are some who regard it as impossible. Smith and Heshusius published a much-quoted paper in 1986 which argued that the 'positivist' and 'constructivist' world-views associated with 'quantitative' and 'qualitative' paradigms respectively are simply incommensurate; therefore reconciliation is inconceivable. Yvonne Lincoln, one of the American evaluation researchers who promoted 'qualitative' methods for intervention evaluation (see chapter 10), argues that: 'The rules for action, for process, for discourse, for what is con-

sidered knowledge and truth, are so vastly different that . . . we are led to
vastly diverse, disparate, distinctive, and typically antithetical ends' (Lincoln
1990:81). This is reminiscent of an exchange between two famous social scientists, C. Wright Mills and Paul Lazarsfeld. Wright Mills opened the conversation by quoting the first sentence of his book *The Sociological Imagination*
(1959:3): 'Nowadays men often feel that their private lives are a series of
traps.' Lazarfeld's response was: 'How many men, which men, how long have
they felt this way, which aspects of their private lives bother them, when do
they feel free rather than trapped, what kinds of traps do they experience, etc.
etc.?' (cited in Elcock 1976:13).[9]

Faced with old-fashioned notions about reality existing and trustworthy
knowledge being needed, one response is clearly for paradigm warfarists to dig
their heels in even further. Francis Bacon described this process accurately in
1620:

> The human understanding, once it has adopted opinions, either because they
> were already accepted and believed, or because it likes them, draws everything
> else to support and agree with them. And though it may meet a greater number
> and weight of contrary instances, it will, with great and harmful prejudice,
> ignore or condemn or exclude them by introducing some distinction, in order
> that the authority of these earlier assumptions may remain intact and unharmed.
> *(Bacon 1994:57)*

Lincoln's view is that the 'socialization processes' and 'emotional and political
commitments' associated with each paradigm are barriers to methodological
integration. Apart from illustrating Bacon's precepts about human obstinacy,
this is an overly cynical view. Socialization is not a determining process; if it
were, all kinds of things would be impossible. In their *Qualitative and Quantitative Methods in Evaluation Research*, Charles Reichardt and Thomas Cook
(1979:20) cite a number of conclusions in the opposite direction, made from
the 1950s onwards, arguing that we should leave paradigm warfare behind us,
and that the 'socialization effect' can be overcome. In 1957, for example, Trow
urged researchers to 'get on with the business of attacking our problems with
the widest array of conceptual and methodological tools that we possess and
they demand. This does not preclude', he noted,

> discussion and debate regarding the relative usefulness of different methods for
> the study of specific problems or types of problems. But that is very different
> from the assertion of the general and inherent superiority of one method over
> another on the basis of some intrinsic qualities it presumably possesses. *(Trow
> 1957:33)*

Reichardt and Cook's discussion (1979:27) is mainly about the desirability
of combining different methods in evaluation research; their exhortation to
researchers to move beyond the dialectical language of 'quantitative' and 'qualitative' (in the second quotation at the head of this chapter) is almost an
incidental remark. But of course, avoiding the language of opposed paradigms

is a solution only on one level. It still leaves the question of how to integrate methods in the design and conduct of research on the practical level. This is not a problem to be solved with an easy shopping list of 'how to do it' procedures.[10] Rather, it is a question of carefully examining the research question, beginning with whether it has been asked and answered before, whether it makes sense to the people who might be asked to take part in the research, and identifying the other 'stakeholders' (including policy-makers); moving on to consider whether it is a question about evaluating the effect of something or about describing processes or events; whether it points to the generation of theory and/or to the production of widely applicable findings, and so on. All research takes place within the context of cost and funding and 'political' constraints; these will inevitably feed into decisions about which methods to use.

At every point, the ethical requirement of treating research participants well means that researchers must constantly bear these perspectives in mind. There are many challenges in all forms of research with respect to involving would-be research participants in setting research agendas, designing research, and contributing to its analysis, dissemination and subsequent use. There is accumulating evidence that including such perspectives brings about fundamental changes in the character, methods and design of research. For example, experimental studies of smoking cessation programmes for pregnant women have convinced doctors, with their focus on birth weight and babies' health (Lumley et al. 1999). But for many women smoking is a strategy which enables them to cope with the stresses of caring in poverty (Graham 1987; Oakley 1989). The usual approach to evaluating smoking cessation interventions ignores these meanings of smoking to women; it isolates physical survival and health from emotional and social well-being in a manner which is not found in most women's accounts of mothering (see Graham 1987; Oakley 1992b; Oliver 1995, 1997, 1998). One consequence of this is that the methods and conclusions of systematic reviews of smoking cessation trials are altered by the inclusion of women's viewpoints (Lumley et al. 1999; Oliver et al. 1999b).

However, in all kinds of research, it is impossible to avoid the conclusion that it is ultimately the researcher who is privileged. But, as the psychologist Jean Baker Miller (1976) has pointed out, there are different kinds of hierarchy. Some kinds of hierarchy are organized and played out in such a way that they inflate and affirm inequality, while others recognize people's different positioning within a relationship, and attempt to minimize the possibly harmful implications of this. The traditional relationship of employer and worker is an example of the first pattern; that of mother and child might be an example of the other. Minimizing disparities in power within the necessarily unequal relationship of researchers and researched would be a laudable aim for all forms of research to pursue.

Experimental research methods present particular challenges. Either ignored in the paradigm war, or associated with the 'worst' kind of 'quantitative' research, prospective experimental studies have had a chequered, and often misunderstood, history. Whoever actually 'invented' them in the modern sense, there is no doubt that they evolved in the work of both social and natural scientists as a means of dealing with uncertainty. There is therefore a strong case (apart from the one outlined above in relation to feminism and women's health) for rehabilitating these as ways of knowing, assigning them a valuable place in relation to certain kinds of research questions, whatever the topic of enquiry and its disciplinary location. Although 'experimental' is usually equated with 'quantitative', there is nothing intrinsic to the design of prospective experimental studies employing control groups which rules out 'qualitative' methods or data. A recent review for the UK Health Technology Assessment Programme looked at the methods used in studies of health programme evaluation focused on organizational change published in 1995. Ten of the twenty-six studies found used both 'qualitative' and 'quantitative' methods; four used solely 'qualitative' methods (the rest were classed as 'quantitative') (Murphy et al. 1998).

In the Health Technology Assessment study, 'qualitative' methods such as interviews and observations tended to be slotted into a prevailing 'quantitative'/experimental paradigm. A similar process happened in evaluation research in the USA in the 1970s, where many researchers took up Donald Campbell's call for case-studies and 'qualitative knowing' as primary adjuncts to systematic experimentation (Campbell 1988b). Describing the use of 'qualitative' research in five policy research projects, Firestone and Herriott (1983) noted that three factors were associated with the different use of 'qualitative' research, only one of which involved the technical requirements of the research; the others were the demands of the research sponsors and the interests and professional networks of the research teams. There had been no systematic attempt to integrate research methods; what happened instead resembled a 'garbage can model' of methodological decision-making (Firestone and Herriott 1983:460).

A central part of the effort needed to address all these challenges will be the actual *doing* of research, which always raises far more interesting and useful issues than *theorizing* about it. Too many methodologists in the past have not understood what it is like to try to follow textbook strictures in the real world.

Conclusion

We may be in the early stages of a paradigm shift in ways of knowing. As Kuhn has sketched such processes, they are normally far from cumulative, and are certainly not achieved by simple extensions of old paradigms. Rather, they involve a 'reconstruction of the field from new fundamentals' (Kuhn 1962:84–5). Whether or not this is happening, it is sorely needed. While academics and researchers make their careers arguing about methodology, people in the 'real' world continue to be disadvantaged and oppressed and to suffer from remediable problems. These issues form the legitimate subject-matter of all forms of science.

13

Challenges of an Experimenting Society

It is, once more, a hypothesis rather than a settled fact that extension and transfer of experimental method is generally possible. But like other hypotheses it is to be tried in action; and the future history of mankind is at stake in the trial.

Dewey, *The Quest for Certainty*

The empiricist character of much British social policy research is a serious weakness which reduces the impact that the social sciences might have upon society . . . The social scientist is a man [sic] with a problem or he is nothing.

Bulmer, *The Uses of Social Research*

Experimental ways of knowing have featured more prominently in this book than in most other accounts of methodology. There are three main reasons for this: first, such approaches to knowledge have played a much larger role in the social sciences than is acknowledged in most existing accounts; second, we lack a history of how experimental ways of knowing developed and were related to other ways of knowing in the social sciences. All histories are selective. This one is so self-consciously, in that certain themes have been highlighted to the exclusion of others. None the less, there are bound to be relevant gaps, silences and differences of opinion which would, if remedied and addressed, make the book more comprehensive in its coverage.[1]

A third reason for this particular focus – on the ways in which people studying society or the natural world have deliberately intervened in it, accompanying their intervention by procedures designed to assess its effects – has to do, not with history, but with the present policy context. In the UK and also in North America and elsewhere in Europe at the moment, there is considerable discussion of something called 'evidence-based public policy'. In essence, this is the same enterprise as that which informed the social policy experiments that burgeoned in the USA from the 1960s to the 1980s (discussed in chapters 9 and 10). The current move to evidence-based policy is paralleled by evidence-based medicine, evidence-based education, evidence-based social work, evidence-based policy making and evidence-based practice. Although a Martian might well find this plethora of 'evidence-based everything' somewhat amazing (unless of course she came from an evidence-based planet in the first place),[2] it is considerably less amazing in view of the story told in this book. Indeed, reading this account, one might well be more impressed by the *absence* rather than the *presence* of evidence-based *anything* in our recent methodological and social policy history.

The cancer of misleading evidence

Table 13.1 shows the findings of eight studies of the hormone diethylstilboestrol (DES) used as a treatment to prevent miscarriage. Many millions of women were prescribed this treatment in the 1940s, 1950s and 1960s; estimates of use by American women alone range from three to six million (Stillman 1982). Its use continued in some countries until at least the early 1980s (Laitman 1990). Of the eight studies listed in table 13.1, the first five used historical matched control designs to look at the effectiveness of DES by comparing women given DES with women not given DES. In this approach, the evaluation is, as it were, done after the event. Those who get an intervention receive it on the usual basis (that their professional advisers believe they will benefit from it). Then, after the outcomes are known, researchers compare these with those in another group of people who were not given the intervention (see Grant and Chalmers 1985). This approach to evaluation, used in the first five studies shown in table 13.1, demonstrated clearly that DES was a success story. The chances of women having a live baby appeared to be more than doubled with DES: 65 per cent of women given the drug had live babies, compared with 32 per cent who were not.

The remaining three studies in table 13.1 used a prospective experimental research design. Women at risk of miscarriage were randomly allocated either to be given DES or not, on the basis that their doctors were prepared to admit uncertainty as to whether the treatment worked. In these three studies the answer about the effectiveness of DES was quite different: no effect could be detected on the chances of having a live baby. These findings later acquired enormous significance when cases began to be reported of rare vaginal cancers in the daughters of women who had taken the drug.[3] Other serious health problems in both daughters and sons also came to light (Beral and Colwell 1981; Buitendijk 1991); DES-users themselves went on to have an increased risk of breast cancer (Beral and Colwell 1980). It became obvious that, not only did DES *not* work for the purpose intended (preventing the death of the baby), it also had harmful long-term consequences. That the harm affected

Table 13.1   Differences in live birth rates among pregnant women given diethylstilboestrol: studies using historical and randomised controls

	Proportion of live births in:	
	DES-treated women (%)	Control group women (%)
Historical controls (N = 5 studies)	65	32
Randomised controls (N = 3 studies)	87	87

Source: Taken from Sacks et al. 1982

innocent people who had not directly taken the drug (the babies) heightened the adverse health warnings people took away from this salutary story.

The DES research is a dramatic instance of a general problem: that well-intentioned interventions can have far from beneficial effects. It is also an example with a particular significance in terms of the autobiographical journey which lies behind the writing of this book (see chapter 1). My own early, sceptical position on experimental research design was considerably weakened by exposure to the DES example. After learning about it, I found it hard to understand how anyone with a concern (either professional or personal) for women's health could fail to find persuasive the lesson that well-designed research is important in revealing unsuspected consequences of courses of action, often inspired by beneficent motives, whose effects would otherwise be unknown. Such unsuspected harmful effects are by no means the prerogative of medicine. Among the examples discussed in this book where evidence of harm was detected following a social intervention are social work counselling for 'problem' boys and girls in the Cambridge–Somerville and Girls at Vocational High studies (chapter 8); income maintenance in the Negative Income Tax studies, financial aid for ex-prisoners in the Transitional Aid Research Project, and privatizing teaching in the Educational Performance Contracting research (chapter 9); and counselling for prisoners in California and intensive social and medical services for older people in New York (chapter 10). In all these instances, the findings of the research surprised those who had launched it, and also the professional groups involved. The research findings appeared 'counter-intuitive', in the sense that people responsible for the various interventions believed that they were doing good, not harm. For this reason, they often found it difficult to take on board the results of the experimental evaluation, seeking instead other explanations (the context of the research, its design, problems with the quality or the implementation of the intervention) which would preserve the possibility that the practice under test *did* actually work.[4]

The 'first do no harm' precept, a critical principle in medical practice, applies to all interventions made in people's lives, whether these are of a professional or a non-professional character, whether they are made in the name of 'qualitative' or 'quantitative' research, and however benign the effects of the intervention are believed to be. It may well be impossible to establish with certainty that no harm is being done. But it is certainly possible to take steps to ensure that any harm is more likely to be detected than not. Research is, in this sense, an activity with which all practitioners of interventions ought to engage, whatever their discipline, and whatever the substance of their intervention. But just doing research is not enough. It is important to do the kind of research that will provide the best evidence possible about what works. *Whether* something works is here the primary question, the question of greatest interest to most practitioners and policy-makers. *How* something works, and theories or behavioural models which might underpin the relationship between intervention and effects, are secondary questions.[5]

The lessons of the DES story with respect to evaluation design have been repeated many times (Kunz and Oxman 1998). Table 10.2, in chapter 10, is one such example, from the crime prevention field, where substantially higher 'success' rates were claimed for interventions evaluated with a design which did not include control groups than for those which did. Tables 13.2 and 13.3, below, are two further examples, from health promotion studies. Without control groups, 95 per cent of studies are said to be effective; with control groups, this reduces to 69 per cent (table 13.2). The second table looks at effectiveness claims made for a particular subset of work-place health promotion studies, those aimed at cholesterol reduction. For studies including 'qualitative' data, 87 per cent are said to be effective; this falls to 58 per cent for well-designed trials.

The general rule here is that studies with control groups generally yield less striking estimates of effect than those without them, and that studies with randomised controls generally yield less striking estimates than studies without them (see I. Chalmers 1997a; T. C. Chalmers et al. 1977, 1983; Devine and Cook 1983; Kleijnen et al. 1997; Sacks et al. 1982). But there is nothing magic about the idea of random allocation. As noted earlier, it is simply the easiest and

Table 13.2 The effectiveness of work-place health promotion interventions by evaluation design

Authors said	Studies with control groups (%)	Studies without control groups (%)
positive effect	69	95
no change	31	5

Based on N = 139 studies.

Source: Peersman et al. 1998

Table 13.3 The effectiveness of work-place health promotion interventions aimed at reducing cholesterol level

	Effective interventions according to authors (%)
Studies including 'qualitative' data	87
All studies	81
All trials	70
Well-designed trials[a]	58

Based on N = 52 studies.
[a] Comparable intervention and control groups, pre- and post-intervention data, reporting on all outcomes.
Source: Peersman et al., 1999.

most efficient way to create comparable research groups. Allocation does not have to be strictly according to random numbers; alternate allocation, for example, works just as well (I. Chalmers 1998). The important issue is whether the sequence of numbers is known in advance to whoever is carrying out the allocation. This is because of the human tendency to want to control what happens; people thought to 'need' the intervention under test will be more likely to be allocated to the group which will get it, thereby destroying the whole logic of the design scheme. Ken Schulz and colleagues (1995), in an analysis of 250 controlled trials in health care, found on average higher estimates of treatment effects in those studies where 'treatment allocation' was not concealed.

But the danger is that all this will come across as a set of highly technical and trivially methodological statements, when actually it is of great *substantive* importance. The lesson that interventions are often less effective when subjected to well-designed evaluation than they seem to be without this means that decisions about policy and practice can be taken on the basis of better evidence and more realistic expectations about the difference that any particular intervention is likely to make. If different interventions are similar in their effectiveness, then other relevant criteria can be used to choose between them. New approaches – in medicine, new drugs or technical procedures – are often hailed as promising miracle answers, when their chances of being more effective than established methods are no better than 50:50 (I. Chalmers 1997b). This tendency to anticipate substantial effects from new approaches helps to explain the disillusionment that set in in some quarters when the results of the large social experiments in the USA became known. Expectations had been too high; it was these that were at fault, not the evaluation design.

As Lipsey and colleagues (1985:24) note: 'The important issue is whether methodologically deficient work in evaluation research is benign in its consequences.' If studies which are designed to minimize the chances of researchers affecting the study findings are *systematically* associated with estimates of greater effectiveness, then there may very well be something unintentionally deceptive about the way in which, on the basis of other kinds of 'evidence', many professionals (and others) would have us believe that they know how to improve our lives. Thus, the 'methodological' lesson is actually a *political* one. In a discussion of conclusions to be drawn from social policy experiments, Henry Aaron, a high-level official active in the US evaluation industry in its 'golden era' (see chapter 10), noted that,

> Consciously, we recognize that it is hard to design experiments and that the results are often needlessly obscure ... But as we sharpen our instruments, we should recognize that ... the social experiment ... is part of an adversary process. ... the adversaries are contending for power, not truth. And deep down, that is what many of us are contending for too. *(Aaron 1978:275)*

One very important value of well-designed experimental ways of knowing inheres in the democratic ends they serve: their capacity to interrupt the 'normal' power relations existing between dominant professional groups and their clients.[6] The accumulation and wider accessibility of evidence produced by this means would bring about nothing short of a revolution in the traditional relationship between the 'lay' public as targets of interventions, on the one hand, and the professionals and others who practise these interventions on them, on the other. In this sense, scientific enquiry is fundamentally anti-authoritarian. This is quite contrary to its emotionally charged historical image as a form of enforced atrocity akin to what happened in the concentration camps of Nazi Germany (see I. Chalmers 1983).

An example to us all?

The history of experimental ways of knowing straddles the two worlds of social and medical research. Moves to put practice and policy on a firmer evidence base are apparent at various stages in this history for both sorts of research. Today, however, the notion of evidence is definitely in the ascendant in the medical domain. The iconoclastic Scottish doctor Archie Cochrane (see chapter 8), laid down a far-reaching challenge to medicine in 1979. In a contribution to a book published by the Office of Health Economics in the UK, he deemed it a great indictment of the medical profession that its work was not based on critical summaries, organized by speciality and periodically updated, of the results of all relevant randomised controlled trials (Cochrane 1979). This built on Cochrane's reflections as a medical student (before the days of the NHS) that 'all effective treatment must be free'. The slogan appealed, but what did 'effective' mean? (Cochrane 1972). In his challenge to medicine, Cochrane ranked specialities in order of their attention to such scientific evidence; the tuberculosis chest physicians came first; obstetrics and gynaecology came last.[7]

After Cochrane died, an ex-obstetrician, Iain Chalmers, helped to found an international network of people committed to the evidence from RCTs, named the Cochrane Collaboration. Iain Chalmers's own early research had looked at the practices of different obstetric teams in Cardiff in relation to what threatened to become an epidemic of intervention applied to child-bearing women: the surgical and medical induction of labour. He found that different obstetric teams had very different rates of induction, but could not detect any evidence of a direct relationship between induction rate and the chances of having a live, healthy baby (I. Chalmers et al. 1976a, 1976b). Chalmers went on to head a new research unit in Oxford, the National Perinatal Epidemiology Unit (NPEU), which quickly established a reputation for high-quality research in the maternity care field. Part of the NPEU's programme of work involved finding relevant randomised controlled trials: by 1985, over 3,000 such reports published in more than 250 journals had been located. A survey of 42,000 obstetricians in eighteen countries sought additional unpublished studies (Cochrane Centre 1992). Systematic reviews of trials by intervention were then carried out, resulting in some 350 separate reviews. These were collated in a 1,500-page, two-volume book called *Effective Care in Pregnancy and Childbirth* (I. Chalmers et al. 1989).[8] The researchers divided interventions into four categories: those shown to reduce the risk of negative outcomes; those promising forms of care requiring further evaluation; interventions with unknown effects; and those so unlikely to be of benefit they ought to be abandoned. A digest of the information in *Effective Care*, called *A Guide to Effective Care in Pregnancy and Childbirth* was written specifically for child-bearing women (Enkin et al. 1989).

Between 1989 and 1992, updated versions of the pregnancy and childbirth reviews and new reviews were published electronically as *The Oxford Database of Perinatal Trials*. By this time the NPEU's efforts were clearly having some effect. A House of Commons Health Committee, for example, reporting in 1992, said the findings of *Effective Care in Pregnancy and Childbirth* had 'profoundly influenced' its deliberations, and had this work been available twenty years earlier, some of the most undesirable developments in the maternity services might never have taken place (Health Committee 1992). The Committee recommended that all relevant health care professionals be supplied with a copy of the book; the Department of Health subsequently sent complimentary copies to all District Health Authorities. The results of the pregnancy and childbirth reviews were also incorporated into training material for health professionals, and were taken up and used by activist groups in the maternity care field (Stocking 1993). Outside the UK, the results were used by health care decision-making bodies in the USA and Australia, by the World Health Organization in its Maternal Health and Safe Motherhood Programme, and by professional bodies in the USA, Canada and New Zealand as the basis of new practice guidelines (Cochrane Centre 1992).

In 1992, Iain Chalmers left the NPEU to head a new research centre in Oxford, the Cochrane Centre, later renamed the *UK* Cochrane Centre when it was cloned in other countries. The Cochrane Centre was opened in October 1992 as part of the new NHS Research and Development Programme in the UK, headed by Michael Peckham (this was the first time the NHS had had such a programme) (Peckham 1991). As others in the UK and world-wide expressed enthusiasm for these developments, they led rapidly to the concept of an *international* research network, the Cochrane Collaboration, which was launched at a meeting in Oxford in October 1993.[9] The Cochrane Collaboration forms a resource for evidence-based health care which attempts to meet the criteria of Archie Cochrane's original vision. According to its mission statement, its aim is helping 'people make well-informed decisions about healthcare by preparing, maintaining and promoting the accessibility of systematic reviews of the effects of healthcare interventions' (Cochrane Library 1999; see I. Chalmers et al. 1997).

The Cochrane Collaboration has many activists and admirers, but also critics and outright enemies, among health care researchers, practitioners and policymakers, and others in other fields. The hostility of its critics is often rather vaguely focused, in part because of the somewhat intangible identity of the collaboration. It is a 'virtual' organization with unknown numbers of members and an unknown amount of funding.[10] Its organizational structure consists of 'registered entities' headed by an elected steering group of fourteen members, which is supported by a small secretariat based in Oxford. 'Registered entities' mean collaborative review groups, which undertake and update systematic reviews (currently forty-nine groups with 576 completed and 538 reviews in preparation), fields or networks (groups with primarily networking and trial-collecting responsibilities – currently nine) and methods groups (currently sixteen) which tackle issues about review methodology. There are now fifteen Cochrane Centres world-wide. For anyone studying the sociology of organizations, the Cochrane Collaboration provides a most extraordinary example of effective international networking, inspired by a shared commitment to a single goal – that of advancing evidence-based health care. The results of the Cochrane Collaboration's considerable endeavours are available electronically in the form of the Cochrane Library, advertised as 'the most powerful single source of evidence about the effects of health care anywhere in the world' (M. Fischer 1996:1), and available for £120 either as a CD-ROM or as an internet licence. The Cochrane Library holds information about the Collaboration, lists of its activities, the results of systematic reviews and other work, and a bibliography of some 225,000 trials, mainly (but not exclusively) in health care.

Criticism of the Cochrane Collaboration includes its focus on RCTs (see e.g. Feinstein 1995; Hunter 1993) and the dubious applicability of systematic review evidence to the real world (see e.g. Black 1996). A cartoon in the June 1996 issue of *Cochrane News* (figure 13.1) shows a man asking, 'What have you learnt from the Cochrane Collaboration?' and a woman answering, 'Life is full of trials'. This may well be a statement of the experience of lay people whose credentials as evidence have yet to be fully established within the Collaboration (see Oliver 1997).

What's so special about health care?

The Cochrane Collaboration is one way of organizing evidence about effectiveness and of collecting research material together so that it is accessible to

Figure 13.1 Lessons from the Cochrane Collaboration.
From *Cochrane News*. Issue no. 7 (June 1996):7.

researchers, practitioners and others, including lay people, who have an interest in using it. But is it a model for how this should be done for interventions
outside the health care field? Among the issues currently being discussed is the
conceptual framework used to organize the huge volume of research data,
which focuses on health *problems*,[11] rather than on types of *intervention*, or on
the *contexts* in which interventions are implemented (which may well affect the
way in which they work).[12] A second bone of contention in some circles is the
focus on controlled trials (whether randomised or not). Although far more of
these have been carried out to evaluate social interventions than the conventional story of experimental ways of knowing would suggest, there are still far
fewer than in the health care field. A recent outgrowth of the Cochrane Collaboration is SPECTR, the Social, Psychological and Educational Controlled
Trials Register, which lists trials collected from various databases covering
social care, education and criminology. SPECTR currently contains some 10,500
trials.[13] The relative lack of trial evidence in the social field raises questions
about whether methods could be found for including well-designed 'qualitative' (non-experimental) studies as sources of evidence to be drawn on in
systematic reviews. Work on this is currently ongoing. But it is not likely to be
an easy task (in view partly of the dissensions documented in chapter 3). When

Matthias Egger and colleagues (1998) carried out a meta-analysis of observational studies and RCTs examining the association between beta-carotene in-
take (found in fruit and vegetables) and heart disease mortality, they found
that the observational studies suggested considerable benefit, whereas the opposite was the case for the pooled trial data: beta-carotene appeared to increase
the risk of death. Meta-analysis of observational studies has been compared, in
a memorable metaphor, to the attempt of a quadriplegic person to climb Mount
Everest unaided (Feinstein 1995).

Many of the arguments and counter-arguments about the applicability of
trial methodology to social interventions have been rehearsed in earlier chapters of this book. This topic is the subject of a particularly keen debate in
social policy circles today. In 1996, Adrian Smith, a Professor of Statistics, in
a presidential address to the Royal Statistical Society in London, threw down
a similar gauntlet to Archie Cochrane's, but for the public policy field: 'But
what is so special about medicine?' Smith asked:

> We are, through the media, as ordinary citizens, confronted daily with contro-
> versy and debate across a whole spectrum of public policy issues. But typically,
> we have no access to any form of a systematic 'evidence base' – and therefore no
> means of participating in the debate in a mature and informed manner. Obvious
> topical examples include education – what *does* work in the classroom? – and
> penal policy – what *is* effective in preventing re-offending?

Smith went on to suggest that the Royal Statistical Society, together with
other learned societies and the media, launch a campaign 'directed at developing analogues to the Cochrane Collaboration', so as to achieve a 'quantal shift'
in public policy debates (A. F. M. Smith 1996).

Also in 1996, David Hargreaves, Professor of Education at Cambridge,
caused considerable controversy in educational circles with his lecture to the
Teacher Training Agency entitled 'Teaching as a research-based profession:
possibilities and prospects'. Hargreaves, like Smith, used the example of medicine to suggest that it behoves social researchers to get their house in order.
Like medicine, teaching is a 'people-centred profession'; like medicine, too,
large amounts of money are spent annually on research (£50–60 million a year
in the case of educational research in the UK); like medical research, educational research has (or ought to have) a broadly cumulative nature. Hargreaves
pointed out that,

> Far less medical practice is based on evidence than lay people commonly sup-
> pose. Medical treatment is not invariably followed by clinical improvement any
> more than classroom teaching is invariably followed by student learning. Indeed
> when doctors concede that, ' . . . a large proportion of treatments, not to say
> investigations and referrals, are no more than a face-saving disguise for medical
> impotence', one is tempted to shout a deeply sympathetic 'snap' with an equiva-
> lent admission that much teaching, specific lessons and acts of individual atten-
> tion to students, are no more than a face-saving disguise for pedagogic impotence.
> *(Hargreaves 1996:3)*

But teaching treats scientific knowledge in a fundamentally different way from medicine: there is no agreed knowledge base. Hargreaves's conclusion that 'there is simply not enough evidence on the effects and effectiveness of what teachers do in classrooms to provide an evidence-based corpus of knowledge' echoes Eisner's statement made twenty years earlier (see chapter 8) to the effect that if teachers had to base their practice on 'hard' data, we would have to close our schools.

Hargreaves's uncompromising challenge to the educational research community drew sharp responses, many in predictable directions. For example, Tony Edwards of the University of Newcastle upon Tyne objected to the 'unfavourable comparisons with medicine' which relies on 'the "scientific", bio-medical end of the research spectrum where experiments are feasible and ethically acceptable' (T. Edwards 1996:9). Martyn Hammersley of the Open University reiterated the line that, in educational research, 'strict experimentation is often ruled out for practical or ethical reasons'; human social life is simply 'quite different in character from the physical world studied by natural scientists [and] . . . investigated by most medical researchers'. Hammersley also noted that educational researchers *had* once used 'the scientific model', but gave it up when it yielded few conclusive findings (Hammersley 1997:145, 144) (see chapter 8).[14] Going back to the DES story, on this basis many more young women would have developed vaginal cancer, as the epidemic of using DES to 'prevent' miscarriage would have continued for much longer: indeed, it is difficult to see what would have stopped it. As Francis Bacon noted in 1620: 'Indeed it generally happens that men [*sic*] conduct experiments . . . and if the thing does not succeed, they grow scornful and abandon the attempt' (Bacon 1994:79).

To anyone who has read the book so far, these are dreadfully familiar arguments (see chapter 2; also R. Booth 1991; R. Walker 1998). Some of the most frequently rehearsed objections to the use of randomised controlled trials for evaluating social interventions were described by Robert Boruch in 1975. His list of 'common contentions' included their unfeasibility in 'real world' settings; their expense and time-consuming character; the view that other methods, especially quasi-experimental studies and statistical modelling, will give us the answer just as well; that randomisation is impossible and/or unethical; that such research designs ignore other useful social data; that 'qualitative' data are disregarded as unimportant; that different people are affected differently by the same intervention; that RCTs are one-shot affairs and therefore limited in usefulness; that they give us no information about how to improve the programme under test; and that their results lack generalizability (Boruch 1975). Boruch argued persuasively against these notions (see also his more recent rebuttal (Boruch 1997)). His arguments are paralleled elsewhere in the evaluation literature (see e.g. Bennett and Lumsdaine 1975; D. T. Campbell 1988a; Campbell and Stanley 1966; Rossi and Freeman 1993; Rossi and Williams 1972; Saxe and Fine 1981; and see also the discussion in Oakley and Fullerton 1996).

Evidence-based everything

The controversies provoked by Smith's and Hargreaves's lectures are part of a
general move in the social intervention field towards taking the notion of
evidence of effectiveness more seriously. Some of these moves are also afoot in
social work, which, as we have seen in earlier chapters of this book, has already
enjoyed – though that is probably not quite the right word – the experience of
being subjected to systematic evaluation. Joel Fischer's 1973 review of selected
social work studies, which showed that in about half of these clients getting
casework services tended to get worse, has been followed by other, similarly
critical reviews and commentaries (see e.g. Gough 1993; Macdonald and Sheldon
1992; Macdonald 1996a, 1996b, 1997; Macdonald and Roberts 1995; Newman
and Roberts 1997). These demonstrate how often claims to social work success
are based on shaky evidence, the lesson (again) that research design matters in
systematically affecting the conclusions drawn, and the proposal that randomised
controlled trials are a useful and possible way forward, because anything else is
ultimately a 'disservice to vulnerable people' (Macdonald 1997:144). Once
again, too, the case for well-designed experimental ways of knowing in social
work research is being contested by contrary voices which speak of 'restrictive
positivist practices' and identify the unpalatable conclusions yielded by rigorously produced research evidence as proving the methodological need to 'shop
elsewhere' (Macdonald 1996b:21, 29; see e.g. Cheetham et al. 1992; D. Smith
1987).

Over the last few years the 'anti-positivism' of some health promotion practitioners and researchers has also had to deal with weighty evidence that design
matters in this field. Tables 13.2 and 13.3 are examples. A programme of work
based at the Social Science Research Unit, University of London Institute of
Education, since 1993 has established databases of relevant studies, developed
guide-lines for assessing evaluation quality, and conducted a number of systematic reviews (see e.g. Oakley et al. 1995a, 1995b, 1996; Oliver et al. 1999b;
Peersman et al., 1999; Harden et al., 1999).[15] In the health promotion and
other social fields, 'comprehensive' evaluations incorporating randomised control groups, preceded by thorough needs assessment and pilot testing, and
including both process and 'qualitative' outcome data, are being proposed as
the most appropriate way forward (see Rossi and Wright 1984).

This does not, however, stop some health promotion researchers from following the 'anti-positivism' moves of their colleagues in education. A large
evaluation project called 'StopAIDs London' has recently been undertaken by
a pressure group called 'Gay Men Fighting AIDS'. Although the research
brief contained a requirement that the intervention be evaluated using the
approach of an RCT, as the project evolved, this was replaced with a method
relying on judgements about effectiveness by a few key actors, chosen because
it was felt that a trial might not yield the results the researchers and other
stakeholders desired (see Bonell 1999). The use of 'connoisseurial impact assessments' was thrown out many years ago in the evaluation literature as being

'among the shakiest of all impact assessment technologies' (Rossi and Freeman 1993:252).[16] In the HIV/AIDS prevention field, such moves are especially worrying in the light of growing evidence that gay men are ignoring safer sex recommendations in favour of 'barebacking' (sex without condoms) (Editorial 1999).

This kind of retreat into 'qualitative' methods has happened before; it was recommended among educational researchers in the 1940s and 1950s, and following the American social experiments by some of those who found the results of experimental evaluation methods disappointing. But using other methods because the results of experimental evaluations are deemed unattractive, and/or their design is considered politically incorrect, is not the answer. There are certain sorts of knowledge that people want to have – knowledge about the actions of others on their lives and the lives of their families – and well-designed experimental methods are the best ways of acquiring and making accessible that knowledge.

Studies of *how* evaluations are done in particular political contexts yield particularly good sources of clues about how best to implement systematic social experimentation. Two instructive examples are Peter Haug's (1992) case-study of an experimental assessment of different school-starting ages in Norway and the evaluation described by Robert Stake (1986) of a programme for disadvantaged youth in America, which produced so few 'hard' data that it was widely regarded as a complete waste of time and money.[17] The prime mover in this evaluation, Charles Murray, was so disheartened by the experience that he subsequently resigned from his research position, wrote an invective against the whole notion of government intervention (see chapter 10), and turned his hand to fiction (Stake 1986:96–7).[18]

Writing fiction seems an unnecessarily desperate response. A more sensible response to some of the challenges noted in this book with regard to the application to the social field of experimental ways of knowing is to try again; to learn what lessons can be learnt from how it was done before, and do better next time. The discussions in chapters 10 and 11 offer particular pointers about issues of design and ethics that need attention.

Other current signs of the move towards evidence-based policy in the UK are two meetings held in 1999 at the School of Public Policy in London (headed by Michael Peckham, who played a key role in establishing the Cochrane Collaboration). The focus of these was the importance of research synthesis in public policy. Among other relevant occasions in the UK were two seminars funded by the Economic and Social Research Council on evaluating social interventions in London in 1995 (Oakley and Roberts 1996) biennial conferences on educational research at Durham University, and two meetings on evidence-based public policy held at St Andrews University in 1998 and the Social Science Research Unit in 1999. Within a number of UK government departments, including the Department for Education and Employment, the Home Office and the Treasury, there is now talk of the need for evidence of effectiveness resources. In the research-funding community, the Medical Research Council and, more recently, the Economic and Social

Research Council are both making investments in this area. The previously
implacable opposition of some well-known charitable funders to experimental research is showing signs of weakening. Outside the UK, there has been
a conference in Germany in 1998 on randomised experiments in criminal
justice research, a report to the US Congress in 1997 on what works in
criminal justice, and also in the US, a Welfare Reform Evaluation Academy
with meetings in 1996–8, a conference on the quality of evidence organized
by the Department of Health and Human Services in 1999, and two conferences convened by the American Academy of Arts and Sciences and the
Department of Education in 1999 on the quality of evidence in educational
research (Boruch et al. 1999). The World Health Organization has recently
set up a 'Cluster on Evidence and Information for Policy', which aims to
invest major resources in rigorous approaches to evidence to underpin its
health politics and programmes.

A Campbell Collaboration?

If there is to be an 'analogue' to the Cochrane Collaboration, it is likely to be
named after Donald Campbell, the 'father' of scientific evaluation (see chapter
9). In 1971 Campbell published a remarkable paper called 'The experimenting
society' (reprinted along with many of Campbell's germinal papers in Campbell
and Overman 1988). The paper extended the argument developed in Campbell's
earlier paper 'Reforms as experiments' (1969), a highly influential and much
quoted argument for seeing the community and the nation (if not the world) as
a laboratory for well-planned experiments that continually test policy and
programme decisions. In his 1971 paper, Campbell reviewed his and his colleagues' past efforts to extend the epistemology of the experimental method to
non-laboratory social science. Two aspects of this experience stood out, in his
view: the resistances of the existing political system to 'social reality-testing'
and the fact that the efforts of evaluation methodologists effectively added up
to new procedures for political decision-making. Campbell derived from these
influences the radical imagery of an experimenting society. Such a society, he
said,

> would vigorously try out possible solutions to recurrent problems and would
> make hard-headed, multidimensional evaluations of outcomes, and when the
> evaluation of one reform showed it to have been ineffective or harmful, would
> move on to try other alternatives. *(D. T. Campbell 1988a:291)*

The experimenting society would be active, preferring innovation to inaction;
it would be an evolutionary, learning society and an honest society, committed
to reality testing, to self-criticism and to avoiding self-deception; it would be
non–dogmatic, accountable, decentralized and scientific 'in the fullest sense of
the word "scientific"', which includes the requirement of what Campbell called
'a disputatious community of "truth-seekers"' as the context for *doing* science;

it would also be a 'popularly responsive' and egalitarian society, providing for individual participation and consent at all levels of decision-making (D. T. Campbell 1988a:293–6).

Campbell's vision is remarkably like Cochrane's; both recommend making policy decisions on the basis of reliable evidence; both caution against the dangers of professional arrogance – in Campbell's case, the tendency of social scientists to cloak their recommendations 'in a specious pseudoscientific certainty' instead of the more humble language of 'wise conjectures' (Campbell 1988a:298). Both visions also recognize that all scientists and all people do in fact deal in the currency of cause in everyday life: causes are so much more interesting than correlations. Unlike Cochrane, however, Campbell admitted that there are significant issues to be tackled in the democratic application of experimental ways of knowing, particularly as regards information and consent.

Campbell derived the concept of 'the experimenting society' from the work of the American social philosopher John Dewey, whose call to apply the experimental method more widely heads this chapter (Dewey 1929:186). Dewey's professional project was to turn philosophy from a contemplative, ivory-tower study into a pragmatic science of action. He saw the point of knowledge as bettering human life, and called on his colleagues in other academic fields to give up metaphysics in favour of social action. Dewey's notion of politics as (ideally) an open, experimental process was a response to what he saw as the increasing regulation of people's lives by industry and other large-scale capitalist activities. This called, he believed, for some opposing mechanism of rationality and accountability (Dewey 1980; see Haworth 1960). Dewey shared with Elijah Jordan, another American philosopher, an astonishingly modern sense of normal political processes as uncontrolled experimentation. As Jordan (1952:411) phrased it:

> the process of public life . . . already follows the experimental method, and the only thing required to make it as fully adequate to public purpose as it could be is to have the method of experimentation consciously and openly and avowedly acknowledged and recognised.

Social science and the experimenting society

Campbell's conception of the social scientist's role in helping society towards his utopian vision was primarily that of the social scientist as methodological servant, giving policy-makers the tools with which to assess what *has* been done as a guide to decisions about what *might* be done in future. This modest scenario is far removed from Martin Bulmer's admonition (in the second quote at the head of this chapter) that 'The social scientist is a man with a problem or he is nothing' (1982:38). Social scientists are women as well as men, and this, as we have seen, has sometimes made a difference to conceptions of social science and its proper methodological concerns. The gendering of social science and of methodology has provided us with a particular *status quo*. We really have no way of knowing how this *status quo* might have been altered had these processes not occurred in the way they did.

But the substantive point that Bulmer was making was about the failures of UK social science to take much of a step, so far, in the direction of Campbell's experimenting society. In referring to the British tradition as 'empiricist', he was using the term in its derogatory sense as factual and atheoretical;[19] a social science that is 'merely' concerned with fact-gathering is unlikely to contribute to anything in a systematic, informed and thoughtful manner. Elsewhere, in a comparative study of British and American poverty research, Bulmer noted the very obvious lack of interest in large-scale social experimentation in British social policy research, attributing this to two main differences between the two countries: the British obsession with social surveys ('empirical' fact-gathering), on the one hand, and the greater permeability of the boundary between social scientists and policy-makers in Britain compared to America, on the other (see Jenkins and Gray 1989). Bulmer observes, candidly, that,

> Whether such close links with policy makers and 'political administrators' are good for the health of the social sciences is rather debatable. They give entrée into government, and the feeling of being able to influence policy quite directly, through having the ear of key politicians. They do, however, divert attention from academic goals such as the improvement of the analytic procedures used to study social processes. To that extent, they contribute to the methodological weakness characteristic of much British social-policy research. Research carried out for explicitly political reasons is not necessarily the most objective or fruitful in its outcome. *(Bulmer 1991:162)*

This seems a reasonable conclusion. But if social science has been complicit with the purposes of government in ways that do not necessarily serve the public interest, then it, in turn, has not been well served (in the recent past) by the conservative anti-social science tendencies manifested by government. Both in the UK and in the USA, social scientists in the 1980s and early 1990s suffered from budgetary cuts, reduced access to statistical and policy information, the privatization of public research, and a general stigmatization as agents of disruptive, self-serving social reform (Kirkpatrick 1984). While 'self-serving' may not be the most accurate term here, social science, like all professions, has a tendency to consider its own interests first, especially during times of external siege (Scott and Shore 1979). But although these threats to social science have been general, the investment of social scientists in different countries has been very different. This book has drawn mainly on the experience in Britain and in the USA, but there is a significant history of experiments with education and health policy in Germany (see Derlien 1989) and also with evidence of policy effectiveness in the Netherlands (see Bemelmans-Videc et al. 1989). There are important lessons to be learnt from cross-cultural studies about the conditions under which systematic social experimentation does, and does not, prosper (see Rist 1989; Wagner et al. 1991a).

Conclusion

We are left with a number of paradoxes. Social science *can* play a role in promoting evidence-based public policy; but often it has not done so. Experimental ways of knowing have a significant, though uneven, history in the social science and policy fields. Many experimental evaluations of social interventions have been designed and implemented in complex and methodologically shaky ways, and this, in a world which places a high premium on simple explanations, has worked to their disadvantage. None the less, the argument for using well-designed experimental ways of knowing is essentially the same as it was in the 1960s, when the 'golden era' of evaluation dawned in the USA: that reliable information about the effectiveness of public policy and social interventions is hard to come by using any other means. Moreover, such formalized approaches to knowledge are needed in order to protect the public from the damaging effects of professional and other forms of arrogance. Significantly, many of the policy issues on the UK agenda at the turn of the century parallel those that were trialled in the American experiments: how to reduce crime, how to encourage young people to stay in education, the costs of welfare dependency, the problem of the long-term unemployed, how to persuade single mothers to re-enter the labour market, and the benefits of early childhood intervention.

Experimental methods can make an important contribution to the kinds of knowledge in which not only academics, practitioners and policy-makers, but also the public at large, are interested. Recent attitudes to evaluation in some quarters have been marked by a retreat into more 'naturalistic' and theory-driven approaches to public policy evaluation, but these serve the interests of academic careers more than they promote the goals of either an emancipatory social science or an informed evidence base for social and policy interventions. But there are countervailing signs of a resistance to epistemological nihilism and a healthy disregard for obscurantist post-modernist escapes. Reality exists, and, although we do not all see it in the same way, we share an interest in being able to live our lives as well as we can, free from ill-informed intervention and in the best knowledge we can gather of what is likely to make all of us most healthy, most productive, most happy and most able to contribute to the common good.

The process of understanding the contribution which experimental methods can make to this endeavour has been interrupted by the unfortunate ideological and political history outlined in this book. Women and social scientists, as groups possessing lesser power than men and natural/medical scientists, have been particular opponents of this ideology, often for understandable reasons. But the confusion of experimental methods with 'bad' science has been part of the social construction of methodology as a gendered configuration. The paradigm war has set us against one another in ways that have been unproductive in answering some of the most urgent social questions facing us today.

There are fashions in all things, including social experimentation. Peter

Rossi and Howard Freeman, who have both played key roles in some of the history reviewed in this book, predicted that by the end of the Clinton era there would be a marked increase in the volume of social programme activity, and a corresponding need to build on what the USA and other countries have already learnt about generating policy-relevant evidence (Rossi and Freeman 1993:25). Donald Campbell cautioned in 1979 that we would need to draw on our past experience of experimental ways of knowing in order to be ready when the political will returns again, which it is bound to do (D. T. Campbell 1979:80). In his essay 'Of Innovations', Francis Bacon, using the medical analogy which has run throughout this book, wrote (1625:123): 'Surely every medicine is an innovation, and he [sic] that will not apply new remedies must expect new evils: for time is the greatest innovator; and if time of course alters things to the worse, and wisdom and counsel shall not alter them to the better, what shall be the end?'

Notes

Chapter 1   Who Knows?

1   I put the terms in quotation marks because referring to them as 'real' differences implies a complicity with this view.
2   See Hoeg 1994.
3   The focus is on 'Western' culture. Oriental ways of knowing may have anticipated by several centuries Western ones in certain ways (see Boruch 1984). For example, scholars in eighteenth-century China developed methods for evaluating research data based on precise criteria (see Spence 1990).
4   This rules out the possibility of any further changes in direction, which would probably be unwise.
5   The larger study was a randomised controlled trial. See Oakley 1992b.
6   This case is outlined in more detail in ch. 12; see also Oakley 1998b.
7   In the same case-study my work is also held up as an exemplar of unreliable qualitative knowing, so there is a sense in which it is simply impossible to win.

Chapter 2   Paradigm Wars

1   The two lists are randomised controlled trials, systematic reviews, meta-analyses, double-blind methods, case-control studies, outcomes measurement, cost–benefit analysis, decision analysis and surveys; and interviewing, action research, case-studies, observational studies and ethnography.
2   E.g. Patton (1978) gives seven, and Guba (1978) fourteen.
3   The twenty-one senses are: a set of achievements, or a concrete achievement; a myth; a philosophy; a classic work; a tradition; an accepted device in common law; a set of political institutions; a device, a source of tools, or a machine tool factory; an anomalous pack of cards; a gestalt figure; an analogy, or a standard illustration; a metaphysical speculation; a scientific standard, or an organizing principle; a general epistemological viewpoint; a new way of seeing, or something which defines a broad sweep of reality (Masterman 1970).
4   Like other features of experimental methods, N-of-1 trials were first used in

psychology before entering medicine in the 1980s. An early report was by the socialist geneticist Lancelot Hogben of a trial on himself of two drug treatments and a placebo for tiredness and mild depression. One of the treatments was clearly inferior to the placebo, and the other (amphetamines, or 'speed') improved mood but not working capacity; Hogben thought this approach to evaluation much superior to group data and 'irrelevant algebra' (Davey-Smith and Egger 1998).

5 Exceptions are Jayaratne (1983), Jayaratne and Stewart (1991), Marsh (1984) and Oakley (1992b and 1998b), whose 'defences' are at least partly addressed to feminist anti-quantitative critics.

6 Hammersley (1995:1) points out that D. Silverman (1989) is an exception.

7 Platt (1985) has observed that it is difficult to trace direct links between Weber's work and that of the early 'qualitative' researchers.

8 Glaser and Strauss's critique of 'verification' theory may even have been sufficiently radical to count as 'feminist' (Reinharz 1984:vii).

9 In its early years ethnomethodology was very like traditional ethnography, although a later repudiation of the latter by the former developed around the issue of the sources of bias in ethnographical fieldwork.

10 'Subjective' is often used in two different ways: to mean 'influenced by human judgement' and 'relating to individual feelings, beliefs and experiences' (see Reichardt and Cook 1979). In everyday parlance, 'subjective' (like 'sentimental') often carries negative connotations.

11 Similarly, in the health care field there has been a change of language – from 'patient' to 'user' (and people who use trains are now known as 'customers'). Whether the change of terminology makes any substantial difference to the way participants/users/customers are treated is, of course, another question.

12 Reinharz (1992) says she discusses psychology on the grounds that there *is* no equivalent sociological tradition.

13 Harding later regretted this analogy (see Nemecek 1997).

14 By and large, they do not (see Oakley and Fullerton 1996).

15 Much of the critique misunderstands the design of RCTs, especially the notion of random allocation, which is often confused with random sampling. One consequence is that survey methods get tarred with the same brush; as Marsh (1984:85) has pointed out, 'The only element of randomness in the survey design comes in random selection of cases; random sampling is not the same as random allocation into control and experimental groups.'

16 Resistance comes sometimes from within medicine (see e.g. Herman 1995); it is a mistake to try to draw party lines in any neat way.

Chapter 3   Hearing the Grass Grow

1 'Duck-rabbit' comes originally from a book by Jastrow called *Fact and Fable in Psychology* (1901).

2 The phrase 'face-to-face' evokes the psychologists' descriptions of the 'en face' position of mother and child.

3 Interestingly, this is not a criterion for validity which appears in tables 3.2 or 3.3.

4 In a later volume, the authors discuss some of the many uses to which their work has been put and some of the criticisms levelled against it, particularly of their neglect of cultural and ethnic differences between the women they interviewed, and the charge of 'essentialism' – that women do have special ways of knowing. A

better title for the book, they say, would have been '*some* women's ways of know-ing'. Goldberger and colleagues argue that they did not claim originally that the five ways of knowing they identified *were* distinctively female: 'We believed that those categories might be expanded or modified with the inclusion of a more culturally and socioeconomically diverse sample of women and men' (Goldberger 1996a:7; see also Goldberger 1996b).

5   The existence of a male menopause has been suggested, but the physiological referents are obviously different.

6   This picture of middle-aged *people* having similar health experiences is supported by other research – for example, a recent study in the Netherlands looked at bone density and hip fracture, finding that the risk of hip fracture by age and bone density is similar for both men and women, as men also suffer a loss of bone density with age (De Laet et al. 1997).

7   This is also an interesting use of statistics in a piece of work which is otherwise ideologically anti-numerate.

8   Thanks to Sandy Oliver for this observation.

9   She was married at the time, but did not tell the Samoans this, because she was unsure about how this information might affect the roles assigned to her in that culture (Mead 1972:161).

10   She lived in a building which housed the medical dispensary and the radio station belonging to the naval government of American Samoa.

11   Gerber's interpretation was that Samoan culture had developed stricter prohibi-tions around sexuality; Holmes's view was that this had not happened (see Free-man 1983).

12   The full list (with the number of mentions in parentheses) is as follows: clear aim(s)/purpose (2); research methods appropriate to the question (3); account of theoretical framework (1); clear description of sample (3); justification of sample (2); clear criteria for data collection (1); clear description of recruitment/sample (4); connection to/location within existing body of knowledge (3); clear descrip-tion of sample characteristics (2); adequate sample (1); independent inspection of evidence possible (1); relationship between researcher and subjects considered (2); research explained to subjects (1); adequate description of fieldwork (2); system-atic data collection (2); systematic/careful record keeping/data retrieval (3); ad-equate/clear description of data collection (1); reference to accepted analytic procedures (1); analysis repeated (1); clear/adequate description of data analysis (3); justification of data analysis procedures (1); systematic analysis (1); use of quantitative evidence to test qualitative conclusions (1); sensitive data collection (1); adequate description of how findings/analytic framework derived from data (4); adequate discussion of contrary interpretations (2); measures to test validity (2); steps taken to see if analysis is comprehensible to participants (1); systematic presentation of data (1); sufficient original material presented (3); efforts to estab-lish reliability (1); clear distinction between data and interpretation (1); clear state-ment of author's own position (2); credible and appropriate results (1); adequate consideration of ethical issues (2); understanding of qualitative paradigm (1); ap-propriate references cited (1); problem clearly defined (1); scope of question man-ageable within study time frame (1); literature review sufficiently comprehensive (1); major concepts defined (1); appropriate initial framework (1); context ad-equately described(1); issues of qualitative sampling addressed (1); knowledge of qualitative research strategies demonstrated (1); importance of study to subject area outlined (1).

13 In the event the study went ahead as planned. Some 68,000 women in five countries took part in the Multi-Centre Fetal Movements Trial. Fetal movement counting was shown to be of some value in predicting health problems, although this did not translate into any detectable reduction in the risk of a baby dying before birth (perhaps because the medical diagnostic tests and/or the interventions available were not effective). The data suggested that formal counting made women more anxious, and also more likely to report reduced fetal movements, and be admitted to hospital (Grant et al. 1989).

14 The full list is as follows (with the number of mentions in parentheses): establishing rapport in order to understand research participants' perspectives (2); full immersion in the situation being studied (2); multiple observations (2); peer debriefing (1); negative case analysis (2); constant monitoring of the researcher's own construction/conceptual orientation (2); checking data/interpretations with research participants (2); understanding the researched in their total environments (2); collecting repeated observations/evidence (2); obtaining 'thick' data and/or using 'thick' description in order to understand fully (3); examining similarities of findings with other comparable situations (2); interpreting one social group to another (1); coherently linking researcher's conceptual orientation to the data (1); acknowledging the relationship between researcher and the researched and examining the impact on the data of this (1); protecting the anonymity and integrity of the researched (1); making sources of data clear (1); collecting adequate, appropriate and broad data (1); ensuring that all research processes are trackable and documentable (2); making explicit the logic of connections between data and interpretations (2); collecting data from different sources (1); exploring and contrasting diverse sources of data (1); writing a literarily competent report (1); the privileging of subjective meaning (1); responsiveness of the research design to social context (1); and typicality (1).

15 This was, in fact, pointed out to Guba and Lincoln shortly after they developed their approach. In response they went on to designate a different set of criteria which were non-concrete and 'non-foundational', relating instead to the 'states of being' of researchers, participants and stakeholders in qualitative research. In later work they took this further (see Lincoln 1990).

16 Other research shows that men are generally more concerned to present a public front of their families as happy, successfully functioning systems (Brannen et al. 1994).

17 Anyone who has ever done research using medical notes understands how misleading is the notion that these represent 'gold standard' information. Gaps and inconsistencies abound.

18 On the other hand, the deception was often spotted by other patients, who said things like 'You're not crazy. You're a journalist or a professor,' when they observed the pseudo-patients taking notes (this was considered by staff an aspect of pathological behaviour) (Rosenhan 1973:252).

19 He disguised his occupation of sociologist after a gay friend told him that sociologists were regarded by the gay community with particular suspicion.

20 See Murphy et al. 1998, ch. 5, for a recent review of ethical issues in 'qualitative' research. They conclude that 'research participants are at risk of significant harm in many qualitative research studies, either to their psychological or emotional wellbeing or to their professional or even legal position' (1998:162).

Chapter 4 Cartesian Nightmares

1 See Cohen 1985a: ch. 4 for a discussion of this.

2 Cohen (1985b:15), with the unconscious sexism of much writing about science, calls it 'a real blow to man's pride'.

3 'Little is known of Galileo's mother beyond the fact that in her widowhood she was a trial to her children, especially Galileo' (Sharratt 1994:24).

4 See Sharratt 1994:45–51.

5 The standard story is that Galileo invented the telescope; but while he certainly improved on the Dutch design, it seems that the original idea was not his (see Sharratt 1994:13 16).

6 This is the translation of the title (*Sidereus Nuncius*) used by Cohen (1985a); Sharratt (1994) calls it *The Sidereal Message*; he argues (1994:18) that Galileo meant 'message' rather than 'messager', and that the mistranslation is the fault of Kepler. However, the idea that Galileo was a messenger bringing news from the heavens was attractive.

7 Cohen (1985b:136) observes that Galileo's astronomical observations did not actually prove that Copernicus was right. They were quite consistent with the theories of Tycho Brahe about the Earth being motionless and the other planets going round the Sun, which in turn revolves round the Earth. This whole issue provides a fascinating instance of paradigm change (the drive to see a 'new' approach as decisively different may triumph over the 'facts' of historical consistency).

8 In his personal life, Galileo remained a committed Catholic, though his irregular domestic life, begetting three out-of-wedlock daughters, whom he sought to place in a convent at the earliest opportunity, hardly made him an exemplary one.

9 On the 'idea' and socio-cultural history of the scientific revolution see Cohen 1985b. The term is said to have been coined by the French mathematician d'Alembert in 1759 (Hankins 1985).

10 The term itself was not coined until 1835, according to V. H. H. Green (1952:30).

11 In France, where it originated, it was called the 'siècle des lumières'. According to Hankins (1985:2) it was the German metaphysician Kant who devised the term 'enlightenment'.

12 This meant that the physician and the physicist were one and the same.

13 The term 'scientist' is said to have been coined by the English scholar William Whewell (1794–1866) in 1834 (Schiebinger 1989:1).

14 Immanuel Kant's *Critique of Pure Reason* (1781) was dedicated to Bacon as the 'godfather' of British empiricism.

15 He claimed the experiment 'succeeded excellently well' (cited in Pettonen 1996a:13). According to John Aubrey in his *Brief Lives* (1898), there is something disingenuous about this story, which comes from a letter Bacon wrote to his friend the Earl of Arundel in between catching the cold and dying; Bacon already knew that flesh would be conserved by the cold, mentioning this in the *Novum Organon* (see Urbach 1994:xii). In their recent biography, Jardine and Stewart (1998) argue that the experiments in the prolongation of life to which Bacon was referring in his letter to Arundel were really experiments on himself, part of his lifelong habit of taking opiates.

16 See ch. 7.

17 Bacon may have been talking about sample size, or about the philosophical problem of 'proving' (for example) that all swans are white simply by observing a large number of white ones. (Thanks to Harvey Goldstein for this observation.)

18 See Cottingham 1986:9–10; Vrooman 1970:56–9; Stern 1966:80–4 for a description of the dreams, and Stern 1966:84–105 and Vrooman 1970:58–64 on their interpretation.

19 Vrooman (1970:212) follows tradition in noting that Christina 'lacked virtually every feminine charm', adding that she was physically 'repellent' and 'her morals were highly suspect'. Stern (1966:97) called her 'one of the first great phallic women in modern history'. He notes that when she was born she was at first thought to be a boy; she may in fact have suffered from adrenogenital syndrome, a condition in which genetic females are born with masculinized external genitalia due to excess production by the adrenal glands of male hormones in the womb and following birth. An alternative explanation, offered by Masson (1968:21), is that Christina was born with a caul from head to knees, so that her sex was not at first evident, and 'the birth of a girl was the last thing anyone wanted'.

20 Vrooman (1970: ch. 7) gives another interpretation – that Descartes caught an infection from his friend Canut.

21 Bacon's mentor, James I, is known to have supported anti-women and anti-witchcraft legislation.

22 He was, on the other hand, brought up by his grandmother, who may well have been a successful substitute.

23 It has been suggested, rather harshly, that Descartes may have embarked on fatherhood by way of an experiment. He was an active experimentator himself: he worked on the circulation of the blood and the dissection of the pineal gland, an organ in which he was much interested, believing it to be the seat of the soul – as naïve an assumption 'as any of the wildest pre-scientific claims which Aristotle made' (Stern 1966:102). Descartes' view of the pineal gland was based on the observation that all other parts of the brain are double; since we 'only have a single and simple thought of a given thing at a given time, there must necessarily be some place where the two images coming through the two eyes . . . can coalesce into one' (Voss 1989:36). He dissected animals from slaughterhouses late into the night in a laboratory he built himself in one of the turrets of his little chateau in Holland (following the example of Copernicus (V. H. H. Green 1952:50)). The year of Francine's conception was also the time when he was working on his *Traité de la Formation du Foetus*. But cause and effect may, of course, have been the other way around.

24 Studying the emotions has always been a marginal aspect of mainstream social science. In view of the eugenic connection (see chs 7 and 11), it is interesting to note that Charles Darwin wrote a book called *The Expression of Emotions in Man and Animals* (1873), which is rarely mentioned.

25 The two domains of nature and science overlapped. Even today, one side of the Nobel Prize medals for physics and chemistry portrays both nature and science as women (Schiebinger 1993:147).

26 Schiebinger attributes the probable origins of feminine science to Christian Neoplatonism, with its notion that the rational soul of the universe is feminine and is what gives form to the whole.

27 See H. Rose 1994 for an 'unpacking' of what 'work' means in this context.

28 The name 'Paracelsus' means 'beside' or 'greater than' Celsus, the Roman physician, and was a nickname Paracelsus acquired in his thirties (Cohen 1985b:183). His given names were Theophrastus Bombastus von Hohenheim; his second name is reputedly the origin of the English word 'bombast'.

29 Their framework was the non-empirical doctrine that disease is the result of an

imbalance in the four humours or body fluids (blood, phlegm, choler or yellow bile, and melancholy, or black bile).

30 See Easlea 1981 for a discussion of this.

31 A sample of Newton's hair analysed in the 1970s showed high levels of these compounds (White 1998:251), but hair analysis, like alchemy, is an imperfect science.

32 The role of grandmothers in the lives of great men is interesting.

33 The full title is *A Description of the Famous Kingdome of Macaria Shewing its excellent government: wherein The Inhabitants live in great Prosperity, Health and Happinesse; the King obeyed, the Nobles honoured, and all good men respected, Vice punished, and Vertue rewarded.*

34 In Sir Thomas More's *Utopia*, the Macarians were the neighbours of the Utopians.

35 This is an original solution to the problem of 'the God complex' from which modern medicine is often said to suffer, with doctors proclaiming a kind of theological certainty for practices which may have little basis in empirical evidence.

36 Webster (1974a) concludes that Plattes was probably the main author, but that Hartlib must have contributed, in view (partly) of Plattes' lack of education. See also Webster 1970.

Chapter 5   Mean Values

1 Information on Hobbes is taken mainly from Martinich 1997; Sorell 1996; and Taylor 1908.

2 Hobbes is described as having been 'magnificently vain' about his achievement (Cohen 1994a:170).

3 Hobbes wrote a verse autobiography which is the source of this information (and the story that his mother gave birth to twins – himself and fear) (see Hobbes 1994).

4 McDonald (1993:93) notes that the situation was somewhat more complicated; apparently Hobbes did carry out experiments of his own in physics; he sent these to the Royal Society, which refused to publish them. His atheistic philosophy could not have helped. But there is no doubt that he minded his exclusion.

5 See Baker 1975; Hankins 1985.

6 Cohen (1994a:xxvi) notes that the American statesman John Adams used the terms 'the social science' and 'the science of society' in 1784–5. He probably did not invent these, so the terms must have been in (relatively) common circulation.

7 He found the marsh inhabitants' risk of death to be 20 per cent higher, after controlling for wealth, occupation, life-style and medical care.

8 Madame Vernet was the widow of a sculptor who kept a hostel for students, and had previously sheltered an enemy of the Revolution (E. S. Pearson 1978:446).

9 On Quételet see McDonald 1993; Stigler 1986.

10 The use of male data to construct descriptions of what is claimed to be biologically 'average' for human populations is a flawed tradition which continues to the present day; see e.g. Floud et al. (1990), whose volume *Height, Health and History* is about *male* height, health and history.

11 He found a sex ratio of 1.15 males to every female (E. S. Pearson 1978:8).

12 Pearson (1978:10) argues that Graunt lived a century before Achenwall, and that it was therefore he, not Achenwall, who invented statistics in the modern sense.

13 Greenwood was a student of Karl Pearson's, and one of the first medical research-

ers to apply mathematical statistical methods to medical problems; he reappears later in this story in the context of disputes about the kinds of inferences that may validly be drawn from experimental trial data.

14   Archie Cochrane was later to work on this. In a study of infancy and childhood mortality rates and seventeen health service, dietary and economic indices, he showed an association between the number of doctors per 1,000 population and mortality, which neither he nor anyone subsequently has been able to explain (St Leger et al. 1979; see also Doll 1997).

15   See ch. 6 for some observations which suggest that some early social investigators were aware of the importance of not treating people merely as sources of quantitative data.

16   Although sometimes she has sufficient strength to assert that she wishes she had never had a family, as this would teach them all the facts of what it would be to do without her (Dickens 1854:76).

17   Both Mill and Dickens wrote for John Black's *Morning Chronicle*; Black was a close friend of Mill's father (Johnson 1952:93–4). (Thanks to Berry Mayall for tracking this association down.)

18   Dickens and the younger Mill were almost exact contemporaries.

19   In a private note she asked once: 'What makes the difference between man and woman? Quételet did his work, and I am so disturbed by my family that I can't do mine' (she was at the time taking care of her confused eighty-six-year-old mother) (cited in Diamond and Stone 1981:73).

Chapter 6   Imagining Social Science

1   According to Beatrice Webb's autobiography the fact that George Eliot was in love with Herbert Spencer was 'an open secret' (Webb 1938:49). Her diaries record the famous conversation in which Spencer declared that he could never have considered marrying George Eliot because of her lack of physical beauty (Cole 1956:313).

2   He always regarded her novels as closer to sociology (Lepenies 1988:152).

3   Some years later Beatrice told her relatives of the deception. They were apparently pleased that she had not told them before they got to know her (Webb 1938:195).

4   Like many early social scientists/social surveyors, Booth's main career was in business; the poverty enquiry was a leisure-time pursuit paid for by his main occupation.

5   Beatrice Potter's radicalism did not at the time extend to the position of women; she joined those who were opposed to the political enfranchisement of women. In her autobiography she puzzles about this, noting that, although she changed her mind about this almost immediately, it took twenty years for her to recant publicly (Webb 1938:400–2).

6   Harriet Martineau probably suffered from a benign ovarian cyst and prolapse of the womb (see Cooter 1991; Porter and Porter 1988:212–17).

7   Today 'empirical' is used with a number of meanings. In the terminology of the methodological paradigm war, it is often used disparagingly by anti-quantitativists to equate with 'positivism' or 'science' as undesirable entities. Within medicine, 'empirical' has both 'bad' ('non-scientific') and 'good' ('based on observation') meanings (see Brewin 1994).

8   In the interwar years, some French sociologists referred to their work as 'sociologie expérimentale' as a way of stressing their concern with empirical/experiential methods (Clark 1973).

9   Comte 1853: 2.58: 'After Montesquieu, the next great addition to Sociology (which is the term I may be allowed to invent to designate Social Physics) . . . '.

10   Durkheim called himself a 'rationalist' rather than a 'positivist', because he wanted to dissociate his views from Comtean metaphysics (Lukes 1973:72–3).

11   Talcott Parsons, a major inheritor of the Durkheimian tradition, puts this in reverse in his *The Structure of Social Action:* 'Experiment is, in fact, nothing but the comparative method where the cases to be compared are produced to order and under controlled conditions' (1949:743).

12   Very little, but it was evident from the tables Rowntree included that larger numbers would be most likely to reduce the chances of sampling error.

13   Rowntree's first survey of York was carried out partly to replicate Booth's London survey with data from a provincial town: his figure for the proportion of the town population living in poverty was 27.8 per cent, close to Booth's of 30.7 per cent (Rowntree 1922:355).

Chapter 7   Chance is a Fine Thing

1   On the later role of agricultural experimental stations as supporters of scientific research see Rosenberg 1976.

2   One explanation of Miss Bristol's acuity is that chemical reactions in a cup of tea differ according to whether the tea or the milk is poured in first. (Thanks to Sandy Oliver for this observation.)

3   See Dehue 1997:655 for a list of typical citations.

4   Although the meanings of the terms are confused, the notions of 'random sampling' and 'random allocation' are linked conceptually through the notion of a probability distribution. (Thanks to Harvey Goldstein for pointing this out.)

5   See Oakley 1991.

6   See ch. 8 for other examples of picking victims by lots. W. A. Silverman (1981) attributes the declining fashion for casting lots partly to the appearance of Judaeo-Christian monotheism, which condemned the practice as magical and demoniacal, attempting instead to bring such decision-making under the control of ecclesiastical procedure. He suggests that this history may underlie modern attitudes to random allocation as inherently sinful (see ch. 2).

7   The cumulative result of these three experiments gives 0.5047, a little over 50 per cent, as the proportion of times the coin fell head uppermost.

8   Using the logic of statistical inference, Peirce also came up with the theories of confidence intervals and hypothesis-testing which were formally advanced much later, in the 1930s.

9   See the internet website, www.rcpe.ac.uk/cochrane, for continuously updated references to early examples of controlled trials.

10   If adhered to strictly, alternate allocation should confer the same advantage as random allocation in generating socially equivalent experimental and control groups.

11   Doctors today remain curiously resistant to the hand-washing lesson. A study in 1995 found that senior doctors washed their hands only twice during twenty-one hours of ward rounds (they also significantly over-estimated their hand-washing rate) (Bartzokas et al. 1995; see also Handwashing Liaison Group 1999).

12   This highlights the need for an understanding of *processes* to accompany the measurement of *outcomes* in trials.
13   Although some resist. Asked what they would do when published data and 'clinical experience' conflict, 53 per cent of doctors in a recent study said they would trust 'my clinical experience' (Fallowfield et al. 1977:2224).
14   Leeches might seem self-evidently a damaging therapy, but this is not the case. For example, they are currently used to considerable effect in plastic surgery as a way of reducing blood congestion (Elder 1998).
15   As Kevles points out, Fisher ignored the fact that about nine out of ten 'mentally deficient' children were the offspring of normal parents.
16   A recent systematic review of three randomised controlled trials of intercessory prayer as an intervention for people with health problems supports Galton's conclusion that prayer may have no observable effect on the risk of dying. In this review there was, however, some evidence of fewer poor outcomes in the prayed-for group of people with heart disease, leading the researchers to conclude that the evidence 'is interesting enough to justify further study' (Roberts et al. 1999).
17   Parts are reproduced in K. Pearson 1930:411–25.
18   Hill's father, Leonard, was a physiologist with whom Greenwood trained in 1905–10.
19   This is an early example of the use of 'qualitative' data to explain quantitative findings.
20   See e.g. Erwin et al. 1994:202–3.
21   See ch. 11.

Chapter 8   Experimental Sociology: The Early Years

1   Cochrane does not say who turned it down. On the resistances of social workers to evaluations of their effectiveness, see Macdonald (1997).
2   Maria Edgeworth was the author of *Lazy Lawrence* (1871), a well-known children's book.
3   A recent review of the class-size literature concluded that 97 per cent of available studies have to be discarded because of methodological flaws (Goldstein and Blatchford 1996).
4   These problems with the method of randomising the military draft were to continue (see Fienberg 1971). In the 1969 draft, the method used was placing pieces of paper with the men's birth dates in order from January to December in an urn which was then shaken. However, the urn was not shaken hard enough, with the result that the dates put in last were more likely to come out first (see Rosenblatt and Filliben 1971).
5   Information on Chapin is taken from Bannister 1987; Odum 1951; S. P. Turner 1986.
6   Sorokin was reputedly responsible for one of the early controlled experiments in sociology in Russia in 1921. It was designed to determine the relative efficiency of 'individualist' and 'communistic' methods of rewarding labour (Sorokin 1928; see Brearley 1931).
7   Against all the forecasts of the critics of 'scientism', all this planning apparently produced a very happy retirement.
8   T stands for time, L for space, P for a human population and I for indicators of their characteristics; the superscript and subscript *s*'s are modifying descriptors.

9 ... 'chronic truants, incorrigibles, serious personality problem children, and children charged with such serious offenses as arson and theft' (F. S. Chapin 1947:85).

10 Chapin does not mention randomisation in his 1931 paper on 'The problem of controls in experimental sociology', or in his 1936 paper on 'Design for social experiments', so presumably it occurred to him after this.

11 He was upgraded two years later when the president offered to pay his salary out of his own pocket (Lipset 1955).

12 Most of the key early figures in American sociology had clear personal links with the Church and with Christian social reformist impulses: Giddings, W. I. Thomas (1863–1947) and George Vincent (1864–1941) (a student of Small's, later President of the University of Minnesota and the Rockefeller Foundation) (all presidents of the American Sociological Society) had minister fathers; Sumner, Small and others, including U. G. Weatherley, J. P. Lichtenberger, J. L. Gillin and J. M. Gillette had their own careers in the ministry before turning to sociology (Weatherly and Ely were co-founders of an American Society for Christian Sociology) (Odum 1951).

13 Moore's methodology was apparently so advanced that he was unable to teach elementary courses in statistics. He accepted a 50 per cent cut in his salary in order to become a research professor (Hoxie et al. 1955:187).

14 The method of allocation was not stated. This is a common occurrence in the social experimentation literature, a problem also found in medical research: in Schulz et al.'s 1995 study of allocation concealment, 75 per cent of medical papers did not report how randomisation was done.

15 'The groups were as much alike as possible' (Menefee 1938:577).

16 Gosnell does not give the method used to decide which blocks should be allocated to which group.

17 Cabot engaged the original study workers, did many of the medical examinations of the boys himself, and arranged for the financing of the study for its first ten years through a foundation set up in the name of his dead wife, who had been interested in social welfare.

18 Such boys were to be recognized by a mix of criteria: persistent truancy, aggressiveness, stealing, 'sex delinquency', excessive lying, extreme timidity, bullying, keeping undesirable company/engaging in gang activity, smoking, lack of emotional control, day-dreaming, reading difficulties, cheating (Powers and Witmer 1951:30).

19 Boys were not randomised either to different lengths of treatment or to different counsellors, so it would have been difficult to interpret any apparent effects of either of these.

20 This is an example of the general phenomenon that people entered into trials tend to do better than expected, irrespective of their group allocation (Stiller 1994). The tendency for this to be the case applies to both physical and psychological outcomes (see Edwards et al. 1998a: ch. 4).

21 More than two years of a close counsellor–boy relationship, contact averaging once a week over two years, counsellors working with families as well as the boys themselves, and correcting medical, material and educational handicaps.

22 See Empey and Lubeck (1971) and Empey and Erickson (1972) for two further examples of 'administrative' problems with randomisation in evaluations of interventions for male delinquents; the first initiated by a private institution for delinquents in California called, suitably 'Boys' Republic'; the second carried out in Utah.

23 This was defined as evidence of unsatisfactory pupil–teacher relationships; class-room discipline problems; excessive or chronic absences without 'reasonable' ex-planations; 'obvious inconsistency' between IQ test scores and school performance; reading retardation; truancy or other violation of school rules; unusual behaviours such as shyness, irritability, tension, defiance, depression, temper tantrums; nega-tive ratings of girls' personalities by teachers; preoccupations with physical health, such as obesity and skin trouble; unusual family situation/family problems; fre-quent changes of residence; parental absence; language or 'acculturation' problems (Meyer et al. 1965:30–1).

24 Using 'a random procedure' (Meyer et al. 1965:33).

25 Aronson notes that the word first appeared in a medical dictionary in 1785 to mean 'a commonplace method or medicine'. The so-called placebo effect is impor-tant in modern-day health care practice, where it accounts for the fact that some people feel better without any specific treatment (see e.g. Beecher 1955).

26 Mayo (1960:56) says they 'dropped out'.

27 L. L. and J. Bernard in their *Origins of American Sociology* (1943) estimated that there were thirty-three communities organized along the lines of Fourierism; oth-ers put the number higher than this (see Odum 1951:66–7).

28 E. Greenwood claimed to have found over 100 different definitions of a sociologi-cal experiment (Greenwood 1945:7).

29 Bernard notes that in many places people felt they could not introduce sociology because it was synonymous with socialism; 'older men of a rather doctrinaire training' were a particular impediment (L. L. Bernard 1909:211).

30 In the 1920s the *Sociological Review* even lapsed into publishing free verse (Kent 1981:20).

31 See ch. 6 for an earlier attempt, by Harriet Martineau.

32 See Rosenberg 1976: ch. 5.

33 The term originally meant someone who was already part of the situation under study whom the researcher asked for descriptions of events (Hammersley 1989:81). This is different from its modern usage.

34 See also Jennifer Platt's *A History of Sociological Research Methods in America 1920–1960* (1996). Platt's chapter 3, called 'Scientism', equates this with 'positiv-ism', treating both as epiphenomena of a particular cultural constellation within US sociology.

Chapter 9   Of NITs and LIFE and Other Things

1 This case-study of Carmen Rodriguez is taken from Appendix D, 'Case-studies of four households' in Struyk and Bendick 1981. Other sources of information about the EHAP drawn on in this chapter are Bradbury and Downs 1981; Carlson and Heinberg 1978; Friedman and Weinberg 1983c; and Jackson and Mohr 1986.

2 Like the examples discussed in chapter 8, neither the account of the experiments nor the lessons drawn in this chapter are derived from a 'systematic' review of the evidence. They are intended to illustrate the range of work that was done and some of the common issues raised.

3 In his autobiographical account, 'Perspective on a scholarly career' (1981) Campbell notes his tendency to suffer from severe, incapacitating depressions. These are, perhaps, the twentieth century's reformulation of the 'neurasthenia' or emotional crises which appear to have afflicted so many of the key figures in the history of

methodology.

4 Many of the studies referred to in this chapter claimed to have used random assignment, but information is often lacking about the method used (see ch. 8, n. 14). Randomisation is stated to have been by random numbers table in the Texas Worker Adjustment Program (Bloom 1990). In the EHAP, the assignment method is not described, but it is acknowledged as 'not entirely random', in that extra low-income limits were set for some treatment cells to avoid many being ineligible or receiving only a low subsidy (Bendick and Squire 1981:54). In the Supported Workers Program, alternate assignment was used, according to Ferber and Hirsch (1982:110); Hollister et al. (1979:144) describe it as 'random'. The method used for random assignment in the Rand Corporation Health Insurance Study is not described (Brook et al. 1983). The Negative Income Tax experiments all used a complex randomisation procedure called the 'Conlisk–Watts model'. This effectively limited the costs of the experiment by ensuring that only the better-off families were assigned to the more generous treatments, thus minimizing the amounts that had to be paid to raise them to the minimum income level (Priest, personal communication). One implication of this is that it may have reduced the chances of showing positive programme effects.

5 Rivlin later held the influential post of Director of the Congressional Budget Office.

6 Many other prospective experimental studies were carried out in the USA over this period using other designs (for example, pre- and post-test only, or some process of generating control or comparison groups that did not meet the requirement of generating socially comparable groups). These are not part of the story told in this chapter, although they do, of course, form part of the whole picture of how experimental modes of knowing have been tried in practice.

7 For a recent systematic review of income supplementation trials see Connor et al., in press. This reviews ten trials – the four income trials, the EHAP, and the TARP and LIFE experiments referred to in this chapter, plus two additional pre-1990 studies; a fifth trial of income supplementation undertaken in Manitoba (Hum et al. 1992) and an unpublished study of the Massachusetts State lottery (lotteries constitute 'informal' randomised controlled trials).

8 In this respect, the TARP experiment contrasted with others – for example, the EHAP, where modelling was hardly used and the evaluators 'fell back on the strength of the experimental design' (Kennedy 1983:53).

9 In three of the nine plans families paid 50 per cent for dental and mental health services and 25 per cent for others; at some sites and in some years the expenditure ceiling was $750.

10 For purposes of analysis the fourteen plans were collapsed into four groups: the first and second became 'free care'; the remaining twelve were classified into three cost-sharing groups.

11 Brook et al. (1983) say that 70 per cent were assigned to three-year and 30 per cent to five-year plans; Manning et al. (1984) give these figures as 75 per cent and 25 per cent.

12 Risk of dying was a proxy for actual death, which was (unfortunately for the researchers) too 'infrequent' in the experimental population 'to allow meaningful analysis' (Brook et al. 1983:1427–8).

13 This is how they were described in the first reports (see e.g. Schweinhart and Weikart 1980); later they became 'African-American' (Schweinhart et al. 1993).

14 There is an inconsistency in the reporting of attrition. Schweinhart and Weikart

(1980:24) say that three were lost in the experimental group and one in the control group due to moves out of the area and that another control group child died. According to Schweinhart et al. (1993:31), the loss was four in the experimental group, all due to moves, and one death in the control group.

15 The process is described by Schweinhart and Weikart (1980:21) as 'a close approximation to random assignment'. It went as follows: children were ranked by initial IQ scores with even and odd rankings assigned to different study groups. Then pairs of similarly matched children were exchanged between groups until the sex ratios and mean socio-economic status scores for the two groups were equivalent. Then one group was 'arbitrarily' assigned to be the experimental and one to be the control group. Berrueta-Clement et al. (1984:xv) call it 'a true experiment with random assignment of subjects'. In the initial assignment, there were sixty-four children in each group. Two children were then moved from the experimental to the control group because they had mothers who were employed away from home who could not participate in the programme's home visits (Schweinhart et al. 1993:31) (this figure is reported as 'approximately five' by Weikart in another report (Lazar and Darlington 1982:75)). The focus on mothers was significant.

16 Information on the educational performance contracting experiment is taken from Gramlich and Koshel (1975).

17 It later transpired that contractors knew which items would be included in the final tests and were teaching the answers to these specific test items (D. T. Campbell 1979).

18 An alternative explanation is that students in the control schools were higher academic achievers anyway, but the pre-test scores show almost no differences.

19 Boruch went as far as to say that 'Randomized field experiments should be explicitly authorized in law' (1985:233).

Chapter 10   Lessons from America

1 Because random allocation is a way of distributing between intervention and control groups not only factors influencing outcome that are known about, but also those that are not.

2 The design of American trials appears to be generally more complex than that of UK trials.

3 See chs 1 and 11.

4 Presumably partly because this was the figure of greatest interest to them.

5 This is another reason why pilot studies and process evaluations are needed as part of experimental design.

6 According to Rossi et al. (1980:93–7) there was no evidence in the TARP evaluation of any difference between the two control groups.

7 See Oakley 1992b for a discussion of this problem.

8 This figure includes all the sites, not only those with control groups.

9 In the New Jersey–Pennsylvania NIT experiment 91 per cent of the screening interviews failed to find eligible intact male-headed families (H. L. Ross 1970:101).

10 In a subsequent analysis the point was made that marital dissolution is not an adverse outcome if it frees people from unsatisfactory marriages (Groeneveld et al. 1980).

11 In the health care field, this is known as 'cluster randomisation'.

12   Allocation was made by random numbers chart (Ares et al. 1963:74).
13   As seems to be the rule, rather than the exception, the process was complex. Responding to a criticism by Larson of the experiment which argued that 'computer-derived' matching of beats could not be superior to the judgement of police officers, Pate et al. (1975:300) describe the process used thus: 'five optimum configurations generated by this [computer] procedure were submitted for consideration by police officers and supervisors. Among these five, the officers selected the one which they felt best suited the department's operational concerns, avoided the clustering of beats of the same experimental condition, and considered the peculiarities of each beat. The configuration selected, as a matter of fact, was the one with the best similarity fit on the basis of the computer-matching procedure'.
14   See Kassebaum et al. (1971): ch. 2, 'Doing time in a pastel prison'.
15   The procedure is described in Kassebaum et al. 1975:79–83. The last two digits of the men's departmental serial numbers were used for allocation. An interesting aspect of the research design and the analysis was that some men were allocated to 'voluntary small group counselling'; those who declined this were treated in the analysis as a 'voluntary control group'. This is an early example of what would later become known in medicine as a 'patient preference trial' (see ch. 11).
16   Towards the end of their report of the study, Kassebaum et al. (1971:247–51) discuss a particular objection put to their findings by the supervisor of group counselling at the California Department of Corrections, who argued that men receiving 'stable' counselling (where there was minimal change in group membership and the same leader for at least a year) would demonstrate the effectiveness of the counselling approach. The researchers therefore carried out an additional analysis. This showed no support for the 'stable counselling' theory: men who were high attenders in stable groups did no better than other counselled men; nor did they do any better than the control group.
17   Forty-six of these were randomly assigned to the experimental and twenty-six to the control group. Randomisation was by a table of random numbers (Welch et al. 1969:213).
18   The effect of this was to create two intervention groups, and thus probably to lower the chances of Harvard Project Physics emerging as successful.
19   This is an example of the 'triangulation' dilemma discussed in ch. 3; data collected from different sources or by different means may give different answers.
20   All public primary schools except those with very few students, those which had already used the radio mathematics approach, and two affiliated with a teacher training school, were randomly assigned as experimental or control. Then first-grade classes were stratified by department and rural/urban location, and in each of the three departments eight classes (four rural, four urban) were randomly designated as control and ten (five rural, five urban) as experimental (Searle et al. 1978:655–6).
21   The main report is an internal publication by the New York Institute of Welfare Research (Blenkner et al. 1964).
22   The idea for an experimental study with a control group came from Jerry Morris, a doctor who was one of the pioneers of social medicine in Britain (Goldberg, personal communication).
23   This was especially the case for studies funded by the Office of Education.
24   One of the principle arguments centred on the speed at which the paper passed through the recording machine – 3 cm per minute in North America compared to 1 cm per minute in Britain. It was argued that the faster speed in America enabled

more beat-to-beat variability to be picked up, and that trials of EFM using this technique would be more likely to demonstrate success (see Parer 1986). Similar arguments about techniques appear in many of the discussions about interpreting the results of the American social experiments.

25   The issue in this and other cases is partly one of a trade-off between reducing the risk of rare events, such as death, and using a technology routinely, with sometimes untoward consequences for healthy people. A more recent review of trials of EFM confirmed the reduction of (rare) neonatal seizures as the only 'significant benefit' of routine continuous EFM, and noted that, 'In view of the increase in Caesarean and operative vaginal deliveries, the long-term benefit of this reduction must be evaluated in the decision reached jointly by the pregnant woman and her clinician' (Thacker and Stroup 1999).

26   See ch. 8.

27   For example, research some years ago in New Zealand showed that short out-patient treatments for alcohol abuse are as effective as longer and more costly in-patient ones; but managers and decision-makers ignored the research on the grounds that the information obtained by RCTs is limited. This did not stop them using the research, however, when they wanted to justify closing in-patient facilities (Howden-Chapman 1988; see also Davis and Howden-Chapman 1996).

28   Cronbach (1982:23) notes that he had no personal experience of undertaking a randomised controlled experiment.

Chapter 11   The Rights of Animals and Other Creatures

1   Chapin was much influenced by his uncle, a paediatrician (see ch. 8) who published a defence of animal experimentation with the title 'What animal experimentation has done for children' in 1915.

2   An instrument used to examine the vagina and the cervix.

3   Passages between the vagina and the bowels or the bladder, usually a result of problems in childbirth.

4   The issue of possible *over*-treatment of diagnosed abnormalities remains an important question in all screening programmes.

5   Interestingly, throughout the study Green continued to offer treatment to women with CIS who came to him as private patients (Cartwright Report 1988:38).

6   One considerable problem here is that many trial reports give little information about the social backgrounds of trial participants (see Oakley et al. 1998a).

7   See Edwards et al. 1998a for a summary of the literature on attitudes to, and understanding of, trials.

8   This would have been some other anti-oestrogen drug or oophorectomy (removal of the ovaries).

9   There is little available information on whether this would be a problem for trials in the 'social' arena (but see chs 9 and 10).

10   See ch. 9.

11   See also Oakley 1990, 1992b for discussions.

12   The opposite possibility, that control groups experience positive feelings as a result of being included in research, is discussed in ch. 10.

13   Other findings were higher rates of operative delivery and maternal infections after birth and a reduced likelihood of babies having fits in the electronically monitored group (D. Macdonald et al. 1985; see ch. 10).

14 If the principle of uncontrolled experimentation as normal practice becomes more widely understood, there is likely to be an increase in those who actively request to be participants in trials (see I. Chalmers 1995).

Chapter 12   People's Ways of Knowing

1   Presumably only sometimes. But softness may thus be seen as undesirable.
2   The tendency to dualistic thought has also been located in statistical procedures which settle on 'yes/no' answers (Eichler 1988). Medical research is ahead of social science research here in favouring the statistical procedures of odds ratios and 'confidence intervals' which, rather than giving dichotomous answers, provide information about the range along which answers to research questions may lie.
3   See Oakley et al. 1998a on the same problem in health promotion research.
4   The titles of such projects often make no reference to the fact that they are studies of men.
5   This would, interestingly, reverse the historical relationship, making the natural sciences a sub-field of the critical social sciences.
6   By another neat inversion of methodological paradigms, these newer understandings of what science 'is' come from the application of observational social science methods to laboratory scientific work.
7   This has given rise to a body of work on 'experimenter' effects (see e.g. Berkowitz et al. 1964; Rosenthal 1963, 1969).
8   These are often seen as groups from whom something beneficial is withheld; but if the intervention were known to be beneficial, the study would be unethical. Since a significant proportion of interventions turn out to be ineffective or harmful, research participants allocated to control groups are protected from ineffective or harmful interventions.
9   Thanks to the anonymous reviewer who drew this story to my attention.
10 For discussions see Black 1996; Brannen 1992; Buchanan 1992; Griffin and Ragin 1994; Ianni and Orr 1979; Mullen and Iverson 1982; Oakley 1992b.

Chapter 13   Challenges of an Experimenting Society

1   In the spirit of openness which is one of the characteristics of the experimenting society discussed in this final chapter, I invite readers who have omissions or differences to report to let me know (email address: a.oakley@ioe.ac.uk).
2   See Carr-Hill (1995) for a discussion.
3   The link between DES and vaginal cancer was first suggested by a woman who had taken DES whose daughter developed the disease. This is one of many examples of 'lay' people suggesting fruitful hypotheses (Ulfelder 1980).
4   Harmful effects may coexist with beneficial ones. Bergin quoted the following analysis of studies of the effectiveness of psychotherapy in 1975: *treated with therapy*: outcome improved 65 per cent, unchanged 25 per cent, worse 10 per cent; *untreated*: outcome improved 40 per cent, unchanged 55 per cent, worse 5 per cent. Although the proportion of people said to have improved increased, the proportion with worse outcomes also doubled.
5   As regards effectiveness, that is; there are, of course, many other important ques-

tions addressed by research for which other designs are more appropriate.

6   The same point applies to non-professional groups, who can, equally, specialize in unevidenced claims (see I. Chalmers 1983; Oakley et al. 1998b).

7   Thus, according to Cochrane's reckoning, the one medical speciality which deals exclusively with women had the worst scientific record.

8   Archie Cochrane wrote the preface.

9   See the internet website http://som.flinders.edu.au/fusa/cochrane/cochrane/ CCHRONOL.HTM for the chronology of the Cochrane Collaboration.

10   A total of 487 sources of support in thirty-two countries (178 of these in the UK) are currently listed on The Cochrane Library.

11   This is a particular issue in health promotion, an activity which is, by definition, not focused on discrete health problems.

12   Sandy Oliver (personal communication) has noted that 'consumers' of health care very often include the social setting in the definition of an intervention. There may be a gender aspect here, in that men (e.g. obstetricians) may be more interested in the kernel of an intervention (e.g. drugs for pain relief in labour), whereas women (e.g. midwives and health advisers) are interested in the role of a supportive environment as the context for an intervention.

13   The effort which has gone into assembling SPECTR is, as yet, far less than has been committed to finding health care trials, so the number is likely to go up considerably.

14   Presumably there would be some sort of public outcry if doctors were to put the evidence of controlled trials on one side on the grounds that they wanted only positive effects, thereafter resorting to (for example) 'qualitative' evidence about what they and their 'patients' believe to be effective interventions.

15   This work uses many of the same methods as the Cochrane Collaboration, and is linked to it through a co-ordination, jointly with McMaster University in Canada, of the Cochrane Field of Health Promotion.

16   Other currently recommended alternatives are to trust the expert (see Speller et al. 1997), or to define effective interventions as those liked by opinion leaders in local communities (see Aggleton 1997).

17   This study did not use an experimental research design with control groups.

18   For another set of somewhat dispiriting reflections by an ex-evaluator on the role of sociology in evidence-based social policy, see Scott and Shore (1979); Shore worked on the Seattle–Denver income maintenance experiments discussed in ch. 9.

19   Raymond Williams (1983:115) calls 'empirical' one of the most difficult words in the language.

References

Aaron, H. J. (1978) *Politics and the Professors: the Great Society in perspective*. Washington, D.C.: Brookings Institution.

Aaron, H. J. (1981) Policy implications: a progress report. In Bradbury and Downs (eds).

Abrams, P. (1968) *The Origins of British Sociology*. Chicago: University of Chicago Press.

Acker, J., Barry, K. and Esseveld, J. (1983) Objectivity and truth: problems in doing feminist research. *Women's Studies International Forum*, 6(4):423–35.

Addams, J. (1912) *The Spirit of Youth and the City Streets*. New York: Macmillan.

Aggleton, P. (1997) Health education. *AIDS Care*, 9(1):35–9.

Alderson, M. (1983) William Farr's contribution to present day vital and health statistics. *Population Trends*, 31:5–8.

Alderson, P., Madden, M., Oakley, A. and Wilkins, R. (1994) *Women's Views of Breast Cancer Treatment and Research*. London: Social Science Research Unit.

Allen, G. E., Fitts, J. F. and Glatt E. S. (1981) The Experimental Housing Allowance Program. In Bradbury and Downs (eds).

Alpert, H. (1961) *Emile Durkheim and his Sociology*. New York: Russell and Russell Inc.

Altman, D. and Bland, J. M. (1995) Absence of evidence is not evidence of absence. *British Medical Journal*, 311:485.

Anderson, G. M., Brook, R. and Williams, A. (1991) A comparison of cost-sharing versus free care in children: effects on the demand for office-based medical care. *Medical Care*, 29:890–8.

Anderson, N. (1967) *The Hobo*. Chicago: University of Chicago Press (originally pub. 1923).

Anderson, R. B., St Pierre, R. G., Proper, E. C. and Stebbins, L. B. (1978) Pardon us, but what was the question again? A response to the critique of the Follow Through evaluation. In Cook et al. (eds).

Anderson, T. W. (1955) The department of mathematical statistics. In Hoxie et al.

Anon. (variously attributed to G. Plattes and G. Hartlib) (1641) *A Description of the Famous Kingdome of Macaria Shewing its excellent government: wherein The Inhabitants live in great Prosperity, Health and Happinesse; The King obeyed, the Nobles honoured, and all good men respected, vice punished and virtue rewarded*. London: Francis Constable.

Antony, L. M. and Witt, C. (eds) (1993) *A Mind of One's Own*. Boulder, Colo.: Westview Press.

Apsler, R. (1972) Effects of the draft lottery and a laboratory analogue on attitudes. *Journal of Personality and Social Psychology*, 24(2):262–72.

Apsler, R. Friedman, H. (1975) Chance outcomes and the just world: a comparison of observers and recipients. *Journal of Personality and Social Psychology*, 31(5):887–94.

Arber, S. (1990) Revealing women's health: re-analysing the General Household Survey. In Roberts (ed.).

Arber, S. and Ginn, J. (1993) Gender and inequalities in health in later life. *Social Science and Medicine*, 36(1): 33–46.

Ares, C. E., Rankin, A. and Sturz, H. (1963) The Manhattan Bail Project: an interim report on the use of pre-trial parole. *New York University Law Review*, 38:67–95.

Aries, P. (1983) *The Hour of Our Death*. Harmondsworth: Penguin.

Aronson, J. (1999) Please, please me. *British Medical Journal*, 318:716.

Assiter, A. (1996) *Enlightened Women: modernist feminism in a postmodern age*. London: Routledge.

Astbury, J. (1996) *Crazy for You: the making of women's madness*. Melbourne: Oxford University Press.

Atherton, M. (1993) Cartesian reason and gendered reason. In Antony and Witt (eds).

Aubrey, J. A. (1982) *Brief Lives*, ed. R. Barber. Woodbridge, Suffock: Boydell Press (originally pub. 1898).

Bacon, F. (1625) *The Essays of Francis Bacon*. London: Thomas Nelson and Sons.

Bacon, F. (1965) *The Advancement of Learning*, ed. G. W. Kitchin. London: Dent (originally pub. 1605).

Bacon, F. (1994) *Novum Organon, With Other Parts of The Great Instauration*, trans. and ed. P. Urbach and J. Gibson. Chicago and La Salle, Ill.: Open Court (originally pub. 1620).

Bailey, W. (1961) *Correctional Outcome: an evaluation of 100 reports*. Los Angeles: University of California School of Social Welfare.

Bain, R. (1931) Behavioristic technique in sociological research. *Proceedings of the American Sociological Society*, 36:155–64.

Bakan, D. (1966) *The Duality of Human Existence*. Chicago: Rand McNally.

Baker, G. and Morris, K. J. (1996) *Descartes' Dualism*. London: Routledge.

Baker, K. M. (1975) *Condorcet: from natural philosophy to social mathematics*. Chicago: University of Chicago Press.

Bannister, R. C. (1987) *Sociology and Scientism: the American quest for objectivity, 1880–1940*. Chapel Hill, N.C.: University of North Carolina Press.

Bannister, R. C. (1991) *Jessie Bernard: the making of a feminist*. New Brunswick, N.J.: Rutgers University Press.

Barker-Benfield, G. J. (1976) *The Horrors of the Half-Known Life*. New York: Harper and Row.

Barnes, B. (1974) *Scientific Knowledge and Sociological Theory*. London: Routledge and Kegan Paul.

Barnett, S. (1993) Cost–benefit analysis. In Schweinhart et al. (eds).

Bartzokas, C. A., Williams, E. E. and Slade, P. D. (1995) A psychological approach to hospital-acquired infections. In *Studies in Health and Human Sciences*. London: Edward Meller.

Bateson, M. C. (1983) A letter from Margaret Mead's daughter. *British Medical Journal*, 287:1628.

Bateson, M. C. (1984) *With a Daughter's Eye*. New York: William Morrow.

Baudrillard, J. (1988) The year 2000 has already happened. In A. Kroker and M. Kroker (eds), *Body Invaders: sexuality and the postmodern condition*. London: Macmillan.

Baum, F. (1993) Deconstructing the qualitative–quantitative divide in health research. In B. S. Turner, L. Eckermann, D. Colquhoun and P. Crotty (eds) *Annual Review of Health Social Science: methodological issues in health research*, Geelong, Australia: Deakin University.

Baum, M. (1994) The value of randomised controlled trials and the questions they raise for consent. In P. Alderson (ed.), *Breast Cancer, Randomised Controlled Trials and Consent*. Consent Conference Series, London: Social Science Research Unit.

Baum, M., Zilkha K. and Houghton, J. (1989) Ethics of clinical research: lessons for the future. *British Medical Journal*, 299.251–3.

Beard, G. M. (1882) *The Psychology of the Salem Witchcraft Excitement of 1692 and its Practical Application to Our Own Time*. New York: Putnam's Sons.

Becker, H. S. (1979) Do photographs tell the truth? In Cook and Reichardt (eds).

Beecher, H. K. (1955) The powerful placebo. *Journal of the American Medical Association*, Dec. 24:1602–6.

Belenky, M. F., Clinchy, B. M., Goldberger, N. R. and Tarule, J. M. (1986) *Women's Ways of Knowing*. New York: Basic Books.

Belson, W. A. (1966) *The Ability of Respondents to Recall their Purchases of Chocolate Confectionery*. London: Survey Research Centre.

Belson, W. A. (1986) *Validity in Survey Research*. Aldershot, Hants. Gower.

Bemelmans-Videc, M. L., Elte, R. and Koolhaus, E. (1989) Policy evaluation in the Netherlands: institutional context and state of affairs. In Rist (ed.)

Bendelow, G. and Williams, S. J. (eds) (1998) *Emotions in Social Life*. London: Routledge.

Bendick, M. and Squire, A. D. (1981) The three experiments. In Struyk and Bendick (eds).

Bendick, M. and Struyk, R. J. (1981) Origins of an experimental approach. In Struyk and Bendick (eds).

Bennett, C. A. and Lumsdaine, A. A. (eds) (1975) *Evaluation and Experiment: some critical issues in assessing social programs*. New York: Academic Press.

Bennett, D. J. (1998) *Randomness*. Cambridge, Mass.: Harvard University Press.

Beral, V. and Colwell, L. (1980) Randomised trial of high doses of stilboestrol and ethisterone in pregnancy: long-term follow up of mothers. *British Medical Journal*, 281:1098–1101.

Beral, V. and Colwell, L. (1981) Randomised trial of high doses of stilboestrol and ethisterone therapy in pregnancy: long-term follow up of the children. *Journal of Epidemiology and Community Health*, 35:155–60.

Berelson, B. (1960) *Graduate Education in the United States*. New York: McGraw-Hill.

Bergin, A. E. (1975) When shrinks hurt: psychotherapy can be dangerous. *Psychology Today*, 9:100–4.

Berk, R. A. and Rossi, P. H. (1976) Doing good or worse: evaluation research politically re-examined. *Social Problems*, 2:337–49.

Berk, R. A., Boruch, R. F., Chambers, D. L., Rossi, P. H. and White, A. D. (1985) Social policy experimentation: a position paper. *Evaluation Review*, 9(4):387–429.

Berk, R. A., Leniham, K. J. and Rossi, P. H. (1980) Crime and poverty: some experimental evidence from ex-offenders. *American Sociological Review*, 45(5):766–86.

Berkowitz, L., Klanderman, S. B. and Harris, R. (1964) Effects of experimenter awareness and sex of subject and experimenter on reactions to dependency relationship. *Sociometry*, 27:327–37.

Bernard, J. (1971) *Women and the Public Interest*. Chicago: Aldine-Atherton.

Bernard, J. (1973) My four revolutions: an autobiographical history of the American Sociological Association. *American Journal of Sociology*, 78:773–91.

Bernard, L. L. (1909) The teaching of sociology in the United States. *American Journal of Sociology*, 15:164–213.

Bernard, L. L. and Bernard, J. (1943) *Origins of American Sociology*. New York: Thomas Y. Crowell.

Bernoulli, J. (1713) *Ars Conjectandi*. Basel: Thurnisiorum.

Bernstein, I. L. and Freeman, H. E. (1975) *Academic and Entrepreneurial Research*. New York: Russell Sage Foundation.

Berrueta-Clement, J. R., Schweinhart, L. J., Barnett, W. S., Epstein, A. S. and Weikart, D. P. (1984) *Changed Lives: the effects of the Perry Preschool Program through age 19*. Ypsilanti, Mich.: High/Scope Press.

Bertaux, D. (1981) From the life-history approach to the transformation of sociological practice. In D. Bertaux (ed.), *Biography and Society: the life history approach in the social sciences*, Beverly Hills, Calif.: Sage Publications.

Bessel, F. W. (1876) Persönliche Gleichung bei Durchgangsbeobachtungen. In R. Engelmann (ed.) *Abhandlungen von Friedrich Wilhelm Bessel*, vol. 3. Leipzig: Wilhelm Engelmann.

Besser, G. R. (1994) *Germaine de Staël Revisited*. New York: Twayne Publishers.

Betsey, C. L., Hollister, R. G. and Papageorgiou, M. R. (eds) (1985) *Youth Employment and Training Programs: the YEDPA years*. Washington, D.C.: National Academy Press.

Bierstedt, R. (1978) Sociological thought in the eighteenth century. In T. Bottomore and R. Nisbet (eds) *A History of Sociological Analysis*. London: Heinemann Educational.

Bifulco, A., Brown, G. W. and Adler, Z. (1991) Early sexual abuse and clinical depression in later life. *British Journal of Psychiatry*, 159:115–22.

Black, N. (1996) Why we need observational studies to evaluate the effectiveness of health care. *British Medical Journal*, 312:1215–18.

Blacker, C. P. (1952) Eugenic experiments conducted by the Nazis on human subjects. *Eugenics Review*, 44:9–19.

Blaikie, N. (1993) *Approaches to Social Enquiry*. Cambridge: Polity Press.

Blaxter, M. (1990) *Health and Lifestyles*. London: Routledge.

Blenkner, M., Bloom, M. and Nielsen, M. (1971) A research and demonstration project of protective services. *Social Casework*, 52:487–9.

Blenkner, M., Bloom, M., Nielsen, M. and Weber, R. (1974) *Final Report. Protective Services for Older People: findings from the Benjamin Rose Institute Study*. Cleveland, Oh.: Benjamin Rose Institute.

Blenkner, M., Jahn, J. and Wasser, E. (1964) *Serving the Aging: an experiment in social work and public health nursing*. New York: Institute of Welfare Research.

Bloom, H. S. (1990) *Back to Work: testing re-employment services for displaced workers*. Kalamazoo, Mich.: W. E. Upjohn Institute for Employment Research.

Bloor, M. (1997) Techniques of validation in qualitative research: a critical commentary. In G. Miller and R. Dingwall (eds), *Context and Method in Qualitative Research*, Thousand Oaks, Calif.: Sage Publications.

Blumer, H. (1937) Social psychology. In E. P. Schmidt (ed.), *Man and Society*, Englewood Cliffs, N.J.: Prentice-Hall.

Bologh, R. W. (1990) *Love or Greatness: Max Weber and masculine thinking – a feminist inquiry*. London: Unwin Hyman.

Bonell, C. (1999) Evidence as a resource of control and resistance in advanced liberal health systems: the case of HIV prevention in the UK. Ph.D. diss., University of London.

Booth, C. (1891) *Labour and Life of the People*, vol. 1: *East London*. 3rd edn. London: Williams and Norgate.

Booth, C. (1902–3) *Life and Labour of the People of London*, 17 vols. London: Macmillan.

Booth, R. (1991) Social experimentation and service evaluation: lessons from the USA. *Research, Policy and Planning*, 9(2):12–18.

Bordo, S. R. (1987) *The Flight of Objectivity: essays on Cartesianism and culture*. Albany, N.Y.: State University of New York Press.

Boring, E. G. (1938) The Society of Experimental Psychologists 1904–38. *American Journal of Psychology*, 51:411.

Boring, E. G. (1954) The nature and history of experimental control. *American Journal of Psychology*, 67:573–89.

Boruch, R. F. (1974) Illustrative randomized field experiments for program planning and evaluation. *Evaluation*, 2:83–7.

Boruch, R. F. (1975) On common contentions about randomized field experiments. In Boruch and Riecken (eds).

Boruch, R. F. (1984) Ideas about social research, evaluation, and statistics in medieval Arabic literature. *Evaluation Review*, 8(6):823–42.

Boruch, R. F. (1985) Implications of the youth employment experience for improving applied research and evaluation policy. In Betsey et al. (eds).

Boruch, R. F. (1997) *Randomized Experiments for Planning and Evaluation*. Thousand Oaks, Calif.: Sage Publications.

Boruch, R. F. and Riecken, H. W. (eds) (1975) *Experimental Testing of Public Policy*. Boulder, Colo.: Westview Press.

Boruch, R. F., McSweeny, A. J. and Soderstrom, E. J. (1978) Randomized field experiments for program planning, development and evaluation. *Evaluation Quarterly*, 2(4):655–95.

Boruch, R., Snyder, B. and DeMoya, D. (1999) The importance of randomized field trials in delinquency research and other areas. In H. Fujita (ed.) *Proceedings of the University of Tokyo Conference on Juvenile Problems and Violence*, 26–8 Feb.

Botein, B. (1965) The Manhattan Bail project: its impact on criminology and the criminal law processes. *Texas Law Review*, 43:319–31.

Botros, S. (1990) Equipoise, consent and the ethics of randomised clinical trials. In P. Byrne (ed.), *Ethics and Law in Health Care and Research*, London: King's Fund.

Boulton, M., Fitzpatrick, R. and Swinburn, C. (1996) Qualitative research in health care II: a structured review and evaluation of studies. *Journal of Evaluation in Clinical Practice*, 2(3):171–9.

Bowles, G. and Duelli Klein, R. (eds) (1983) *Theories of Women's Studies*. London: Routledge.

Bowley, A. L. (1915) *Livelihood and Poverty*. London: Bell.

Box, J. F. (1978) *R. A. Fisher: the life of a scientist*. New York: John Wiley.

Bradbury, K. L. and Downs, A. (eds) (1981) *Do Housing Allowances Work?* Washington, D.C.: Brookings Institution.

Bradford Hill, A. (1962) *Statistical Methods in Clinical and Preventive Medicine*. Edinburgh: E. & S. Livingstone.

Bradley, C. (1993) Designing medical and educational intervention studies. *Diabetes Care*, 16(2):509–18.

Brannen, J. (1992) Combining qualitative and quantitative approaches: an overview. In Brannen (ed.).

Brannen, J. (ed.) (1992) *Mixing Methods: qualitative and quantitative research.* Aldershot: Avebury.

Brannen, J., Dodd, K., Oakley, A. and Storey, P. (1994) *Young People, Health and Family Life.* Buckingham: Open University Press.

Brearley, H. C. (1931) Experimental sociology in the United States. *Social Forces,* Dec.:196–9.

Brewin, T. B. (1994) Empirical: one word, two meanings. *Journal of the Royal College of General Practitioners of London,* 28(1):78–9.

Briscoe, M. E. (1985) Men, women and mental health. *Health Education Journal,* 44(3):151–3.

Brook, R. H., Ware, J. E., Rogers, W. H., Keeler, E. B., Davies, A. R., Donald, C. A., Goldberg, G. A., Lohr, K. N., Masthay, P. C. and Newhouse, J. P. (1983) Does free care improve adults' health? *New England Journal of Medicine,* 309(23):1426–34.

Brown, R. H. (1977) *A Poetic for Sociology.* Cambridge: Cambridge University Press.

Brown, G. W. and Harris, T. (1976) *Social Origins of Depression.* London: Tavistock.

Bruner, J. S. (1966) *On Knowing: essays for the left hand.* Cambridge, Mass.: Belknap Press of Harvard University Press.

Bruzzi, P. (1998) Tamoxifen for the prevention of breast cancer. *British Medical Journal,* 316:1181–2.

Bryant, C. G. A. (1985) *Positivism in Social Theory and Research.* London: Macmillan.

Bryman, A. (1988) *Quantity and Quality in Social Research.* London: Unwin Hyman.

Bryman, A. (1992) Quantitative and qualitative research: further reflections on their integration. In Brannen (ed.).

Buchanan, D. R. (1992) An uneasy alliance: combining qualitative and quantitative research methods. *Health Education Quarterly,* 19(1):117–35.

Buckle, H. T. (1859) *History of Civilisation in England.* New York: D Appleton.

Buitendijk, S. E. (1991) Current treatments for miscarriage and preterm labour in DES daughters and other women: a review. *European Journal of Public Health,* 1:94–9.

Bulbrook, R. D. (1996) Long term adjuvant therapy for primary breast cancer. *British Medical Journal,* 312:389–90.

Bulmer, M. (1982) *The Uses of Social Research.* London: Allen and Unwin.

Bulmer, M. (ed.) (1986) *Social Science and Social Policy.* London: Allen and Unwin.

Bulmer, M. (1991) National contexts for the development of social-policy research: British and American research on poverty and social welfare compared. In: Wagner et al. (1991a).

Bungay, G. T., Vessey, M. P. and McPherson, C. K. (1980) Study of symptoms in middle life with special reference to the menopause. *British Medical Journal,* 281:181–3.

Bunkle, P. (1988) *Second Opinion: the politics of women's health in New Zealand.* Auckland: Oxford University Press.

Burrows, R., Burton, R., Muncer, S. and Gillen, G. (1995) The efficacy of health promotion, health economics and late modernism. *Health Education Research,* 10(2):241–9.

Burtless, G. and Haveman, R. H. (1984) Policy lessons from three labor market experiments. In R. T. Robson (ed.), *Employment and Training R & D: lessons learned and future directions,* Kalamazoo, Mich.: W. E. Upjohn Institute for Employment Research.

Butler, J. (1991) *Gender Trouble: feminism and the subversion of identity.* New York: Routledge.

Campbell, D. T. (1969) Reforms as experiments. *American Psychologist,* 24 (Apr.):409–

29.

Campbell, D. T. (1979) Assessing the impact of planned social change. *Evaluation and Program Planning*, 2:67–90.

Campbell, D. T. (1981) Perspective on a scholarly career. In M. B. Brewer and B. E. Collins (eds), *Scientific Inquiry and the Social Sciences: a volume in honor of Donald T. Campbell*, San Francisco: Jossey-Bass.

Campbell, D. T. (1988a) The experimenting society (originally pub. 1971). In Campbell and Overman (ed.).

Campbell, D. T. (1988b) Qualitative knowing in action research. In Campbell and Overman (ed.).

Campbell, D. T. and Boruch, R. F. (1975) Making the case for randomized assignment to treatments by considering the alternatives: six ways in which quasi-experimental evaluations in compensatory education tend to underestimate effects. In Bennett and Lumsdaine (eds).

Campbell, D. T. and Erlebacher, A. (1970) How regression artifacts in quasi-experimental evaluations can mistakenly make compensatory education look harmful. In J. Hellmuth (ed.) *Disadvantaged Child*, vol. 3, New York: Brunner/Mazel.

Campbell, D. T. and Overman, E. S. (eds) (1988) *Methodology and Epistemology for Social Science*. Chicago: University of Chicago Press.

Campbell, D. T. and Stanley, J. C. (1966) *Experimental and Quasi-experimental Designs for Research*. Boston: Houghton Mifflin (originally pub. 1963).

Campbell, D. W. and Stover, G. F. (1933) Teaching international-mindedness in the social studies. *The Journal of Educational Sociology*, 7(4):244–8.

Caplan, P. (1988) Engendering knowledge: the politics of ethnography, part I. *Anthropology Today*, 4(5):8–17.

Cardinal, M. (1991) *Devotion and Disorder*. London: The Women's Press.

Carlson, D. B. and Heinberg, J. D. (1978) *How Housing Allowances Work: integrated findings from the Experimental Housing Allowance Program*. Washington, D.C.: Urban Institute.

Caro, F. G. (ed.) (1977) *Readings in Evaluation Research*. New York: Russell–Sage Foundation.

Carr, L. J. (1929) Experimental sociology: a preliminary note on theory and method. *Social Forces*, 8:63–75.

Carr-Hill, R. (1995) Welcome? to the brave new world of evidence-based medicine. *Social Science and Medicine*, 41(11):1467–8.

Carter, G. M., Coleman, S. B. and Wendt J. C. (1983) Participation under open enrollment. In Friedman and Weinberg (eds).

Cartwright Report (1988) *The Report of the Committee of Inquiry into Allegations Concerning the Treatment of Cervical Cancer at National Women's Hospital and into Other Related Matters*. Auckland: Government Printing Office.

Casti, J. L. (1989) *Paradigms Lost: images of man in the mirror of science*. London: Scribners.

Cavendish, M. (1655) *World's Olio*. London.

Cavendish, M. (1656) *Nature's Pictures Drawn by Fancies Pencil to the Life*. London.

Cavendish, M. (1662) *Orations of Divers Sorts*. London.

Cavendish, M. (1664) *Philosophical Letters*. London.

Cavendish, M. (1666) *Observations upon Experimental Philosophy to which is added the Description of a New Blazing World*. London: A. Maxwell.

Cavendish, M. (1668) *Grounds of Natural Philosophy*. London.

Cavendish, M. (1992) *The Description of a New World Called the Blazing-World* (ed. K.

Lilley). London: Pickering and Chatto (originally pub. 1668).

Chalmers, I. (1983) Scientific inquiry and authoritarianism in perinatal care and education. *Birth*, 10(3):151–66.

Chalmers, I. (1986) Minimizing harm and maximizing benefit during innovation in health care: controlled or uncontrolled experimentation? *Birth*, 13(3):155–64.

Chalmers, I. (1994) Public involvement in research to assess the effects of health care. Paper presented to the Harveian Society of London.

Chalmers, I. (1995) What do I want from research and researchers when I am a patient? *British Medical Journal*, 310:1315–18.

Chalmers, I. (1997a) Assembling comparison groups to assess the effects of health care. *Journal of the Royal Society of Medicine*, 90:379–86.

Chalmers, I. (1997b) What is the prior probability of a proposed new treatment being superior to established treatments? *British Medical Journal*, 314:74–5.

Chalmers, I. (1998) Unbiased, relevant and reliable assessments in health care. *British Medical Journal*, 317:1167–18.

Chalmers, I., Enkin, M. and Keirse, M. J. N. C. (eds) (1989) *Effective Care in Pregnancy and Childbirth*. Oxford: Oxford University Press.

Chalmers, I., Lawson, J. G. and Turnbull, A. C. (1976a) Evaluation of different approaches to obstetric care, I. *British Journal of Obstetrics and Gynaecology*, 83:921–9.

Chalmers, I., Lawson, J. G. and Turnbull, A. C. (1976b) Evaluation of different approaches to obstetric care, II. *British Journal of Obstetrics and Gynaecology*, 83:930–3.

Chalmers, I., Sackett, D. and Silagy, C. (1997) The Cochrane Collaboration. In Maynard and Chalmers (eds).

Chalmers, T. C., Celano, P., Sacks, H. S. and Smith, H. (1983) Bias in treatment assignment in controlled clinical trials. *New England Journal of Medicine*, 309:1358–61.

Chalmers, T. C., Matta, R. J., Smith, H. and Kunzler, A. M. (1977) Evidence favoring the use of anticoagulants in the hospital phase of acute myocardial infarction. *New England Journal of Medicine*, 297:1091–6.

Chapin, F. S. (1913) *An Introduction to the Study of Societal Evolution*. New York: Century Co.

Chapin, F. S. (1917) *Historical Introduction to Social Economy*. New York: Century Co.

Chapin, F. S. (1920) *Field Work and Social Research*. New York: Century Co.

Chapin, F. S. (1931) The problem of controls in experimental sociology. *Journal of Educational Sociology*, 4 (May):541–51.

Chapin, F. S. (1936) Design for social experiments. *American Sociological Review*, 3:786–800.

Chapin, F. S. (1938) The effects of slum clearance and re-housing on families and community relationships in Minneapolis. *American Journal of Sociology*, Mar.:744–63.

Chapin, F. S. (1947) *Experimental Designs in Sociological Research*. New York: Harper and Row.

Chapin, H. D. (1915) What animal experimentation has done for children. *Popular Science Monthly*, Jan.:55–62.

Chard, J. A., Lilford, R. J. and Court B. V. (1997) Qualitative medical sociology: what are its crowning achievements? *Journal of the Royal Society of Medicine*, 90:604–9.

Cheetham, J., Fuller, R., McIvor, G. and Perth, A. (1992) *Evaluating Social Work Effectiveness*. Buckingham: Open University Press.

Chodorow, N. (1978) *The Reproduction of Mothering: psychoanalysis and the sociology of gender*. Berkeley: University of California Press.

Cicirelli, V. (1977) The impact of Head Start: executive summary. In Caro (ed.).

Cicirelli, V. G. et al. (1969) *The Impact of Head Start: an evaluation of the effects of Head Start on children's cognitive and affective development*, vol, 1. Report to the US Office of Economic Opportunity by Westinghouse Learning Corporation and Ohio University.

Cicourel, A. V. (1964) *Method and Measurement in Sociology*. New York: Free Press.

Clark, T. N. (1973) *Prophets and Patrons: the French university and the emergence of the social sciences*. Cambridge, Mass.: Harvard University Press.

Cobb, A. K. and Hagemaster, J. N. (1987) Ten criteria for evaluating qualitative research proposals. *Journal of Nursing Education*, 26(4):138–43.

Cobbe, F. P. (1894) *Life of Frances Power Cobbe by Herself*. Boston: Houghton Mifflin.

Cochrane A. L. (1972) *Effectiveness and Efficiency: random reflections on health services*. London: Nuffield Provincial Hospitals Trust.

Cochrane, A. L. (1979) 1931–1971: a critical review with particular reference to the medical profession. In Office of Health Economics *Medicines for the Year 2000*, London: Office of Health Economics.

Cochrane, A. L. with Blythe, M. (1989) *One Man's Medicine: an autobiography of Professor Archie Cochrane*. London: BMJ Publications.

Cochrane Centre (1992) Brochure. Oxford: Cochrane Centre.

The *Cochrane Library* (1999) Issue 1. Oxford: Update Software.

Code, L. (1991) *What Can She Know? Feminist theory and the construction of knowledge*. Ithaca, N.Y.: Cornell University Press.

Codell Carter, K. (trans. and ed.) (1983) *Ignaz Semmelweiss. The Etiology, Concept, and Prophylaxis of Childbed Fever*. Madison, Wis.: University of Wisconsin Press.

Cohen, I. B. (1985a) *The Birth of a New Physics*. Harmondsworth: Penguin.

Cohen, I. B. (1985b) *The Revolution in Science*. Cambridge, Mass.: Belknap Press of Harvard University Press.

Cohen, I. B. (1994a) A note on 'social science' and 'natural science'. In Cohen (ed.) 1994c.

Cohen, I. B. (1994b) The scientific revolution and the social sciences. In Cohen (ed.) 1994c.

Cohen, I. B. (ed.) (1994c) *The Natural Sciences and the Social Sciences*. Dordrecht: Kluwer Academic.

Cole, M. (ed.) (1956) *Beatrice Webb's Diaries 1924–1932*. London: Longmans Green and Co.

Cole, S. (1972) Continuity and institutionalization in science: a case study of failure. In Oberschall (ed.).

Collier, G. Minton, H. C. and Reynolds, G. (1992) *Currents of Thought in American Social Psychology*. New York: Oxford University Press.

Comte, A. (1853) *The Positive Philosophy of Auguste Comte* (trans. H. Martineau), 2 vols. London: John Chapman.

Comte, A. (1877) *Cours de philosophie positive*. Paris: Baillière.

Condorcet, le Marquis de (1785) *Essai sur l'application de l'analyse à la probabilité des décisions rendues à la pluralité des voix*. Paris: Imprimerie Royale.

Coney, S. (1988) *The Unfortunate Experiment*. Auckland: Penguin Books.

Connor, J., Rodgers, A. and Priest, P. (in press) Randomised studies of income supplementation: a lost opportunity to assess health outcomes. *Journal of Epidemiology and Community Health*.

Cook, E. R. (1913) *The Life of Florence Nightingale 1820–1910*. London: Macmillan.

Cook, T. D. (1997) Lessons learned in evaluation over the past 25 years. In E. Chelimsky and W. R. Shadish (eds), *Evaluation for the 21st Century: a handbook*, Thousand Oaks, Calif.: Sage Publications.

Cook, T. D., Del Rosario, M. L., Hennigan, K. M., Mark, M. M. and Trochim, W. M. K. (eds) (1978) *Evaluation Studies Review Annual*, vol. 3. Beverly Hills, Calif.: Sage Publications.

Cook, T. D. and Campbell, D. T. (1979) *Quasi-experimentation: design and analysis issues for field settings*. Chicago: Rand McNally.

Cook, T. D. and Reichardt, C. S. (eds) (1979) *Qualitative and Quantitative Methods in Evaluation Research*. Beverly Hills, Calif.: Sage Publications.

Coole, S. (1976) *The Sociological Method*, 2nd edn. Chicago: Rand McNally.

Cooper, H. M. and Rosenthal, R. (1980) Statistical versus traditional procedures for summarizing research findings. *Psychological Bulletin*, 87:442–9.

Cooter, R. (1991) Dichotomy and denial: mesmerism, medicine and Harriet Martineau. In M. Benjamin (ed.), *Science and Sensibility: gender and scientific enquiry 1780–1945*, Oxford: Blackwell.

Cottingham, J. (1986) *Descartes*. Oxford: Blackwell.

Cotton, P. (1990a) Examples abound of gaps in medical knowledge because of groups excluded from scientific study. *Journal of the American Medical Association*, 263(8):1051–2.

Cotton, P. (1990b) Is there still too much extrapolation from data on middle-aged white men? *Journal of the American Medical Association*, 263(8):1049–50.

Crawford, M. (1989) Agreeing to differ: feminist epistemologies and women's ways of knowing. In M. Crawford and M. Gentry (eds).

Crawford, M. and Gentry, M. (eds) (1989) *Gender and Thought*. New York: Springer Verlag.

Creswell, J. W. (1994) *Research Design: qualitative and quantitative approaches*. Thousand Oaks, Calif.: Sage Publications.

Critchlow, D. T. (1985) *The Brookings Institution 1916–1952*. DeKalb, Ill.: Northern Illinois University Press.

Cronbach, L. J. (1982) *Designing Evaluations of Educational and Social Programs*. San Francisco: Jossey-Bass.

Cronin, F. J. and Rasmussen, D. W. (1981) Mobility. In Struyk and Bendick (eds).

Curthoys, J. (1997) *Feminist Amnesia*. London: Routledge.

Danzinger, K. (1990) *Constructing the Subject: historical origins of psychological research*. Cambridge: Cambridge University Press.

Darwin, C. (1873) *The Expression of the Emotions in Man and Animals*. London: John Murray.

Davey-Smith, G. and Egger, M. (1998) Lancelot Hogben on speed: the forgotten history of the n-of-1 trial. Abstract for Society for Social Medicine Annual Conference, Cardiff.

Davies, J. K. and Macdonald, G. (1998a) Beyond uncertainty: leading health promotion into the twenty-first century. In Davies and Macdonald (eds) (1998b).

Davies, J. K. and Macdonald, G. (eds) (1998b) *Quality, Evidence and Effectiveness in Health Promotion*. London: Routledge.

Davis, K. B. (1929) *Factors in the Sex Life of Twenty-two Hundred Women*. New York: Harper and Brothers.

Davis, P. and Howden-Chapman, P. (1996) Translating research findings into health policy. *Social Science and Medicine*, 43(5):865–72.

Davy, H. (1802) *A Discourse Introductory to a Course of Lectures on Chemistry*. London.

Deegan, M. J. (1988) *Jane Addams and the Men of the Chicago School*. New Brunswick,

N.J.: Transaction.

De Laet, C. E. D. H., van Hout, B. A., Burger, H., Hofman, A. and Pols, H. A. P. (1997) Bone density and risk of hip fracture in men and women: cross-sectional analysis. *British Medical Journal*, 315: 221–5.

de Tocqueville, A. (1835) *Democracy in America*, trans. H. Reeve. London: Saunders and Otley.

Dehue, T. (1997) Deception, efficiency, and random groups. *Isis*, 88:653–73.

Dennis, M. L. (1988) *Implementing Randomized Field Experiments: an analysis of criminal and civil justice research*. Evanston, Ill.: Northwestern University Press.

Derlien, H.-U. (1989) Program evaluation in the Federal Republic of Germany. In Rist (ed.).

Descartes, R. (1644) *Principles of Philosophy*. In *The Philosophical Writings of Descartes*, trans. J. Cottingham, R. Stoothoff and D. Murdoch. 2 vols. Cambridge: Cambridge University Press, 1985.

Descartes, R. (1968) *Discourse on the Method and The Meditations*, trans. by F. E. Sutcliffe. Harmondsworth: Penguin (originally pub. 1637 and 1641).

Descartes, R. (1970) *Descartes: Philosophical Letters*, trans. and ed. A. Kenny. Oxford: Oxford University Press (originally published 1645).

Desrosières, A. (1991) How to make things which hold together: social science, statistics and the state. In Wagner et al. (eds) (1991b).

Devine, E. C. and Cook, T. D. (1983) A meta-analytic analysis of effects of psychoeducational interventions on length of post-surgical hospital stay. *Nursing Research*, 32:267–74.

Dewey, J. (1980) *The Quest for Certainty*. New York: Perigee (originally pub. 1929).

Dex, S. (1987) *Women's Occupational Mobility*. London: Macmillan.

Diamond, M. and Stone, M. (1981) Nightingale on Quételet. *Journal of the Royal Statistical Society*, 144(1):66–79.

Dickens, C. (1854) *Hard Times*. London and Glasgow: Collins.

Dodd, S. C. (1934) *A Controlled Experiment on Rural Hygiene in Syria*. Publication of the Faculty of Arts and Sciences, Social Science Series, no. 7. Beirut: American University of Beirut.

Dodd, S. C. (1942) *Dimensions of Society: a quantitative systematics for the social sciences*. New York: Macmillan.

Doll, R. (1997) Cochrane and the benefits of wine. In Maynard and Chalmers (eds).

Donovan, J. (1990) Animal rights and feminist theory. *SIGNS: Journal of Women in Culture and Society*, 15(21):350–75.

Dorfman, J. (1955) The department of economics. In Hoxie et al.

Downie, R. S., Tannahill, C. and Tannahill, A. (1996) *Health Promotion: models and values*. Oxford: Oxford University Press.

Dreher, M. (1994) Qualitative research methods from the reviewer's perspective. In Morse (ed.).

DuBois, B. (1983) Passionate scholarship: notes on values, knowing and method in feminist social science. In Bowles and Duelli Klein (eds).

Duelli Klein, R. (1983) How to do what we want to do: thoughts about feminist methodology. In Bowles and Duelli Klein (eds).

Dunkle, R. E., Poulshock, S. W., Silverstone, B. and Deimling, G. T. (1983) Protective services reanalyzed: does casework help or harm? *Social Casework*, 144:195–9.

Durkheim, E. (1938) *The Rules of the Sociological Method*. Chicago: the Free Press of Glencoe (originally published 1895).

Durkheim, E. (1952) *Suicide: a study in sociology*, trans. J. A. Spaulding and G. Simpson.

London: Routledge, (originally pub. 1897).

Early Breast Cancer Trialists' Collaborative Group (1992). Systemic treatment of early breast cancer by hormonal, cytotoxic and immune therapy: 133 randomized trials involving 31,000 recurrences and 25,000 deaths among 75,000 women. *Lancet*, 339:1–15, 71–85.

Easlea, B. (1981) *Science and Sexual Oppression*. London: Weidenfeld and Nicolson.

Edgeworth, F. Y. (1885) *Logic of Statistics*. London.

Edgeworth, M. (1871) *Lazy Lawrence and the White Pigeon: stories for children*. London.

Edgeworth, M. and Edgeworth, R. L. (1798) *Practical Education*. London: J. Johnson.

Editorial (1991) MRC to go ahead with controversial tamoxifen trial. *Bulletin of Medical Ethics*, Oct.:3–5.

Editorial (1999) Dangerous liaisons. *Big Issue*, 15–21 Mar.:14–15.

Edwards, R. (1990) Connecting method and epistemology: a white woman interviewing black women. *Women's Studies International Forum*, 13(5):477–90.

Edwards, S. J. L., Lilford, R. J., Braunholtz, D. A., Jackson, J. C., Hewison, J. and Thornton, J. (1998a) Ethical issues in the design and conduct of randomised controlled trials. *Health Technology Assessment*, 2(15).

Edwards, S. J. L., Lilford, R. J. and Hewison, J. (1998b) The ethics of randomised controlled trials from the perspectives of patients, the public, and healthcare professionals. *British Medical Journal*, 317:1209–12.

Edwards, T. (1996) The research base of effective teacher education. *British Educational Research Association Newsletter*, no 57, July:7–12.

Egger, M., Schneider, M. and Smith, G. D. (1998) Spurious precision? Meta-analysis of observational studies. *British Medical Journal*, 316:140–4.

Egger, M. and Smith, G. D. (1998) Bias in location and selection of studies. *British Medical Journal*, 316:61–6.

Eichler, M. (1988) *Nonsexist Research Methods*. Boston: Allen and Unwin.

Eiseley, L. (1961) *The Man Who Saw Through Time*. New York: Charles Scribner's Sons.

Eisner, E. W. (1979) *The Educational Imagination: on the design and evaluation of school programs*. New York: Macmillan.

Elbourne, D. (1987) Subjects' views about participation in a randomized controlled trial. *Journal of Reproductive and Infant Psychology*, 5:3–8.

Elcock, H. (1976) *Political Behaviour*. London: Methuen.

Elder, C. (1998) A vein-glorious future for leeches. *Hampstead and Highgate News*, 28 Aug.:20.

Elesh, D. (1972) The Manchester Statistical Society: a case study of discontinuity in the history of empirical social research. In Oberschall (ed.).

Eliot, G. (1994) *Middlemarch*. Harmondsworth: Penguin (originally pub. 1872).

Elshtain J. B. (1981) *Public Man, Private Woman*. Oxford: Martin Robertson.

Elston, M. A. (1987) Women and anti-vivisection in Victorian England 1870–1900. In Rupke (ed.).

Ely, R. T. (1938) *Ground Under Our Feet: an autobiography*. New York: Macmillan.

Empey, L. T. and Erickson, M. L. (1972) *The Provo Experiment*. Lexington, Mass.: D. C. Heath and Company.

Empey, L. T. and Lubeck, S. G. (1971) *The Silverlake Experiment*. Chicago: Aldine Publishing Company.

Enkin, M., Keirse, M. J. N. C. and Chalmers, I. (eds) (1989) *A Guide to Effective Care in Pregnancy and Childbirth*. Oxford: Oxford University Press.

Erwin, E., Gendin, S. and Kleiman, L. (eds) (1994) *Ethical Issues in Scientific Research*.

New York: Garland Publishing Inc.

Evans, C. (1983) *The Making of the Micro*. Oxford: Oxford University Press.

Evans, J. W. (1977) Head Start: comments on the criticisms. In Caro (ed.).

Fallowfield, L. J., Jenkins, V., Brennan, C., Sawtell, M., Moynihan, C. and Souhami, R. L. (1998) Attitudes of Patients to Randomised Clinical Trials of Cancer Therapy. *European Journal of Cancer*, 34(10):1554–9.

Fallowfield, L., Ratcliffe, D. and Souhami R. (1977) Clinicians' attitudes to clinical trials of cancer therapy. *European Journal of Cancer*, 33(13):2221–9.

Faris, R. I. (1967) *Chicago Sociology*. Chicago: University of Chicago Press.

Farkas, G., Olsen, R., Stromsdorfer, E. W., Sharpe, L. C., Skidmore, F., Smith, D. A. and Merrill, S. (1984) *Post-Program Impacts of the Youth Incentive Entitlement Pilot Projects*. New York: Manpower Demonstration Research Corporation.

Farr, W. (1837) Vital statistics; or the statistics of health, sickness, disease and death. In J. R. McCulloch (ed.), *Statistical Account of the British Empire*, London: C. Knight and Co.

Faules, D. (1982) The use of multi-methods in the organizational setting. *Western Journal of Speech Communication*, 46:150–61.

Fechner, G. T. (1860) *Elements der Psychophysik*. Trans. H. E. Adler as *Elements of Psychophysics*, (ed.) D. H. Howes and E. G. Boring. New York: Holt, Rinehart and Winston.

Feinstein, A. R. (1995) Meta-analysis: statistical alchemy for the 21st century. *Journal of Clinical Epidemiology*, 48:71–9.

Ferber, R. and Hirsch, W. Z. (1982) *Social Experimentation and Economic Policy*. Cambridge: Cambridge University Press.

Fetterman, D. M. (1982) Ibsen's baths: reactivity and insensitivity. *Educational Evaluation and Policy Analysis*, 4(3):261–79.

Fibiger, J. (1898) Om serumbehandling af difteri. *Hospitalstidende*, 6:309–25.

Fienberg, S. E. (1971) Randomization and social affairs: the 1970 draft lottery. *Science*, 171:255–61.

Filstead, W. J. (1979) Qualitative methods: a needed perspective in evaluation research. In Cook and Reichardt (eds).

Finch, J. (1984) 'It's great to have someone to talk to': the ethics and politics of interviewing women. In C. Bell and H. Roberts (eds), *Social Researching: politics, problems, practice*, London, Routledge.

Finch, J. (1986) *Research and Policy*. Lewes, East Sussex: Falmer Press.

Firestone, W. A. and Herriott, R. E. (1983) The formalization of qualitative research: an adaptation of 'soft' science to the policy world. *Evaluation Review*, 7(4):437–66.

Fischer, J. (1973) Is casework effective? A review. *Social Work*, Jan.:5–20.

Fischer, M. (1996) Introducing the Cochrane Library. *Cochrane News*. 7 (June).

Fisher, B., Bauer, M., Margolese, R., Poisson, R., Pilch, Y., Redmond, C., Fisher, E., Wolmark, N., Deutsch, M. and Montague, E. et al. (1985a) Five year results of a randomized clinical trial comparing total mastectomy and segmental mastectomy with and without radiation. *New England Journal of Medicine*, 312(11):665–73.

Fisher, B., Redmond, C., Fisher, E. R., Bauer, M., Wolmark, N., Wickerham, D. L., Deutsch, M., Montague, E., Margolese, R. and Foster, R. (1985b) Ten-year results of a randomized trial comparing radical mastectomy and total mastectomy with and without radiation. *New England Journal of Medicine*, 312(11):674–81.

Fisher, R. A. (1913–14) Some hopes of a eugenist. *Eugenics Review*, 5:309–15.

Fisher, R. A. (1930) *The Genetical Theory of Natural Selection*. Oxford: Clarendon Press.

Fisher, R. A. (1935) *The Design of Experiments*. Reissued in *Statistical Methods, Experimental Design and Scientific Inference*. Oxford: Oxford University Press, 1990.

Fisher, R. A. (1956) *Statistical Methods and Scientific Inference*. Reissued in *Statistical Methods, Experimental Design and Scientific Inference*. Oxford: Oxford University Press, 1990.

Fitzpatrick, E. (1990) *Endless Crusade: women social scientists and progressive reform*. New York: Oxford University Press.

Fletcher, C. (1974) *Beneath the Surface*. London: Routledge and Kegan Paul.

Floud, R., Wachter, K. and Gregory, A. (1990) *Height, Health and History: nutritional status in the United Kingdom 1750–1980*. Cambridge: Cambridge University Press.

Folkenflik, V. (trans.) (1987) *An Extraordinary Woman: selected writings of Germaine de Staël*. New York: Columbia University Press.

Fonow, M. M. and Cook, J. A. (eds) (1991) *Beyond Methodology: feminist scholarship as lived research*. Bloomington, Ind.: Indiana University Press.

Frame, J. (1980) *Faces in the Water*. London: Women's Press.

Frame, J. (1990) *An Autobiography*. London: Women's Press.

France-Dawson, M., Holland, J., Fullerton, D., Kelley, P., Arnold, S. and Oakley, A. (1994) *Review of Effectiveness of Workplace Health Promotion Interventions*. London: Social Science Research Unit.

Franke, R. H and Kaul, J. D. (1978) The Hawthorne experiments: first statistical interpretation. *American Sociological Review*, 43(5):623–43.

Freeman, D. (1983) *Margaret Mead and Samoa: the making and unmaking of anthropological myth*. Cambridge, Mass.: Harvard University Press.

Freeman, F. N. (1933) The technique used in the study of the effect of motion pictures on the care of the teeth. *Journal of Educational Sociology*, Jan.:309–11.

Freeman, F. N., Holzinger, K. J. and Mitchell, B. C. (n.d.) The influence of environment on the intelligence, school achievement and conduct of foster children. Cited in Murphy et al. 1937.

Freidson, E. (1970) *Profession of Medicine*. New York: Dodd Mead.

Friedman, J. and Weinberg, D. H. (1983a) History and overview. In Friedman and Weinberg (eds).

Friedman, J. and Weinberg, D. H. (1983b) Introduction. In Friedman and Weinberg (eds).

Friedman, J. and Weinberg, D. H. (eds) (1983c) *The Great Housing Experiment*. Beverly Hills, Calif.: Sage.

Friedman, M. (1962) *Capitalism and Freedom*. Chicago: University of Chicago Press.

Furumoto, L. (1988) Shared knowledge: the experimentalists, 1904–1929. In Morawski (ed.).

Gage, N. L. (1972) *Teacher Effectiveness and Teacher Education: the search for a scientific basis*. Palo Alto, Calif.: Pacific Books.

Galton, F. (1892) *Hereditary Genius*, 2nd edn. London: Watts (originally pub. 1869).

Galton, F. (1909) *Memories of my Life*, 3rd edn. London: Methuen.

Galtung, J. (1967) *Theory and Methods of Social Research*. London: Allen and Unwin.

Garcia, J., Corry, M., MacDonald, D., Elbourne, D. and Grant, A. (1985) Mothers' views of continuous electronic fetal heart monitoring and intermittent auscultation in a randomized controlled trial. *Birth*, 12(2):79–85.

Garfinkel, H. (1967) *Studies in Ethnomethodology*. Englewood Cliffs, N.J.: Prentice-Hall.

Garry, A. and Pearsall, M. (eds) (1989) *Women, Knowledge and Reality*. London: Unwin Hyman.

Geertz, C. (1973) Thick description: towards an interpretive theory of culture. In C. Geertz, *The Interpretation of Cultures*, New York: Basic Books.

Gellner, E. (1979) *Spectacles and Predicaments: essays in social theory*. Cambridge: Cambridge University Press.

General Accounting Office (1972) Legislative references to evaluation 1967–1972. Memo, Report from the Comptroller General's Office. Washington, D.C.: US General Accounting Office.

Gerber, E. R. (1975) The Cultural Patterning of Emotions in Samoa. Ph.D. diss., University of California, San Diego.

Giddens, A. (1978) Positivism and its critics. In T. Bottomore and R. Nisbet (eds), *A History of Sociological Analysis*, London: Heinemann.

Giddings, F. H. (1898) *The Elements of Sociology: a textbook for colleges and schools*. New York: Macmillan.

Giddings, F. H. (1901) *Inductive Sociology: a syllabus of methods, analyses and classifications, and provisionally formulated laws*. New York: Macmillan.

Gilbert, J. P., Light, R. J. and Mosteller, F. (1975) Assessing social innovations: an empirical base for policy. In Bennett and Lumsdaine (eds).

Gillespie, R. (1988) The Hawthorne experiments and the politics of experimentation. In Morawski (ed.).

Gilligan, C. (1982) *In a Different Voice: psychological theory and women's development*. Cambridge, Mass.: Harvard University Press.

Gillis, M. B. (1927) An experimental study of the development and measurement of health practices of elementary school children. *Journal of Educational Sociology*, 1 Nov.:164–5.

Glaser, B. G. and Strauss, A. L. (1967) *The Discovery of Grounded Theory*. Chicago: Aldine.

Glass, G. V. (1976) Primary, secondary, and meta-analysis of research. *Educational Researcher*, 5:3–8.

Glass, G. V., McGaw, B. and Smith, M. L. (1981) *Meta-analysis in Social Research*. Beverly Hills, Calif.: Sage Publications.

Glassner, B. and Moreno, J. D. (1989) Introduction: quantification and enlightenment. In B. Glassner and J. D. Moreno (eds), *The Qualitative–Quantitative Distinction in the Social Sciences*, Dordrecht: Kluwer.

Glueck, E. T. (1936) *Evaluative Research in Social Work*. New York: Columbia University Press.

Glueck, S. and Glueck, E. T. (1959) *Predicting Delinquency and Crime*. Cambridge, Mass.: Harvard University Press.

Goldberg, M. (1970) *Helping the Aged: a field experiment in social work*. London: Allen and Unwin.

Goldberger, N. (1996a) Introduction: looking backward, looking forward. In Goldberger et al. (eds).

Goldberger, N. (1996b) Cultural imperatives and diversity in ways of knowing. In Goldberger et al. (eds).

Goldberger, N., Tarule, J., Clinchy, B. and Belenky, M. (eds) (1996) *Knowledge, Difference and Power*. New York: Basic Books.

Goldstein, H. and Blatchford, P. (1996) *Class Size and Educational Achievement: a methodological review*. Draft paper for UNESCO.

Goodare, H. (1996) Fighting Spirit: the story of women in the Bristol Breast Cancer Survey. London: Scarlet Press.

Gordon, G. and Morse, E. V. (1975) Evaluation research. *Annual Review of Sociology*,

1:339–61.

Gosnell, H. F. (1927) *Getting Out the Vote: an experiment in the stimulation of voting.* Westport, Conn.: Greenwood Press.

Gough, D. (1993) *Child Abuse Interventions.* London: HMSO.

Gould, S. J. (1981) *The Mismeasure of Man.* London: Penguin.

Graham, H. (1983) Do her answers fit his questions? Women and the survey method. In E. Garmarnikow, S. Morgan, J. Purvis and D. Taylorson (eds), *The Public and the Private,* London: Heinemann.

Graham, H. (1987) Women's smoking and family health. *Social Science and Medicine,* 25(1):47–56.

Graham, H. (1994) Surviving by smoking. In S. Wilkinson and C. Kitzinger (eds), *Women and Health: feminist perspectives,* London: Taylor and Francis.

Gramlich, E. M. and Koshel, P. P. (1975) *Educational Performance Contracting.* Washington, D.C.: Brookings Institution.

Grant, A. and Chalmers, I. (1985) Some research strategies for investigating aetiology and assessing the effects of clinical practice. In R. R. Macdonald (ed.), *Scientific Basis of Obstetrics and Gynaecology,* 3rd edn, London: Churchill Livingstone.

Grant, A., Elbourne, D., Valentin, L. and Alexander, S. (1989) The effect of a policy of routine formal fetal movement counting on the risk of antepartum late death among normally-formed singleton fetuses: a multicentre randomized controlled trial. *Lancet,* 2:345–9.

Grant, J. (1993) *Fundamental Feminism.* New York: Routledge.

Grant, J. (1661) *Natural and Political Observations made upon the Bills of Mortality.* London.

Gray, J., White, M. and Barton, A. (1995) *Investigating the Dissemination of Public Health Research.* Unpublished report. Newcastle-upon-Tyne: Department of Epidemiology and Public Health, University of Newcastle-upon-Tyne.

Green, F. H. K. (1954) The clinical evaluation of remedies. *Lancet.* 27 Nov.:1085–90.

Green, J. and Britten, N. (1998) Qualitative research and evidence based medicine. *British Medical Journal,* 316:1230–2.

Green, V. H. H. (1952) *Renaissance and Reformation.* London: Edward Arnold.

Greene, J. C., Doughty, J., Marquart, J. M., Ray, M. L. and Roberts, L. (1988) Qualitative evaluation audits in practice. *Evaluation Review,* 12(4):352–75.

Greenwood, E. (1945) *Experimental Sociology.* New York: Octagon Books (repr. 1976).

Greenwood, M. (1948) *Medical Statistics from Graunt to Farr.* Cambridge: Cambridge University Press.

Greer, G. (1999) *The Independent,* 3 Mar. 1999.

Griffin, L. and Ragin, C. C. (1994) Some observations on formal methods of qualitative analysis. *Sociological Methods and Research,* 23(1):4–21.

Griffin, S. (1980) *Women and Nature: the roaring inside her.* New York: Harper Colophon.

Groeneveld, L. P., Tuma, N. B. and Hannan, M. T. (1980) The effects of negative income tax programs on marital dissolution. *Journal of Human Resources,* 15(4):654–74.

Grossman, M. and Bart, P. (1979) Taking the men out of menopause. In R. Hubbard, M. S. Henifen and B. Fried (eds), *Women Looking at Biology Looking at Women,* Boston: G. K. Hall.

Guarnieri, P. (1987) Moritz Schiff (1823–96): experimental physiology and noble sentiment in Florence. In Rupke (ed.).

Guba, E. G. (1978) *Towards a Methodology of Naturalistic Inquiry in Educational Evalu-*

ation. Los Angeles: University of California, Center for the Study of Evaluation.

Guba, E. G. (ed.) (1990) *The Paradigm Dialog*. Newbury Park, Calif.: Sage Publications.

Guba, E. G. and Lincoln, Y. S. (1981) *Effective Evaluation*. San Francisco: Jossey-Bass.

Guba, E. G. and Lincoln, Y. S. (1989) *Fourth Generation Evaluation*. Newbury Park, Calif.: Sage Publications.

Guyatt, G., Sackett, D., Taylor, D. W., Chong, J., Roberts, R. and Pugsley, S. (1986) Determining optimal therapy – randomized trials in individual patients. *New England Journal of Medicine*, 314:889–92.

Hacking, I. (1988) Telepathy: origins of randomization in experimental design. *Isis*, 79:427–51.

Hacking, I. (1990) *The Taming of Chance*. Cambridge: Cambridge University Press.

Halfpenny, P. (1982) *Positivism and Sociology: explaining social life*. London: Allen and Unwin.

Halpern, E. S. (1983) Auditing Naturalistic Enquiries: the development and application of a model. Ph.D. diss., Indiana University.

Hammersley, M. (1989) *The Dilemma of Qualitative Method: Herbert Blumer and the Chicago tradition*. London: Routledge.

Hammersley, M. (1995) *The Politics of Social Research*. London: Sage Publications.

Hammersley, M. (1997) Educational research and teaching: a response to David Hargreaves' TTA lecture. *British Educational Research Journal*, 23(2):141–61.

Hancock, B. W., Aitken, M., Radstone, C. and Vaughan Hudson, G. (1997) Why don't cancer patients get entered into clinical trials? Experience of the Sheffield Lymphoma Group's collaboration in British National Lymphoma Investigation studies. *British Medical Journal*, 314:26–7.

Handwashing Liaison Group (1999) Hand washing: a modest measure – with big effects. *British Medical Journal*, 318:686.

Hankins, T. L. (1985) *Science and the Enlightenment*. Cambridge: Cambridge University Press.

Harden, A., Peersman, G., Oliver, S., Mauthner, M. and Oakley, A. (1999) A systematic review of the effectiveness of health promotion interventions in the workplace. *Occupational Medicine*, 49:1–9.

Harding, S. (1986) *The Science Question in Feminism*. Milton Keynes: Open University Press.

Harding, S. (1991) *Whose Science? Whose Knowledge?* Buckingham: Open University Press.

Hargreaves, D. H. (1996) Teaching as a research-based profession: possibilities and prospects. Teaching Training Agency Annual Lecture, 1996.

Harper, E. (1943) Sociology in England. *Social Forces*, 11:335–42.

Hart, H. (1921) Science and sociology. *American Journal of Sociology*, 27:364–83.

Harvey, W. (1963) *The Circulation of the Blood and Other Writings*. New York: Dutton (originally pub. 1628).

Haslanger, S. (1993) On being objective and being objectified. In Antony and Witt (eds).

Haste, H. (1993) *The Sexual Metaphor*. Hemel Hempstead: Harvester Wheatsheaf.

Haug, P. (1992) *Educational Reform by Experiment*. Stockholm: HLS Förlag.

Haveman, R. H. (1987) Policy analysis and evaluation research after twenty years. *Policy Studies Journal*, 16(2):191–218.

Hawkesworth, M. E. (1989) Knowers, knowing, known: feminist theory and claims of truth. *SIGNS: Journal of Women in Culture and Society*, 14(3):533–57.

Haworth, L. (1960) The experimenting society: Dewey and Jordan. *Ethics*, 71:27–40.

Health Committee (1992) *Second Report, Session 1991–2: Maternity Services*. London: HMSO.

Hedges, L. V. (1987) How hard is science, how soft is science? *American Psychologist*, 42(2):443–55.

Heller, F. (ed.) (1986) *The Use and Abuse of Social Science*. Beverly Hills, Calif.: Sage Publications.

Hemminki, E. and McPherson, K. (1997) Impact of postmenopausal hormone therapy on cardiovascular events and cancer – pooled data from clinical trials. *British Medical Journal*, 315:149–53.

Hemminki, E, Topo, P. and Kangas, I. (1995) Experience and opinions of climacterium by Finnish women. *European Journal of Obstetrics and Gynaecology and Reproductive Biology*, 62:81–97.

Henshaw, R. C., Naji, S. A., Russell, I. T. and Templeton, A. A. (1993) Comparison of medical abortion with surgical vacuum aspiration: women's preferences and acceptability of treatment. *British Medical Journal*, 307:714–17.

Herbst, J. (1965) *The German Historical School in American Scholarship*. Ithaca, N.Y.: Cornell University Press.

Herman, J. (1995) The demise of the randomized controlled trial. *Journal of Clinical Epidemiology*, 48(7):985–8.

Hey, V. (1994) *Elderly People, Choice and Community Care*. London: Social Science Research Unit.

Hill, C. (1974) William Harvey and the idea of monarchy. In Webster (ed.).

Hill, R. (1944) An experimental study of social adjustment. *American Sociological Review*, Oct.:481–94.

Hobbes, T. (1994) *Leviathan*, ed. D. Curley. Indianapolis: Hackett Publishing Company (originally pub. 1668).

Hobbes, T. (1656) *Elements of Philosophy, (Concerning Body)*, ed. W. Molesworth, *English Works*, vol. 1. London.

Hodnett, E. (1999) Support from caregivers during childbirth (Cochrane Review). In *The Cochrane Library*, Issue 1. Oxford: Update Software.

Hoeg, P. (1994) *Miss Smilla's Feeling for Snow*. London: Flamingo.

Hollister, R. G., Kemper, P. and Wooldridge, J. (1979) Linking process and impact analysis: the case of Supported Work. In Cook and Reichardt (eds).

Holmes, L. D. (1957) A Restudy of Manu'an Culture: a problem in methodology. Ph.D. diss., Northwestern University.

Holmes, L. D. (1983) A tale of two studies. *American Anthropologist*, 85(4):929–35.

Holte, A. (1991) Prevalence in climacteric complaints in a representative sample of middle aged women in Oslo, Norway. *Journal of Psychosomatic Obstetrics and Gynaecology*, 12:303–17.

Hood-Williams, J. (1996) Goodbye to sex and gender. *The Sociological Review*, 1–6.

Horkheimer, M. and Adorno, T. W. (1972) *Dialectic of Enlightenment*. New York: Herder and Herder.

Hoshmand, L. S. T. (1989) Alternative research paradigms: a review and teaching proposal. *Counselling Psychologist*, 30:3–79.

House, E. R. (1993) *Professional Evaluation: social impact and political consequences*. Newbury Park, Calif.: Sage Publications.

Hovland, C., Lumsdaine, A. A. and Sheffield, F. D. (1949) *Studies in Social Psychology in World War II*, vol. 3. *Experiments in Mass Communications*. Princeton, N.J.: Princeton University Press.

Howden-Chapman, P. (1988) The demise of Wolfe Home: a case study of the closure of an inpatient alcoholism unit. *Community Health Studies*, 12:453–60.

Howe, K. and Eisenhart, M. (1990) Standards for qualitative (and quantitative) research: a prolegomenon. *Educational Researcher*, 19(4):2–9.

Hoxie, G., Moore, S. F., Dorfman, J., Hofstadter, R., Anderson, T. W., Millett, J. D. and Lipset, S. M. (1955) *A History of the Faculty of Political Science, Columbia University*. New York: Columbia University Press.

Hudelson, R. (1928) *Class Size at the College Level*. Minneapolis: University of Minnesota Press.

Hum, D. P. J. and Choudhry, S. (1992) Income, work and marital dissolution: Canadian experimental evidence. *Journal of Comparative Family Studies*, 23:246–65.

Humphreys, L. (1970) *Tearoom Trade: a study of homosexual encounters in public places*. London: Duckworth and Co.

Hunt, M. (1985) *Profiles of Social Research: the scientific study of human interactions*. New York: Russell Sage Foundation.

Hunter, D. (1993) Let's hear it for R & D. *Health Service Journal*, 15 Apr.: 17.

Hunter, M. (1990) Emotional well-being, sexual behaviour and hormone replacement therapy. *Maturitas*, 12:299–314.

Ianni, F. A. J. and Orr, M. T. (1979) Toward a rapprochement of quantitative and qualitative methodologies. In Cook and Reichardt (eds).

Illich, I. (1975) *Medical Nemesis*. London: Calder and Boyars.

Independent (1997) Breast cancer drug trial in jeopardy. 23 Oct.

Inlander, C. B., Levin, L. S. and Weiner, E. D. (1988) *Medicine on Trial*. New York: Prentice-Hall.

Irigaray, L. (1985a) *Speculum of the Other Woman*. Ithaca, N.Y.: Cornell University Press.

Irigaray, L. (1985b) *This Sex Which is Not One*. Ithaca, N.Y.: Cornell University Press.

Isler, M. L. (1981) Policy implications: moving from research to programs. In Struyk and Bendick (eds).

Jackson, B. O. and Mohr, L. B. (1986) Rent subsidies: an impact evaluation and an application of the random–comparison group design. *Evaluation Review*, 10(4):483–517.

Jaggar, A. M. (1983) *Feminist Politics and Human Nature*. Brighton: Harvester Press.

Jardine, L. and Stewart, A. (1998) *Hostage to Fortune: the troubled life of Francis Bacon*. London: Gollancz.

Jastrow, J. (1901) *Fact and Fable in Psychology*. London: Macmillan.

Jay, N. (1981) Gender and dichotomy. *Feminist Studies*, 1:35–56.

Jayaratne, T. E. (1983) The value of quantitative methodology for feminist research. In Bowles and Duelli Klein (eds).

Jayaratne, T. E. and Stewart, A. J. (1991) Quantitative and qualitative methods in the social sciences: current feminist issues and practical strategies. In Fonow and Cook (eds).

Jeannie Campbell Breast Cancer Radiotherapy Appeal (n.d.) Fact-sheet, available from 29 St Luke's Avenue, Ramsgate, Kent, CT11 7JZ.

Jenkins, B. and Gray, A. (1989) Policy evaluation in British government: from idealism to realism? In Rist (ed.).

Jenkins, R. (1985) Sex differences in minor psychiatric morbidity. Psychological Medicine, Monograph Supplement 7. Cambridge: Cambridge University Press.

Jessor, R, Colby, A. and Schweder, R. A. (eds) (1996) *Ethnography and Human Devel-*

opment: context and meaning in social enquiry. Chicago: University of Chicago Press.

Johnson, E. (1952) *Charles Dickens: his tragedy and triumph*, vol. 1. London: Hamish Hamilton.

Jones, G. (1986) *Social Hygiene in Twentieth Century Britain*. London: Croom Helm.

Jones, J. H. (1981) *Bad Blood*. New York: Free Press.

Jones, K. (1988) *A Glorious Fame: the life of Margaret Cavendish, Duchess of Newcastle 1623–1673*. London: Bloomsbury.

Jones, O. G. (1928) Laboratory work in municipal citizenship. *National Municipal Review*, Oct.:580–5.

Jordan, E. (1952) *Theory of Legislation: an essay on the dynamics of public mind*. Chicago: University of Chicago Press.

Jordanova, L. (1989) *Sexual Visions*. Hemel Hempstead: Harvester Wheatsheaf.

Josefson, D. (1997) FDA insists on more women in drug trials. *British Medical Journal*, 315:833.

Josefson, D. (1998) Breast cancer trial stopped early. *British Medical Journal*, 316:1187.

Josefson, D. (1999) Women with heart disease cautioned about HRT. *British Medical Journal*, 318:753.

Kant, I. (1855) *A Critique of Pure Reason*, trans. J. M. D. Meiklejohn. London: Henry G Bohn (originally pub. 1781).

Kaplan, A. (1965) Noncausal explanation. In D. Lerner (ed.), *Cause and Effect*, New York: Free Press.

Kassebaum, G. G., Ward, D. A. and Wilner, D. A. (1971) *Prison Treatment and Parole Survival*. New York: Wiley.

Kaufert, P. A., Gilbert, P. and Hassard, T. (1988) Researching the symptoms of menopause: an exercise in methodology. *Maturitas*, 10:117–31.

Kean, H. (1998) *Animal Rights: political and social change in Britain since 1800*. London: Reaktion Books.

Kearney, H. F. (1974) Puritanism, capitalism and the scientific revolution. In Webster (ed.).

Kehrer, K. C. (1978) The Gary income maintenance experiment: summary of initial findings. In Cook et al. (eds).

Kehrer, K. C. and Wolin, C. M. (1979) Impact of income maintenance on low birthweight: evidence from the Gary experiment. *The Journal of Human Resources*, 14(4):434–62.

Keirse, M. J. N. C. (1987) Electronic monitoring in labor: too good to be put to the test. *Birth*, 13(4):256–8.

Keller, E. F. (1980) Baconian science: a hermaphroditic birth. *The Philosophical Forum*, 11(3):299–308.

Keller, E. F. (1983) *A Feeling for the Organism: the life and work of Barbara McClintock*. New York: W. H. Freeman and Company.

Keller, E. F. (1985) *Reflections on Gender and Science*. New Haven: Yale University Press.

Keller, E. F. (1990) Gender and science. In J. Nielsen (ed.), *Feminist Research Methods: exemplary readings in the social sciences*. Boulder, Colo.: Westview Press.

Kelling, G. L., Pate, T., Dieckman, D. and Brown, C. R. (1974) *The Kansas City Patrol Experiment: a technical report*. Washington, D.C.: Police Foundation.

Kelling, G. L., Pate, T., Dieckman, D. and Brown, C. R. (1977) *The Kansas City Preventive Patrol Experiment: a summary*. In Caro (ed.).

Kellor, F. (1901) *Experimental Sociology*. New York: Macmillan.

Kennedy, I. (1988) The law and ethics of informed consent and randomised controlled trials. In I. Kennedy, *Treat Me Right*, Oxford: Clarendon Press.

Kennedy, S. D. (1983) The demand experiment. In Friedman and Weinberg (eds).

Kent, R. A. (1981) *A History of British Empirical Sociology*. Aldershot: Gower.

Kevles, D. J. (1985) *In the Name of Eugenics*. New York: Alfred A. Knopf.

Keynes, J. M. (1947) Newton the man. In The Royal Society, *Newton Tercentenary Celebrations*, Cambridge: Cambridge University Press.

Keynes, J. M. (1966) *The Life of William Harvey*. Oxford: Clarendon Press.

Kinsey, A. C., Pomeroy, W. B., Martin, C. E. and Gebhard, P. H. (1953) *Sexual Behavior in the Human Female*, Philadelphia: W. B. Saunders.

Kirkpatrick, S. A. (1984) Social science research under siege: scarcity or conspiracy? *Social Science Quarterly*, 64(4):705–17.

Kleijnen, J., Gøtzsche, P., Kunz, R. A., Oxman, A. and Chalmers, I. (1997) So what's so special about randomisation? In Maynard and Chalmers (eds).

Kline, M. (1972) *Mathematics in Western Culture*. Harmondsworth: Penguin.

Kmietowicz, Z. (1998) Latest studies fail to show that tamoxifen prevents breast cancer. *British Medical Journal*, 317:162.

Knorr-Cetina, K. and Mulkay, M. (eds) (1981) *Science Observed: perspectives on the social study of science*. Beverly Hills, Calif.: Sage Publications.

Kolakowski, L. (1972) *Positivist Philosophy: from Hume to the Vienna Circle*. Harmondsworth: Penguin.

Komarovsky, M. (1967) *Blue Collar Marriage*. New York: Vintage Books.

Kramer, P. E. and Lehman, S. (1990) Mismeasuring women: a critique of research on computer ability and avoidance. *SIGNS: Journal of Women in Culture and Society*, 16:158–72.

Kreft, I. G. G. and Brown, J. H. (1998) Zero effects of drug prevention programs: issues and solutions. *Evaluation Review*, 22(1):3–14.

Kristeva, J. (1981) Woman can never be defined. In E. Marks, I. de Courtivron (eds), *New French Feminisms: an anthology*, New York: Schocken Books.

Krug, G. and Hepworth, J. (1997) Poststructuralism, qualitative methodology and public health: research methods as a legitimation strategy for knowledge. *Critical Public Health*, 7 (1 & 2):50–60.

Kuhn, T. S. (1962) *The Structure of Scientific Revolutions*. Chicago: University of Chicago Press.

Kuhn, T. S. (1996) *The Structure of Scientific Revolutions*, 3rd edn. Chicago: University of Chicago Press.

Kunz, R. and Oxman, A. (1998) The unpredictability paradox: review of empirical comparisons of randomised and non-randomised clinical trials. *British Medical Journal*, 317:1185–90.

Laitman, C. (1990) DES on prescription: it's time for Europe to act. *Scientific European*, Oct.: 27–9.

Lakatos, I. and Musgrave, A. (eds) (1970) *Criticism and the Growth of Knowledge*. Cambridge: Cambridge University Press.

Lana, R. E. (1969) Pretest sensitization. In R. Rosenthal and R. L. Rosnow (eds), *Artifact in Behavioral Research*, New York: Academic Press.

Lansbury, C. (1985) *The Old Brown Dog: women, workers and anti-vivisection in Edwardian England*. Madison, Wis.: University of Wisconsin Press.

Larson, R. C. (1978) What happened to patrol operations in Kansas City? In Cook et al. (eds).

Lather, P. (1988) Feminist perspectives on empowering research methodologies. *Women's Studies International Forum*, 11(6):569–81.

Latour, B. and Woolgar, S. (1979) *Laboratory Life: the social construction of scientific facts.* Beverly Hills, Calif.: Sage Publications.

Lavoisier, A. and Franklin, B. (1784) *Rapport des Commissaires Chargés par le Roi du Magnetisme Animal.* Paris: Imprimerie Royale.

Lazar, I. and Darlington, R. (1982) *Lasting Effects of Early Education: report from the Consortium for Longitudinal Studies.* Chicago: University of Chicago Press.

Learmonth, A. and Watson, N. (1997) The search for the gold standard: mapping the evidence for health promotion. Paper presented at British Sociological Association Annual Medical Sociology Conference. Cardiff, Wales.

Leavey, C. (1997) In conversation with Ann Oakley. *Journal of Contemporary Health,* 5:18–20.

Leininger, M. (1994) Evaluation criteria and critique of qualitative research studies. In Morse (ed.).

Leiss, W. (1972) *The Domination of Nature.* New York: George Braziller.

Lenzer, G. (1975a) Introduction: Auguste Comte and modern positivism. In Lenzer (ed.).

Lenzer, G. (ed.) (1975b) *Auguste Comte and Positivism: the essential writings.* Chicago: University of Chicago Press.

Leonard, M. (1988) *The Life of Kathleen Ferrier.* London: Futura Publications.

Lepenies, W. (1988) *Between Literature and Science: the rise of sociology.* Cambridge: Cambridge University Press.

Levin, H. M. (1978) A decade of policy developments in improving education and training for low-income populations. In Cook et al. (eds).

Levin, H. M. (1987) Cost-benefit and cost-effectiveness analyses. In D. S. Cordray, H. S. Bloom and R. J. Light (eds), *Evaluation Practice in Review. New Directions for Program Evaluation,* no. 34, San Francisco: Jossey-Bass.

Leviton, L. C. and Boruch, R. F. (1983) Contributions of evaluations to education programs and policy. *Evaluation Review,* 7(5):563–98.

Lewis, S. (1925) *Arrowsmith.* New York: Grosset and Dunlap (originally pub. 1924).

Lidbetter, E. J. (1933) *Heredity and the Social Problem Group.* London: E. Arnold and Company.

Light, R. J. (1983) Introduction. In R. J. Light (ed.) *Evaluation Studies Review Annual,* vol. 8. Beverly Hills, Calif.: Sage Publications.

Light, R. J. and Pillemer, D. B. (1984) *Summing Up: the science of reviewing research.* Cambridge, Mass.: Harvard University Press.

Lincoln, Y. S. (1990) The making of a constructivist. In Guba (ed.).

Lincoln, Y. S. and Guba, E. G. (1985) *Naturalistic Inquiry.* Beverly Hills, Calif.: Sage Publications.

Lind-af-Hageby, L. and Shartau, L. (1913) *The Shambles of Science: extracts from the diary of two students of physiology.* London: Ernest Bell (originally pub. 1903).

Lindquist, E. F. (1940) *Statistical Analysis in Educational Research.* Boston: Houghton Mifflin.

Lipsey, M. W., Crosse, S., Dunkle, J., Pollard, J. and Stobart, G. (1985) Evaluation: the state of the art and the sorry state of the science. In D. S. Cordray (ed.), *Utilizing Prior Research in Evaluation Planning,* San Francisco: Jossey-Bass.

Lipset, S. M. (1955) The department of sociology. In Hoxie et al. (eds).

Llewellyn-Thomas, H. A., McGreal, M. J., Thiel, E. C., Fine, S. and Erlichman, C. (1991) Patients' willingness to enter clinical trials: measuring the association with perceived benefit and preference for decision participation. *Social Science and Medicine,* 32:35–42.

Lloyd, G. (1982) *The Man of Reason.* London: Methuen.

Lofland, J. (1971) *Analyzing Social Settings: a guide to qualitative observation and analysis.* Belmont, Calif.: Wadsworth.

Lofland, J. (1974) Styles of reporting qualitative field research. *American Sociologist,* 9:101–11.

Logan, C. H. (1972) Evaluation research in crime and delinquency: a reappraisal. *Journal of Criminal Law, Criminology and Police Science,* 63(3):378–87.

Lottin, J. (1912) *Quételet: statisticien et sociologue.* Louvain.

Louis, P.-C.-A. (1836) *Researches on the Effects of Bloodletting in Some Inflammatory Diseases,* trans. C. G. Putnam, Boston: Hilliard, Gray.

Louis, P.-C.-A. (1837) De l'examen des malades et de la recherche des fait généraux. *Mémoires de la Société Médicale d'Observation,* vol. 1. Paris: Crochard.

Lukes, S. (1973) *Emile Durkheim: his life and work.* London: Allen Lane.

Lumley, J., Oliver, S. and Waters, E. (1999) Interventions for promoting smoking cessation during pregnancy (Cochrane Review). In *The Cochrane Library,* Issue 1. Oxford: Update Software.

Lundberg, G. (1933) Is sociology too scientific? *Sociologus,* 9 (Sept.):298–323.

Lundberg, G. (1964) *Foundations of Sociology.* New York: McKay.

Lynd, R. S. and Lynd, H. M. (1929) *Middletown: a case study in American culture.* New York: Harcourt Brace.

Lynn, L. E. (1980) *Designing Public Policy.* Santa Monica, Calif.: Scott, Foresman.

Lynöe, N., Sandlund M., Dahlqvist G. and Jaconsson, L. (1991) Informed consent: study of quality of information given to participants in a clinical trial. *British Medical Journal,* 303:610–13.

McCall, W. A. (1923) *How to Experiment in Education.* New York: Macmillan.

McCord, J. (1981) Consideration of some effects of a counselling program. In S. E. Martin, L. B. Sechrest and R. Redner (eds), *New Directions in the Rehabilitation of Criminal Offenders,* Washington, D.C.: National Academy Press.

McCord, W. and McCord, J. (1959) *Origins of Crime: a new evaluation of the Cambridge–Somerville Youth Study.* New York: Columbia University Press.

McCormack, T. (1981) Good theory or just theory? Toward a feminist philosophy of social science. *Women's Studies International Quarterly,* 2:1–12.

McDill, E. I., McDill, M. S. and Sprehe, J. T. (1972) Evaluation in practice: compensatory education. In Rossi and Williams (eds).

Macdonald, D., Grant, A., Sheridan-Pereira, M., Boylan, P. and Chalmers, I. (1985) The Dublin randomized controlled trial of intrapartum fetal heart rate monitoring. *American Journal of Obstetrics and Gynecology,* 152:524–39.

Macdonald, G. (1996a) Evaluating the effectiveness of social interventions. In Oakley and Roberts (eds).

Macdonald, G. (1996b) Ice therapy? Why we need randomised controlled trials. In Barnardos, *What Works? Effective Social Interventions in Child Welfare,* Ilford, Essex: Barnardos.

Macdonald, G. (1997) Social work: beyond control? In Maynard and Chalmers (eds).

Macdonald, G. and Davies, J. K. (1998) Reflection and vision: proving and improving the promotion of health. In Davies and Macdonald (eds).

Macdonald, G. and Roberts, H. (1995) *What Works in the Early Years?* Ilford, Essex: Barnardos.

Macdonald, G. and Sheldon, B. (1992) Contemporary studies of the effectiveness of social work. *British Journal of Social Work,* 22(6):615–43.

McDonald, L. (1993) *The Early Origins of the Social Sciences.* Montreal and Kingston: McGill-Queen's University Press.

McDowall, M. (1983) William Farr and the study of occupational mortality. *Population Trends*, 31:12–14.

McIndoe, W. A., McLean, M. R., Jones, R. W. and Mullins, P. (1984) The invasive potential of carcinoma in situ of the cervix. *Obstetrics and Gynecology*, 64(4):451–8.

Macintyre, S. and Hunt, K. (1997) Socio-economic position, gender and health. *Journal of Health Psychology*, 2(3):315–34.

McKay, J. R., Alterman, A. I., McLellan, A. T., Snider, E. C. and O'Brien, C. P. (1995) Effect of random versus nonrandom assignment in a comparison of inpatient and day hospital rehabilitation for male alcoholics. *Journal of Consulting and Clinical Psychology*, 63:70–8.

MacKenzie, D. (1976) Eugenics in Britain. *Social Studies of Science*, 6:499–532.

McKie, L. (1996) Getting started. In L. McKie (ed.), *Researching Women's Health*, Dinton, Wilts.: Quay Books.

McNemar, Q. (1940) Sampling in psychological research. *Psychological Bulletin*, 37(6):331–63.

McPherson, K. (1994) What do we know about breast cancer, and what do we need to know? In P. Alderson (ed.), *Breast Cancer, Randomised Controlled Trials and Consent*, Consent Conference Series, London: Social Science Research Unit.

McPherson, K. (1995) Breast cancer and hormonal supplements in postmenopausal women. *British Medical Journal*, 311:699–700.

McPherson, K., Britton, A. R. and Wennberg, J. E. (1997) Are randomized controlled trials controlled? Patent preferences and unblind trials. *Journal of the Royal Society of Medicine*, 90:652–6.

McRae, R. F. (1974) Introduction. In J. S. Mill, 1973–4.

Macready, N. (1997) US to encourage more black people to join research trials. *British Medical Journal*, 314:696.

Madge, J. (1963) *The Origins of Scientific Sociology*. London: Tavistock.

Mahl, M. R. and Koon, H. (eds) (1977) *The Female Spectator: English women writers before 1800*. Old Westbury, N.Y.: Feminist Press.

Mahon, J. L., Feagan, B. G. and Laupacis, A. (1995) Ethics of n-of-1 trials. *Lancet*, 345:989.

Mainland, D. (1950) Statistics in clinical research: some general principles. *Annals of the New York Academy of Sciences*, 52:925.

Malinowski, B. (1922) *Argonauts of the Western Pacific*. London: Routledge and Kegan Paul.

Mallar, C. (1977) The educational and labor supply responses of young adults on the urban graduated work incentive experiment. In Watts and Rees (eds).

Mandel, S. and Solnick, L. (1979) *A Preliminary Estimate of the Impact of Youth Entitlement on School Behavior*. New York: Manpower Demonstration Research Corporation.

Manicas, P. (1987) *A History and Philosophy of the Social Sciences*. Oxford: Blackwell.

Manicas, P. (1991) The social science disciplines: the American model. In Wagner et al. (eds).

Manning, W. .G., Leibowitz, A., Goldberg, G. A., Rogers, W. H. and Newhouse, J. P. (1984) A controlled trial of the effect of a prepaid group practice on use of services. *New England Journal of Medicine*, 310:105–10.

Manpower Demonstration Research Corporation (1980) *Summary and Findings of the National Supported Work Demonstration*. Cambridge, Mass.:Ballinger.

Manuel, D. (1987) Marshall Hall (1790–1857): vivisection and the development of experimental physiology. In Rupke (ed.)

Marquis, D. (1986) An argument that all prerandomized clinical trials are unethical. *Journal of Medical Philosophy*, 11(4):367–83.

Marsh, C. (1984) Problems with surveys: methods or epistemology? In M. Bulmer (ed.), *Sociological Research Methods: an introduction*, London: Macmillan.

Marshall, D., Johnell, O. and Wedel, H. (1986) Meta-analysis of how well measures of bone mineral density predict occurrence of osteoporotic fractures. *British Medical Journal*, 312: 1254–9.

Martin, E. (1987) *The Woman in the Body*. Boston: Beacon Press.

Martineau, H. (1834) *Illustrations of Taxation*. London: C. Fox.

Martineau, H. (1837) *Society in America*. London: Saunders and Otley.

Martineau, H. (1838) *How to Observe Morals and Manners*. London: Charles Knight and Co.

Martineau, H. (1849) *Household Education*. London, E. Moxon.

Martineau, H. (1853) Preface. In Comte.

Martineau, H. (1877) *Autobiography*, 3 vols. London: Smith, Elder and Co.

Martinich, A. P. (1997) *Thomas Hobbes*. London: Macmillan.

Martinson, R. (1970) *The Treatment Evaluation Survey*. New York: Office of Crime Control Planning.

Masson, G. (1968) *Queen Christina*. London: Secker and Warburg.

Masterman, M. (1970) The nature of a paradigm. In Lakatos and Musgrave (eds).

Mastroianni, A. C., Faden, R. and Federman, D. (eds) (1994) *Women and Health Research*, vol. 1. Washington, D.C.: National Academy Press.

Matthews, J. R. (1995) *Quantification and the Quest for Medical Certainty*. Princeton, N.J.: Princeton University Press.

Mattson, M. E., Curb, J. D., McArdle, R. and the AMIS and BHAT Research Groups (1985) Participation in a clinical trial: the patients' point of view. *Controlled Clinical Trials*, 6:156–67.

Mayhew, H. (1851) *London Labour and the London Poor*, vol. 1: *The London Street-Folk*. London: George Woodfall and Son.

Maynard, A. and Chalmers, I. (eds) (1997) *Non-random Reflections on Health Services Research*. London: BMJ Publishing Group.

Maynard, R. A. (1977) The effects of the rural income maintenance experiment on the school performance of children. *American Economic Review*, 67:370–5.

Maynard, R. A. and Murnane, R. J. (1981) The effects of a negative income tax on school performance. In H. E. Freeman and M. A. Solomon (eds), *Evaluation Studies Review Annual*, vol. 6. Beverly Hills, Calif.: Sage Publications.

Mayo, E. (1960) *The Human Problems of an Industrial Civilisation*. New York: Viking Press (originally published 1933).

Mays, N. and Pope, C. (1995) Rigour and qualitative research. *British Medical Journal*, 311:109–12.

Mazumdar, P. M. H. (1992) *Eugenics, Human Genetics and Human Failings*. London: Routledge.

Mead, M. (1928) *Coming of Age in Samoa*. New York: William Morrow.

Mead, M. (1972) *Blackberry Winter: my earlier years*. New York: William Morrow.

Medawar, P. (1982) *Pluto's Republic*. Oxford: Oxford University Press.

Meddin, J. R. (1986) Sex differences in depression and satisfaction with self: findings from a United States national survey. *Social Science and Medicine*, 22(8):807–12.

Medical Sociology Group (1996) Criteria for the evaluation of qualitative research papers. *Medical Sociology News*, 22(1): 69–71.

Meehl, P. E. (1986) What social scientists don't understand. In Fiske, D. W. and

Shweder, R. A. (eds), *Metatheory in Social Science*, Chicago: Chicago University Press.

Meek, E. B. (1933) The effect of the study of Latin upon character traits. *The Journal of Educational Sociology*, 7(4):241–3.

Melhuish, E. C. and Wolke, D. (eds) (1991) Special issue on international perspectives on day care for young children. *Journal of Reproductive and Infant Psychology*, 9(2/3).

Melvin, B. L. (1925) Laboratory work in rural social problems. *The Journal of Social Forces*, 3:261–3.

Menefee, S. C. (1938) An experimental study of strike propaganda. *Social Forces*, 16:574–82.

Merchant, C. (1982) *The Death of Nature*. London: Wildwood House.

Merriam, C. E. and Gosnell, H. F. (1924) *Non-voting: causes and methods of control*. Chicago: University of Chicago Press.

Meyer, J. and Sandall, J. (1997) Medical sociology and health services research: has Armstrong gone native and will Bury miss the stop? *Medical Sociology News*, 23(3):50–4.

Meyer, H. J., Borgatta, E. F. and Jones, W. C. (1965) *Girls at Vocational High: an experiment in social work intervention*. New York: Russell Sage Foundation.

Meyrick, J. and Swann, C. (1998) *An Overview of the Effectiveness of Interventions and Programmes Aimed at Reducing Unintended Conceptions in Young People*. London: Health Education Authority.

Mies, M. (1983) Towards a methodology for feminist research. In Bowles and Duelli Klein (eds).

Mill, J. S. (1869) *The Subjection of Women*. London: Longmans, Green, Reader and Dyer.

Mill, J. S. (1973–4) *A System of Logic*, ed. J. M. Robson. Toronto: University of Toronto Press (originally pub. 1843).

Mill, J. S. (1981) *Autobiography and Literary Essays*, ed. J. M. Robson. Toronto: University of Toronto Press (originally pub. 1873).

Miller, J. B. (1976) *Toward a New Psychology of Women*. Boston: Beacon Press.

Millman, M. and Kanter, R. M. (eds) (1975a) *Another Voice: feminist perspectives on social life and social science*. New York: Anchor Books.

Millman, M. and Kanter, R. M. (1975b) Editorial introduction. In Millman and Kanter (eds).

Mills, E. S. and Sullivan, A. (1981) Market effects. In Bradbury and Downs (eds).

Mitroff, I. I., Jacob, T. and Moore, E. T. (1977) On the shoulders of the spouses of the scientists. *Social Studies of Science*, 7:303–27.

Moivre, A. de (1718) *The Doctrine of Chances: – or, a method of calculating the probability of events in play*. London: W. Pearson.

Morawski, J. (ed.) (1988) *The Rise of Experimentation in American Psychology*. New Haven: Yale University Press.

Morse, J. M. (1994a) Qualitative research: fact or fantasy? In: Morse (ed.).

Morse, J. M. (ed.) (1994b) *Critical Issues in Qualitative Research Methods*. Thousand Oaks, Calif.: Sage Publications.

Muecke, M. A. (1994) On the evaluation of ethnographies. In Morse (ed.).

Mulford, J. E. (1983) Earmarked income supplements. In Friedman and Weinberg (eds).

Mullen, P. D. and Iverson, D. (1982) Qualitative methods for evaluative research in health education programs. *Health Education*, May/June:11–18.

Munson, C. E., Robins, P. K. and Stieger, G. (1980) Labor supply and childcare arrangements of single mothers. In Robins et al. (eds).

Murphy, F., Dingwall, R., Greatbatch, D., Parker, S. and Watson, P. (1998) Qualitative research methods in health technology assessment: a review of the literature. *Health Technology Assessment*, 2(16).

Murphy, G., Murphy, L. B. and Newcomb, T. M. (1937) *Experimental Social Psychology: an interpretation of research upon the socialization of the individual*. New York: Harper.

Murray, C. (1984) *Losing Ground: American social policy 1950–1980*. New York: Basic Books.

Murray, G. (1997) Agonize, don't organize: a critique of postfeminism. *Current Sociology*, 45(2):37–47.

Nathan, R. P. (1988) *Social Science in Government*. New York: Basic Books.

Navarro, V. (1976) *Medicine Under Capitalism*. New York: Prodist.

Neilson, J. P. (1999) Ultrasound for fetal assessment in early pregnancy (Cochrane Review). In *The Cochrane Library*, Issue 1. Oxford: Update Software.

Nemecek, S. (1997) The furor over feminist science. *Scientific American*, Jan.:83–4.

Newby, H. (1977) In the field: reflections on the study of Suffolk farm workers. In C. Bell and H. Newby (eds) *Doing Sociological Research*, London: Allen and Unwin.

Newman, T. and Roberts, H. (1997) Assessing social work effectiveness in child care practice: the contribution of randomized controlled trials. *Child-care, Health and Development*, 23(4):287–96.

Newton, I. (1729) *The Mathematical Principles of Natural Philosophy*. London: Motte (originally pub. 1687).

Nicholson, R. H. (ed.) (1986) *Medical Research with Children: ethics, law and practice*. Oxford: Oxford University Press.

Nightingale, F. (1858) *Notes on Matters affecting the Health, Efficiency, and Hospital Administration of the British Army*. London: Harrison and Sons.

Nightingale, F. (1871) *Introductory Notes on Lying-in Institutions: together with a proposal for organising an institution for training midwives and midwifery nurses*. London: Longmans, Green and Co.

Nightingale, F. (1969) *Notes on Nursing: what it is and what it is not*. London: Constable and Company (originally pub. 1860).

Nisbet, R. (1976) *Sociology as an Art Form*. London: Heinemann.

Oakley, A. (1972a) Introduction. In Oakley (1972b).

Oakley, A. (1972b) *Sex, Gender and Society*. London: Maurice Temple Smith.

Oakley, A. (1974) *The Sociology of Housework*. London: Martin Robertson (repr. with new introduction, Oxford: Blackwell, 1985).

Oakley, A. (1979) *Becoming a Mother*. Oxford: Martin Robertson.

Oakley, A. (1980) *Women Confined: towards a sociology of childbirth*. Oxford: Martin Robertson.

Oakley, A. (1981) Interviewing women: a contradiction in terms? In H. Roberts (ed.), 1981.

Oakley, A. (1984) *The Captured Womb: a history of the medical care of pregnant women*. Oxford: Blackwell.

Oakley, A. (1989) Smoking in pregnancy – smokescreen or risk factor? *Sociology of Health and Illness*, 11(4):311–35.

Oakley, A. (1990) Who's afraid of the randomised controlled trial? Some dilemmas of the scientific method and 'good' research practice. In Roberts (ed.).

Oakley, A. (1991) Eugenics, social medicine and the career of Richard Titmuss in Britain, 1935–50. *British Journal of Sociology*, 42(2):165–94.

Oakley, A. (1992a) Informed consent and the cervical cancer 'trial' in New Zealand. In P. Alderson (ed.), *Consent to Health Treatment and Research: differing perspectives*, Consent Conference Series, London: Social Science Research Unit.

Oakley, A. (1992b) *Social Support and Motherhood*. Oxford: Basil Blackwell.

Oakley, A. (1996) *Man and Wife: my parents' early years*. London: HarperCollins.

Oakley, A. (1997) A brief history of gender. In Oakley and Mitchell (eds).

Oakley, A. (1998a) Experimentation in social science: the case of health promotion. *Social Sciences in Health*, 4(2):73–89.

Oakley, A. (1998b) Science, gender and women's liberation: an argument against postmodernism. *Women's Studies International Forum*, 21(2):133–46.

Oakley, A. (1999) Health visiting and social support. Presentation to Systematic Reviews in Child Health Conference, Manchester.

Oakley, A., Rajan, L. and Robertson, P. (1990) A comparison of different sources of information about pregnancy and childbirth. *Journal of Biosocial Science*, 22:477–87.

Oakley, A. and Fullerton, D. (1995) *Young People and Smoking*. London: Social Science Research Unit.

Oakley, A., Fullerton, D. and Holland, J. (1995a) Behavioural interventions for HIV/AIDS prevention. *AIDS*, 9:479–86.

Oakley, A., Fullerton, D., Holland, J., Arnold, S., France-Dawson, M. and Kelley, P. (1995b) Sexual health interventions for young people: a methodological review. *British Medical Journal*, 310:158–62.

Oakley, A. and Fullerton, D. (1996) The lamppost of research: support or illumination? In Oakley and Roberts (eds).

Oakley, A, France-Dawson, M., Fullerton, D., Holland, J., Arnold, S., Cryer, C., Doyle, Y., Rice, J., Hodgson, C. R., Sowden, A., Sheldon, T., Fullerton, D., Glenny, A.-M. and Eastwood, A. (1996) Preventing falls and subsequent injury in older people. *Quality in Health Care*, 5:243–9.

Oakley, A. and Roberts, H. (eds) (1996) *Evaluating Social Interventions*. Ilford, Essex: Barnardos.

Oakley, A. and Mitchell, J. (eds) (1997) *Who's Afraid of Feminism?* London: Hamish Hamilton.

Oakley, A., Peersman, G. and Oliver, S. (1998a) Social characteristics of participants in health promotion research: trial and error? *Education for Health*, 11(3):305–17.

Oakley, A., Rajan, L. and Turner, H. (1998b) Evaluating parent support initiatives: lessons from two case studies. *Health and Social Care in the Community*, 6(5):318–30.

Oberschall, A. (1972a) The institutionalisation of American sociology. In Oberschall (ed.).

Oberschall, A. (1972b) Introduction: the sociological study of the history of social research. In Oberschall (ed.).

Oberschall, A. (ed.) (1972c) *The Establishment of Empirical Sociology*. New York: Harper and Row.

Odum, H. E. (1951) *American Sociology: the story of sociology in the United States through 1950*. New York: Longmans, Green and Co.

Office of Technology Assessment, US Congress (1993) *Benefit Design in Health Care Reform: patient cost-sharing*. OTA-BP-H-112. Washington, D.C.: US Government Printing Office.

Ogburn, W. F. (1930) The folkways of a scientific sociology. *Publications of the American Sociological Society*, 24:2.

Ogburn, W. F. (1964) *On Culture and Social Change: selected papers*, ed. O. D. Duncan. Chicago: University of Chicago Press.

Okely, J. (1994) Thinking through fieldwork. In A. Bryman and R. G. Burgess (eds), *Analyzing Qualitative Data*, London: Routledge.

Oldenhave, A., Jaszmann, L. J. B., Haspels, A. A. and Everaerd, W. T. A. M. (1993) Impact of climacteric on well-being. *American Journal of Obstetrics and Gynecology*, 168:772–80.

Oleson, A. and Voss, J. (eds) (1979) *The Origins of Knowledge in Modern America 1860–1920*. Baltimore: Johns Hopkins University Press.

Oliver, S. R. (1995) How can health service users contribute to the NHS research and development programme? *British Medical Journal*, 310:1318–20.

Oliver, S. (1997) Exploring lay perspectives on questions of effectiveness. In Maynard and Chalmers (eds).

Oliver, S. (1998) Users of health services: following their agenda. In B. Mayall, S. Hood and S. Oliver (eds), *Critical Issues in Social Research: power and prejudice*, Buckingham: Open University Press.

Oliver, S., Rajan, L., Turner, H., Oakley, A., Entwhistle, V., Watt, I., Sheldon, T. A. and Rosser, J. (1996) Informed choice for users of health services: views on ultrasonography leaflets of women in early pregnancy, midwives, and ultrasonographers. *British Medical Journal*, 313:1251–3.

Oliver, S., Peersman, G., Harden, A. and Oakley, A. (1999a) Discrepancies in findings from effectiveness reviews: the case of health promotion for older people. *Health Education Journal*, 58(1):77–88.

Oliver, S., Lumley, J., Waters, E. and Oakley, L. (1999b) Observational and qualitative research: increasing a review's relevance to practitioners and consumers. Unpublished paper.

Olsen, T. (1980) *Silences*. London: Virago.

Orshansky, M. (1968) The shape of poverty in 1968. *Social Security Bulletin*, 31:5.

Osborn, A. F. (1987) Assessing the socio-economic status of families. *Sociology*, 21(3):429–48.

Oudshoorn, N. (1994) *Beyond the Natural Body: an archaeology of sex hormones*. London: Routledge.

Palmer, B. V., Walsh, G. A., McKinna, J. A. and Greening, W. P. (1980) Adjuvant chemotherapy for breast cancer: side effects and quality of life. *British Medical Journal*, 281:1594–7.

Pappworth, M. H. (1967) *Human Guinea Pigs*. London: Routledge and Kegan Paul.

Parer, J. T. (1986) The Dublin trial of fetal heart rate monitoring: the final word? *Birth*, 13:119–21.

Park, R. E., Burgess, E. W. and McKenzie, R. D. (1925) *The City*. Chicago: University of Chicago Press.

Parr, J. (1998) Theoretical voices and women's own voices. In J. Ribbens and R. Edwards (eds), *Feminist Dilemmas in Qualitative Research*, Thousand Oaks, Calif.: Sage Publications.

Parsons, T. (1949) *The Structure of Social Action*. Glencoe, Ill.: Free Press.

Pate, T., Kelling, G. L. and Brown, C. (1975) A response to 'what happened to patrol operations in Kansas City?' *Journal of Criminal Justice*, 3:299–320.

Patten, S. C. (1994) On the supposed indispensability of deception in social psychology. In E. Erwin, S. Gendin and L. Kleiman (eds), *Ethical Issues in Scientific Research*, New York: Garland Publishing.

Patton, M. Q. (1978) *Utilization-Focused Evaluation*. Beverly Hills, Calif.: Sage Publications.

Patton, M. Q. (1980) *Qualitative Evaluation Methods*. Beverly Hills, Calif.: Sage Publications.

Patulin Clinical Trials Committee, Medical Research Council (1944) Clinical trial of patulin in the common cold. *Lancet*, 16 Sept.:373–5.

Pawson, R. (1989) *A Measure for Measures: a manifesto for empirical sociology*. London: Routledge.

Pawson, R. and Tilley, N. (1997) *Realistic Evaluation*. Thousand Oaks, Calif.: Sage Publications.

Pawson, R. and Tilley, N. (1998) Caring communities, paradigm polemics, design debates. *Evaluation*, 4(1):73–90.

Pearson, E. S. (1938) *Karl Pearson: an appreciation of some aspects of his life and work*. Cambridge: Cambridge University Press.

Pearson, E. S. (ed.) (1978) *The History of Statistics in the 17th and 18th Centuries: lectures by Karl Pearson*. London and High Wycombe: Charles Griffin and Company.

Pearson, K. (1892) *Grammar of Science*. London: Walter Scott.

Pearson, K. (1904) Report of certain enteric fever inoculation statistics. *British Medical Journal*, 1:1243–6.

Pearson, K. (1914) *The Life, Letters and Labours of Francis Galton*, vol. 1. Cambridge: Cambridge University Press.

Pearson, K. (1924) *The Life, Letters and Labours of Francis Galton*, vol. 2. Cambridge: Cambridge University Press.

Pearson, K. (1930) *The Life, Letters and Labours of Francis Galton*, vol. 4. Cambridge: Cambridge University Press.

Pechman, J. A. and Timpane, P. M. (eds) (1975) *Work Incentives and Income Guarantees: the New Jersey Negative Income Tax Experiment*. Washington, D.C.: Brookings Institution.

Peckham, M. (1991) Research and development for the National Health Service. *Lancet*, 338:367–71.

Peel, J. D. Y. (1971) *Herbert Spencer*. London: Heinemann.

Peersman, G., Harden, A. and Oliver, S. (1998) *Effectiveness of Health Promotion Interventions in the Workplace: a review*. London: Health Education Authority.

Peersman, G., Oakley, A. and Oliver, S. (1999) Evidence-based health promotion? Some methodological challenges. *International Journal of Health Promotion and Education*, 37(2):59–64.

Pérez-Ramos, A. (1996) Bacon's legacy. In Pettonen (ed.).

Perry, W. G. (1970) *Forms of Intellectual and Ethical Development in the College Years*. New York: Holt, Rinehart and Winston.

Peterson, I. (1998) *Jungles of Randomness*. Harmondsworth: Penguin.

Peto, R. (1987) Why do we need systematic overviews of randomized trials? *Statistics in Medicine*, 6:233–40.

Pettonen, M. (1996a) Introduction. In Pettonen (ed.).

Pettonen, M. (ed.) (1996b) *The Cambridge Companion to Bacon*. Cambridge: Cambridge University Press.

Phillips, D. C. (1992) *The Social Scientist's Bestiary*. Oxford: Pergamon Press.

Pickering, A. (ed.) (1992) *Science as Practice and Culture*. Chicago: Chicago University Press.

Pittman, M. S. (1921) *The Value of School Supervision*. Baltimore: Warwick and York, Inc.

Platt, J. (1985) Weber's *verstehen* and the history of qualitative research: the missing link. *British Journal of Sociology*, 36(3):448–66.

Platt, J. (1996) *A History of Sociological Research Methods in America 1920–1960*. Cambridge: Cambridge University Press.

Popay, J. (1992) 'My health is all right, but I'm just tired all the time'. In H. Roberts (ed.), *Women's Health Matters*, London: Routledge.

Popay, J., Rogers, A. and Williams, G. (1998) Rationale and standards for the systematic review of qualitative literature in health services research. *Qualitative Health Research*, 8(3):341–51.

Popay, J. and Williams, G. (1998) Qualitative research and evidence-based healthcare. *Journal of the Royal Society of Medicine*, 91 (suppl. 35):32–7.

Pope, C. and Mays, N. (1993) Opening the black box: an encounter in the corridors of health services research. *British Medical Journal*, 306:315–18.

Porter, R. and Porter, D. (1988) *In Sickness and in Health: the British experience 1650–1850*. London: Fourth Estate.

Porter, T. (1995) *Trust in Numbers: the pursuit of objectivity in science and public life*. Princeton, N.J.: Princeton University Press.

Powers, E. and Witmer, H. (1951) *An Experiment in the Prevention of Juvenile Delinquency: the Cambridge–Somerville Youth Study*. New York: Columbia University Press.

Powles, T., Eeles, R., Ashley, S., Easton, D., Chang, J., Dowsett, M., Tidy, A., Viggers, J. and Dewey, J. (1998) Interim analysis of the incidence of breast cancer in the Royal Marsden Hospital tamoxifen randomised chemoprevention trial. *Lancet*, 352:98–101.

Quételet, A. (1837) *Correspondance Mathématique et Physique*, vol. 9. Paris: Bachelier.

Quételet, A. (1962) *A Treatise on Man and the Development of his Faculties*, trans. R. Knox. New York: Burt Franklin, Research Source Works Series.

Quételet, A. (1869) *Physique sociale: ou 5 Essai sur le developpement des facultes de l'homme*. Brussels: C. Muquardt.

Qureshi, H. (1992) Integrating methods in applied research in social policy: a case study of carers. In Brannen (ed.).

Raffle, A. (1996) Presentation to National Cervical Screening Conference. Oxford, Sept.

Raffle, A. E., Alden, B. and Mackenzie, E. F. D. (1995) Detection rates for abnormal cervical smears: what are we screening for? *Lancet*. 345:1469–73.

Rainwater, L. (1987) Sociological lessons from the Negative Income Tax Experiments: a sociological view. In A. H. Munnell (ed.), *Lessons from the Income Maintenance Experiments*, Boston: Federal Reserve Bank of Boston.

Rainwater, L., Coleman, R. P. and Handel, G. (1959) *Workingman's Wife*. New York: Oceana Publications.

Rajan, J. and Turner, H. (1997) Daycare Trial Feasibility Study Report. Unpublished report, London: Social Science Research Unit.

Rangachari, P. K. (1997) Evidence-based medicine: old French wine with a new Canadian label? *Journal of the Royal Society of Medicine*, 90:280–4.

Rapoport, R. and Rapoport, R. (1971) *Dual-Career Families*. Harmondsworth: Penguin.

Rapoport, R. and Rapoport, R. (1976) *Dual-Career Families Re-examined*. London: Martin Robertson.

Rees, D. A. (1992) Restricted entry to the tamoxifen trial (letter) *British Medical Journal*, 304:844.

Reichardt, C. S. and Cook, T. D. (1979) Beyond qualitative *versus* quantitative methods. In Cook and Reichardt (eds).

Reid, M. (1983) Review article: a feminist sociological imagination? Reading Ann Oakley. *Sociology of Health and Illness*, 5(1):83–94.

Rein, M. and White, S. (1978) Can policy research help policy? In Cook et al. (eds).

Reinharz, S. (1984) *On Becoming a Social Scientist*. New Brunswick, N.J.: Transaction Books.

Reinharz, S. (1992) *Feminist Methods in Social Research*. New York: Oxford University Press.

Reiser, S. J. (1978) *Medicine and the Reign of Technology*. Cambridge: Cambridge University Press.

Residents of Hull House (1895) *Hull-House Maps and Papers: a presentation of nationalities and wages in a congested district of Chicago. Together with comments and essays on problems growing out of the social conditions*. Boston: Thomas Crowell and Co.

Ribbens, J. (1989) Interviewing – an 'unnatural' situation? *Women's Studies International Forum*, 12(6):579–92.

Riecken, H. W. (1975) Introduction. In: Boruch and Riecken (eds).

Riecken, H. W. and Boruch, R. F. (1974) *Social Experimentation: a method for planning and evaluating social intervention*. New York: Academic Press.

Ripa, C. (1593) *Iconologia*. Rome.

Rist, R. C. (1980) Blitzkrieg ethnography: on the transformation of a method into a movement. *Educational Researcher*, Feb.:8–10.

Rist, R. C. (ed.) (1989) *Program Evaluation and the Management of Government*. New Brunswick, N.J.: Transaction Publishers.

Rivlin, A. M. (1971) *Systematic Thinking for Social Action*. Washington, D.C.: Brookings Institution.

Robb, E. K. and Faust, J. F. (1933) The effect of direct instruction. *The Journal of Educational Sociology*, 7(4):237–40.

Roberts, H. (ed.) (1981) *Doing Feminist Research*. London: Routledge.

Roberts, H. (ed.) (1990) *Women's Health Counts*. London: Routledge.

Roberts, I., Oakley, A. and Laing, G. (1997) Effects of out-of-home daycare on the health and welfare of socially disadvantaged families with children: a randomised controlled trial. Unpublished protocol.

Roberts, L., Ahmed, I., Hall, S. and Sargent, C. (1999) Intercessory prayer for the alleviation of ill health (Cochrane Review). In *The Cochrane Library*, Issue 1. Oxford: Update Software.

Roberts, M. M. (1989) Breast cancer screening: time for a rethink? *British Medical Journal*, 299:1153–5.

Robins, P. K., spiegelman, R. G., Weiner, S. and Bell, J. G. (eds) (1980) *A Guaranteed Annual Income: evidence from a social experiment*. New York: Academic Press.

Robinson, J. (1998) Was it 'informed'? Was it 'consent'? Lessons from the ECMO trial. *British Journal of Midwifery*, 6(3):175.

Roethlisberger, F. J. (1941) *Management and Morale*. Cambridge, Mass.: Harvard University Press.

Roethlisberger, F. J. and Dickson, W. J. (1939) *Management and the Worker*. Cambridge, Mass.: Harvard University Press.

Romito, P. (1997) Studying work, motherhood and women's well-being: a few notes about the construction of knowledge. *Journal of Reproductive and Infant Psychology*, 15:209–220.

Rose, H. (1993) Rhetoric, feminism and scientific knowledge, or from either/or to both/and. In R. H. Roberts and J. M. M. Good (eds), *The Recovery of Rhetoric*, Bristol: Classical Press.

Rose, H. (1995) Learning from the new priesthood and the shrieking sisterhood: debating the life sciences in Victorian England. In L. Birke and R. Hubbard (eds), *Reinventing Biology: respect for life and the creation of knowledge*, Bloomington, Ind.: Indiana

University Press.

Rose, H. (1994) *Love, Power and Knowledge*. Cambridge: Polity Press.

Rose, H. and Rose, S. (1976) (eds) *The Political Economy of Science*. London: Macmillan.

Rose, P. (1984) *Parallel Lives: five Victorian marriages*. London: Chatto and Windus.

Rosenberg, C. E. (1976) *No Other Gods: on science and American social thought*. Baltimore: Johns Hopkins University Press.

Rosenblatt, J. R. and Filliben, J. J. (1971) Randomisation and the draft lottery. *Science*, 171:306–8.

Rosenhan, D. L. (1973) On being sane in insane places. *Science*, 179:250–8.

Rosenthal, R. (1963) On the social psychology of the psychological experiment: the experimenter's hypothesis as unintended determinant of experimental results. *American Scientist*, 51:268.

Rosenthal, R. (1969) Interpersonal expectations: effects of the experimenter's hypothesis. In Rosenthal and Rosnow (eds).

Rosenthal, R. (1979) The 'file drawer problem' and tolerance of null results. *Psychological Bulletin*, 86:638–74.

Rosenthal, R. and Rosnow, R. L. (eds) (1969) *Artifact in Behavioral Research*. New York: Academic Press.

Ross, D. (1979) The development of the social sciences. In Oleson and Voss (eds).

Ross, D. (1991) *The Origins of American Social Science*. Cambridge: Cambridge University Press.

Ross, H. L. (1970) An Experimental Study of the Negative Income Tax. Unpublished Ph.D. diss., Massachusetts Institute of Technology.

Rosser, S. V. (1988) Good science: can it ever be gender free? *Women's Studies International Forum*, 11(1):13–19.

Rossi, P. H., Berk, R. A. and Lenihan, K. J. (1980) *Money, Work and Crime: experimental evidence*. New York: Academic Press.

Rossi, P. H. and Freeman, H. E. (1993) *Evaluation: a systematic approach*. Newbury Park, Calif.:Sage publications.

Rossi, P. H. and Lyall, K. C. (1976) *Reforming Public Welfare*. New York: Russell Sage Foundation.

Rossi, P. H. and Williams, W. (eds) (1972) *Evaluating Social Programs: theory, practice and politics*. New York: Seminar Press.

Rossi, P. H. and Wright, J. D. (1984) Evaluation research: an assessment. *Annual Review of Sociology*, 10:331–52.

Rossi, P. H. (1987) The iron law of evaluation and other metallic rules. In J. L. Miller and M. Lewis (eds), *Research in Social Problems and Public Policy*, Greenwich, Conn.: JAI Press.

Rossiter, M. W. (1982) *Women Scientists in America: struggles and strategies to 1940*. Baltimore: Johns Hopkins University Press.

Rowntree, B. S. (1922) *Poverty: a study of town life*. London: Macmillan (originally pub. 1901).

Rowntree, B. S. (1941) *Poverty and Progress: a second social survey of York*. London: Longmans, Green and Co.

Rupke, N. A. (1987a) Introduction. In Rupke (ed.).

Rupke, N. A. (ed.) (1987b) *Vivisection in Historical Perspective*. London: Croom Helm.

Rusk, R. R. (1919) *Experimental Education*. London: Longmans, Green and Co.

Sacks, H., Chalmers, T. C. and Smith, H. (1982) Randomised versus historical controls for clinical trials. *American Journal of Medicine*, 72:233–40.

Saint-Exupéry, A. de (1974) *The Little Prince*. London: Pan Books (originally pub.

1943).

St Leger, A. S., Cochrane, A. L. and Moore, R. (1979) Factors associated with cardiac mortality in developed countries with particular reference to the consumption of wine. *Lancet*, 1:1017–20.

Salvesen, K. A., Vatten, L. J., Eik-Nes, S. H., Hugdahl, K. and Bakketeig, L. S. (1993) Routine ultrasonography in utero and subsequent handedness and neurological development. *British Medical Journal*, 307:159–64.

Sandelowski, M. (1994) The proof is in the pottery: toward a poetic for qualitative inquiry. In Morse (ed.).

Saxe, L. and Fine, M. (1981) *Social Experiments: methods for design and evaluation.* Beverly Hills, Calif.: Sage Publications.

Schapiro, J. S. (1934) *Condorcet and the Rise of Liberalism.* New York: Harcourt Brace and Co.

Schatzman, L. and Strauss, A. L. (1973) *Field Research: strategies for a natural sociology.* Englewood Cliffs, N.J.: Prentice-Hall.

Scherer, J. C. (1975) 'You can't believe your eyes: inaccuracies in photographs of North American Indians.' *Studies in the Anthropology of Visual Communication*, 2:67–86.

Schiebinger, L. (1989) *The Mind Has No Sex.* Cambridge, Mass.: Harvard University Press.

Schiebinger, L. (1993) *Nature's Body.* London: HarperCollins.

Schnare, A. B. (1981) Comments. In Bradbury and Downs (eds).

Schulz, K. F., Chalmers, I., Hayes, R. J. and Altman, D. G. (1995) Empirical evidence of bias: dimensions of methodological quality associated with estimates of treatment effects in controlled trials. *Journal of the American Medical Association*, 273(5):408–12.

Schutz, A. (1967) *Collected Papers*, vol. 2, ed. M. Natanson. The Hague: Martinus Nijhoff.

Schutz, A. (1972) *The Phenomenology of the Social World.* London: Heinemann Educational (originally pub. 1932).

Schweinhart, L. J., Barnes, H. V. and Weikart, D. P. (1993) *Significant Benefits: the High/Scope Perry Preschool Study through age 27.* Ypsilanti, Mich.: High/Scope Press.

Schweinhart, L. J. and Weikart, D. P. (1980) *Young Children Grow Up: the effects of the Perry Preschool Program on youths through age 15.* Ypsilanti, Mich.: High/Scope Press.

Schwendiger, J. and Schwendiger, H. (1971) Sociology's founding fathers: sexists to a man. *Journal of Marriage and the Family*, Nov.:783–99.

Scott, R. A. and Shore, A. R. (1979) *Why Sociology Need Not Apply: a study of the use of sociology in public policy.* New York: Elsevier.

Seale, C. and Silverman, D. (1997) Ensuring rigour in qualitative research. *European Journal of Public Health*, 7:379–84.

Searle, B., Friend, J. and Suppes, P. (1976) *The Radio Mathematics Project: Nicaragua 1974–5.* Stanford, Calif.: Stanford University Institute for Mathematical Studies in the Social Sciences.

Searle, B., Matthews, P., Suppes, P. and Friend, J. (1978) Formal evaluation of the Radio Mathematics Instructional Program, Nicaragua – Grade 1, 1976. In Cook et al. (eds).

Searle, G. R. (1979) Eugenics and politics in Britain in the 1930s. *Annals of Science*, 36:159–69.

Seidler, V. J. (1998) Masculinity, violence and emotional life. In Bendelow and Williams (eds).

Senn, R. (1958) The earliest use of the term social science. *Journal of the History of Ideas*, 19:568–70.

Sewell, A. (1877) *Black Beauty*. London.

Seymour-Jones, C. (1993) *Beatrice Webb: woman of conflict*. London: Pandora Press.

Shadish, W. E., Cook, T. D. and Leviton, L. C. (1991) *Foundations of Program Evaluation*. Newbury Park, Calif.: Sage Publications.

Shapiro, M. F., Ware, J. E. and Sherbourne, C. D. (1986) Effects of cost sharing on seeking care for serious and minor symptoms: results of a randomized controlled trial. *Annals of Internal Medicine*, 104:246–51.

Sharf, A. (1964) *The British Press and Jews under Nazi Rule*. London: Oxford University Press.

Sharratt, M. (1994) *Galileo*. Cambridge: Cambridge University Press.

Sherif, C. W. (1987) Bias in psychology. In S. Harding (ed.), *Feminism and Methodology*, Bloomington, Ind.: Indiana University Press.

Sherman, J. A. and Beck, E. T. (eds) (1979) *The Prism of Sex: essays in the sociology of knowledge*. Madison, Wis.: University of Wisconsin Press.

Shulman, H. M. (1945) Delinquency treatment in the controlled activity group. *American Sociological Review*. June:405–14.

Sidell, M. (1993) Interpreting. In P. Shakespeare, D. Atkinson and S. French (eds), *Reflecting on Research Practice*, Buckingham: Open University Press.

Silverman, D. (1985) *Qualitative Methodology and Sociology*. Aldershot: Gower Press.

Silverman, D. (1989) Telling convincing stories: a plea for cautious positivism in case studies. In B. Glassner and J. D. Moreno (eds), *The Quantitative–Qualitative Distinction in the Social Sciences*, Dordrecht: Kluwer.

Silverman, W. A. (1980) *Retrolental fibroplasia: a modern parable*. New York: Grune and Stratton.

Silverman, W. A. (1981) Gnosis and random allotment. *Controlled Clinical Trials*, 2:161–4.

Silverman, W. A. (1990) *Human Experimentation: a guided step into the unknown*. Oxford: Oxford University Press.

Simey, T. S. and Simey, M. B. (1960) *Charles Booth: social scientist*. London: Oxford University Press.

Simkin, P. (1987) Is anyone listening? The lack of clinical impact of randomized controlled trials of electronic fetal monitoring. *Birth*, 13(4):219–20.

Simms, M. (1985) In Betsey et al. (eds).

Simon, W. M. (1963) *European Positivism in the Nineteenth Century*. Ithaca, N.Y.: Cornell University Press.

Singer, D. W. (1924) *Selections from the Work of Ambroise Paré, with short biography and explanatory and bibliographic notes*. London: John Bale and Sons and Danielson, Ltd.

Singer, P. (1976) *Animal Liberation*. London: Jonathan Cape.

Sklar, K. K. (1991) Hull-House Maps and Papers: social science as women's work in the 1890s. In M. Bulmer, K. Bales and K. K. Sklar (eds), *The Social Survey in Historical Perspective*, Cambridge: Cambridge University Press.

Slevin, M., Mossman, J., Bowling, A., Leonard, R., Steward, W. and Harper, P. et al. (1995) Volunteers or victims: patients' views of randomised cancer clinical trials. *British Journal of Cancer*, 71:1270–4.

Small, A. W. (1924) *Origins of Sociology*. Chicago: University of Chicago Press.

Smart, B. (1993) *Postmodernity*. London: Routledge.

Smith, A. (1759) *The Theory of Moral Sentiments*. London: A. Millar.

Smith, A. F. M. (1996) Mad cows and ecstasy: chance and choice in an evidence-based society. *Journal of the Royal Statistical Society*, 159(3):367–83.

Smith, D. (1987) The limits of positivism in social work research. *British Journal of Social Work*, 17:401–16.

Smith, D. E. (1979) A sociology for women. In Sherman and Beck (eds).

Smith, D. E. (1988) *The Everyday World as Problematic*. Milton Keynes: Open University Press.

Smith, F. T. (n.d.) An experiment in modifying attitudes towards the Negro. Cited in Murphy et al. (1937).

Smith, J. K. (1984) The problem of criteria for judging interpretive inquiry. *Educational Evaluation and Policy Analysis*, 6(4):379–91.

Smith, J. K. and Heshushius, L. (1986) Closing down the conversation: the end of the quantitative–qualitative debate among educational inquirers. *Educational Researcher*, 4–12.

Smith, M. L. (1980) Publication bias and meta-analysis. *Evaluation in Education*, 4:22–4.

Smith, M. L. and Glass, G. V. (1977) Meta-analysis of psychotherapy outcome studies. *American Psychologist*, 32:752–60.

Snowden, C., Elbourne, D. and Garcia, J. (in press) Zelen randomization: attitudes of parents participating in a neonatal clinical trial.

Snowden, C., Garcia, J. and Elbourne, D. (1997) Making sense of randomization: responses of parents of critically ill babies to random allocation of treatment in a clinical trial, *Social Science and Medicine*, 45(9):1337–55.

Solomon, R. L. (1949) An extension of control group design. *Psychological Bulletin*, 46:137–50.

Sorell, T. (ed.) (1996) *The Cambridge Companion to Hobbes*. Cambridge: Cambridge University Press.

Sorokin, P. (1928) An experimental study of efficiency under various specified conditions. *American Journal of Sociology*, 25:765–82.

Speller, V., Learmonth, A. and Harrison, D. (1997) The search for evidence of effective health promotion. *British Medical Journal*, 315:361–3.

Spence, J. D. (1990) *The Search for Modern China*. London: Hutchinson.

Spencer, H. (1903) *The Study of Sociology*. London: Kegan Paul, Trench, Trübner and Co.

Spencer, H. (1904) *An Autobiography*, vol. 2. London: Williams and Norgate.

Spencer, H. (1850) *Social Statics: or, the conditiones essential to human happiness specified and the first of them developed*. London: John Chapman.

Spender, D. (ed.) (1981) *Men's Studies Modified: the impact of feminism on the academic disciplines*. Oxford: Pergamon Press.

Spender, D. (1985) Model knowledge-making: Ann Oakley's research. In *For the Record: the making and meaning of feminist knowledge*, London: Women's Press.

Sprague, J. and Zimmerman, M. K. (1989) Quality and quantity: reconstructing feminist methodology. *American Sociologist*, spring: 71–86.

Stacey, J. (1988) Can there be a feminist ethnography? *Women's Studies International Forum*, 11(1):21–7.

Staël, Madame de (1788) *Letters on Rousseau*. Repr. in Folkenflik (1987).

Staël, Madame de (1796) *The Influence of the Passions on the Happiness of Individuals and Nations*. Repr. in Folkenflik (1987).

Staël, Madame de (1800) *On Literature Considered in its Relationship to Social Institu-*

tions. Repr. in Folkenflik (1987).

Stael, Madame de (1813) *Reflections on Suicide.* Repr. in Folkenflik (1987).

Stake, R. E. (1981) Case study methodology: an epistemological advocacy. In W. Welch (ed.), *Case Study Methodology in Educational Evaluation,* Minneapolis: Minnesota Research and Evaluation Center.

Stake, R. E. (1986) *Quieting Reform: social science and social action in an urban youth program.* Urbana and Chicago: University of Illinois Press.

Stanley, J. C. (1957) Controlled experimentation in the classroom. *Journal of Experimental Education,* 25:195–201.

Stanley, J. C. (1966) The influence of Fisher's 'The Design of Experiments' on educational research thirty years later. *American Educational Research Journal,* 3(3):223–9.

Stanley, J. C. (1972) Controlled field experiments as a model for evaluation. In Rossi and Williams (eds).

Stanley, L. and Wise, S. (1983) *Breaking Out: feminist consciousness and feminist research.* London: Routledge.

Stanley, L. and Wise, S. (1993) *Breaking Out Again: feminist ontology and epistemology.* London: Routledge.

Stark, A. (1997) Combating the backlash: how Swedish women won the war. In Oakley and Mitchell (eds).

Stebbins, L. B., St Pierre, R. G., Proper, E. C., Anderson, R. B. and Cerva, T. R. (1978) An evaluation of Follow Through. In Cook et al. (eds).

Stephan, A. S. (1935) Prospects and possibilities: the New Deal and the New Social Research. *Social Forces,* 13(May):515–21.

Stern, K. (1966) *The Flight from Woman.* London: Allen and Unwin.

Stevenson, H. M. and Burke, M. (1991) Bureaucratic logic in new social movement clothing: the limits of health promotion research. *Health Promotion International,* 6(4):281–9.

Stigler, S. M. (1978) Mathematical statistics in the early States. *Annals of Statistics,* 6:239–65.

Stigler, S. M. (1986) *The History of Statistics: the measurement of uncertainty before 1900.* Cambridge, Mass.: Belknap Press of Harvard University Press.

Stiller, C. (1994) Centralized treatment, trial entry and survival. *British Journal of Cancer,* 70:352–62.

Stillman, R. J. (1982) *In utero* exposure to diethylstilboestrol: adverse effects on the reproductive tract and reproductive performance in male and female offspring. *American Journal of Obstetrics and Gynecology,* 142:905–21.

Stocking, B. (1993) Implementing the findings of Effective Care in Pregnancy and Childbirth in the United Kingdom. *Milbank Quarterly,* 71(3):497–521.

Storr, A. (1985) Isaac Newton. *British Medical Journal,* 291:1779–84.

Stouffer, S. A., Suchman, E. A., DeVinney, L. C., Star, S. A. and Williams, R. M. (1949) *The American Soldier,* vol. 1. Princeton, N.J.: Princeton University Press.

Struyck, N. (1746) *Calculations of the Chances in Games, by aid of Arithmetic and Algebra, together with a Memoir on Lotteries and Interest.* In *Les œuvres de Nicolas Struyck* (1912), Amsterdam.

Struyk, R. J. and Bendick, M. (eds) (1981) *Housing Vouchers for the Poor.* Washington, D.C.: Urban Institute.

Sutherland, I. (1960) The statistical requirements and methods. In Council for International Organizations of Medical Sciences, *Controlled Clinical Trials,* Oxford: Blackwell Scientific Publications.

Taggart, R. (1972) *The Prison of Unemployment: manpower programs for offenders.* Baltimore: Johns Hopkins University Press.

Tate, H. C., Rawlinson, J. B. and Freedman, L. S. (1979) Randomised cooperative studies in the treatment of cancer in the United Kingdom: room for improvement? *Lancet*, 2:623–5.

Taylor, A. E. (1908) *Thomas Hobbes*. London: Archibald Constable and Co.

Thacker, S. B. and Stroup, D. F. (1999) Continuous electronic heart rate monitoring versus intermittent auscultation for assessment during labor (Cochrane Review). In *The Cochrane Library*, Issue 1. Oxford: Update Software.

Thorndike, E. L. and Woodworth, R. S. (1901) The influence of improvement in one mental function upon the efficiency of other functions. *Psychological Review*, 8:247–61, 384–95, 553–64.

Thrasher, F. H. (1927) *The Gang: a study of 1,313 gangs in Chicago*. Chicago: University of Chicago Press.

Tiffany, S. W. and Adams, K. J. (1985) *The Wild Woman: an inquiry into the anthropology of an idea*. Cambridge, Mass.: Schenkman Pub. Company.

Titmuss, R. M. (1970) Foreword. In Goldberg et al.

Titmuss, R. M. (1997) *The Gift Relationship: from human blood to social policy*, ed. A. Oakley and J. Ashton. London: LSE Books (originally pub. 1970).

Tones, K. (1996) Conflict and compromise in health promotion research: a quest for illumination. Paper presented at Conference on the Status of Nordic Health Promotion Research, Bergen, Norway.

Topo, P. (1997) Dissemination of climacteric and post-menopausal hormone therapy in Finland. Helsinki: STAKES National Research and Development Centre for Welfare and Health Research Reports, 78.

Torgerson, D. J. and Sibbald, B. (1998) What is a patient preference trial? *British Medical Journal*, 316:360.

Trend, M. G. (1979) On the reconciliation of qualitative and quantitative analysis: a case study. In Cook and Reichardt (eds).

Tröhler, V. and Maehle, A.-H. (1987) Anti-vivisection in nineteenth century Germany and Switzerland: motives and methods. In Rupke (ed.).

Trow, M. (1957) Comment on 'Participant observation and interviewing: a comparison'. *Human Organization*, 16:33–5.

Tuana, N. (ed.) (1989) *Feminism and Science*. Bloomington, Ind.: Indiana University Press.

Tucker, J. S., Hall, M. P. H., Howie, P. W. , Red, M. E., Barbour, R. S., Florey, C. du V. and McIlwaine, G. M. (1996) Should obstetricians see women with normal pregnancies? A multicentre randomised controlled trial of routine antenatal care by general practitioners and midwives compared with shared care led by obstetricians. *British Medical Journal*, 312:554–9.

Turner, E. S. (1992) *All Heaven in a Rage*. Fontwell, Sussex: Centaur Books.

Turner, S. P. (1986) *The Search for a Methodology of Social Science*. Dordrecht: D. Reidel Publishing Company.

Turner, S. P. and Turner, J. H. (1990) *The Impossible Science: an institutional analysis of American Sociology*. Newbury Park, Calif.: Sage Publications.

UK Collaborative Trial Group (1996) UK collaborative randomised trial of neonatal extracorporeal membrane oxygenation. *Lancet*, 348:75–82.

Ulfelder, H. (1980) The stilbestrol disorders in historical perspective. *Cancer*, 45(12):3008–11.

Urbach, P. (1994) Editor's introduction to Francis Bacon's *Novum Organon, With Other Parts of The Great Instauration*, trans. and ed. P. Urbach and J. Gibson. Chicago and

La Salle, Ill.: Open Court.

van Fraassen, B. C. (1980) *The Scientific Image*. Oxford: Clarendon Press.

van Helmont, J. A. (1662) *Oriatrike, or Physik Refined: the common errors therein refuted and the whole are reformed and rectified*, (trans. J. Chandler). London: Lodowick-Loyd.

Vaughan, T. (1919) *The Works of Thomas Vaughan*, ed. A. E. Waite. London: Theosophical Publishing House (originally pub. 1650).

Verbrugge, L. (1986) From sneezes to adieux: stages of health for American men and women. *Social Science and Medicine*, 22(11):1195–212.

Verbrugge, L. and Wingard, M. (1987) Sex differentials in health and mortality. *Women and Health*, 12(2):103–43

Veronesi, V., Maisonneuve, P., Costa, A., Sacchini, V., Maltoni, C., Robertson, C., Rotmensz, N. and Boyle, P. (1998) Prevention of breast cancer with tamoxifen: preliminary findings from the Italian randomised trial among hysterectomised women. *Lancet*, 352:93–7.

Vesalius, A. (1543) *De Humani Corporis Fabrica*. Basel.

Viney, L. L., Benjamin, Y. N., Clarke, A. M. and Bunn, T. A. (1985) Sex differences in the psychological reactions of medical and surgical patients to crisis intervention counseling: sauce for the goose may not be sauce for the gander. *Social Science and Medicine*, 20(11):1199–205.

Voss, S. (trans.) (1989) *The Passions of the Soul* by René Descartes. Indianapolis, Ind.: Hackett Publishing Company.

Vrooman, J. R. (1970) *René Descartes: a biography*. New York: G. P. Putnam's Sons.

Wagner, M. (1994) *Pursuing the Birth Machine*. Camperdown, N.S.W., Australia: ACE Graphics.

Wagner, P. and Wollmann, H. (1986) Fluctuations in the development of evaluation research: do 'regime shifts' matter? *International Social Science Journal*, 38:205–18.

Wagner, P., Weiss, C. H., Wittrock, B. and Woolman, H. (eds) (1991a) *Social Sciences and Modern States: national experiences and theoretical crossroads*. Cambridge: Cambridge University Press.

Wagner, P., Wittrock, B. and Whitley, R. (eds) (1991b) *Discourses on Society: the shaping of the social science disciplines*. Dordrecht: Kluwer Academic Publishers.

Walden, R. and Walkerdine, V. (1981) *Girls and Mathematics: the early years*. London: Bedford Way Paper no. 8.

Walker, L. (1984) Sex differences in the development of moral reasoning: a critical review. *Child Development*, 55:667–91.

Walker, R. (1998) The scope for experimentation in the evaluation of social security policies in Britain. Paper presented to the Franco-British Evaluation Seminar, Paris, 29–30 January.

Walkerdine, V. (1989) *Counting Girls Out*. London: Virago.

Walters, M. (1976) The rights and wrongs of women: Mary Wollstonecraft, Harriet Martineau, Simone de Beauvoir. In J. Mitchell and A. Oakley (eds), *The Rights and Wrongs of Women*, Harmondsworth: Penguin.

Ward, D. A. (1973) Evaluative research for corrections. In L. E. Ohlin (ed.), *Prisoners in America*, Englewood Cliffs, N.J.: Prentice-Hall.

Ward, V. M., Bertrand, J. T. and Brown, L. F. (1991) The comparability of focus group and survey results. *Evaluation Review*, 15(2):266–83.

Warner, M. (1985) *Monuments and Maidens: the allegory of the female form*. London: Weidenfeld and Nicolson.

Watts, H. W. (1981) A critical review of the program as a social experiment. In Bradbury and Downs (eds).

Watts, H. W. and Rees, A. (eds) (1977) *The New Jersey Income-Maintenance Experiment*, vol. 3: *Expenditures, Health and Social Behavior; and the Quality of the Evidence*. New York: Academic Press.

Webb, B. (1938) *My Apprenticeship – I & II*. Harmondsworth: Penguin.

Webb, S. and Webb, B. (1932) *Methods of Social Study*. London: Longmans, Green and Co.

Weber, M. (1947a) *A Theory of Social and Economic Organization*. Glencoe, Ill.: Free Press.

Weber, M. (1947b) *From Max Weber: essays in sociology*, trans. and ed. H. H. Gerth and C. Wright Mills. London: Kegan Paul, Trench, Trubner and Co.

Webster, C. (ed.) (1970) *Samuel Hartlib and the Advancement of Learning*. Cambridge: Cambridge University Press.

Webster, C. (1974a) The authorship and significance of 'Macaria'. In Webster (ed.).

Webster, C. (ed.) (1974b) *The Intellectual Revolution of the Seventeenth Century*. London: Routledge and Kegan Paul.

Weeks, H. A. (1958) *Youthful Offenders at Highfields*. Ann Arbor, Mich.: University of Michigan Press.

Weininger, O. (1975) *Geschlecht und Charakter (Sex and Character)*. New York: AMS Press (originally pub. 1903).

Weiss, C. H. (1972) *Evaluation Research: methods for assessing program effectiveness*. Englewood Cliffs, N.J.: Prentice-Hall.

Weiss, C. H. (1973) Where politics and evaluation research meet. *Evaluation*, 1:37–45.

Weiss, C. H. (1987) Evaluating social programs: what have we learned? *Society*, 25(1):40–45.

Weiss, C. H. (1991) Policy research: data, ideas, or arguments? In Wagner et al. (eds) (1991a).

Weiss, R. S. and Rein, M. (1970) The evaluation of broad-aim programs: experimental design, its difficulties, and an alternative. *Administrative Science Quarterly*, 15:97–109.

Welch, W. W. and Walberg, H. J. (1970) Pretest and sensitization effects on curriculum evaluation. *American Educational Research Journal*, 7(4):605–14.

Welch, W. W., Wahlberg, H. G. and Ahlgren, A. (1969) The selection of a national random sample of teachers for experimental curriculum innovation. *School Science and Mathematics*, March:210–6.

Wells, H. G. (1907) The so-called science of sociology. In *Sociological Papers 1906 Volume 3*:357–77, London: Macmillan.

Wenger, N. K. (1997) Coronary heart disease: an older woman's major health risk. *British Medical Journal*, 315:1085–90.

West, R. W. (1980) The effects on the labor supply of young nonheads. *Journal of Human Resources*, 15(4):574–89.

Weström, L. (1986) Treatment of salpingitis acuta with antibiotics solely or in combination with an antiphlogistic drug. Protocol for the research ethics committee, University of Lund, Sweden.

White, M. (1998) *Isaac Newton: the last sorcerer*. London: Fourth Estate.

Williams A. S. (1997) *Women and Childbirth in the Twentieth Century: a history of the National Birthday Trust Fund 1928–1993*. Stroud, Glos.: Sutton Publishing.

Williams, G. and Popay, J. (1997) Social science and public health: issues of method, knowledge and power. *Critical Public Health*, 7(1,2):61–72.

Williams, N. (1981) An eclectic approach to evaluation. In C. Lacey and D. Lawton (eds), *Issues in Evaluation and Accountability*, London: Methuen.

Williams, R. (1983) *Keywords*. London: HarperCollins.

Williams, S. J. and Bendelow, G. (1998). Introduction. In Bendelow and Williams (eds).

Williams, W. and Elmore, R. F. (1976) *Social Program Implementation*. New York: Academic Press.

Williams, W. and Evans, J. W. (1972) The politics of evaluation: the case of Head Start. In Rossi and Williams (eds).

Willson, V. L. and Putnam, R. R. (1983) A meta-analysis of pretest sensitization effects in experimental design. In R. J. Light (ed.), *Evaluation Studies Review Annual*, 8:623–31.

Wilner, D. M., Walkley, R. P., Pinkerton, T. C. and Tayback, M. (1962) *The Housing Environment and Family Life*. Baltimore: Johns Hopkins University Press.

Winch, W. H. (1908) The transfer of improvement in memory in school-children. *British Journal of Psychology*, 2:284–93.

Wirth, L. (1928) *The Ghetto*. Chicago: University of Chicago Press.

Wise, J. (1996) HRT use in high risk women should be reviewed. *British Medical Journal*, 313:1102.

Witt, P. L., Bauerle, C., Derouen, D., Kamel, F., Kelleher, P., McCarthy, M., Namenwirth, M., Sabatini, L. and Voytovich, M. (1989) The October 29th Group: defining a feminist science. *Women's Studies International Forum*, 12(3):253–9.

Wittgenstein, L. (1977) *Philosophical Investigations*. Oxford: Basil Blackwell (originally pub. in English 1953).

Wittrock, B. and Wagner, P. (1996) Social science and the building of the early welfare state: toward a comparison of statist and non-statist western societies. In D. Rueschemeyer and T. Skocpol (eds), *States, Social Knowledge and the Origins of Modern Social Policies*, Princeton, N.J.: Princeton University Press.

Wittrock, B., Heilbron, J. and Magnusson, L. (1997a) The rise of the social sciences and the formation of modernity. In Wittrock et al. (eds).

Wittrock, B., Heilbron, J. and Magnusson, L. (eds) (1997b) *The Rise of the Social Sciences: conceptual change in context, 1750–1850*. Sociology of the Sciences. A Yearbook. Dordrecht: Kluwer Academic Publishers.

Wolf, D. L. (1996) Situating feminist dilemmas in fieldwork. In D. L. Wolf (ed.), *Feminist Dilemmas in Fieldwork*, Boulder, Colo.: Westview Press.

Wollstonecraft, M. (1792) *Vindication of the Rights of Woman*. London.

Woodham-Smith, C. (1950) *Florence Nightingale 1820–1910*. London: Reprint Society.

Woods, R. A. (1923) *The Neighbourhood in Nation-Building*. Boston: Houghton Mifflin, Riverside Press of Cambridge.

Woolgar, S. (1996) Psychology, qualitative methods and the ideas of science. In J. T. E. Richardson (ed.), *Handbook of Qualitative Research Methods for Psychology and the Social Sciences*, London: British Psychological Society.

World Health Organization European Working Group on Health Promotion Evaluation (1998) *Health Promotion Evaluation: recomendations to policymakers*. Copenhagen: WHO Regional Office for Europe.

Wortman, C. B. and Rabinowitz, V. C. (1979) Random assignment: the fairest of them all. *Evaluation Studies Review Annual*, 177–85.

Wortman, C. B., Hendricks, M. and Hillis, J. W. (1976) Factors affecting participant reactions to random assignment in ameliorative social programs. *Journal of Personality and Social Psychology*, 33(3):256–66.

Wright, A. E. (1904) *A Short Treatise on Anti-Typhoid Inoculation*. Westminster: Archibald

Constable.

Wright Mills, C. (1959) *The Sociological Imagination*. New York: Oxford University Press.

Wright, W. E. and Dixon, M. C. (1977) Community prevention and treatment of juvenile delinquency. *Journal of Research in Crime and Delinquency*, 35(Jan.):67.

Wysowski, D. K., Kennedy, D. L. and Gross, T. P. (1990) Prescribed use of cholesterol-lowering drugs in the United States, 1978 through 1988. *Journal of the American Medical Association*, 263(16):2185–8.

Yeo, E. J. (1996) *The Contest for Social Science: relations and representations of gender and class*. London: Rivers Oram Press.

Young, S. (1997) *Changing the Wor(l)d: discourse, politics and the feminist movement*. New York: Routledge.

Zaretsky, E. (1976) *Capitalism, the Family and Personal Life*. New York: Harper and Row.

Zeisel, H. (1982) Disagreement over the evaluation of a controlled experiment. *American Journal of Sociology*, 88(2):378–89.

Zelditch, M. (1962) Some methodological problems of field studies. *American Journal of Sociology*, 67:566–76.

Zelen, M. (1979) A new design for randomized clinical trials. *New England Journal of Medicine*, 300:1242–5.

Ziglio, E. (1996) How to move towards evidence-based health promotion interventions. Paper given to Third European Conference on Effectiveness: Quality Assessment in Health Promotion and Health Education, Turin, Italy.

Zorbaugh, H. W. (1929) *The Gold Coast and the Slum: a sociological study of Chicago's near North Side*. Chicago: University of Chicago Press.

Zoritch, B., Oakley, A. and Roberts, I. (1998) The health and welfare effects of daycare: a systematic review of randomised controlled trials. *Social Science and Medicine*, 47(3):317–27.

Index

Printed in the United Kingdom
by Lightning Source UK Ltd.
134006UK00001BA/6/P